# THE STUDY OF
# ECONOMICS

*This book is dedicated to my sister
and best friend, Ruby Browning.*

ABOUT THE AUTHOR: Dr. Turley Mings received his undergraduate degree in economics from Occidental College and his Ph.D. in economics from the University of California at Berkeley. He is Professor Emeritus of economics at San Jose State University where he taught the introductory course for 30 years. He served as director of the Center for Economic Education for 20 years, developing strategies for teaching economics and conducting in-service workshops at all levels.

ABOUT THE COVER: Charles Sheller's *General Motors Research* (1965) expresses the technological strength of the United States in the twentieth century. Reprinted with kind permission of General Motors Research Laboratories.

# 4th EDITION

# THE STUDY OF
# ECONOMICS
## Principles, Concepts & Applications

**TURLEY MINGS**

The Dushkin Publishing Group, Inc.

# Credits and Acknowledgments

The illustrations in this book reflect the work of many professional artists and photographers. We, however, would particularly like to thank and acknowledge the following American and international corporations, institutions, and government agencies that have provided us with complimentary illustration material: American Cancer Society, American Egg Board, American Heritage Center at the University of Wyoming, American Iron and Steel Institute, American Red Cross, Banta, Cadillac, Chase Manhattan Bank, Chrysler Corporation, Congressional News Photos, Corrections Corporation of America, CPC International, Inc., Crafted with Pride in America, Department of Agriculture, Department of Defense, Department of the Treasury, Dole Food Company, Environmental Protection Agency, EPA Documerica, Farm Sanctuary, Federal Aviation Administration, Federal Reserve Bank/Charlotte Branch, Florida News Bureau, Ford New Holland, General Electric, General Motors, Greenpeace, IBM, Krause Publications, Library of Congress, Matsushita Electric, Merck & Co., Inc., Morrison Knudsen Corporation, Motorola, National Gallery of Art, National Institute of Standards and Technology, New York Convention and Visitors' Bureau, Northrop Corporation, Port Authority of New York and New Jersey, Sony Corporation, Soviet Mission to the UN, StarKist Seafood Company, TRW, TVA Washington Office, UAW Solidarity, Union Electric, United Nations, University of Texas, Austin/News and Information Service, World Health Organization.

The following is a list of sources by chapter:

**Chapter 1**  4 © Plowden 1989—Greenpeace; 8 Mike Eagle; 10 Pamela Carley Petersen—DPG; 12 UN photo by Antoinette Jongen; 13 USDA; 15 Pamela Carley Petersen—DPG; 16 Steve Delaney—EPA; 17 University of Texas Austin/News and Information Service; 23 Steve Delaney—EPA; 24 Greenpeace; 25 courtesy Paul Samuelson

**Chapter 2**  34 M. Christopher Zacharow—Tania; 38 Mike Eagle; 39 courtesy American Egg Board; 40 courtesy Northrop Corporation; UN photo by P. Sudhakaran; 43 Pamela Carley Petersen—DPG; 46 courtesy Stuart L. Shalat; 47 Reuters/Bettmann; 52 Terry Husebye; 53 Punch magazine; 54 M. Christopher Zacharow—Tania; 55 John Kenneth Galbraith

*(continued on page xlvii)*

Printed in the United States of America

Library of Congress Catalog Card Number 91-70272

International Standard Book Number (ISBN) 0-87967-921-2

Fourth Edition, First Printing

The Dushkin Publishing Group, Inc., Sluice Dock, Guilford, Connecticut 06437

# PREFACE

This edition of *The Study of Economics* contains the most extensive revisions since the book's original publication. In the 15 years since the first edition appeared, much has changed in economics. The world economy has become more integrated, and its impact on the domestic economy of the United States much greater. This change is reflected by an expansion of Unit IV on World Economics from 3 to 4 chapters for this edition. The new chapter on "International Finance and the National Economy" shows the interrelationship between the U.S. balance of payments deficits and the government budget deficits, a relationship that is important to the understanding of domestic economic developments in recent years and crucial to the problems facing the economy in the 1990s.

Another major change in the intervening years has been the relative decline of the competitive position of the United States economy. A discussion of the causes of this descent and the efforts to reverse it appears in a new chapter 7 on "Industry Performance."

In response to requests from users of the previous edition, the material on graphs and the construction and use of diagrams has been moved from an appendix at the end of the book to a new first chapter on "Economic Methods." It incorporates a discussion of the use of the scientific method in economics with coverage of the tools of the economic discipline that appeared in the earlier first chapter.

The book retains the basic features that have characterized it since the first edition. One of these features is the presentation of economic concepts in the context of real-world situations that introduce each chapter.

This is done to give the beginning student, for whom economics all too frequently seems abstract, a concrete setting to which new concepts can be related, since a principle of learning theory is that the learner needs familiar intellectual pegs on which to hang unfamiliar ideas.

The concepts in each chapter are grouped into three or four sections, and there is a different case application at the conclusion of each section. The intention is to integrate the explanations of economic concepts very closely with their applications. Each of the case applications is followed by questions which encourage the student to practice economic analysis and to apply the newly learned concepts. An important objective of this structure is to teach students to approach problems as an economist would. The numerous applications included in the text and the additional applications in the student workbook should help students to master basic concepts and increase their ability to transfer economic skills and knowledge to new problems as they arise in the real world.

Although the text makes extensive use of case applications, *The Study of Economics* is not a casebook. It presents economic theory in as systematic a framework of organization as more traditional texts. Each of the major areas of economics is discussed thoroughly, starting with economic methods and the fundamental choices about the use of resources and proceeding to deal in turn with markets, consumers, business and industrial organization and performance, government, labor and income distribution, money, economic instability, national income, public finance, policies for stabilization and growth, international trade and finance, alternative economic systems, and world economic development. Thus the text provides an evenly balanced presentation of the full range of economics. Although microeconomics is treated first in the text's organization, macroeconomics can just as easily be covered before microeconomics without any loss in student understanding.

It has been alleged that economics is the only discipline in which we try to teach everything we know about the subject in the beginning course. The rule in this text has been to include only those tools of economic analysis which will be useful to a student in understanding the real economic world. The book avoids purely technical devices that are relevant to advanced economic theory but have no immediate value to the beginning student. The close integration of concepts and models with real-world applications has helped to exclude theory that does not have concrete applicability. When a simple model serves as well to explain a set of relationships, it has been used in place of a more complicated model. An example is the use of the GNP tank model in Chapter 12 rather than the more abstract Keynesian cross diagram.

The questions following each case application and the study questions at the end of each chapter are designed to be useful for class discussion, either as a whole class with the teacher leading the discussion or in small discussion groups. There is a consistent pattern for the three questions that follow each case application. The first question of the three is one that a student who has read the material should not have too much difficulty in answering. Taxonomically, the first question is a concept recognition/simple applica-

tion question. The second question is generally more difficult, requiring analytical thinking. It is a complex application/analysis-type question. The third question is an open-ended question involving the student's own personal belief system and attitudes as well as the concepts in the text. These questions are of the integrative/valuation type.

Suggested answers to all of the application questions and to the study questions at the end of the chapter are given in the instructor's guide, *Teaching with The Study of Economics*. The instructor's guide also includes additional discussion of the text presentation and teaching strategies. It provides schematic outlines for each chapter that can be used as transparency masters for every section of the chapter. Also included are transparency masters for all of the charts and graphs in the text.

Supplementary materials include a testing program and a microcomputer test generator, a set of instructional color transparencies with overlays for overhead projection, and a student workbook, *Working With The Study of Economics*. The workbook contains review exercises, additional case applications with questions for each section of the chapters, self-test multiple-choice questions, and schematic outlines of every chapter section.

The schematic outlines serve a variety of purposes: as a preview of the material in the chapter, as an aid to the student in understanding the relationships between the economic concepts and models discussed, as a review, and, when displayed on an overhead projector, as a means for the teacher to orient the students to the material being covered in class.

Turley Mings

# CONTENTS SUMMARY

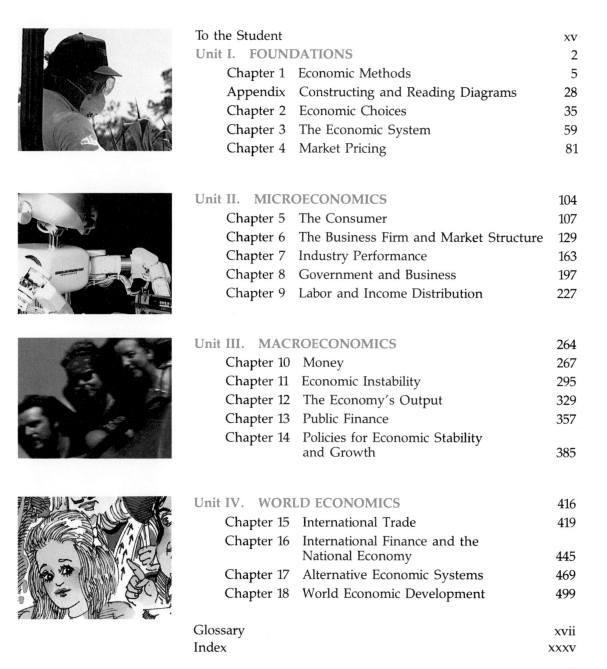

# CONTENTS

# TO THE STUDENT

Welcome to the study of economics. I hope that you will find it interesting and worthwhile; I have done my best to make it so. Interest in economics is higher today than it has ever been, at least since the depression era of the 1930s. Today's daily newspapers, weekly newsmagazines, and nightly newscasts are full of reporting on the latest economic developments and expert analysis of what those developments mean for us.

In order to help you gain an economic understanding of current events and problems, I have incorporated many applications of the economic concepts in the text. The applications are continuously interwoven with the explanations of economics to make it easier for you to see the relevance of the economic ideas and to make them more interesting. Economics sometimes has the reputation of being a difficult, dull, and abstract subject. I hope that this book will convince you that this does not have to be the case. Certainly economics is complicated, but by taking it one step at a time and being clear on just what each idea means and how it is used, you can enjoy it, master it, and find it useful.

What is economics? One definition is given in the cartoon panel below. "Economics is the social science concerned with how resources are used to satisfy people's wants." The

subject matter of economics is divided into two major fields. One deals with the individual units in an economy, the individual businesses, workers, consumers, and so forth. This is called microeconomics because it takes a detailed look at the economic decisions made by individuals and businesses and the effect government policies have on them. The other major area is macroeconomics, which deals with the broad measurements of economic activity such as the average price level, employment, and total output. *The Study of Economics* is divided into four parts. The first part consists of 4 chapters on the fundamentals of economics. This is followed by 5 chapters on microeconomics, 5 chapters on macroeconomics, and 4 chapters on the world economy.

The organization of each chapter of the text follows a consistent pattern, and each part of the chapter has a specific function. The chapters begin with an introductory article on some event or problem related to the economic topics covered in the chapter. Chapter 4, for example, which deals with how markets work and how prices are set, begins with an article on what happened to the price and availability of peanut butter when there was a failure of the peanut crop. The economic concepts that explain how markets behave are then introduced in the context of what actually occurred in the peanut butter market. The introductory articles conclude with a preview of the content of the chapter and a set of learning objectives that give you an idea of what the main things are that you should look for in the chapter. The next feature of the chapters is one that we hope you will enjoy. These pointed (and, we hope, amusing) cartoons relate the topic of the introductory article to the economic content of the body of the chapter.

The economic topics of the chapters are broken down into 3 or 4 *analysis sections,* each headed by an organizing question, such as *"What forces determine prices in the marketplace?"* Each of these sections is further subdivided into discussions of the individual concepts that are relevant to answering the organizing question. The contents explained under the above question are *demand, supply,* and *equilibrium.* When new concepts and unfamiliar terms are introduced, they are underlined in blue in the text, as microeconomics and macroeconomics are on the previous page, and defined in the *marginal glossary.* There is also an *end-of-the-book glossary* keyed to the text pages, arranged alphabetically, incorporating all of these terms.

Each analysis section concludes with a short case that illustrates the application of the concepts covered in the section. The *case application* for the section on "What forces determine prices in the marketplace?" deals with the market for student academic talent. Following each case application

**microeconomics** the area of economic studies that deals with individual units in an economy, households, business firms, labor unions, and workers.

**macroeconomics** the area of economic studies that deals with the overall functioning of an economy, total production output, employment, the price level.

are three questions which ask you to apply the economic concepts in the preceding section to the case application. The first of the three questions should be fairly easy for you to answer if you have read the section carefully. The second question will usually be somewhat more difficult, requiring you to employ your reasoning powers in applying economic concepts. Question number three calls for your opinion based on your own attitudes and judgments, as well as what you have learned about the topic.

There is a *Putting It Together* summary of the chapter's principal economic ideas at the end of each chapter. There is also an essay on some *perspective* of the topic covered in the chapter from the viewpoint of an influential economist or from a relevant historical event that has shaped our view. The chapters then conclude with the *For Further Study and Analysis* section which includes study questions, analytical exercises, and references to books for pursuing the material in more depth. The study questions are not review questions as such, but are intended to expand and reinforce your understanding of the material and, where appropriate, to give you a chance to apply it in your own locality.

There is available a study guide, *Working With The Study of Economics*, that contains review exercises, additional applications, practice questions, and a schematic outline of each section of the chapters. To get the most out of reading the text, it is recommended that you look over the schematic outline of a chapter section before you read it and then review the outline when you have finished reading the section.

The introductory articles and case applications in the chapters are similar to those reported in the news media. They have been selected with two things in mind: their interest and relevance and their suitability for applying the economic concepts in the chapter. In some cases, the names of people and their experiences are composites of the experiences of different individuals and do not refer to an actual person.

We hope that you will look for opportunities to apply the economic understandings you gain from this book to stories currently in the news. There is a valuable collection of analytical tools in the intellectual toolbox of economics that, once you have learned how to use them, can be applied to the understanding and solution of new problems as they arise. The trick is to recognize which tools of analysis are useful for a particular problem. The knowledge and practice you get from this book should enable you to do that.

*Turley Mings*

# Unit I
# FOUNDATIONS

## Chapter 1. Economic Methods

Economics is a social science that is concerned with how resources are used to satisfy people's wants. By use of the scientific method and economic reasoning, economics enables us to understand and deal with problems that arise. The economics discipline has a set of factual and theoretical tools to apply to the solution of those problems. Descriptive charts and analytical diagrams are particularly useful tools in economics.

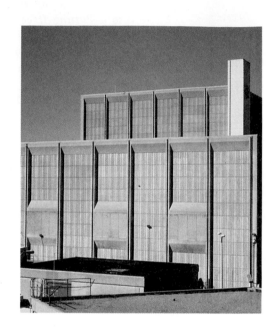

## Chapter 2. Economic Choices

Scarcity of resources relative to our needs and wants requires that we make choices about the alternative uses of those resources. In allocating resources, an economy must resolve the basic economic questions of what, how, and for whom to produce. Societies make choices in accordance with certain economic and socioeconomic goals.

The foundations of economics are the ideas that form the basis of the discipline. They are fundamental to the different areas of economic applications.

## Chapter 3. The Economic System

Societies need a system to organize and coordinate economic activities in an efficient way. This makes the different elements in an economy interdependent. There are three principal types of economic systms, but modern economies are a mixture. The United States economy is predominantly market-directed.

## Chapter 4. Market Pricing

In a market system, prices are determined by the demand for and the supply of goods and services. At the equilibrium price there is no shortage or surplus. If the conditions that determine demand or supply change, the equilibrium price and the quantity bought and sold will change.

# ECONOMIC METHODS

*The study of economics entails a special way of looking at the world around us and the way things work. It has been described as "the economic way of thinking." Once you learn it, it will come in handy in dealing with many types of situations, even some that are not necessarily thought of as being "economics." On the face of it, the subject of the introductory article for this first chapter might appear to be in the area of such natural sciences as meteorology or climatology rather than economics. But, as we shall see, its underlying causes and its ultimate effects are very much in the economics field.*

## There's Something in the Air

There is something in the air. In fact, there is a great deal too much in the air. There is too much carbon dioxide, too much methane, too much nitrous oxide, too many chlorine gases (CFCs). In short, there is too much pollution.

Air pollution is nothing new. In the first half of this century, the air in many of the industrial cities of the East and Midwest was gritty with soot particles from the coal-burning furnaces of factories and homes. This type of air pollution was replaced in the years after World War II by smog from auto exhausts and manufacturing operations. According to the Environmental Protection Agency, some 150 million people in this country live in areas where the air is unfit to breathe.

While still wrestling with the problem of what to do about the growing smog problem, we have become aware that acid rain is killing our lakes and forests. The effects of air pollution are felt in rural wilderness areas as well as in the big cities.

Now we are faced with potentially the most destructive forms of air pollution yet. There is a depletion of the ozone layer that protects us from harmful rays of the sun and a threat of global warming that could bring catastrophic changes, both environmental and economic.

The old saying that "Everybody talks about the weather, but nobody does anything about it" is, unfortunately, no longer true. We have attained the capacity to cause worldwide changes in the weather. Accumulation of gases released into the atmosphere produces a "greenhouse effect" by trapping heat near the surface of the earth. This may be likened to the way glass in a greenhouse traps heat from the sun. There is continuing research and controversy concerning the timing and expected severity of the greenhouse effect. Various climate experts predict that average temperatures will rise by anywhere from 3 to 9 degrees Fahrenheit by the middle of the next century. That would be an unprecedented change in such a short period. If it is the lower figure, it will be the largest change in recorded history. If it is the higher figure, it will make the world's climate hotter than it has been since the time of the dinosaurs, over 65 million years ago.

The consequences of such a global warming would be enormous. It would bring extreme conditions of heat, drought, and floods. There would be increased rainfall on coastal regions, with more violent storms and hurricanes. The most devastating effects could result from a melting of the Antarctic, Greenland, and Alpine glaciers. If these melted, a thermal expansion of ocean waters could raise the level of the oceans and cover low-lying coastal territories around the world. This would flood large areas, including rich agricultural land in Bangladesh, the Nile delta, China, Japan, and the Netherlands. It would displace an estimated 25 to 40 million people. Masses of environmental refugees would be forced to migrate.

In the United States, such cities as New York, New Orleans, and San Francisco would be flooded. Even whole states such as Delaware and Florida would be covered by water. Meanwhile, continental interiors would experience drought conditions. The corn and wheat belts would become deserts. The northern forests would be destroyed by insects and diseases. As rainfall declined by 40% in the central part of the country, the evaporation of Lake Michigan would leave acres of reeking mud flats around Chicago.

This is a worst-case scenario, projected by computer models. Since there has never been such a drastic climatic change in human experience, we don't know if these extreme outcomes would be lessened by offsetting effects in nature. For example, drought conditions in the interior could be reduced by increasing cloud cover.

Nonetheless, even smaller climate changes would have great effects on our way of life and on economic conditions. And we may not have to wait 50 years to see those changes. We may already be experiencing them. The six hottest years ever recorded have all occurred in the last decade. Also, according to the National Oceanic and Atmospheric Administration, the temperature of the world's oceans has risen about 0.2 degrees a year since 1982. Perhaps this is the first scientific evidence of the consequences of the greenhouse effect.

Whether or not it has actually started, there is no question that we have created the conditions for a greenhouse effect. The pri-

mary cause is the increased amount of carbon dioxide released into the air. It accounts for about half of the greenhouse gas buildup. Carbon dioxide is a natural component of air, but the amount of atmospheric carbon dioxide has increased 25% since the 1850s. From the beginning of the Industrial Revolution we have dumped some 185 billion tons of carbon dioxide into the atmosphere as a result of burning fossil fuels—coal and petroleum in particular—in factories, power plants, homes, and vehicles. Other gases contributing to the greenhouse problem are methane, nitrous oxides, and chlorofluorocarbons (CFCs).

The CFCs are doubly dangerous because not only do they add to the greenhouse effect, but their chlorine content eats away the ozone in the outer atmosphere that serves to shield us from the sun's damaging ultraviolet rays. These CFCs come mainly from refrigeration gases used in refrigerators and air conditioners. They come also from insulation and packaging materials such as the plastic boxes containing fast foods.

The Environmental Protection Agency has estimated that 60% of the global warming is the result of burning fossil fuels to generate electricity, process raw materials and manufacture goods, heat homes and offices, and power automobiles. The CFCs account for another 20%.

The problem of carbon dioxide accumulation is made worse by the destruction of the world's rain forests. Forests help to prevent carbon dioxide buildup by absorbing large quantities of it from the atmosphere. But according to Stanford University's Center for Conservation Biology, 74,000 acres of rain forest are destroyed every day. The trees are cut down for heating and cooking fuel in poor countries and to make way for agriculture. Such agriculture is usually unproductive due to the low nutrient quality of rain forest soil. Burning the trees, or letting them decay, releases their stored carbon dioxide into the air.

This reduction of forests accounts for another estimated 10% of the greenhouse effect. The remaining 10% comes largely from agri-

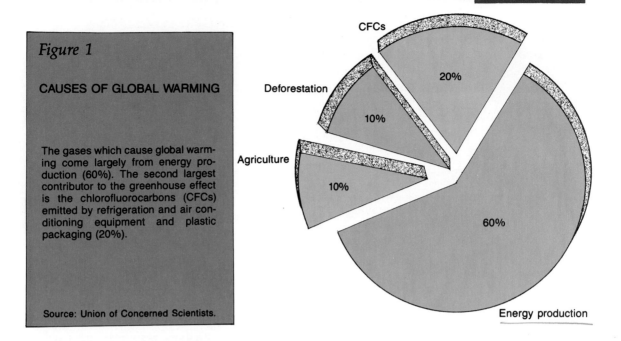

**Figure 1**

**CAUSES OF GLOBAL WARMING**

The gases which cause global warming come largely from energy production (60%). The second largest contributor to the greenhouse effect is the chlorofluorocarbons (CFCs) emitted by refrigeration and air conditioning equipment and plastic packaging (20%).

Source: Union of Concerned Scientists.

cultural operations, such as the use of artificial fertilizer.

Solving the greenhouse problem will require major changes and unprecedented worldwide cooperation. A start on this cooperation was made at a meeting in 1987 when three dozen nations signed the Montreal Protocol. They promised to cut the production of CFCs by 50% by 1998. In May 1989, the signatory countries informally pledged to ban CFCs altogether by the year 2000.

In 1990 the United States enacted a comprehensive clean air bill that greatly strengthened the 1977 Clean Air Act. It was primarily aimed at reducing smog, acid rain, and other toxic chemicals in the air. But its provisions will also reduce the amount of gases from automobile exhausts and industries that contribute to global warming.

It may even now be too late to stop the greenhouse effect and ozone depletion altogether. The gases already released into the air will continue to affect the atmosphere for years to come. The most we can hope for is to minimize future damage. Because of what the required changes mean for nations' economies and individuals' life-styles, nobody thinks that it is going to be easy.

## Chapter Preview

*Examining the problem of air pollution and its consequences provides a good illustration of economic methods. It is not an easy problem to resolve because it involves conflicting interests of different groups and public as well as private decisions. We will use it as a reference case for the questions: What is economics? What are the tools of economics? What are the uses of graphs? The chapter is followed by an appendix on how to construct and interpret line graphs.*

## Learning Objectives

*After completing this chapter, you should be able to:*

1. *Explain scarcity as an economic term.*
2. *List the factors of production.*
3. *Describe the steps in the scientific method.*
4. *Describe three types of factual tools used in economics.*
5. *Describe the theoretical tools used in economics.*
6. *Give four examples of different types of charts.*
7. *Explain what an analytical diagram is used for.*
8. *Draw and label an analytical diagram showing the relationship between two variables.*

*Scarcity: the limited resources for production relative to the wants and limits.*

## What Is Economics?

*factor of production (resources used to produce goods and services):*
*- land*
*- labor*
*- capital*
*- entrepreneur.*

A standard definition of economics is that "economics is the social science concerned with how <u>resources</u> are used to satisfy people's wants." This section discusses the basis of economics as a science and the methods it uses.

**Scarcity**   Global warming and the destruction of the ozone layer are problems that naturally lend themselves to the study of economics because their underlying causes are economic. They have enormous economic consequences. They involve dealing with <u>scarcity</u>. The need for a science of economics comes from scarcity. We have only a limited amount of resources to satisfy our unlimited wants for goods and services. As a result, we need to economize on the use of those resources, to get the greatest benefit out of the resources available.

Resources used to produce goods and services, called the <u>factors of production</u>, consist of <u>land</u>, <u>labor</u>, and <u>capital</u>. Land includes all natural resources—the minerals under the surface, the forests on it, and even the air above it. Labor refers to all types of human resources, managers and professionals as well as manual and clerical workers. <u>Entrepreneurs</u> are a particular type of human resource. They are individuals who see the possibility of profitable production and organize the resources to produce a good or service.

Capital refers to the machinery, factories, and office buildings used in production. <u>Technology</u> and information, both of which have increasing importance in today's economy, are also classified as capital resources. Financial capital is not a real resource like the factors of production, but it enables entrepreneurs and managers to purchase any of the factors of production.

**resources**   the inputs that are used in production. Includes natural resources (minerals, timber, rivers), labor (blue collar, white collar), and capital (machinery, buildings).

**scarcity**   the limited resources for production relative to the wants for goods and services.

**factors   of   production**   another name for the production resources of land (natural resources), labor, and capital (machinery and buildings).

**land**   all natural resources including fields, forests, mineral deposits, the sea, and other gifts of nature.

**labor**   all human resources including manual, clerical, technical, professional, and managerial labor.

**capital**   the means of production including factories, office buildings, machinery, tools, and equipment; alternatively, it can mean financial capital, the money to acquire the foregoing and employ land and labor resources.

**entrepreneur**   a business innovator who sees the opportunity to make a profit from a new product, new process, or unexploited raw material and then brings together the land, labor, and capital to exploit the opportunity, risking failure.

**technology**   the body of skills and knowledge that comprises the processes used in production.

**financial capital**   the money to acquire the factors of production.

**SIZE OF THE UNITED STATES LABOR FORCE**
**1950–1990**

*Figure 2*

Labor force (millions)

Source: U.S. Bureau of Labor Statistics, *Employment and Earnings.*
*1990 projected on the basis of 10-year trend.

Labor is the most important factor of production. The United States labor force grew twice as much in the last twenty years as it did in the previous two decades.

Even in such a wealthy country as the United States, we do not have enough of these resources to satisfy all of our wants. How does resource scarcity apply to the case of air pollution? If there is one thing that you would think there is enough of, it is air. And there would be sufficient air if only it were not used as a garbage dump for the by-products of our production activities.

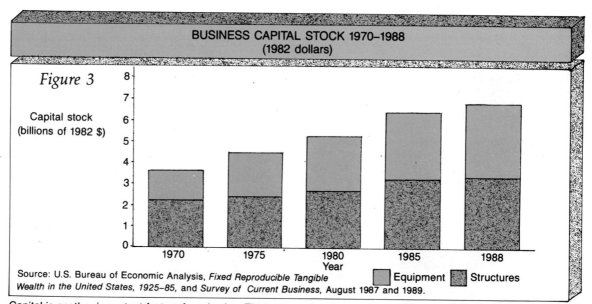

**BUSINESS CAPITAL STOCK 1970–1988**
**(1982 dollars)**

*Figure 3*

Capital stock (billions of 1982 $)

Source: U.S. Bureau of Economic Analysis, *Fixed Reproducible Tangible Wealth in the United States, 1925–85,* and *Survey of Current Business,* August 1987 and 1989.

Equipment    Structures

Capital is another important factor of production. The amount of real capital has almost doubled since 1970. The stock of equipment has increased faster than structures.

There must be a demand for an item in order for it to be scarce in the economic sense. These one-clawed lobsters are more rare than lobsters with two claws, but because there is no great demand for them they are not considered as scarce.

This example underlines the fact that, in economics, scarcity is not the same thing as rarity. We have more air than anything else on the planet. But because of competing uses for it, air, at least pure air, has become very scarce. On the other hand, a thing could be rare; but if no one wants it, it is not scarce. For example, radioactive waste is rare but not scarce.

**The scientific method** Economics, like other sciences, makes use of the scientific method. This consists of (1) observing an event, (2) devising an explanation (hypothesis) that accounts for that event, (3) testing the hypothesis by gathering additional information and observing whether a repeat of the conditions assumed by the hypothesis leads to the same result, and (4) tentatively accepting, revising, or rejecting the hypothesis, depending on whether it correctly predicts a repetition of the event.

For the study of the greenhouse effect, the scientific

**scientific method** a procedure used by scientists to develop explanations for events and test the validity of those explanations.

**hypothesis** a tentative explanation of an event; used as a basis for further research.

*Table 1*                                   THE SCIENTIFIC METHOD

| Procedure | Example |
| --- | --- |
| 1. Observe event. | 1. Observe global warming. |
| 2. Make hypothesis to explain the event. | 2. The accumulation of gases in the atmosphere traps the sun's heat. |
| 3. Test the hypothesis by performing experiments (if that is possible), gathering additional evidence on the relationship between the effects and the assumed cause, predicting future events on the basis of the hypothesis, and observing whether or not the predictions are accurate. | 3. Gather information on atmospheric gases; experiment on the effects of those gases; study data on the relationship between temperature change and pollution; predict future temperature increases based on the increasing pollution; observe whether or not the predictions are accurate. |
| 4. Tentatively accept, or revise, or reject the hypothesis, depending on whether it explains the event. | 4. Tentatively accept the greenhouse effect hypothesis to explain global warming. |

The scientific method of investigation can be applied to the specific case of global warming.

method involved observing the steady increase in average global temperatures. It required forming a hypothesis. The hypothesis was that the increase in temperature is due to the buildup of gases in the atmosphere that trap the sun's heat. The scientific method involved testing this hypothesis.

The testing itself necessitated gathering information on the types and quantities of gases. It involved performing experiments on the effects of those gases on the retention of the sun's heat. It also involved studying data from the past on temperature changes and atmospheric pollution. It included measuring the relationship between the continuing accumulation of gases in the atmosphere and rising global temperatures.

The increase detected in ocean temperatures is further evidence consistent with the greenhouse hypothesis. With the evidence supporting the hypothesis, it is tentatively accepted. It is accepted until there is any new information that might lead to a different conclusion.

Economics makes use of the scientific method, but it differs from some of the other sciences—laboratory sciences such as chemistry—because it is a social science. Economists are not usually able to conduct controlled experiments in order to test hypotheses. They must depend on the observation of real-world events, which seldom occur under exactly the same conditions from one time to the next. Economics is not, therefore, an exact science.

**Economic reasoning** An alternative definition of economics is that economics is the way an economist thinks. The science of economics is characterized by a particular way of analyzing problems. It is called the economic way of

In poor countries, the need to use forests for firewood often outweighs the economic—and environmental—consequences. Economic policies must take such value judgments into consideration.

*Economics – not an exact science but depend on logical analysis, using principles of economics. (take inconsideration objective facts,*

**economic reasoning** the application of theoretical and factual tools of economic analysis to explaining economic developments or solving economic problems.
**free good** a production or consumption good that does not have a direct cost.
**economic good** any good or service which sells for a price; that is, not a free good.

thinking or economic reasoning. Whatever their personal and political views, economists have a similar approach to examining the way the world works. They make use of a common set of tools of economic analysis. (We will discuss what these tools are in the next section.)

The case of air pollution provides an illustration of what is unique about the economic way of thinking. Air pollution has reached serious levels because individuals, businesses, and frequently even governments treat air as a free good. Since it does not have a direct cost, as do economic goods, air is freely used to dispose of exhaust gases, without regard to its scarcity. According to the economic way of thinking, on the other hand, all costs should be included as costs of production, whether they are paid by the producer or not.

The economic way of thinking would generally prefer an antipollution policy that forces producers to bear all of the social costs of production. This includes the pollution costs. To most economists, that would be a better policy than one that imposes an outright ban on pollution. (Antipollution policies are discussed in chapter 8 on Government and Business.)

Since economics is not an exact science, economists depend to a great extent on logical analysis, making use of the principles of economics. These principles include assumptions about how people, businesses, and governments behave. On the basis of these assumptions, economists predict the results of particular events or policies; for example, what the results would be of taxing pollution. Economic reasoning consists of applying economic principles to explain events, predict outcomes, and recommend policies.

Because of differences in individual preferences and belief systems, economics must also take value judgments into account. A policy which makes sense economically may not be acceptable if it violates people's sense of what is right or just. For example, poor countries may not prevent their citizens from cutting down trees for firewood, despite the economic consequences, if that is the only source of heat they can afford. Policies to reduce global warming must take this value judgment into account.

Economic reasoning is similar to the process of critical thinking. You will have a chance to practice critical thinking skills frequently as you go through this book. For example, the Economic Reasoning questions following the Case Applications at the end of each chapter analysis section call for critical thinking. The first question in each set of three is a comprehension question. The second question involves economic analysis and critical thinking skills. The third question calls for you to apply your own value judgments, along with economic reasoning, in arriving at an answer.

# case application

## The Vanishing Land

In the United States land is disappearing at a rapid rate. Millions of acres have disappeared in the last decade. In Western Europe 1% disappears every 4 or 5 years. Land is disappearing at an even faster rate in much of the less-developed areas of the world.

The vanishing land has not ceased to exist, of course. It is disappearing because it is being covered over by expanding cities, highways, and reservoirs, or it is being stripped away for mining. Many of these activities serve a useful purpose, but much of the land that is "disappearing" is farmland, and the production of food is a basic necessity.

Every year the United States loses about 1.4 million acres of agricultural land to development, and the rate is increasing. Unless the situation changes, urban development in this country in the next 25 years will consume a land area equivalent to that of New Hampshire, Vermont, Massachusetts, and Rhode Island combined.

Additional croplands are being lost to erosion because of farming methods that do not practice conservation. According to a report by the Department of Agriculture, about 3 billion tons of topsoil are being eroded from U.S. croplands every year. For every ton of grain produced, 6 tons of soil are lost to erosion. In Iowa, before the land was cultivated, there was a layer of topsoil that averaged about 16 inches. Today that layer is down to 8 inches, and it continues to diminish.

The conversion of cropland to urban uses and the erosion of topsoil is happening in countries around the globe. Worldwide, erosion is destroying 23 million acres of cropland every year. India may be losing its topsoil at four times the U.S. rate and China even faster: the Yellow River carries 1.6 billion tons

Every year the United States loses about 1.4 million acres of agricultural land to development, and the rate is increasing.

of sediment to the sea each year. Some population experts predict that the earth's population will double in the next generation. If world food output is barely adequate for present needs, what will happen in the future when more food will have to be produced on less available agricultural land?

### Economic Reasoning

1. Which factor of production is becoming more scarce as a result of urban development and wasteful farming practices?
2. Present a hypothesis that explains the reduction in cropland around the world. Can your hypothesis be tested? How?
3. Do you think that the government should force farmers to use farming methods that reduce soil erosion, even though those methods might lower farmers' income? Why or why not?

13

*[handwritten: Statistic = data — tool in finding an average.]*

# What Are the Tools of Economics?

Important in the economic way of thinking are the factual and theoretical tools of economics. Many of them are useful in analyzing the problem of air pollution.

**Factual tools**  The factual tools used by economists are statistics, history, and how institutions operate.

The term "statistics" has a couple of meanings. First, statistics are the data, the figures that economists use in various economic measurements such as production, prices, or unemployment. Second, statistics can refer to the methods employed in studying the data, such as finding an average.

Statistics are often essential to understanding a problem and determining what to do about it. For example, data on the destruction of the rain forests and the contribution it makes to global warming is important in forming interna-

**statistics**  the data on economic variables; also the techniques of analyzing, interpreting, and presenting data.
**institutions**  decision-making units, established practices, or laws.

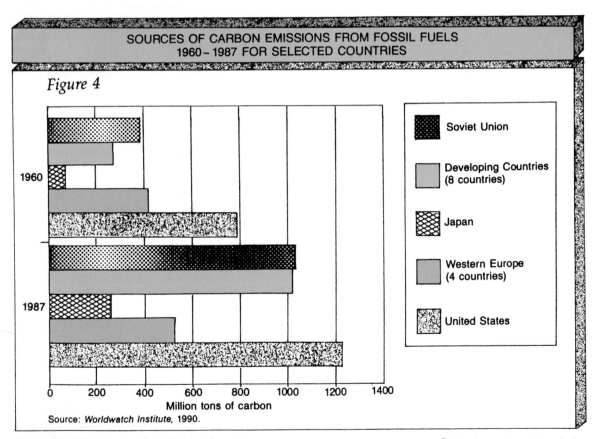

**SOURCES OF CARBON EMISSIONS FROM FOSSIL FUELS 1960–1987 FOR SELECTED COUNTRIES**

Figure 4

Legend:
- Soviet Union
- Developing Countries (8 countries)
- Japan
- Western Europe (4 countries)
- United States

Million tons of carbon

Source: *Worldwatch Institute*, 1990.

Carbon dioxide pollution has been increasing from sources around the world. The most rapid increases have come in the Soviet Union and the developing countries of Asia, Africa, and Latin America. The major source, however, is still the United States because of the quantity of its energy production, industrial output, and motor vehicles.

tional policies to slow the greenhouse effect. But obtaining accurate statistical information can be difficult.

History, especially economic history, is another useful tool in helping economists understand what is going on and how to deal with current problems. The experience of the industrial countries of North America and Western Europe has been that their economic growth was accompanied by greatly increased use of fossil fuels to power their economic expansion. If the developing countries of Asia, Africa, and Latin America follow the same path to economic growth, global warming will speed up. The worst-case scenario will likely occur sooner. Figure 4 shows that as the total amount of carbon dioxide in the atmosphere has increased, a rising proportion of it has come from the developing countries.

Institutions are important organizations, customs, or patterns of behavior in a society. In economics, institutions can be a wide variety of things. They may vary from the banking system to labor unions, from the legal principle of private property ownership to the federal bureaucracy. They include the military, the media, accounting practices, and the zero population movement.

The institution of private property has permitted the owners of automobiles and factories to use their property in such a way that public welfare is injured by air pollution. To reduce the pollution problem, the institution of private property is now being modified. Owners are being restricted from using their property without regard to how the environment is affected.

**Theoretical tools**  The principal theoretical tools that are used in economics are concepts and models. Economic concepts are ideas. They are words or phrases that convey a specific meaning in economics. The sub-sections in the chapters of this book are organized by major concepts that are shown in **bold type.**

Other concepts are underlined in blue and defined in the marginal glossary, especially if their meaning in economics is different or more precise than the meaning of the word in general. Usually a concept means the same in economics as it does in ordinary usage. But sometimes it has a particular meaning. In economics, for instance, the concept of scarcity does not indicate that there is necessarily only a small amount of something. Instead, it takes into account the amount available relative to the amount desired.

The most important theoretical tools of economists are economic models, which are simplified representations of the real world. Models are abstractions, reflecting only the most important aspects of a situation. A model of the greenhouse effect would show the relationship between the

The capitol building in Washington, D.C., symbolizes an important American institution, Congress.

economic concept  a word or phrase that conveys an economic idea.
economic model  a simplified representation of the cause and effect relationships in a particular situation. Models may be in verbal, graphic, or equation form.

Owners of private property are being restricted from using it without regard to how the environment is affected. This North Carolina farmer is not free to spray his corn with whatever pesticide he chooses.

accumulation of gases in the atmosphere and global warming. It would not include other factors that might cause temperatures to vary from one year to the next such as upper atmosphere winds, particles from volcanic activity, and so forth.

Models can be stated in words, or as mathematical equations. They can be shown visually as graphs. The graphic form is the most common and useful in studying economics. We will examine different types of graphs and how they are used in the next section.

# case application

## Does It Pay to Go to College?

It has long been assumed that the investment of time and money in a college education is justified by the increased earning power that results from having a college degree. This view came into question in the 1970s when there was a decrease in the relative value of a college degree. Between 1970 and 1980, the earnings advantage of a college degree over a high school degree decreased by 40%.

But during the 1980s the trend was reversed. A study by Frank S. Levy, an economist at the University of Maryland, shows that in the last decade there was a rapidly widening gap between the value of a high

More is involved in judging the value of a college education than a simple comparison of incomes with costs.

school and college degree. In 1979 male college graduates between the ages of 25 and 34 earned, on the average, 18% more than high school graduates of the same age. By the late 1980s the "college premium" had jumped to 43%. There was a similar increase in the earnings advantage of female college graduates, though not as large.

Not only do college graduates earn more, they are more likely to have a job. Richard B. Freeman of Harvard University found that male workers aged 25 to 34 with less than a high school education had a 12.1% unemployment rate in 1988. The unemployment rate for those with a high school degree was 6.7% and for college graduates a low 2.1%.

Although statistics show that college graduates make more money and have better job security than high school graduates, are the extra earning power and security enough to offset the high cost of a college education? Something that would help answer this question is an economic model called a *cost-benefit analysis*. A cost-benefit model compares the costs of a project (in this case, a college education) with the value of the benefits of the project. If the value of the benefits exceeds the costs, the project is worthwhile.

What would be included in a simple form of cost-benefit model of a college education? The most obvious benefit is the increased earning power of a college degree projected over a person's lifetime. The average expected lifetime earnings of a high school graduate is $1,667,000. By comparison, college graduates can expect to earn $4,142,000, on the average.

On the other side of the cost-benefit calculation, the largest costs are the direct costs of attending college and the sacrificed income that would have been earned by the student if he or she had not attended college.

Taking the college premium of increased earnings accumulated over a lifetime and dividing it into the sum of the direct and sacrificed earnings costs of attending college, the investment in college appears to have a higher return than that of other long-term personal financial investments.

But for the individual student, whether or not it pays to get a college degree may depend on considerations other than purely financial ones. Does a degree provide more job opportunities? Do college graduates express more job satisfaction than high school graduates? Is there more job security? More is involved in judging the value of a college education than a simple comparison of incomes with costs. A model is only as good as the assumptions on which it is built and the data which is fed into it, but in economics it is an essential analytical tool.

## Economic Reasoning

1. What factual tools of economic reasoning do you find in this application?
2. What theoretical tools of economic analysis do you find in this application?
3. What additional nonmonetary benefits of attending college might be included in a complete model of the advantages of a college education? Are there nonmonetary costs as well? What are they? In your view, would a complete cost-benefit model of a college education justify it or not? Why?

# What Are the Uses of Graphs?

It is increasingly important to be able to read and use graphs. Besides being important in studying economics, it helps you understand a great deal of what appears in the news media. It also is becoming more necessary for today's occupations.

**Descriptive charts**  <u>Charts</u> are widely used to present information, frequently statistical data, visually. One type of chart commonly seen is the *pie chart*. Pie charts are used to show the relative size of the components of a whole. An example is the chart on page 7 showing the amounts contributed by different sources to the greenhouse buildup. That chart is reproduced below, in its basic form, as Figure 5 (it is renumbered for simplicity's sake, to avoid being confused with Figure 1).

The graph showing the size of the United States labor forces reproduced on the next page as Figure 6, represents another type of chart. It is a *line graph* which shows how the number of workers in the labor force has changed over the years. The number of workers is a <u>variable</u> with the quantity measured on the left vertical axis of the graph. The years are shown on the bottom horizontal axis. This type of graph, with the values of the variable measured on the vertical axis and the years shown on the horizontal axis, is called a <u>time series</u>.

**chart** a graphic representation of statistical data or other information.
**variable** a quantity—such as number of workers, amount of carbon dioxide, interest rate, amount of cropland, etc.—whose value changes in relationship to changes in the values of other associated items.
**time series** the changes in the values of a variable over time; a chart in which time—generally years—is one of the variables.

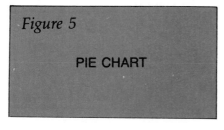

*Figure 5*

PIE CHART

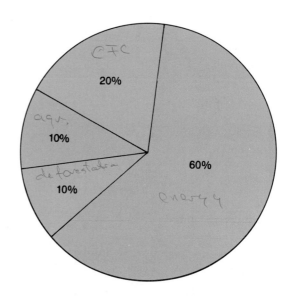

CFC
20%
agr.
10%
deforestation
10%
60%
energy

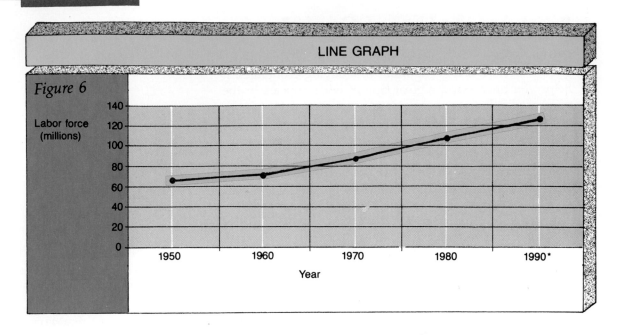

**LINE GRAPH**

*Figure 6*

Labor force
(millions)

Year

Another commonly seen graph is the *column chart*. It is useful in comparing the value of one variable with another or comparing the values of a variable over a period of time. An example of the column chart is Figure 3 on page 9. This is a stacked column chart which shows how the quantity of capital used by industries has increased over time. It also shows how much of the capital stock consists of machinery

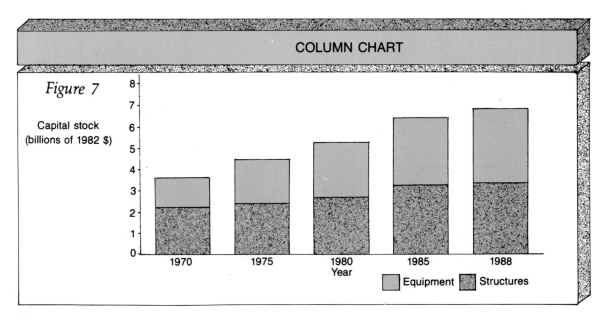

**COLUMN CHART**

*Figure 7*

Capital stock
(billions of 1982 $)

Year

Equipment    Structures

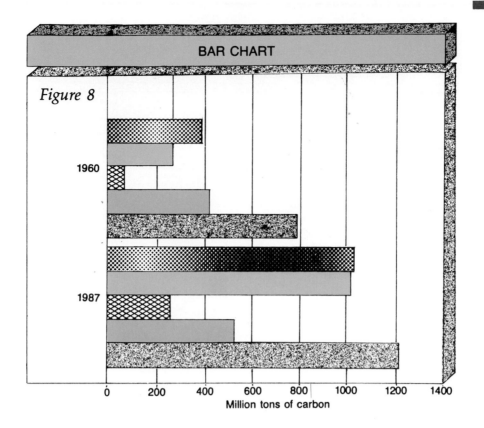

**BAR CHART**

*Figure 8*

1960

1987

0    200    400    600    800    1000    1200    1400
Million tons of carbon

and equipment. It shows how much consists of factory buildings and other commercial structures. The basic form of the chart is shown as Figure 7.

*Bar charts* are like column charts turned on their side. Figure 4 on page 14, reproduced in Figure 8 above, shows how much the total amount of carbon dioxide emissions has increased since 1960. It also shows how the relative amounts contributed by different countries has changed.

An *area chart* is particularly suited to demonstrating how the relative importance of different components of a variable change over time. The chart on page 302 is an area chart showing how the composition of total unemployment has changed. There are additional types of charts—scatter charts, range charts, three-dimensional charts—but the ones described above are those most commonly encountered.

**Analytical diagrams** Economic diagrams are visual models. They resemble line charts, but instead of showing how a variable changes over time or with respect to a country or industry or other category, a diagram shows how two or more variables relate to each other. They are graphic models based on observation and economic reasoning.

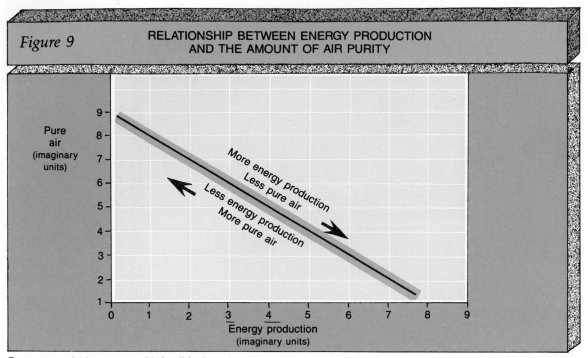

**Figure 9** — RELATIONSHIP BETWEEN ENERGY PRODUCTION AND THE AMOUNT OF AIR PURITY

Because producing energy with fossil fuels emits carbon dioxide and other gases, the more energy that is produced, the less pure air there is.

As an example of such a model, let us take the relationship between energy production and air purity. In Figure 9 above, we measure the amount of energy production on the horizontal axis and the amount of pure air on the vertical axis. The measurements of the amounts of energy production and pure air both begin at 0 in the lower left corner of the diagram. The amount of energy production increases to the right on the horizontal axis and the amount of pure air increases as we move up the vertical axis. The purpose of the diagram is to show the interaction between energy production and air purity.

Figure 9 shows that the more energy that is produced, the less pure air there is. The relationship between the two variables is an inverse relationship; as the amount of one increases, the amount of the other decreases. (If two variables were to increase together and decrease together, they would have a direct relationship.) We will make more use of this type of model in the next chapter.

Diagrams are used a great deal in studying economics to illustrate economic principles. If you are not experienced with diagrams, you should read the appendix to this chapter and practice drawing diagrams to become familiar with them.

**inverse relationship** a relationship between two variables in which the value of one decreases as the value of the other increases.
**direct relationship** a relationship between two variables in which their values increase and decrease together.

# case application

## The Energy Gluttons

When we looked to see who the enemy was, it was us. In our growing concern over the greenhouse effect, we must recognize that the United States is the major contributor to the problem. We emit the most carbon dioxide and other greenhouse gases into the atmosphere. This country is responsible for over 20% of the carbon dioxide buildup in the atmosphere, although we have only 5% of the world's population. The explanation lies in our high energy consumption, energy that is produced mainly by burning fossil fuels. The United States consumes almost one-quarter of world energy production.

The U.S. share of world energy consumption is down, however, from earlier years. In 1960 it was 37% (see Table 2 below). Our high energy consumption correlates with our large amount of production of goods and services. This country is responsible for nearly one-quarter of the world's output of goods and services.

Nevertheless, on an individual basis, we consume an excessive amount of energy. On the average, each American consumes twice the amount of energy consumed by someone in West Germany or Japan. The largest portion of our energy consumption goes for transportation. Cars and trucks account for some 67% of the oil burned in this country.

Cars and trucks account for some 67% of the oil burned in the United States, which consumes almost one-quarter of world energy production.

By contrast, only 44% of the oil used in Western Europe and 35% in Japan is linked to transportation.

To conserve oil and reduce carbon dioxide emissions, it has been proposed that we sharply increase the gasoline tax, to as much as $1.00 a gallon. It is hoped that such an increase would cause us to go on an energy diet and give up our gluttonous ways.

### Economic Reasoning

1. Which type of graph would be appropriate to show the information in Table 2? Why? *Bar chart. Different countries in different years.*
2. Draw the graph and label it. Explain what the graph shows.
3. Are you in favor of raising the federal gas tax from 14¢ a gallon to $1.00 a gallon? Why or why not?

---

*Table 2*      PERCENT OF WORLD ENERGY CONSUMPTION BY REGION
1960–1987

| Year | United States | Europe | Soviet Union | Asia | Other |
|------|---------------|--------|--------------|------|-------|
| 1960 | 37 | 27 | 15 | 13 | 8 |
| 1970 | 34 | 27 | 16 | 14 | 9 |
| 1980 | 28 | 25 | 17 | 19 | 11 |
| 1987 | 24 | 23 | 19 | 22 | 12 |

Source: Statistical Office of the United Nations, *Energy Statistics Yearbook*, annual.

The U.S. share of world energy consumption is down from earlier years.

Seventy-four thousand acres of rain forest are being destroyed every day. This reduction of forests accounts for an estimated 10% of the greenhouse effect.

# Putting It Together

Economics is the social science concerned with how resources are used to satisfy people's wants. The science of economics arises from the need to overcome *scarcity*. The *resources* available for production are not sufficient to satisfy all our wants. We need therefore to use them in such a way as to maximize output. These *factors of production* are *land* (all natural resources), *labor* (including managerial and professional), and *capital* (machinery, buildings, technology, and information). *Financial capital* is used by *entrepreneurs* and managers to purchase the factors of production.

The *scientific method* is a process of observing events, forming *hypotheses* concerning their causes, testing the hypotheses, and rejecting, revising, or tentatively accepting them. Economics makes use of the scientific method; but it is a social science, not a laboratory science, and cannot do controlled experiments. It applies logical analysis based on economic principles to explain events, predict outcomes, and recommend policies. Economic policies must take into account an individual's and a society's value judgments as well.

*Economic reasoning* is based on the application of economic principles and the use of a common set of tools of economic analysis. *Free goods* do not have a direct cost, while *economic goods* do.

Economics makes use of factual and theoretical tools. The factual tools are *statistics*, history, and the functioning of *institutions*. The theoretical tools are *economic concepts*, words that may have a more specialized meaning in economics than they do in general use, and *economic models*, simplified representations of the real world. Models may be in verbal, mathematical, or visual form.

Graphs may be charts that visually present statistical information, or they may be diagrams that show the relationship of *variables* to each other in an economic model. It depends on the nature of the information to be shown. Charts may take the form of pie charts, line charts, columnar charts, bar charts, or others. Charts that show the values of a variable over a succession of years are called *time series*.

Diagrams are visual models based on observation and economic reasoning. In the case of energy production and air purity, the two variables have an *inverse* rather than a *direct relationship*.

# Perspective

## The Master Model Builder

**Paul Anthony Samuelson (born 1915)**
Born in Gary, Indiana, Samuelson attended the University of Chicago, the temple of conservative economics. He studied under a number of the leading economists of the time, some with well-deserved reputations as tyrants in their classes. The young Samuelson had the guts and the knowledge to challenge them when he thought they had made a mistake—and get away with it.

He graduated in 1935 and would have been happy to pursue a doctoral degree at Chicago. But the scholarship that he received required him to change schools, so he went to Harvard, where he received his Ph.D. in 1941. Since 1940 he has been on the faculty of the Massachusetts Institute of Technology.

In 1947, at the age of 32, he published *Foundations of Modern Economics*. Milton Friedman, himself a University of Chicago product and quite conservative (see Perspective, p. xx), wrote *Foundations* that "immediately established his [Samuelson's] reputation as a brilliant and original mathematical economist" (*Newsweek*, November 9, 1970, p. 80).

Samuelson's introductory economics text was published a year later. It was subsequently translated into other languages and published in a number of countries. In 1958, in collaboration with two coauthors, he published *Linear Programming and Economic Analysis*.

In 1970, the second year that the Nobel Prize in economics was awarded, it went to an American, Paul Samuelson. It was in recognition of his outstanding work in constructing economic models. According to the Nobel Prize citation: "By his many contributions, Samuelson has done more than any other contemporary economist to raise the level of scientific analysis in economic theory."

Samuelson got off to a fast start in becoming the first American to win a Nobel Prize in economics. As an undergraduate student at the University of Chicago, he was allowed to attend graduate economics classes. Some leading economists today, who were then graduate students in those classes, report that they were intimidated by his intellectual ability. Remembering the "shock" of encountering Samuelson as a competitor in class, one of those graduate students, Martin Bronfenbrenner, now a renowned economist himself, has said of the course instructor, "I shall always be grateful for [the professor's] kindly assurances that one need not really be another Samuelson to pass muster as an economist" (Feiwel, p. 349. See Further Reading). Before he finished graduate school, Samuelson had published two papers that set forth models that were major contributions to economic theory. His subsequent articles fill four large volumes of *The Collected Scientific Papers of Paul Samuelson*.

The mathematical models in those papers are not easy reading, even for other economists. But Samuelson proved his versatility by writing an introductory textbook that was the most successful economics text of all time. *Economics: An Introductory Analysis* (1948) was the leading introductory economics text for two decades, selling over 3 million copies.

In addition to his activities as a researcher and textbook writer, Samuelson has been a columnist for *Newsweek* magazine and an adviser to the government during the Kennedy administration. He has been a teacher most of his life and an occasional speculator in the commodities market. The success of his textbook and commodities speculation made Samuelson a millionaire. By excelling in the world of finance as well as scholarship, he joins another great economist of the past, John Maynard Keynes, who is the subject of the Perspective in chapter 12.

Samuelson the scientist and capitalist is also Samuelson the social critic who believes that government economic activities have been too much "suppressed—so that we have public squalor along with private, really decadent, opulence" (*Science News*, Oct 31, 1970, p. 348).

# For Further Study and Analysis

## Study Questions

1. Give all of the examples of scarcity that you can find in the introductory article on air pollution.
2. Name something, in addition to radioactive waste, that is rare but is not scarce.
3. What productive resources are used in your school? Do any of them appear to be more scarce than others? Which ones?
4. On the basis of your observation of which factors of production are especially scarce in your school, devise a hypothesis to explain their scarcity. How could that hypothesis be tested?
5. Why is information listed as a factor of production?
6. Name another "free good" besides air. Does excessive use of that good lead to problems in the way that unrestricted use of air has led to global warming and depletion of the ozone layer?
7. What example of each of the three factual tools used in economics do you find in the case application on "Energy Gluttons" (p. 23)?
8. Do you find any economic concepts or models in that application? What are they?
9. What type of chart would be most appropriate for showing how your time is allocated during a weekday between attending school, traveling, eating, studying, engaging in leisure activities, sleeping, and other? Draw such a graph in its basic form and label it.
10. What variables are involved in the case application on "The Vanishing Land" (p. 13)? Pick two of those variables that have an inverse relationship and draw a diagram that shows that inverse relationship.

## Exercises in Analysis

1. Visit a local business and gather information on the factors of production used in that business. Ask the manager if there have been any recent technological improvements in the operations of the business. Write a short paper describing what resources are used in the business.
2. Prepare a short paper describing the school that you attend using the factual tools of economic analysis.
3. Prepare a cost-benefit analysis model of your own education.
4. Find examples in newspapers or magazines of the following types of graphs: pie charts, line charts, column charts, and bar charts. For each type, identify what the variable is that is being measured and what it is being measured with respect to (time, industries, states, etc.).

## Further Reading

Abrahamson, Dean Edwin, ed. *The Challenge of Global Warming*. Washington, D.C.: Island Press, 1989. This book contains articles on the impacts of the greenhouse effect, the biology of global warming, its physical consequences, the greenhouse gases, and alternate policy responses. The articles tend to be more technical than the Schneider selection listed below concerning global warming.

Bisconti, Ann Staufer, and Lewis C. Solomon. *Job Satisfaction After College: The Graduates' Viewpoint*. Bethlehem, Pa.: The CPC Foundation, 1977. Covers attitudes toward work and the relationship between occupational choice and job satisfaction.

Brown, E. Cary, and Robert M. Solow, eds. *Paul Samuelson and Modern Economic Theory*. New York: McGraw-Hill, 1983. This book is a *festschrift*, a collection of articles published to honor a scholar, which the Feiwel book (see below) claims not to be. The lead monograph is by Samuelson himself and provides an insight into his personality.

Feiwel, George R., ed. *Samuelson and Neoclassical Economics*. Boston: Kluwer-Nijhoff Publishing, 1982. A varied selection of monographs by representative scholars of widely divergent perceptions discussing, sometimes critically, Samuelson's "history-making contributions to and impact on the economics of our age."

Flavin, Christopher. "Slowing Global Warming" in Worldwatch Institute Report *State of the World-1990*. New York: W. W. Norton, 1990. The Worldwatch Institute publishes an annual report on "progress toward a sustainable society" which surveys the status of environmental and food conditions in the world. This article describes the causes of the greenhouse effect and alternative strategies for lessening its impact.

Logue, A. W. *The Psychology of Eating and Drinking*. New York: W. H. Freeman and Co.,

1986. Describes scientific inquiries into food consumption, both normal and abnormal behaviors such as overeating and obesity.

McAllister, Donald M., ed. *Environment: A New Focus for Land-use Planning*. Washington, D.C.: National Science Foundation, 1973. Monographs and Conference Committee reports on the social, economic, and environmental factors in land-use planning.

McKibben, William. *The End of Nature*. New York: Random House, 1989. A popular and personalized treatment of the greenhouse effect problem. The author suggests that we can follow one of two paths in dealing with environmental problems: we can defy nature and continue with our customary practices or we can humble ourselves to nature's requirements.

Quay, Richard H. *The Costs and Benefits (Mainly Economic) of a College Degree*. Monticello, Ill.: Vance Bibliographies, 1979. A selective bibliography of publications on the subject. Available from Vance Bibliographies, P.O. Box 229, Monticello, Ill. 61856.

Rhoads, Steven E. *The Economist's View of the World*. Cambridge, U.K.: Cambridge University Press, 1985. "This book is written, first and foremost, for intelligent, educated readers who are interested in domestic public policy and who know little or nothing about economics." (From the preface.)

Schneider, Stephen H. *Global Warming: Are We Entering the Greenhouse Century?* San Francisco: Sierra Club Books, 1989. Examines the impact of human activity on the environment. Evaluates the arguments favoring climate stability due to negative feedback processes that offset climatic changes.

*The Encyclopedic Dictionary of Economics*. 4th ed. Guilford, Conn.: Dushkin Publishing Group, 1991. Explanations of economic terms, theories, and institutions, organized alphabetically.

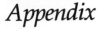

# *Appendix* CONSTRUCTING AND READING DIAGRAMS

Here is how the points on a diagram are constructed. Let us take a noneconomic example that is familiar—an automobile trip. Our destination is 200 miles away. We are interested in how long it will take us to get there and where we will be at different times along the way.

In order to show this information graphically, let us draw a diagram that measures the driving time in hours on the horizontal axis and the distance covered in miles on the vertical axis. The axes with their appropriate scales are shown in Figure A.

How far we travel in a given amount of time depends, of course, on our driving speed. If we drive at a constant 40 miles per hour, at the end of the first hour we will have covered 40 miles, at the end of the second hour 80 miles, and so forth. The relationship between time and distance traveled is plotted in Figure B on the opposite page. At the 1-hour mark on the horizontal axis, a vertical line is drawn—referred to as a perpendicular. At the 40-mile mark on the vertical axis, an intersecting line is drawn—also called a perpendicular because it is perpendicular to that axis. Where the two lines cross at point A is the first point plotted on the time-distance diagram.

If we plot the additional distances traveled at the end of each subsequent hour of driving time in the same fashion,

Measurement scales for the items being compared are put on the horizontal and vertical axes of the diagram.

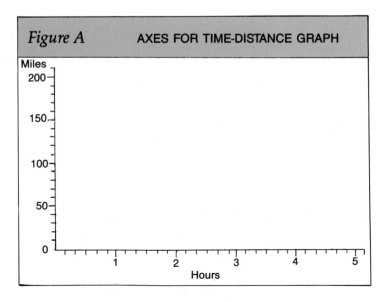

Figure A — AXES FOR TIME-DISTANCE GRAPH

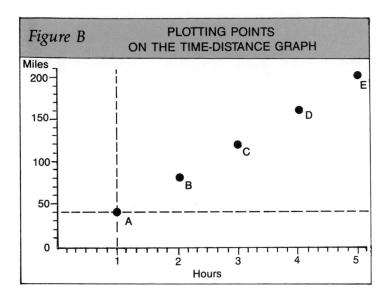

Points are plotted on the diagram showing the distance traveled each hour at a speed of 40 miles per hour.

we find points B, C, D, and E. At the end of 5 hours, we will reach our destination 200 miles away.

The dots in Figure B show how far we have gone at the end of each hour. Since we are traveling at a constant rate of speed, a line connecting the dots shows the distance traveled at any point in time. Such a line showing the relationship between two variables—here time and distance—is generally referred to as a curve, even when it is a straight line as it is in this case. The line in Figure C we can label the 40-mph Travel Curve.

To find how far we have traveled at any particular time, we draw a perpendicular from the horizontal axis to the

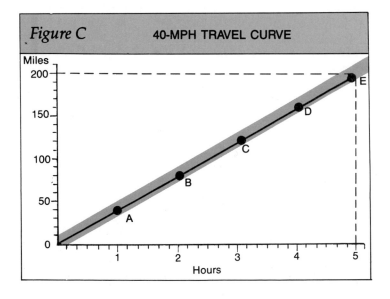

A line on a diagram showing the relationship of the variables is referred to as a curve, even when it is a straight line.

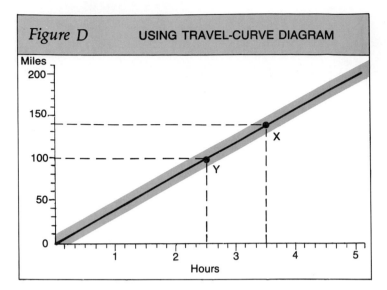

**Figure D**     USING TRAVEL-CURVE DIAGRAM

Information is obtained from a diagram by finding corresponding points on the axes with the use of perpendiculars.

travel curve and locate the corresponding point on the vertical axis. If we want to know how far we will have traveled in 3¹/₂ hours, we draw a perpendicular from the 3¹/₂-hour point on the horizontal axis to the travel curve in Figure D. This gives point X on the curve. From point X we draw a perpendicular across to the vertical axis. The perpendicular intersects the vertical axis at 140 miles.

From the graph we could similarly find how long it would take to reach any particular place along the way. If we wished to know when we would pass through a town 100 miles from home, we draw a perpendicular in Figure D from the vertical axis at 100 miles to the travel curve. It intersects the travel curve at point Y. From that point we drop a perpendicular to the horizontal axis. It shows that we would pass through the town 2¹/₂ hours after we leave home.

If we wish to make the trip in less time, we can increase our speed. Figure E, on the opposite page, shows the travel curve for a speed of 50 miles an hour. Because more distance is covered each hour, the new travel curve rises more steeply than the previous one. It shows that we would reach our destination in 4 hours instead of 5. It also shows that we would pass through the town 100 miles from home in 2 hours.

In these diagrams we have assumed a constant rate of speed during the whole trip, so the travel curve rises at a constant slope. What will happen if the rate of speed changes during the trip? Let us say that the first two hours we can only drive 40 miles per hour because of congested traffic, but the third hour we can drive 50 and after that 65 miles an hour. The travel curve based on those speeds is

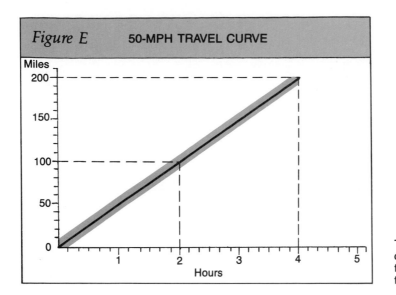

The travel curve relating the distance covered to the driving time is steeper for a speed of 50 miles per hour than for a speed of 40 miles per hour.

shown in Figure F below. As speed increases, the slope of the curve becomes steeper. To find the time required to reach the destination, we draw a perpendicular from the 200-mile mark on the vertical axis to the travel curve. From that point we draw a perpendicular down to the horizontal axis where it intersects the time scale at 4 hours and 5 minutes.

The relationship of time to distance in the travel curve is positive (or direct). As one increases, so does the other. Therefore, the curve slopes upward to the right. The relationship of other variables may be negative (or inverse). As one increases, the other decreases. For example, the distance

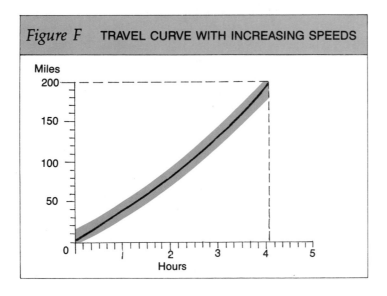

As the driving speed increases over time, the travel curve becomes steeper.

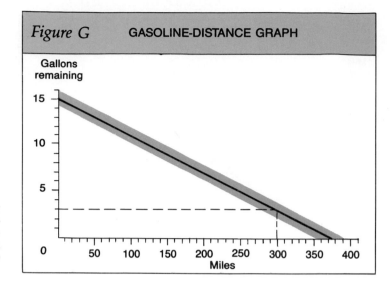

*Figure G*      **GASOLINE-DISTANCE GRAPH**

The relationship between the number of miles driven and the amount of gasoline remaining in the tank is a negative (or inverse) relationship. As a result, the curve slopes downward to the right.

driven and the amount of gas remaining in the tank are inversely related. In Figure G the miles driven are shown on the horizontal axis and the amount of gasoline in the tank on the vertical axis. Assuming that the car has a 15-gallon tank and gets 25 miles to a gallon, the amount of gas remaining at any point on the trip can be determined from the curve. If we wish to find the amount of gasoline remaining in the tank after 300 miles, we draw a perpendicular from the 300-mile mark on the horizontal axis up to the intersection with the curve and from that point draw a perpendicular across to the vertical axis. It shows that we have 3 gallons left and had better start looking for a filling station.

Because the relationship between miles driven and the amount of gas left in the tank is negative—as one increases the other decreases—the curve slopes downward to the right. The curve ends at the horizontal axis because you cannot have less than zero gas in the tank.

However, there are some variables that can have negative values—become less than zero. Let us suppose that this trip we have been discussing is to visit some friends and we have notified them that we expect to arrive at 4 P.M. We plan on leaving at noon and driving at a speed of 50 miles per hour. However, we encounter bad weather and are only able to average 40 miles an hour. The vertical axis in Figure H shows the amount of time remaining before our anticipated arrival. The distance driven is shown on the horizontal axis. We expected to cover the 200 miles in 4 hours, but due to the weather delay we only cover 160 miles at the end of 4 hours. The amount of time by which we are late in arriving is shown below the horizontal axis where the values are

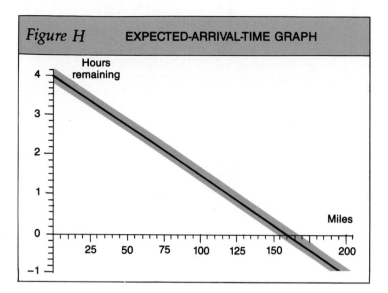

Figure H — EXPECTED-ARRIVAL-TIME GRAPH

The part of a curve that falls below the horizonal axis indicates negative values of the variable measured on the vertical axis.

negative. We arrive at our destination an hour later than expected.

In becoming better acquainted with graphs and how to use them, it is helpful to draw diagrams yourself. You will be given the opportunity to do this in some of the Economic Reasoning questions following the Case Applications.

Here is a suggestion for a diagram that you could practice on now. Draw a graph showing the relationship of the number of weeks in your economics course and the number of chapters that you are going to cover in the text. Put the number of weeks on the horizontal axis scale and the number of chapters on the vertical axis scale. Draw a curve showing the relationship between the number of weeks and the number of chapters if you were to cover the chapters at a constant rate. Draw another curve on the same diagram showing the relationship between the number of weeks and the number of chapters covered if you instead spend more time on the early chapters and less time on later chapters. (For the second curve don't bother to plot specific points; just make a freehand drawing of the curve showing its general shape and location in relation to the first curve.)

Practice using the diagram by locating, with the use of perpendiculars, in which weeks you will complete the first third of the chapters under each of the two assumptions—a constant rate of covering the material and an increasing rate.

# ECONOMIC CHOICES

*Making economic choices is something we all do as consumers, as producers, and as members of society. Many personal and business choices are important—whether to buy a house, what product to produce— but among the most important are the choices citizens make about the use of the nation's resources. This chapter's introductory article deals with choices we face about the best uses for the "peace dividend."*

## Swords Into Plowshares

Did you ever ask yourself "What couldn't I do with an extra $100 billion?" Well, you may get a chance to find out. Not the whole hundred billion for you personally, of course, but you may share in it if proposals for scaling back military spending are carried through. The thaw in the cold war and the disarmament agreements between the Soviet Union and the Western nations have created the promise of a "peace dividend," extra resources available to the civilian economy that were previously allocated to the military. Savings on the military budget in the 1990s could reach $100 billion or more per year.

If such a reduction in defense spending occurs, it will result in a massive redirection of resources away from preparation for war to civilian uses. There will be controversy over how to allocate the savings. The alternatives are (1) reducing the government deficit, (2) lowering taxes, and (3) increasing govern-

ment spending on civilian programs. But however the defense savings are allocated, there will be $100 billion of resources available for civilian production each year that were not available before. Your per capita share of that $100 billion of resources would be about $400.

If you were allowed to decide how the resources were to be used, what would you choose? You might consider that if the defense budget savings were applied to reducing the deficit or cutting taxes, the resources could be used by the private sector—individuals and businesses—to purchase consumption or investment goods. If, instead, the savings in military spending were shifted to nonmilitary government programs, the resources could be used for such purposes as repairing our deteriorated highways and bridges; improving and expanding the nation's airports; cleaning up the polluted environment; providing more prenatal care, nutrition, and Head Start programs for chil-

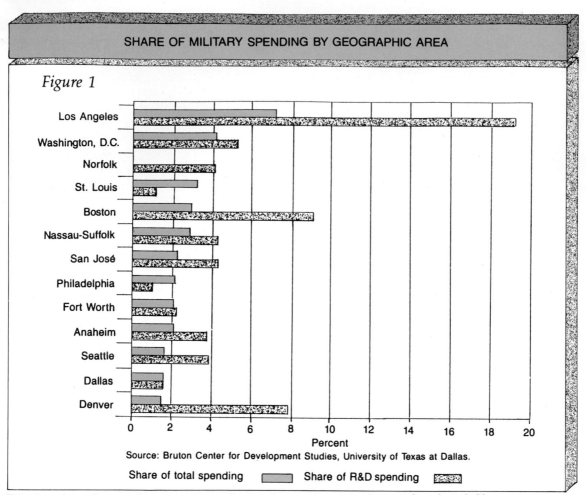

**SHARE OF MILITARY SPENDING BY GEOGRAPHIC AREA**

*Figure 1*

Source: Bruton Center for Development Studies, University of Texas at Dallas.

Share of total spending  Share of R&D spending

This chart shows the spending on goods, services, and research and development for selected cities. Military payrolls are excluded.

dren; expanding the number of Pell grants for technical and collegiate education for youths from needy families; and so forth.

One advantage of applying the peace dividend to the government deficit would be a reduction of interest rates. Lower interest rates, in turn, would encourage investment. This would increase our production capacity and improve the competitiveness of U.S. firms in world markets. Equally important, the reduction in defense spending would free research and development (R&D) resources for use in the civilian sector. There is

a limited amount of skilled scientific and technical labor available, and a sizeable amount of the most highly trained labor is engaged in R&D work for military projects. Making those scarce resources available for consumer product development and increased production efficiency would help American industry to compete with foreign producers.

Allocating resources to repairing and improving our transportation, water, and energy systems would also make the nation more productive. It is estimated that the country is about $15 billion short of the amount that needs to be spent each year on public works for the economy to produce at its potential.

Others advocate using the peace dividend to reduce taxes or for social programs. There is no scarcity of ideas about what to use the money and resources for. But the shift of that much spending from defense to civilian purposes will not be without stresses and dangers. Those industries heavily dependent on defense contracts and the regions in which they are located will be faced with a loss of jobs and income. Areas such as Los Angeles, St. Louis, and Dallas–Fort Worth, with their large concentrations of defense contractors, will be especially affected.

In addition to the jobs lost in defense industries, the reduction in military spending will result in the discharge of a million, more or less, servicemen and women and civilian employees of the military. If we were to cut the defense budget by the full $100 billion in one year, there would not be an opportunity for the reallocation of those service personnel and defense workers and other resources from military to nonmilitary production. Mass unemployment would occur.

For this reason, as well as due to caution in moving toward disarmament for strategic reasons, the cutback in military spending is expected to be gradual, perhaps involving reductions of around $15 billion each year. Getting even this amount of cuts in defense spending through the Congress may be a difficult process, since every program reduction means a loss of jobs in some legislator's district. Congress has already refused to cut back some programs that the military considered unnecessary: additional F-14D fighter planes and the Osprey tilt-rotor aircraft, for example. These two programs could cost $51 billion in the 1990s, an expenditure that the secretary of defense has said is not justified by military necessity.

The crisis in the Middle East dampened expectations for the peace dividend. It provided ammunition for defense industry lobbyists and others opposed to sharp reductions in military spending. On the other hand, it increased public and congressional interest in greater defense burden sharing by our allies.

Countries such as Japan and West Germany have shown that a large defense budget is not necessary for a prospering economy. Part of the reason for their economic success in recent years has been that they allocated a much smaller part of their resources to the military than did the United States. The peace dividend offers us an opportunity to convert some of our resources to more productive uses.

## Chapter Preview

*Decisions about what to do with the peace dividend are examples of the kinds of choices that an economy must continually make regarding the use of resources. How successful we are at choosing the best allocation of our available resources determines how well we can achieve our economic goals. This chapter examines the questions:* How do we make economic choices? What are the basic economic questions? What are society's economic goals?

## Learning Objectives

*After completing this chapter, you should be able to:*

1. *Define and give examples of economic trade-offs.*
2. *Explain opportunity cost.*
3. *Explain the production possibility frontier and increasing costs.*
4. *Give examples of the three basic economic questions.*
5. *List the four primarily economic goals of society.*
6. *Show the effect on output of increasing employment to full employment.*
7. *Show the effect on economic growth of producing more capital goods.*
8. *Give examples of trade-offs between economic and socioeconomic goals.*

## How Do We Make Economic Choices?

An abundant supply of everything relative to the demand for it would mean that individuals and society could be as wasteful as they pleased and not have to consider making choices. But because of scarcity, our choices involve trade-offs.

**Trade-offs**    Because resources are scarce in relation to the demand for them, using resources for one purpose means that other things will not be produced. The allocation of 6% of the nation's production to the military in recent years has meant that resources were drawn away from production for civilian use. Being strong militarily has involved a trade-off economically. Making our defense capability stronger has made our economy weaker and our standard of living lower. This is sometimes referred to as the guns-for-butter trade-off.

Most trade-off decisions are made by individual consumers and producers, rather than by government. Every time you go to the store to shop, you affect the decisions about how resources are allocated. If consumers buy fewer eggs because of concern over their cholesterol content, resources flow out of the poultry businesses and into some other occupation. True, laying hens are not much good for anything but egg production, but the labor, feed, and capital in the industry can be transferred to other industries that better meet our needs.

When we turn from war production to peace, we do not literally beat our swords into plowshares, as may have been

**trade-off**  the choice between alternative uses for a given quantity of a resource.

Egg production represents a trade-off in the allocation of resources. The resources (land, labor, and capital) that go into egg production are unavailable for other uses. If customers buy fewer eggs, resources flow out of the poultry businesses and into some other occupation.

done in biblical times, or directly transform an armaments factory into a dairy in trading off guns for butter. But the trade-off consists of reallocating the land, labor, and capital—the factors of production—used to produce military goods, and those employed in the military services themselves, to increase output for civilian purposes.

**Opportunity costs**  To make the best possible use of our limited resources, we need to compare the trade-off possibilities to find out what is gained and what is lost. If resources are used for armaments, they cannot be used for consumption or investment. The value of the sacrificed alternative is called the opportunity cost of whatever is produced. To give an idea of what the opportunity costs of our military spending are, the $70 billion B-2 Stealth bomber program is the approximate cost of what the Ford Foundation estimates is needed to repair the "safety net" of social programs during the next five years. Or if we cut the Stealth bomber program by only 3.5%, it would provide the resources for airport capital improvements and airline safety requirements for the next decade.

The guns-to-butter trade-off is shown by the diagram in Figure 2 (p. 41). In this type of diagram, called a production possibility frontier, we can compare the opportunity costs of our alternative choices by showing the varying amounts of the two types of outputs that can be produced by the same fixed amount of resources. Figure 2 shows the amounts of armaments that could be produced in relation to the

**opportunity cost** real economic cost of a good or service produced measured by the value of the sacrificed alternative.
**production possibility frontier (PPF)** the line on a graph showing the different maximum output combinations of goods or services that can be obtained from a fixed amount of resources.

The opportunity cost of a program is the value of the sacrificed alternative. Military spending for such programs as the B-2 Stealth bomber (top) has an opportunity cost affecting spending on social programs, such as for the homeless (bottom).

amounts of civilian goods that could be produced with a given amount of a hypothetical country's resources. The units of civilian goods are measured from left to right along the horizontal axis and the units of armaments are measured from bottom to top on the vertical axis.

If all of the available resources were put into military production, the country could produce 5 million units of armaments. If, instead, all of those same resources were put into increasing civilian goods, 10 million more units could be produced. (These units and quantities are imaginary; they are simply used to illustrate the principle of opportunity cost.) If we allocate part of the resources to produce armaments and the other part for civilian output, and if we assume that the trade-off between the two outputs is constant, the line marked PPF shows the different combinations of armaments and civilian goods that could be produced. PPF stands for production possibility frontier. It represents the maximum combinations of the two outputs that could be produced with the available resources.

If the nation chose to allocate its resources to produce the

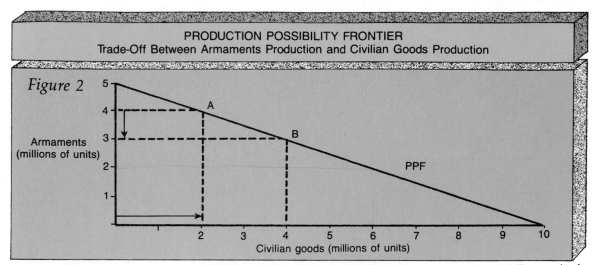

**PRODUCTION POSSIBILITY FRONTIER**
Trade-Off Between Armaments Production and Civilian Goods Production

*Figure 2*

Armaments
(millions of units)

PPF

Civilian goods (millions of units)

Moving from point A to point B on the production possibility frontier results in an increase in production of civilian goods of 2 million units, with an opportunity cost of 1 million units reduction in armaments production.

combination shown at point A, it could produce 4 million units of armaments and 2 million units of civilian goods. If it allocated its resources to produce at point B, it could produce 3 million units of armaments and 4 million units of civilian goods. The opportunity cost of changing the composition of output from A to B, of increasing civilian production by 2 million units, is reducing armaments production by 1 million units. Similarly, if you go from B to A, the opportunity cost of increasing armaments production by 1 million units is decreasing civilian production by 2 million units. The opportunity costs would be the same wherever we moved the composition on the PPF because we assumed that the trade-off ratio was constant at 2:1.

**Increasing costs**  In the real world, however, trade-off ratios are seldom constant. The opportunity costs depend on what combination of outputs the country is producing, where it is on the production possibility frontier. If government spending goes largely for armaments and little for civilian output, it is likely that a large increase in civilian production can be had for a relatively small opportunity cost in military preparedness. At the other extreme, if resources were all being used for civilian production and none for armaments, the opportunity cost of increased military purchases would be a relatively small decline in civilian production.

This situation is pictured in Figure 3 on the next page. Here the trade-offs are not constant. Still employing a given amount of resources, the opportunity costs of armaments and civilian goods vary, depending on where you are on the

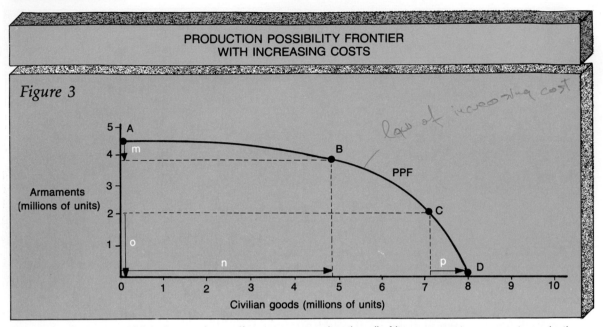

## PRODUCTION POSSIBILITY FRONTIER WITH INCREASING COSTS

*Figure 3*

With increasing costs, which is the usual case, if a country were devoting all of its resources to armaments production (point A), it could have a great deal more civilian goods (n) by sacrificing a small amount of armaments output (m). On the other hand, if it were already producing mostly civilian goods (point C) and moved to total production of civilian goods (point D), the increased amount of civilian goods output (p) would be small in comparison to the reduced armaments production (o).

production possibility frontier. The closer you are to one axis or the other, the greater the opportunity cost of obtaining more of the output measured on that axis, and the smaller the opportunity cost of obtaining the other output. If the country were spending its whole budget on armaments and nothing on civilian output (point A), it could obtain a large increase in units of civilian production with only a small sacrifice in arms (point B). It might, for example, give up a small amount of bomber production (m) to expand transportation facilities by a large amount (n). On the other hand, if it were at point C and changed output composition to point D there would be a large opportunity cost in military preparedness (o) to obtain a small increase in civilian output (p).

The situation of increasing opportunity costs as resources are allocated exclusively to one output is the usual case. The more resources are devoted to the production of one good, the higher becomes its opportunity cost in the sacrifice of an alternative good because some resources are better suited for the production of that other good. The typical production possibility frontier is more like Figure 3 rather than Figure 2.

# case application

## Dieting—The National Pastime

Even in America, a land of relative plenty, there are people who have insufficient food. And there would be millions more hungry if it were not for government and private food programs for the needy.

But in this country there is an even larger number of people who are overfed. According to the National Center for Health Statistics, there are in excess of 34 million Americans between the ages of 20 and 74 that are more than 20% above desirable body weight. It has been demonstrated that such overweight constitutes a health hazard for those individuals.

Although only a little over one-quarter of the population is clinically obese, about 100 million adult Americans are overweight and an even larger number think they are. Overweight has been an increasing problem among adolescents. According to statistics, there are 50% more obese young people in the United States than there were 10 years ago.

In response to social and self-image pressures, as well as health considerations, dieting has become a national pastime. It is estimated that Americans spent $33 billion in 1989 attempting to lose weight, and the amount increases by some 10% a year. The sales of diet books, diet drugs, prepared diet foods, health club and "fat farm" memberships are booming. Weight-loss firms have been known to advertise their rates by the pound. Along with the waste disposal industry, the "waist disposal" industry is one of the few businesses that charges you for what you give up rather than what you receive.

However, despite the money and the physical and psychological energy expended, few dieters have had lasting success in weight reduction. There are many theories about why it proves so difficult for most people to

lose weight and keep it off. Is it due to heredity, to childhood eating habits, to hormonal balance, to an automatic "starvation metabolism" reaction of the body to dieting, to psychological tensions that are released by eating, or to a combination of factors?

Most people find it difficult to stay on a diet. Many succumb to their craving for food, especially carbohydrates and fats, in response to anxiety, depression, or loneliness. Eating gives them a temporary feeling of well-being. A doughnut or a bag of potato chips is psychologically irresistible, even though the person may be well fed.

It has been shown that the most successful long-term weight loss programs are those that combine diet, exercise, and behavior therapy. Despite all of the advertised new diet drugs and systems, the outcome of the weight battle is resolved, as it always has been, by hard choices—the chocolate chip cookie versus the waistline.

### Economic Reasoning

1. What is an example of a trade-off in this case application?  *Money spent vs. success in dieting.*
2. Where a dieter is concerned, are there different types of opportunity costs of a chocolate chip cookie? What are they?
3. Is the $33 billion and more spent each year on losing weight justified? Why or why not?  *Not. Less costing success.*

# What Are the Basic Economic Questions?

In allocating resources, there are three basic economic questions that must be resolved. How we resolve these questions determines to a large extent what kind of economic system we have.

**What to produce?** Because of the scarcity of resources, a society cannot produce everything it wants. Therefore, the economy must continually decide what mix of goods and services it is going to produce with the available resources. It must find the most efficient resolution of the "what" question.

How we allocate the peace dividend between deficit reduction, tax cuts, public works, and social programs will determine what is produced. If the savings are directed toward deficit reduction, there will be a reduction of interest rates, which will encourage investment. This will mean more resources used in producing equipment, factories, and office buildings. There will also be more home construction and automobile production because there will be more money for lending to finance these purchases.

Using the savings to finance a tax cut will redirect resources into the production of consumer goods and services. Consumers will be able to purchase more electronic items, restaurant meals, and vacations. If it is instead directed into public works, the construction industry will greatly expand. If it goes into social programs, there will be an increase in government services. What will the peace dividend be used to produce?

**How to produce?** Once an economy determines what mix of goods and services it is going to allocate its resources to produce, it must determine what production methods are going to be used. The resolution of the "how" question depends on the technology of production and on the particular combination of resources that will be used to produce each good or service.

How the peace dividend is allocated will affect production methods in the economy. If the resources go into investment, nonmilitary production will become more capital-intensive. In the civilian sectors of the economy, there will be more capital used in production relative to the amount of labor. There will also be more real capital, in this case public rather than private capital, if the savings go toward better

**"what" question** the question concerning the decisions made by an economy about how much of the different alternative goods and services will be produced with the available resources.

**"how" question** the question concerning the decisions made by an economy about the technology used to produce goods and services.

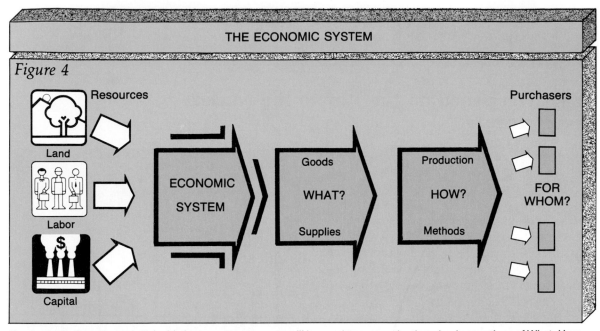

THE ECONOMIC SYSTEM

Figure 4

Resources

Land

Labor

Capital

ECONOMIC SYSTEM

Goods
WHAT?
Supplies

Production
HOW?
Methods

Purchasers

FOR WHOM?

Every economic system must decide how scarce resources will be used to answer the three basic questions of What, How, and For Whom to produce.

highways, bridges, airports, and public transportation facilities—the infrastructure of the economy. This will similarly make the economy more productive.

An increase in capital investment, either private or public, would increase the competitiveness of the U.S. economy relative to Asia and Western Europe. An economic system needs to use the most efficient production methods that are available to it, given its particular combination of resources, in resolving the "how" question.

**For whom to produce?**    The third basic economic decision every economic system must make is how to allocate finished goods and services among its population. The resolution of the "for whom" question determines who gets how much of what is produced. Because the economy can't produce as much of everything as we would like it to produce, the output must be rationed in some fashion.

The "for whom" question does not imply that a particular item is produced for a particular consumer, but rather that different groups will benefit from the peace dividend depending on how it is allocated. If it is used for deficit reduction, borrowers will benefit from lower interest rates to buy real estate or invest in capital goods. If it is allocated to social programs, the benefits will go more to the lowest income groups in society.

**infrastructure**   an economy's stock of capital—much of it publicly owned—that provides basic services to producers and consumers. Includes highways, electric power, water supplies, educational facilities, health services, etc.
**"for whom" question**   the question concerning the decisions made by an economy about income distribution—who gets how much of the goods and services produced.

# case application

## What Happened on the Way to the Nuclear Power Future?

Electricity is a vital input for a modern industrial economy. Factories, businesses, and homes could hardly function without it, as anyone well knows who has experienced a power blackout. As the evidence mounts that the electric generating plants powered by fossil fuels spew unacceptable pollutants into the air, contributing to global warming as well as to acid rain, how are we going to meet our future electricity needs?

In the 1960s the obvious answer was nuclear power. The energy contained in atoms had been vividly demonstrated by the atomic and hydrogen bombs. Having learned how to harness that energy to produce electricity, we expected to satisfy a limitless appetite for electricity at costs so low that it would be unnecessary even to meter the amounts used. Two decades later, after spending $112 billion constructing 100 nuclear power plants and some $25 billion more on 111 nuclear power projects that were cancelled or mothballed, we hit a wall of cost overruns and hazardous installations that stopped nuclear power dead in its tracks. There has not been an order placed for a new nuclear plant since 1978. What happened on the way to our bright future of cheap, clean, plentiful nuclear power?

The problems began showing up in the mid-1970s when there was a serious accident at the Brown's Ferry nuclear reactor in Alabama and an escalation of construction expenses for new nuclear plants. The costs per kilowatt of electric capacity rose from an approximate parity with the construction costs of coal-burning plants in the early 1970s to twice the cost of coal-fired plants by 1985.

But the real turning point was the accident at the Three Mile Island nuclear plant in 1979

Pilgrim Station nuclear power plant, Plymouth, Massachusetts.

near Harrisburg, Pennsylvania, which very closely approached the ultimate disaster—a meltdown of the radioactive core. That incident focused attention on widespread weaknesses in construction and operations in the industry. A number of plants under construction could not be licensed without expensive redesign or extensive repairs on shoddy work. Many became uneconomical. The Marble Hill nuclear power station in Indiana, for example, had been projected to cost $1.4 billion when construction began in 1978. By the time work was abandoned on the half-finished plant at the end of 1983, some $2.5 billion had already been spent; the estimated final cost would have been $7.7 billion or more. As a result of its losses on Marble Hill, the utility company increased the rates charged to the customers of its other electric

generating facilities and reduced the dividend payments to its stockholders by 67%.

The future of nuclear power was dealt a further blow by an accident at Chernobyl in the Soviet Union. On April 26, 1986, there was an explosion and fire in one of the Chernobyl nuclear reactors. The short-term consequences were the deaths from radiation of 30 people in the weeks immediately following the accident. But no one can say what the number of casualties will be in future years from the lingering effects. Some 100,000 people in the vicinity of the plant had to be evacuated, and the area became uninhabitable for miles around for an indefinite period due to high levels of radiation. Nuclear fallout, carried in the atmosphere over western Europe, forced the destruction of crops in a number of countries because of poisonous contamination.

The cost and safety problems of nuclear power cast doubts on whether it is an acceptable energy alternative. Further complicating the problem is what to do with the nuclear waste from the plants. But in view of the mounting concern over the environmental damage from conventional power generators—and with tantalizing hints of breakthroughs in nuclear fusion, hot or cold—it may be premature to pronounce nuclear power dead and buried.

A youngster swallows an antiradiation solution in a Warsaw clinic in March 1986 as part of a precaution against fallout from the Chernobyl nuclear power plant accident in the neighboring Soviet Union.

## Economic Reasoning

1. Which of the basic economic questions are involved in this case? In what way?
2. Using this case as an example, how does changing technology affect the "how" question?
3. Who should pay the costs of failed nuclear projects? The customers of the utility company? The stockholders or bondholders of the company? The government (taxpayers)? What are the advantages and disadvantages of putting the burden on each group?

# What Are Society's Economic Goals?

We make economic choices in the light of certain goals. There are four goals that societies aim to achieve that are principally economic in nature. In addition to these economic goals, there are other social goals with important economic dimensions. This section examines the goals that often underlie decisions as to what trade-offs a society will make and what opportunity costs it will bear in resolving the three basic economic questions.

**Efficiency**   Military production is notoriously inefficient. There are horror stories of $435 hammers, $7,622 coffee pots, and $449 pairs of pliers produced for the military. One way to achieve efficiency is to avoid waste. A part of the peace dividend would be the reallocation of resources to industries that are less wasteful than the defense industries. Given the scarcity of resources, it is important to use them with maximum efficiency to obtain the greatest output possible from the resources consumed.

Another way to achieve efficiency is to use the limited resources for their most important purposes. We need to resolve the "what" question in allocating peace dividend resources in the way that will best serve our needs. How much should be directed toward investment in capital goods versus how much into consumer goods? The production possibility frontier in Figure 5 presents us with these choices. Which is the better combination of outputs for the peace dividend, combination A with more capital goods or combination B with more consumer goods? Combination B would provide a higher current standard of living, but combination A would increase the economy's production capacity (see discussion under **Growth** on p. 50).

Finally, one of the most important ways we achieve increased efficiency is by improving the technology of production. Since much highly skilled labor is employed in the defense sector of the economy—scientists, engineers, technical personnel—and much capital is tied up in those industries, technology has been held back in the civilian sectors. This is one of the reasons why the U.S., the world technology leader in the first half of the century, has fallen behind other countries that do not allocate as large a percentage of output to their military, such as Japan and West Germany, in the technology of production.

**Price stability**   Another economic goal is to maintain price stability. Price stability is the avoidance of rapid changes in the general price level of goods and services. Prices of individual goods and services go up and down in response

**efficiency**   maximizing the amount of output obtained from a given amount of resources or minimizing the amount of resources used for a given amount of output.

**price stability**   a constant average level of prices for all goods and services.

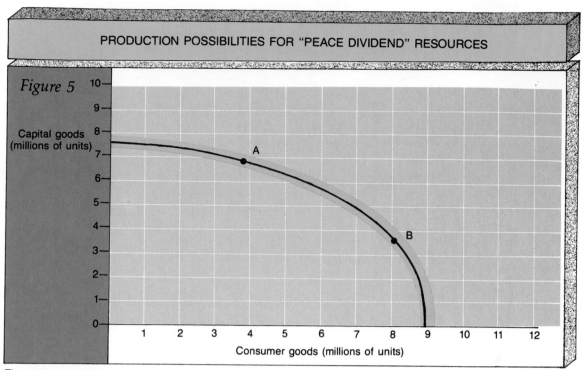

*Figure 5*

PRODUCTION POSSIBILITIES FOR "PEACE DIVIDEND" RESOURCES

Capital goods (millions of units)

Consumer goods (millions of units)

The resources that are made available by a decrease in military spending can be used to produce consumer goods and capital goods. Selecting the best combination of consumer and capital goods to produce with the available resources will result in efficiency in resource allocation.

to changes in the costs of producing them and the demand for them. When there is inflation, however, with the prices of most things rising rapidly at the same time, it can disrupt the economy.

The stop-and-go nature of military production—rapid increases in our defense output whenever the cold war heated up—tended to create price instability. The smaller the defense sector, the easier it will be to maintain stable prices.

**Full employment**   A stable price level is only one aspect of economic stability. The other is job stability at full employment. This means that nearly everyone who wants to work can find a job. Full employment is an important economic goal for two reasons. It is important because jobs are the main source of most people's incomes, and it is important because full employment is necessary for an economy to utilize fully its limited resources. Labor is a resource, and unemployed labor means loss of production from a resource that can never be recovered.

Unemployment is shown on the PPF diagram by operating at a point inside the production possibility frontier. In Figure 6 on the next page, point A is less than full employ-

**inflation**   a continuously rising general price level, resulting in a loss of the purchasing power of money.
**full employment**   employment of nearly everyone who desires to work. In practice, an unemployment level of not more than 4–5% is considered full employment.

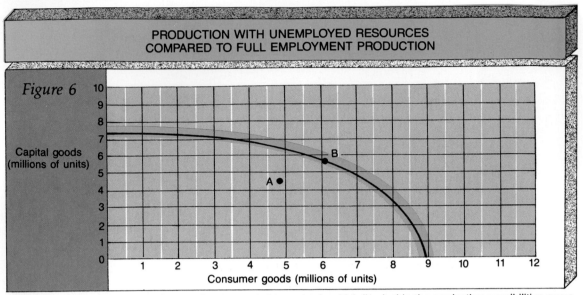

**PRODUCTION WITH UNEMPLOYED RESOURCES COMPARED TO FULL EMPLOYMENT PRODUCTION**

*Figure 6*

Capital goods (millions of units)

Consumer goods (millions of units)

Production at less than full employment is represented by point A, which lies inside the production possibilities curve. Point B on the PPF is full employment, with more output of consumer goods and capital goods. Maintaining full employment while demilitarizing the economy will be easier if the economy is healthy to begin with.

ment output. Moving to point B on the curve gives us full employment and increased production of both capital goods and consumer goods.

The trick in shifting resources from military to civilian production will be to minimize unemployment as labor moves from defense industries to industries producing for the civilian sector, to stay as close as possible to the PPF. This will be easier if the economy is healthy to begin with. It will also be easier if the shift is spread out over a number of years; however, this will delay the benefits of the peace dividend.

**Growth**  Efficiency, price stability and full employment contribute to achieving the fourth economic goal—growth. Economic growth means a continuing increase in the capacity of an economy to produce goods and services.

Channeling capital resources from defense industries into research and development for the civilian sector will speed up economic growth through new products and the use of advanced production methods. Growth will also be promoted by a lowering of the deficit and the resulting reduction in interest rates, which encourages investment in new capital equipment. (The relationship between capital investment and output is covered in more depth in chapter 7.) Improvement in the economy's infrastructure will also facilitate growth by making investment more profitable.

**economic growth**  an increase in the production capacity of the economy.

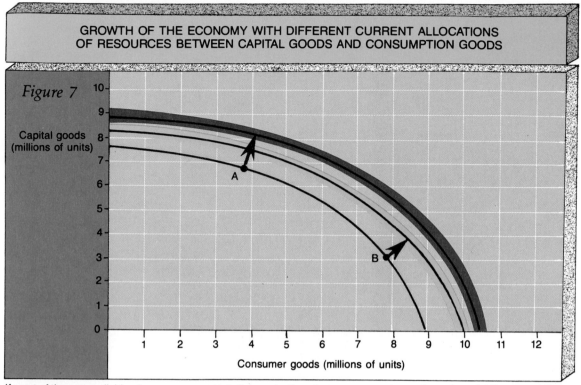

**GROWTH OF THE ECONOMY WITH DIFFERENT CURRENT ALLOCATIONS OF RESOURCES BETWEEN CAPITAL GOODS AND CONSUMPTION GOODS**

*Figure 7*

Capital goods (millions of units)

Consumer goods (millions of units)

If most of the peace dividend resources went into the production of consumer goods, as shown by point B, we would have a higher current standard of living; but economic growth during the next few years would only expand to the green line. If the resources were allocated as shown by point A, however, the economy would expand to the red line, making even higher future living standards possible.

Figure 7 illustrates that how we allocate the peace dividend will affect the rate of growth. If all of it were used for a tax cut, most of the increased output would be consumer goods (point B in Figure 7). This would give us a lower rate of growth, shown by the outward shift of the PPF curve only as far as the green line. On the other hand, if we used the peace dividend to reduce the deficit, a larger amount of investment would occur (point A). This larger investment would give us a higher growth rate, as shown by the outward shift of the PPF curve to the red line.

**Socioeconomic goals** There is not much disagreement over the desirability of the four primarily economic goals discussed above (although there is a great deal of debate over how best to achieve them). There are some additional goals of society that are to a large degree economic in nature—what we might term <u>socioeconomic goals</u>—about which there is less universal agreement. An examination of public policies indicates that the following might be included among socioeconomic goals: protection of the environment

**socioeconomic goal** the type of social goal that has important economic dimensions.

The peace dividend could help us achieve socioeconomic goals by reallocating resources from defense industries to the civilian sector. For example, the radar shown above, which was originally developed by Westinghouse for the military, now finds new uses: when attached to a dirigible, it can detect drug smugglers' aircraft crossing the border between the United States and Mexico.

from pollution, financial security for individuals, economic equity, just treatment for all individuals in economic matters, and freedom to carry out economic choices.

The peace dividend should help us to achieve some of these socioeconomic goals. For example, conversion of government spending from defense against foreign attack to defense of the environment will help to solve some of the problems discussed in chapter 1. Conversion of spending to repair the safety net of social programs will help to meet some of the other socioeconomic goals.

# case application

## Replaced by R₂D₂?

The current generation of robots, relatively dumb brutes that perform repetitive tasks, may replace up to 1.3 million American workers by the year 2000. The industrial robot market was born in the United States some 30 years ago, but little happened in the industry until the late 1970s and early 1980s, when there was a surge of growth in the use of robots to meet competition from overseas, particularly in the automobile industry. Robots were assigned such jobs as welding, painting, and drilling motor blocks.

But sales flattened after the mid-1980s, and in 1990 there were still less than 50,000 robots at work in this country, compared to twice that number in Japan. Now, however, a new generation of robots, relatives of R₂D₂, the robot of *Star Wars* fame, with senses of vision, touch, and hearing, is coming on the scene and could have an impact on as many as 3.8 million jobs. Robots are performing a remarkable variety of tasks, everything from sorting parts (a worker can teach the robot's "eyes" to recognize a new part in less than 10 minutes) to acting as night watchmen at factories, patrolling the buildings and grounds to detect intruders.

The automobile industry is still the major employer of robots, and General Motors even has its own company to produce them. One of the things that delayed the spread of the use of robots was their high cost, but the price for the cruder type of robots has fallen. A welding robot that originally cost $150,000 now costs half that.

More sophisticated robots, such as the night watchmen, cost $100,000 and up. But robots can frequently save money in the long run compared to the cost of human workers. Not only can they do some jobs with more precision and less fatigue, but they don't have to be paid wages, don't get fringe benefits, don't take coffee breaks, and have very low absenteeism rates.

### *Economic Reasoning*

1. Which primarily economic goals are served by the use of production robots?
2. Does the use of robots involve a trade-off among different economic or socioeconomic goals? Which?
3. Do you favor or oppose a rapid increase in the use of robots to replace human workers? Why?  *High unemployment*

Bad news, Cromwell—you're being replaced by a machine.

# Putting It Together

Because resources are insufficient to produce all the things we want, we have to choose how best to use those resources. In deciding how to use our limited resources, certain *trade-offs* are necessary.

The value of what we give up when resources are used to produce one thing rather than another is the *opportunity cost* of what is produced. In order to get the greatest benefits from our limited resources, we should use them for the outputs that best serve our needs. If we don't, then the opportunity costs of what we produce will be too high.

A *production possibility frontier* (PPF) shows the trade-off between two alternative uses of a resource. (See Figures 2 and 3 on pages 41 and 42.) The PPF shows the opportunity cost of producing more of one good by showing the amount of the alternative good that is sacrificed. Production possibility frontiers generally curve outward because of *increasing opportunity costs* incurred as more of one good is produced. Production possibility frontiers are economic tools helpful in analyzing the opportunity costs of trade-offs.

All economic systems must resolve three basic economic questions: *what to produce; how to produce; for whom to produce.* Scarcity cannot efficiently be dealt with unless the economy allocates its resources to producing the goods and services most needed and desired. An economic system needs also to utilize the most efficient production methods with the resources available. Finally, an economic system must determine who gets how much of what is produced.

There are four principally economic goals by which the effectiveness of an economy can be judged: *efficiency, price stability, full employment* and *growth.* Some socioeconomic goals of our society are: *protection of the environment, financial security,* and *equity, justice, and freedom in economic matters.*

Decisions about what to do with the peace dividend are examples of the kinds of choices that an economy must continually make regarding the use of resources. How successful we are at choosing the best allocation of our available resources determines how well we can achieve our economic goals.

# Perspective

## The Affluent Society

**John Kenneth Galbraith (born 1908)**
Galbraith is a lofty economist in more than one sense. At 6' 8", he towers over colleagues and debate opponents. Born on a farm in Ontario, Canada, he graduated from an agricultural college in the depths of the Depression in the 1930s. He came to the United States for graduate study and remained to teach at the University of California, Berkeley, at Princeton, and mainly, until he retired in 1973, at Harvard. He gave up the Harvard classroom to embark on a three-and-a-half-year project which took him to many locations around the world narrating a television series called, "The Age of Uncertainty," which he wrote. "The Age of Uncertainty" was a broad, sweeping overview of the history of economic ideas.

Of the twenty-some books he has written, *The Affluent Society* and two others form an important triad on the functioning of our capitalist economy. The second book in the triad is *The New Industrial State* (1967), which examines the way decisions are made in modern corporations, their relationship to government, and the consequences for society. The third book is *Economics and the Public Purpose* (1973), in which Galbraith argues the necessity for government to act as a "countervailing power" against the economic and political power of big business and labor.

John Kenneth Galbraith, one of the most provocative modern economists, wrote a book in 1958 entitled *The Affluent Society*. In it he argued that the problem that had traditionally been of primary concern to economists, how to increase production, was no longer the most important problem in industrially advanced countries like the United States. He maintained that the problem of production had been so well solved that all citizens could have enough to satisfy their needs if output were distributed more equally. Furthermore, he said, a lot of what we produced was intentional waste, such as oversized cars. He noted that most of us eat too much, not too little.

Other social scientists have made the same point. Vance Packard maintained in *The Waste Makers* that the American economy has come to depend on consumption for the sake of consumption, planned obsolescence, and "progress through the throwaway spirit."

In the 1970s, the energy crunch, the decline in productivity and income growth, the shift to smaller cars, and the increased emphasis on conservation led to talk about "an age of limits" and cast doubt on the affluent society thesis. But in the fourth edition of his book, published in 1984, Galbraith sticks by his argument. Total output, in his view, is not the main concern. Of more importance is the uses to which output is allocated. Poverty and hunger continue to persist in an economy of abundance. Public squalor in the streets of our cities contrasts with the opulence of the offices in the skyscrapers above. Many types of jobs are unnecessarily arduous, boring, or dangerous for the sake of maximizing total output.

Galbraith's thesis is contrary to the current movement in economic policy—the emphasis on increasing productivity and total output, the reduction of government spending in favor of private spending, the cutbacks in Occupational Safety and Health Agency activities, and the truce in the war on poverty, both at home and abroad. Being out of step with the popular parade is not unusual for Galbraith. He notes in his introduction to *The Affluent Society*, "I have read on occasion that I find perverse pleasure in attacking the conventional myth. I do not, and on the contrary, it is very hard work. Some day for recreation I intend to write a book affirming fully all the unquestioned economic truths."

For
Further
Study
and
Analysis

## Study Questions

1. Why are trade-offs necessary in our modern economic system?

2. Give an example of a personal economic choice you have made recently. What was the opportunity cost?

3. Give an example of an economic choice made by society as a whole. How was the choice made?

4. What are three examples of differences in the resolution of the "what" question in the United States today compared to five years ago?

5. How has the increased use of production robots affected the resolution of the "how" question?

6. What determines how much of the nation's output of goods and services is allocated to you?

7. Points on a production possibility frontier, such as points "A" and "B" in Figure 2, show the different combinations of two goods that could be produced with the available resources. Would it be possible to produce at a point outside the PPF curve? What would such a point mean?

8. Some economic and socioeconomic goals are complementary; achieving one goal helps to achieve another goal. What is one example where economic and socioeconomic goals are complementary?

9. In other cases, there are conflicts between different goals: efforts to achieve one make it more difficult to achieve another. What is an example of a conflict between economic goals?

10. What goals does Galbraith consider the most important in the United States today?

## Exercises in Analysis

1. Prepare an analysis of the alternative uses of any selected natural resource (pine trees, for example) by considering the following questions: (a) What are three alternative uses of this resource? (b) What are the trade-offs for any one of the three uses you have selected? (c) What is the opportunity cost of using the natural resource for any one of the three uses you chose?

2. Select a local business and discuss how it resolves the "what," "how," and "for whom" questions.
3. Find out where the nearest nuclear power plant is located and what utility company owns it. Write to the utility company and request a copy of its latest annual report, a prospectus on any recent bond or stock issues, and a summary of any recent rate increase

proposals submitted to the public utilities commission. On the basis of those reports, write a short paper on the economic effects of the nuclear power plant.
4. Prepare a list of government policy measures that promote goals of our society such as full employment, economic growth, protection of the environment, or financial security.

## Further Reading

Ayres, Robert U., and Steven M. Miller. *Robotics: Applications and Social Implications.* Cambridge, Mass.: Ballinger, 1983. Discusses the technology and the costs and benefits of robots. Examines also the impact of robotization on employment and productivity and its policy implications.

Bolton, Roger E., ed. *Defense and Disarmament: The Economics of Transition.* Englewood Cliffs, N.J.: Prentice Hall, 1966. In the introduction, the editor examines whether defense spending is a burden or a prop to the economy. The articles cover a wide range of problems of the guns-to-butter transition.

Burns, Grant. *The Atomic Papers.* Metuchen, N.J.: Scarecrow Press, 1984. A guide to selected books and articles on nuclear power and other aspects of the atomic age.

Campbell, John E. *Collapse of an Industry: Nuclear Power and the Contradictions of U.S. Policy.* Ithaca, N.Y.: Cornell University Press, 1988. Discusses the problems of the nuclear power industry, including its financial crisis.

Chester, Michael. *Robots: Facts Behind the Fiction.* New York: Macmillan, 1983. In contrast to the Hunt book (see below), this is an extremely simple examination of robots and their future.

Hunt, V. Daniel. *Smart Robots: A Handbook of Intelligent Robotic Systems.* New York: Chapman and Hall, 1985. A somewhat technical book on advanced types of robots. Discussion includes their social impacts and their impact on the work force.

Lynch, John E., ed. *Economic Adjustment and Conversion of Defense Industries.* Boulder, Colo.: Westview Press, 1987. Chapters on such topics as community adjustments to defense plant closings, conversion of plants to nonmilitary production, civilian product market opportunities for defense plants, and worker assistance and placement.

Patterson, Walter C. *Nuclear Power.* Baltimore, Md.: Penguin Books, 1983. This book covers various aspects of nuclear power.

Ullman, John E. *The Prospects of American Industrial Recovery.* Westport, Conn.: Quorum Books, 1985. The author argues that "The military preemption of resources [leads] to inadequate investment, incompetent management, and, an early economic consequence, to an inability to hold back inflation." This has caused countries such as Great Britain and Argentina to "de-industrialize" and become "fifth-world" countries, ex-great powers. He believes that this is the direction in which the United States is headed.

# THE ECONOMIC SYSTEM

*Every society, even the most primitive, has an economic system that organizes the production and distribution of goods and services. Although these systems have basic identifiable characteristics that remain consistent over long periods of time, change in the systems inevitably takes place.*

## Ranch to Table: A Different Story Now

In 1856 a Texan named Bill Hayden went on a cattle-buying trip to Oklahoma. Hayden bought a few dozen head of longhorn cattle from different ranchers until he had a herd of about 600 head of cattle. Hayden's plan was to drive the cattle east and sell them in New York, where the price of beef was high.

It was spring when Hayden's cowhands started the longhorns on their trek. The rains were heavy and the steers often had to be pulled out of thick mud holes. When the summer sun baked the mud, the cattle stirred up huge dust clouds, and the cowhands had to cover their faces with neckerchiefs in order to breathe. Many of the longhorns died along the way from hunger, thirst, and exhaustion. When winter came, the drive halted and the cattle had to be penned up and fed corn.

The following spring, Hayden and his trailhands pushed the longhorns on until they reached a railroad in Illinois. The steers were loaded onto cattle cars and shipped the rest of the way to New York. The drive had taken Hayden a year and a half, but the price he got

for his cattle in New York was high enough to make the trip worthwhile.

Today, cross-country cattle drives are a thing of the past, and modern beef cattle are not much like Bill Hayden's longhorns. José and Maria Ruiz have a cattle ranch in the high plateau country of northwest Texas. They raise short, heavy cattle that yield large amounts of high quality beef. A century ago, the longhorn was a tough, rangy animal that could survive bad weather, scarce water, and long drives. The Ruizes' cattle require protection from bad weather, plentiful water and feed, and a relatively calm existence.

The Ruizes' cattle rarely walk more than a few hundred yards at a time. They are kept on the ranch until they reach 450 to 500 pounds, then they are trucked to feedlots. In the feedlots, the cattle may eat up to 24 pounds of especially prepared feed and gain three pounds a day—about a pound of beef for each eight pounds of feed. The feed is a rich mixture of wheat, barley, corn, chopped alfalfa, corn silage, cottonseed hulls, molasses, tallow, and other ingredients. The ideal mixture of ingredients for each stage of the steer's development is determined by nutritionists. In five months each steer doubles in weight to a total of 1,000 pounds or more.

Cattle are sent from the ranch to feedlots where they double in weight to 1,000 pounds or more. This specialization in modern beef production increases the supply and lowers prices to consumers.

A century ago it took Bill Hayden over a year to move his longhorns to market. Today, cattle are trucked from feedlots to slaughterhouses in a matter of hours. Within a few more hours they are slaughtered, loaded into refrigerated trucks, and shipped to butcher shops or supermarkets.

Although beef is relatively expensive to produce when compared to many other foods, specialization of various tasks in beef production has made it possible to keep beef prices low enough so that most of us can afford to eat at least some beef. From the birth of the calf on the ranch to the sale of packages of meat in a supermarket, each stage of production is handled by specialists. The result is a better product at a lower price.

## Chapter Preview

*The way cattle is produced and brought to market has changed over the past 100 years in an effort to better satisfy the economic goal of efficiency. The manner in which society organizes production to deal with the problem of scarcity is continually evolving. In some countries it has evolved in different directions than in others. But every society has to resolve the same basic economic questions. This chapter will examine the way societies are organized to deal with scarcity by asking the following questions:* Why are economic systems needed? What are the principal types of economic systems? How does a market system resolve the three basic economic questions?

## Learning Objectives

*After completing this chapter, you should be able to:*

1. *Distinguish between absolute and comparative advantage.*
2. *Explain why specialization based on absolute or comparative advantage results in greater economic efficiency and interdependence.*
3. *Identify the three major types of economic systems, and explain how they differ.*
4. *Explain how a market system resolves the three basic economic questions.*
5. *Distinguish between goods and services sold in product markets and those sold in factor markets.*
6. *Diagram the circular flow of a market economy.*

# Why Are Economic Systems Needed?

Back in 1856, Bill Hayden and his cowhands were largely on their own when they drove their cattle from Oklahoma to Illinois. Today, José and Maria Ruiz depend on many different people to help them raise cattle. They depend on feed suppliers, veterinarians, gasoline distributors, and government cattle inspectors, among others. In many ways the Ruizes' cattle ranch is much like the economy as a whole. In achieving greater efficiency in production, we have become more dependent on others, thereby increasing the need for an economic system to organize and coordinate diverse economic activities of our society.

**Specialization**   A century ago many Americans raised their own beef cattle. In rural areas there was a high degree of self-sufficiency in food production. But people in large cities did not raise their own cattle. Thus, cattlemen like Bill Hayden found a profitable opportunity in that particular specialization—raising cattle in an area well suited for it and supplying the beef to city dwellers.

Today, the modern cattle business is very highly specialized. Ranchers such as the Ruizes concentrate on raising cattle. Truckers ship the cattle to feedlots. Nutritionists use computers to create diets for the cattle. At slaughterhouses, people with specialized skills dispatch the cattle with efficiency, and butchers at supermarkets trim various cuts for the consumer. In the production of beef and most other products there is a division of labor into specialized tasks that results in greater efficiency and a lower cost product.

One reason why this division of labor results in greater

**specialization**   concentrating the activity of a unit of a production resource—especially labor—on a single task or production operation. Also applies to the specialization of nations in producing those goods and services that their resources are best suited to produce.

New York City obviously lacks the grazing space necessary to cattle production that is found in the western plains states. Thus, our western states have an absolute advantage over New York City in cattle raising. However, New York City has an absolute advantage over some cattle-producing areas in banking and finance due to its location.

efficiency and lower costs is that specialization enables the producer to concentrate on only one job. A veterinarian, for example, is much better at keeping cattle healthy than the Ruizes because the veterinarian has specialized knowledge and experience.

**Absolute and comparative advantage**  In addition to the advantages of specialization as such, specialization is most efficient when it is based on natural advantages. The residents of New York City cannot very well produce beef there. Grazing cattle in Manhattan would be difficult, to say the least. City dwellers must get their beef from a place where the conditions are more suitable for producing it, such as on the plains of the western states. That area has an absolute advantage over New York City in beef production because the resources are more suitable for the production of cattle, and the production costs are therefore much less. New York, for its part, has an absolute advantage over the western plains states in such things as banking and finance because New York is a hub of commerce. Its advantages were originally due to its strategic geographical location on a natural harbor and then to the historical development of its institutions.

Oklahoma obviously has an absolute advantage over New York City in raising cattle, but absolute advantage does not account for all, or even most, specialization. It's apparent why you wouldn't raise cattle in New York City. But why not produce the beef for New Yorkers someplace closer than Oklahoma or Texas? It is possible, for example, to raise cattle

**absolute advantage**  when each of two producers can produce a different good or service more efficiently than can the other producer, each of the producers has an absolute advantage in the good or service that he produces most efficiently.

just across the Hudson River in New Jersey, and, in fact, some cattle are raised there. But most of the limited agricultural land in New Jersey is better allocated to farming and dairying because cattle grazing takes too much room in a state where land is scarce. New Jersey can make better use of its scarce land resources in farming and dairying, which take less space. It has a greater advantage in these economic activities than it does in raising beef cattle. Although New Jersey with its fertile land has the resources to produce either vegetables and dairy products or beef, it has a comparative advantage relative to the plains states in farming and dairying because those activities take less space than raising beef cattle. The plains states, on the other hand, have a comparative advantage in cattle raising because their vast land resources are better suited to that activity.

The distinction between specialization based on comparative advantage rather than absolute advantage is important. Assume that the best surgeon in town is also the best auto mechanic. Such a person would have an absolute advantage in both surgery and auto repairing, but that person's time would be spent more valuably in healing sick people than sick automobiles because the economic value of a surgeon's time is greater than the economic value of an auto mechanic's time. Although the surgeon has an absolute advantage in both endeavors, the comparative advantage lies in surgery. Individuals, regions within a country, and nations all tend to produce those things in which they have a comparative advantage.

**Interdependence**  Specialization results in interdependence—the reliance of different individuals and businesses on each other. José and Maria Ruiz could not specialize in raising cattle without the help and cooperation of others. They depend on the veterinarian to keep the cattle healthy; on various manufacturers to supply trucks, gasoline and equipment; and on the feedlot operator to fatten the cattle for market. They depend on the government to protect their herd from epidemics of hoof-and-mouth disease. And they depend on consumers in cities to buy the beef produced.

This interdependence requires an economic system to coordinate the various activities. As the degree of specialization and interdependence has increased over the years, so has the complexity of the economic system. When Bill Hayden drove his longhorns across the country, our economic system was much simpler than it is today. People were not as dependent on each other or on government services. Now, because of interdependence, it is more important than ever that the economic system should function effectively.

*Comparative advantage = efficiency advantage*

**comparative advantage**  when one producer has an efficiency advantage over another producer in both of two products, but has a greater relative advantage in one product than in the other, the efficient producer has a comparative advantage in the product in which he has the greater relative efficiency; and the inefficient producer has a comparative advantage in the product in which he has the lesser relative efficiency.

**interdependence**  the relationship between individuals and institutions in a country or between countries that arises because of specialization of production.

# case application

## The Efficiencyburger

In 1948, the McDonald brothers opened a small restaurant in San Bernardino, California, specializing in the production of hamburgers. They developed a method of producing hamburgers so easily and inexpensively that they could be sold profitably at fifteen cents each.

Today, the McDonald's chain of restaurants (the original McDonald brothers are no longer associated with it) sells more hamburgers than any comparable operation. The key to the McDonald method of hamburger production is specialization. The menu at a McDonald's restaurant is limited to a select number of items. This cuts food waste to a minimum and eliminates much of the expense of a full-line restaurant.

For the sake of efficiency, each job in the McDonald operation has been refined and simplified. Workers have one speciality, although they can also perform other jobs. A typical restaurant has a fry specialist, a grill specialist, and a shakes specialist, all coordinated by a production control specialist. To learn the system of operation, owners and operators of individual restaurants attend McDonald's "Hamburger University" in Elk Grove, Illinois, where they take a 19-day course that leads to a "Bachelor of Hamburgerology, with a minor in French Fries."

The McDonald's operation is dedicated to speed. A hamburger, french fries, and a shake can be turned out in 50 seconds. Production is tightly controlled in an effort to maintain freshness. Unsold burgers are to be destroyed if not sold within 10 minutes, french fries after 7 minutes.

Everything is done the same way at each of the McDonald's restaurants—the way hamburgers are made, the napkins used, even the greetings used by the salespeople are the same.

Everything is even done the same way at the Moscow McDonald's, opened in 1990. The first fast-food restaurant in the Soviet Union, it is the biggest McDonald's in the world, capable of serving over 15,000 customers a day. At first, the Russian patrons had to adjust to the McDonald's system. On opening day they attempted to line up in one line for the 27 cash registers, until they were encouraged to go to whichever cash register had the shortest line. Even more unusual were the pleasant greetings from the service workers, the result of hours of drills by McDonald's trainers, something Soviet customers were quite unaccustomed to.

## *Economic Reasoning*

1. What economic principle did McDonald's adopt that was so successful that it was copied by others? *Specialization of labor and menu.*
2. How does the McDonald's operation reflect the relationship between specialization and interdependence? *They are dependent on Hamburger University?*
3. One objective of economics is to avoid waste, but McDonald's policy is to destroy hamburgers if not sold within 10 minutes. Is this a good idea? Why or why not? *"Quality"*

# What Are the Principal Types of Economic Systems?

The greater the specialization and interdependence in economic activities, the more important is the development of an economic system to organize and coordinate production and distribution. Different types of economic systems have evolved. All of them must resolve the questions of what to produce, how to produce it, and how to allocate what is produced. But different economic systems make these determinations in different ways.

**Market economies**  The key to allocating resources and finished products in a market economy is the function of the price system in the marketplace. In 1856 beef sold for such a high price in New York that it made it worthwhile for Bill Hayden to spend a year and a half bringing cattle all the way from Oklahoma to market them there. Today, the Ruizes

*(handwritten margin notes:)*
*market economy: ec. syst. in which the ec. basic questions what how for whom are solved by buyers and sellers who interact in markets*

*marketplace = network = location*

Resources and finished products in a market economy are allocated by the functioning of the price system in the marketplace.

**market economy**  an economic system in which the basic questions of what, how, and for whom to produce are resolved primarily by buyers and sellers interacting in markets.

**marketplace (market)**  a network of dealings between buyers and sellers of a resource or product (good or service); the dealings may take place at a particular location or they may take place by communicating at a distance with no face-to-face contact between buyers and sellers.

Centrally-directed economies have often concentrated on the production of heavy industrial goods, tractors, and trucks, rather than on the production of consumer goods.

decide how many head of cattle to breed on the basis of beef prices in the marketplace, and they decide how to raise their cattle on the basis of feed prices and other production costs. Prices also determine who will consume the beef; namely, those who can afford it and are willing to pay the price.

Market economies are often called capitalist or free enterprise economies. We will examine in more detail how such an economic system resolves the what, how, and for whom questions in the next section of this chapter.

**Centrally directed economies** In centrally directed or command economies, most production is controlled by the government. The major decisions concerning what to produce, how to produce, and for whom to produce are made

**centrally directed (command) economy** an economic system in which the basic questions of what, how, and for whom to produce are resolved primarily by governmental authority.

by centralized authoritarian agencies. Typically, a central planning commission draws up a master plan, which is then put into effect by regional and local government agencies. The natural resources and capital goods are owned by the government. Workers are generally employed in government enterprises or in the government agencies that plan and administer the system.

Resources are allocated in a much different way in a centrally directed economy than they are in a market economy. In a market economy, ranchers like the Ruizes, responding to signals from the market for beef, decide how much beef will be produced. In a command economy, the central planning authority decides how much beef will be produced. The ranchers are given production goals and permission to buy the supplies necessary to produce the amount of beef decided upon. They may also be given directions about most of the details involved in cattle production from the selection of feed to the number of steers to be slaughtered.

Once the beef is produced, it is placed on sale in government-owned stores. The price, rather than being determined by the interplay between sellers and buyers in the marketplace, is determined by the government. When there is an insufficient quantity available to satisfy all who would like to purchase it, meat may be allocated to buyers by a formal rationing system, with each customer limited to buying a certain amount of meat each week or month. Or it may be allocated on a "first come, first served" basis, resulting in lines of customers at stores when there are supplies available. The operation of centrally directed economies is covered in chapter 17.

**Traditional economies**   In earlier ages, and, to some extent in nonindustrialized countries today, basic economic decisions depended on tradition and not on the function of markets or the commands of a centralized authority. In traditional economies goods are produced and distributed in certain ways because that is the way it has always been done.

We have seen how the raising of beef cattle can be controlled by decisions based on market considerations or by the decisions of a centrally directed planning authority. In India, which in many ways has a traditional economy, the business of raising beef cattle is very limited because the majority of people are Hindu and it is against Hindu tradition and religion to eat beef. Cattle are numerous in India, but most of them are not slaughtered and marketed due to the power of traditional religious beliefs. Another example of tradition at work in India is the way jobs are

**traditional economy** an economic system in which the basic questions of what, how, and for whom to produce are resolved primarily by custom and tradition.

Tradition can often determine what goods and services are available. In India, strong religious taboos limit beef production.

allocated. For centuries, India's population was divided by a caste system, a way of classifying people according to the social class, or caste, into which they were born. People born into certain castes could only do the kind of jobs those castes traditionally did. Although now prohibited by Indian law, the tradition of the caste system maintains a strong hold over the behavior of the people. It still determines to an extent what kinds of occupations are open to which people, how much they earn, and, therefore, how much income they will have to purchase goods and services.

Experience has shown that tradition is still very strong in many nonindustrial nations that are trying to industrialize. Even the lure of profits, an almost irresistible force in most places, is frequently unable to overcome the force of custom in traditional societies. The nonindustrialized countries are the subject of chapter 18.

**Mixed economies** The actual systems in existence throughout the world are not pure market, pure centrally directed, or pure traditional economies. They are mixtures of the three, and these mixed economies take many different forms. Some, such as that of the United States, are basically market economies with a mixture of government regulation and government ownership. For example, in the cattle industry the government encourages beef production by favorable tax benefits for investment in the industry. The government inspects cattle for disease and regulates sani-

**mixed economy** an economic system in which the basic questions of what, how, and for whom to produce are resolved by a mixture of market forces with governmental direction and/or custom and tradition.

A hydroelectric dam is an example of the type of goods produced by government in mixed economies such as the United States.

tary conditions in meat processing. There have been times when it even imposed price controls on meat. The U.S. government does not produce the beef, but it does own many dams that supply water and electricity to the ranches. The government also owns land that it leases to ranchers for cattle grazing.

Other economies, such as that of China, are primarily centrally directed, but with some private ownership and sales. The Soviet Union and the countries of Eastern Europe are in transition from centrally directed economies to market economies. As for India, its economy combines all three forms—market, command, and traditional—in a very mixed system.

Most of this book, with the exception of the last two chapters, describes the operation of the type of economic system found in the United States and other western industrialized countries. They are basically market economies in which the government plays a significant but secondary role.

# case application

## Capitalists in the U.S.S.R.

Until late 1986, the only legal private enterprise in the Soviet Union was the raising of agricultural produce on "private plots" of land, only 1.5% of Soviet farmland. There was, however, an underground market economy producing a variety of services and products. Repair people, carpenters, and mechanics, with regular jobs at state agencies, moonlighted on the side, often for customers that they contacted at their jobs. Frequently, those extracurricular services were performed with tools and materials illegally "borrowed" from government agencies.

Perhaps the most surprising parts of the underground economy were the illegal private manufacturing activities and the widespread marketing of illicitly produced goods through regular retail outlets. Those so-called "left-hand" goods were often produced on the sly in the same government factories that produced official goods, and by the same workers. The raw materials needed for this extra production were acquired by padding the orders for official goods or by skimping on the materials used in producing those goods. Individuals caught engaging in such activities were severely punished with long prison terms or even, in a few extreme cases, execution.

In changing over from a centrally directed to a market system, the Soviet workers were permitted to form cooperatives to produce goods or provide services. There must be at least three persons involved in the ownership of the enterprise. This regulation is presumably aimed at preventing "capitalist exploitation," a traditional target of communism. However, since the three people can all be from the same family, say a mother, father, and child, the regulation is not very meaningful.

More of a problem for the co-ops is the tax imposed on them, which ranges from 20% to as high as 40%. Another problem is the Soviet Mafia that extorts money from many co-ops and controls others.

The reason that the Mafia has moved into the co-ops in a big way is that they are so profitable. Given the hunger that Soviet consumers have for goods and services in short supply, co-ops that can satisfy that demand take in a great deal of money.

Their profitability has resulted in much resentment on the part of other Soviet citizens. Workers accuse the co-ops of making money either by supplying high-cost luxury services, such as restaurants to which the average Russian cannot gain entrance, or obtaining scarce goods and reselling them at extremely high markups.

### *Economic Reasoning*

1. What type of economic system do Soviet co-ops represent? How can you tell? *centrally directed*
2. What led individuals to take the risks of engaging in illegal private manufacturing activities when the penalties were so great if they were caught?
3. Would you approve of or condemn the co-ops if you were a Soviet consumer? Why? How about if you were a government official? What effect do they have on the efficiency of the economy?

70

# How Does a Market System Resolve the Three Basic Economic Questions?

As we have seen, there are three basic types of economic systems. The one we are most familiar with is that of the United States—the market economy. A market economy determines (what) to produce, (how) production will take place, and how output will be allocated to individuals largely on the basis of market forces. What these forces are and how they form the answers to the basic questions are surveyed here and examined more closely in the following chapters.

**Markets**   The word "market" can have a variety of meanings. Markets differ in the way they are structured and the way they operate. Some are highly organized and are found in particular locations to which the buyers and sellers come. José and Maria Ruiz sell their cattle at a cattle auction—a market where the buyers and sellers of beef cattle come together. The buyers bid against each other for the animals offered for sale by the sellers. The highest bidder gets the cattle. Both buyers and sellers get what they want at the best prices they are able to obtain, and the market is usually cleared of all merchandise.

based on auction

Other markets are more dispersed and unorganized. The hamburger meat that is made from the Ruizes' cattle is sold in many different supermarkets at various prices. Sometimes a supermarket does not sell all of its hamburger, while at other times it may sell out its stock, which means its customers have to look elsewhere or do without.

**Product and factor markets**   Hamburger meat sold by a supermarket to its customers is sold in what economists call a product market—a market in which a finished product is sold to the consumer. However, if the hamburger meat is sold to McDonald's or to other commercial buyers, it is then part of a factor market—a market in which goods and services are purchased and then used to make final products. The land, labor, and capital resources used in production are sold in factor markets.

The Ruizes buy their cattle feed, hire their ranch hands, and acquire stud bulls in factor markets. They also sell their fattened cattle in a factor market, because the cattle are part of the production input for a slaughterhouse. The butchered beef is sold in the factor market to supermarket chains, and it is not until the hamburger, roasts, or steaks are sold to the consumer that the beef is finally sold in a product market.

**product market**   a market in which finished goods and services are exchanged.
**factor market**   a market in which resources and semifinished products are exchanged.

Retail stores are primary examples of product markets that sell finished products such as the packaged meats found in supermarkets.

**Incentives** Why do markets function in the first place? What is it that makes them work? Bill Hayden's story provides some of the answers to these questions. In 1856, Hayden felt that New Yorkers would pay enough for beef to make his cross-country cattle drive profitable for him. The high prices New Yorkers were willing to pay for beef provided Hayden with an incentive. In a market system, the opportunity to make a profit is the usual incentive for providing a good or service.

The profit incentive also motivates the Ruizes. Today, just as 100 years ago, if there are people who are able and willing to pay a price high enough to cover production costs and yield some profit, an incentive exists for someone to produce the good or service wanted. A rise in price is generally an incentive to produce more. A decrease in price generally brings a decrease in production.

A rise in beef prices would probably provide the incentive needed for ranchers to increase their cattle stocks and encourage more ranchers to raise cattle. It might also induce feedlot operators to fatten their beef for a longer time in order to get heavier animals to sell at the higher prices. A decline in beef prices would be a signal to ranchers to produce fewer cattle and perhaps cause some ranchers to stop raising cattle altogether. Ranch hands would be laid off, and there would be less investment in breeding stock because of poorer profit prospects. In the market system, prices and the profit motive determine what will be produced, how it will be produced, and for whom.

**Circular flow of the economy** In a market economy, the factor and product markets support each other and keep the system going. Owners of resources provide the production inputs—the land, labor, and capital—that business firms need to function, and business firms provide the finished goods and services consumers want. The owners of resources are also the consumers, who are sometimes referred to as households. Firms pay money to the households for the use of the factors of production. These payments are rent for land, wages and salaries for labor, and interest for

**incentive** a motivation to undertake an action or to refrain from undertaking an action; in a market economy profits are the incentive to produce.
**production inputs (inputs)** the factors of production used in producing a good or service.
**household** an economic unit consisting of an individual or a family.
**rent** a factor payment for the use of land.
**wage or salary** a factor payment for labor service.
**interest** a factor payment for the use of capital.

the use of capital. Households, for their part, use the factor incomes they receive to purchase the goods and services they want from the business firms. Everyone's receipts are someone else's expenditure.

The basic functioning of a market economy can be shown as a circular flow diagram with two complementary circles flowing in opposite directions. The outer circle shows the flow of inputs and outputs from firms and households—the production inputs provided by the households to the firms and the finished outputs provided by the firms to the households. The inner circle shows the corresponding money payments made for the inputs—the rents, wages, and interest—and the money payments for the finished goods and services purchased.

The model of the market system shown here is overly simplified. The transactions between firms in the business sector are not shown in our diagram, nor are the effects of government, foreign trade, or the banking system. The diagram shows a closed, static system without growth. It is a useful model, however, for illustrating the interdependence of economic sectors and the self-sustaining operation of a market economy. We will make use of a more elaborate model for studying how the economy works in later chapters.

**factor incomes**   the return to factors of production as a reward for productive activity.
**circular flow diagram**   a schematic drawing showing the economic relationships between the major sectors of an economic system.

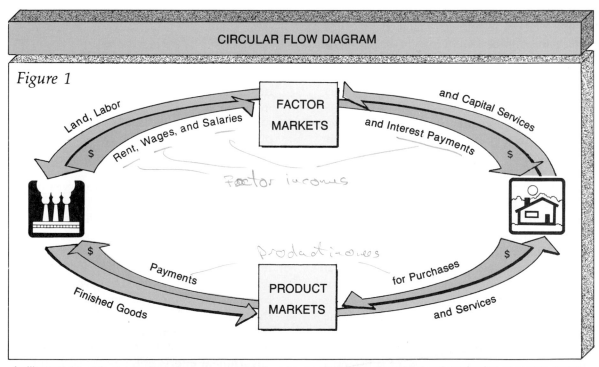

## CIRCULAR FLOW DIAGRAM

*Figure 1*

Land, Labor — Rent, Wages, and Salaries — FACTOR MARKETS — and Interest Payments — and Capital Services

Factor incomes

Payments — Finished Goods — PRODUCT MARKETS — for Purchases — and Services

Production

As illustrated by this circular flow diagram, a constant exchange of goods and services and production resources occurs between businesses and individuals (households) in a self-sustaining market economy.

# What Is the Answer to Power Brownouts?

The nation's electric utilities are facing a serious shortage of capacity in the 1990s. Growing demand on one side and the high costs and environmental obstacles of new power generators on the other have left the industry with very little reserve capacity entering the decade.

Considering the problems of the nuclear power industry (chapter 2, p. 46) and the fact that the world's reserves of petroleum, currently our major energy resource, are expected to be increasingly scarce and expensive in coming years, what will provide us with energy in the future?

For the United States, coal is one obvious answer because we have so much of it. It is estimated that we have a 200-year supply of coal reserves in the ground. Will coal again become, as it was earlier in our history, the "king" of energy?

The main problem with coal is that it is not a "clean" source of energy. To begin with, coal mining operations despoil the landscape, especially strip mining in which scoops gouge out the coal from enormous pits. But the most serious drawback of coal is that when it is burned in utility generating plants or factory furnaces it pollutes the air with particles and gases that cause "acid rain" and contribute to the greenhouse effect (chapter 1, p. 5).

Another possible candidate to take over from petroleum is natural gas. It is much cleaner and neater to obtain, to transport, and to burn than coal. Until recently, however, it was believed that supplies of natural gas would disappear along with our dwindling petroleum. In the past, natural gas has been obtained as a coproduct from the same wells as the oil. But recent findings of geological surveys and developments of new drilling technologies give promise of substantial additional supplies of natural gas in this country. It has been estimated that in one area alone, along the Texas and Louisiana coasts, there exists 24 quadrillion cubic feet of gas. (That is the number 24 followed by 15 zeros.) In energy output, that is equivalent to 4 trillion barrels of oil, which is about twice the currently estimated petroleum reserves of the whole world. Comparably immense natural gas reserves are thought to exist deep underground in an arc stretching across southern Oklahoma and the Texas Panhandle and in the Overthrust Belt of the Rocky Mountains.

Other possible sources of future energy supplies are synthetic fuels (gas or liquid made from coal), oil shale, and renewable resources from solar power, wind power, and the ocean's tides. None of these, however, is expected to provide a very significant portion of our energy needs in the foreseeable future.

## Economic Reasoning

1. Natural gas piped to a homeowner for heating a house is sold in what kind of a market? Natural gas piped to a factory for heating its boilers is sold in what kind of a market? Why can the same good be sold by the same supplier in two different types of markets?

2. If the United States has vast reserves of both coal and natural gas, what will determine which of the two will replace petroleum as our principal source of energy?

3. If natural gas is less polluting than coal when burned, should the government promote the use of gas and discourage the use of coal, or should the government leave the determination entirely to the marketplace? Indicate what forms government intervention might take and give the reasons for your answer.

# Putting It Together

In attempting to overcome the problem of scarcity, *specialization* in production has developed in order to increase efficiency and enlarge output. Workers, regions, and nations get the largest returns for their efforts by concentrating on the economic activity that they perform most efficiently.

A producer who can produce a good or service with a smaller amount of factor inputs of land, labor, and capital than another producer has an *absolute advantage* in the production of that good or service.

If one producer has an absolute advantage in the production of two or more goods or services, it would pay for that producer to specialize in that good or service produced with the greatest efficiency relative to another producer of the same goods or services. The second producer, who is less efficient in producing both outputs, should specialize in producing that good or service which is produced with the least relative inefficiency. This is a case of *comparative advantage*.

Specialization results in *interdependence*. Workers and firms are dependent on each other and on the buyers of the finished products. They are often dependent on government services as well. The more specialized and interdependent economic activities become, the greater is the importance of a smoothly functioning economic system to coordinate production and distribution.

There are three basic types of economic systems and each resolves the "what," "how," and "for whom" questions in a different way. In a *market economy*, the interplay of buyers and sellers in many various markets determines what will be produced, how it will be produced, and for whom it will be produced. Markets are places or arrangements for the exchange of goods and services. In a *command economy*, a centrally directed, authoritarian agency decides what to produce, how to produce it, and for whom to produce it. *Traditional economies* use custom to resolve these basic questions. Most economic systems today are actually *mixed economies* with elements of traditional, command, and market economies.

The United States has basically a market economy. Producers in this economic system react to price signals from markets and the desire to make a profit when deciding what to produce and how to produce it. The prices of goods and services and individuals' ability to pay for them determine who will get these products.

There are basically two types of markets in our market economy—*product markets* and *factor markets*. A factor is anything that is used to produce goods and services. Factor markets deal in goods and services that will be used in production. Product markets provide goods and services used directly by the consumer. It is the *households* which provide the *production inputs* to the business firms which supply semifinished and finished products.

In our market economy, each person's spending is another person's income. The *rent, wages,* and *interest* paid out by business firms to households are spent by households in exchange for the goods and services produced by business firms. The flows of finished goods and services and factor inputs are paid for by the counterflows of *factor incomes* and sales revenues. Together they form a *circular flow* in our economy that is self-perpetuating.

The manner in which society organizes production to deal with the problem of scarcity is continually evolving, to better satisfy the economic goal of efficiency.

# Perspective

## The Industrial Revolution

**James Watt** and his improved steam engine, which was perhaps the most important invention of the Industrial Revolution.

Additional information on the Industrial Revolution can be found in *The Industrial Revolution* by T. S. Ashton (New York: Oxford University Press, 1961); *The Industrial Revolution and Economic Growth* by R. M. Hartwell (Oxford: Blackwell, 1970); and *Workers in the Industrial Revolution* by P. N. Stearns (New Brunswick, N.J.: Transaction Books, 1974).

The Industrial Revolution was a period of great change during which basically agricultural countries with small, home-based "cottage industries" were transformed into industrial societies characterized by machine-dominated factory production centered in heavily populated cities.

The Industrial Revolution first took place in Great Britain between 1750 and 1850. It did not become widely diffused in the rest of Europe and in North America until the last half of the nineteenth century and is only now spreading to some parts of the world as the nonindustrialized nations strive to change from agricultural economies to industrial economies.

During the century between the mid-1700s and the mid-1800s drastic changes in production methods and in the products themselves occurred. The changes were initiated by the invention of spinning and weaving equipment in the textile industry that took textile production out of homes and put it into factories. Perhaps the most important invention was the improved steam engine developed by James Watt in 1769 because it provided an efficient motive source to power the other new inventions. It also advanced the art of machine toolmaking.

The production of textiles, metal products, and other goods with the use of power equipment instead of hand tools gave Great Britain such a large competitive edge over other countries that it became the wealthiest and most powerful country of the nineteenth century.

The wealth created by the Industrial Revolution at first did not benefit the workers. In fact, many workers viewed the new machinery as a competitive threat to their livelihood. They feared machines would put them out of work. There were riots, and factories and machinery were destroyed. As a result, laws were passed which made the willful destruction of any building containing machinery an offense punishable by death. Working conditions were very bad; and labor, especially child labor, was grossly exploited in the early factory system of the Industrial Revolution.

In our time, we have reaped the benefits of the Industrial Revolution—high consumption levels and increased leisure time—along with its costs, such as pollution of the environment and depletion of our energy and other resources. The slowing of productivity growth of recent decades has led to calls for a "new Industrial Revolution," which might again transform not only production methods but society itself.

For
Further
Study
and
Analysis

## Study Questions

1. Does the operation of the Ruizes' cattle ranch represent specialization according to absolute advantage or comparative advantage or both? Why?

2. What is an example of a specialized job with which you are personally familiar? How is that job performed efficiently as a result of specialization?

3. Specialization and interdependence increase efficiency, but what disadvantage might result from interdependence? Give an example.

4. What instances of interdependence can you identify in the cattle industry?

5. Was the 1856 cattle drive of Bill Hayden representative of a traditional economy or a market economy? Why?

6. How does tradition in the United States affect the resolution of any one of the three basic economic questions?

7. What is an example of a relatively well organized market in your area? What is an example of a relatively unorganized market in your area?

8. What changes in the Soviet Union are making use of incentives?

9. Give an example of a factor market in which you have participated. What factor did you provide and what was the factor income called?

10. How did the Industrial Revolution affect the outcome of the three basic economic questions?

## Exercises in Analysis

1. Visit a local fast-food restaurant and observe the job specialization in production there. Write a short paper on what you observe.
2. The case application "Capitalists in the U.S.S.R." demonstrated how elements of a market economy have been introduced into the command economy of the Soviet Union. Prepare a short paper showing how elements of command and traditional economies can be found in the United States.
3. On the basis of what you know about different countries and using any available resource materials, make a list of countries that would be classed as basically market economies, centrally directed economies, or traditional economies.
4. Write a short essay on what will determine the type of energy production that will be used in the future in a market economy.

## Further Reading

Fishwick, Marshall, ed. *Ronald Revisited: The World of Ronald McDonald.* Bowling Green, Ohio: Bowling Green University Popular Press, 1983. A collection of essays on McDonald's and the fast-food industry.

Goldman, Marshall I. *U.S.S.R. in Crisis: The Failure of an Economic System.* New York: W. W. Norton, 1983. A critical look at the Soviet economy.

Goldman, Minton F., ed. *Global Studies: The Soviet Union and Eastern Europe.* Third edition. Guilford, CT: Dushkin Publishing Group, 1990. A comprehensive volume providing a foundation of information—geographic, cultural, economic, political, and historical—allowing students to better understand the current and future problems within this region.

Haveman, Robert, and Kenyon Knopf. *The Market System,* chapters 1 and 2. New York: John Wiley & Sons, 1981. These two chapters discuss the basic model of a market economy.

Lachmann, Ludwig M. *The Market as an Economic Process.* Oxford, U.K.: Blackwell Scientific Publications, 1986. An examination of how markets function and what they accomplish, looked at from an economic doctrines approach.

Oppenheimer, Harold L. *Cowboy Arithmetic: Cattle as an Investment.* Danville, Ill.: The Interstate Printers and Publishers, 1961. Explains the operations and economics of cattle ranching.

Stobaugh, Robert, and Daniel Yergin, eds. *Energy Future.* New York: Vintage Books, 1983. An examination of alternative energy sources to satisfy our future needs.

White, Colin. *Russia and America: The Roots of Economic Divergence.* London: Croom Helm, 1987. Compares the resources, history, institutions, and interactions of market and government in the U.S. and the U.S.S.R.

# MARKET PRICING

*The American economy is run basically by the marketplace, with each individual helping to direct the economy by the market choices he or she makes. The marketplace, however, sets its own terms; and both consumers and producers are forced to adjust their decisions to market changes. This chapter's introductory article illustrates how an act of nature can alter the market and our behavior.*

## The Peanut Butter Crunch

Peanut butter sandwiches are almost as much a part of American food culture as apple pie. Generations of children have been raised on them. It was therefore a blow to American families and their budgets when the great peanut butter shortage hit, emptying grocery shelves and causing prices to double in a single year.

Who was responsible for this rapid rise in peanut butter prices? Was there a sinister international peanut conspiracy manipulating the market to drive prices up? No, not really. Actually, it was just nature playing tricks with agricultural production again. A summer drought in Georgia, Texas, and other peanut-growing states reduced the peanut crop by 42%. This shortage raised peanut prices from the government-supported price level of $45 a ton to as high as $2,000 a ton.

Faced with such high peanut butter prices, some buyers turned to a substitute made with cotton nut kernels flavored with peanut oil. While this substitute had fewer calories and was more nutritious than peanut butter, the substitute's best attribute was its price, which was about one-third less than peanut butter.

However, those with a real passion for peanut butter stuck to the high-priced original in such numbers that the shelves in many stores were cleared of it. Although there was a good deal of consumer resistance to the high price, not everyone was willing to settle for a substitute. Actually, the decline in peanut butter sales was proportionally smaller than the decline in the peanut harvest. This was probably because peanut butter manufacturers purchased more of the available peanuts than the customary 50% of the crop they normally used.

The peanut butter crunch focused public attention on the fact that the federal government had, as part of its price-support programs for many agricultural products, a system of regulating the size of the nation's peanut crop. The agricultural price supports were enacted before World War II, but of all the price-supported crops only peanuts and tobacco had specific parcels of land designated for growing them. There were some 59,000 pieces of land allotted to peanut grow-

Droughts are not the only reason for higher peanut butter prices. Federal government restrictions on the amount of acreage allowed for commercial peanut growing squeeze the supply and push prices higher.

ing, and despite the shortage, anyone growing more than one acre of peanuts elsewhere could be fined or sent to prison.

A consumer group claims that government regulators cost consumers $250 million a year more than they would otherwise pay for peanut products. But efforts in Congress to remove the acreage restrictions on peanut raising have been strongly resisted by the peanut lobby, even though an expansion of peanut production and a lowering of prices to the consumer might very well result. The removal of those restrictions would also reduce the chances of a future drought causing yet another peanut butter crunch.

## Chapter Preview

*Market prices are the result of many influences, including consumer preferences, available supplies, and government price supports. The prices of agricultural products are especially sensitive to these influences. They are affected by weather conditions, damage from insects or disease, changes in foreign demand for agricultural products from the United States, changes in the prices of products that can be used as close substitutes, and, of course, government regulations. This chapter will explore how market influences interact to establish prices. We shall investigate the following questions: What forces determine prices in the marketplace? What determines demand? What determines supply? Why do prices change?*

## Learning Objectives

*After completing this chapter, you should be able to:*

1. *Explain the laws of demand and supply.*
2. *List the determinants of demand.*
3. *List the determinants of supply.*
4. *Distinguish between short-run and long-run supply.*
5. *Identify the causes of shifts in demand and how they affect market equilibrium.*
6. *Identify the causes of shifts in supply and how they affect market equilibrium.*
7. *Explain why prices move toward an equilibrium price.*
8. *Distinguish between a change in demand and a change in quantity demanded.*

# What Forces Determine Prices in the Marketplace?

The key element in the functioning of a market economy is the allocation of resources through the voluntary exchange of goods and services. These goods and services are not directly traded for each other in our modern economy, as they would be in a primitive barter economy. Instead they are bought and sold in markets where each good and service has its price. This analysis section examines how prices are determined.

**Demand**  Households in the United States consume about 540 million pounds of peanut butter every year. It is a staple of the American diet. When the price of peanut butter nearly doubled, some people cut back their purchases. The quantity demanded decreased because of the higher price. For virtually every product or service, an increase in price results in a smaller amount demanded. This is the law of demand: a rise in price causes a fall in the quantity demanded, while a decline in price causes an increase in the quantity demanded.

There are two reasons why people behave according to the law of demand. One reason is that when the price of a product goes down, people can afford to buy more of it, and when the price goes up, they can't afford to buy as much. This is the income effect.

The second reason why people behave according to the law of demand is that when price of a product rises, people tend to buy less of that product and buy a cheaper substitute instead. This is the substitution effect, replacing a more costly item with a less costly one.

Let's take a look at a hypothetical family—the Smiths—buying peanut butter at alternative prices. At $1.25 a jar, the

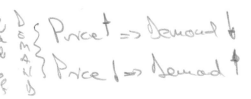

**quantity demanded**  the amount of a good or service that consumers would purchase at a particular price.
**law of demand**  the quantity demanded of a good or service varies inversely with its price; the lower the price the larger the quantity demanded, and the higher the price smaller the quantity demanded.
**income effect**  the effect of a change in the price of a good or service on the amount purchased which results from a change in purchasing power of the consumer's income due to the price change.
**substitution effect**  the effect of a change in the price of a good or service on the amount purchased which results from the consumer substituting a relatively less expensive alternative.

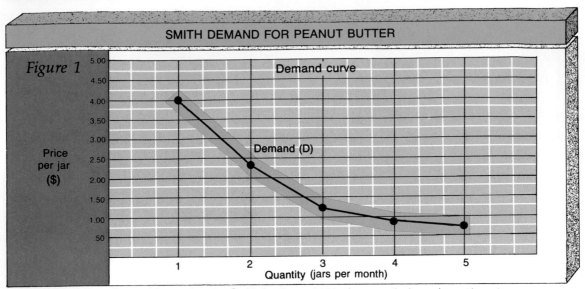

**SMITH DEMAND FOR PEANUT BUTTER**

*Figure 1*

Price per jar ($)

Demand curve

Demand (D)

Quantity (jars per month)

The number of jars of peanut butter that the Smith family would buy in a month depends on the price.

**Table 1**

### SMITH DEMAND SCHEDULE

| Price per jar | Number of jars per month |
|---------------|--------------------------|
| $ .75         | 5                        |
| .90           | 4                        |
| 1.25          | 3                        |
| 2.35          | 2                        |
| 4.00          | 1                        |

**demand** the relationship between the quantities of a good or service that consumers desire to purchase at any particular time and the various prices that can exist for the good or service.
**demand schedule** a table recording the number of units of a good or service demanded at various possible prices.
**demand curve** a graphic representation of the relationship between price and quantity demanded.

Smiths buy three jars of peanut butter a month. If the price rises to $2.35 a jar, they cut back their purchases to two jars a month. If another year's drought caused the price to go up to $4.00 a jar, the Smiths cut down to one jar a month. At prices higher than $4.00 a jar, the Smiths give up peanut butter altogether as a luxury they can't afford.

On the other hand, if the government eliminates price supports, and the price of a jar of peanut butter falls to $.90 a jar, the Smiths increase their consumption to four jars a month. With a further drop to $.75 a jar, the Smiths would increase consumption to five jars a month.

The Smiths' demand for peanut butter is given in Table 1, which shows the number of jars they would buy each month at different possible prices. This is the Smiths' demand schedule for peanut butter.

A demand schedule also can be shown in the form of a diagram as in Figure 1. In this diagram of the Smiths' demand schedule for peanut butter, the alternative prices for peanut butter are shown on the vertical axis and the corresponding quantities of peanut butter that they would buy on the horizontal axis. This is the customary way to diagram a market situation. Prices are always on the vertical axis, and quantities are always on the horizontal axis.

If we locate for each price on the vertical axis the corresponding quantity demanded at that price on the horizontal axis, given in Table 1, and then draw a line connecting these points we have a demand curve. (We locate points on the demand curve by drawing perpendiculars from corresponding prices and quantities, as shown in the appendix to

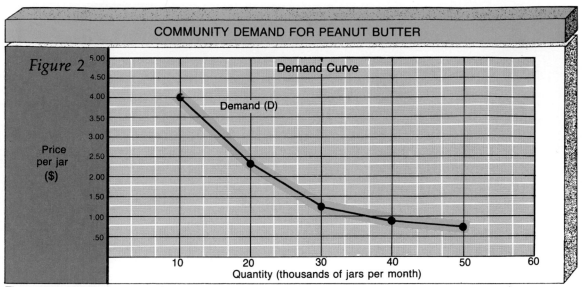

**COMMUNITY DEMAND FOR PEANUT BUTTER**

*Figure 2*

Demand Curve

Demand (D)

Price per jar ($)

Quantity (thousands of jars per month)

The number of jars that 10,000 families similar to the Smiths would buy in a month depends on the price.

chapter 1, page 29.) Just as the law of demand dictates, the quantity demanded increases when the price decreases. The demand curve on our chart slopes downward from upper left to lower right. The lower the price, the more the Smiths would buy; the higher the price, the less the Smiths would buy.

That is the individual household demand for peanut butter. How about the whole market demand for peanut butter? Let us assume that in the town where the Smiths live there are 10,000 other families who have the same demand for peanut butter that the Smiths have. If we multiply the number of jars that the Smith family would buy at different prices by 10,000, we get a hypothetical community demand schedule for peanut butter. This is shown in Table 2. To assume that all the families have the same demand for peanut butter is, of course, a simplification. In real life, different families have different demands for peanut butter as well as for other products and services. (We will see in the next analysis section what determines each individual's demand.)

The data in Table 2 is plotted on the diagram in Figure 2. This shows how much peanut butter would be demanded at different prices ranging from $.75 to $4.00 per jar in a community composed of 10,000 families, each with the same demand for peanut butter as the Smiths.

**Supply**   Demand schedules are economic models that help us understand consumer reaction to various prices of a product. To see the behavior of supply on the sellers' side of the market, we make use of a supply schedule. Sellers have

| Table 2 COMMUNITY DEMAND SCHEDULE | |
|---|---|
| Price per jar | Number of jars per month |
| $ .75 | 50,000 |
| .90 | 40,000 |
| 1.25 | 30,000 |
| 2.35 | 20,000 |
| 4.00 | 10,000 |

**community demand schedule**   the sum of all the individual demand schedules in a particular market showing the total quantities demanded by the buyers in the market at each of the various possible prices.
**supply**   the relationship between the quantities of a good or service that sellers wish to market at any particular time and the various prices that can exist for the good or service.
**supply schedule**   a table recording the number of units of a good or service supplied at various possible prices.

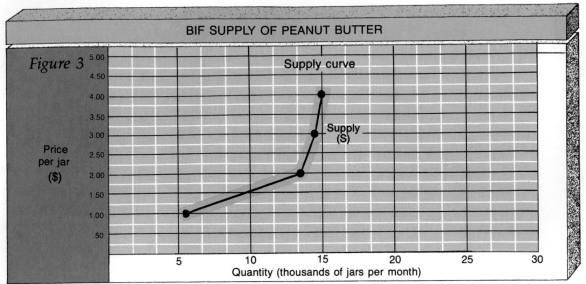

*Figure 3*

**BIF SUPPLY OF PEANUT BUTTER**

Price per jar ($)

Supply curve

Supply (S)

Quantity (thousands of jars per month)

The number of jars of peanut butter that the Bif Company would like to sell in a month depends on the price.

## Table 3
### BIF SUPPLY SCHEDULE

| Price per jar | Number of jars per month |
|---------------|--------------------------|
| $1.00         | 5,625                    |
| 2.00          | 13,125                   |
| 3.00          | 14,500                   |
| 4.00          | 15,000                   |

**supply curve** a graphic representation of the relationship between price and quantity supplied.
**law of supply** the quantity supplied of a good or service varies directly with its price; the lower the price the smaller the quantity supplied, and the higher the price the larger the quantity supplied.

just the opposite attitude towards prices that consumers have. The higher the price of a product, the more of the product sellers are willing to offer for sale. Table 3 shows the amounts of peanut butter one hypothetical seller, Bif Peanut Butter, would have offered at different prices before the drought. At low prices, Bif is not willing to supply much peanut butter. At higher prices, the company offers more for sale. Table 3 is the supply schedule for one producer of peanut butter. (In the third section of this chapter we will examine what determines the quantities sellers are willing to offer at different prices.)

If we plot the points indicating how much peanut butter Bif will supply at different prices, and then connect these points, we get the supply curve shown in Figure 3 above. Note that the supply curve slopes upward to the right indicating that higher prices are associated with larger quantities supplied. In providing more peanut butter at higher prices, Bif is complying with the law of supply: the higher the price of a good or service the more will be offered for sale.

If we assume that there are three other peanut butter suppliers similar to Bif in the market, we create the market supply schedule shown in Table 4 and the market supply curve shown in Figure 4. Note that the supply curves indicate only what quantities sellers would like to sell at various prices, not how much they *can* sell. How much they can sell depends on the demand schedule. Supply and demand schedules are determined independently by differ-

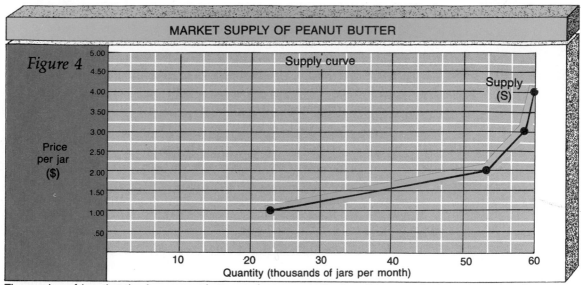

**Figure 4**

MARKET SUPPLY OF PEANUT BUTTER

Supply curve

Supply (S)

Price per jar ($)

Quantity (thousands of jars per month)

The number of jars that the four peanut butter producers would like to sell in a month depends on the price.

ent considerations, but they jointly determine price as shown in the following section.

**Equilibrium**  The Smith family, along with all of the other potential peanut butter customers in their community, determine the demand by their willingness to buy a certain number of jars at any particular price. It may not be until they see what the price is on the supermarket shelf that they decide how many jars they are going to buy. But the community demand schedule accurately describes their behavior on the average. If the Smith family doesn't buy any peanut butter one month because they are on vacation, another family is just as likely to buy twice as much because they are having a picnic. With demand curves, as with many economic variables, individual variations from the norm tend to cancel each other out when you are dealing with large numbers.

Bif and the other peanut butter suppliers determine what the supply will be at different prices by their willingness to produce and market a certain number of jars. The sellers are likely to plan in advance how much they will offer for sale depending upon the price they can get. The market supply schedule gives the total amounts they will offer to sell at different prices.

The actual market price is determined when the two sides of the market, the buyers and the sellers, come together. Out of all the possible prices, only one price can exist in a market at a given time when all of the selling conditions are identical. Normally, that is the price that "clears" that mar-

**Table 4**

MARKET SUPPLY SCHEDULE

| Price per jar | Number of jars per month |
|---------------|--------------------------|
| $1.00 | 22,500 |
| 2.00 | 52,500 |
| 3.00 | 58,000 |
| 4.00 | 60,000 |

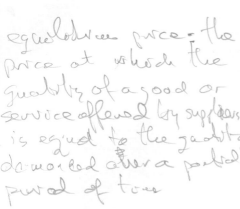

*equilodvee price - the price at which the quality of a good or service offered by suppliers is equal to the quantity demanded over a period of time*

ket—the price at which the amount the buyers are willing to purchase just equals the amount the sellers are willing to supply. That price is called the equilibrium price.

Market equilibrium is shown when we put the demand curve and the supply curve on the same diagram. The point at which they cross shows the price that clears the market. The equilibrium price for peanut butter in our example is $1.25, as shown in Figure 5.

At $1.25 the families in the community wanted to buy 30,000 jars of peanut butter a month, which the suppliers were willing to sell. If the market price had been less than $1.25, the buyers would have wanted more, but the suppliers would not have been willing to sell as much. As a result, a shortage would have developed. Whenever there is a shortage, the price goes up. Buyers, in effect, would have been bidding against each other for the short supply. This would have raised the price to the equilibrium level.

If the market price had been higher than $1.25, there would have been a surplus of peanut butter and the higher price would not have been maintained. Competition among sellers to get rid of their overstock would have driven the price down to $1.25. Whenever there is a surplus, the price goes down. Freely competitive markets are self-equilibrating, with the price always adjusting to the level which clears the market over a period of time. However, in our economy we sometimes find markets that are not freely competitive, as in the case of government regulated prices. In such noncompetitive markets, surpluses or shortages can persist for a long time.

**equilibrium price** the price at which the quantity of a good or service offered by suppliers is exactly equal to the quantity that is demanded by purchasers in a particular period of time.

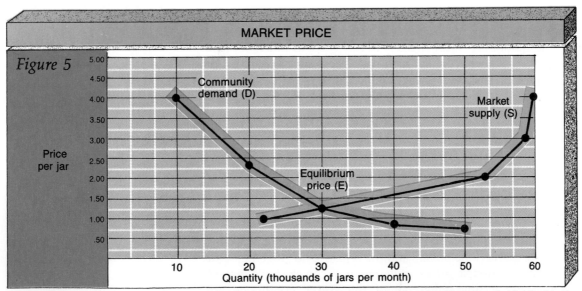

The equilibrium price in the market is the price at which the quantity that consumers would like to buy is identical to the quantity that suppliers would like to sell.

# case application

## How Much Is a Good Student Worth?

Colleges have long recognized the value to the school in having outstanding athletes. This recognition takes the form of scholarships, part-time jobs, and other inducements. Vigorous competition among colleges for star high school athletes has created a market in which the athlete, in a sense, "sells" his or her services to the highest bidder, although there are many restrictions on what the school can offer.

In recent years a similar market has developed for top academic students. For prestige purposes and to strengthen their academic programs, colleges are trying to attract high academic achievers by offering monetary inducements. It is not new for colleges to give academic scholarships, but the competition and the size of the offerings have greatly increased as the result of two developments in the past decade. One of these developments is the leveling off of college enrollments. The other is the decline in the supply of top students as evidenced by SAT scores and other tests.

As a result of the competition, some colleges have begun to engage in recruiting practices for top scholars that formerly were reserved for star quarterbacks. College officials now visit students' homes and bid against rival schools for the students. Sometimes the money inducement can be substantial. Every year one "Big Ten" university gives a number of special academic scholarships that are worth more than $20,000. A small university in Kentucky does even better, awarding 25 merit scholarships, valued at over $40,000 each. And the graduating seniors of a prestigious New Orleans high school received a total of nearly half a million dollars in scholarships.

As a result of high-pressure recruiting practices by some schools, regional college associations have begun to establish rules and limitations on the recruiting of scholars that are similar to those on recruiting athletes.

## Economic Reasoning

1. In the market for scholarly talent, what are the two sides of the market? Who is represented on the two sides of the market?
2. What has happened to the equilibrium price for top high school scholars? Why?
3. Is the effort of college associations to regulate the recruitment of outstanding student scholars an unwarranted interference in the marketplace? Why or why not?

Bologna is one of the more popular ingredients found in sandwiches. Consumer preference for meat and an affordable price keep demand high.

## What Determines Demand?

We have seen that there is a predictable relationship between the price of a good or service and the quantity demanded—the lower the price, the larger the quantity. But what determines how much demand there will be for a good or service at any particular price? Or, for that matter, whether there will be any demand at all? This analysis section examines the determinants of demand.

**Tastes and preferences** Consumer tastes and preferences are particularly important determinants of demand. Eating peanut butter is a taste that many people acquire when they are young and retain to a greater or lesser extent throughout their lives. The fact that people like or dislike peanut butter is the first thing that determines their demand for the product. As they grow older, their tastes may change, and they may not want as much peanut butter as before.

**Income** In order for demand to exist for a product, the desire for the product must be backed up by the ability to pay for it. This is sometimes called effective demand. Without the ability to pay for a product, demand for that product does not exist. Our income determines how much money we have to spend; therefore, a person's income plays an important role in determining that person's demand for a product. Increases in income enable people to purchase more goods and services, including more peanut butter, if that is what they choose to spend part of their increased income for.

**Substitutes and complements** A third determinant of demand for a particular product is the availability and price of

**consumer tastes and preferences** individual liking or partiality for specific goods or services.

**effective demand** the desire and the ability to purchase a certain number of units of a good or service at a given price.

substitutes and complements. There are some close substitutes for peanut butter that are made from other nuts, such as almonds, or from cotton nut kernels or sunflower seeds. More general substitutes—not in looks or taste, but in function—are cheese, salami, and eggs. With these substitutes available, many families might not be willing to pay higher prices for peanut butter, at least not for as many jars of peanut butter as they had been purchasing.

Among the products that complement peanut butter, a favorite one is jelly. A rise in the price of jelly would result in less peanut butter being demanded, since peanut butter and jelly are used together so often. While a rise in the price of a substitute, cheese for example, generally results in an increase in the demand for a product like peanut butter, a rise in the price of a complement such as jelly results in a decrease in the demand for the product. Conversely, a drop in the price of cheese would cause the demand for peanut butter to go down, while a fall in jelly prices would cause it to go up.

**Population**  Finally, the demand for a product depends on the number of people in the market area. Since peanut butter is eaten in every part of the United States, and is an easily transported, nonperishable item, the potential domestic market population is over 250 million, excluding peanut butter haters. Increases in population result in greater demand for virtually everything that is produced. Selling domestically produced goods in other countries also results in larger demand.

The demand for one product is influenced by the availability of others. These meats and sausages offer many substitute choices.

**substitute**  a product that is interchangeable in use with another product.
**complement**  a product that is employed jointly in conjunction with another product.

# case application

## Pedal Power

Bicycling was already the third most popular sports activity in the United States (after swimming and fishing), but the televising of the sport during the 1984 Olympic Games in Los Angeles gave it a further boost. A 1985 Gallup poll found that 33% of all Americans bicycled at least once during the year. And when American Greg LeMond won the Tour de France, the "super bowl" of world cycling competition, U.S. interest in the sport reached an even higher pitch and continues to grow.

There has been a generally increased interest in sports activities and in the sales of sports equipment in recent years as people became more aware of the relationship between exercise and good health. As a result, bicycles and bicycle accessories have become big business. There are now 6,500 bicycle shops in the United States, where some of the more fancy bicycles are priced in four figures.

The most rapidly growing part of the market is not the bikes themselves but the accessories, especially cycle clothing. Sales of eye-catching uniforms, shoes, and headgear for cycling enthusiasts are growing at a rate of 25% each year. The popularity of the hip-hugging shorts and flashy jerseys is such that stores are springing up which sell only cycling-style clothing but not bicycles.

As with participants in such other sports as jogging, skiing, and health spa training, cyclists not only want to get in shape, but they want to look good while doing it. The leaders in this trend are the young urban professionals, the so-called Yuppies. Typically, the incomes of Yuppies have increased faster than their financial responsibilities, leaving them with a large amount of disposable income to satisfy their leisure-time

wants. Yuppies show a preference for high-end quality in their purchases, and they have transformed the bicycle market from its traditional sales to a trendy commodity.

## Economic Reasoning

1. Which of the determinants of demand have been responsible for the booming market in bicycles and accessories?
2. If higher import taxes increased the prices of bicycles, how would this affect the demand for cycle clothing? Why?
3. Are the changes in the bicycle market, with a trend toward higher quality expensive bicycles and fashionable accessories, a good thing or a bad thing? Why?

# What Determines Supply?

The determinants of supply are totally different from the determinants of demand. It should be noted from the outset that demand does not determine supply. Of course if there is no demand for a product it will not be produced. But the amounts that producers are willing to offer for sale at different prices are not the same as the amounts that are demanded at those prices. The supply schedule, as we have seen, is independent of the demand schedule.

The most important determinant of supply is the cost of production. In the peanut butter industry, the price of peanuts, the wages of factory workers, and the price of jars, as well as how efficiently these factors are used in production, are among the things that determine production cost.

**Short run**   How costs behave also depends on the time period under consideration. At any given time, peanut butter producers can adjust their output only over a limited range. They have only so many ovens for roasting peanuts, just so much factory space for processing them, and only so many canning machines for filling jars. In the short run they can vary their output only within the limits of their existing plant and equipment. They can increase production by purchasing more peanuts and jars and hiring more workers. They can put on a night shift of workers to increase output. But in the short run, they cannot add to their existing plant and equipment to increase the amount of output.

Increasing the output in the short run generally increases the cost of producing each unit. More workers in the plant means that each one has a smaller amount of capital equipment to work with, so average labor output falls. Consequently, producers will have to get higher prices to induce them to expand production.

**Long run**   Production costs in the long run differ from short run costs in that the size of the plant and the amounts and types of equipment can be altered. If market conditions justify it, a producer in the long run can expand output by building larger production facilities. Additional outputs can then be produced more efficiently in the long run than they can in the short run.

The exact time period that divides the short run from the long run varies from industry to industry. A copy firm which duplicates printed materials for customers may have a long run of a few weeks—only as long as it takes to rent additional floor space and install some more copying machines. For an electric power company, however, the long run is a matter of years. Building additional electric power production capacity takes a long time.

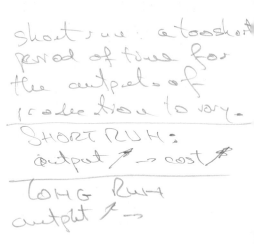

> **short run**   a period of time so short that the amount of some factor inputs cannot be varied.
> **long run**   a period of time sufficiently long that the amount of all factor inputs can be varied.

The expansion of a plant can increase product output in the long run.

# case application

## Jojoba: A Desert Weed That Smells Like Money

Before sperm whales came under the protection of international whaling agreements, millions of pounds a year of sperm whale oil were used in the production of leather, textiles, carbon paper, drugs, and polishes. Much whale oil also was used as a lubricant. It prevented corrosion in tractor and automobile transmissions, gears, and machine parts. There was no close substitute. Sperm oil was so vital that it was stockpiled against emergencies. However, in the early 1970s, the United States and Canada banned the import of any whale products because sperm whales were in danger of extinction, and a search for substitutes for whale oil began.

A desert bush called the jojoba ("ho ho ba"), native to the southwestern United States and to Mexico, provides one of best of these substitutes. Peanut-sized seeds from the jojoba contain a colorless liquid wax with properties that are very similar to whale oil. Jojoba oil is significantly purer than whale oil and is nearly odorless. It never gets rancid and does not deteriorate even after long periods of high-pressure, high-temperature use. The jojoba is a workable substitute for animal oils and waxes, which are difficult to synthesize commercially. Ancestors of the American Indians in this region used jojoba wax as a hair conditioner, and modern cosmetics manufacturers have been the biggest customers for seeds of the wild plants.

The jojoba is a renewable resource. Each bush lives for 100 to 200 years and apparently is not subject to serious insect damage or disease. It responds well to cultivation. But it takes five years for the plant to produce harvestable numbers of seeds. The supply of wild seeds was so limited that, when its uses as a substitute for sperm whale oil were first

recognized, the price of jojoba oil nearly tripled in one year to over $7,000 per barrel.

Now, however, commercial growing of jojoba, which got under way with the first commercial farm planted in 1978, has brought down the cost substantially. A jojoba harvesting machine shakes beans off of the rows of bushes onto a conveyer belt where a blower removes the chaff, and the beans are bagged for transport to the processing plant. Rising supply is matching demand as more uses are found for the versatile jojoba.

## *Economic Reasoning*

1. What period of time is the long run for increasing jojoba oil production?
2. How much did jojoba oil cost in the short run? Why was it so expensive? Why did it become cheaper in the long run?
3. Investment in commercial jojoba farms was encouraged by especially favorable tax credits. Should jojoba farm investors be given special tax benefits? Why or why not?

*100 - 200*

*$ 7,000*

*raising supply*

# Why Do Prices Change?

Prices generally do not remain constant for very long in our economy. They are always changing because the factors determining demand change, or the factors determining supply change, or both do. Changes in demand and supply cause prices to change, and not the other way around. In this section of the chapter we will examine why prices change.

**Shifts in demand** If there is a change in any of the four determinants of demand for a good or service—tastes, incomes, the prices and availability of substitutes and complements, or population size—there will be a <u>shift in the demand</u> schedule. More or less of the item will be demanded at each and every price.

Assume, for example, that research were to show peanut butter was a major cause of acne. Publication of this news would probably result in a significant decline in the quantity of peanut butter demanded at every price. Such a demand shift is shown in Figure 6. The original equilibrium price of a jar of peanut butter, as reflected in Figure 5, was $1.25. Let us assume the news story causes the demand to fall by 5,000 jars per month. This is reflected by a shift of the demand schedule from $D_1$ to $D_2$. As a result of this shift, the price of a jar of peanut butter drops to $1.16 and the number of jars purchased to 27,500.

**shift in demand** a change in the quantity of a good or service that would be purchased at each possible price.

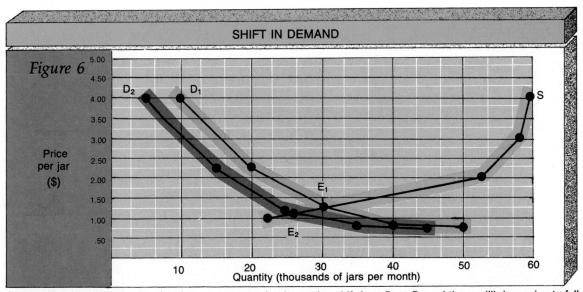

A report that peanut butter is related to acne causes the demand to shift from $D_1$ to $D_2$ and the equilibrium price to fall from $1.25 to $1.16.

Notice that the decrease in quantity purchased is less than the decrease in demand. The news story caused demand to decrease by 5,000 jars. At any given price, the consumers wanted 5,000 fewer jars than before. However, the quantity purchased fell from 30,000 to 27,500, a decline of only 2,500 jars. The reason that the decrease in the quantity purchased was not as great as the decrease in demand is because of the price reduction. Decreasing demand causes suppliers to cut their prices. This is shown in Figure 6 by the movement down the supply curve (which has not changed) from $E_1$ to $E_2$. Suppliers cut their price because with smaller output their short-run production costs are lower.

In summary, the news story about the alleged relationship between peanut butter and acne caused a downward shift in demand from $D_1$ to $D_2$, a reduction of 5,000 jars. This fall in demand caused a reduction of the price of a jar of peanut butter from $1.25 to $1.16. At this new equilibrium price the quantity demanded and supplied is 27,500 jars. The demand shift caused a reduction in the quantity demand and the quantity supplied of 2,500 jars. Note that there has been no change in the supply schedule. At any given price, suppliers would be willing to sell as much as before the demand shift.

**Shifts in supply** The rise in the cost of peanuts because of the drought caused a shift in the supply schedule for peanut butter. In Figure 7, the original hypothetical supply of peanut butter is represented by $S_1$. The rise in production costs because of higher peanut prices in the drought re-

**shift in supply** a change in the quantity of a good or service that would be offered for sale at each possible price.

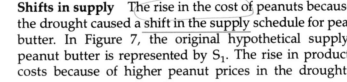

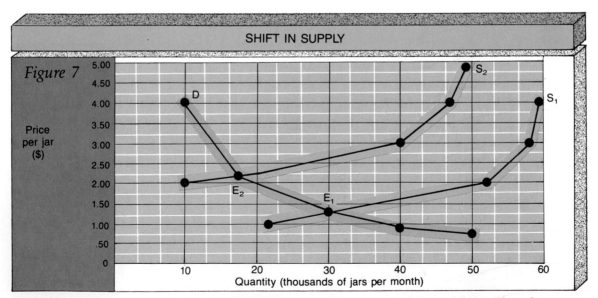

Figure 7

Price per jar ($)

SHIFT IN SUPPLY

The higher costs of peanuts during the shortage causes the supply of peanut butter to shift from $S_1$ to $S_2$ and the equilibrium price to increase from $1.25 to $2.35.

sulted in a fall in the peanut butter supply to $S_2$. At each price, sellers were offering a smaller quantity for sale than the year before.

As a result, the market equilibrium as shown in Figure 7 moved from $E_1$ to $E_2$. The jump in prices from $1.25 to $2.35 a jar caused families to cut back on their peanut butter consumption. This did not represent a shift in demand, but rather a movement back along the existing demand curve to a smaller quantity at the higher price. The quantity demanded decreased because of the change in supply, not because of any change in demand (shift in the demand schedule).

It is easy to confuse the causes of market changes between changes in demand and changes in supply. If peanut prices were to decline because of reform of the government agricultural price support program and as a result families began consuming more peanut butter, people might refer to this increased consumption as an increase in demand. The real reason for the changed consumption, however, would be the increase in supply. An increase in supply, by reducing the market price, causes an increase in the *quantity demanded*—represented by a movement downward to the right on the existing demand curve. This is different from an increase in *demand*—represented by a shift upward to the right of the whole demand curve.

To determine whether a market change is the result of a change in demand or a change in supply, look at the cause of the change. If it is due to a change in tastes, incomes, the availability or prices of substitutes and complements, or population size, the cause is a change in demand. If the market change is due to a change in production costs, the cause is a change in supply.

Like many farmers, Peggy Ward Moser found her hopes of cashing in on the oat bran craze frustrated by the forces of demand and supply. As more farmers began to grow the sought-after crop, the oat supply grew and the price per bushel dropped. Despite her investment of 13 acres of land, months of labor, and thousands of dollars in capital, in the end Farmer Moser was able to reap a net profit of only $812 for her entire harvest—before taxes.

## Oat Bran Fettuccini?

Oat bran is the outer part of the oat kernel, surrounding the oat flour center. In the past, oats were frequently used as animal feed and were not as profitable a crop as wheat, corn, or soybeans, which receive higher federal subsidies.

But attitudes toward the cereal changed in 1988. An article in the American Medical Association journal reported test results showing that oat bran included in a person's diet reduced cholesterol, a cause of heart attacks. As a result of this report, and other articles and books praising the health benefits of oat bran, the sales of oat bran cereals

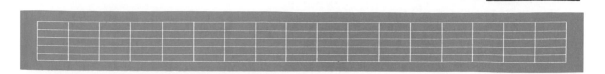

jumped 240%. Grocers' shelves were cleared of oat bran. A name-brand of hot oat bran cereal, which cost 99 cents for a one-pound box before the health reports, disappeared from stores for awhile. When it reappeared, the price had doubled to $1.98 a box. In the meantime, the scarcity gave rise to numerous off-brands, available in health food stores at premium prices.

As a result of the new-found popularity of oats, many other products containing them appeared. There was heavy advertising promotion of the oat bran contents, not only of cereals, but of a large variety of foods to which oat bran was added, including cookies, muffins, bread, pretzels, popcorn, and fettuccine. The advertising did not mention that these foods contain so little oat bran fiber—only a few grams per serving—that one would need to eat great quantities of them to significantly affect the cholesterol level in the blood. Even eating pure oat bran cereal requires the consumption of two normal-size servings a day to get a 10% reduction in high cholesterol levels.

Because of the boom in oat bran popularity, coming at the time of an unusually small 1988 oat crop, the price received by farmers for their oats reached as high as $4.25 a bushel. To meet the demand, cereal companies actively encouraged farmers to plant oats in 1989, guaranteeing to buy their oat harvest and offering them prize incentives in addition. With favorable weather, the oat crop harvest that year rose 92% above the 1988 level. This expansion of production caused the price of oats to fall to $1.15 a bushel.

Then, in 1990, a new study published by the *New England Journal of Medicine* reported that oat bran apparently did not have any special ability to lower cholesterol levels after

all. It appeared that the reductions in cholesterol reported on in the earlier studies were not due to the oat bran itself, but merely to the fact that when the subjects ate so much oat bran, they reduced their consumption of foods containing saturated fats which the body turns into cholesterol. Substituting foods made of plain flour in the diet had the same effect.

The American Oat Association and the cereal companies have questioned the validity of that study because of its small sample size and the fact that the participants did not have high levels of cholesterol to begin with. While research produces conflicting claims about whether oat bran has any magical properties as a cholesterol fighter, it *is* a healthy food; and, hey, the fettuccini isn't half bad.

## Economic Reasoning

1. Which of the four determinants of demand caused a shift in the demand curve for oat bran in 1998–89? Which way did the demand curve shift?

2. What happened to the equilibrium price received by farmers for the 1988 oat crop? What happened to the equilibrium price for the 1989 crop? Explain these changes using diagrams to illustrate your explanation.

3. Should producers of food products be permitted to make health claims for their products? Why or why not?

Agricultural products like peanut butter are particularly sensitive to the influences that cause shifts in demand and supply.

# Putting It Together

In our economic system resources are allocated through the exchange of goods and services between producers and consumers. Each good or service commands a price. These prices are determined by the interplay between the *demand* for a product and its *supply*.

A *demand schedule* and its graphic representation, the *demand curve*, show the amounts of a good or service buyers would purchase at different prices. For almost any item, the higher the price, the smaller the *quantity demanded*. This is referred to as the *law of demand*. People buy less of an item at higher prices because of the *income effect*—they can't afford to buy as much—and because of the *substitution effect*—they buy relatively less costly substitutes instead.

A *supply schedule* and its graphic representation, the *supply curve*, show the amounts of a good or service sellers would offer for sale at different prices. For virtually any good or service, the higher the price, the larger the quantity that will be offered for sale. This is referred to as the *law of supply*.

When buyers and sellers come together in the market, an *equilibrium price* is established where the quantity demanded equals the quantity supplied. This is the market-clearing price at which there are no shortages and no surpluses. In competitive markets, prices cannot stay above or below the equilibrium point for very long. Competitive pressures push prices back down or up to the equilibrium point.

The determinants of demand are *consumer tastes and preferences,* income levels, the availability and prices of substitutes and *complements,* and the population size of the market.

Supply is determined by production costs. The *short-run* situation assumes that plant size, equipment, and technology do not change; the *long-run* situation assumes production capacity and technology can change.

A change in demand or supply is reflected by changes along the entire demand or supply schedule. This causes the schedule to shift left or right. *Shifts in demand* and *shifts in supply* cause equilibrium prices to change in the marketplace. In contrast to shifts in the whole schedule, changes in the quantity demanded or the quantity supplied reflect movements by sellers or buyers along existing demand or supply curves. These changes in quantity demanded or supplied are the result of price changes.

An increase in demand will raise prices and cause suppliers to offer more for sale in the short run. If they expect the increased demand to be permanent, they will invest in new plant and equipment and thereby increase production capacity and long-run supply.

# Perspective

## Adam Smith's Marketplace

**Adam Smith (1723–1790)**
Smith was born in Scotland. At the age of three, he was kidnapped by gypsies. He was, however, soon rescued. He was sickly as a child and was in the habit of talking to himself when alone. Absent-minded throughout his life, he nevertheless had an extraordinary memory. At the age of 28 he became Professor of Moral Philosophy at the University of Glasgow in Scotland. He was a popular lecturer, and his classes were very well attended. When he was 40, after the publication of his first book, *The Theory of Moral Sentiments*, he accepted an appointment as traveling tutor to the young duke of Buccleuch. He accompanied the duke to France, where he became acquainted with the intellectual leaders of the country, including a number of Physiocrats. When he returned to England, Smith worked on his masterpiece, *The Wealth of Nations*, for a decade before its publication in 1776. Two years later he was appointed Commissioner of Customs in Scotland. Not long before his death in 1790, he expressed the regret that he had "done so little" in his lifetime.

Adam Smith is considered the father of economics. Before him, economics was studied either as a branch of politics called political economy, or as an area of philosophy. Economics was born as a distinct discipline with the publication of Smith's *The Wealth of Nations* in 1776. It was a remarkable book setting forth expositions of basic economic ideas, which hold up very well today, along with a mind-boggling amount of factual data.

Among the most important and enduring contributions to economic thought was Smith's explanation of the beneficial workings of the free marketplace. He explained market equilibrium as follows:

> The quantity of every commodity brought to market naturally suits itself to the effectual demand. It is the interest of all those who employ their land, labour, or stock [capital] in bringing any commodity to market, that the quantity never should exceed the effectual demand; and it is the interest of all other people that it never should fall short of that demand.

A major thrust of *The Wealth of Nations* was that market prices and quantities should be permitted to adjust to their equilibrium levels without any interference from the government. Smith was arguing in opposition to the system of mercantilism under which the government exercised a great deal of control over economic life. The government regulated production and trade with the objective of bringing gold and silver into the coffers of the state.

Smith contended that a nation's real wealth would be maximized by allowing individuals to make economic decisions based on the forces of the marketplace, unhindered by government regulations. He maintained that in pursuing their own self-interest, people would be guided by an *invisible hand* to maximize their personal contribution to the economy. Smith's views had been greatly influenced by the three years he spent in France associating with the French Physiocrats. The Physiocrats promoted a policy of *laissez-faire,* which called for the government to keep its hands off trade and allow prices to seek their natural levels.

Because of his *laissez-faire* doctrine, Adam Smith is greatly admired by economic conservatives today. But Smith was anything but a conservative in his day. He was, in fact, someone that today we might call a consumer advocate, protesting the special interests backed by governments that profited at the expense of the general public.

For
Further
Study
and
Analysis

## Study Questions

1. "Retail Chain Stores Increase Sales of Tennis Balls." Does this headline reflect a change in demand for tennis balls? Explain.

2. "Lobsters Found to Contain Harmful Levels of Mercury." How would this discovery affect your demand for lobster meat? Explain how some consumers might actually buy more lobster after the market adjusted to the news.

3. "Cane Sugar Prices Rise Dramatically." How would this price rise affect the demand for beet sugar?

4. "Record Number of Hockey Fans Paid Higher Prices." Explain how this situation could have occurred, and then use supply and demand curves to illustrate your answer.

5. "Pollution Curbs on Steel Mill Urged." What effect would this proposal to curb pollution have on the supply of steel? How would such a law affect the long-run planning for steel production?

6. "New Auto Sales Off by 25%." What changes in demand and/or supply might have accounted for this headline?

7. If a friend said to you, "I really need a new car, but I can't afford one for at least six months," does your friend have an automobile demand in economic terms? What is the meaning of demand in economics?

8. Is the time period that divides the short run from the long run in a particular industry different according to whether firms in the industry are increasing production capacity or decreasing production capacity? In the case study on jojoba oil production, does it take the same number of years to increase the quantity of jojoba beans grown as to decrease the quantity of jojoba beans grown?

9. What is the difference between a "change in demand" and a "change in the quantity demanded"? What is the cause of each? How is each represented on a diagram of the market?

10. Adam Smith strongly believed that governments should not interfere in the marketplace. What examples of government interference in the marketplace do you find in this chapter?

## Exercises in Analysis

1. Make a table of the number of times you would attend the movies at different possible admission prices from $1 to $10 in steps of $1. Then draw a diagram of your demand for theater movies. Total the demand schedules for a group of seven students to obtain a community demand schedule; then draw the demand curve. Save the results for use in an exercise at the end of chapter 5.

2. Take a disc or tape of a popular singer or group to campus and ask a sample of ten students how much they would pay for the disc or tape at a store. Assuming each student in the sample represents one-tenth of the total number of students at your school, use the data to draw a demand schedule of the campus demand for that disc or tape. (Keep in mind that the students who name a particular price are also willing to buy the disc or tape at any price less than that.)

3. From a financial publication, such as the *Wall Street Journal*, find the current world market price of a barrel of petroleum. What has caused the change in the price from what it was in 1980? Diagram the change in market conditions which has resulted in the price change.

4. Look up "Physiocrats" in the encyclopedia. Write an explanation of their beliefs in your own words.

## Further Reading

Deutschman, Alan. *Winning Money for College.* 2nd ed. Princeton, N.J.: Peterson's Guides, 1987. This is a "how-to" book on the strategies for winning college scholarships. For each scholarship program, it gives the rules and procedures, helpful hints, program deadlines, and where to obtain more information.

Dooley, Peter. *Elementary Price Theory,* chapter 1. 2nd ed. Englewood Cliffs, N.J.: Prentice Hall, 1973. A simple explanation of how markets determine prices.

Dorfman, Robert. *Prices and Markets,* chapters 2, 3, and 5. 3rd ed. Englewood Cliffs, N.J.: Prentice Hall, 1978. A more sophisticated and thorough, but understandable, treatment of the market model.

Earnest, Barbara, and Sarah Schlesinger. *The Low Cholesterol Oat Plan.* New York: Hearst, 1988. The preface describes the book as "a short course in everything you could ever hope to know about this fibrous wonder." The largest part of it, however, is devoted to recipes using oats and oat bran.

Goeller, Priscilla S. *The A's and B's of Academic Scholarships.* Alexandria, Va.: Octameron Associates, 1987. Lists 1200 colleges and 100,000 awards.

Lehman, Andrea E. *College Money Handbook.* 6th ed. Princeton, N.J.: Peterson's Guides, 1988. Gives cost and aid profiles for all accredited institutions that offer baccalaureate degree programs in the United States and territories.

# Unit **II**
# MICROECONOMICS

## Chapter 5. The Consumer

In a market economy, consumers dictate what is produced by their spending decisions. They make their spending and saving decisions in the way that obtains the most satisfaction from their incomes, based on the information available.

## Chapter 6. The Business Firm and Market Structure

Business firms are of three different types of organization, each with its particular advantages and disadvantages. Firms decide what prices to charge and how much to produce in order to obtain the largest profit possible. The market outcome depends on the structure of the industry they are in.

The field of economics is divided into two major areas, microeconomics and macroeconomics. Microeconomics includes the topics that have to do with the individual units of the economy, the households and the firms, and with the way markets for products and resources behave.

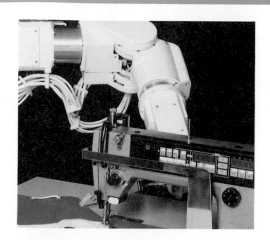

## Chapter 7. Industry Performance

The performance of industries is measured by their efficiency, the quality of their product, their responsiveness to the market, and their responsiveness to social concerns. There are various ways that American industries can improve their performance. The amount of industry concentration affects performance.

## Chapter 8. Government and Business

The government intervenes in business in various ways, regulating industries and sometimes producing goods and services. There are a variety of government agencies that enforce laws and regulations to protect consumers, workers, and the environment.

## Chapter 9. Labor and Income Distribution

The price of labor is wages or salaries, which are determined by forces in the labor market. One of these forces is labor unions. Other income shares come from rents, interest, and profits. Incomes are unequally distributed because of differences in productivity, opportunity, and the ownership of assets. Public policy is particularly concerned with household income levels below the poverty line.

## chapter 5

# THE CONSUMER

*The end result of nearly all economic activity is consumption. The consumer in our economy is said to be king (or queen). Consumer demand in the market is presumed to dictate what will be produced. But sometimes, it seems, there is a Madison Avenue Merlin behind the scenes manipulating the king's decisions.*

## Blowing Smoke Rings

In 1964 the Surgeon General of the United States published a report on medical findings that indicated cigarette smoking is linked to lung cancer. Additional research since then has also implicated cigarettes in heart disease, emphysema, and other health problems. A RAND Corporation study estimates that for each pack of cigarettes smoked, a person's life expectancy is reduced by more than 2 hours.

Tobacco companies are now required to put warning labels on their packages that caution the buyer about the health hazards of the product. Tobacco use causes the deaths of as many as 390,000 people a year in the United States alone. Nonsmokers, especially children, subjected to long-term exposure to secondhand smoke are also at significant risk for smoking-related diseases.

As the public became aware of the dangers of cigarette smoking, per capita consumption declined. The proportion of the U.S. population that smokes has fallen from 40% at the time of the Surgeon General's report to under 30% today. But about 1 million Americans take up smoking each year, half of them by age 13; and the total number of smokers is almost the same as it was in 1964—just over 50 million.

The wholesale value of cigarette sales is more than $20 billion a year; and, despite the industry's recent setbacks, cigarette makers are still among the most profitable companies in the nation. If most other products had experienced the bad press that cigarettes have had in the last three decades, we would expect the producers to be in big trouble financially. How is it, then, that the cigarette companies are doing so well?

One important reason is that their customers have a particular type of loyalty not found in most products: namely, addiction. This has helped make tobacco a very profitable industry in the face of a shrinking market. Even with a decline in the number of packs sold due to a doubling of federal taxes on cigarettes, the operating profits of the tobacco companies nevertheless ranged from 11% to 24% of sales. Whether measured as a percentage of sales or as a percentage of the amount invested in the companies, the profits of cigarette manufacturers have always been, and still continue to be, among the highest for any industry.

One way the tobacco companies have ensured that profits continue to roll in is by spending large sums on promoting their product, half a billion dollars on magazine and newspaper cigarette advertisements alone. The largest cigarette producer, Phillip Morris, got to the top of the heap with successful advertising campaigns that created images of the macho, tattooed Marlboro man and the liberated Virginia Slims woman. Ironically, the original model for the Marlboro man died in 1987 of emphysema, a lung disease caused by smoking. Nevertheless, the companies continue to combat the medical attacks on their product by putting even more of their revenues—some $2.5 billion a year—into advertising, packaging, developing new brand "images" aimed at particular segments of the market, and giving away cigarettes to attract new customers. One segment that they have successfully targeted is young women, the only group among whom the rate of smoking has increased since the Surgeon General's report.

The combination of physical and psychological addiction to smoking plus heavy advertising promotion enables the tobacco companies to raise prices, even in the face of the negative health reports. The average price of a pack of cigarettes was raised 50% in just 5 years. The cigarette makers believe that, because their customers are hooked on the product anyhow, price is not as important as image in purchasing decisions. However, a study by the National Bureau of Economic Research shows that those assumptions are not true for all groups of smokers and potential smokers. It determined that for those in whom the cigarette habit is well established, smokers over 25 years old, a rise in the price of cigarettes causes them to reduce their consumption by only 10% as much as the price increase. But for younger people between the ages of 20 and 25, for whom the habit is not as ingrained, the effect of higher prices is much greater. Their consumption of cigarettes decreases by nearly 90% of the amount of the price increase. Another study shows that for beginning smokers in the 12–17 age range, consumption decreases by 140% of the price rise. In other words, a 10% increase in price results in a 14% decrease in cigarette smoking among the youngest smokers.

Possibly with that group of future hard-core customers in mind, and because of increased competition among the producers for customers in a shrinking market, some companies have in recent years begun selling less-expensive brands, discounted, and "generic" cigarettes. So far, this price cutting has affected only a small fraction of the market. Philip Morris, the most successful producer, and others still think that image is more important than price. They are convinced that blowing advertising smoke rings will distract smokers both from the unpleasant medical reports and from concerns about how much their habit costs.

## Chapter Preview

*When consumers spend a part of their income on cigarettes, they must give up some other use for the money—a trade-off. Just as the economy doesn't have enough resources to produce everything desired, people do not have enough income to purchase everything they want. Their spending reflects their priorities. Those priorities are conditioned by the information made available to them, notably by advertising. In this chapter we will examine the decisions consumers make and how they make them. The questions to be discussed are:* What choices do consumers make? How do consumers make choices? How can consumers make better choices?

## Learning Objectives

*After completing this chapter you should be able to:*

1. *Define elasticity of demand.*
2. *Define the terms perfectly elastic, relatively elastic, unitary elasticity, relatively inelastic, and perfectly inelastic.*
3. *Compute elasticity ratios.*
4. *Define consumer sovereignty and show how it is related to the allocation of resources.*
5. *Define average propensity to consume and average propensity to save.*
6. *Show the relationship of marginal utility to total utility.*
7. *Explain the principle of diminishing marginal utility.*
8. *State the conditions necessary for consumer equilibrium.*
9. *Explain the effects of product information and advertising on consumer choices.*

## What Choices Do Consumers Make?

The interplay between demand and supply in a market economy determines the prices of goods and services. Prices, in turn, influence consumer choices between different goods and services. They also affect consumer decisions about how much to save rather than spend.

**Spending choices**   People are faced with spending choices every day. They make these spending decisions to satisfy their consumption needs and desires.

Spending decisions depend on personal preferences and the prices of different goods and services in the marketplace. Consumption purchases can be classified as necessities—items people must have, including food, clothing, shelter and medical care—or luxuries—items they would like to have but don't necessarily need. For the average household, about $7 of every $10 they spend is used for necessities. The other $3 goes for nonessential luxuries such as VCRs, hobby equipment, shows, and holiday trips.

In their spending decisions, consumers react differently to price changes depending on whether a good or service is a necessity or a luxury. When the price of a luxury rises, consumers are more likely to cut back their purchases of the item much more than they would if it were a necessity. An item such as cigarettes would normally be considered a luxury purchase. But because of the addictiveness of cigarettes, smokers react to changes in the price of cigarettes more as if they were necessities than luxuries.

The extent to which the quantity demanded of a good or service varies with small changes in its price is its price elasticity of demand, a term usually shortened to elasticity of demand. If demand for an item is very elastic, the quantity demanded will decrease a great deal with a small

**necessity**   a good or service which is considered essential to a person's well-being.

**luxury**   a good or service which increases satisfaction but is not considered essential to well-being.

**price elasticity of demand**   the relative size of the change in the quantity demanded of a good or service as a result of a small change in its price.

**elastic**   a demand condition in which the relative size of the change in quantity demanded is greater than the size of the price change.

Americans require more income each year to buy the necessities of life. The growth of home entertainment, however, demonstrates that the demand for recreational products remains high.

**inelastic** a demand condition in which the relative size of the change in the quantity demanded is less than the size of the price change.

increase in its price. The demand for cigarettes, however, is inelastic, especially among established smokers. Younger smokers, who are not as hooked on smoking, have a more elastic demand for cigarettes. If the price increases, their purchases of cigarettes will decrease by anywhere from 90% to 140% as much as the increase in price. For example, take a 20-year-old smoking 10 packs a week with cigarettes costing $2 a pack. If the price went to $2.20 a pack, the 20-year-old would cut back approximately 1 pack to purchase about 9 packs a week. Established smokers, by contrast, would on

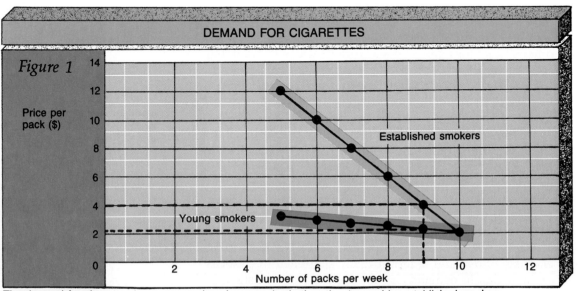

**DEMAND FOR CIGARETTES**

*Figure 1*

Price per pack ($)

Established smokers

Young smokers

Number of packs per week

The demand for cigarettes by young smokers is more elastic than the demand by established smokers.

the average reduce their purchases by only 1/10 pack per week. To get established smokers to reduce their smoking by one pack a week the price of a pack of cigarettes would have to go to over $4.00.

The cigarette demand by established smokers is thus much more inelastic than the demand by younger smokers. The amount of cigarettes they purchase is less responsive to changes in the price. The difference in the behavior of demand for the two groups is shown in Figure 1. The more vertical demand curve represents the demand by established smokers. Changes in price, shown on the vertical axis, result in only very small changes in the amounts purchased, shown on the horizontal axis. The curve showing the demand by younger smokers indicates that a change in price results in a larger change in the quantity purchased.

A very elastic demand curve is more horizontal. It shows that small changes in price result in large changes in the amounts purchased. At the extreme, an absolutely flat demand curve indicates that a rise in the price would reduce purchases to zero. This is perfectly elastic demand. At the other extreme, if changes in price resulted in no change whatsoever in the amounts purchased, the demand is perfectly inelastic, shown by a curve that is straight up and down. The various degrees of elasticity are represented in Figure 2.

Price elasticity of demand is an important characteristic of consumer behavior. It is vital to understanding spending decisions by consumers and pricing decisions by producers.

**perfectly elastic** a demand condition in which the quantity demanded varies from zero to infinity when there is a change in the price.
**perfectly inelastic** a demand condition in which there is no change in the quantity demanded when price changes.

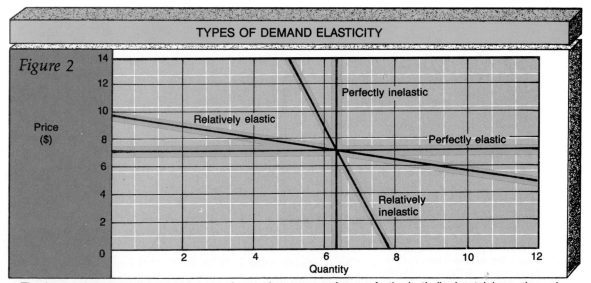

## TYPES OF DEMAND ELASTICITY

Figure 2

The degree of elasticity of demand for a good or service can range from perfectly elastic (horizontal demand curve) to perfectly inelastic (vertical demand curve). The elasticity of demand is usually somewhere in between these extremes.

Elasticity is also important to such governmental decisions as what fares to charge on public transit systems and what taxes to levy on goods such as gasoline, cigarettes, and liquor. It is important to understand what the effects are of governmental regulations on prices and thus on demand. It is useful, therefore, to have a measurement of elasticity. If we know how much change there is in the amount of an item people will buy when its price changes, we can calculate its demand elasticity by dividing the percentage change in the quantity demanded by the percentage change in price. This is the elasticity ratio.

$$\text{Elasticity Ratio} \quad = \quad \frac{\% \text{ change in Q (quantity)}}{\% \text{ change in P (price)}}$$

From this equation it can be seen that if the percentage change in quantity demanded is greater than the percentage change in price, the elasticity ratio will be greater than one (1). If the elasticity ratio is greater than one, demand is elastic. If it is less than one, demand is inelastic. If the ratio is exactly one, the demand elasticity is unitary. Unitary elasticity exists when the relative change in quantity is identical to the relative change in price, when demand is neither elastic nor inelastic but right in between. If the demand for cigarettes were unitary, doubling the price would cut consumption in half.

But the study by the National Bureau of Economic Research on the reactions of smokers to higher cigarette prices showed that elasticity was much less than unitary. Established smokers cut back on purchases of cigarettes only one-tenth as much as prices increased. If prices increased 100% from $2 a pack to $4, a 10-pack-a-week confirmed smoker would cut down to nine packs, a 10% decrease.

$$\text{Elasticity Ratio} \quad = \quad \frac{\% \text{ change in Q}}{\% \text{ change in P}} \quad = \quad \frac{10\%}{100\%} \quad = \quad 0.1$$

The established smoker's elasticity of demand for cigarettes is 0.1 or one-tenth. The average 20- to 25-year-old smoker's elasticity of demand is much greater; it is 0.9 or nine-tenths. Nevertheless, it is still inelastic, at that price, because the elasticity ratio is less than one.

For the 12–17 age group, however, the percentage change in quantity is greater than the percentage change in price. A rise in the price of 10% causes a 14% decrease in purchases. The elasticity ratio is thus 14/10 or 1.4. Since the ratio is greater than one, those very young smokers have an elastic demand for cigarettes. This has implications for the types of

**elasticity ratio** a measurement of the degree of the response of a change in quantity to a change in price.
**unitary elasticity** a demand condition in which the relative change in the quantity demanded is the same as the size of the price change.

Since 1964, the surgeon general of the United States has required all advertising and packaging of cigarettes to carry a warning of the health hazards of smoking, like the one on this billboard.

public policies which might discourage teenagers from taking up smoking.

In general, goods and services for which demand tends to be inelastic are those which are necessities, those for which there are either no or few close substitutes, and those which take an insignificant part of our total spending. Salt is a very good example of an item with highly inelastic demand. It has few close substitutes and the amount we pay for salt is an insignificant part of our total spending. Those goods and services which tend to have an elastic demand are luxuries, those that have many close substitutes, and those which cost us a significant amount of money. Silk shirts are a good for which there is an elastic demand. Silk shirts are very expensive and many other types of shirts can be used as close substitutes.

**Consumer sovereignty** Consumer spending decisions are crucial in the functioning of a market economy because they are the most important determinant of the allocation of resources. These decisions are the basis of resolving the "what to produce" question. Producers generally provide goods and services for which there is sufficient consumer

Savers try to find the most advantageous way to save in order to get the largest returns (interest, dividends, growth) from the part of their incomes that they allocate for savings.

demand and stop producing goods and services for which demand is insufficient. In this way producers reflect the will of the consumer. Consumer sovereignty exists when the choices of consumers in the market determine what producers make.

When the news first appeared about the effects of cigarette smoking on health, many concerned smokers switched to cigarettes with less tars and nicotine, suspected causes of damage. Encouraged by cigarette company advertisements, they thought that by switching to reduced-tar brands they could have their cigarettes and their health too. As a result, the manufacturers increased production of reduced-tar cigarettes until they constituted 53% of the total amount produced. As it turned out, a lot of those who switched found that they were smoking more of the less-tasteful brands, thus defeating the purpose, and went back to the stronger cigarettes. Even though consumers sometimes aren't sure *what* they want, consumer sovereignty, influenced by advertising, determines what is produced.

**Savings choices** Consumers have two alternatives for their after-tax income: they can spend it, or they can save it. On the average, we in the United States currently spend about 95% of our disposable income on goods and services. This is the average propensity to consume. Propensity means inclination. In this case, we are inclined to spend 95 cents of every after-tax dollar we receive. We put the remaining 5 cents of each dollar of after-tax income into savings. Our average propensity to save is 5%.

Savers try to find the best way to save in order to get the largest returns (interest, dividends, or growth) from their savings for the amount of risk they are willing to take. At one time some people kept their savings in old shoes or under floorboards, and maybe there are some who still do. But this is an expensive way to save, because the savings earn no returns. There is a wide choice of alternative ways to save with differing rates of return and different degrees of risk, ranging from passbook savings accounts to stocks and bonds. For most people, the largest amount of savings they have is the equity in their house. Equity is the money value of a property less the amount of outstanding mortgages.

Deciding how to save is important to the individual and to the economy as a whole because savings provide the funds other individuals and business firms borrow to begin or expand production. Savings are channeled by banks, brokerage firms, pension funds and insurance companies into productive investments. Therefore, individual consumer decisions on saving can have a significant impact on the entire economy.

**consumer sovereignty** the condition in a market economy by which consumer decisions about which goods and services to purchase determine resource allocation.
**average propensity to consume** the percentage of after-tax income which, on the average, consumers spend on goods and services.
**average propensity to save** the percentage of after-tax income which, on the average, consumers save.
**equity** the owner's share of the value of property or other assets, net of mortgages or other liabilities.

# The American Dream

Owning one's own home has been called "the American dream" for good reason. Buying a house is an unusual type of expenditure because it represents both a form of consumption and a form of saving. On the consumption side, mortgage payments take the place of paying rent. At the same time, they enable homeowners to save by accumulating equity. The value of their house is the largest savings most families have. Sixty-four percent of households own their own home, with a median sales price of over $90,000. By comparison, only 10% of households own stock portfolios exceeding $5,000 in value.

Besides appreciation in the value of their homes, homeowners also get tax breaks. Both interest payments and real estate taxes can be deducted from income when calculating income taxes.

In the 1970s and 1980s houses were virtual money machines. Housing demand was boosted by the large numbers of "baby boomers" entering the housing market and by the impetus of the 1970s inflation. As a result, the median value of an average home more than quadrupled between 1969 and 1990, from $21,800 to $93,100.

In the 1990s the market has changed. Construction of new housing is lower than in the 1980s and is not expected to return soon to previous levels. The much smaller "baby bust" generation will be reaching the age of establishing households. They will form only 1.1 million households a year in the 1990s, compared with 1.7 million in the 1970s. Also, inflation has lessened, reducing speculation in real estate. Some of the super-heated real estate markets of the 1980s, such as the Northeast, have experienced an actual decline in housing prices. The declines are even

spreading to markets that have been traditionally stable, such as Chicago.

Purchasing a home may not be the profitable investment that it was in the past two decades, but is still a good combination of consumption and saving. And houses may be more affordable for the first-time buyer.

## Economic Reasoning

1. How did changes in the housing market reflect consumer sovereignty?
2. From the behavior of the housing market in the 1970s and 1980s, can you draw any conclusions about the elasticity of demand for housing? How did the quantity demanded appear to be related to price changes? How can you explain this behavior of demand?
3. Which is the better situation in the housing market, the rapid escalation of housing prices in the 1970s and 1980s or the relatively static housing prices in the 1990s? Why?

# How Do Consumers Make Choices?

There are two types of choices facing consumers. First they must decide how to allocate their income between spending and saving. Second, they must determine exactly what specific spending and saving choices they want to make. People are not necessarily conscious of why they make the choices they do. There are psychological and economic factors involved in all spending and saving decisions. This section explores how consumers make these choices.

**Utility** In deciding what to spend their incomes on, consumers may purchase a particular item for a wide variety of reasons: because it adds to their comfort or convenience; because they get pleasure from it; or because it satisfies their egos. Whatever the individual reasons, people buy something because they derive satisfaction from it. The amount of satisfaction that they obtain from a purchase is its utility. Utility is the ability of a good or service to provide satisfaction to its consumer. People purchase the necessities and luxuries that they think will provide them with the greatest utility.

Smokers buy cigarettes because they expect the cigarettes to provide them with a certain amount of satisfaction. The amount of satisfaction they derive from smoking a certain number of packs is the total utility they receive from their cigarette purchases.

But since they have limited income and other needs and desires, how do smokers decide how many packs of cigarettes to buy in a certain time period? The answer to this question lies in how smokers perceive the marginal utility of each additional pack they buy. Marginal utility is the value or satisfaction received by a consumer from one more unit of consumption—in this case, an additional pack of cigarettes. Up to a point, each pack purchased adds to the total utility of cigarettes for a smoker. But each pack will add less utility than the one before.

For a smoker, the first cigarette of the day has a very high utility. If he or she only smoked one cigarette a day, the marginal utility of that one cigarette would be very large. Additional cigarettes would add to total utility, but the second would have less satisfaction than the first, the third less than the second and so on. This characteristic of diminishing marginal utility is true not only for cigarettes but for virtually everything else.

Figure 3 shows the utility a smoker might derive from packs of cigarettes in a day. There are no actual measurements of utility, but we can use a hypothetical unit and call it a "util." Each additional pack purchased adds so many utils

**utility** the amount of satisfaction a consumer derives from consumption of a good or service.

**total utility** the amount of satisfaction a consumer derives from all of the units of a particular good or service consumed in a given time period.

**marginal utility** the amount of satisfaction a consumer derives from consuming one additional unit (or the last unit consumed) of a particular good or service.

**diminishing marginal utility** the common condition in which the marginal utility obtained from consuming an additional unit of a good or service is smaller than the marginal utility obtained from consuming the preceding unit of the good or service.

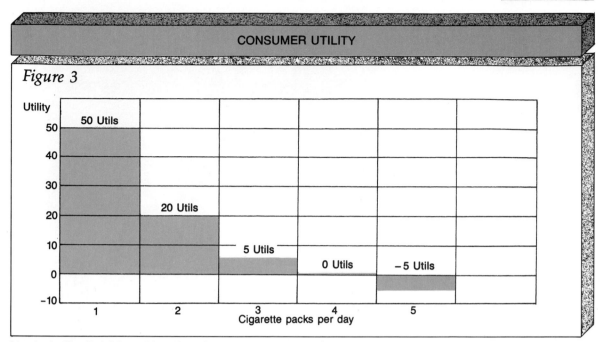

**CONSUMER UTILITY**

*Figure 3*

Marginal utility diminishes with each additional pack purchased. Generally, the more we have of a good or service the less we will be willing to pay for an additional amount.

to the total utility the smoker obtains from smoking cigarettes during the day.

We will assign the first pack 50 utils of utility. We will assume a second pack adds 20 utils. The third pack adds 5 utils more, and the fourth zero utils, since even confirmed cigarette addicts seldom enjoy smoking that many cigarettes a day, not to mention the devastating health effects of such heavy smoking. We can suppose that, even for this hypothetical heavy smoker, a fifth pack of cigarettes in a day would have negative marginal utility. The smoker would not only not enjoy the fifth pack, but would have to be paid to smoke it.

As Figure 3 shows, the marginal utility is less for each additional pack purchased than for the preceding pack. The principle of diminishing marginal utility means that, all other things being equal, the more we have of a good or service, the less we will be willing to pay for an additional amount of the same good or service.

The total utility a consumer gets from a good or service is the sum of the marginal utilities. If the smoker in the above example bought three packs of cigarettes a day, the total utility would be 50 plus 20 plus 5, a total of 75 units of utility.

**Consumer equilibrium**   How many packs of cigarettes, or anything else, a consumer buys depends on comparing the

Because of the devastating health effects, the principle of diminishing marginal utility may apply even more to cigarette smoking than to most types of consumption.

marginal utility of the good or service to its price. The objective is to obtain the largest amount of utility possible with our limited incomes. This is accomplished when the last dollar spent on any item provides the consumer with the same marginal utility as the last dollar spent on any other good or service. That spending allocation results in consumer equilibrium because the consumers obtain more satisfaction from whatever they spend their money on than from any other pattern of spending.

Consumer equilibrium is reached for smokers when the last dollar they spend on additional packs of cigarettes provides as much added satisfaction as the last dollar spent on gasoline, hamburgers, movie tickets, rent, or anything else. Also, the marginal utility per dollar spent on the various goods and services our hypothetical smoker buys should be equal to the marginal utility received from an additional dollar saved. When consumers have allocated their incomes so that the marginal utility of every item purchased divided by its price is equal to the marginal utility of every other item divided by its price, the consumers are doing as well as they can with their incomes. If they can't do any better, they are at consumer equilibrium. They have maximized the satisfaction they can get from their income because any other allocation of their income would result in lower total utility.

**consumer equilibrium** the condition in which consumers allocate their income in such a way that the last dollar spent on each good or service and the last dollar saved provide equal amounts of utility.

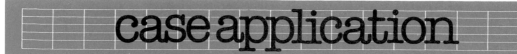

# case application

## The Channel Race

A lot of competitors have plunged into the channel race on cable television. Subscribers now have their choice of all-news, all-sports, all-children's, all-music-video, all-religious, and all-cultural channels, among others. In some cities, you can add a channel that allows you to push a button to respond electronically to questions asked in the broadcast studio.

In addition to paying a basic service fee, many cable subscribers are subscribing to additional "premium" channels at extra cost. Some are paying for more than one movie channel, although the channels often show the same films. Even with the increase in cable subscribers, many of the companies that supply programs to the cable stations operate at a loss, and some have gone broke. But these losses have not deterred new companies from entering the field. Two new all-comedy channels plunged into the swim in 1990. The lure of potential profits is attractive; nobody yet knows how many pay channels the viewing public will support.

### Economic Reasoning

1. How would adding a second movie channel to a cable subscription affect the subscriber's total and marginal utility from pay television?
2. What criteria would you use, in economic terms, in deciding how many premium cable channels to subscribe to?
3. Do you think that there is a danger that people might spend too much of their income on pay television? Why or why not?

Information, such as an automobile's gas mileage, is an essential requirement for making wise consumer spending decisions.

# How Can Consumers Make Better Choices?

Consumers try to get the most they can out of the dollars they spend or save. However, obtaining the maximum utility from our income is not always easy. This analysis section examines under what conditions consumers can make proper consumption or savings decisions.

**Information**  An essential requirement for making wise consumer spending and saving decisions is to have sufficient and accurate information about your choices. For product information, the consumer should know what goods and services are available, where they can be obtained, what prices they are selling for, their quality and serviceability, and their distinctive characteristics.

With respect to cigarettes, an important piece of information consumers did not have prior to the Surgeon General's report was the effects of smoking on health. Smokers who died of lung cancer or other smoking-related diseases were not able to make informed decisions about the allocation of their spending in the absence of information concerning the relationship between cigarette consumption and health. With that information, they might decide to continue smoking, to cut down on the amount, to switch to lower-tar cigarettes, or to quit smoking. Whatever their choice, it would be a more efficient allocation of income if based on full knowledge about the product.

> SURGEON·GENERAL'S WARNING: Smoking By Pregnant Women May Result in Fetal Injury, Premature Birth, And Low Birth Weight.

Similarly, in making savings decisions consumers need to know how secure the savings are against being reduced in value, how easily they can be turned into cash (their liquidity), and how much the earnings on the savings will be. In the case of borrowing, it is important to know what the real interest rate is as well as all the loan repayment conditions.

Ideally, consumers can achieve the greatest total utility from their incomes by having complete information about all goods and services. But there is a cost to obtaining information—the opportunity cost of the time involved in seeking the information. If you were in the market for an automobile, it would be wise to visit a number of dealers, get comparative prices, read brochures and test reports on the

**real interest rate**  the quoted interest rate calculated on an annual basis and adjusted for changes in the purchasing power of money during the duration of the loan.

characteristics and quality of the different makes, and talk to car owners. On the other hand, if you are buying a can of tomatoes, it doesn't pay to put that much time into deciding which brand to buy and where to buy it.

Even with such an insignificant purchase as a can of tomatoes, however, we would like to know that the quality of the product is good. For this information we often depend on the reputation of the brand name and the producer's desire to maintain a good reputation. For some products, especially foods and drugs, we also depend on government-imposed standards and testing. The government requires firms in certain industries to make information available about their products, such as the contents of mattresses, pillows, and sleeping bags, the energy efficiency of home appliances, and the ingredients in packaged foods. Cigarette manufacturers must print warnings about the health dangers of their product on the packages and in their advertisements. The government also requires lending institutions to inform borrowers in writing of the actual rates of interest they will be paying and other conditions of the loan. A major purpose of these government requirements is to reduce information costs for consumers and enable them to obtain greater utility from their income.

**Advertising**  The most prevalent source of information about products and services is advertising. There is a good deal of dispute over the merits of advertising. Some of advertising's benefits are that it informs consumers of what is available, where, and at what price. Advertisements also often present the distinguishing characteristics of different products and services. This is essential information in making consumer choices. In some cases, advertising may lower production costs per unit by expanding a producer's market. By identifying producers, it may encourage them to maintain the quality of and service for the product.

On the negative side, advertising generally adds to the cost of products and thus reduces consumers' purchasing power. It may help eliminate all but the biggest firms from production—the ones that can afford the high advertising costs in certain industries. It also helps create wants and fads and thereby affects consumer sovereignty. If the advertising is false or misleading, it will reduce consumer satisfaction.

The heavy advertising by cigarette companies is credited for maintaining a large market for their product in the face of information about its detrimental effects on health. The image created by advertising that smoking is sophisticated, sexy, macho, or whatever the advertising firms think people might identify with, has been effective in offsetting the health warnings, especially in inducing those who have not yet developed the habit to begin smoking.

The American Cancer Society publishes combative advertisements.

# case application

## That's No Alligator; It's a Chameleon

When you buy a shirt with an alligator insignia on the front, it may not have been made by Izod Lacoste. The alligator is a trademark of Izod Lacoste clothing, but counterfeit copies of clothes with the well-known trademark symbol have been produced by others and sold in regular retail outlets as the legitimate article.

What is worse, you could be driving your car after having the brakes relined and have an accident because the brake linings that were installed were inferior imitations of a name brand. Automobile parts have long been a favorite target of counterfeit manufacturers. A car company executive collected over 225 different parts that were sold with Ford company markings but were not legitimate Ford products.

Other favorites of the counterfeiters have been Rolex watches, Gucci leather goods, Levi's jeans, Spaulding sporting goods, Apple computers, and pirated music and videotapes and computer software. More recently, the product forgers have moved on to new industry targets such as over-the-counter pharmaceuticals, industrial parts, and electronic components. Since the fake products generally do not meet the quality standards of the originals, there are potential health and safety problems. Counterfeit birth-control pills labeled as G. D. Searle brand were delivered to pharmacists, forcing the company to recall more than 1 million pills to find the bogus ones. The cause of a helicopter crash and the death of its pilot has been traced to a defective counterfeit part in the rotor assembly.

Most of these imitation goods are produced by countries in the Far East. Pressured by United States officials, who are in turn being pressured by the legitimate American manufacturers, those countries have begun to crack down on the counterfeit manufacturers. Taiwan, once the capital of counterfeit goods production, has recently led this fight by passing tough new anticounterfeiting laws. But sidewalk hustlers still hang around the tourist hotels in Taipei, offering fake Rolex watches for $25.

The laws in this country have also been strengthened. In 1984 Congress passed legislation bolstering the trademark laws and giv-

The destruction of fake Cartier watches in La Chaux-de-Fonds, Switzerland.

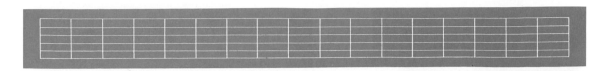

ing customs agents more powers to search out and confiscate imitation products coming into the country. However, with the Customs Service concentrating on narcotics smuggling, only a small fraction of the counterfeit imports are caught.

The merchandise counterfeiters are taking advantage of the reputation and market success of name brand producers. The public's familiarity with manufacturers' trademarks was built up by a great amount of promotional advertising, as well as by the quality of the products themselves. The prices of the legitimate products include those advertising costs. Thus, even if the imitation products were of as high a quality as the originals, they could be sold at lower prices because they do not have to cover the promotional costs.

Name brand producers have good reason to protect the rights to their trademarks jealously. When a customer buys a counterfeit Izod Lacoste shirt, not only might the alligator change color like its cousin the chameleon, but the whole shirt might change color in the wash. This would not be good for Izod Lacoste's image, on which they have lavished so much promotional investment.

## Economic Reasoning

1. What consumer information is conveyed by a trademark?
2. How does counterfeiting of trademarks affect consumer utility?
3. Would you knowingly buy an imitation Apple computer made in Hong Kong if you could get it at a greatly discounted price, say one-half the price of a legitimate Apple, and try it out before you bought it? Why or why not?

Counterfeit computers being crushed in Taipei, Taiwan.

**WORLD HEALTH**

**Smoking or Health the choice is yours!**

The decision to smoke or not to smoke is an economic as well as a health choice, involving such concepts as trade-offs and utility.

## Putting It Together

Consumers dictate what will be produced in a market economy. They express their wants through their purchases of the goods and services they desire at the prices they are willing to pay. This is *consumer sovereignty*.

Some goods such as food, housing, clothing, and medical care are *necessities* for all consumers. Other goods and services, on which we may choose to spend our incomes, are *luxuries*.

If we do not change the amount we buy of something by very much when its price changes, it has an *inelastic demand*. If the amount demanded varies a great deal with changes in the price, the item has an *elastic demand*. The *elasticity ratio* is measured by dividing the percentage change in the quantity demanded of a good or service by the percentage change in its price. If the elasticity ratio is less than one, demand is inelastic. If the elasticity ratio is greater than one, demand is elastic. If the elasticity ratio is exactly one, demand elasticity is *unitary*.

The percentage of our total disposable income that we spend on goods and services is our *average propensity to consume*. The percentage that we put into savings is our *average propensity to save*.

The amount of satisfaction that a good or service provides to its purchaser is called its *utility*. The total satisfaction provided by all units of the item consumed is its *total utility*. The extra satisfaction provided by one additional unit of the item is its *marginal utility*. The marginal utility diminishes as more units are purchased because our wants for the item are more fully satisfied.

The consumer is getting the maximum satisfaction possible when income is allocated so that the marginal utility from the last dollar of expenditure on a good or service is the same as the marginal utility from the last dollar of expenditure on every other item consumed and also the same as the marginal utility from the last dollar put into savings. This situation is called *consumer equilibrium*.

In order to obtain the maximum utility from our spending and saving, we need full and accurate information on which to base our decisions. Commercial advertising is one source of product information, and, to the extent that it provides useful information, it is helpful in making consumer choices. However, it may add to the cost of products; and when it does not provide accurate, useful information, it is wasteful at best and sometimes misleading.

# Perspective

## Conspicuous Consumption

**Thorstein Veblen (1857-1929)**
Of Norwegian parentage, Veblen was raised in a Wisconsin farm community. He was educated at some of the country's best universities (Johns Hopkins, Yale, and Cornell), but his agricultural background gave him an appreciation for the realities of life which shaped his thinking about economics. He mistrusted the theoretical formulations of the marginalist school of economists who held that the economy worked according to certain economic "laws" and automatically made adjustments "at the margin" to give the optimum outcome. Instead, Veblen emphasized the importance of the way a society's culture and institutions dictate economic outcomes, and he is credited with being the founder of the institutionalist school of economics.

In addition to *The Theory of the Leisure Class* (1899), Veblen's books on economics include: *The Theory of Business Enterprise* (1904), *The Engineers and the Price System* (1921), and *Absentee Ownership and Business Enterprise* (1923). He also wrote on such diverse subjects as the way universities are run in his book, *The Higher Learning in America* (1918), along with articles on sociology and anthropology, and translations of ancient Nordic sagas, *The Laxdoela Saga* (1925).

Consumers are supposed to be calculating buyers, spending their limited income to get the most utility. But are they? Why do they spend $100 for a pair of designer jeans with a particular label on the back or $50 for a knit shirt with a cute animal on the pocket when for about half the price they could buy very similar items without the identifying trademarks? How can shops on exclusive Rodeo Drive in Beverly Hills charge so much more for merchandise than stores do only a few blocks away on Wilshire Boulevard in West Los Angeles?

These phenomena were explained as far back as 1899 by an American economist, Thorstein Veblen. In his best-known work, *The Theory of the Leisure Class*, Veblen pointed out that people at the high end of the income ladder, whom he referred to as the "leisure class," set the consumption standards that other income classes try to emulate. "Conspicuous consumption of valuable goods is a means of reputability to the gentleman of leisure," Veblen said, and ". . . members of each [social] stratum accept as their ideal of decency the scheme of life in vogue in the next higher stratum, and bend their energies to live up to that ideal." In other words, people try to copy the life-style of those above them on the income ladder, and the ones at the top display their purchasing power by *conspicuous consumption* of expensive things. Purchasing things because they are expensively chic has been termed "the Veblen effect."

A similar but somewhat different consumption behavior is "the snob effect." The snob effect depends on the consumption of a good being confined to a very limited number of people. Buying a Mercedes automobile might be an example of the Veblen effect at work, while buying a gold-plated Mercedes would be an example of the snob effect.

We have another type of consumer motivation at work at the other extreme, "the bandwagon effect." The bandwagon effect arises when people purchase a good because "everyone else has one." An example of the bandwagon effect is the popularity of hi-tech sneakers.

Do these various psychological motivations that drive people to buy certain goods undermine the idea of maximizing total utility? Not at all. Utility comes from psychological satisfaction as well as from satisfaction in use. In the words of Veblen, we derive satisfaction from "the utility of consumption as an evidence of wealth."

# For Further Study and Analysis

## Study Questions

1. What goods and services do you consider to be necessities in your own consumption? How do you differentiate between a necessity and a luxury?

2. What luxuries do you think would have a higher price elasticity of demand than others? Give three examples and explain why you think they would have an exceptionally high elasticity.

3. Besides salt and drinking water, what other items that you use regularly have an inelastic demand? Pick one of those items and explain why if its price went up 10% you would reduce your consumption of the item by less than 10%.

4. If you were the owner of a business and trying to decide what price to charge for your product or service, why would the elasticity of demand be an important consideration?

5. A hamburger stand raised the price of its hamburgers from $2.00 to $2.50. As a result, its sales of hamburgers fell from 200 per day to 180 per day. Was the demand for its hamburgers elastic or inelastic? How can you tell?

6. Why would something that has many close substitutes tend to have an elastic demand?

7. If the average propensity to consume was 90% of after-tax income, what would the average propensity to save be?

8. How does tobacco company advertising affect the cigarette market? Does it influence the elasticity of demand for cigarettes? How?

9. Chemically, all aspirin is the same, but some aspirin sells for much more than other aspirin. Why do consumers often purchase the higher-priced aspirin when all aspirin is chemically the same?

10. What are examples of purchases you have made because of the Veblen effect, the snob effect, and the bandwagon effect?

## Exercises in Analysis

1. In the first exercise at the end of chapter 4 you constructed the demand schedule of a group of students for movie theater tickets. Using the data from that demand schedule, calculate the elasticity of demand for movie theater tickets when the price falls from $7 to $6. Then calculate the elasticity of demand when the price is reduced from $3 to $2. How do the two elasticity ratios compare? Compare the elasticity ratios for your group's demand with those calculated by the other groups for their demand schedules. Can you draw any generalizations from these comparisons about the behavior of elasticity of demand at high prices compared

to low prices? Save the results of this exercise for use in an exercise at the end of chapter 6.

2. Sometimes things that are considered luxuries at one time come to be looked upon as necessities by later generations. Using the recent past, demonstrate how a good or service once considered a luxury might become a necessity.

3. The theory of consumer sovereignty holds that only those goods and services consumers want are produced. Prepare a report showing the principle of consumer sovereignty at work in the automobile industry in recent years.

4. Write a paper comparing the advertising in a section of the daily newspaper with the advertising in an hour of prime-time television. Which has the most useful information for the consumer? Which has the most uninformative, repetitive, and/or misleading advertising?

## Further Reading

Charles, Susan. *Housing Economics.* London: Macmillan, 1977. An examination of housing as a consumer durable, what determines housing demand, supply, and prices, and the financing of house purchase.

Earl, Peter. *Lifestyle Economics.* New York: St. Martin's Press, 1986. Analyzes the processes of consumer choice-making.

Fritschler, A. Lee. *Smoking and Politics.* 4th ed. Englewood Cliffs, N.J.: Prentice Hall, 1989. The book examines the response of the government bureaucracy to the health threat posed by smoking and the administrative politics in rule-making.

Neuberger, Maurine B. *Smoke Screen: Tobacco and the Public Welfare.* Englewood Cliffs, N.J.: Prentice Hall, 1963. Chapter 7 of this book discusses the differences between the impetus for teenagers to smoke as compared to adults.

O'Shaughnessy, John. *Why People Buy.* New York: Oxford University Press, 1987. Examines consumer behavior with respect to what motivates people to buy specific products and brands. It makes use of a social science survey approach, based on buyers' statements.

Otnes, Per, ed. *The Sociology of Consumption.* Atlantic Highlands, N.J.: Humanities Press International, 1988. A study of consumer behavior from the standpoint of economic and sociological doctrines.

Penz, G. Peter. *Consumer Sovereignty and Human Interests.* Cambridge, U.K.: Cambridge University Press, 1986. A view of the operation of consumer sovereignty with respect to private-want satisfaction, social wants, and human interests and deprivation.

Thorelli, Hans Birger, Helmut Becker, and Jack Engledow. *The Information Seekers.* Cambridge, Mass.: Ballinger, 1974. A look at advertising from the consumer's point of view.

White, Larry C. *Merchants of Death: The American Tobacco Industry.* New York: William Morrow, 1988. This book attacks "the big lie" put forth by the cigarette companies that there is no proof that smoking kills. It investigates the role of advertising in promoting and romanticizing smoking.

Whitside, Thomas. *Selling Death: Cigarette Advertising and Public Health.* New York: Liveright, 1971. The author believes that "the selling of cigarettes is symbolic of the mass merchandising of consumer products in this country."

## chapter 6

# THE BUSINESS FIRM AND MARKET STRUCTURE

*In the American economy decisions about what, how, and for whom to produce are made primarily by private business firms. Their decisions are dictated by the marketplace; but for some the market is more dictatorial than for others. For farmers the market is often fickle, as the following article shows.*

## Let the Good Times Roll Down On the Farm

Just a few short years ago the nation's farmers were in such deep trouble that benefit concerts were conducted on their behalf. The first concert, organized by singer Willie Nelson, was held in the fall of 1985 in the University of Illinois football stadium. Although the amount of money raised was not very important, about $10 million—equivalent to barely a few hours' interest payments on the $213 billion debt owed by farmers—it served to call attention to their plight.

Many farmers were losing their life's savings in foreclosure sales of their farms and equipment. Some 400,000 farmers either went into bankruptcy in 1985 or quit before the creditors took over. Between 1980 and 1986 the farm population fell by 13.6%. Farm-

ing has always been a chancy business, but conditions in the farm economy in the mid-1980s were the worst since the Great Depression of the 1930s. The farmers' main problem was their large indebtedness at high interest rates, combined with depressed crop prices and the falling value of farmland. The value of some Iowa and Nebraska farmland fell by half from its peak in 1980.

Sales were down to overseas markets, which normally absorb more than half of U.S. wheat output, as a result of large crops in the grain-producing regions abroad and the high cost of the dollar. Agricultural exports fell from a peak value of $43 billion in 1981 to $26 billion in 1986.

But in 1987 the farm economy turned around. Agricultural exports were boosted by the weakening value of the dollar, which made U.S. farm products cheaper for foreign buyers, and by government export subsidies.

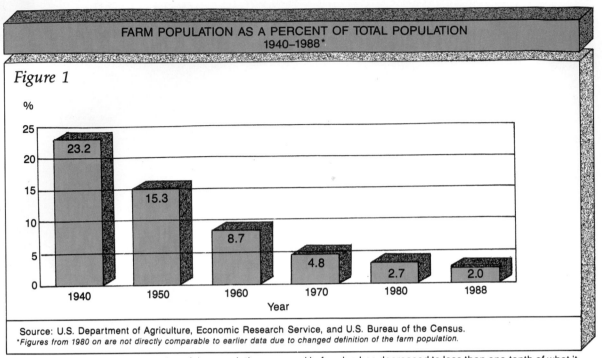

**FARM POPULATION AS A PERCENT OF TOTAL POPULATION**
**1940–1988***

*Figure 1*

%

Source: U.S. Department of Agriculture, Economic Research Service, and U.S. Bureau of the Census.
*Figures from 1980 on are not directly comparable to earlier data due to changed definition of the farm population.*

In the last half-century the proportion of the population engaged in farming has decreased to less than one-tenth of what it was.

Net farm income in 1987 reached a record level of $57 billion, up from $37.5 billion in 1986.

Over two-thirds of the 1987 net income, however, was accounted for by the $26 billion pumped into the farm economy that year by the government. Under provisions of the 1985 Food Security Act, the government provided deficiency payments to farmers to cover the difference between the "target price" set for a number of basic crops and the price they received in the marketplace.

These farm subsidies under the Food Security Act continue a policy of farm price supports that dates back to the Depression of the 1930s. The policy was intended to help family farms stay in business and smooth out crop price fluctuations from year to year. But despite the government price support programs, there has occurred a massive exodus of the population from agriculture (see Figure 1). Even the general prosperity of the farm economy since 1987 and the continuing

government agricultural subsidy program have not succeeded in stopping the exodus.

The agricultural sector is more and more dominated by large farmers and corporate farms. The largest 95,000 or so farm operators account for 51% of the total agricultural sales, while the million and a half smallest farmers generate less than 10% of sales. Despite the stated goal of the farm price support program to sustain the family farm, most of the benefits go to the largest operators who need the assistance the least. In 1987 there was a survey of 1,920 Kansas farms that showed the 480 most profitable farms, averaging $104,000 in profits, receiving an average $41,000 in government payments. On the other hand, the 480 farms with the smallest net income, losing an average $3,000 each, averaged only $20,000 in subsidies per farm.

It appears from the evidence in Figure 1 and the data on farm incomes by size that the good times are mainly for the large farmers and corporate farms. Modern technology in

farming may dictate large operations; but if so, we need to rethink our 60-year-old agricultural policy.

## Chapter Preview

*Farmers traditionally represent the epitome of free enterprise in action. In a market economy, the private business firm is the principal supplier of goods and services. Consumers express their will in the marketplace, and it is up to the individual enterprises to put together the labor, capital, and natural resources to satisfy these consumer demands.*

*This chapter will explain how the business sector of our economy works. The market structure of an industry determines the quantity of goods or services produced and the prices charged. These matters are explored under the questions:*

What are the forms and economic functions of business firms? What determines a firm's profits? How does industry market structure affect price and output decisions?

## Learning Objectives

*After completing this chapter, you should be able to:*

1. *List the three main forms of business organization and cite the advantages and disadvantages of each.*
2. *Describe the four economic functions of business firms.*
3. *Distinguish between fixed costs and variable costs.*
4. *Show the relationship of total cost and total revenue to output.*
5. *Locate the break-even point and point of maximum profit.*
6. *Distinguish between normal rate of return and economic profits.*
7. *List the characteristics of purely competitive industries.*
8. *Explain the principle of diminishing returns.*
9. *Explain the short-run and long-run adjustments to changes in demand in a purely competitive industry.*
10. *Differentiate between pure monopoly, shared monopoly, and differentiated competition.*

## What Are the Forms and Economic Functions of Business Firms?

The three basic allocation questions an economic system must resolve were described in chapter 2 as the "what to produce," "how to produce," and "for whom to produce" questions. In a market economy, it is the interplay of demand and supply in the marketplace that resolves these three allocation questions by directing the decisions of business firms. In this section, we will first examine what the different forms of business organization are, and then discuss what economic functions businesses perform.

**Forms of business organization**   By far the overwhelming majority of farms are individual proprietorships, owned and operated by one individual or one family. This type of business organization accounts for some 87% of the total number of farms and 70% of farm real assets (value of land and buildings). About 10% of farms are partnerships, which own 16% of farm real assets. Only 3% are corporations, but they have about 11% of the real assets. These are the three main forms of business organization. In addition, there are some farm cooperatives.

There is a trend toward fewer and larger farms. This has led to concerns about the consequences if family farms are allowed to go under and be replaced by corporate farming. Since food is a necessity of life, what would be the results if all agriculture fell into the hands of a few giant corporations? Can this happen, and would they then raise food prices to levels people couldn't afford? Will the agricultural industry

**proprietorship** a business enterprise with a single private owner.

**partnership** a nonincorporated business enterprise with two or more owners.

**corporation** a business enterprise that is chartered by a state government or, occasionally, by the federal government to do business as a legal entity.

**cooperative** producer and worker cooperatives are associations in which the members join in production and marketing and share the profits. Consumer cooperatives are associations of consumers engaged in retail trade, sharing the profits as a dividend among the members.

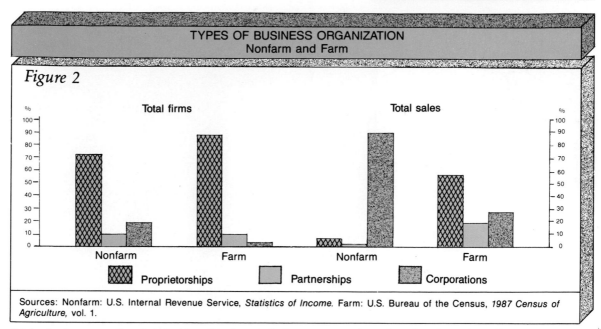

**TYPES OF BUSINESS ORGANIZATION**
Nonfarm and Farm

*Figure 2*

Sources: Nonfarm: U.S. Internal Revenue Service, *Statistics of Income.* Farm: U.S. Bureau of the Census, *1987 Census of Agriculture,* vol. 1.

Total sales by corporations in industries other than agriculture are many times the sales of proprietorships, even though the number of corporations is only about one-fourth the number of proprietorships. In farming, however, proprietorships dominate the industry in sales as well as in numbers.

end up like the automobile industry, with just a handful of giant producers?

The economic organization of agriculture differs from the economic organization of manufacturing industries. In nonfarm industries taken together, 71% of the firms are proprietorships, but those proprietorships account for only 6% of total industry sales, while corporations account for 90%. In agriculture, on the other hand, proprietorships receive 56% of the revenue from farm sales, compared with only 26% for farm corporations. At present the corporate form of business does not dominate in agriculture as it does in manufacturing. Whether it will in the future depends on the relative advantages of the different types of business organization in agriculture.

Proprietorships, partnerships, and corporations each have their advantages and disadvantages which are of varying importance in different industries. One of the advantages of a proprietorship is that, depending on the type of business, it can be relatively inexpensive to start. Over one-fourth of all farms are less than 50 acres in size. The average investment in land and buildings for a family farm is less than $300,000, not a big investment compared to a manufacturing plant. Another advantage of proprietorships is that the owner-operator makes all of the decisions and keeps all of the profits, on which only a personal income tax is paid.

Single proprietorships are often small businesses such as this farm market.

On the other side, a major disadvantage of a proprietorship business is that the owner is personally responsible for the debts of the business if it goes bankrupt. Some of the other disadvantages are that the business is legally terminated when the owner dies, and a single owner often does not have access to enough capital to make the business succeed.

For all businesses outside of farming, there are only 15% as many partnerships as there are individual proprietorships; but since partnerships tend to be larger in size than proprietorships, their total sales are over half of the total sales of proprietorships. The principal advantage partnerships have over proprietorships is that they enable two or more people to pool their capital and/or talents to make a business successful. A disadvantage is that each individual is personally liable for all decisions made and for all financial obligations of the company. Another drawback of the partnership form of business organization is that if one of the partners dies, the business is dissolved in the eyes of the law, just as a proprietorship is when the owner dies.

Proprietorships and partnerships allow individuals with ideas, talent, and a willingness to work the opportunity to take a risk on their abilities. If they succeed, they reap the financial and personal rewards of their efforts, and the economy benefits from the availability of a product or service at a price people are willing to pay. If they fail, they suffer the brunt of the failure. It is a ruthless process because the overwhelming majority of new businesses do fail, but it serves an economizing function. Businesses normally do not continue in operation when they do not satisfy a demand efficiently.

The corporate form of business is one in which ownership is represented by stock purchases. A corporation is a legal "person" in the eyes of the law. As such, one of the big advantages of a corporation is the limited liability of the stockholders. Unlike proprietorships and partnerships, the owners of a corporation are normally not personally liable for debts of the company. The corporation is legally treated as an individual and is responsible for its financial obligations. If it fails, its stockholders can only lose the amount they have invested in their stock. Furthermore, when ownership of a corporation changes through the sale of shares in the company, the corporate firm is not legally dissolved.

Some of the disadvantages of the corporate form of business organization are: corporations are more regulated by the government than other businesses; they must pay corporation taxes on their earnings; there are state and legal fees charged for incorporation. Corporations must be chartered by the state in which they are legally headquartered or, in some cases, they are chartered by the federal government. The costs of incorporation tend to discourage small firms from incorporating. There are some small corporations, including professionals such as doctors that incorporate, but the typical corporation is quite large. Although only 20% of the nation's businesses are corporations, they account for 90% of total business receipts.

When a large corporation fails, the economy tends to suffer more than when a small proprietorship fails. More jobs are lost by corporate failure, more suppliers are hurt, more buildings and equipment are wasted, and the government loses more potential tax revenue. If the company is sufficiently important, the government may step in to save it, as it did with Lockheed in 1971, Chrysler in 1980, and Continental Illinois in 1984, by guaranteeing new loans extended by creditors to keep the firm functioning.

**Identifying consumer wants**   The first function of any type of business firm is to determine what will be produced by identifying what consumers want and will pay for. Farmers have a particularly difficult time predicting this because they must make their production decisions at planting time on the basis of what they think the market will be the following year at harvest time. And because American farmers are so dependent on foreign markets in which to dispose of a large part of their output, their decision about what to produce is complicated by the need to know what world demand will be as well as what domestic demand will be.

**limited liability** a legal provision that protects individual stockholders of a corporation from being sued by creditors of the corporation to collect unpaid debts of the firm.

The sprawling Chrysler headquarters and plant illustrate the large amount of capital and labor involved in a major corporate enterprise. Government loan guarantees saved Chrysler from a possible permanent shutdown.

But producers in other industries have different problems in identifying consumer wants. At least farmers are producing necessities that are always in demand—food and fibers. Producers of luxury goods are at the mercy of changing fads. Identifying what new products consumers will buy is the first task of the entrepreneur.

**Organizing production** The second function of businesses is to organize production—to resolve the "how" question. It is the most complex function of business firms. How effectively they perform it usually determines whether the business succeeds or fails. Business firms must decide what mix of the factors of production—land, labor, and capital—will best achieve the desired output.

Many farmers invested too heavily in farm equipment in the 1970s and found themselves capital-poor as well as land-poor when markets weakened in the 1980s. They had so much invested in expensive equipment and land that they couldn't meet their current bills. Farmers who had invested less in land and capital equipment, depending more on their labor for cultivating and harvesting and hiring the large machinery when it was needed, fared better. Corporate farms, on the other hand, are able to make efficient use of capital equipment because with their large size they can employ it more intensively; it is not idle as much of the time.

**Allocating revenues** As part of the circular flow of economic activity, businesses allocate the revenue they receive from sales to pay their employees, suppliers, and investors. When farmers are in an economic squeeze, it spreads to their suppliers—the farm equipment dealers, the fertilizer companies, the banks that lend them money—and to the whole farm communities. And when the good times come to the farm, they also come to the farm suppliers.

Businesses not only decide what will be produced and how, but they also decide how purchasing power is allocated. This is their third function. In resolving the "for whom" question, they do not decide who will purchase their products. Consumers decide for themselves what they will purchase under the principle of consumer sovereignty. But businesses do determine how much will be paid to the suppliers of inputs and therefore how much purchasing power each supplier has. The income received by the firm's employees and other factor inputs is spent, in turn, on other goods and services, or it is saved. In a freely functioning market economy, it is purchasing power that determines the answer to the "for whom" question.

**Real capital investment** The fourth function of business firms is to increase the economy's stock of real capital—the barns, factories, office buildings, machinery, tools, and equipment used to produce goods and services. This investment in real capital is an important economic function because it makes possible the expansion and modernization of production. One thing that has led to such an increase in agricultural production in this country that it can supply its food needs with fewer and fewer farmers is the investment in real capital. American agriculture is the most productive in the world. Although this has not always benefited the farmers, it has been very good for consumers.

Investment is an aspect of the resolution of the "what" question because if all resources were allocated to the production of consumption goods and none used for capital goods, the economy would not grow. By investing in real capital, business firms shift some resources from production for present consumption to production for increasing future consumption. This is sometimes referred to as the "when to produce" question.

Real capital investment is also important in resolving the "how" question. It may be possible to change production methods to increase efficiency without new capital investment, perhaps by organizing workers into production teams and giving the teams broad decision-making authority. But most changes in production methods are associated with the installation of new, more technologically advanced machinery and equipment, which is expensive and calls for new investment capital.

**real capital** the buildings, machinery, tools, and equipment used in production.

# case application

## Running With the Bulls

The "Great Bull Market" of the 1980s set new records for daily and weekly advances in stock prices and numbers of shares traded. The "bulls"—speculators who expect rising stock prices—were buying on every price increase and contracting for future deliveries of stock, expecting to turn around and sell the stock for more than they paid. In that kind of market it was hard not to make a profit, unless of course you were a "bear," expecting prices to fall and selling short—contracting to make future delivery of stock you didn't own in hopes the price would drop before you had to cover the transaction. The market was pushed to ever-higher levels as the bulls routed the bears and drove them into hibernation.

But the bears had their days, notably October 19, 1987, when the Dow Jones index of prices of a group of major industrial corporation stock prices fell by a record 508 points. The fall was another instance of the stock market adage that what goes up must come down. The only questions are when and how far. Anyone having the answers to those questions would hold the keys to the capitalist kingdom. There is no shortage of "experts" who profess to know the answers—and sell them for a price. However, examinations of the predictions of stock market analysts suggest that one can do just as well by consulting the stars, or the length of women's skirts, or which professional football conference wins the Super Bowl. All of these have been better indicators of the direction stock prices will take in the following year, presumably by pure coincidence, than the predictions of security analysts.

Furthermore, stock market analysts' predictions of the performance of individual stocks have been no better than their predictions of market trends. As Burton Malkiel has shown in his book *A Random Walk Down Wall Street* (see Further Reading at the end of the chapter), one could do just as well at picking stocks by throwing darts at a page of stock listings as by following the advice of the market experts.

Why are the security analysts no better at predicting the direction of stock prices than simply taking the recent trend and no better at picking individual stocks than pure chance? The explanation is not analysts' incompetence, but the nature of the stock market. Analysts are unable to predict accurately the direction of stock prices because what the market does depends less on the real factors affecting the market—profits, interest rates, inflation, employment—than it does on the psychological factors—how investors think other investors will react to economic and market developments. The "Great Bull Market" was propelled less by actual economic conditions than it was by the desire of investors, particularly institutional investors, not to be left behind when stock prices rose.

In their ability to pick individual stocks, market analysts can do no better than random chance because securities are traded in a "perfect" market. A perfect market is one in which all relevant information is available to everyone. As a result, the price of a stock reflects any good or bad news that is likely to affect its future earnings, or what people think its value will be. Because stocks are traded in a perfect market, their prices correspond to their relative expected values. Except in retrospect, there are no bargains in the stock market. The current market price of a stock is the best estimate of what it is worth. If it turns out to be worth more, it was a bargain at that price. But it will just as often turn out to be worth less.

One contribution of stock market analysts is to help make it a perfect market. After surveying the performance of Wall Street security analysts and fund managers, Anne

## HOW TO READ THE DAILY STOCK MARKET REPORT

| High | Low | Stock | Div. | Yld% | P-E Ratio | Sales 100s | High | Low | Close | Net Chg. |
|------|-----|-------|------|------|-----------|------------|------|-----|-------|----------|
| 123¹/₈ | 93³/₈ | IBM | 4.84 | 4.3 | 16 | 19689 | 114 | 112¹/₂ | 113¹/₂ | + 1-1/2 |
| The price of IBM shares in current year. | | | Annual dividend per share in dollars to stock-holders | Yield = Div. × 100 ₁ closing price | Price-earnings ra-tio: the number of times the current market value of the company exceeds its annual profits. | Number of shares that changed hands (1,968,900). | | In day | | Net price change from pre-vious day's closing price (ex-pressed as a fraction of a dollar). |

B. Fisher writes: "All in all, the record doesn't really refute the widespread suspicion that security analysts aren't very good at picking stocks. . . . [But] in gathering and dissem-inating huge gobs of information about com-panies and stocks that investors wouldn't otherwise have, the analysts over the long run help to insure that stocks are fairly val-ued. Maybe that's all we can ask of them" (*Fortune*, October 1, 1984, p. 136).

The only advantage anyone can have in the market—so-called expert or not—is to know something about a company that others do not know. For example, if someone knew that a company was about to be acquired by another firm at a price for its stock higher than the current market price, the person could buy a large block of the company's stock and sell it at a profit when the merger took place. But the use of such "insider" information is illegal. The Securities and Ex-change Commission, the government watch-dog agency over the securities business, investigates reports or indications of "insider trading" and prosecutes offenders.

Does all of this mean that you can't make a profit in the stock market or that it is just a gamble? Attempting to "play" the market by short-term trading in stocks is definitely a gamble, more likely to enrich the brokers with commissions than to enrich the inves-tors. But long-term investment in stocks, the so-called "buy and hold" strategy, can be profitable. On the average, over a long period of time stock ownership has provided a real return to investors, after taking inflation into account, of 6%. This may not appear to be a high figure, but when you consider that it is in addition to increases in the consumer price level and that the earnings compound if you leave them invested, a real return of 6% can mount up significantly over a period of years. It doubles the purchasing power of your investment in 12 years and triples it in 19 years, minus any income taxes on the earnings.

In order to avoid the risk of selecting a stock or stocks that, for some unexpected reason, do worse than anticipated, it is con-sidered good investment strategy to diversify investments into different companies in a variety of industries. A convenient way for investors to do this is by purchasing shares in mutual funds. Mutual stock funds are pools of stocks in a variety of companies, where the investment decisions are made by a professional fund manager. Some funds charge a sales fee, ranging up to 8% of the amount invested; others are "no-load" funds, meaning that they charge the buyer no sales fee. For both load and no-load funds, the fund managers collect administrative fees from the fund assets at regular intervals, and frequently also collect "performance" fees based on increases in the value of the fund shares.

Different funds have varying investment objectives. The aggressive growth funds in-vest in stocks with greater risk but with the potential to return higher profits. More con-servative funds frequently have at least a part of their portfolio invested in bonds, which

have a fixed return and are considered safer than stocks. Some journals, such as *Forbes* magazine, annually publish reports on the performance of mutual funds by type of fund, showing their returns over the past year, five-year, and ten-year periods. The funds themselves publish prospectuses which give their investment objectives, the fees they charge, the names of fund administrators, etc. They must provide this prospectus to anyone interested in investing in the fund before selling them any shares.

The rapid growth of mutual funds in recent years has contributed to the volatility of the stock market. Institutional investors—mutual funds, pension funds, insurance companies—have increasingly dominated the market. Their enormous buy and sell orders cause wild swings in the prices of stocks. The small investor who engages in short-term trading can be tripped up by the rapid price movements.

Most institutional investment takes place in stocks traded on the two major exchanges: the New York Stock Exchange, where stocks of the nation's largest companies are traded, and the smaller American Stock Exchange, also located in New York. In addition, there are half a dozen regional exchanges around the country that trade many of the same stocks listed on the major exchanges. But the stocks of the overwhelming number of companies, the tens of thousands of small corporations that have publicly traded stocks, are not sold on any stock exchange floor. They are sold by individual brokers "over the counter."

The stock exchanges do not handle new issues of stock. When a company wishes to issue new shares of stock, it negotiates a sale of the stock to an investment bank; or, if it is a major corporation raising a very large amount of money, to a group of investment banks referred to as a consortium. Invest-

ment banks then sell the stocks through brokers to the public.

Small "start-up" companies are frequently financed by venture capitalists, financiers who provide funds for promising new ventures in return for part ownership in the company. If the company succeeds well enough to "go public," that is, make a stock offering to the general public, the venture capitalist can reap rewards many times the amount of the capital invested in the company.

Although the stock exchanges do not trade new issues of stock, they are important to the ability of companies to raise investment capital. Investors would be reluctant to buy stock in a company if there were no ready way to dispose of it when they want to get their money out. The efficiency of the U.S. stock market is important to the dynamism of our economy. However, excessive speculation in the stock market can create big problems, as it did in the financial collapse of 1929. Running with the bulls is exciting, but a bull can cause havoc in a china shop economy.

## *Economic Reasoning*

1. Are shares of ownership of most business organizations traded in the stock market? What types of businesses are traded there?

2. Which of the functions of business firms are most affected by the stock market? How?

3. Should the Securities and Exchange Commission reduce the amount of speculation in the stock market by prohibiting investors from buying stock on credit, paying only a fraction in cash and pledging the stock as collateral on the balance owed? Why should such "buying on the margin" be allowed or why should it be prohibited?

# What Determines a Firm's Profits?

The objective of producers in all types of business organizations is to make the largest possible profit. Profit is the difference between the revenue a firm takes in and the costs it incurs. For the smallest farmers included in the 1987 Kansas study, their profits were negative—costs were greater than revenues. Like other producers, farmers try to maximize profits or minimize losses. This is accomplished by producing the most profitable quantity of output with the resources available. We will use a farm operation to illustrate how costs and revenue are determined and how they determine profits.

**Costs**  To illustrate how a firm's costs affect production decisions we will use the example of a chicken farm. A chicken farm with 300,000 laying hens might have three employees and an owner-manager. A large percentage of the hens have to be replaced each year because hens have a limited time of productivity. During its productive span a hen will lay, on the average, about 250 eggs a year. Modern chicken farms keep the hens in environmentally controlled cages, with feeding equipment and egg collection both automated. In contrast to farms that grow crops, they do not need much land, just a few acres.

As with other businesses, chicken farms have two categories of costs: fixed and variable. Fixed costs are those that do not change with changes in the quantity of goods or services produced. The principal fixed costs of a business are the costs of its buildings, equipment, and land—the real capital invested. When a building is constructed and machinery and equipment purchased, they are expected to have specified lifetimes before needing replacement. If a building is expected to have a useful lifetime of 40 years, one-fortieth of the cost of the building is charged as a fixed cost of the business each year. This is called depreciation. If a piece of equipment is expected to have a productive life of 10 years, one-tenth of the cost of the equipment is charged as a fixed cost for depreciation for each year of its expected productive life. The productive life of machinery and equipment usually depends more on the rate of technological advances in an industry than it does on actual physical wear and tear. If an industry is undergoing rapid technological change, the capital goods used in the industry usually become obsolete and inefficient and have to be replaced long before they wear out.

The fixed costs of a chicken farm include depreciation of the buildings and equipment and replacement of the hen flock. Unlike machinery, laying hens do not become obso-

**fixed costs**  production costs which do not change with changes in the quantity of output.
**depreciation**  the costs of buildings, machinery, tools, and equipment which are allocated to output during a given production period.

A major cost of chicken farming is hen depreciation.

lete, but they do wear out and have to be replaced—hen depreciation.

The monthly fixed costs of a representative chicken farm with 300,000 laying hens are:

| | |
|---|---|
| Depreciation on buildings and equipment | $18,800 |
| Hen depreciation | 59,100 |
| Total fixed costs/month | $77,900 |

Variable costs of a business are those costs which increase with each additional unit of a product that is provided. Variable costs include the labor, raw materials, and other costs which increase with the quantity of goods produced and sold. Variable costs are calculated on a per unit basis.

The largest cost item in producing eggs is feed, which amounts to about two-thirds of the total cost. Other variable costs include labor, energy for lighting and temperature control of the henhouses, medication, litter, and other supplies.

The variable costs per dozen eggs are:

| | |
|---|---|
| Feed | $0.28 |
| Labor | 0.03 |
| Energy and miscellaneous | 0.02 |
| Variable costs/dozen eggs | $0.33 |

Total costs are the fixed costs plus the variable costs for a particular level of output. At zero output, total costs equal fixed costs. Total costs rise with output by the amount of additional variable costs. An equation measuring total costs would be:

Total Cost (TC) = Fixed Costs (FC) + Variable Costs (VC)

The total monthly costs of the chicken farm when it is producing 520,000 dozen eggs per month are:

TC = FC + (VC/doz. eggs × # of doz.)

TC = $77,900 + ($0.33 × 520,000) = $77,900 + $171,600 = $249,500.

**variable costs** production costs that change with changes in the quantity of output.
**total costs** the sum of fixed costs and variable costs.

The total costs of the chicken farm are $249,500. Its average cost (AC) per dozen is the total costs divided by the output (Q).

AC = TC/Q = $249,500/520,000 doz. = $0.48/doz.

The farm could produce less or more than 520,000 dozen eggs per month by culling (that is, disposing of) more or fewer hens at a time, changing the amount or mixture of feed, or altering the length of time the henhouses are lit each day (light makes the hens lay more eggs). However, the most efficient output for this size of farm with the existing buildings and equipment is 520,000 dozen eggs, and increasing or decreasing the output would raise the production costs per dozen. Doing that would make it difficult for the farm to sell its eggs in competition with other egg producers.

**Revenue** The money that a firm receives from the sale of its products or services is the company's revenue. Total revenue is the price of the product times the number of units sold.

Total Revenue (TR) = Price (P) × Quantity (Q)

For an egg farm, the monthly revenue is the price it receives for a dozen eggs times the number of dozen sold in the month. Because there are a number of farms trying to sell their eggs to the same buyers and eggs are a standardized commodity, the egg producer (the farm owner, that is, not the hen) has little control over the price. The producer must sell eggs of a given size and type from that farm at the going market price, whatever the price is and however small or large the farm's egg production.

If the average wholesale market price for eggs is $0.53 a dozen and the farm produces 520,000 dozen eggs per month, the farm's total revenue per month is:

TR = P × Q
TR = $0.53 × 520,000 doz. = $275,600

**Profits** Profits are determined by subtracting total costs from total revenue.

Profit (P) = Total Revenue (TR) − Total Cost (TC).

The egg farm we have been looking at would appear to have profits of $26,100 a month.

P = TR − TC
P = $275,600 − $249,500 = $26,100

However, this profit figure does not take into account some economic costs to the owner of operating the farm. It does not, for instance, take into account the managerial costs of running the farm. Since the owner is the manager, unless

**average costs** total costs divided by the number of units produced.
**revenue** the receipts from sales of goods and services.
**total revenue** the sum of receipts from all of the units sold; price × quantity.
**profits** the net returns after subtracting total costs from total revenue. If costs are greater than revenue, profits are negative.

he or she pays himself or herself a salary the accounting profit figure overstates the actual profitability of the business. Part of that $26,500 is really compensation to the owner for performing the managerial functions of running the farm. If we assume that the value of the management service provided by the owner—the salary and benefits that would have to be paid to someone else to manage the operation or the amount the owner could earn managing some other egg farm—is $5200 a month, the profit figure is reduced to $21,300.

Another cost not included in computing the farm's profits is a fair return on the money the owner has invested in the business. If the investment in land, buildings, equipment, and hens were financed with borrowed money, the interest on the loan would appear as a fixed cost along with depreciation. But if the investment is the owner's own capital, which is the case here, there is no actual interest payment. Nevertheless, there is a cost to the owner of the capital tied up in the business—an opportunity cost of the money which could otherwise be earning a return on loan to another business or in some other investment.

The return calculated on the owner's invested capital should be what the capital would earn on the average if put into some other investment having the same degree of risk. This expected return on the capital invested in the business is the normal rate of return and is included as a cost when determining the firm's economic profits.

The chicken farm has a capital investment of $1,800,000. If the normal rate of return on investments with a similar amount of risk is 15%, the monthly cost to the owner of having his or her capital tied up in the chicken farm is $22,500. When this is added to the other costs of the business, total costs are greater than the revenue. The economic profits are a minus—a loss of $1,200 a month. In effect, the owner is subsidizing the business with his labor and the use of his capital. This is not unusual where proprietorships are concerned. Small business owners frequently pay a price for being their own boss.

As with other branches of farming, the egg business is undergoing consolidation. Since 1980 about half of the egg growers with more than 10,000 laying hens have left the business. The industry is becoming dominated by corporate firms such as Cargill—the nation's largest egg company, with a flock under contract of about 9 million birds—Rose Acre Farms, and Michael Foods. Cargill achieved its dominant position in part because it is an integrated company, producing the chicken feed purchased by its own and other growers and marketing its eggs under the Sunny Fresh label.

**normal rate of return** the rate of earnings on invested capital that is normal for a given degree of risk.
**economic profits** earnings on invested capital that are in excess of the normal rate of return.

# case application

## Aging Rockers Hit the Road One More Time

Two decades after they rode the wave of rock and roll popularity to the top of the charts, aging rock stars such as the Who, the Rolling Stones, and Jefferson Starship staged "reunion tours" to cash in on the nostalgia of the 1960s generation and the curiosity of that generation's children. In the sad absence of John Lennon, there could be no Beatles reunion, but Paul McCartney performed a hugely successful 1990 tour on his own.

These superstars of the past, and a few of the more transient current rock and roll groups, can still sell out performances. But many concert promoters have discovered that lesser-known groups don't draw well enough to cover expenses. Costs have greatly increased. The cost of liability insurance, for example, has multiplied many times over. If promoters have to guarantee the performers $80,000, lay out another $20,000 for rental of the arena, purchase liability insurance, rent sound and lighting systems, and pay for radio and newspaper advertisements, they face at least a $150,000 outlay before they even start to sell tickets. Performance costs such as hiring ushers, security guards, and the many ticket checkers needed to counter widespread counterfeiting of concert tickets add to promoters' expenses. They also have to pay the ticket agencies a percentage of each ticket sold and pay state taxes on the tickets.

The costs for a medium-size rock concert are shown in Table 1.

With these high costs for a less-established group that may or may not draw a capacity crowd, it is not surprising that promoters turn to the '60s rock stars who can draw on two generations of fans to fill the arenas.

*Table 1*     COSTS OF A ROCK CONCERT

| Expense | Cost |
| --- | --- |
| Performers | $ 80,000 |
| Arena rental | 20,000 |
| Insurance | 9,500 |
| Sound system | 5,700 |
| Lighting system | 3,250 |
| Radio advertising | 9,800 |
| Newspaper advertising | 6,700 |
| Personnel (ushers, etc.) | 3.40 per ticket sold |
| Ticket agency | 1.50 per ticket sold |
| State taxes | 1.80 per ticket sold |

## Economic Reasoning

1. What are the fixed costs shown for a rock concert? What are the variable costs?
2. About how many tickets would the promoter have to sell at $30 each to cover the above costs of a concert?
3. If the promoter could only count on selling enough tickets to cover those costs, do you think it would be a good idea to go ahead and put on the concert? Why or why not?

# How Does Industry Market Structure Affect Price and Output Decisions?

Although the egg industry discussed in the previous section is becoming more dominated by giant corporate firms, there are still well over a thousand large-scale egg farmers. In other types of farming, there are even more producers in the market. Other industries, however, have different market characteristics from those of farming. There are four types of industry market structure and, although firms in each of the four types attempt to maximize their profits, the results are different in the four different types of industries.

**Pure competition** Agriculture represents an industry that is as close to pure competition as one can find. Purely competitive industries are those in which there are a large number of producers supplying a standardized product. Firms in such industries don't have any choice about what price they charge. It is relatively easy for new producers to get into the purely competitive industries or for existing producers to drop out. If a wheat farmer tries to charge more for wheat than the going price in the wheat market, he won't find any buyers. Nor would it pay wheat farmers to set their price below the market price because they can sell all of their wheat at that price. Wheat farmers, therefore, because they sell a standardized product in competition with many other suppliers, have no control over price. The only choice they

**pure competition** a condition prevailing in an industry in which there are such a large number of firms producing a standardized product that no single firm can noticeably affect the market price by changing its output; also an industry in which firms can easily enter or leave.

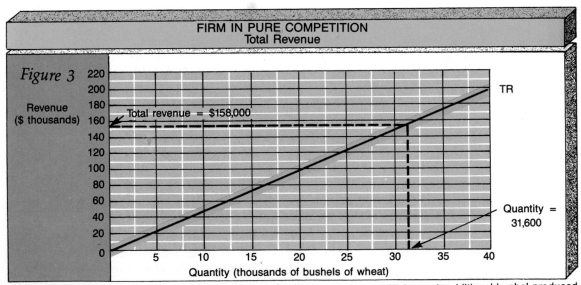

*Figure 3*

**FIRM IN PURE COMPETITION**
Total Revenue

Revenue ($ thousands)

Total revenue = $158,000

TR

Quantity = 31,600

Quantity (thousands of bushels of wheat)

If the market price of wheat is $5 a bushel, the farmer's total revenue rises by $5 for each additional bushel produced and sold. In pure competition, the total revenue of the individual firm increases at a constant rate with increasing output.

have is how much wheat to sell at the going price. If wheat is selling for $5 a bushel, their total revenue will be $5 multiplied by the number of bushels they sell, as shown by the total revenue curve in Figure 3.

The yearly quantity of wheat produced on the farm is shown along the bottom axis. The revenue from sale of the wheat is shown on the vertical axis. The total revenue is the price per bushel times the number of bushels sold (TR = P × Q). This is shown by the TR curve on the diagram. The farmer's revenue, beginning at zero with zero output, would rise at a constant rate with each additional bushel of wheat produced and sold. At an output of 31,600 bushels the total revenue is $158,000 ($5 × 31,600 bushels).

The wheat farmer's costs are shown in Figure 4. The fixed costs are $62,000, whatever the level of output. This fixed cost includes not only depreciation on the buildings and equipment and interest on the borrowed capital, but also an allowance for the normal rate of return on the farmer's own capital invested in the farm and his management input. The variable costs are added to the fixed costs, depending on how much wheat is produced. They include seed, fertilizer, irrigation water, and hired labor costs. The total costs are the sum of the fixed and variable costs. Total costs are $140,000 at an output of 31,600 bushels of wheat.

Notice that costs go up at an increasing rate, especially after about 25,000 bushels, as shown by the TC curve rising more and more steeply. Wheat farmers can increase wheat production by using more seed, fertilizer, and irrigation; and by cultivating land more intensively. But if the amount

This combine can harvest enough wheat in 9 seconds to provide flour to make 70 loaves of bread. Wheat farming is a purely competitive business, and wheat farmers cannot raise prices to increase revenues.

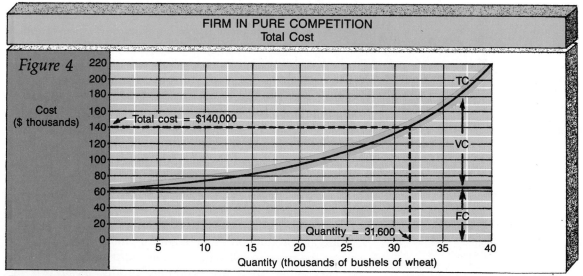

The total costs for each level of output are the fixed costs plus the variable costs. Variable costs go up at an increasing rate because of diminishing returns.

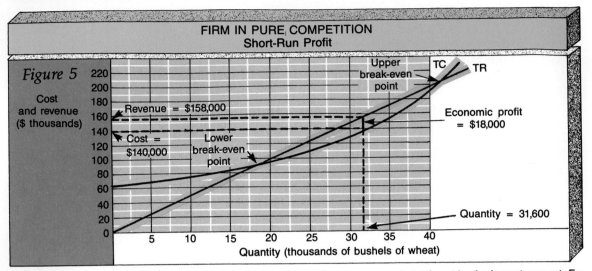

**FIRM IN PURE COMPETITION**
**Short-Run Profit**

*Figure 5*

Cost and revenue ($ thousands)

Revenue = $158,000

Cost = $140,000

Lower break-even point

Upper break-even point

TC    TR

Economic profit = $18,000

Quantity = 31,600

Quantity (thousands of bushels of wheat)

A firm can maximize profits by producing the output at which total revenue exceeds total cost by the largest amount. For a firm in pure competition, economic profits are only possible in the short run because they attract new entry into the industry.

of land on which they are growing wheat is fixed, costs per bushel of wheat grown increase as they cultivate the land more intensively. This is due to the principle of <u>diminishing returns</u>. When one factor input is fixed, in this case, land, it requires successively larger amounts of the other inputs to obtain an additional unit of output. As a result of diminishing returns, a farmer's costs go up faster than output.

Total cost and total revenue together determine profits ($P = TR - TC$). This is shown in Figure 5. The levels of output where total revenue equals total cost are the <u>break-even points</u>. The lower break-even point is just under 20,000 bushels of wheat and the upper break-even point is around 40,000 bushels. Producing any output between the lower and upper break-even points will give the farm a profit. But the <u>maximum profit level</u> will be at an output of 31,600 bushels where total revenue exceeds total cost by the greatest amount. At that output the total cost is $140,000 and the total revenue is $158,000, providing a profit of $18,000.

Since the costs were calculated to include a normal rate of return on the capital invested by the farmer and a salary for the farmer's labor input, the $18,000 is pure profit—economic profit. However, in pure competition, where entry into the industry is easy, any profit earnings in the industry greater than the normal rate of return on capital attracts additional production. The resulting increase in supply causes the price to fall. This is what happens in the wheat industry when there are economic profits, as shown in Figure 6.

**diminishing returns** the common condition in which additional inputs produce successively smaller increments of output.

**break-even point** the output level of a firm where total revenue equals total costs (TR = TC).

**maximum profit level** the output level of a firm where the revenue from one additional unit of production (marginal revenue) is equal to the cost of producing that unit (marginal cost).

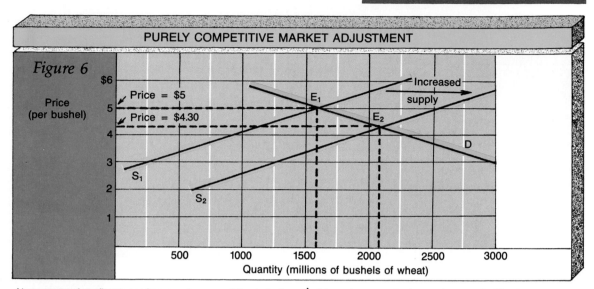

PURELY COMPETITIVE MARKET ADJUSTMENT

*Figure 6*

Price (per bushel)

Price = $5

Price = $4.30

Above-normal profit returns in a purely competitive industry result in an increase in the market supply. The increased supply causes the price to fall to the level at which producers no longer make economic profits.

With the supply of wheat $S_1$ and the demand D, the equilibrium price was $5 a bushel. At this price wheat farmers were making above-normal profits. This short-run situation does not last in purely competitive industries. It results in an increase in the production of wheat, shifting the supply to $S_2$. The new market equilibrium, $E_2$, lowers the price for wheat to $4.30 a bushel. At this price, wheat farmers are just covering their costs, as shown in Figure 7.

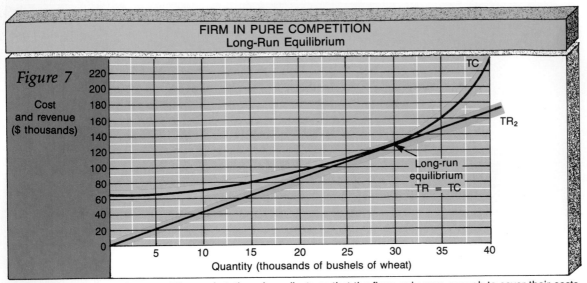

**FIRM IN PURE COMPETITION**
Long-Run Equilibrium

*Figure 7*

Cost and revenue ($ thousands)

Quantity (thousands of bushels of wheat)

In the long run in a purely competitive market, the price adjusts so that the firms only earn enough to cover their costs, including a normal return on the capital invested.

The new total revenue curve, TR₂, reflects the lower wheat price of $4.30. At this price, total revenue equals total cost, including a normal rate of return on the farmer's capital. With no economic profits to attract more farmers into wheat production, the supply is stabilized. This is the long-run equilibrium in pure competition where the producers are just covering their costs, including a normal return on their investment. They must produce at the level of output which minimizes their costs per unit. If their average costs are higher than for other producers in the industry, they can not stay in business.

**Pure monopoly** At the opposite end of the spectrum from pure competition is the industry with only one firm, pure monopoly. Except for public utilities—industries such as electricity, gas, water, and local telephone service—there are not many examples of pure monopolies. One industry that is a virtual monopoly is the diamond industry. De Beers Consolidated Mines, Ltd., a South African company, controls over 80% of the world wholesale diamond business. As a result, it is able to manipulate prices by controlling the supply.

In the early 1980s there was a break in the diamond market because of a sharp drop in the demand for diamonds by investors. In just one year diamond prices fell by one-third. The price of a flawless, one-carat diamond dropped from $63,000 to $40,000. To stop the slide in prices, De Beers cut back sales of diamonds to dealers. The changes in the diamond market are shown in Figure 8.

**pure monopoly** an industry in which there is only one firm.
**public utility** an industry that produces an essential public service such as electricity, gas, water, and telephone service; normally, a single firm is granted a local monopoly to provide the service.

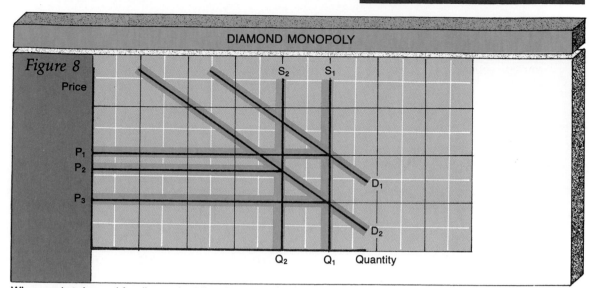

DIAMOND MONOPOLY

*Figure 8*

When market demand for diamonds shifted from $D_1$ to $D_2$, De Beers reduced the supply from $S_1$ to $S_2$ in order to keep the equilibrium price from falling to $P_3$.

Because of the lessened demand for diamonds by investors and speculators, the market demand fell from $D_1$ to $D_2$. To stop the price decline, De Beers reduced the supply of uncut diamonds offered to dealers from $S_1$ to $S_2$. De Beers might have attempted to raise the price back to $P_1$ by reducing the supply even further. But they felt that the March 1980 price, inflated by speculation, was too high to maintain a healthy diamond market and maximize profits. To get the price of a flawless, one-carat diamond back up to $60,000, they would have to have cut production by more than 60%.

Although there are few pure monopolies, most industries have some degree of of monopolistic pricing. Unlike producers in a purely competitive industry who have to sell their product at the prevailing market price, firms in monopolistic industries can raise or lower their prices to maximize their profits. If they lower prices they will sell more because their product has a downward-sloping demand curve—the lower the price, the more of the product customers will buy. If they raise prices they will sell less but receive more per unit sold. As a result, their total revenue does not rise at a constant rate with increasing output as it does under pure competition. The amount of revenue at different prices depends on the demand schedule.

Table 2 shows the quantities that a hypothetical monopolist could sell at different prices and the resulting total revenue.

*Table 2*

### DEMAND SCHEDULE AND TOTAL REVENUE FOR A HYPOTHETICAL MONOPOLISTIC FIRM

| Price | × Quantity | = Total Revenue |
| --- | --- | --- |
| $15 | 0 | 0 |
| 14 | 50 | 700 |
| 13 | 100 | 1,300 |
| 12 | 150 | 1,800 |
| 11 | 200 | 2,200 |
| 10 | 250 | 2,500 |
| 9 | 300 | 2,700 |
| 8 | 350 | 2,800 |
| 7 | 400 | 2,800 |
| 6 | 450 | 2,700 |
| 5 | 500 | 2,500 |
| 4 | 550 | 2,200 |
| 3 | 600 | 1,800 |
| 2 | 650 | 1,300 |
| 1 | 700 | 700 |
| 0 | 750 | 0 |

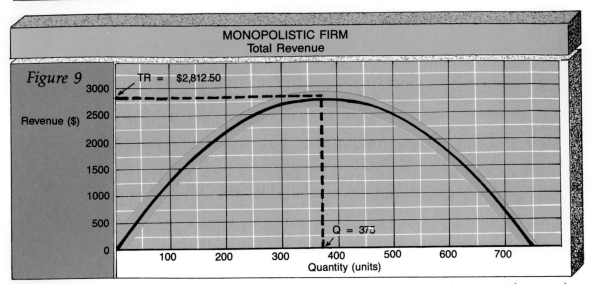

**MONOPOLISTIC FIRM**
Total Revenue

*Figure 9*

TR = $2,812.50

Revenue ($)

Q = 375

Quantity (units)

Monopolistic firms can increase sales by reducing the price. As the price declines and sales increase, total revenue rises to a maximum point and then it falls with further price cuts.

The data in Table 2 is shown as a diagram in Figure 9 with the revenue measured on the vertical axis and the number of units produced on the horizontal axis.

The firm could maximize its revenue by producing 375 units which it could sell at $7.50 each for a total revenue of $2,812.50. However, the purpose is not to maximize revenue but to maximize profit, $P = TR - TC$. The maximum profit output is shown in Figure 10 on the opposite page.

Because diminishing returns cause costs to rise more rapidly for outputs greater than 300 units, it does not pay to produce more even though revenue would be greater. At an output of 375, which provides the highest revenue, the firm would be losing money because costs are even higher than revenue.

The rule for maximizing profits is to produce the quantity at which total revenue is rising at the same rate as total cost. For this firm, as output is increased up to about 300 units, total revenue is rising more rapidly than total cost for each additional unit produced and profits are getting larger. Up to this point costs increase at a diminishing rate—the TC curve rises less steeply—because of an increase in plant efficiency. But as output exceeds the most efficient production level of the plant and equipment, total costs rise more rapidly. Beyond an output level of 300 units, total revenue is not rising as fast as total cost and profits are shrinking, as shown by the narrowing difference between TR and TC in

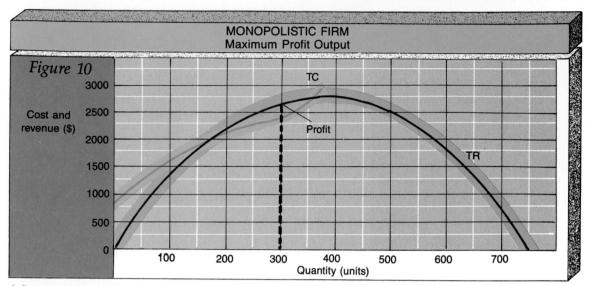

**MONOPOLISTIC FIRM**
**Maximum Profit Output**

Figure 10

Cost and revenue ($)

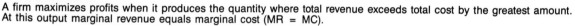

A firm maximizes profits when it produces the quantity where total revenue exceeds total cost by the greatest amount. At this output marginal revenue equals marginal cost (MR = MC).

Figure 10. At more than 340 units of output (the upper break-even point) costs exceed revenue and profits become negative.

The increase in total revenue from producing one more unit is called marginal revenue (MR). The increase in total cost from producing that one additional unit is marginal cost (MC). The output level at which revenue and cost are increasing at the same rate (MR = MC) is the maximum profit level of output.

**Shared monopoly** Single-firm monopolies like De Beers are rare, but there are many industries in which the market is controlled by only a few firms. According to the most common measurement, any industry in which four firms or less account for over 50% of industry sales is considered a shared monopoly. If there is a formal agreement among the firms regarding pricing and/or dividing up the market, the group of firms is called a cartel. OPEC is a prominent example of a cartel. If there is no formal agreement among the firms, the industry is called an oligopoly. Many industries in the United States are oligopolistic, including the steel, aluminum, cigarette, metal can, and automobile industries. The steel and aluminum industries produce homogeneous products, while the cigarette and automobile industries produce differentiated products.

As in pure monopolies, above-normal profit returns in shared monopoly industries can be maintained over the

**marginal revenue** the addition to total revenue from the sale of an additional unit of output.
**marginal cost** the addition to total cost from the production of an additional unit of output.
**shared monopoly** an industry in which there are only a few firms; more specifically, an industry in which four or fewer firms account for more than 50% of industry sales.
**cartel** an industry in which the firms have an agreement to set prices and/or divide the market among members of the cartel.
**oligopoly** a shared monopoly in which there is no explicit agreement among the firms.
**homogeneous products** identical products produced by different firms.
**differentiated products** similar but not identical products produced by different firms.

McDonald's used to package their hamburgers in distinctive styrofoam containers. Now, bowing to concern about the environment, the company has changed its packaging to biodegradable paper.

long run by restricting output. Because it is difficult or impossible for new competitors to enter the industry, there is no increase in supply to lower the price. The smaller the number of firms in the industry, the easier it is for them to maintain maximum monopoly profits.

It benefits the firms in a shared monopoly to cooperate and produce the quantity and charge the price that a pure monopolist would. But where there is no formal agreement among the firms in the industry, and sometimes even when there is, this cooperation is difficult to sustain because of the desire of each firm to get a larger share of the market.

The danger of a price war among the different firms is a threat to profits in a shared monopoly. As a result, we frequently see a practice of price leadership in this type of industry. One firm, usually the most powerful, takes the lead in setting the price. The other firms follow its price leadership and avoid price competition.

**Differentiated competition**  An industry with differentiated competition, sometimes called monopolistic competition, is one in which there are many firms. But, unlike pure competition, the product is not standardized. Each firm differentiates its product to make it unique and to appeal to customers. The fast-food industry is a good example of differentiated competition. The "Big Mac," the "Whopper," and Wendy's burger are all hamburgers which the producers attempt to differentiate from the competition.

As a result of the relative ease of entry into differentiated competition industries, monopolistic profits tend not to last in the long run. Firms in these industries spend a lot of money on advertising and packaging in order to differentiate their product and carve out a mini-monopoly position in the industry. But since other firms in the industry are doing the same thing, profits tend to fall to the normal rate of return on capital, and economic profits disappear over time.

**price leadership**  a common practice in shared monopoly industries by which one of the firms in the industry, normally one of the largest, changes its prices, and the other firms follow its lead.

**differentiated competition**  an industry in which there are a large number of firms producing similar but not identical products; sometimes called monopolistic competition.

# case application

## Hard Decisions for the Software Industry

It is always a difficult problem knowing how best to price a product when it is first brought to market. When the product is one in a new and rapidly evolving industry, the decision is doubly difficult.

The microcomputer software industry did not exist until the 1980s. At first the owners of personal computers were so hungry for software to use on their new machines that nearly any useful software could be sold at whatever price, reasonable or not. Software industry sales doubled every year. Major software programs—word processing, spreadsheet, database—sold for hundreds of dollars, although the direct production costs were only a few dollars for each disk. The major costs of the programs were the developmental expenses—the labor hours (number of programmers times the hours worked) required to write and de-bug the programs. Those fixed costs had to be recovered from sales of the disks, of course. But there was little relationship between the costs of producing the software and the price charged, and successful programs could be priced well above their total costs.

As more software developers entered the industry—over 3,000 at one point—competition forced a reassessment of pricing policies. Was it best to charge a high price and sell a smaller number of disks or charge a lower price and aim for volume? One software producer decided to find out what price would give it the most profits by actually testing the market at different prices.

The firm, Noumenon Corporation, had initially priced its Intuit program for the IBM PC at $395. In spite of extensive advertising, the program wasn't selling. In order to find the best price, the company first reduced the price to $50 and then each week raised it by an additional $20. After trying prices in increments of $20 all the way up to $210, at which point sales virtually dried up, they found that total revenue was maximized at a price of $90. As a result of this experiment they decided to advertise and market Intuit at $89.95, much lower than the prices of competing software programs.

Other software producers also began to adopt competitive pricing policies. Dac Software set a price of $70 for an accounting package that was equivalent to programs for which some companies were charging $300 or more. Even the major software firms—Microsoft, Lotus, Ashton-Tate—felt the heat of competition, and their programs often sold at deep discounts from list prices.

It is unusual for a company to actually experiment with a wide range of prices for their product as Noumenon did for Intuit. But computer software is not an ordinary industry. It is continually innovating and developing new types of programs, even programs to determine the best price to charge for new products.

A different approach to pricing is taken by airline, hotel, and other businesses that can separate their market into segments and charge each segment a different price. When a firm can charge a price in each separate segment of its market so that the marginal cost equals the marginal revenue for that segment, it can obtain more profits than if it charges all customers the same price. It charges the customers with the most inelastic demand curves a higher price than it charges customers with lower elasticity of demand.

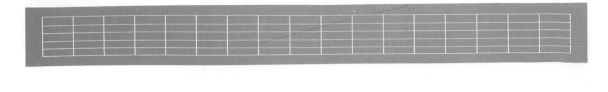

The airlines first employed this practice by offering discounts to passengers who made reservations a minimum time in advance of the flight and who stayed over a Saturday night on the trip. This segmented their market into business passengers, who had no scheduling flexibility and who generally returned home for weekends, and nonbusiness discretionary fliers. As a result of their more inelastic demand, business travelers paid higher fares.

With the use of computerized reservation systems, the airlines have become more sophisticated in discriminatory pricing. Early bookings are used to gage the price sensitivity of the market. If, on the basis of the number of early reservations, a particular flight is projected to fill, the airline reduces the number of discounted seats available on that flight. This is called yield management. The objective is to fill all of the seats by the time the plane takes off, and at the same time fill the largest number of seats possible with full-fare passengers.

Besides the airlines, other businesses that are making use of yield management are car rentals, hotels, cruise ships, resort condominiums, and even a blood bank.

## *Economic Reasoning*

1. What type of market structure exists in the software industry? How can you tell?
2. Is a software company likely to price its programs near the price that maximizes total revenue? Why? Diagram the total cost and total revenue situation of a hypothetical software producer and show whether maximum profit output is close

### DESKTOP PUBLISHING & GRAPHICS

| | |
|---|---|
| Autosketch | 139 |
| Corel Draw | 309 |
| DrawPerfect | 265 |
| Freelance Plus | 307 |
| GEM Desktop Pub. | 159 |
| Generic Cadd Level 2 Starter Kit | 109 |
| Generic Cadd Level 3 | 199 |
| Harvard Graphics | 275 |
| Pagemaker | 479 |
| PC Paintbrush IV Plus | 109 |
| Perspective Jr. | 69 |
| PFS:First Publisher | 89 |
| Publisher's Paintbrush | 149 |
| Publish It! | 104 |
| Ventura Publisher Gold | 519 |

### FINANCIAL

| | |
|---|---|
| Bedford Integrated Acct. | 145 |
| DAC Accounting 4.0 | 79 |
| DAC Bonus Pack 4.0 | 157 |
| Dollars & Sense | Call |
| Managing Your Money | 113 |
| Peachtree Complete III | 139 |
| Peachtree with Data Query | 209 |
| Quicken | 35 |

### INTEGRATED

| | |
|---|---|
| First Choice | 105 |
| SmartWare II | 417 |
| LotusWorks | 89 |
| Windows 3.0 | 89 |
| Works | 89 |

### MICE

| | |
|---|---|
| Keytronics Professional | 65 |
| Logitech HiRes C9 Serial | 65 |
| Logitech HiRes C9 Bus | 76 |
| Logitech Trackman Serial | 75 |
| Microsoft Serial or Bus w/ paint | 95 |
| Microsoft with Windows 3.0 | 147 |

**LOGITECH Hi-Res Mouse $65**
C-9 Serial Ver. Our best mouse-includes Pop-Up Dos & LogiMenu. Add $15 for PaintShow .

### WORD PROCESSORS

| | |
|---|---|
| Grammatik IV | 49 |
| Multimate 4.0 | 267 |
| Professional Write | 149 |
| Rightwriter 4.0 | Call |
| Sprint | 117 |
| Word | 209 |
| Word for Windows | 309 |
| Word Perfect 5.1 | 239 |
| Word Perfect Add'l Station | 153 |
| Word Perfect Office | 79 |
| WordStar Professional | 239 |

## WordPerfect 5.1 $239

WordPerfect 5.1 adds even more to its top-rated product. Pull-down menus, mouse support, table functions, expanded graphics, and much more have been added. Yet, it retains its classic ease-of-use!

### UTILITIES

| | |
|---|---|
| Control Room | 69 |
| CoreFast | 60 |
| Carbon Copy Plus | 109 |
| Desqview | 68 |
| Desqview 386 | 115 |
| Direct Access | 54 |
| Fastback Plus | 109 |
| Formtool Gold | 52 |
| Formfiller | 85 |
| Headroom | 59 |
| Laplink III | 85 |
| MS-Dos 3.3 or 4.01 | 59 |
| Mace Utilities 1990 | 85 |
| Norton Advanced 5.0 | 109 |
| PC Anywhere III | 59 |
| PC Tools Deluxe | 79 |
| ProComm Plus | 52 |
| QEMM 386/QRAM | 54 / 43 |
| SideKick Plus | 119 |
| Sideways | 37 |
| Super PC Kwik | 43 |
| XTree Pro Gold | 75 |

to maximum revenue output. (It is unnecessary to put in quantity and revenue figures. Only the relative positions of the TR and TC curves are important.)

3. Do you think that airlines and other businesses should be allowed to charge different prices to different customers on the basis of their elasticity of demand? Why or why not? How about pharmaceutical companies?

# Putting It Together

Businesses may be organized as individual *proprietorships, partnerships,* or *corporations.* Proprietorships are the most numerous, but because they are typically small, they account for only a minor percentage of total business sales. Partnerships make possible the pooling of capital and/or abilities of two or more people. The advantages of proprietorships and partnerships are that they are easily and inexpensively started and the owners have the responsibility for success or failure of the business and reap the rewards or suffer the losses. The disadvantages of proprietorships and partnerships are: owners are personally responsible for the debts of the business if it goes bankrupt; the business legally terminates if an owner dies or withdraws; and owners may not have sufficient capital to enable the business to succeed.

The corporate form of business organization is one in which the ownership is represented by stock. Corporations, although fewer in number than proprietorships, do most of the nation's business because of their large size. Stockholders are not personally responsible for actions of the firm or for its indebtedness. The selling of stock makes it possible for corporations to pool large amounts of capital. Change of ownership does not terminate the life of the firm, since a corporation is a legal entity (or "person"). The disadvantages of the corporate form are: it costs money to get a corporate charter; corporations are more regulated than other businesses, especially in that they must publicly disclose information about the firm; corporations must pay corporation taxes on their earnings.

The economic functions of business firms are: to identify needs (what to produce), organize production (how to produce), allocate revenues (for whom to produce), and invest in real capital (plant and equipment).

The costs of production are divided into *fixed costs* and *variable costs.* Fixed costs are those which are paid regardless of the level of output. Even if the firm stops production altogether, fixed costs continue in the short run. In general, fixed costs are the costs of depreciation on plant and equipment and interest charges on borrowed funds. In economic analysis, fixed costs also include the opportunity cost of the owners' capital invested in the business. This is calculated as the *normal rate of return* on investments with similar risks. Variable costs are the costs which increase with each additional unit produced. They are generally the costs of labor

Whether they are owned by individuals or by corporations, farms represent the free-enterprise system in action. The market structure of an industry will determine the quantity of goods or services produced and the prices charged.

and raw materials. *Total costs* are the fixed costs plus the variable costs for a particular level of output. At zero output, total costs are the amount of fixed costs. As output increases, total costs rise by the amount of additional variable costs.

In agriculture, and in fact in industries in general, firms encounter *diminishing returns* with expanding output. In the short run, with fixed size of plant and equipment, adding variable inputs results in smaller and smaller additions to output. These diminishing returns cause costs to rise at an increasing rate for a firm.

*Total revenue* is the price of the product multiplied by the number of units sold. If the firm can sell more without lowering its price, as is the case with a firm in a purely competitive industry, total revenue rises at a constant rate with increasing output.

*Profits* are total revenue minus total cost. The output level at which total revenue just equals total cost is the *break-even point*. Profits are maximized at the output level where total revenue exceeds total cost by the greatest amount.

*Purely competitive* industries are those in which there are a large number of firms producing a standardized product. Each firm in the industry produces such a small part of the total industry output that it cannot noticeably affect the market price. Purely competitive firms can earn *economic profits* in the short run. But the ease of entry of new firms into the industry will result in an increased supply. Prices drop, and profits will fall to the normal rate of return in the long run. Because of competition, purely competitive firms must operate at their most efficient level of output, which is also their break-even point.

A *pure monopoly* is an industry in which there is only one firm producing a product with no close substitutes. Monopolistic firms, unlike purely competitive firms, can adjust the price to obtain maximum profits. They produce the quantity of output that provides the greatest difference between total revenue and total cost. At this output total revenue is rising at the same rate as total cost so that *marginal revenue* equals *marginal cost*.

A *shared monopoly* is an industry in which there are only a few firms that account for the majority of industry sales. They may produce a *homogeneous product* such as aluminum or a *differentiated product* such as automobiles. Firms in these industries tend to avoid price competition. They may establish a *cartel* with a formal agreement, like OPEC, or they may be an *oligopoly* and follow a practice of *price leadership*.

An industry with *differentiated competition* has many firms producing a similar but not identical product. Promotional costs tend to be high in these industries, while profits tend to be low in the long run because of competition.

# The Evolution of the Modern Corporation

A Dutch East India Company seashore market in Batavia, N.Y. (about 1682) represents the activities of one of the world's earliest corporations.

Additional information about the evolution of corporations can be found in: *The Modern Corporation and Private Property* by Adolf A. Berle and Gardner Means (Buffalo, N.Y.: W. S. Hein, 1982 [reprint of 1933 edition]); *Essays in the Earlier History of American Corporations* by Joseph S. Davis (Cambridge, Mass.: Harvard University Press, 1917); *Great Enterprise: Growth and Behavior of the Big Corporation* by Herrymon Maurer ( New York: Macmillan, 1955); and *The Corporation in the Emergent American Society* by William L. Warner (New York: Harper & Row, 1962).

Technological changes in production techniques associated with the Industrial Revolution (see Perspective in chapter 3) are generally credited with establishing the nature of our present economy. But changes in business organization and management have also played a crucial role. If it were not for a parallel revolution in business organization, the mass production methods of the Industrial Revolution could not have been as extensively implemented as they were.

The most important aspect of this business revolution was the development of the modern corporation. The corporate form of business organization actually existed in Roman times, although it was not well evolved. It first achieved some importance as the form of organization for trading companies of the sixteenth and seventeenth centuries.

The Dutch East India Company, chartered in 1602, used the capital of its investors to finance voyages to procure spices and other exotic merchandise from Asia for sale in Europe. The British government chartered private trading companies, such as the Hudson's Bay Company (chartered in 1670), to develop trade and settlements in the New World in order to secure its colonization. Until well into the nineteenth century, corporate charters in Europe were granted by the king or parliament only for special purposes. In 1800, England and France together had only a few dozen such corporations.

It was in the United States that the corporate form of business first obtained widespread importance. By 1800 there were already some 300 private business corporations. At first, state legislatures, like the kings and parliaments of Europe, granted individual corporate charters. But in 1811 New York enacted a general incorporation law providing for corporate charters to be issued by New York's secretary of state. State governments grant most corporate charters, but the federal government also charters firms in some fields such as banking (federal savings and loan banks), transportation (railroads), and communications (Comsat).

Today, there are over 2 million corporations in the United States. About 100 of them own one-half of the total corporate wealth, and the trend is continuing toward fewer and larger corporations.

# For Further Study and Analysis

## Study Questions

1. Why isn't it a good idea to join in a partnership if you do not know the other partners very well? Does the same consideration apply to buying shares in a corporation?

2. Why would the capital equipment of a firm in a dynamic industry such as electronics depreciate more rapidly than in an industry such as textile manufacture?

3. What is the difference between accounting profits and economic profits?

4. Why does the total revenue of an egg farmer rise at a constant rate with increasing sales, while the total revenue of a monopolistic firm rises at a decreasing rate, reaches a maximum, and then declines with increasing sales?

5. If a firm increases its output beyond the level where MR = MC, what happens to its profits? Why?

6. Why is a firm more likely to encounter diminishing returns in the short run than in the long run?

7. Why do economic profits tend to disappear in pure competition in the long run?

8. Why do purely competitive firms in the long run have to operate at the level of output that minimizes their average cost while monopolists do not?

9. What are examples of firms in your area that represent each of the four types of industry structure? If there are not any firms that correspond exactly to one or more of the four types, what firm comes closest to the industry type?

10. What are three examples of industries in which advertising expenditures appear to be especially large? Are these industries purely competitive, monopolies, shared monopolies with standardized products or with differentiated products, or differentiated competition industries?

## Exercises in Analysis

1. Select a corporation, preferably one in your community, and request a copy of its annual report. Using the report as a source, write a short paper on the operations of the company including such information as the amount of capital investment, annual sales, fixed and variable costs, and profits.

2. Interview the owner of a business in your area. Find out what type of industry the business is in, whether it is purely competitive, monopolistic, shared monopoly, or differentiated competition. Find out how the business decides what price to charge. Ask the owner if he or she experiments with different prices to see the effect on total revenue and profits. Write a report on the interview.

3. From the demand schedule computed for your group's demand for movie theater tickets in the first exercise at the end of chapter 4, construct a total revenue

curve for sales of movie tickets to the group.

4. In Exercise 1 at the end of chapter 5, you calculated the elasticity of demand of your group for movie theater tickets for price changes from $7 to $6 and from $3 to $2. Calculate the effect of these same price changes on total revenue. Compare the results for your group with the results found by other groups in the class. From this information, can you make any generalizations about the relationship between elasticity of demand and the effect of price changes on total revenue?

## Further Reading

Adams, Walter, ed. *The Structure of American Industry*. 7th ed. New York: Macmillan, 1985. Separate chapters on the economics of a number of industries, including agriculture and computers.

Caves, Richard. *American Industry: Structure, Conduct, Performance*. 6th ed. Englewood Cliffs, N.J.: Prentice Hall, 1987. A short book on the economics of industrial organization.

Fite, Gilbert. *American Farmers: The New Minority*. Bloomington, Ind.: Indiana University Press, 1981. Traces the changes in farming and the struggles of farmers to keep up.

Frank, Werner. *Critical Issues in Software: A Guide to Software Economics, Strategy, and Profitability*. New York: John Wiley & Sons, 1983. Covers the economics of the computer software industry, including the effects on profits of alternative pricing policies for microcomputer software.

Goodman, George J. W., Jr. *The Money Game*. New York: Random House, 1976. Written under the pseudonym "Adam Smith," a market insider tells what motivates stock players. It is an amusing account of winners and losers, the cocoa game, and the Gnomes of Zurich.

Kamphuis, Robert W., Jr., Roger C. Kormendi, and J. W. Henry Watson, eds. *Black Monday and the Future of Financial Markets*. This collection of essays on the causes and implications of the October 19, 1987, stock market collapse concentrates on the technical and institutional factors that affect stock markets today.

Malkiel, Burton G. *A Random Walk Down Wall Street*. 4th ed. New York: W. W. Norton, 1985. "Taken to its logical extreme, [the random walk principle] means that a blindfolded monkey throwing darts at a newspaper's financial pages could select a portfolio that would do just as well as one carefully selected by the experts" (page 16).

Rogers, Kenny, and Len Epand. *Making It With Music: Kenny Rogers' Guide to the Music Business*. New York: Harper & Row, 1978. An examination of the economic aspects of the music business from the standpoint of the performer.

Shover, John. *First Majority—Last Minority: The Transforming of Rural Life in America*. De Kalb, Ill.: Northern Illinois University Press, 1976. Traces the revolution in American agriculture that has transformed a one-time majority of the population into a vanishing minority—the parts played by technology, agribusiness, and the federal government.

Sokoloff, Kiril. *The Thinking Investor's Guide to the Stock Market*. New York: McGraw-Hill, 1984. A serious discussion of the principles of stock market investment. Less technical than many others.

Tweeten, Luther. *Causes and Consequences of Structural Change in the Farming Industry*. Washington, D.C.: National Planning Association, 1984. Discusses farm size and technology with respect to the causes and consequences of structural change in agriculture.

Weiss, Leonard. *Case Studies in American Industry*. 3rd ed. New York: Macmillan, 1980. An economic analysis of market structure and performance using information on specific industries.

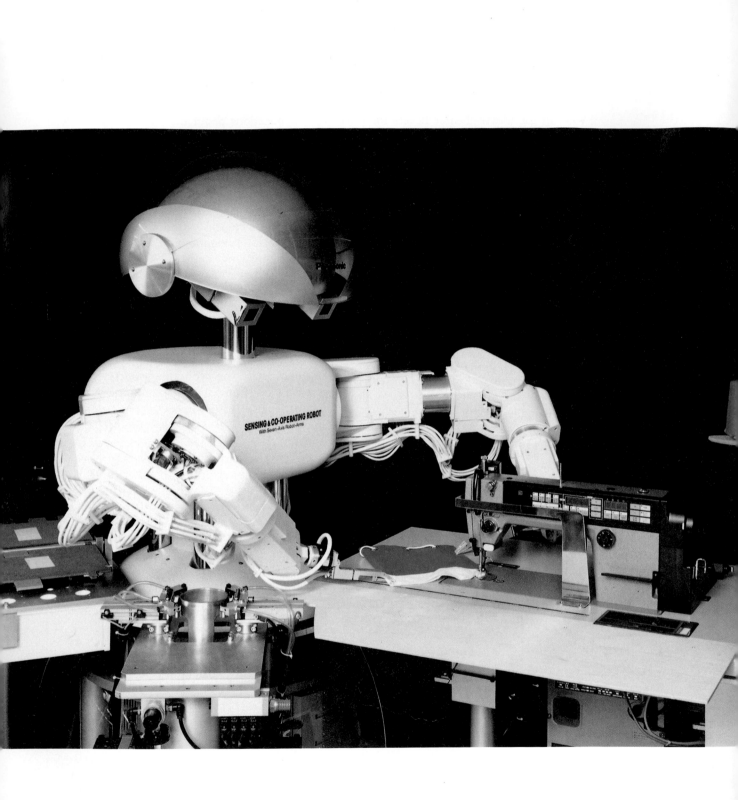

# INDUSTRY PERFORMANCE

*Economics was defined in chapter 1 as a social science. But since some American industries such as automobiles, television sets, VCRs, computer chips, and machine tools were kicked in the head by Japanese producers in the 1980s, industry economics may seem more like a form of a martial art—kung-fu economics.*

## Industry Economics as a Martial Art

Many of the Japanese industrial combines that powered her economic success following World War II—Mitsui, Mitsubishi, Sumitomo, among others—are descendants of the *zaibatsu*. The *zaibatsu* were holding companies established in the nineteenth century to develop the then-feudal Japanese economy. They were combines of interlocking manufacturers and banks that assisted each other. This type of holding company was abolished by the American occupation authorities at the end of the war. Its power has been resurrected, however, in the form of the *keiretsu*, giant integrated companies whose various divisions support each other.

These Japanese companies have proved formidable competitors in world markets. In the 1980s a number of U.S. industries lost out

in the competition, both at home and abroad. Between 1978 and 1988, for example, the U.S. share of world automobile production fell from 29% to 18%. Its share of world machine tools production declined by half, from 14% to 7%. In the new high-tech industries, mostly pioneered by U.S. firms, the losses were even more striking. United States production of DRAMs (dynamic random-access memory chips) fell from 73% of the world supply to 17%, and its output of floppy disks for computers dropped from 66% to just 4%.

In one case, an American firm invented a major consumer electronics product—the home videotape recorder—only to forfeit its production to Japan. The original patents for videotape recording machines were held by Ampex Corporation of Redwood City, California. In the 1960s Ampex produced videotape equipment for the broadcast industry and attempted to develop a model for the consumer market. Due to inadequate engineering know-how and managerial indecision, it failed to mass-produce its videotape recorder design successfully. Even though Ampex put $90 million into the VTR venture, the company failed to produce a machine that was small enough, reliable enough, and cheap enough to sell in the consumer market. Other U.S. companies, such as RCA and Cartrivision, also attempted to develop home VTRs. Cartrivision even got as far as marketing a model in 1972, but it was unsuccessful.

Meanwhile, Sony and other Japanese companies were working to improve the design and simplify the production process in order to make videorecorders acceptable and affordable to consumers. In 1975, when Sony put its first Betamax on the market, Japan added the videotape industry to its trophy case of consumer electronics industries, along with audio cassettes, television sets, calculators, and digital watches.

How did Japan succeed in taking one market after another away from U.S. industries? A number of volumes have been written about this question in recent years (see Further Reading at the end of the chapter). The answer to the question is still not resolved. It involves differences between Japan and the United States in business organization and philosophy, in the relationship of a firm to its workers, in the relationship between business and government, and even in the very fabric of each society.

There has emerged, however, a consensus on the importance of certain differences in the way economic affairs are conducted in the two countries. These differences include the short-term profit objectives of American business management compared to the patient market development of their Japanese rivals; the low level of savings, both household and governmental, in the United States compared to Japan; the separation between management and labor in U.S. plants compared to the cooperation in Japanese firms; and the division between product design decisions and production methods in this country versus the integration of the two in Japan.

An irony in the story of the development of Japanese industrial might is the role played by American tutors. During the occupation of Japan by the U.S. Army following World War II, General Douglas MacArthur sent for a U.S. electronics engineer to restart the Japanese radio industry. There was a need for the occupation authorities to communicate with the Japanese people. The engineer, Homer Sarasohn, found that of the first batch of radio vacuum tubes produced by the Japanese factories, 99% were defective. "The idea of quality they did not understand," he said. Discovering that the Japanese lacked any knowledge of modern business practices, he and a colleague, with MacArthur's blessing, set up a course of instruction for Japanese managers. Among the principles taught in the course were that a company must have a concise and complete statement of the purpose of the company, providing direction for the efforts of management and labor; that quality is the first consideration and profits follow; and that every employee deserves the same respect accorded to managers, since democratic management is good management. Out of the course came the future leaders of some of Japan's most successful companies: Sony, Matsushita, and Mitsubishi, among others. The course was still being taught to Japanese executives 25 years after Sarasohn departed.

During the postwar period, the Japanese put to use the principles taught in the course and stayed with them. Meanwhile, American businesses, led by the graduates of elite U.S. business schools, turned their attention from production to finance and marketing. Increasingly, top management in U.S. industry came from the accounting or sales departments of a company rather than from the production side.

The outstanding success of the Japanese export industries, and of their manufacturing in general, is only one side of the story, however. There are sectors of the Japanese economy that are quite unproductive. This is especially true of the agricultural and distribution systems. Japanese laws protect uneconomical small farms and "mom and pop" retail stores to keep them in business. As a result, the Japanese pay up to three times as much as Americans for food and staples. Rice in Japan costs 10 times the world price because of government subsidies to the politically powerful farm bloc. A multilayered, high-cost distribution system adds as much as 60% to the price of Japanese products. As a result, a third of the country's export industry goods cost more in Japan than in the United States—a camera that cost $380 in New York City, for example, was priced at $539 in Tokyo.

As a consequence of such large markups and the inflated price of land in Japan, where it takes a family an average of 17 years before they can afford to buy their own home, the costs of living in Japan are very high. The desire for a better standard of living makes Japanese workers put in an average of 300 more hours on the job per year than workers in the United States. This includes a great deal of overtime. There are recent indications that the Japanese are beginning to rebel against the austerity of high living costs and long work hours.

Other problems have cropped up for the Japanese economy: rising interest rates, a falling value of the yen, scandals in government and finance, and wild movements on the stock market. The *zaibatsu* type of mutual support among the industrial combines and their allied banks is breaking down as a result of a greater diversity of interests of the individual firms. Whether Japanese industry will be able to carry its phenomenal successes of the 1980s into the decade of the 1990s remains to be seen. There is a common assumption abroad that the world economy of the 1990s will belong to Europe as a result of the consolidation of the European Economic Community (see chapter 15). Past experience, however, has shown that Japan should not be discounted.

As for the United States, Japanese export aggression can be viewed as having done us a favor by forcing U.S. industries to refocus on quality and productivity. With an increasing interdependence of world markets, the lessons in kung-fu economics administered by Japanese producers in the 1980s may prove invaluable to American industries in the years ahead.

## Chapter Preview

*The relative decline of American industrial might in recent years has drawn attention to what determines the competitiveness of producers, to their ability to produce quality products at low costs. We will look at that concern in the context of these questions:* What determines industry performance? How can industry performance be improved? What are the effects of industry concentration on performance?

## Learning Objectives

*After completing this chapter, you should be able to:*

1. *Describe four factors that determine industry performance.*
2. *Define productivity and state how it is usually measured.*
3. *Explain why product quality is important and how it can be improved.*
4. *Describe why and how businesses respond to social concerns, and give three examples.*
5. *Explain the importance of investment in capital equipment, why the investment rate is low in the United States, and how it can be increased.*
6. *Describe investment in human capital and show how it affects the learning curve.*
7. *Explain R&D spending and its importance.*
8. *Describe process innovations and explain how they improve productivity.*
9. *List and give an example of three types of EI teams.*
10. *Describe market concentration and define the degree of market concentration in terms of the concentration ratio.*
11. *Explain the difference between market concentration and aggregate concentration.*
12. *Describe four consequences of high concentration in industries.*

# What Determines Industry Performance?

In chapter 2 we noted that one of the principal goals of an economic system is efficiency. How do we achieve efficiency in production? Why do the Japanese and other producers appear to be outdistancing the U.S. in efficiency? In this section we will examine those things that affect the efficiency of firms, and why American producers have fallen behind in some industries.

**Productivity** United States industrial productivity overall has been stagnating since 1973. During the 15 years up to 1973 it grew at an average of 2.5% a year, and increases averaged 2% a year from the very beginning of the century. From 1974 to 1988, on the other hand, productivity rose on the average just 1% per year.

While the difference between 1% and 2% per year may not sound like much, it has a great impact over a period of time. With annual increases in productivity of 2%, output per person doubles every 35 years due to compounding. At 1% productivity growth, it takes twice as long, 70 years, to get the same increase in output. Consequently, low productivity growth in this country in the 1970s and 1980s put us years behind the Japanese and other producers with higher rates of productivity growth.

Low productivity growth in the United States is particularly a problem in the service industries, such as finance, business services, and wholesale and retail trade. In these industries productivity grew at only about half a percent a

**productivity** a ratio of the amount of output per unit of input; denotes the efficiency with which resources (people, tools, knowledge, and energy) are used to produce goods and services; usually measured as output per hour of labor.

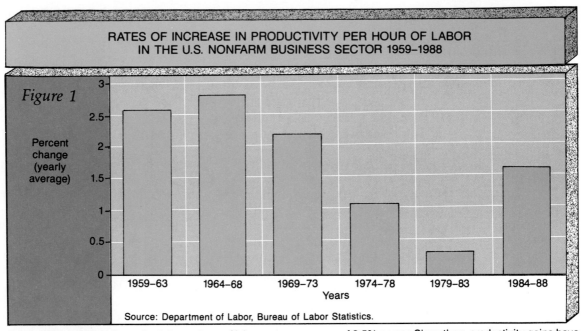

RATES OF INCREASE IN PRODUCTIVITY PER HOUR OF LABOR
IN THE U.S. NONFARM BUSINESS SECTOR 1959–1988

*Figure 1*

Percent change (yearly average)

Years

Source: Department of Labor, Bureau of Labor Statistics.

From 1959 to 1973, U.S. productivity per hour of labor rose an average of 2.5% a year. Since then, productivity gains have averaged only 1% a year.

year during the 1980s. Manufacturing industries, on the other hand, had higher productivity increases in the last half of the decade. It is sometimes said that high rates of productivity growth cannot be attained in service industries. This assertion is not supported by the experiences of Western European countries and Japan. There, productivity in the service sectors has increased two to four times as fast as in this country. This is significant, since the service-producing industries now account for 70% of U.S. private employment. (One of the reasons for slow productivity growth in the service sectors is discussed in chapter 9.)

**Quality**   In addition to the problem of lagging productivity in the 1980s, American industry suffered in comparison with other producers in the matter of quality. This was especially obvious in the case of U.S. automobiles compared to Japanese. The number of defects of Japanese cars sold in the U.S. in 1990 averaged 1.2 per vehicle, while the number of defects per vehicle built by U.S. auto makers was 1.7. Although the U.S. figure was an 8% improvement over two years previous, the Japanese producers continued to improve the quality of their cars at the same time.

The concern with quality starts with the parts purchased from suppliers. The U.S. suppliers of parts for cars produced by Nissan in this country averaged 2 defects per 1,000 parts in 1989 compared to only 1 defect per 1,000 parts from its

THE POWER OF BELIEF: #1 in a series

**When you aim for perfection, you discover it's a moving target.** Every advance in quality raises new expectations. The company that is satisfied with its progress will soon find its customers are not. It is this belief that has spurred Motorola to a 100-fold improvement in quality since 1981. ■ Our formula is a simple one: First, banish complacency. Second, set heroic goals that *compel* new thinking. Finally, "raise the bar" as you near each goal. Set it out of reach all over again. ■ Today, Motorola's standard is Six Sigma quality in all we do by 1992. In statistical terms: 99.9997 percent perfect. Our progress has been swift. Recently, Motorola shared the first Malcolm Baldrige National Quality Award, given by the President. ■ Total customer satisfaction, our goal, is now on the horizon. We dare not rest in its pursuit.

OUR FUNDAMENTAL OBJECTIVE
(Everyone's Overriding Responsibility)
**Total Customer Satisfaction**

MOTOROLA INC.

Over 100,000 Motorolans carry this card at all times...a constant reminder of everyone's overriding responsibility.

Winner 1988 Malcolm Baldrige National Quality Award

Motorola semiconductor defects, once measured in parts per thousand, are now measured in parts per million and even parts per billion.

In 1988 Motorola was a winner of the Malcolm Baldrige National Quality Award.

**Building On Beliefs**

© 1989 MOTOROLA INC. Motorola and Ⓜ are registered trademarks of Motorola, Inc.

Ⓜ **MOTOROLA**

One way that industry performance and efficiency can be improved is by increasing the quality of the product.

Japanese suppliers. Japanese manufacturers are more demanding of quality from suppliers than their American counterparts. Honda examined over 250 potential suppliers of metal stampings before choosing 6. Mazda was in contact with 1,000 U.S. suppliers when setting up its manufacturing facilities in this country, but only found 65 that satisfied its standards.

After Japanese firms have chosen a supplier, they work closely with the supplier to reduce the defect rate even further. The practice of American producers, on the other hand, has been to maintain a distance from their suppliers, constantly bidding them against competing firms to get the lowest possible prices. An exception is Motorola, an American company that in recent years has adopted many of the practices used by Japanese management. In the early 1980s it bought from 5,000 suppliers. By 1989 it had reduced the number of suppliers to 1,600, and planned eventually to use only 400.

In order to promote attention to quality by American firms, Congress established the Malcolm Baldrige National Quality Award, given annually. Of the tens of thousands of firms eligible to compete for the award, only 106 applied in the first 2 years. Those that entered, and even some who didn't yet feel ready, found that the standards for the competition brought an urgency to the firm's concern with quality improvements. Motorola, a winner in the first year, insisted that all of its eligible suppliers also prepare to compete. It dropped 200 who refused.

**Responsiveness to the market**   Producing a quality product efficiently is not good enough unless it is a product that people want to buy. What features does a customer want in a product? When does the customer need delivery? What level of support, including maintenance, does the customer require after delivery? Firms that respond quickly to such questions are more likely to be successful. Japanese producers take pains to satisfy their clients, possibly because their Japanese customers in the domestic market are very particular. They demand not only high-quality products, but good service to back them up. If the car of a Japanese purchaser breaks down, the dealer will often pick it up, repair it promptly, and return it free of charge.

Japanese manufacturers respond to changes in market preferences more quickly than U.S. firms. The lead time for producing a new model automobile from design to production is only 3 to 4 years for Japanese car companies compared to 5 years for American manufacturers. This gives the Japanese greater flexibility in responding to changing consumer tastes and introducing advanced engineering and styling features.

More and more products are being targeted at specific market niches. Producers in the United States have traditionally planned for long production runs in order to reduce the average cost of a product. Japanese firms, on the other hand, build flexible plants that can readily be shifted between the production of differentiated products according to market demand. This enables them to satisfy customer preferences quickly and at the same time hold down the costs of inventory storage.

**Responsiveness to social concerns**   Another measure of industry performance today is the responsibility shown by firms with respect to such social concerns as environmental protection, resource conservation, product safety, and equal opportunity for employees. To a large extent, these concerns are forced upon firms by government regulations, about which more will be said in the next chapter.

Public opinion and liability suits are also causing businesses to clean up their acts. Polls show that 83% of the American public is concerned about the environment and only 36% think that industry is doing an adequate job of protecting it. The *Exxon Valdez* spill of 240,000 barrels of oil

Responsiveness to social concerns is another measure of industry performance. Businesses, such as Starkist, often find it makes economic sense to pay attention to public opinion on issues like environmental protection, rather than risk being boycotted.

**boycott** refusal by consumers to buy the products or services of a firm.

into Alaska's scenic Prince William Sound in 1989 catalyzed citizen anger over environmental damage. The rising voice of concern by the citizenry over air and water pollution, accumulation of garbage—especially nonbiodegradable plastics—and waste of natural resources has led to changes in corporate behavior.

In the past, businesses tended to ignore environmental problems and oppose environmental protection laws because of the costs involved. But in the face of aroused public opinion and legal pressures, corporations are showing more environmental awareness. In April 1990, under threat of a consumer boycott of all of its products, the H. J. Heinz Company announced that its Starkist cannery would no longer buy tuna from fishing boats using gill nets. Such gill nets killed thousands of dolphins each year. Other tuna canners immediately followed suit. IBM gave notification that by 1993 it would stop using CFC chemicals that destroy the ozone layer and contribute to global warming (see chapter 1). The American Paper Institute, an industry association, says that 40% of all paper produced in 1995 will be recycled, thereby saving millions of trees.

Social responsibility is one area of industry performance in which the Japanese have not done any better than the United States. The Japanese whaling industry, along with that of the Soviet Union, refused to abide by international agreements to stop the killing of whales. Industrial plants in Japan have dumped toxic wastes into the environment, resulting in many deaths. Japanese businesses exclude women and non-Japanese from high executive positions.

Does the improved social behavior on the part of American firms represent a basic attitude change by business or only a temporary accommodation to the pressures? A survey of top MBA candidates at the nation's business schools found 89% of them saying that corporations should become more directly involved in solving the country's major social problems. By comparison, only 69% of current business executives believe that. Many business schools have introduced ethics courses into the curriculum. They have been encouraged to do this by those in the corporate community who see an urgent need to prepare future business leaders to deal with complex ethical questions. The large accounting firm Arthur Andersen & Co. is spending $5 million over 5 years to produce ethics case studies and other ethics teaching materials for business schools. A donor has pledged $20 million to Harvard to improve the teaching of ethics. There are those, however, including some teachers that have taught such courses, who are skeptical about whether ethics can be instilled by a course in school.

# case application

## A Rough Road for the U.S. Auto Industry or, "If You Can't Beat 'em, Join 'em"

No industry better exemplifies the decline in American industrial supremacy than the automobile industry. In the 1920s U.S. automobile producers held close to 90% of the global market. Today the U.S. automobile industry produces less than one-third of the cars sold in the world and less than two-thirds of those sold in the United States. There was a 13% reduction in the share of the domestic market held by U.S. producers in the 1980s. That meant a loss in sales of over 1 million vehicles and the closing of 13 North American car and truck assembly plants.

The industry practices that led to this decline can be traced back to the 1950s. At the time Detroit, the capital of the automobile

In the General Motors–Toyota joint venture plant in Fremont, California, new management techniques come to the traditional assembly line. Here an assembly-line worker pulls a rope to halt production temporarily—a decision made only by senior managers in traditionally run plants.

industry, concerned itself only with producing for the North American market. It manufactured almost exclusively large, powerful cars suited to the vast spaces of the U.S. marketplace with its open roads and cheap gas. Auto companies maximized their earnings by a system of "planned obsolescence" in which there were minor annual restylings of car bodies and a major restyling every 3 years or so. This restyling of car exteriors, accompanied by heavy advertising promotion, encouraged customers to buy new cars frequently, even though the car they were buying was not basically different from the one they were replacing. Mechanical and safety improvements were few and far between.

Safety improvements were never high on the list of priorities for auto executives. In the 1930s when Du Pont tried to interest the auto companies in using its newly invented safety glass, Alfred P. Sloan, president and chairman of General Motors from 1923 to 1956, replied: "It is not my responsibility to sell safety glass. . . . You can say, perhaps, that I am selfish. We are not a charitable institution—we are trying to make a profit for our stockholders." In succeeding decades, the auto companies vigorously opposed proposals for new safety standards, from stronger bumpers to secured gas tanks to air bags. (The attitude that safety doesn't sell cars has changed in the 1990s, with U.S. producers leading the Japanese in installing air bags and promoting safety features in their advertising.)

Meanwhile, European auto makers were engineering a greater diversity of cars to appeal to different segments of the market. Volvo and Peugeot were designing safer cars,

case application

Volkswagen and Fiat economical cars, MG and Triumph sports roadsters, and Porsche and Mercedes high-performance cars. The European producers were the first to introduce disc brakes, rack-and-pinion steering, unitized bodies, front-wheel drive, and fuel injection systems, among other technological improvements. As a result, by 1970 auto exports from western Europe were 25 times higher than American exports.

With a continually expanding domestic market and healthy profit margins on the large cars that they produced, U.S. companies were not concerned about foreign competition. The first sign of trouble was the large number of Volkswagen "Beetle" imports in the 1960s. Their popularity showed that there was a market for an economical small car in the United States, a fact that the domestic car companies for years had denied.

But the real problems for the industry started with the oil crisis of the 1970s that drove up gas prices sharply. American buyers turned to small, gas-efficient Japanese models, a type of car that U.S. producers were unable to supply. And by the time Detroit got such models to the market, buyers had discovered that Japanese cars were not only cheaper, but better made. They had fewer defects, a better fit and finish, and were more dependable. And after a decade of U.S. firms trying to catch up, such is still the case. Examining 100,000 repairs to recent cars and trucks, an automobile industry consulting firm found that U.S. makes required the replacement of 42% more critical parts—water pumps, transmissions, alternators—than did Japanese imports.

In the late 1980s the fall in the value of the dollar compared to the yen made U.S. cars relatively cheaper. This and rising wages in Japan went a long way toward closing the price gap between American cars and imports. Further, U.S. automobile companies learned a number of lessons from the Japa-

nese about how to build better cars more efficiently. In 1980 the average American car cost $2,000 more than its Japanese counterpart. Today two-thirds of that cost difference has been eliminated. But despite the improved performance by American producers, a 1989 study showed that the average auto plant in Japan turns out a car with 19.5 hours of labor compared with 26.5 hours for U.S. plants. Even in Japanese "transplant" factories in the United States, production costs are about $700 a car less and defects 21% fewer than in the plants of U.S. firms.

In order to take advantage of Japanese know-how, U.S. auto companies have formed joint ventures with Japanese producers. General Motors has established a joint venture, New United Motor Manufacturing, with Toyota in a previously shut-down G. M. plant in Fremont, California. Chrysler and Mitsubishi have a joint venture at Normal, Illinois, said to be the world's most advanced assembly plant—a robot wonderland—to produce Plymouth Lasers and Mitsubishi Eclipses. If you can't beat 'em, join 'em.

## Economic Reasoning

1. What comparisons between the quality of American cars and Japanese cars do you find in this case application?

2. What is the relative productivity of labor in automobile plants in Japan and in the United States in percentage terms? If U.S. auto workers are paid $18 an hour, including benefits, how much does the difference in productivity increase the cost of a car produced by an American manufacturer?

3. Do you think that it is a good idea for American automobile companies to form joint ventures with Japanese companies to produce cars in this country? Why or why not?

# How Can Industry Performance Be Improved?

American industry is attempting to get back into shape in order to fight off the challenge of Japanese and European producers. In this section we will investigate the factors that increase productivity and improve other aspects of industry performance.

**Investment in capital equipment**  Although productivity is commonly measured as output per hour of labor, the quantity of output depends greatly on the amount of investment in capital equipment. This includes machine tools, robots, computers, and the like that labor works with. In the early 1980s investment by American business in durable equipment declined. It did not recover its 1979 level until 1984 (Figure 2). Since the size of the labor force was expanding during those years, productivity suffered from an insufficient amount of investment per worker.

Real investment in equipment has been steadily increasing since 1984, resulting in sizable increases in manufactur-

**capital equipment** the machinery and tools used to produce goods and services.

**real investment** the purchase of business structures and capital equipment; investment measured in dollars of constant value to adjust for inflation.

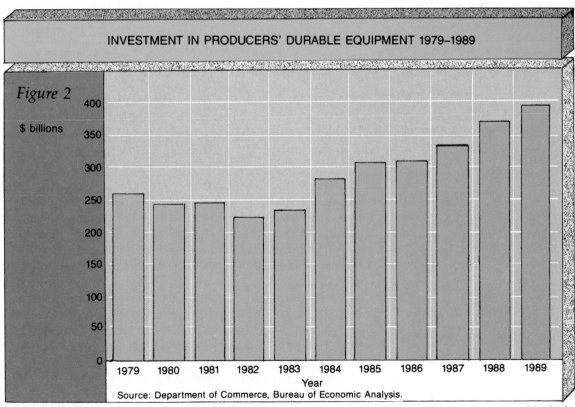

INVESTMENT IN PRODUCERS' DURABLE EQUIPMENT 1979–1989

Figure 2

$ billions

Year

Source: Department of Commerce, Bureau of Economic Analysis.

Investment by U.S. industries in capital equipment tailed off in the early 1980s. Because there were more workers in the labor force each year, labor productivity suffered.

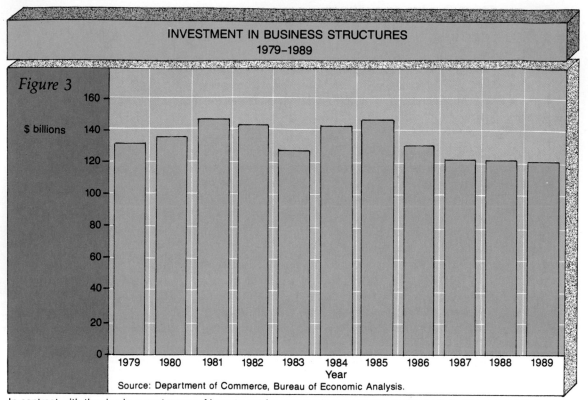

**INVESTMENT IN BUSINESS STRUCTURES**
**1979–1989**

*Figure 3*

$ billions

Source: Department of Commerce, Bureau of Economic Analysis.

In contrast with the rise in recent years of investment for new equipment shown in Figure 2, business spending on new structures has been falling. This represents a changed philosophy in American industry—to invest for increased productivity in order to expand output rather than enlarge plant size.

ing productivity. One of the lessons learned from the Japanese was that purchasing equipment that increases labor productivity is a better use of investment funds than expanding the size of plants. As a result, spending by business firms on new structures fell each year from 1985 to 1989, despite strong economic expansion (Figure 3).

Although manufacturing productivity has been higher in recent years, service industry productivity remains low, and overall productivity gains still lag behind those in Japan and some western European countries. Japan allocates twice as large a percentage of its output to investment as does the United States. One of the reasons for the low investment rate in the United States is the high cost of financial capital— the high interest rate for borrowed money. A study by B. Douglas Bernheim of Northwestern University and John B. Shoven of Stanford University showed that U.S. firms in the 1980s incurred the highest after-tax costs of capital among all of the leading industrialized nations, over 5%. At the same time, capital cost Japanese firms less than 3%, while the cost to British and West German companies was in between.

Financial capital is cheaper in Japan in large part because of their high savings rate. Savings are the major source of funds for investment, and the savings rate in the United States, both private and public, reached historic lows in the decade of the eighties. (Public savings, the difference between government revenues and government spending, are covered in chapter 13.)

Another reason for the low rate of real capital investment in the 1980s was the diversion of financial capital from the purchase of new plant and equipment into the purchase of existing firms. These buyouts, financed in great measure by junk bonds (see "Corporate Raiders, LBOs, and the Feeding Frenzy," p. 190), drove interest rates higher and made real investment less attractive.

The investment rate by U.S. firms also tends to be lower than that of their Japanese counterparts because of the shorter time horizon of corporation objectives in this country. If corporate executives do not see the likelihood that an investment in new plant and equipment will pay for itself and return a profit in a very few years, they will not undertake it. Japanese business leaders, on the other hand, are willing to invest for the long term. They believe that increasing their company's market share by reducing production costs and improving the product will pay off in the future. The heads of American corporations are not in a position to be as patient. They are under pressure from stockholders and Wall Street analysts to show good earnings reports every quarter. If they do not, the value of the company's stock may fall and the president be ousted, or at the least not given the customary year-end bonus.

Some of the ways that real capital investment can be increased, thus raising productivity and lowering production costs, are

1. to lower interest rates by increasing private and public savings,
2. to redirect capital from financial speculation to new investment, and
3. to shift the pressures on corporate executives from short-term to long-term performance objectives.

**Investment in human capital**   Another lesson that American industry needs to learn from the Japanese is the value of investing in its workers. The investment in productive equipment must be accompanied by training of workers to use the equipment. Studies have shown that investment in human capital is actually more effective in raising productivity than investment in physical facilities. American firms,

**junk bonds**  bonds that are issued paying higher than normal interest rates because they have a greater risk of default.

**human capital**  labor which is literate, skilled, trained, healthy, and economically motivated.

Investment in human capital is an important way of improving industry performance. Training workers to use new equipment and increasing their literacy skills improves their productivity. At Texas Instruments, above, immigrant workers receive training in English.

however, invest ten times more in new plant and equipment than they do in employee training. According to research conducted by Martin K. Starr of Columbia University, Japanese companies in the United States spend twice as much on training as U.S. companies. A report by the American Society for Training and Development for the U.S. Department of Labor says that industry needs to double the $30 billion a year it currently spends on employee training.

Studies of increasing labor productivity in specific firms have shown the existence of a learning curve. A plant with new equipment and new technology will achieve increasing labor productivity for a period of time as the total number of units produced increases. However, the successive increases of output per worker will be greater at first and then gradually diminish as the learning curve flattens out. The steeper the learning curve, the faster costs of production will drop and the more profitable the investment will be. One reason that Japanese firms are able to be so competitive in world markets is that the learning curve in Japanese industries appears to be steeper than it is in American industries, as the hypothetical learning curves in Figure 4 illustrate. The steepness of the learning curve depends upon the amount and quality of the training given to workers, attitudes of workers towards their jobs and the employer, and the degree of flexibility of work rules.

**learning curve** a diagram showing how labor productivity or labor costs change as the total number of units produced by a new plant or with new technology increases over time.

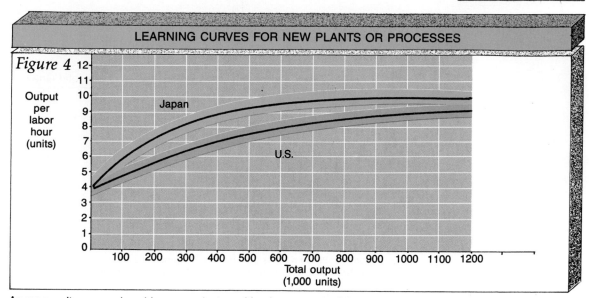

**LEARNING CURVES FOR NEW PLANTS OR PROCESSES**

*Figure 4*

Output per labor hour (units)

Japan

U.S.

Total output (1,000 units)

As more units are produced in a new plant or with a new process, labor productivity increases at a diminishing rate.

One of the first companies to get the message on the importance of worker training was Motorola. In order to compete with global challengers to its electronics business, it invested heavily in computer-controlled robots in its factories. To operate the high-tech equipment it needed workers with higher skill levels than those of its existing work force. The company determined that employees should have at least fifth-grade math skills and seventh-grade reading skills to work in its plants. It discovered, however, that fully half of its workers needed remedial training to reach this level. To retrain its existing work force and train new employees, it established a $10 million center for training and education where workers attended classes five hours a day for four months. To upgrade performance on a continuing basis, the company has set a goal that every employee from janitor up to the president of the company receive 40 hours of training each year.

IBM is another company that spends heavily on employee training, $900 million a year. On any given day, 18,000 IBM employees are receiving education or training.

Some companies have adopted the Japanese practice of cross-training workers for different jobs. This provides a more flexible work force that can switch from one operation to another as production demands require, detect flaws in each other's work, and jointly solve production problems. It also has the side benefit of reducing worker boredom, a problem on traditional assembly lines where the worker does one repetitive job all day long, day after day.

**cross-training**  giving workers training in performing more than one task.

*Table 1*  **FACTORS RESPONSIBLE FOR PRODUCTION GROWTH IN THE UNITED STATES 1929–1982**

| Factor | % Total Growth |
|---|---|
| Labor input | 32 |
| Technology | 28 |
| Capital input | 19 |
| Education | 14 |
| Economies of scale | 9 |
| Improved resource allocation | 8 |
| Negative growth factors<br>costs of pollution abatement, protecting worker<br>safety and health, dishonesty and crime, etc. | – 10 |
| | 100 |

Source: Based on data from Edward F. Denison, *Trends in American Economic Growth, 1929–1982* (Washington, D.C.: The Brookings Institution, 1985).

**Research and development**  A statistical analysis commissioned by *Business Week* in 1989 "demonstrated beyond any doubt" that the companies which were most successful in their markets were those that spent the most on research and development per dollar of sales and per employee. But industry-funded R&D spending in the United States as a percentage of total output has lagged behind both Japan and West Germany for two decades. In 1989 it was 1.8% in the United States compared to 2.6% in West Germany and 2.8% in Japan. In industries such as electrical equipment and ceramics, Japanese companies regularly spend 30% to 60% more on R&D than their U.S. counterparts.

Investment in R&D may result in new products or in new production technologies. The importance of earlier R&D spending for new technology is demonstrated in a study by Edward F. Denison on the factors contributing to production growth in the United States from 1929 to 1982. It shows that technology made the second largest contribution to increased output. It ranked just behind the amount of labor input and ahead of both the quantity of capital and the contribution of education (Table 1).

The importance of increased private R&D spending in this country is greater as a result of declining government spending on R&D for the military. Also, a higher level of cooperation between industry and universities is necessary, particularly to stimulate more applied research. Scientific discoveries in university research are too slowly implemented in industry production.

**Organization of production**  Research and development results in product innovation, but the real secret of Japanese industry success seems to be their process innovation. This entails improvements in the methods of organizing production to reduce costs, improve quality, and satisfy the demands of customers. Process innovation can take different forms, such as the incorporation of manufacturing feasibility in product design decisions; the automation of production with the use of computer-controlled equipment; the integration of ordering, scheduling, accounting, and production operations with the aid of a computer network; the use of just-in-time manufacturing methods; and, most important of all, the inclusion of workers in decision-making, generally by forming one or more types of worker teams or worker-management teams.

Industry studies show that as much as 75% of all manufacturing costs are locked in by the product design. In Japanese firms the product design engineers work closely with the manufacturing departments to avoid designs that will present manufacturing problems or be costly to make. In the United States, conversely, it has been traditional for the white-collar design people to have little contact with the blue-collar manufacturing people. Ford was the first American auto company to adopt a new approach to product development called design for manufacturability and assembly (DFMA). It is estimated that in one year alone DFMA trimmed manufacturing costs by more than $1.2 billion at Ford. This helped Ford edge out General Motors as the nation's most profitable auto maker, despite a lower sales volume.

Some companies—Lockheed, Caterpillar, Hughes, General Electric, and Borg-Warner, to name a few—have installed flexible manufacturing systems (FMS). These systems, which use automated equipment controlled by computers, are costly—the average outlay for a FMS is $4 million—but efficient. A General Electric plant in Somersworth, New Hampshire, can be programmed to make up to 2,000 variations of 40 basic models of an electric meter. American companies were pioneers in FMS development in the 1970s. Nevertheless, it was competition from the Japanese, who custom-tailor their products for buyers, that stimulated heavy new investment by U.S. firms in FMS.

More expensive yet are totally computer-integrated manufacturing (CIM) plants. With CIM, all of the various production operations of the company are fed into a mainframe computer. This provides a common pool of data for the various departments—ordering, scheduling, accounting, and production—where factory versions of personal computers, communicating through local networks, control the operations. It is estimated that about 30% of Japanese companies have CIM installed now and that the number will expand to 70% within 10 years.

**process innovation**   introducing improved methods of organizing production.

**automation**   production techniques that adjust automatically to the needs of the processing operation by the use of control devices.

**just-in-time**   a system that provides for raw materials and subassemblies to be delivered by suppliers to the location where they will be processed at the time they are needed rather than being stored in inventories.

**design for manufacturability and assembly (DFMA)**   a system of designing products in which the design engineers consult with manufacturing personnel during the designing process to avoid designs that will be difficult or costly to manufacture.

**flexible manufacturing systems (FMS)**   the use of computer-controlled capital equipment that can be readily shifted from the production of one part to a different part.

**computer-integrated manufacturing (CIM)**   a system of integrating all the operations of different departments in a plant by means of a central computer and a network of workstation computers.

Even before CIM, Japanese producers made use of just-in-time manufacturing methods. Under this system, raw materials and sub-assemblies from suppliers are delivered to the plant at the time they are needed. This eliminates investment in inventories, and it reduces warehouse and distribution costs. Incoming supplies can often be delivered directly to their processing area. Many U.S. firms have implemented just-in-time methods in recent years.

Much less expensive than CIM—and possibly providing even larger productivity and quality returns—are employee involvement (EI) programs. These programs provide for worker participation in organizing production. This concept was first introduced in the United States in the 1920s under the title of "industrial democracy." But it remained for the Japanese to make extensive use of the idea.

Employee involvement can take different forms, from self-contained teams of workers that operate without direct supervision to worker participation in such managerial decisions as what types of investment to undertake. There are three basic types of EI teams:

1.  Self-managing teams. These are customarily made up of 5 to 15 employees who produce an entire product, rather than make subunits. Team members learn all jobs and rotate from job to job. They take on such managerial functions as work and vacation scheduling and materials ordering. The Volvo auto company in Sweden led in the use of this type of EI team.
    Example: Teams at a General Mills cereal plant in Lodi, California, operate production and maintain the machinery so effectively that the factory runs with no managers present during the night shift.

2.  Problem-solving teams. These consist of hourly and salaried volunteers, generally 5 to 12, from different areas of a department. They meet one or two hours a week to discuss ways of improving quality, efficiency, and work environment. Known as "quality circles," this type of EI team was developed and used widely in Japan. Now the system is in use in thousands of American companies.
    Example: A team of Federal Express clerks, meeting weekly, spotted and solved a billing problem that was costing the company $2.1 million a year.

3.  Special-purpose teams. These teams are made up of workers and managers who undertake such tasks as designing and introducing work reforms and new technology, meeting with suppliers and customers, or link-

**employee involvement (EI)** various programs for incorporating hourly-wage workers in decision-making; may involve decisions on production methods, work scheduling, purchase of capital equipment, etc.

Participation by labor in management decisions is practiced in "quality circles" in Japan.

ing separate functions within the plant. This type of team is more common in the United States than in Japan.

Example: A team of Chaparral Steel mill-workers examined new production machinery in other countries before selecting and installing machines that helped make their mill one of the world's most efficient.

There has in the past been a basic difference in philosophy about the use of labor in Japanese and U.S. companies. Japanese companies view their workers as valuable assets, the use of which should be maximized. Management in this country, on the other hand, has tended to view workers as expensive inputs, the cost of which should be minimized. The nature of relationships within a company is also different in the two countries. U.S. companies have vertical lines of authority like the military. Communications between different departments in a company go up a chain of command to a high level and back down another chain of command. In Japanese companies there are continual communications between members of different departments at the same level and levels above and below as well. This is a flatter system of organization than that of U.S. businesses.

Employee involvement programs have been very helpful to some U.S. companies in increasing productivity and improving quality. A study of 101 industrial companies found that the EI companies outscored those that had no participative management programs on 13 of 14 financial measures.

Despite the benefits from employee involvement, EI programs have not had an easy time in this country. According to one study, about 75% of all EI programs introduced in the early 1980s failed. Another survey, conducted by the U.S. General Accounting Office, found that among 476 large companies some 27% were using work teams. But even in those companies, the programs usually involved less than a fifth of their employees.

Opposition to EI has come from labor unions and from middle management. Some labor leaders see EI as just a cover for management to get more work out of its employees for the same wages—a new version of the old work speed-up routine. The president of a paper-workers' union local was quoted as saying:

> What the company wants is for us to work like the Japanese. Everybody go out and do jumping jacks in the morning and kiss each other when they go home at night. You work as a team, rat on each other, and lose control of your destiny. That's not going to work in this country.*

Many unions have gone along with EI in the hope that it would enable the company to compete more effectively with imports and save union jobs. Other unions have pushed for employee stock ownership plans (ESOPs) as the ultimate form of employee involvement. An increasing number of companies are totally owned by their employees—Avis Car Rental, Health Trust hospital management, Amsted Manufacturing, Weirton Steel, and Dan River Textiles, to name a few.

More damaging to EI programs than unions has been the opposition of middle managers and foremen. They see worker participation as a threat not only to their authority but to their jobs, and not without reason. Changing from a vertical system of management to a flatter organizational system often means that half or more of the middle management positions are eliminated.

*John Brodie, President, United Paperworkers Local 448, Chester, Pa. Quoted in *Business Week*, July 10, 1989, p. 56.

# case application

## The New Industrial Revolution

The first Industrial Revolution (see Perspective, page 77) was the second most important economic event in humankind's history, exceeded in significance only by the change from nomadic wandering to settled agriculture. We are now in the midst of a second Industrial Revolution, which also may have far-reaching effects. At the heart of this new revolution is a tiny piece of silicon, a "chip," less than the size of a fingernail. This chip is a microprocessor, which can do everything from controlling the shutter speed on a camera to weighing the cargo of a truck. When linked to input-output and programming units on separate chips, it forms the central processing unit (CPU) of a computer.

The public is most familiar with the uses of microprocessors in consumer goods such as pocket calculators, automobile controls, and personal computers, but it is their industrial applications that may ultimately have a greater impact on our lives. A Kansas City firm, manufacturing air conditioning refrigeration systems for buildings, formerly needed months of engineering work and production time to custom design and fabricate a system for a new building. Now it can do the job in a few weeks with only one-fourth the personnel formerly needed. It is able to do this through the use of CAD/CAM (computer-aided design/computer-aided manufacturing). CAD/CAM is to the second Industrial Revolution what the steam engine was to the first. The ultimate in CAD/CAM is the factory totally automated by computer-integrated manufacturing.

What effect will CIM have on workers' jobs? Is the U.S. labor force going to be

thrown out of work en masse? Will we see workers riot as they did when machines were installed in factories at the beginning of the Industrial Revolution? The answer to these questions is probably not. Just as the first Industrial Revolution was responsible for creating more jobs than the total number of workers employed when it began, this second revolution will very likely create more than enough new opportunities to offset the jobs eliminated. However, this technological revolution will radically alter the types of jobs available and most likely cause temporary dislocations. There will be jobs in the industries that produce the new equipment, jobs in operating and maintaining the equipment, and, most of all, jobs in a variety of new industries created by the reduction in costs due to CIM.

The transition will not occur overnight. Only one-quarter of all industrial plants in the U.S.—mainly auto and auto parts, aerospace, electronics, electrical and mechanical engineering, food, and paper companies—were making use of CAD/CAM by 1990.

The adoption of computerized automation is slow because of the high cost of the equipment. It can cost anywhere from $100,000 to $1,000,000 for one device. The vast sums of money needed to finance the second Industrial Revolution will be difficult to find. But firms that do not make the investments will not be able to compete. CIM enables companies to produce custom-made products of the highest quality to the customer's order at the least cost. Increasingly, as time goes on, companies that do not install CIM systems will not be able to match the quality and

# case application

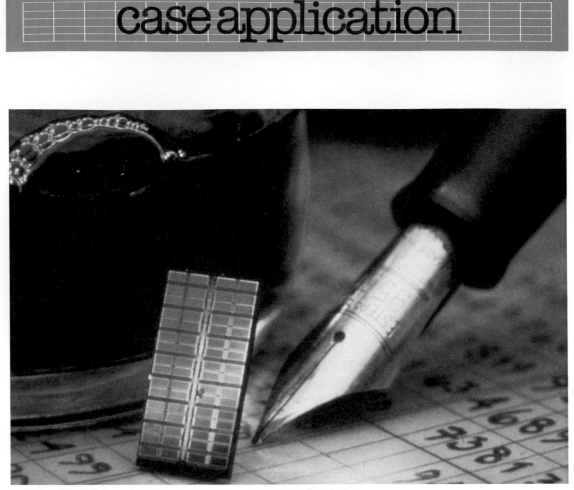

The tiny silicon chip is at the heart of the second Industrial Revolution.

prices of those producers that do, both domestic and foreign.

Another cost of automation is the extensive retraining of workers and managers required. Since only 30% or 40% of the costs of production have anything to do with actually producing a part, the main impact of CIM will be on planning, scheduling, and controlling the use of equipment. This change will totally transform the functions of management. In the second Industrial Revolution, the managers may resist the introduction of the new production techniques more than the workers.

## Economic Reasoning

1. What is an example of investment in real capital improving industry performance in this application?
2. Why does automation of production require investment in human capital?
3. Do you think EI teams of workers and managers should decide on investments in CAD/CAM, or should investment decisions be left to management and owners? Why? If such decisions do include workers, which of the three types of EI teams would be involved?

# What Are the Effects of Industry Concentration on Performance?

In the last section of chapter 6 we examined the different types of industry structure from pure competition to pure monopoly. Industry performance can be affected by how monopolistic the industry is—how close it is to pure monopoly.

**Market concentration**   The degree of concentration in an industry is determined by the number of firms in the industry that are competing for customers. The degree of market concentration ranges from pure monopoly as the most concentrated to pure competition as the least concentrated. Reduction of the number of firms in an industry increases market concentration and enables the firms in the industry to exert more control over prices. When there are fewer firms, each firm faces a demand curve for its output that is more inelastic. As a result, it can raise prices without as much loss in sales. Also, the more concentrated an industry is, the more likely it is to follow the practice of price leadership and avoid price competition.

The degree of concentration in an industry is measured by the proportion of total sales accounted for by the largest firms in that industry. The percentage of industry sales accounted for by the four largest firms is the most commonly used concentration ratio. Industries in which the four largest firms account for over 50% of sales can be considered shared monopolies. In the United States these include the motor vehicle, photographic equipment, tire, aircraft, and soap industries. When the concentration ratio is less than 25%, industries are assumed to be competitive. This is the case with such industries as printing, sawmills, fluid milk, meat packing, plastics, and papermills.

Approximately one-third of the sales of American industry fall into the shared monopoly category and another third is competitive. The remaining third, those with concentration ratios between 25% and 50%, are neither clearly monopolistic nor clearly competitive.

The extent of monopoly power in American business as defined by the concentration ratio, however, is perhaps understated. There can be local monopolies that have as much power in their area as national monopolies do in the nation as a whole. Furthermore, the way industries are defined frequently masks the actual amount of monopoly that exists in the economy. For example, the largest four producers of salt account for 80% of salt sales. But in the data on which concentration ratios are based, salt producers are lumped together with firms producing other chemical com-

**market concentration**   a measure of the number of firms in an industry.
**concentration ratio**   the percentage of total sales of an industry accounted for by the largest four firms. An alternative measure is the percentage of sales accounted for by the largest eight firms.

| Rank | Company | Industry | Sales ($ millions) | Profits[2] ($ millions) | Rank | Profitability[3] (% Return) | Rank |
|------|---------|----------|-------|---------|------|------|------|
| 1. | General Motors | Motor vehicles | 126,974.3 | 4,224.3 | 1 | 12.1 | 277 |
| 2. | Ford Motor | Motor vehicles | 96,932.6 | 3,835.0 | 3 | 16.9 | 186 |
| 3. | Exxon | Petroleum refining | 86,656.0 | 3,510.0 | 5 | 11.6 | 287 |
| 4. | I.B.M. | Computers | 63,438.0 | 3,758.0 | 4 | 9.8 | 317 |
| 5. | General Electric | Electronics | 55,264.0 | 3,939.0 | 2 | 18.9 | 142 |
| 6. | Mobil | Petroleum refining | 50,976.0 | 1,809.0 | 11 | 11.1 | 294 |
| 7. | Philip Morris | Food | 39,069.0 | 2,946.0 | 6 | 30.8 | 41 |
| 8. | Chrysler | Motor vehicles | 36,156.0 | 359.0 | 74 | 5.0 | 375 |
| 9. | E.I. du Pont | Chemicals | 35,209.0 | 2,480.0 | 8 | 15.7 | 207 |
| 10. | Texaco | Petroleum refining | 32,416.0 | 2,413.0 | 9 | 26.3 | 53 |
| 11. | Chevron | Petroleum refining | 29,443.0 | 251.0 | 107 | 1.8 | 394 |
| 12. | Amoco | Petroleum refining | 24,214.0 | 1,610.0 | 13 | 11.8 | 283 |
| 13. | Shell Oil | Petroleum refining | 21,703.0 | 1,405.0 | 15 | 8.8 | 334 |
| 14. | Procter & Gamble | Soaps & cosmetics | 21,689.0 | 1,206.0 | 17 | 19.4 | 138 |
| 15. | Boeing | Aerospace | 20,276.0 | 973.0 | 21 | 15.9 | 205 |

*Table 2*     THE 15 LARGEST U.S. INDUSTRIAL CORPORATIONS IN 1989[1]

[1]From *Fortune* magazine, April 23, 1990.

[2]Net income after taxes.     [3]Profits as a percentage of stockholders' equity.

pounds. As a result of including salt producers with producers of other chemicals that do not compete with salt, the entire industry is classified as competitive.

**Aggregate concentration** If instead of market concentration we look at the aggregate concentration of all industries we see that there has been a dramatic increase in the overall amount of concentration in American industry. Aggregate concentration is the percentage of total sales of all industries accounted for by the nation's largest corporations. Today, fewer than 200 corporations control the same proportion of business assets that the 1,000 largest corporations controlled in 1941.

The idealized concept of a market economy is one in which large numbers of small firms compete for customers by offering better products and lower prices. This market model does not correspond to the real world of concentrated industries.

**aggregate concentration** a measure of the proportion of the total sales of all industries accounted for by the largest firms in the country. There is no common standard for measuring the aggregate concentration ratio.

**Concentration and industry performance** Concentration in an industry may result from mergers, barriers to entry, or predatory business practices, including such illegal ones as price discrimination, sales below cost, and kickbacks.

In the last decade a controversy arose among economists regarding the effects of industry concentration. Up until then there was general agreement, at least among economists in industrialized countries, that unregulated monopolies have undesirable effects on the economy and on consumer welfare. One of the most obvious effects is monopolistic pricing. With only a few firms in an industry, barriers to entry of new firms, and a lack of close substitutes for products sold under monopolistic conditions, firms can charge prices substantially above their costs of production and make monopoly profits. The Federal Trade Commission once estimated that eliminating concentration in industries would reduce prices by 25% or more.

Another unfortunate result of concentration is misallocation of resources. Monopolies keep prices high by limiting the supply of the product on the market. As a result, monopolistic industries have less need for labor, raw materials, and capital equipment than they would if they were more competitive. The resources squeezed out of monopolistic industries by restricting output are diverted to other industries where they are in surplus. The surplus of these factors in the other industries lowers the incomes of the households that provide them. Too few resources are used in a particular industry when that industry is monopolistic. Our resources would be used more efficiently if prices were more competitive. One estimate is that the misallocation of resources, resulting from monopoly pricing, costs the economy between $48 billion and $60 billion a year in lower total output.

Although large firms can have lower costs than small firms because of economies of scale, monopoly may instead result in higher costs. Firms in competitive industries are forced by market pressures to operate at or near their most efficient production levels. Monopolistic firms are not subject to this pressure, and may therefore permit costs to rise above the lowest possible cost per unit.

One reason for higher costs in shared monopoly and differentiated competition industries is the amount of money they spend on advertising. If advertising provides useful information to buyers, it is not wasteful of resources. Advertising that describes real attributes of the product, where it can be purchased, and at what price is a productive service that improves the operation of markets. This is the case with most newspaper advertising. But much advertising is repetitive, and purchased only for the purpose of

**merger** a contractual joining of the assets of one formerly independent company with another; may be a horizontal merger of companies producing the same product, a vertical merger of companies producing different stages of a product in the same industry, or a conglomerate merger of companies producing in different industries.
**barrier to entry** an obstacle to the entry of new firms into an industry.
**predatory business practice** any action on the part of a firm carried out solely to interfere with a competitor.
**price discrimination** selling a product to two different buyers at different prices where all other conditions are the same.
**kickback** the return of a portion of a payment or commission in accordance with a secret agreement.
**monopolistic pricing** setting a price above the level necessary to bring a product to market by restricting the supply of the product.
**misallocation of resources** not producing the mix of products and services that would maximize consumer satisfaction.
**economies of scale** decreasing costs per unit as plant size increases.

countering a rival's advertising claims, such as in many national television ad campaigns.

Competitive firms selling a standardized product do not have large advertising budgets. They do not need them because there are buyers at the market price for all that they can produce, and they cannot afford large advertising outlays because they must keep their costs down to be able to sell at the market price.

Other forms of non-price competition that drive up costs are product differentiation and packaging. In differentiated competition industries, a firm will often attempt to differentiate its product in the mind of consumers from that of its competitors in order to segment the market and make the demand for its product more inelastic. Product differentiation purely for the sake of promotion is found extensively in the detergent, soft drink, and cosmetics industries, among others. Differentiation may take the form of "additives," product appearance, or packaging. Distinctive packaging for the sake of product differentiation adds greatly to the cost of many products. A University of California study showed that $1 of every $11 spent on products goes for packaging, and in one-fourth of the industries studied the packaging cost more than the contents.

Industry concentration may also result in greater economic instability, due to the pricing practices in monopolistic industries. During periods of good business with booming sales, all businesses are likely to raise prices. During times of depressed business conditions, firms in competitive industries are forced by falling sales and the resulting price competition to reduce prices. This helps to maintain sales and cushion the amount of unemployment. But such is not the case in monopolistic industries. When sales decline, shared monopolies are likely to hold their prices stable or even raise them in order to increase their margin of profit on each unit sold to compensate for the reduction in sales volume.

Against this view of the drawbacks of concentration in industry, some economists now argue that the emergence of global competition has made national monopolies irrelevant. If domestic monopolies charge prices that are higher than costs of production, including a normal profit, foreign producers will enter the market and drive prices down.

Furthermore, they maintain, global competition calls for companies that are very large and also for cooperation among the firms in a country's industries. Small, independent firms do not have the financial resources to develop and market products in competition with aggressive manufacturing giants outside the United States.

According to these economists, cooperation among firms

**product differentiation** a device used by business firms to distinguish their product from the products of other firms in the same industry.

Finding a new way to package a product will help differentiate it from its competitors, but can also add greatly to the cost of the product.

plays a large part in the Japanese national competitive advantage. In the semiconductor industry, for example, such *keiretsu* companies as Hitachi, NEC, and Fujitsu are <u>vertically integrated</u>. Individual firms are associated with industrial groups in which they have close ties with each other, with large Tokyo banks, with their suppliers, and with the government. Industrial policies and export strategies are devised and promoted by the Ministry of International Trade and Industry (MITI). It encourages cooperation among firms to carry out the strategies.

But the idea that Japan's success in world markets is due to cartel practices in its industries, aided and abetted by MITI, is challenged by Michael Porter of the Harvard Business School in *The Competitive Advantage of Nations* (see Further Reading at the end of the chapter). Porter maintains that the success of Japanese firms is not due to their cooperation or to assistance by the government, but rather to vigorous domestic rivalry among companies in their home market. The Japanese industries in which there is the fiercest competition among the firms in the domestic market—autos, consumer electronics, televisions, cameras—are the very ones that have been the most successful abroad. On the other hand, in those Japanese industries in which there are strong cartels and government restrictions on competition—construction, agriculture, food, paper, commodity chemicals, and fibers—costs are so high that Japan cannot compete with other countries. According to Porter, this is no accident. It is competition at home that has made Japanese companies lean and mean for kung-fu assaults on foreign markets.

**vertically integrated**  separate divisions of one company producing the different stages of a product and marketing their output to one another.

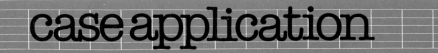

## Corporate Raiders, LBOs, and the Feeding Frenzy

Of the companies that were on the *Fortune* 500 list of the nation's largest industrial corporations in 1983, 143 had disappeared from the list by 1988. In 102 of those cases the reasons were acquisition or merger.

We are accustomed to thinking of acquisitions in terms of large, successful companies buying up small, less successful companies—big fish swallowing little fish. In the 1980s there was a lot of this going on, but more characteristic of the decade was the acquisition of one giant corporation by another—big fish swallowing other big fish. Gulf Oil, the 11th largest company in 1983, was acquired by Standard Oil of California (now Chevron), the 9th largest; General Foods, 38th on the list of the 500 largest in 1985, was purchased by Phillip Morris, number 27, as was Kraft in 1987 when it was 31st and Phillip Morris 12th; and number 54 in 1984, Nabisco, was acquired by R. J. Reynolds, number 23.

In the latter part of the decade, the feeding frenzy increased as a result of corporate raiders and leveraged buyouts (LBOs). Leading raiders such as T. Boone Pickens, Sir James Goldsmith, and Irv ("the Liquidator") Jacobs were constantly on the lookout for likely takeover targets with undervalued assets or complacent managements. Sometimes the raiders succeeded in getting control of the company's assets. Other times they arranged to be bought off by management with "greenmail," payments for the raider's stockholdings at far above the market price for the stock.

Leveraged buyouts are a means of financing the takeover of a corporation by selling securities which are secured by the assets of the company. Since the price raiders pay for a company is often well above the previous market value of the company's stock, the LBO saddles the company with a large debt burden. By the end of the decade, U.S. corporations on the average were paying over half of their pretax earnings in interest on their debts.

In order to induce investors to buy the risky security issues that financed LBO transactions, interest rates on the securities were higher than normal. These securities acquired the name "junk bonds" because of their high risk. If the company did not earn enough to pay the large interest charges on its debt, it could be forced into bankruptcy, leaving the bond purchasers holding the bag.

The "inventor" of junk bonds to finance LBOs was Michael Milken, a 40-year-old financier employed by the investment banking firm of Drexel Burnham Lambert. He first used junk bonds to raise money for small, start-up companies that had trouble borrowing sufficient capital. He then turned to using the technique for raising the billions of dollars needed by corporate raiders to get control of large corporations. Milken is credited for almost singlehandedly creating the junk-bond market. For his efforts he was paid hundreds of millions of dollars, $550 million in 1987 alone.

But in 1989, about the time some of the mega-deals that he arranged were coming apart as a result of defaults on the bonds, Milken and Drexel Burnham Lambert were indicted for fraud. Drexel Burnham Lambert pleaded guilty to six felony counts of mail, wire, and securities fraud. It paid a fine of $650 million, and the following year the firm was dissolved. Milken also copped a plea to six felony counts. He agreed to pay $600 million in fines and restitutions and was sentenced to a 10-year prison term.

*Economic Reasoning*

1. What effect effect did Chevron's acquisition of Gulf Oil have on market concentration?
2. How could the acquisition of General Foods, Kraft, and other food companies by Philip Morris affect the price of food and the allocation of resources?
3. Was the creation of the junk-bond market good for American business? Why or why not?

# Putting It Together

A principal determinant of industry performance is *productivity*. Productivity is customarily measured by the amount of output per hour of labor. Productivity growth in the United States was lower in the 1970s and 1980s than in Japan and a number of other countries.

Another indication of performance is the quality of goods and services produced by industry. In order to encourage U.S. firms to devote more effort to improving quality, Congress established the Malcolm Baldrige National Quality Award in 1988.

The level of industry performance also depends on the responsiveness of companies to market preferences and changes. Production is increasingly targeted at specific market niches, which necessitates flexible plants.

Today industry performance is also measured by the extent to which businesses act responsibly in environmental protection, resource conservation, product safety, and equal opportunity for employees.

A means of raising productivity is increasing the amount of *real investment* in *capital equipment*. Financial capital is more costly in the United States than in Japan because the savings rate is lower here both for households and government, because financial capital has been diverted from real investment to financial speculation, and because of the short time horizon of U.S. corporation executives who are under pressure to show good profit reports every quarter.

Another way of increasing productivity and also improving quality is investment in *human capital*. When new equipment and technology are introduced in a plant there is a *learning curve* of rising productivity.

The learning curve for Japanese companies is steeper than for American companies in part because the Japanese invest more in training their workers than do U.S. firms. *Cross-training* workers provides a more flexible labor force and reduces worker boredom.

Spending on research and development has in the past been the second most important factor responsible for growth in the U.S. economy. Private R&D spending takes on increased importance today as the government cuts back on military-related R&D, and more cooperation between industry and universities is needed.

A sewing robot from Matsushita Electric symbolizes the innovative approach that Japanese companies have brought to many industries.

The most successful Japanese business innovations have not been their product innovations but their *process innovations*. These include the inclusion of manufacturing feasibility considerations in product design, installing flexible manufacturing systems, integrating the various operations in a plant by means of a computer network, using just-in-time manufacturing methods, and including workers in decision-making.

*Design for manufacturability and assembly (DFMA)* is a system of product design that reduces production costs. *Flexible manufacturing systems (FMS)* enable workers and equipment to shift quickly from producing one item to producing a different one. *Computer-integrated manufacturing (CIM)* plants tie together the different production operations by means of a computer network. *Just-in-time* manufacturing methods allow raw materials and sub-assemblies to be delivered by suppliers to the location where they are needed at the time they are needed.

A process innovation first introduced in the United States but extensively put to use in Japan is *employee involvement (EI)*. EI programs may be self-managing teams, problem-solving teams, or special-purpose teams.

Japanese firms view their workers as valuable assets to be maximized, while U.S. firms have been inclined to view their workers as expensive inputs to be minimized. In U.S. firms the organization is vertical, while in Japanese firms it is flatter, resulting in closer communications.

Some labor leaders in the United States and middle managers have opposed EI programs.

*Market concentration* is determined by the number of firms in an industry. The *concentration ratio* is customarily measured by the percentage of industry sales accounted for by the four largest firms. If it is over 50%, the industry is a shared monopoly. If it is less than 25%, the industry is competitive.

*Aggregate concentration* is the share of total output of all industries accounted for by the nation's largest firms.

Concentration may result from *mergers, barriers to entry*, or *predatory business practices* such as *price discrimination*, sales below cost, and *kickbacks*.

The consequences of high industry concentration include *monopolistic pricing, misallocation of resources* (despite *economies of scale*), uneconomical *product differentiation*, and greater economic instability.

Contrary to conventional wisdom in this country about the reasons for Japanese success in exporting, it is not so much the result of cartels and government help, but due more to the vigorous competition between Japanese firms in their home markets.

# Perspective

## An Imperfect World

**Robinson, Joan Violet (1903–1984)**
The daughter of a British major-general, Joan Robinson received an "upper class" education in exclusive English schools. She taught at Cambridge University for 42 years until her retirement in 1973. She visited the United States to deliver lectures to various groups, including the American Economic Association, and she spent a few months at Stanford University in 1969 as a Special Professor.

Referred to at times by other economists as "the magnificent queen" and "the magnificent tigress," her small stature belied the force of her presence. In face-to-face debates, the rigor of her uncompromising intellectual honesty was a match for such leading American economists as Nobel Prize-winners Paul Samuelson and Robert Solow.

In addition to her work on the structure of industry and capital theory, she wrote on such subjects as Marxian economics (*Essay on Marxian Economics*, 1942) and China (*The Cultural Revolution in China*, 1969).

Classical economists, starting with Adam Smith (1723–1790) and culminating in the neoclassical writings of Alfred Marshall (1842–1924), formulated their economic ideas around the concept of pure competition and its antithesis, pure monopoly. But the world is not composed of purely competitive and purely monopolistic markets. In the real world, industries lie somewhere between these extremes.

One of the first economists to light the way through the murky regions of imperfect competition was Joan Robinson. In her classic work, *The Economics of Imperfect Competition* (1933), she developed a model of an economy consisting of shared monopolies. Reversing the approach of earlier economists, she treated pure competition as a special case, just as it is in the real world.

In her subsequent writings, Robinson explored the relationship of the market behavior of business enterprises and labor unions to the economic growth and stability of the capitalist system. In her view, the desire of capitalists to retain as much as they can of sales revenues for reinvestment and growth is in conflict with the desire by labor unions to obtain a larger share of the proceeds for the workers.

The struggle between these two monopolistic forces, big business and big labor, creates uncertainty in the business world and causes fluctuations in economic growth. Also, Robinson believed the efforts of businesses and unionized workers to increase their respective shares of business income contributes to inflation.

Robinson was one of the century's leading economic theorists and was considered a prime candidate for the Nobel Prize in economics. Nonetheless, she had a disdain for the abstract mathematical manipulations that are so common in modern economic theory. She described the mathematical economists' models as being "such a thin story that they have to put it into algebra."

More than most of her contemporaries, Robinson's approach to economics was strongly tied to the realities of market practices. She made significant contributions to economics by wedding the theoretical models of the neoclassical and marginalist schools of economics to the pragmatism of Veblen and the institutionalists.

# For Further Study and Analysis

## Study Questions

1. According to Figure 1, page 167, what was the period of highest productivity growth in the past 30 years? What was the period of lowest productivity growth? Approximately what was the difference in productivity growth rates during those two periods?

2. Why did Motorola insist that its suppliers compete for the Malcolm Baldrige Award?

3. What is a recent example of a product, domestic or imported, that was targeted at a specific market niche?

4. If the increase in new producer's durable equipment does not keep pace with the increase in the size of the labor force, what will happen to productivity? Why?

5. Table 1 lists some negative growth factors that have reduced the growth of output. Should businesses avoid these costs? How are they related to the socio-economic goals discussed in chapter 2, page 51?

6. What sorts of worker skills are necessary in order for EI programs to work successfully?

7. In 1989, total sales of the aerospace industry in the United States amounted to $132.4 billion. The largest producers were Boeing with $20.3 billion in sales, United Technologies with $19.8 billion in sales, McDonnell Douglas with $15 billion in sales, and Rockwell International with $12.6 billion in sales. What was the concentration ratio in the aerospace industry? Was the industry monopolistic, competitive, or in between?

8. How do monopolies manage to keep prices higher than they would be in a competitive market? Why do they not raise their prices even higher?

9. Do the companies that have the largest sales also have the largest profits? What might explain differences between the sales rank of a company and its profits rank?

10. What are examples of informative advertising? What are examples of non-informative advertising?

## Exercises in Analysis

1. From the most recent Economic Report of the President or another source find the productivity increase for the previous year and compare it with the average for 1984–88 shown in Figure 1.

2. Survey local industries or firms that you know about through personal contacts and write a paper on their worker training programs.

3. Select an industry that is important in your state or province and write a short paper on the extent to which that industry is concentrated.

4. Write a short paper defending or attacking the results of concentration of industry in the United States over the past 25 years.

## Further Reading

Dertouzos, Michael L., Richard K. Lester, and Robert M. Solow. *Made in America: Regaining the Productive Edge.* Cambridge, Mass.: MIT Press, 1989. This is a thorough examination of the performance of American industry and how it can be improved, the results of a two-year study by a Massachusetts Institute of Technology Commission on Industrial Productivity.

Fallows, James. *More Like Us: Making America Great Again.* Boston: Houghton Mifflin, 1989. This book emphasizes the cultural factors in economic performance, comparing the U.S. and Japanese economies.

Goddard, Walter E. *Just-in-Time.* Essex Junction, Vt.: Oliver Wright, 1986. More than merely a description of the just-in-time system, it discusses the building of a "just-in-time environment" with chapters on "The Thinking Worker—The Secret Weapon" and "Taking the Quality High Road," among other topics.

Green, Mark, and John F. Berry. *The Challenge of Hidden Profits : Reducing Corporate Bureaucracy and Waste.* New York: William Morrow, 1985. This book reports on studies of corporate mismanagement and provides interviews with executives and others.

Ishinomori, Sho-taro. *Japan Inc.: An Introduction to Japanese Economics.* Berkeley, Calif.: University of California Press, 1988. This book explores the operation of the Japanese economy and its economic relations with other countries in an unusual format—as a comic book. It was written for the Japanese people, especially students, and subsequently translated for U.S. publication.

Lardner, James. *Fast Forward: Hollywood, the Japanese, and the Onslaught of the VCR.* New York: W. W. Norton, 1987. A very readable book detailing the story of how an American invention was lost to Japanese producers by default.

Porter, Michael. *The Competitive Advantage of Nations.* New York: The Free Press, 1990. The results of a four-year study of the degree of success in global markets of ten countries shows that the ability to compete internationally depends on improvements in technology and productivity that result from vigorous competition in a nation's markets.

Prestowitz, Clyde V., Jr. *Trading Places: How We Allowed Japan to Take the Lead.* New York: Basic Books, 1988. Examines the factors in the Japanese economy that have led to its ascendancy and the factors in the U.S. economy that have led to its descendancy. Presents future prescriptions for both countries.

Rutledge, John, and Deborah Allen. *Rust to Riches: The Coming of the Second Industrial Revolution.* New York: Harper & Row, 1989. The authors begin this book with a futuristic look backwards from the year 2041 on the reasons for the demise of General Motors. Despite this dour introduction, the book's outlook is optimistic. Its authors believe that the baby boomers will rescue the U.S. economy as they mature and shift from consumption to savings, thus providing more capital for investment. At the same time, the Japanese economy is expected to slow because of increased consumer materialism and decreased savings there.

Sobel, Robert. *Car Wars.* New York: E. P. Dutton, 1984. The story of how the U.S. auto industry succumbed to foreign competition, then rebounded.

## chapter 8

# GOVERNMENT AND BUSINESS

*One industry in which corporate fish have been swallowing other corporate fish at a rapid rate in recent years is long-distance telephone service. The telephone service industry provides a good example of government intervention in a market economy—and the rationale and problems involved.*

## Reach Out and Swallow Someone

For over a century, the American Telephone and Telegraph Company, known as "Ma Bell," held a virtual monopoly over the provision of telephone service to the nation's households and businesses. It began in 1876 when Alexander Graham Bell first spoke over a wire to his assistant: "Mr. Watson, come here! I want to see you!" and took out a patent on the telephone.

The hold of AT&T over the telephone industry was legally approved by the Communications Act of 1934, which made it an "authorized monopoly." Although a few thousand local telephone companies continued to exist, those that were not absorbed into the AT&T system were but a small fraction of the telephone business. AT&T also had exclusive rights to provide long-distance service. In return for this government approval to operate as a monopoly, and to prevent it from exploiting its monopoly power, AT&T's rates and services were regulated by a government agency, the Federal Communications Commission (FCC).

Under this arrangement, Ma Bell prospered mightily. At the time its monopoly reign ended, AT&T, classified as a service company, had more assets than the top three industrial corporations combined. With some 1,100,000 employees, it was the largest private employer in the world. The company also had the largest number of stockholders, over 3 million. Its dividend payments were so dependable that its stock was referred to as "the widows and orphans stock."

Ma Bell connected over 800 million telephone calls a day among 186 million telephones. It did so with an efficiency that was the envy of the rest of the world. Comedians got a lot of mileage out of Ma Bell jokes; but in other countries, even the most industrially advanced, telephone service was no laughing matter. It was more likely to incite fury than humor.

Despite all its success, AT&T was beset by increasing problems from different quarters. One of its problems was with the government. The Justice Department believed that AT&T was abusing its monopoly position. The first action against the company was taken in 1949 when the government brought suit to force it to detach itself from its manufacturing subsidiary, Western Electric.

Unlike the telephone services provided by Bell, the prices of the equipment manufactured by Western Electric were not regulated. But since AT&T had a monopoly over telephone service and got all its equipment from Western Electric, in effect Western Electric was in a monopoly position as well. This

Telephone companies use fiber optics like the ones pictured at the beginning of this chapter to connect telephones all over the world—even a cordless phone in a car.

meant that other companies were virtually frozen out of the telephone equipment business. Over 90% of telephone equipment production was in the hands of Western Electric, the remainder produced by others for private exchanges. It also meant that AT&T was able to charge high prices for the equipment sold to its local service companies, the costs of which could then be incorporated into their rate base and passed on to customers in their telephone bills.

The antitrust suit dragged on in the courts for seven years before the government and the company reached a compromise. AT&T was allowed to keep Western Electric, but it had to agree to license its equipment technology to competitors and to confine its operations to the telephone business. In 1956 this

restraint from entering other fields did not seem very important. But by the 1980s, with the growing importance of computers and other technologies in the newly emerging "information industry," AT&T was chafing at the bit.

In 1974, the Justice Department again filed suit to break off Western Electric from the rest of AT&T, charging the company with continuing abuse of its monopoly. This case lasted even longer than the first; and, like the first, was ultimately resolved by a compromise agreement, a so-called "consent decree." On January 1, 1984, AT&T was divorced from the local telephone service companies, which were reorganized into seven independent regional firms.

Ma Bell was left with its long-distance

services, its equipment manufacturing, and the freedom to pursue such newly emerging markets as computers and data processing. But in all of these it faced something unfamiliar to the Goliath of the communications industry—competition. New providers of long-distance services undercut AT&T rates by 15% to 20%—MCI, Sprint, Telecom, Skyline, and Metrofone, to name a few. In the equipment market, private branch exchanges (PBXs) using new electronic technologies became more important. Equipment manufacturers such as West Germany's Siemens and Sweden's L. M. Ericsson siphoned off Western Electric's business. As for its Data Systems division, it incurred annual losses of over $200 million in the late 1980s.

As the new decade dawned, however, things were looking up for the dowdy dowager. A complete corporate reorganization in December 1988 divided the company into 19 separate semi-autonomous divisions, each one competing for customers and responsible for its bottom-line results. Rising equipment sales and a projected 1990 break-even point for Data Systems improved the company's overall profit margin.

But the most promising change for AT&T was in the long-distance phone service market. The differential in rates between AT&T and its competitors diminished to less than 5%. More significantly, there were fewer and fewer competitors to exert downward pressure on prices. Between 1984 and 1989 AT&T had lost 17 points in its share of the long-distance calling market to competitors. But it still retained 68% of the market. And mergers and acquisitions by MCI and Sprint were turning the industry into an oligopoly dominated by only three firms.

As a result, the price wars that followed immediately after deregulation have given way to competition in promoting quality and service instead, forms of competition less hazardous to profits. The long-distance telephone service industry, once a monopoly tightly controlled by the government, is transformed into a maturing oligopoly with "pricing discipline." For an industry provid-

ing an essential service, and in which there can be no competition from Japanese suppliers to hold down prices, that may be good news for its stockholders but bad news for its customers.

## Chapter Preview

*In the mixed economy of the United States, government plays a large role in the nation's business. In this chapter we shall examine the relationship between government and business by asking: What does the government do to regulate monopoly? Why, in a market economy, does the government produce goods and services? What is the role of government in protecting consumers, workers, and the environment?*

## Learning Objectives

*After completing this chapter, you should be able to:*

1. *Explain the purposes of the Interstate Commerce Act and the Sherman, Clayton, and Celler-Kefauver Acts.*
2. *Explain the purpose of industry R&D consortiums and why they are exempt from the antitrust laws.*
3. *List the causes of natural monopoly and indicate what industries fall under that classification.*
4. *Explain how public policy deals with natural monopolies.*
5. *Discuss the positive and negative aspects of regulation.*
6. *Explain the reasons for and the consequences of deregulation.*
7. *Identify the kinds of goods and services that constitute collective goods, and explain why the government provides them.*
8. *Explain the concepts of external economies and external costs.*
9. *Explain how the government protects workers and consumers.*
10. *Describe three alternative ways by which the government can reduce pollution by getting firms to internalize the external costs of environmental pollution.*

crops

## What Does the Government Do to Regulate Monopoly?

The last section in the preceding chapter discussed the economic consequences of monopolistic industries. The disadvantages for the economy of monopoly behavior were recognized at least as early as the eighteenth century, pointed out by Adam Smith in *The Wealth of Nations*. But it wasn't until the end of the nineteenth century that government undertook measures to curb monopolies.

**Antitrust legislation**  Much as AT&T dominated the modern business scene, the powerhouses of the previous century were the railroad trusts. They generated a great deal of public resentment because of their monopolistic behavior. Especially angry were the farmers, who were almost totally dependent on railroads to transport their crops to market. Because farmers had little choice of transportation services, the railroads serving particular farming regions could charge extremely high rates. This enabled the railroads to give rebates (partial returns of payments) to large industrial shippers as a means of attracting their business. These and other abuses led to the passage of the Interstate Commerce Act by Congress in 1887. This law required that all rail rates for railroad traffic between states be fair and reasonable. The Interstate Commerce Act strictly forbade competing railroads from making arrangements for sharing traffic and earnings. It required that all rates be published and adhered to, thus limiting rate discrimination. To oversee the application of the Interstate Commerce Act, Congress established the Interstate Commerce Commission (ICC).

**trust**  a combination of producers in the same industry under one direction for the purpose of exerting monopoly power.
**rate discrimination (price discrimination)**  charging different customers different rates for services of equal production cost.

The Interstate Commerce Act was the first antitrust legislation, but because the railroads were not the only businesses abusing monopoly powers, a more comprehensive law soon followed. The Sherman Antitrust Act was passed in 1890 declaring illegal all contracts, combinations of business firms, and conspiracies that were in restraint of interstate or foreign trade. Any person who monopolized, attempted to monopolize, or conspired with others to monopolize any part of commerce between the states or with foreign countries was guilty of a misdemeanor.

The Sherman Act formed the basic national antitrust legislation. However, lack of enforcement funding, nonaggressive attorneys general, and conservative interpretation of the law by the courts made the Sherman Act relatively ineffective in the years following its passage. In fact, many monopoly practices became more apparent after its enactment. The Clayton Antitrust Act (1914) helped to remedy this situation by putting teeth in the Sherman Act. Among other things, it prevented firms from acquiring stock in competing companies and it prohibited price discrimination if the price discrimination injures competition. Later, price discrimination that injures buyers was also outlawed, unless the difference in prices charged to two buyers could be justified by actual differences in the costs of supplying the buyers.

The Sherman and Clayton Acts were aimed at preventing collusion among firms to raise prices and at practices that reduced competition in the marketplace. But the merger of two competing firms into a single company was not prohibited, and there were many such mergers following the end of World War II. As a result, the Celler-Kefauver Antimerger Act was passed in 1950 to slow down the wave of mergers. Congress was concerned about the increasing amount of concentration in American industry. The Celler-Kefauver Act forbids mergers by a company acquiring the assets of another company when this would lessen competition. It has greatly reduced horizontal mergers, but not vertical and conglomerate mergers, which do not directly increase the concentration ratio.

The government has not attempted to prevent the acquisition by MCI and Sprint of competing telephone companies because it sees their growth as a means of reducing the dominance of AT&T.

**Industrial consortiums**   In order to meet the challenge of global competition described in the last chapter, there has been some modification of antitrust policy. The government has initiated a program of actively encouraging collaboration among the firms in certain industries in research and development. The most important instance was in 1989 when the

Been Rolling a Little too High.

Policing the railroad monopoly was the first mandate of the ICC as shown in this early cartoon.

**antitrust legislation**   laws which prohibit or limit monopolies or monopolistic practices.

Commerce Department organized the leading semiconductor companies into an industry consortium for development of advanced chipmaking technology. The consortium, Sematech, was formed of 14 companies and partly funded by the Pentagon.

The National Co-operative Research Act of 1984 exempts companies engaged in joint R&D projects from some antitrust provisions. In the 5 years following its passage there were 134 joint ventures registered under the act, shielding the companies against civil antitrust suits for triple damages.

In other actions to facilitate cooperative research efforts, the government has created more than 30 research centers at universities with the goal of promoting rapid application of the most recent technological discoveries to production. Since 1985 the government-funded National Science Foundation has set up 18 Engineering Research Centers at universities to encourage academic research specifically related to the needs of industry.

Legislation passed in 1986 permits the government's own laboratories to collaborate with industries in turning the results of their research into useful products.

There is pressure from business to relax the antitrust laws further in order to allow for joint manufacturing and marketing activities as well as research. Such a liberalization of antitrust policies, however, could be expected to result in less domestic competition, higher prices, a greater rate of inflation, rising interest rates, and ultimately lower investment as a consequence.

**Public utility regulation** There are some industries in which competitive conditions, having a number of firms competing in the same market, would be inefficient. These are industries where natural monopolies exist, industries where the market is best served when there is only one firm. Public utility companies fall in this category.

Local telephone service is an example of a natural monopoly. Two or more telephone companies serving the same city would have to string duplicate telephone wires on duplicate telephone poles or lay duplicate underground cables. Furthermore, subscribers to one telephone company could not call friends subscribing to a different company. As a matter of fact, this happened in the early days of the telephone industry. It is more efficient to have only one company provide service in a natural monopoly industry. Local telephone service, electrical power service, and the supplying of water and natural gas are all examples of natural monopolies.

Natural monopolies arise when there are economies of scale in production that encompass the market. One large utility company serving a city or region is considered more

**industry consortium** a combination of firms in an industry to carry out a common purpose.

**natural monopoly** an industry in which the economies of scale are so extensive that a single firm can supply the whole market more efficiently than two or more firms could; natural monopolies are generally public utilities.

Due to economies of scale, electricity is often more efficiently provided by one utility. The utility is then considered a natural monopoly and is subject to regulation by a public utility commission.

efficient than a number of smaller ones. Because of the lower costs that result when one firm supplys the whole market, the government treats public utilities differently from other industries. It either grants a franchise to a single firm and then closely regulates it, or provides the service itself, as with community-owned utilities.

In order to prevent privately owned public utilities from charging monopolistic prices or providing inadequate service, public utility commissions are appointed to regulate the companies. When the utility wants to raise its rates or reduce the level of its service, the commission holds public hearings at which concerned parties, including consumers, give testimony. It then approves, disapproves, or modifies the proposed changes. If a commission finds that a utility company has been overcharging customers, it can order refunds to be made.

Government regulation of public utilities faces the problem of reconciling adequate service with a fair return to the investors. Up until 1989 AT&T was allowed a profit rate of 12.75% on its investment in interstate transmission facilities. This was considered a fair return for a public utility, for which the investment risks are less than for other businesses. Such calculations, however, are beset with pitfalls. If the equipment that AT&T invested in was produced by its subsidiary, Western Electric, and was overpriced, AT&T would make more than a fair return. Also, there was no way

**public utility commission** a regulatory body whose members are appointed by government to set rates and services provided by public utility firms.

to determine how much of AT&T's central administrative costs should be allocated to its long-distance telephone services.

But the greatest drawback to the fair-return principle of regulation is that it discourages improvements in efficiency and innovation because any resulting increase in profits is eliminated by offsetting rate reductions. As a result of these concerns, on July 1, 1989, the Federal Communications Commission (FCC) switched from setting a cap on AT&T's profit return to capping the prices it could charge for types of service. By permitting price increases less than the rate of inflation, the FCC hopes to encourage efficiency and innovation. This allows the company to keep larger profits and at the same time pass on some of the benefits to consumers.

**Deregulation** The difficulty of establishing rates that return no more or less than a fair profit on a regulated company's investment is only one of the problems faced by government regulation. With respect to regulated industries other than public utilities, the original purpose of government regulation was to prevent monopoly and foster competition. However, in many cases, regulation resulted in restricting competition rather than promoting it. The airline and trucking industries are examples of industries which were regulated in such a way as to prevent competition.

Growing dissatisfaction with the results of regulation has led to widespread deregulation in recent years. Railroad regulatory reform acts in 1976 and 1980 allowed railroads to set prices, start new services, abandon old services, and sign long-term contracts without Interstate Commerce Commission approval. Under the Airline Deregulation Act of 1978, the airlines were freed to select their routes and set their prices for the first time in 40 years. The Motor Carrier Act of 1980 did the same thing for the interstate trucking industry, despite opposition by the large trucking firms and the Teamsters Union. Both feared that increased competition would reduce hauling rates, profits, and wages in the industry. Partial deregulation has also been applied to banks, savings and loan associations, and other financial services firms.

Deregulation has not been accomplished without pain. Some older firms could not meet the new competition and failed, putting their employees out of work. Some new firms expanded too aggressively and also failed. Labor unions in industries where regulation limited competition enjoyed high wages by forcing the firms to share their monopolistic revenues. After deregulation introduced competitive pricing into an industry, many union members were forced to take pay cuts. Others lost their jobs due to cost-cutting reorganizations by the firms. Even customers sometimes suffered.

**deregulation** the process of eliminating government regulations and reducing the scope and power of regulatory bodies.

Airline passengers were left stranded with useless tickets when an airline could no longer pay its bills and had to shut down. Bank depositors were hit with large increases in service charges when banks had to pay competitive interest rates and made up the revenue losses by raising their service fees. Families, whose basic telephone service had been subsidized by revenue from business long-distance calls under AT&T, found bigger telephone bills after decentralization of the industry.

Despite these numerous problems, deregulation has in general achieved its aims. It has revitalized industries, providing consumers with a wider selection of services, usually at lower prices. Where prices have gone up—local telephone service charges, for example—the increases can be attributed to an end to artificial pricing structures that do not reflect actual costs. It is a basic tenet of economics that prices should be in accord with costs in order to obtain the most efficient allocation of resources. If prices are higher than production costs, not enough can be sold to employ sufficient resources in the industry. Consumer wants will not be satisfied as fully as with a price system that reflects actual production costs. Achieving a more rational allocation of our resources is one of the main objectives of deregulation.

*[Handwritten margin notes: Deregulation: process of eliminating government regulations and the power of regulations still remaining. Aim of deregulation: - revitalized industry - wider variety of the products]*

Deregulaton of the airlines provided consumers with a wider selection of services at lower prices. But when an airline went bankrupt in the competitive market, passengers were sometimes left stranded with useless tickets.

# case application

## Less-Friendly Skies?

Developments in the airline industry after deregulation have paralleled those in long-distance telephone service. Prior to the Airline Deregulation Act of 1978, the domestic airline industry was a government-controlled cartel. Routes between cities were allocated to specific carriers by the Civil Aeronautics Board (CAB) and competition from other airlines was not permitted. The CAB set fares according to the distance flown.

Following deregulation, a number of new airlines entered the industry, and existing airlines expanded their services to routes that that had previously been closed to them. There were constant fare wars to attract passengers to these expanded services.

Not all areas of the country benefited from more air service. Under CAB regulation, airlines had been forced to provide unprofitable service to small cities in order to be granted routes to service major markets. After deregulation, some small cities lost all airline service.

There was concern that safety would also suffer under deregulation. With cutthroat price competition and rapid expansion of routes, it was feared that airlines would skimp on equipment maintenance and allow unsafe planes to take off. These fears have proved groundless. Although the CAB was phased out of existence, the Federal Aviation Administration (FAA) has responsibility for inspecting airline equipment maintenance and safety procedures.

The safety record for air travel has actually improved significantly since deregulation. In the decade following deregulation, the average number of commercial airline accidents decreased by more than one-third compared to the decade before deregulation. Considering the great increase in the number of people flying, the safety improvement was even more striking. There was a decrease of 57% in fatal accidents per million passenger miles traveled. These safety improvements are credited to advancing technology and better understanding of dangers like wind shear rather than to deregulation, but deregulation apparently has not been detrimental to safety.

Other aspects of air travel have not fared as well under deregulation. The increased number of flights, especially during the popular morning and evening departure and arrival hours, has resulted in frequent delays. There is flagrant overbooking, causing passengers to be bumped from flights. Complaints about lost and battered luggage have increased faster than passenger traffic. And complaints about inedible airline food are louder than ever.

But the prime consideration for most passengers is what happens to fares. Deregulation clearly made flying more affordable and to a large extent was responsible for the great expansion of air travel. Adjusted for inflation, air fares declined 21% between 1978 and 1988, and at least 43% more people were flying than before deregulation. The Brookings Institution calculated that consumers saved about $100 billion in fares during that 10-year period.

But in the latter 1980s the air transportation industry began to change. Numerous mergers and takeovers resulted in decreased competition; and the smaller, weaker airlines that were not absorbed by large carriers were driven out of business. By 1989 there had been more than 50 mergers and 150 bankruptcies since deregulation. Price wars diminished, and fares began to rise faster than the general inflation rate.

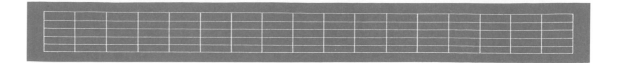

market. At nine major airports, over 60% of all traffic is controlled by a single airline. The effect on prices of this lack of competition is clear. A Department of Transportation study found that between 1985 and 1988, while air fares rose 11% nationwide, in 7 of the hub cities fares went up between 21% and 35%. Another study of airline pricing, conducted by Severin Borstein of the University of Michigan, revealed a strong link between prices and the amount of competition in a particular market. He found, for example, that USAir, whose hub is Pittsburgh, charges 20.5 cents per mile on flights to and from Pittsburgh where it has an 85% share of the market, while it charges only 15.8 cents per mile on flights to other destinations. Similar differences exist in pricing for TWA in St. Louis (83% market share), Northwest in Minneapolis (79%), American in Dallas (63%), Delta in Atlanta (59%), and United in Chicago (51%).

As a result of consolidation of the industry into a small number of large carriers, we can expect higher fares and more profits for the airlines. For the ticket buyer, the skies may not be as friendly.

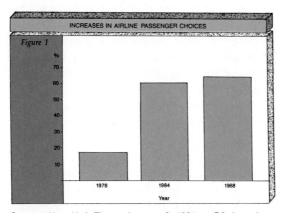

Source: *New York Times*, January 2, 1991, p. D8, based on data from U.S. Transportation Department. Reprinted by permission.

This figure shows the percentages of passengers with a choice of three or more airlines on the route they want to fly. Passengers have these choices because even carriers that dominate hubs must still compete with airlines that fly to the same destinations through other hubs. However, residents of cities that have become hubs for single carriers and who are therefore beginning and ending their flights in those cities are paying more.

Fare increases were especially noticeable in those cities where one carrier dominated the market. Following deregulation, airlines went to a route system based on hub cities. Major carriers have one or two hub cities for their fleet. They fly passengers from their point of origin to the airline's hub city, where they are consolidated into planes flying to a passenger's final destination. This is cost-effective for the airlines, though for passengers it is more time-consuming than nonstop flights.

Another advantage the hub-and-spoke system gives the airlines is more control over prices. Since flights into and out of each hub city are dominated by the airline that uses that hub, it has a near monopoly on that

## *Economic Reasoning*

1. Is air transportation a natural monopoly? Explain.
2. What benefits resulted from deregulating the airline industry? What drawbacks?
3. Should the Celler-Kefauver Act be rigorously applied to the airline industry? Why or why not?

# Why Does the Government Produce Goods and Services?

In a market economy, consumer sovereignty is supposed to dictate what is produced. Consumers voting with their dollars in the marketplace decide how resources will be allocated: this product or service will be supplied because it can be sold at a profit, and that product or service won't be supplied because it can't be sold at a profit. If that is the way the system is supposed to work, why does the government provide a variety of goods and services that do not produce profits? Why does it provide mail service, highways, bridges, dams, lighthouses, harbors, air traffic controls, national defense, and, at the local level, schools and police and fire departments? This next section examines these questions.

**Collective goods**  Among major countries, a privately owned and operated telephone system serving the nation is unique to the United States. In other countries, the telephone system, like the postal system here, is a government

Air traffic controllers are trained and paid by the Federal Aviation Administration.

agency. In many countries, in fact, the telephone and postal systems are operated by the same government agency. The railroad, electric power, and various other industries are also government-owned in most countries, even those countries that are considered capitalist.

Goods and services produced by the government are collective goods. One reason for the existence of collective goods is that, for some types of production, it is not feasible or efficient to recover the full costs by charging the people directly who use the product or service. If the good or service is considered of sufficient importance to society to justify its production, but it cannot be sold for a price which covers its production and distribution costs, it may be supplied by the government. Since the profit-making private sector is not motivated by profit to provide these goods or services, the government does. It pays for them, in whole or in part, out of tax money. Collective goods are also called public goods.

Some things are clearly public goods. National defense is an obvious case. It is not feasible for individuals to purchase their own ICBMs to protect their homes against attack from foreign enemies. In the case of other collective goods, such as sidewalks, it might be possible to collect user fees to pay for the service, but the collection costs would be too great to make it workable. In earlier times, some towns had privately owned, for-profit fire departments. When the fire truck arrived at a fire, homeowners sometimes had to negotiate the fee for putting out the fire while they watched their house burn.

National defense, sidewalks, and fire departments are obvious cases of collective goods. Other collective goods such as Amtrak, the postal service, libraries, museums, and public schools, are not so obvious. There have been proposals to turn each of these services over to the private sector of the economy, or in some cases, if they can't pay their way, abolish them altogether. The issue of the movement for privatization of government services as a way of saving tax dollars and reallocating resources will be examined in more detail in chapter 13.

**External economies**  Goods and services sometimes benefit people other than the purchasers. A telephone, for instance, not only benefits the subscriber, but also provides benefits to everyone who places a call to that number. The subscriber pays for the telephone and pays the monthly service charges, but all of the callers receive benefits from that telephone as well, even though they do not pay for it. Of course, most of them have telephones of their own which they do pay for. But the more people that have telephones, the more useful a telephone is to each person. A telephone is

The Peacekeeper, a four-stage intercontinental ballistic missile, is an example of a government-owned collective good. Shown above is a test launch of the Peacekeeper by the U.S. Air Force at Vandenberg AFB, California.

**collective good (public good)** an economic good (includes services) that is supplied by the government either with no direct payment by the recipient or at a price less than the cost of providing it.
**privatization** the process of selling government assets to private buyers and/or relinquishing government services to the private sector.

The National Gallery represents a greater value than what some consumers would be willing to pay for its services. Governments often support museums and other institutions that benefit all of society.

a good that has <u>external economies</u>; it benefits not only the purchaser, but other people as well.

The existence of external economies is often a reason for governments to provide collective goods. If goods and services are supplied by private enterprises, the price must cover their costs. Buyers must pay for the total costs of production and distribution. If people are unwilling to pay the price, the goods and services are not produced. However, there are some products for which the external economies are so significant that their production is justified, even if buyers are unwilling to pay the price.

External economies, for example, are a justification for the

**external economies** benefits which accrue to parties other than the producer and purchaser of the good or service; benefits for which payment is not collected.

government to pay for education. If our country did not have a literate population it could not operate its industries efficiently or provide the professional services needed by people. Also, the public could not effectively participate in the political process. As a result, the country would be less productive and probably less politically stable. Because of the external economies resulting from education, families are not required to pay the full costs of their children's schooling. The government pays most of the costs for public education. Public health services, medical research, postal services, and city transit systems are other instances where services benefit people other than those directly receiving the services.

Libraries and museums are a variation of this type of collective good. They are considered merit goods. They enrich our entire culture, not just individuals. Because the social value of such services is greater than the price buyers will pay, the government provides the services either for free or at less than full cost.

**Collective goods and equity**   Sometimes collective goods are provided in order to meet the goal of greater equity. Public transportation, for example, is most heavily used by lower-income groups, including young people and the elderly. This is one of the justifications for government subsidies to public transit systems. It helps to achieve the socioeconomic goal of greater economic equity.

An alternate way to achieve the goal of greater equity would be direct subsidies to low-income people. In some ways, this would satisfy the goal of equity more efficiently. Income supplements might help low-income people more than subsidized bus fares because such supplements permit them to choose the best transportation means for their particular circumstances. The same reasoning has led to rent supplements for the poor as an alternative to public housing.

The argument over which is the best approach, income supplements or public services, continues. The answer may depend on whether providing a particular public service satisfies other objectives as well as equity. It is possible that direct income supplements to low-income families to help them pay for private transportation could be less expensive than maintaining public transit. But it would also result in more pollution, greater traffic and parking congestion, and more vehicle accidents.

It has been proposed that collective goods be subjected to cost-benefit analyses to balance total costs against total benefits. Such analyses are difficult, however, where externalities and equity considerations are involved.

**merit goods**  goods (including services) which have a social value over and above their utility for the individual consumer.

**externalities**  external economies or external dis-economies (external costs).

# case application

## Private Participation in Public Education

Education is the most important collective good provided by state and local governments. It absorbs over one-third of all state and local government spending (see chapter 13).

There is widespread concern over the condition of education in this country today. Over one-fourth of students drop out of school before graduation. Some 13% of the nation's 17-year-olds are functionally illiterate. Achievement tests given to students in 13 industrialized countries show American students rank 11th in chemistry, 9th in physics (for students who have taken two years of physics), and last in biology. Average Japanese 12th graders have a better command of mathematics than the top 5% of their American counterparts.

This situation disturbs parents, educators, and politicians. It also disturbs leaders of American industry, who wonder where they are going to get the workers they need in coming years for their high-tech factories and offices. As an example, Baldor Electric Company installed a new "flexible flow" manufacturing system at its Columbus, Mississippi, plant. Production was disrupted because, although computer-generated work orders clearly told employees *not* to weld motor shafts to rotors, they were welding them anyhow. Investigation turned up the fact that many of Baldor's employees simply couldn't read those orders. At a new Motorola factory that makes cellular phones in Schaumburg, Illinois, using highly automated equipment, just 25 out of 200 workers passed a basic skills test for jobs. Japanese automakers that have opened U.S.

plants found that they have to hire college graduates to fill assembly jobs that would have been filled by high school graduates in Japan.

In coming years there will be a shortfall of skilled labor at all levels. The fastest-growing job category in the 1990s will be technicians, with a growth of 38% in job openings by the end of the century. The National Science Foundation estimates that the United States will experience a shortage of 700,000 scientists by the year 2010. Currently, more than half of engineering Ph.D. degrees awarded in this country go to foreign nationals.

Concern over meeting the needs of American business for a competent labor force has led a number of companies and executives to get involved in the effort to improve education. A 1990 *Fortune* magazine poll of its list of 500 largest industrial corporations and 500 largest service corporations revealed that 98% of the companies responding to the poll contributed to public education. The principal form of assistance was contributing money (78% of the companies). Sizable percentages also provided students with summer jobs (76%), contributed materials or equipment to schools (64%), participated in school partnerships (48%), and encouraged employees to run for school boards (59%) or to tutor or teach (50%).

In the past, most corporate contributions have been at the college level, but businesses are increasingly getting involved in public education in the high schools and lower grades. They have come to understand that worker competency in basic skills is as im-

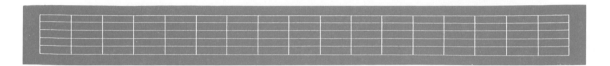

Businesses are becoming increasingly involved in public education. Some retail chains, for example, sponsor programs in which store receipts may be redeemed for computers to benefit students in kindergarten through high school.

portant to them as the contribution of the highly trained part of the labor force. They realize that they need to be part of the solution.

## *Economic Reasoning*

1. Is all education a collective good? Explain. *No*

2. Do corporations contribute to education because of the external benefits? Explain. *yes*

3. There are those who argue that education would have better results if it were not a collective good, but instead turned over to private enterprise, with government subsidies for families with schoolchildren. Do you think that "privatizing" education would be a good idea? Why or why not? *opportunity cost.*

213

# What Is the Role of Government in Protecting Consumers, Workers, and the Environment?

*It sets up regulations, and commisions who conduct research and dutys in order to protect - costumers - workers - environment*

Beginning in the 1960s, there has been a large increase in government involvement in the welfare of consumers, workers, and the environment. The activities of government in these respects are discussed in this analysis section.

**Consumer protection**   As civilized society developed, the dangers we face have become more of our own making than from nature—poisonous chemicals, polluted air, automobile accidents, defective products. And as the nature of the dangers has changed, so has the way we respond. We have increasingly looked to government to protect us from man-made dangers that we feel incapable of protecting ourselves from.

The U.S. Department of Transportation conducts crash tests such as this to evaluate automobile safety, in response to increasing consumer concerns. This is one example of how consumer protection has become a function of government.

*Table 1*          SELECTED GOVERNMENT REGULATORY AGENCIES

| Agency | Year Created | Regulates |
|---|---|---|
| *Agencies that regulate specific industries:* | | |
| Interstate Commerce Commission (ICC) | 1887 | Railroads, trucking, pipelines, barges, express carriers |
| Food and Drug Administration (FDA) | 1906 | Food, drugs, cosmetics |
| Federal Reserve Board (FRB) | 1913 | Banks |
| Federal Power Commission (FPC) | 1930 | Public utilities |
| Federal Communications Commission (FCC) | 1934 | Radio, television, telephone, telegraph |
| Federal Aviation Administration (FAA) | 1967 | Airline safety |
| National Highway Traffic Safety Administration (NHTSA) | 1970 | Motor vehicles |
| Nuclear Regulatory Commission (NRC) | 1975 | Nuclear power plants |
| *Agencies that regulate specific functions:* | | |
| Federal Trade Commission (FTC) | 1914 | Unfair business practices |
| Securities and Exchange Commission (SEC) | 1934 | Sales of securities |
| National Labor Relations Board (NLRB) | 1935 | Labor-management relations |
| Equal Employment Opportunity Commission (EEOC) | 1964 | Hiring practices |
| Environmental Protection Agency (EPA) | 1970 | Pollution of the environment |
| Occupational Safety and Health Administration (OSHA) | 1971 | Conditions in workplaces |
| Consumer Product Safety Commission (CPSC) | 1972 | Design and labeling of goods |

One dangerous place in modern society is the highway. Over 50,000 people are killed in automobile accidents in the United States each year. In order to reduce the death and injury rate, the Department of Transportation (DOT) has required automobile manufacturers to provide certain safety features such as seat belts, secure fuel tanks, and bumpers that meet federal standards. The DOT conducts crash tests on new car models to determine which ones give the passengers the most protection.

One of the most important government agencies dealing with product safety is the Food and Drug Administration (FDA). If foods or medicines are found to be unsafe, the FDA has the power to order them off the market. The agency conducts tests on prepared foods to find out if any of the ingredients are cancer-causing. No new drugs may be put on the market without the FDA's approval.

Another federal agency concerned with consumer safety is the Consumer Product Safety Commission. It has issued a recall of asbestos-insulated hair dryers, put an end to the use of benzene in paint removers, banned the use of Tris—a cancer-causing flame retardant in children's clothing—and required that slats on baby cribs be set close together to prevent strangulation.

There are government agencies not only to protect our health, but to protect our pocketbooks. The Federal Trade Commission tries to prevent deceptive advertising. It has made producers of aspirin pills, diet breads, toothpastes, cigarettes, and numerous other products either prove their claims or change their advertisements.

To protect the interests of investors and provide more stability to the financial markets, the Securities and Exchange Commission was set up in 1934 to regulate the stock market. It requires full disclosure of a company's financial condition when new stock is issued, and has helped eliminate stock swindles. (cheating)

In recent years there has been legislation requiring financial institutions and companies extending credit to provide the borrower with complete information about the true interest charges and payment conditions. In some states, customers are allowed to cancel certain kinds of purchase contracts within a few days after signing them. Some of the types of contracts which can be cancelled are land purchases in undeveloped land promotions and contracts signed with door-to-door salespeople. These laws are designed to protect consumers from being manipulated into hasty, unwise decisions by high-pressure sales techniques.

**Worker protection**   Over 10,000 workers are killed on the job each year and nearly 2 million suffer disabling injuries. As large as these figures are, they are less than they were in the 1960s, despite a near doubling of the size of the labor force.

Improved safety on the job is credited at least in part to the establishment of the Occupational Safety and Health Administration (OSHA) in 1971. The Occupational Safety and Health Act gave OSHA, in the Department of Labor, the power and responsibility to set standards for the workplace to protect workers from work-caused injury and illness. Since 1970, the year before OSHA was established, the rate of job fatalities has been cut in half and disabling injuries have declined from 30 to 16 for every million workers during the year. The improvement in the rates of workplace casu-

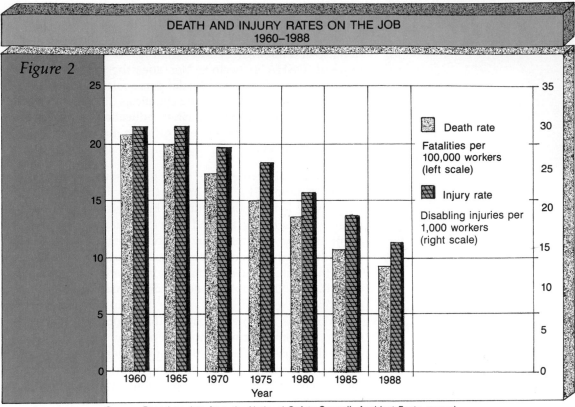

**DEATH AND INJURY RATES ON THE JOB**
**1960–1988**

Figure 2

Death rate

Fatalities per
100,000 workers
(left scale)

Injury rate

Disabling injuries per
1,000 workers
(right scale)

Year

Source: Based on data from the National Safety Council, *Accident Facts*, annual.

The rates of worker fatalities and disabling injuries on the job have been steadily decreasing, especially since the establishment of the Occupational Safety and Health Administration in 1971.

alties is even greater than the data indicates due to more complete reporting of casualties now than earlier.

However, OSHA regulations and plant inspections have been vigorously opposed by some businesses. It has been claimed that OSHA regulations cost industry too much, that they drive some companies out of business, and that they make competition with imports difficult because the increased costs must be reflected in higher prices. The American Textile Manufacturers Institute and twelve textile companies filed suit to overturn OSHA standards requiring mills to reduce cotton-dust levels in the plants. Cotton dust causes brown-lung disease among the workers. The textile firms maintained that the air-filtration systems needed to meet the standards would impose unreasonable costs on the firms. But the Supreme Court rejected the arguments of the textile industry. The Court held that the law only required that the needed safety measures be "feasible," not that they meet cost-benefit criteria; and therefore the textile plants were required to install the filtration equipment.

This toxic waste worker tests the chemicals in a stream in New York State. A tanning factory has made the water so polluted that no fish live downstream from the factory.

**external costs**  costs of the production process that are not carried by the producer unit or by the purchaser of the product and are therefore not taken into consideration in production and consumption decisions.
**internalize external costs**  the process of transforming external costs into internal costs so that the producer and consumer of a good pay the full cost of its production.

OSHA is prevented from regulating the greater part of the most dangerous industry of all—farming—where the annual death rate is 48 per 100,000 workers, higher than construction (34) and mining (25). More than 95% of all farms are off-limits to OSHA inspectors. Nor does the government do much to inform farmers of the dangers a farm family faces in operating machinery and using chemicals. It spends only 30 cents a year per farmer on safety education, while at the same time spending $4.48 per worker in industry and $244 per mine worker.

**Environmental protection**  The greenhouse effect discussed in chapter 1 is only one of the environmental problems with which the country has become concerned recently. Others are air and water pollution, toxic waste dumping, the accumulation of nonbiodegradeable plastic and other garbage, and urban noise pollution.

As the United States becomes more aware of the dangers of pollution, the public is demanding that the sources of pollution be curbed. One of the principal reasons why pollution has become so bad is that producers and consumers in some circumstances do not pay the full costs of what they use, including the environmental costs. Consumers of electricity do not have to pay on their utility bills the costs of environmental damage done by smoke from the power plants. Motorists do not have to include in the cost of running their cars the health and environmental damage resulting from automobile exhaust emissions. Airlines, and their passengers, do not generally have to pay for the noise pollution that they create in the neighborhoods of airports when landing and taking off. These costs, which are not paid by the user, are called external costs because they are imposed on other people.

The existence of external costs means that too much of a good is being produced and used. External costs often arise because the environment is treated as a free good (see chapter 1, p. 12). From the standpoint of economic efficiency, prices should always reflect the full production costs of a good or service. When there are external costs that are not covered by the market price, the equilibrium price is too low and the quantity produced too large for the most efficient allocation of resources. Just as prices should not be higher than production costs, as we've seen in the case of monopoly, neither should they be lower than the costs of the good, including the costs of any environmental damage resulting from its use.

The solution for this problem is to internalize the external costs by requiring producers and buyers to shoulder the full costs of production. In the case of electric power generation, this is accomplished by requiring the installation of smoke scrubbers on power plant stacks. For auto exhaust pollution, installation and proper maintenance of exhaust emission control devices is required. In the case of airport noise, the solutions are to require airlines to fly planes with quieter engines, restrict their hours of takeoffs and landings, and restrict their flight patterns. The cost of these pollution abatement requirements raises prices to consumers. But without such regulations, society subsidizes the production of pollution. Somebody has to pay the costs, and it is more resource-efficient for the user to pay than to allow external costs to shift the burden to others.

The above examples of direct regulation are the most common means used by government to protect the environment. Alternatives to these command-and-control regulations have been proposed as more economically efficient, saving costs.

One way to force an internalization of external environmental costs is to impose an emission charge on firms for the environmental damage they do. These are sometimes referred to as eco-taxes. The electric utility industry, for example, might be taxed $2 billion a year or more for spewing pollutants into the air. This would provide a strong incentive for the utilities to internalize their external costs by reducing smokestack emissions. Eco-taxes would be a more flexible, market-directed, less bureaucratic means of reducing industry environmental damage than regulation. The emission charges could be set high enough to get the level of environmental compliance desired. There would be the additional benefit that whatever amount of pollution remained would provide a source of government revenue.

A similar and even more market-oriented approach, one that is favored by many economists, would be for the government to sell emission allowances—so much per ton of emissions. This method would encourage those firms that found emission control less costly than buying the permits to clean up. At the same time it would enable other companies, for whom emission control was more costly, to purchase the right to continue polluting. There would be a market for emission allowances, allowing firms to buy and sell them. As with eco-taxes, the price of the permits could be set to achieve any desired level of environmental cleanliness, given that a totally pure environment is not technically or economically feasible. The comprehensive clean air bill that was passed in 1990 permits, among other things, sale of emission allowances granted to plants faced with heavy pollution control costs. The receipts from sale of the allowances allow the firms to recover some of the costs imposed on them by the bill.

The worker above covers toxic waste with plastic. Adding to the problem of pollution is the fact that producers and consumers often do not pay the full costs of what they use, including the environmental costs.

**command-and-control regulations** a system of administrative or statutory rules that requires the use of specific control devices to reduce pollution.
**eco-tax** a fee levied by the government on each unit of pollutant emitted.

# Environmental Murder

Residents of urban areas, hoping to flee pollution by a visit to pristine wilderness, are likely to be in for an unpleasant surprise. Even in the most remote locations, far from factories and highways, our forests and bodies of water are sick and dying from pollution. Once lush green mountaintops are denuded or sparsely covered by sickly trees that have ceased growing. Lakes in remote locations that formerly provided anglers with choice fishing are now dead, unable to support any life.

Tree damage is most apparent in the Appalachian mountain range, stretching from New England to the southern states. In recent years, some species of trees have declined by 25%. An environmental disaster threatens the important timber-products industry; among other effects, this could raise the cost of housing.

Although it is most obvious in the eastern part of the country, the environmental destruction is widespread. Excessive quantities of trees are dying in the San Bernardino Mountains of southern California, where harvests of ponderosa pines have declined by 80% in the last few decades. Lakes high in the Rocky Mountains no longer support the numbers of trout they once did. Salamanders are disappearing from their water habitats in the mountains of Arizona and New Mexico.

The principal suspect in this environmental murder is acid rain. Although the process is as yet not completely understood, acid rain is the result of sulfur dioxide and nitrogen oxide emissions, which are highly toxic to nature. Major sources of the emissions are coal-burning furnaces in the electric utility and metal smelting industries. The chemicals are carried by clouds until they fall in rain, poisoning the soil and bodies of water. As the clouds envelop mountaintops in their passage, the tree foliage combs some of the pollutants out of the air. This explains why the first and most serious forest damage is seen on the tops of mountains.

There are other theories about what is killing the forests. Disease, drought, ozone, airborne metallic particles, and natural growth cycles have all been proposed as possible causes. But air pollution, acid rain in particular, is the most likely villain.

In order to stop the damage to our forests before it becomes as destructive as it has already been in West Germany and other parts of Europe, more strict restrictions are proposed for smokestack emissions. To prevent air pollution in the area nearby, coal-burning plants built high smokestacks, some as tall as the Empire State building, to disperse the pollutants into the atmosphere. This prevented local air pollution, but created the acid rain problem.

The 1990 clean air legislation requires that electric utility companies must halve the amount of sulphur dioxide and nitrogen oxides that they spew into the air. These new requirements will cost the electric utility companies billions of dollars in equipment outlays and additional annual operating expenses. These costs will be added, of course, to customers' electricity bills.

## Economic Reasoning

1. What external costs are produced in the electric power industry? Why are they considered external costs?
2. How can external costs in the industry be internalized?
3. Of the three means available to bring about an internalization of the external costs in the industry, which means do you advocate, if any? Why?

# Putting It Together

In the last quarter of the nineteenth century, the growth of industries in which there were a few large firms conspiring to fix prices inspired legislation to curb their monopolistic behavior. The Interstate Commerce Act of 1887 put an end to the railroad *trust's* market-sharing agreements and *rate discrimination*. In 1890 the passage of the fundamental *antitrust legislation*, the Sherman Antitrust Act, made monopolies and attempts to monopolize illegal. The generality and vagueness of the Sherman Act made its enforcement difficult, so the Clayton Act (1914) spelled out specific anticompetitive practices which were prohibited. The wave of mergers after World War II led to the Celler-Kefauver Antimerger Act (1950) which prohibits one firm from acquiring the assets of another when this would substantially lessen competition.

To assist U.S. industry in meeting foreign competition, strict application of the antitrust laws has been modified by the National Co-operative Research Act. It permits companies to form an *industry consortium* for purposes of sharing the costs and results of R&D. Also, the government has established research centers at universities to promote a rapid application of new technology in production and permits government laboratories to collaborate with industries.

Certain types of monopolies are not illegal. These are *natural monopolies* such as *public utility* companies, which, for technological reasons, are more efficiently operated as single firms.

In the last decade, some regulated industries, such as railroads, trucking, airlines, petroleum, and banking, have been either partly or totally deregulated. One of the principal reasons for this *deregulation* was that the regulatory agencies were in some instances protecting and enforcing monopolization. Deregulation is aimed at increasing competition, lowering prices and increasing service in these industries.

Some types of goods and services do not lend themselves to distribution through normal market channels. National defense, highways and bridges, police and fire protection, and public transportation systems are examples of *collective goods*. One reason for the government supplying goods and services not provided by the private sector is the existence of

The breakup of the long-distance telephone service industry provides one example of the reasons for government intervention in a market economy, and the problems involved.

*external economies. Merit goods* such as libraries and museums are provided by the government because they enrich the culture. Another justification for publicly provided goods and services is that such actions help achieve the goal of greater economic equity.

Among the numerous government agencies that establish and enforce regulations to protect consumers are the Food and Drug Administration, Consumer Product Safety Commission, Department of Transportation, Interstate Commerce Commission, Federal Trade Commission, and Securities and Exchange Commission. Protection of workers on the job is provided under the Occupational Safety and Health Act, which is enforced by the Department of Labor.

One of the reasons for the extent of environmental pollution is that the environment is considered a free good by consumers and producers. They do not have to pay for dumping their wastes into it. Pollution can be reduced and resources, including the environment, more efficiently used if these *external costs* are *internalized*. Forcing industries to internalize the external costs of pollution can be accomplished by regulating the amount of pollution, imposing *eco-taxes,* or selling pollution permits.

# Perspective

## The Interstate Highway to Serfdom

**Friedrich August von Hayek (born 1899)**

Friedrich Hayek, as he is known in the United States, was born in Vienna, Austria. He began his teaching career there but in 1931 went to teach at the University of London, where he stayed for nearly two decades. In 1950 he moved to the University of Chicago where he was appointed Professor of Social and Moral Sciences. This impressive title reflected the expanse of Hayek's interests and writings, the scope of which includes economic theory and policy, political philosophy, legal theory, social and moral values, and experimental psychology. After 12 years at Chicago, Hayek taught for 7 years in Germany before returning to Austria to live. Some of his major publications include *Prices and Production* (1931), *The Pure Theory of Capital* (1941), *The Road to Serfdom* (1944), *Individualism and Economic Order* (1948), *The Constitution of Liberty* (1960), and *The Fatal Conceit: The Errors of Socialism* (1989).

*[handwritten notes:]*
*– non constructivist philosopher*
*– non government supporter.*
*– cost-benefit believer*

According to an old saying, "The road to hell is paved with good intentions." According to Friedrich von Hayek, the Nobel Prize–winning economist, the road to totalitarian slavery is paved with government planning. His views have gained a wide following, and *Business Week* magazine has referred to him as "the intellectual godfather of today's conservative economics."

Hayek was awarded the Nobel Prize for his work in theoretical economics dating back to the 1930s, but he is best known for his 1944 book on political philosophy, *The Road to Serfdom.* In that book he warns of the dangers of government intervention in the economy. He maintains that government planning and economic control are incompatible with competition and individualism. If the government attempts to manipulate the economy to achieve some objective such as greater equity, says Hayek, it will increasingly resort to totalitarian measures until all freedom is lost and democracy is extinguished.

In later writings, Hayek has labeled those who advocate collectivist ideas and urge government intervention in the economy as "constructivists." Constructivists are those who think that society can consciously devise policies and programs to change the way the system works and achieve certain goals. Constructivist programs do not work, according to Hayek, because they ignore fundamental rules of behavior that have evolved in society over a long period of time. Disregarding these rules, which have enabled existing societies to survive and prosper, will lead to social and economic decline. Hayek believes in an economic Darwinism by which the fittest have survived.

In his latest book, *The Fatal Conceit: The Errors of Socialism*, published when he was 89, Hayek states that man's "fatal conceit" is his belief that he "is able to shape the world around him according to his wishes."

Hayek is not altogether dogmatic, however, in his opposition to government regulations and programs. In *The Road to Serfdom* he allows that some types of government intervention might be justified as long as they do not unduly diminish competition.

"The only question here," Hayek wrote, "is whether in the particular instance the advantages gained are greater than the social costs they impose."

In other words, Hayek would apply a type of cost-benefit analysis to any regulation.

For
Further
Study
and
Analysis

## Study Questions

1. In what ways did monopolistic practices in the late nineteenth century frustrate the functioning of a free market?
2. How did the various laws passed by the federal government deal with the monopolistic abuses of certain industries?
3. Would you agree or disagree with the statement, "Once a natural monopoly, always a natural monopoly"? Why?
4. How are natural monopolies, such as utility companies, prevented from indulging in monopolistic practices?
5. Why should investors in utility companies be guaranteed a fair return on their investments? How would a fair return be determined?
6. Have you used any public goods (services) in the past week? What are they? Could you have obtained them from the private sector?
7. Why does the government subsidize public transportation when most people do not use it?
8. What would happen if the government got out of the lighthouse business? Would lighthouses be provided by private industry?

9. What are some external economies derived from goods or services that you have benefited from, but have not used or paid for yourself?
10. Prior to the 1970s, it was common practice for utility companies to give discounts on quantity consumption by large users of electrical power, thus promoting increased power consumption. Today, utility companies give their lowest rates to their smallest consumers—thereby promoting conservation of electrical power. Why do you think this reversal of policy has taken place?

## Exercises in Analysis

1. Long-distance telephone companies may charge different rates for phone calls at different times of the day. Does this practice reflect price discrimination? Defend your answer with facts and logic.
2. Locate at least five business firms in your community that have had to internalize previously external costs. What effects

did these newly internalized costs have on profits and on the prices charged for the companies' goods or services?

3. Use your library or media center to research the history of federal government regulations in the past year. List any new regulations that went into effect and any older regulations that were dropped.

4. Investigate the operations of the nearest mass transit system. How is it funded? What percentage of costs comes from fares? What percentage from subsidies? From what level of government do the subsidies come? What is the financial condition of the mass transit system you have investigated?

## Further Reading

Asch, Peter. *Consumer Safety Regulation: Putting a Price on Life and Limb.* New York: Oxford University Press, 1988. A technical treatment of the need for public protection and policies to provide it.

Barrows, Paul. *The Economic Theory of Pollution Control.* Cambridge, Mass.: The MIT Press, 1980. Discusses external costs, market failure, and pollution control policies.

Gould, Roy. *Going Sour: Science and the Politics of Acid Rain.* Boston: Birkhauser, 1985. Presents causes, effects, and strategies for reducing acid rain, and the political and legal aspects of control.

Harrison, Bennett, and Barry Bluestone. *The Great U-Turn: Corporate Restructuring and the Polarizing of America.* New York: Basic Books, 1988. Examines what has happened to American business and living standards in recent years, the reasons for U. S. economic reversals, and the role of government in turning the economy around.

Hills, Jill. *Deregulating Telecoms: Competition and Control in the United States, Japan, and Britain.* Westport, Conn.: Quorum Books, 1986. Reviews the history of deregulating the telecommunications industry in three countries and considers the impact of liberalization and privatization of the industry.

Irwin, Manley Rutherford. *Telecommunications America: Markets Without Boundaries.* Westport, Conn.: Quorum Books, 1984. Takes the position that technology and government regulation are not compatible, and that "the

world of regulation and the world of technology stand in sharp contrast." (From the Conclusion, p. 125.)

Petulla, Joseph M. *Environmental Protection in the United States.* San Francisco: San Francisco Study Center, 1987. Reviews the history of environmental protection, the roles of industry and government in environmental protection, the problems associated with it, and what can be done.

Regens, James L., and Robert W. Rycroft. *The Acid Rain Controversy.* Pittsburgh: University of Pittsburgh Press, 1988. Examines the scientific, economic, and political aspects of the acid rain problem.

Samuels, Sheldon W., ed. *The Environment of the Workplace and Human Values.* New York: Alan R. Liss, 1986. Various dimensions of the health conditions of workplaces are considered from labor, business, legal, moral, economic, and political viewpoints.

Siebert, Horst, and Ariane Antel. *The Political Economy of Environmental Protection.* Greenwich, Conn.: JAI Press, 1979. Discusses costs and benefits of a cleaner environment, and "public bads" as opposed to "public goods."

Simon, Samuel. *After Divestiture: What the AT&T Settlement Means for Business and Residential Phone Service.* White Plains, N.Y.: Knowledge Industry Publications, 1985. An analysis of the pressures for change, the divestiture agreement, and telecommunications after divestiture.

## chapter 9

# LABOR AND INCOME DISTRIBUTION

*Measured by its contributions to the output of business and to the income of households, labor is the most important factor of production. Therefore, labor problems are of great concern to the economy. The introductory article deals with a controversial aspect of the labor market.*

## Immigrants—Part of the Problem or Part of the Solution?

There are over 600,000 immigrants admitted to the United States each year. Most of them need a job, and they need public services such as health care, schools, transportation facilities, and other collective goods. In addition to the legal immigrants, there are annually another half million or so illegal immigrants for whom there is no accounting and little control.

Many of the illegals enter by crossing the Mexican border, sometimes with the help of a "coyote" who is paid to sneak them across and transport them to a city where they can disappear into the Mexican barrio. The majority of illegal immigrants, an estimated 60%, arrive in this manner. The remainder enter the country on temporary visitor visas and then simply disappear. When the Immigration and Naturalization Service (INS) computerized its records, it found that of the approximately 10 million visitors who arrive each year, there was no record of some 2 million of them having departed. How many of those that overstay their visas become illegal residents no one knows.

Concern over illegal immigration led to the passage of the Immigration Reform and Control Act of 1986. It was known as the Simp-son-Mazzoli Bill after its two congressional sponsors. The law was counted on to reduce illegal immigration by providing that employers can be fined for knowingly hiring an illegal alien. The penalties are stiff—from $250 to $10,000—and employers must keep accurate records of the citizenship documentation of every worker hired or face additional fines of up to $1,000 for each incomplete record. In order to meet the objections of farm owners, fruit and vegetable growers in particular, who complained that they could not operate without low-cost immigrant farm workers, a special provision was included in the bill. It granted amnesty to alien workers who were employed in agriculture for at least 90 days during the preceding year.

Despite the penalties on employers for hiring illegal immigrants and the occasional highly publicized raids by the INS on businesses suspected of using illegals, there has been no lessening of the inflow of illegal workers. It remains an estimated 500,000 a year.

The current surge of immigrants, legal and illegal, is the largest in our history in total numbers. The nearest comparable period was 1901–1910, when there was an inflow averaging 879,500 per year. As a percentage of the population, however, immigration is much smaller now than it was then. During that first decade of the century, the number

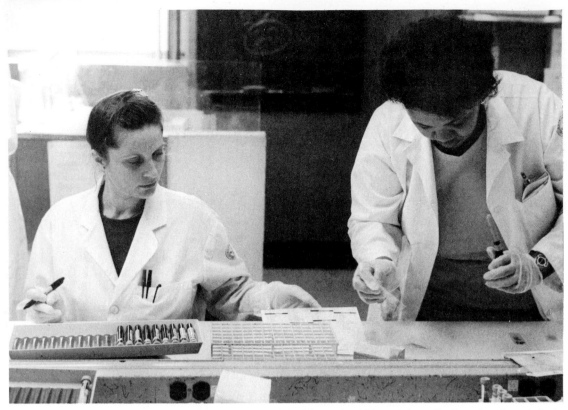

Cornelia Ghincea, left, who came from Romania to the United States in 1989, and Janet Davis, a Jamaican émigré, analyze blood samples in the hematology laboratory of Mount Sinai Hospital in Manhattan.

of immigrants each year averaged more than 1% of the population. Today it is less than half that.

The concerns about immigration are that the immigrants take jobs from native-born workers, put downward pressure on wages, and increase the cost of public services. It was such considerations that led to the passage of the Simpson-Mazzoli Bill. The bill was backed by labor unions, fearful that immigrants willing to work for low wages deprive union members of jobs and make it more difficult to get pay raises.

What is the validity of these concerns? A number of studies have been done and are summarized by Julian Simon in *The Economic Consequences of Immigration*. (See Further Reading. Chapters 5 and 12 of Simon's book are particularly relevant.) The studies generally conclude that immigrants generate as many new jobs as the number of jobs that

they occupy, that their effect on wages is small or nonexistent, and that they pay more in federal, Social Security, state, and local taxes than the amount they cost in social services.

Some studies found adverse local effects where there were sizable concentrations of immigrants. For example, in some southwestern cities the costs of increased educational services required by immigrant families with large numbers of school-age children may exceed the state and local taxes that the families pay, although their total tax payments, including federal and Social Security taxes, exceed the amount of their overall drain on public finances. This situation leads to a proposal for the federal government to subsidize states and localities that are affected by immigration, as it does those impacted by military bases.

Conclusions about the effects of immigrant

competition on native workers similar to those reported by Simon are reached by economist George Borjas of the University of California at Santa Barbara (*Friends or Strangers: The Impact of Immigrants on the U.S. Economy*). He finds not "a single shred of evidence" that American workers suffer from immigration.

Rather than being part of the problem, as assumed by the Simpson-Mazzoli legislation, immigrants may be part of the solution to our production problems in coming years. According to the U.S. Bureau of Labor Statistics, the number of job openings in this country will increase 19.2% by the end of the century, while the labor force will increase only 17.8%. The bureau predicts severe labor shortages in such sectors as health care, retailing, and business-support services.

Immigration can help to close the gap between the needs for labor and the supply of native-born workers available. But there is a call for changing the criteria by which immigrants are selected for admission. Since 1952, immigration laws have given preference to the relatives of current residents—the spouses, children, and siblings of earlier immigrants. Once becoming citizens, they in turn bring in their families.

It is proposed that, to meet the nation's occupational needs and increase productivity, immigration policies be altered to favor those with skills that are in short supply, as Canada and Australia have done. Of the 650,000 immigrants allowed into the United States in 1989, only 54,000 qualified solely on the basis of their education and ability.

Although the studies cited above show that immigrants have little direct effect on wage rates, there may be a long-term effect on labor productivity and wages. An expanding labor supply means that there is less incentive for companies to invest in laborsaving equipment. As a result, labor productivity and wages would not increase as rapidly as if there were more investment. In Japan, with an aging population—the oldest industrial labor force in the world by the end of the century—and little immigration, there will be much worse labor shortages than in the United States. Japanese companies are expected to compensate by increasing their investment rate above its already high level.

Another aspect of immigration is the impact of a growing population on crowding and the environment. Although the population density of the United States is only about two-thirds of the world average, the Zero Population Growth organization and others concerned with protecting the environment are opposed to immigration because of negative effects on the quality of life.

## Chapter Preview

*The effect of immigrant labor on the economy is a subject of continuing debate. To help understand how immigration and various other forces affect income distribution, we will examine the following questions: What determines wages? What determines other incomes? What causes unequal distribution of income? Who is poor in the United States?*

## Learning Objectives

*After completing this chapter, you should be able to:*

1. *Explain what determines the demand for and supply of labor and how demand and supply influence wages.*
2. *Discuss how capital availability affects labor demand and wages.*
3. *Describe the effects of minimum wage laws.*
4. *Explain what labor unions do.*
5. *Explain what "sticky" wages are and discuss their impacts in labor markets.*
6. *Describe the different income sources that make up the functional distribution of income.*
7. *Identify the unique characteristics of the determination of rent compared to the determination of other sources of income.*
8. *Describe how the personal distribution of income is measured, how it has changed over time, and how the distribution is shown on a Lorenz curve.*
9. *Describe the causes of unequal distribution of personal income.*
10. *Explain how poverty is defined and describe the programs for reducing poverty.*

## What Determines Wages?

Wages, the price of labor services, are determined in much the same way other prices are determined—by demand and supply. But many factors enter into this determination including the amount of capital goods available, natural resources, the level of technology, the education and training of the labor force, and the number of workers in the labor force.

**Derived demand**  The demand for labor services is a derived demand because it is dependent upon consumer demand for goods and services. For example, as the consumer demand for electronic products increases or decreases, the demand for parts-assembly labor shifts as well. The demand for labor to pick crops depends on the consumer demand for fruits and vegetables. The demand for restaurant workers depends on desires of consumers to go out to eat and how much income they have to satisfy those desires.

**Labor supply**  If there is a large supply of unskilled workers as a result of illegal immigration, wages tend to be lower in agriculture, restaurant and hotel service, parts-assembly work, and other unskilled and semi-skilled occupations. The effect of immigrant labor on the agricultural labor supply and farm wages is illustrated in Figure 1, where the number of workers hired in agriculture is on the bottom axis and the farm workers' wage is on the vertical axis. The figures are hypothetical.

The demand for labor in agriculture is derived from the demand for farm produce and also depends on the productivity of the workers. The supply of native farm labor is shown by $S_1$. With this limited supply, the wage rate in agriculture would be $6 an hour. Immigrant labor inflow

**derived demand**  the demand for a factor of production, not because it directly provides utility, but because it is needed to produce finished products which do provide utility.

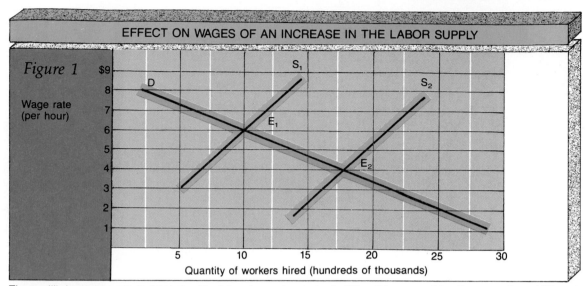

EFFECT ON WAGES OF AN INCREASE IN THE LABOR SUPPLY

*Figure 1*

Wage rate
(per hour)

The equilibrium wage rate is determined by labor demand and supply. Other things remaining the same, the addition of immigrant workers to the labor supply shifts the supply curve from $S_1$ to $S_2$ and lowers the equilibrium wage rate from $E_1$ to $E_2$.

increases the supply to $S_2$. This results in an equilibrium wage rate of $4 an hour, other things remaining the same.

However, if the studies referred to in the introductory article are correct in finding that wages are not lowered by an increase in immigrant labor, other things do not remain the same. For one thing, there will be an increase in the demand for food as a result of the larger population. This explains a part but not all of an upward shift in demand, since the new agricultural workers produce more food than the amount eaten by themselves and their families. An additional cause of increasing demand for agricultural labor may be an increase in food exports as prices are reduced.

The demand for immigrant labor is also increased by the number of immigrants who start small businesses, including farming. The proportion of immigrants that start their own business is larger than that for the population as a whole.

But the main reason immigrant labor does not result in lower wages is that, by spending their income on a wide variety of goods and services, the immigrant workers increase the incomes of other workers who in turn spend more on food and other products.

The increase in demand resulting from immigration is shown in Figure 2 on the next page. Demand shifts from $D_1$ to $D_2$, offsetting most of the effect on wages from the increase in labor supply. There is a small net reduction in agricultural wages from $6 an hour to $5.50 an hour. (The figures, again, are hypothetical.) This outcome is in accord with some studies that show the effect of additional new

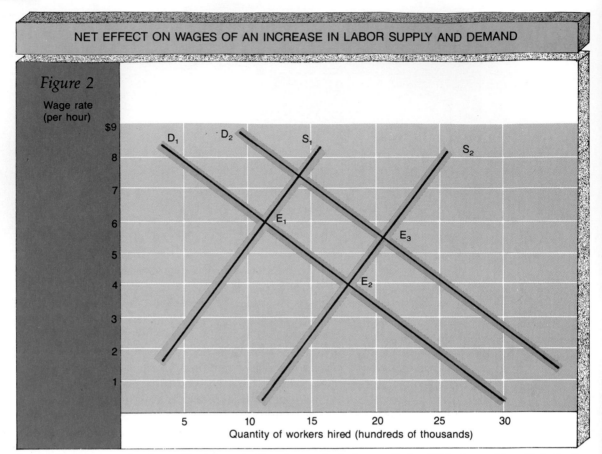

**NET EFFECT ON WAGES OF AN INCREASE IN LABOR SUPPLY AND DEMAND**

*Figure 2*

Wage rate
(per hour)

Quantity of workers hired (hundreds of thousands)

Immigration increases the demand for labor as well as the supply. As the result of a shift in demand from $D_1$ to $D_2$, the equilibrium wage rate in the labor market in which the immigrants are employed is $E_3$, a 50-cent reduction from the wage rate before immigration. Wages overall in the economy are not reduced as a result of immigration because of the increase in demand for other goods and services.

immigrants on wages is a small reduction in the income of the immigrants that preceded them. This does not result in an overall reduction in incomes because of the increased demand for goods and services generated by the immigrants.

**Capital available**   The amount and quality of capital goods available in an industry affect the wages workers are paid. The tools, machines, and other capital goods labor has to work with are a major determinant of labor productivity and wages. In modern industrial plants this capital equipment is frequently controlled by computers (see chapter 7, p. 183). Such automation increases labor productivity and makes the workers more valuable. As automation increases a worker's productivity, more workers will be demanded by industries. More workers will be hired so long as the net value of an additional worker's output exceeds the wage rate.

**net value**   the market value of a worker's output after subtracting the other production costs, such as raw materials.

If there is a shortage of labor in an industry and wages increase, firms in the industry find it profitable to invest more in laborsaving equipment. In coming years the shortage of labor in Japan will likely bring about a change in the competitive relationship between U.S. and Japanese industries. In earlier times, Japanese producers depended on low-wage labor to be competitive. Now, and to an even greater extent in the future, increasing investment in automation by Japanese firms to compensate for the declining availability of new workers will raise the productivity of workers and their wages. Japan will depend more on capital-intensive, high-wage, high-productivity industries to be competitive.

Minimum wage laws are also a stimulus for producers to substitute capital equipment for labor. If the minimum wage is higher than the net value of worker output in an industry, the number of workers employed in the industry will be reduced. When it is possible to offset the higher labor price by increased investment in capital equipment, labor productivity will rise. The current low level of minimum wages provides little incentive for employers to invest in capital equipment if there is a sufficient supply of unskilled labor available.

**Unions**   Labor unions affect wages, although perhaps not as much as people think. Through collective bargaining, the unions negotiate better wages and working conditions. Collective bargaining was established as the basis of labor-management relations by the National Labor Relations Act in 1935, generally referred to as the Wagner Act. This law states that employers cannot "interfere with, restrain, or coerce employees," or "dominate or interfere with the formation or administration of any labor organization or contribute financial support to it." Employers are also forbidden to discriminate against union employees in hiring or firing policies. Most importantly, the Wagner Act established the National Labor Relations Board (NLRB) to enforce and administer the law.

Collective bargaining allows workers to bargain as a group rather than as individuals. The result of collective bargaining is the signing of a contract between the union and the employer regarding pay and working conditions for a specified period of time, generally 1 to 3 years. When labor and management cannot reach agreement on a contract, the union may undertake job actions such as strikes and, occasionally, boycotts of the firm's products.

Union membership as a percentage of the labor force has been declining since the 1940s when it reached a peak of 35%. By 1989 it had fallen to only 12.4% of the private work force. However, unions represent an equal number of

Children were a source of cheap labor shortly after the Industrial Revolution began. They often worked 72-hour weeks at low pay until passage of the Fair Labor Standards Act of 1938 prohibited such practices.

**minimum wage laws**   federal or state laws that prohibit employers from paying less than a specified hourly wage to their employees.
**collective bargaining**   a process by which decisions regarding the wages, hours, and conditions of employment are determined by the interaction of workers acting through their unions and employers.
**job action**   a concerted action by employees to disrupt production or distribution in order to put pressure on employers to grant concessions. They may consist of lesser actions such as work slowdowns or work-to-rule (performing the minimum tasks stipulated in the job description) as an alternative to a strike.
**strike**   a collective refusal by employees to work.

| Table 1 | LEGISLATION CONCERNING LABOR |
|---|---|

| Legislation (Year enacted) | Provisions |
|---|---|
| Clayton Act (1914) | Exempts labor organizations from antitrust law prohibitions against concerted actions, thus making strikes legal. |
| Norris-La Guardia Act (1932) | Makes yellow-dog contracts (by which employers prevent their workers from joining unions) unenforceable. Limits court injunctions that restrict strikes and other union activities. |
| Wagner Act (1935) | Guarantees workers the right to join unions and bargain collectively. Prohibits management from engaging in unfair labor practices such as organizing company unions, discriminating against union members, or failing to bargain in good faith. |
| Fair Labor Standards Act (1938) | Established the minimum wage, originally 25 cents an hour. Also regulates child labor and the length of the work week. |
| Taft-Harley Act (1947) | Prohibits unfair union practices such as secondary boycotts or strikes against firms doing business with a struck company, jurisdictional strikes, and closed shops (requiring that a person must already be a member of the union in order to be hired). It permits states to pass right-to-work laws outlawing union shops (requiring employees to join the union after they are hired). |
| Landrum-Griffen Act (1959) | Regulates the administration of unions, such as governing the election of union officers, prohibiting felons from holding union office, and requiring the filing of union financial reports with the secretary of labor. Also requires employers to file reports on any payments they make to union officers. |
| Civil Rights Act (1964) | Prohibits discrimination in hiring, firing, or promotion on the basis of race, color, religion, sex, or national origin. Established the Equal Employment Opportunity Commission to enforce the Act. |
| Age Discrimination Act (1967) | Provides protection against discrimination based on age to workers between the ages of 40 and 65. |

workers who are not union members in contract negotiations. Since unions represent one-fourth of the labor force in wage bargaining, it would be useful to know the effect they have on wages.

According to the traditional theory of wage determination, with no unions and a perfectly competitive labor market wage rates were determined by equilibrium between the demand for and supply of labor. It was assumed that if there were unemployed workers wage rates would fall until all of the unemployed had jobs. Figure 3 shows a hypothetical demand and supply for hospital orderlies in a competitive labor market. The original point of equilibrium, $E_1$, represents a situation in which the wage rate is at a level where the number of workers that employers demand equals the amount of labor willingly supplied. Anybody willing to work for $5.00 an hour would be working.

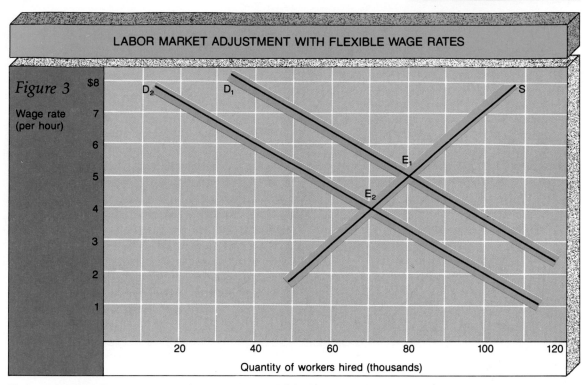

**Figure 3**

LABOR MARKET ADJUSTMENT WITH FLEXIBLE WAGE RATES

Wage rate (per hour)

Quantity of workers hired (thousands)

Under early twentieth-century economic assumptions, a shift in the demand for hospital orderlies from $D_1$ to $D_2$ would lead to a fall in the equilibrium wage rate from $E_1$ to $E_2$ and voluntary exodus from the occupation.

Suppose a reduction in the demand for hospital services reduces the net value of hospital orderlies' labor. Hospitals would no longer find it profitable to hire as many orderlies as before, and the wage rate would fall until the last worker hired produced a net value equal to the new lower wage rate.

As shown in Figure 3 above, hospital administrators cut back their demand for orderlies from $D_1$ to $D_2$. As a result, the wage rate for orderlies falls from $5.00 an hour to $4.00 an hour, equal to the net value of the work performed by the 70,000th orderly employed in the industry. At $E_2$, the new equilibrium, 10,000 orderlies would quit their jobs because they chose not to work at that job at the lower wage rate. Those workers would be rehired elsewhere at wages between $4.00 and $5.00. The costs of hospital care would fall.

Modern economic analysis interprets the labor market differently. When demand falls off, wages seldom drop rapidly. They tend to be rigid or, in economists' terminology, "sticky." Workers, both union and nonunion, strongly resist any lowering of wages.

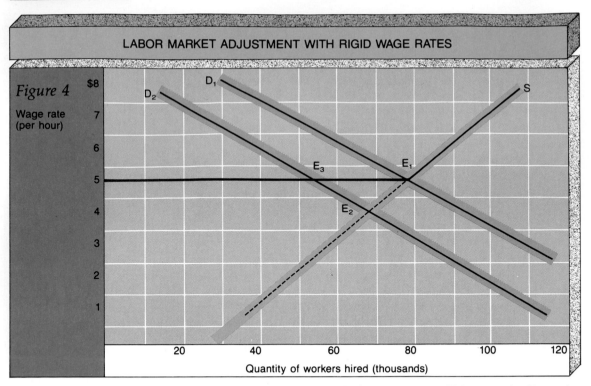

*Figure 4*

Wage rate (per hour)

LABOR MARKET ADJUSTMENT WITH RIGID WAGE RATES

Quantity of workers hired (thousands)

When the wage rate is fixed, the decrease in demand from $D_1$ to $D_2$ forces a new equilibrium at point $E_3$ causing involuntary unemployment.

Figure 4 demonstrates the concept that if wages are rigid, a fall in the demand for a good or service brings an initial reduction in the quantity produced rather than in its price. If the demand for hospital orderlies declines from $D_1$ to $D_2$, wages do not fall to a new equilibrium at $E_2$. Instead, if the orderlies are unionized and the union refuses to let the wage rate fall below $5.00 per hour, 25,000 orderlies will be laid off. The new equilibrium will be at $E_3$, where hospitals would only be willing to hire 55,000 workers, since that is the employment level at which the net value of the last worker is $5.00 per hour. The costs of hospital care will not decline. If there is adequate demand in other fields, and labor is mobile between jobs, workers may find other jobs. In the meantime, there is involuntary unemployment.

The actual effect of unions on wages, although the subject of numerous studies, remains unclear. Members of strong unions, those with a large amount of monopoly power in the labor market, do receive higher wages than nonorganized or weakly represented workers, as shown in Figure 5. The "union effect" on wages may be in the neighborhood of 20% for blue-collar workers, much less for white-collar workers. But it is uncertain how much of this effect is due strictly to

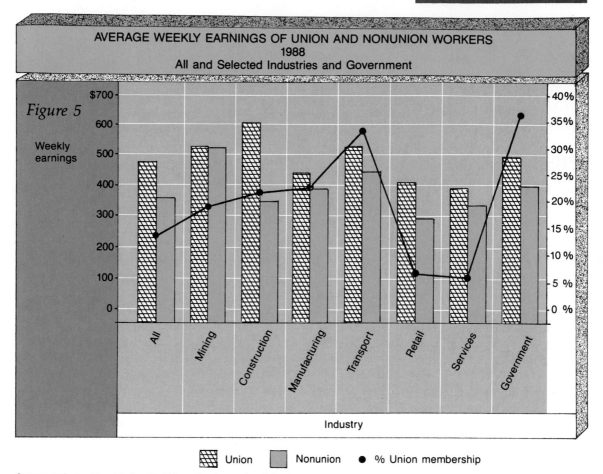

AVERAGE WEEKLY EARNINGS OF UNION AND NONUNION WORKERS
1988
All and Selected Industries and Government

*Figure 5*

Union   Nonunion   ● % Union membership

Source: U.S. Bureau of Labor Statistics, *Employment and Earnings.*

The wages of union workers are higher than those of nonunion workers, but the specific effects of unions on wages are unclear; and the percentage of union membership in an industry is not correlated with the wage differences between union and nonunion workers.

wage bargaining and how much to other factors. In some ways, the effect of unions on wages is similar to that of minimum wage laws. By forcing wages up, they accelerate the introduction of laborsaving technology. This increases labor productivity and the value of an hour of labor. High wages also encourage employers to seek to hire the most productive workers and attract such workers to the job. But the ability of labor unions to increase the relative wage rates of their members in the long run has been questioned. Some observers suggest that unions only enable their membership to hold their own in relation to nonunion employees in the marketplace.

# case application

## "Baby Bust" Generation Replacing "Baby Boom" Generation

The last members of the "baby boom" generation have entered the labor market, and the earlier ones will reach their peak earning years in the 1990s. This surge of humanity was born between 1946 and 1961, and totalled 64 million. They dominated the culture in their youth, as evidenced by the popularity of rock and roll, jeans, and junk food. As they mature, their consumer preferences are similarly dictating trends—golden oldies, take-out food, and minivans. But in one area, their sheer power of numbers has worked against them. The large number of available workers in the labor force has held wage increases below earlier levels, despite a record pace of 2 million jobs created each year. Promotions are more difficult to obtain because of the crowding at their experience level.

As a group, the baby boomers have a great deal of power, but as individuals they see themselves as lacking power and opportunities. They have lower expectations regarding their incomes and living standards than did the previous generation. Surveys of college graduates in the 1980s, for example, indicated that they did not expect to be earning more in five years than their parents' current incomes. This was a change in expectations from those of earlier generations.

The generation behind the baby boom group has been called the "baby bust" generation. Born between 1962 and 1977, this group of individuals is much smaller (Figure 6). About one-quarter fewer babies were born in 1975 than in 1960, the peak of the boom. The number of baby bust entrants into the job market will shrink each year until the mid-1990s, with the growth rate of the work force falling to just 1% a year, the lowest since the 1950s.

The relatively small numbers in the baby bust generation should prove beneficial to their wage rates insofar as the supply of labor is concerned. However, wages depend not only on labor supply but on labor productivity as well. A report by the U.S. Department of Labor estimates that 21.4 million jobs will be created by the year 2000. More than half of the jobs being created today require at least a high school education, and the proportion of new jobs requiring at least one year of college will increase dramatically, according to the report.

There is a closer correlation between income and education now than ever before. High school dropouts in the work force are earning 42% less in constant dollars than they were 15 years ago. The earnings for the bottom quarter of young male high school graduates fell at almost the same rate as the dropouts' earnings did. This fall in real earnings is probably the largest decline in this century for any income group.

There are two labor market models for the 1990s, one for workers with education and another for those without. The one for workers with marketable skills shows a lower labor supply than in the baby boom years and a high demand for skilled labor, resulting in a labor shortage and high wages. The other, for workers lacking education and training, shows a low supply combined with an even lower demand, resulting in low wages.

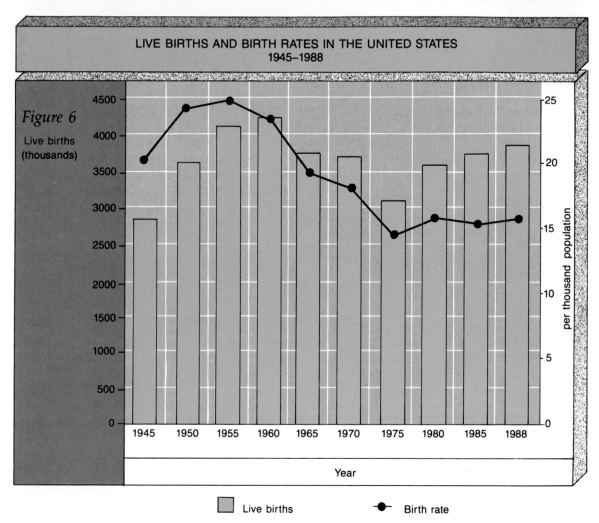

**LIVE BIRTHS AND BIRTH RATES IN THE UNITED STATES**
**1945–1988**

*Figure 6*

Live births
(thousands)

Source: U.S. National Center for Health Statistics, *Vital Statistics of the United States.*

Changing birth rates following World War II affect the number of workers at different age and experience levels in the work force.

*Economic Reasoning*

1. How did the baby boom generation affect the supply of labor? How did it affect the demand for labor?
2. How would you graph the two labor market models for the 1990s, one for educated workers and one for those lacking adequate education? Compare the graphs of the two models, without regard to numerical scales on the axes.
3. Speaking as a member of the baby bust generation, do you see any economic problems arising from the small size of that generation? If so, what are they?

# What Determines Other Incomes?

In the last analysis section we examined the factors that determine wage levels. Variations in labor income are only one, and not the major, explanation for differences in people's incomes. Income from sources other than wages and salaries results in greater inequalities in income distribution. In this section we shall look at the other types of income and what determines them.

**Functional income distribution**   Incomes are received from various sources. Most people earn the largest part of their income from wages and salaries. Other types of income are rent, interest, and profits. The functional distribution of income is the allocation of income according to type—wages and salaries, rent, interest, or profits. Figure 7 shows the relative proportions of different types of income that made up the nation's income in 1989. It shows that nearly three-quarters of total national income came from wages and salaries.

Looked at in economic rather than accounting terms, the proportion is somewhat greater. Part of the income of proprietors, generally the largest part, is implicit wages. Implicit wages measure the value of the owners' time that is spent in running their businesses. The balance of proprietors' income should be added to corporate profits, a 7% share, to give the total share of profits in the nation's income.

**functional income distribution**   the shares of total income distributed according to the type of factor service for which they are paid, e.g., rent as a payment for land, wages for labor, and interest for capital.

**implicit wages**   income which is the result of labor input but is not received in the form of wages or salaries, but in some other form such as net proprietor's income (profits).

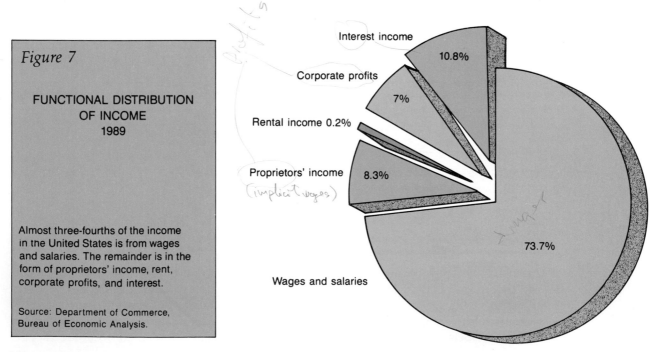

*Figure 7*

FUNCTIONAL DISTRIBUTION
OF INCOME
1989

Almost three-fourths of the income in the United States is from wages and salaries. The remainder is in the form of proprietors' income, rent, corporate profits, and interest.

Source: Department of Commerce, Bureau of Economic Analysis.

Interest income 10.8%

Corporate profits 7%

Rental income 0.2%

Proprietors' income 8.3%

Wages and salaries 73.7%

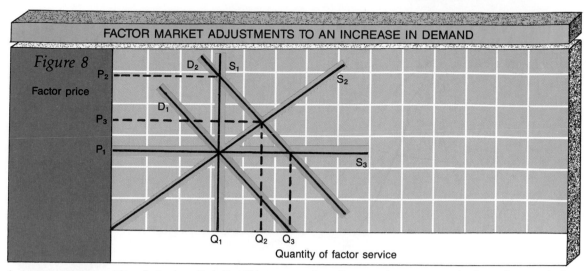

FACTOR MARKET ADJUSTMENTS TO AN INCREASE IN DEMAND

Figure 8

Factor price

Quantity of factor service

An increase in demand for a factor from $D_1$ to $D_2$ will have more of an effect on price or on quantity depending on whether the factor supply is perfectly inelastic like $S_1$ which represents land, or more elastic like $S_2$ which might be skilled labor, or perfectly elastic like $S_3$ which might be unskilled labor.

**Rent** Rent received by persons, not including rent receipts of businesses, is the smallest of the income shares, accounting for only two-tenths of one percent of national income. The total amount of rent people receive is about eight times as large, but the depreciation on their property is deducted in calculating net rental income.

In economic analysis, rent is the payment made for the use of land. Because land is pretty much fixed (unchanging) in supply, the level of rent depends almost entirely on the demand for the resource. A big demand results in a very high rent, and a small demand results in a low rent. This is so because the supply is fixed and can't expand or contract in response to the price changes. The effect of an increase in demand on rent is compared with the effect of an increase in demand on the prices of other types of factors in Figure 8.

The supply schedule for land is shown by $S_1$. It is perfectly inelastic because the quantity of land is fixed and does not change with changes in the price of using it (rent). If the demand for land increases from $D_1$ to $D_2$, the rent on land will increase from $P_1$ to $P_2$ but the quantity transacted stays at $Q_1$. With land, the whole adjustment to an increase in demand is accommodated by an increase in rent. With other types of factor inputs that do not have a perfectly inelastic supply, an increase in demand is partly accommodated by an increase in the quantity supplied. If the factor has a supply schedule such as $S_2$, an increase in demand from $D_1$ to $D_2$ results in a smaller price increase from $P_1$ to $P_3$

Right fielder Jose Canseco's income can be considered to be more like a rent than a salary. Whenever there is a unique talent involved and the supply cannot be increased, the wage may go very high to reflect demand.

and some increase in the quantity transacted from to $Q_2$. If the factor has a perfectly elastic supply such as $S_3$, the increase in demand results in no change in the price. The increased demand is accommodated by an increase in the quantity supplied, reflected in the move from $Q_1$ to $Q_3$.

Although rents compose the smallest share of income receipts, rent-type earnings are frequently found in other factor shares. This helps explain why such large differences can exist in wages and salaries. The $5 million paid to right fielder Jose Canseco by the Oakland A's in 1990 was more like a rent than a salary. The same is true of the income of movie and pop music stars.

For most occupations, an increase in demand only raises wages by a small amount. The increase in the supply of workers attracted by higher wages accommodates the balance of the increased demand. But when there is a unique talent involved and the supply cannot be increased, the wage may go very high as demand increases. The market adjustment to an increase in the demand for a scarce or

**factor share** the part of national income received by a particular factor of production.

unusual talent such as hitting well in baseball is shown by the $S_1$ outcome in Figure 8. By comparison, the adjustment to an increase in the demand for unskilled labor would be more like that for $S_3$, while an increase in the demand for a skilled occupation would lie in between, as in the $S_2$ case.

**Interest** Interest income accounts for nearly 11% of total income. Interest is the factor payment for the use of financial capital. Financial capital comes mainly from savings, and the interest rate depends on the amount of capital available relative to the demand for capital for investing or for financing personal or government debt.

Generally, a rise in the interest rate should make more capital available by making it more profitable for people to save a larger percentage of their income rather than to spend it. However, people who have a specific savings goal for retirement or for some other specified amount such as the down payment on a house will receive more interest income on their savings if interest rates go up. Consequently, they can achieve their goal with a smaller amount of savings each month. The net effect of a change in the interest rate on the amount of savings is not predictable.

Interest rates, like other prices, play an important rationing function. Higher interest rates discourage some uses of capital. When capital is scarce, only the most productive types of investment can justify using the expensive capital.

**Profits** Profits are often the least-understood type of income. It is clear what the other factor payments are for: wages are the payment for labor services, rents for the use of land, and interest for the use of financial capital. But for what factor service are profits paid? Profits are sometimes said to be the payment to entrepreneurs for perceiving a need for a new or better good or service, organizing the factors of production to satisfy that need, and taking the necessary financial risks.

When proprietors use their own capital in their business, there is an implicit interest cost which should be charged against revenues in calculating economic profits. As we saw in chapter 6, accounting profits are the difference between the total revenue of a company and its total costs. But much of accounting profits is actually an implicit interest payment to owners for the use of their capital which they have invested in their business. Only the profits in excess of the normal rate of return on capital are considered economic profits.

In markets where there is no monopoly control, economic profits tend to disappear in the long run because of the entry of new firms, which increases supply and reduces the profit rate. Economic profits only persist in cases of monopoly.

**implicit interest** income which derives from the use of capital but is not paid as interest but rather as a part of accounting profits.

243

# case application

## Rent Control

When members of the Henderson family take a bath in their South Bronx apartment, the bathtub must be emptied with a pan because the water won't drain out of the tub. When the landlord didn't respond after numerous requests to have the plumbing repaired, the Hendersons complained to the Conciliation and Appeals Board of New York's Rent Stabilization Association. It took 45 minutes of steady dialing to get through because the telephone lines to the Board were constantly busy. The stopped-up plumbing was not the only complaint the Hendersons had. They also wanted the landlord to repair a hallway light fixture, which had been broken for over a year, and replace a section of railing missing from the stairway banister.

Why didn't the Hendersons move to an apartment building that was better maintained? Because if they moved from their $325 per month rent-controlled apartment, they would have to pay twice that much for another one with the same amount of space. If they could find one, that is.

The plight of the Henderson family is just one example of the horror stories that are laid at the doorstep of rent control. Its critics, among whom are many economists, point out that when you set a price below the equilibrium level, you create a shortage. Rent control discourages the construction of new rental housing and the maintenance of existing units, these critics say. Many of the apartment buildings in the South Bronx are abandoned and boarded up.

Supporters of rent control, on the other hand, claim that it is instituted only in areas where there is already a housing shortage that results in "rent gouging" by landlords. They argue that most rent control programs allow landlords to pass on the full costs of improvements to the property in increased rents, and therefore rent controls actually encourage upgrading the units. They maintain that run-down and abandoned housing in New York results from social and economic conditions other than rent controls.

Studies show that there is a higher percentage of abandoned housing in St. Louis, Cleveland, Chicago, and Hoboken, New Jersey, all non–rent-controlled cities, than in New York. Pro-control advocates claim that without some limit on rents, low and moderate income families will be unable to afford to live in metropolitan areas. The Hendersons are currently paying 25% of their income in rent, considered to be the normal budget limit for housing costs. They cannot afford to pay twice that amount. In Los Angeles, before rent control was instituted in 1979, rents had risen to consume 34% of the average tenant's salary, compared with 25% in 1970.

Who has the balance of truth on their side, those in favor of rent control, or those against it? In addition to Los Angeles, the cities of Boston, Washington, D.C., San Francisco, and Santa Monica, among others, have adopted rent stabilization programs in recent years. Their experiences may provide some answers.

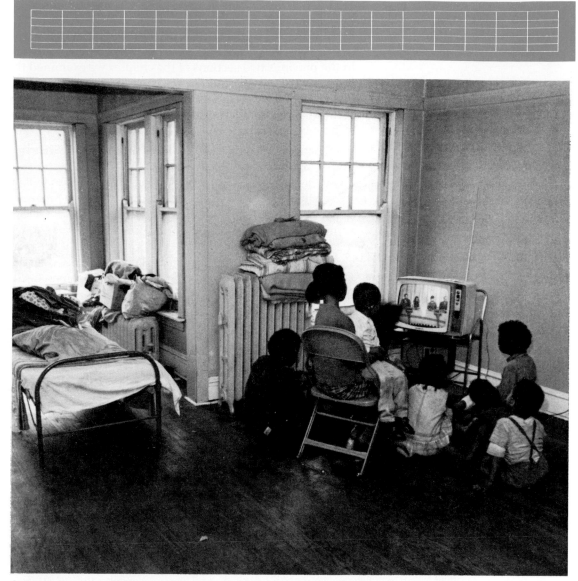

Children sit around a television set in an abandoned apartment building in Chicago. The building was taken over by families on public assistance to protest the substandard conditions in their previous apartments.

## Economic Reasoning

1. Why do rents tend to be higher in central cities than in the suburbs, despite the fact that population in the suburbs has grown more rapidly than in the cities?
2. For most types of goods and services, a reduction in supply costs is followed by a decrease in price. Why isn't this necessarily true for rent? Why would a reduction in property taxes, for example, not necessarily lower rents?
3. Are you in favor of or opposed to rent control measures? What considerations should you take into account?

# What Causes Unequal Distribution of Income?

In the previous two sections of the chapter we examined the functional distribution of income according to its source. In this section we will take a look at the distribution of income according to those who receive it and what causes income differences.

**Personal income distribution**   Functional income distribution is one way of looking at how income is distributed. Another way of looking at income distribution is to look at the pattern of distribution according to the relative size of people's income—personal income distribution. Table 2 shows the distribution of personal income in the United States according to five income classes for the years 1960–1987. Each class represents 20% of all income receivers, ranging from the 20% receiving the lowest incomes to the 20% receiving the highest incomes. The numbers in the table show the percentage of total income received by that group of income receivers. Comparing the percentage of total income received by the people in each fifth of the income scale, we can see the distribution of income in the United States between lower and upper income groups.

A good way to make this comparison is with a Lorenz curve diagram as shown in Figure 9. The bottom axis shows households divided into five equal groups according to

**personal income distribution** the pattern of income distribution according to the relative size of people's income.

**Lorenz curve** a diagram showing the distribution of income among groups of people; an indicator of the degree of inequality of income distribution.

*Table 2*

### INCOME DISTRIBUTION 1960–1987
### MONEY INCOME OF FAMILIES
(percentage distribution of total income)*

| Year | Lowest fifth | Second fifth | Third fifth | Fourth fifth | Highest fifth |
|------|-------------|--------------|-------------|--------------|---------------|
| 1960 | 4.8 | 12.2 | 17.8 | 24.0 | 41.3 |
| 1965 | 5.2 | 12.2 | 17.8 | 23.9 | 40.9 |
| 1970 | 5.4 | 12.2 | 17.6 | 23.8 | 40.9 |
| 1975 | 5.4 | 11.8 | 17.6 | 24.1 | 41.1 |
| 1980 | 5.1 | 11.6 | 17.5 | 24.3 | 41.6 |
| 1984 | 4.7 | 11.0 | 17.0 | 24.4 | 42.9 |
| 1987 | 4.6 | 10.8 | 16.9 | 24.1 | 43.7 |
| Income classes | 1987 | below $14,450 | $14,451 to $25,100 | $25,101 to $36,600 | $36,601 to $52,910 | above $52,911 |

*Row totals may not add to 100% because of rounding.

Source: U.S. Bureau of the Census, *Current Population Reports*.

During the 1960s income distribution became somewhat more equal. Since then it has become more unequal than it was in 1960. In the 1980s the highest fifth of income receivers gained at the expense of the other four-fifths.

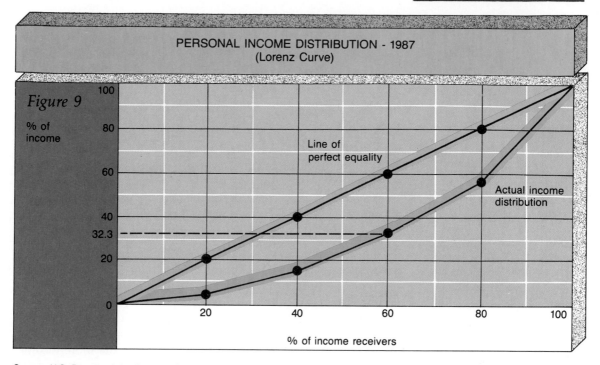

PERSONAL INCOME DISTRIBUTION - 1987
(Lorenz Curve)

*Figure 9*

% of income

Line of perfect equality

Actual income distribution

% of income receivers

Source: U.S. Bureau of the Census, *Current Population Reports*.

The degree of inequality of income distribution is shown by the extent of deviation from the straight line. In 1987 the lower 60% of income receivers got 32.3% of the income, while the highest 40% got 67.7%.

amount of income received. The vertical axis shows the percentage of total income that is earned by each fifth of the population. Perfect equality of income distribution would be represented by a diagonal straight line from the lower left corner to the upper right corner, with 20% of the population earning 20% of total income, 40% of the population earning 40% of the income, and so forth.

The extent to which the actual income distribution shown by the Lorenz curve varies from a diagonal straight line indicates the extent of inequality in income distribution. The more the curve bows away from the straight line, the greater is the inequality in income distribution.

Figure 9 shows the Lorenz curve for income distribution in 1987. The bottom 20% of income receivers earned 4.6% of total income, while the top 20% of income receivers earned 43.7% of total income. The lowest 40% of the population received 15.4% of the income, while the highest 40% received 67.7% of the income.

During the 1960s, as Table 2 shows, income distribution was becoming somewhat more equal. The lowest 20% of income receivers increased their share of total income while

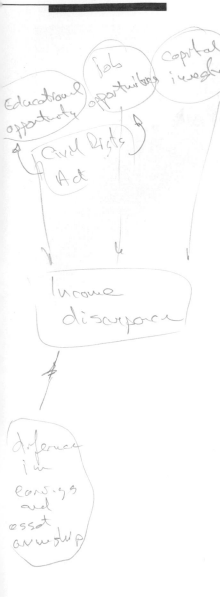

the shares received by the highest groups declined. During the 1970s the highest two-fifths regained their earlier relative shares at the expense of the second fifth, the lower middle income group.

In the 1980s income distribution became more unequal than at any time since the data has been published. The highest fifth of income receivers increased their share of income at the expense of the other four-fifths of families. Between 1970 and 1987 the share of total income going to the upper fifth of income receivers increased 2.8%. It represented a shift of income of $105.8 billion from the lower 80% of income receivers to the top 20%. This amounted to an average of $2,030 less income per family in the lower 80% and $8,120 more income per family in the upper 20%.

**Differences in productivity**   One of the causes of inequality in income distribution is differences in productivity. Labor incomes in particular are closely related to productivity. As we saw in the last chapter, the wages of workers are determined by the net value of the output of the last worker it pays an employer to hire. The greater the value of the output of a particular type of worker, the more income such workers will receive. Workers in low-productivity jobs generally receive small incomes. Workers in high-productivity jobs generally earn relatively high incomes. The productivity of skilled workers is greater than that of unskilled workers and their earnings are related to their productivity.

Some of the differences in productivity between occupations are due to differences in education, training, and ability. However, productivity also depends on the amount of capital equipment that a worker has to work with. Labor in automated firms is more productive than labor in firms that do not have much capital investment per worker. The high-wage industries generally have a great deal of capital equipment per worker, while the low-wage industries generally have much smaller amounts of capital investment per worker.

**Differences in opportunity**   While differences in productivity explain differences in income between different types of jobs, productivity does not explain differences in income between different population groups. Men are not inherently more productive than women, yet median pay for females is only 68% that for white males. Nor are there any innate racial or ethnic productivity differences, but the median weekly earnings of white full-time workers in 1988 were $394, while black full-time workers earned only $314.

The income discrepancies between sexes and between racial and ethnic groups result from differences in opportunities—educational opportunities and job opportunities.

Workers who move clothing in New York's garment industry can earn $7.00 an hour. Unfortunately, the garment industry is expected to diminish in the coming years as retailers move toward large suppliers with out-of-town manufacturing plants.

Title VII of the Civil Rights Act of 1964 prohibits employers from discriminating in the hiring, firing, promotion, job assignment, compensation, training, and other "terms, conditions, or privileges of employment." It is the task of the Equal Employment Opportunity Commission (EEOC) to enforce those provisions of the law.

Discriminatory attitudes and practices, however, cannot be easily reversed. Lack of educational opportunities and motivations in the past are one explanation of current differences in earnings between population groups. While 14.4% of all white males have completed college, only 8.4% of white females, 4.2% of black males, and 5.9% of Hispanic males have college degrees. The most educationally disadvantaged group is Hispanic females, of whom only 3.2% have four-year college educations.

**Differences in asset ownership**   While there are wide differences in income between different occupations, the greatest income variations result from differences in earnings from asset ownership. Of those people with incomes of more than $1 million a year, the largest source of income, by far, is the capital gains on their assets. The second largest source of their incomes is dividends on stock.

The third largest source of income among millionaires is salaries. They receive less than one-fifth as much in salaries, on the average, as the sum of their capital gains and dividend income. Most people who receive incomes at the top of the scale earn them from assets rather than from wages and salaries.

**capital gain** net income realized from an increase in the market value of a real or financial asset when it is sold.

# case application

## Created Equal, But . . .

When the 1964 Civil Rights Act made it illegal for employers to discriminate on the basis of race, religion, or sex, the focus of public attention was on the discrimination against black and other minority workers. The better-paying jobs were frequently open to white workers only. The median weekly earnings of black workers were only 70% as large as the earnings of white workers. The income gap has since been reduced for black workers to 80% as much as whites. But the relative income of women was and still is the lowest of all, in 1990 only 70% as large as that of white males.

In terms of family income rather than weekly earnings, which is a better measure of economic welfare, women are at an even greater disadvantage. Families with women as head of the household have an average income that is only 52% as much as households headed by men. This discrepancy is even larger than the interracial differences in family income: black families average 57% and Hispanic families 64% of the median income of white families.

The main reason for the low earnings of women is that women workers are concentrated in low-wage occupations. A study by the National Academy of Sciences has shown that the more an occupation is dominated by women, the less it tends to pay. Women constitute over 80% of the work force in six of eight low-paying jobs: practical nurses, stitchers and sewers, child-care workers, hairdressers, nurse's aids, and health care workers. The only two of the low-paying jobs in which they do not predominate are cooks (50% are women) and farm laborers (less than 15%).

The principal reason for the slow growth of productivity in the 1980s discussed in chapter 7 (p. 166) was the low rate of productivity growth in the service industries, less than 1% a year. This was in part due to the availability of female labor to fill the low-paying jobs in that sector of the economy. Large numbers of women entered the labor force during the decade, increasing the labor force participation rate of women by 6 percentage points and adding some 15 million workers. The great majority of these new female workers went into service occupations.

The availability of this pool of cheap labor meant that service industries did not have to invest in new capital equipment to meet rising demand. In western Europe and Japan, which did not have such a pool of cheap labor available, service companies invested heavily in new technology that resulted in productivity gains of 2% to 4% per year. The difference in productivity growth between other industrialized countries and the United States has left the United States at a disadvantage in global competition. Substandard pay for women is not only a hardship for them, but a drag on the economy as well.

### Economic Reasoning

1. In which income classes of Table 2 would you expect to find an unusually large proportion of women?
2. Considering the causes of income inequality, why do women predominate in six of the eight low-paying jobs?
3. Do you think that affirmative action in the hiring and promotion of women and minorities is a good idea? Why or why not?

# What Is the Answer to Poverty?

As we have seen, unequal distribution of income can be the result of a variety of causes. The result for those at the bottom of the income distribution ladder is poverty. This section of the chapter looks at what constitutes poverty and some of the methods used to combat it.

**The poverty line**   The dividing line between those officially considered poor and those not officially considered poor is called the poverty line. The initial poverty line was established in 1964 and was based on the cost of an economical food expenditure budget for a family. The poverty income threshold was calculated at three times a family's economical food budget. This income level has been adjusted each year for changes in the cost of living. In 1975 the poverty line was $5,500 for a family of four. In 1980 the poverty line for such a family was $8,414, and in 1988 it was $12,092. By adjusting the poverty line to reflect inflation, the government can keep the poverty threshold constant in real purchasing power.

The total number of people below the poverty threshold declined from almost 40 million in 1960 to a low of 23 million in 1973. Since then it has been increasing, and in 1988 stood at 31.9 million. This comprised 13.1% of the population.

This poverty line measurement, however, may actually

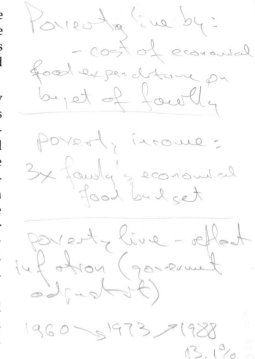

*Handwritten margin notes:*
Poverty line by:
- cost of economical food expenditure on budget of family

poverty income:
3x family's economical food budget

poverty line - reflect inflation (government adjust it)

1960 → 1973 → 1988
13.1%

Over 100 million people around the world have no home at all. These homeless residents of New York City are eating a meal provided by the Church of the Holy Apostles at Ninth Avenue and 28th Street. The church provides food for 1,000 people each weekday from 10:30 A.M. to 1:30 P.M.

**poverty line**   the family income level below which people are officially classified as poor.

*by housing-based poverty rate & poverty line 10%*

understate the increase in the amount of poverty. Consumption patterns, living standards, and relative costs have changed since the measure was devised. Food's share of family budgets has shrunk from one-third of family income to one-fifth of income. Meanwhile, housing's share has risen from one-third of income to over two-fifths of income for the average family, two-thirds for poor families. As a consequence, the poverty threshold based on food expenditures does not reflect a family's actual living costs today. Using a housing-based poverty measure in place of the food-based poverty line would raise the poverty rate some 10 percentage points.

Another objection to the poverty line measurement is the different criteria used in computing the needs of the elderly compared to those used for the rest of the population. Because the food needs of the elderly were about 10% below those of the nonelderly, the poverty threshold was set lower for those 65 and older. This adjustment, which is still made, ignores the higher health care costs for the aged. The aged spend more than twice as much of their budgets on health costs not covered by Medicare than other households spend on health care. If the same poverty criterion is used for the elderly as for others, the percentage of elderly living in poverty is higher than average, rather than lower as shown by the existing poverty line.

**Increased opportunity** A major objective of the Civil Rights Act of 1964 and the Age Discrimination Act of 1967 was to remove obstacles to economic opportunity caused by racial, religious, sex, or age discrimination. The actions of the Equal Employment Opportunity Commission have opened doors of increased opportunities that were previously closed to minorities, women, and older people.

The antipoverty programs initiated by the Johnson administration in 1965 and expanded under following administrations reduced the percentage of people living below the poverty line from 22.2% of the population in 1960 to 11.1% in 1973. This was accomplished in part by equal employment opportunities and affirmative action programs in government and private employment, and by government-funded jobs for the hard-core unemployed.

Reductions in federal government funding for the antipoverty programs in the 1980s, decreases in work training opportunities, and elimination of day-care centers, which gave mothers of young children more opportunity to work, slowed progress on increasing opportunities for economically disadvantaged groups.

**Transfer payments** Providing increased employment and educational opportunities is one way of raising people out of

**affirmative action program** a program devised by employers to increase their hiring of women and minorities; frequently mandated by government regulations.

The Food Stamp Program, one of the government's largest transfer payment programs, enables low-income persons to buy more groceries.

poverty. But this approach misses many of those currently in need. A more direct method of assisting those living in poverty is transfer payments. Government transfer payments to low-income households are subsidies paid out of tax receipts to supplement the income of impoverished families. These transfers include money payments such as welfare, Social Security benefits, and unemployment compensation.

One of the largest entitlement programs to supplement the cash income of the poor is federally financed food stamps. The Food Stamp Program was authorized by Congress in 1964 with the stated goal of helping low-income households obtain more balanced and nutritious diets. Stamps that can be used to purchase food vary in cost depending on the income of the recipient. The program is administered by the Department of Agriculture through state and local welfare offices. Many cities also have federally funded programs that provide hot meals to the elderly each day. In order to ensure nutrition for the young, schoolchildren of low-income families are provided free or discounted lunches and, in some cases, breakfasts.

Another major entitlement program is Aid to Families With Dependent Children (AFDC). This program was begun to provide income maintenance and social services for that most needy of all groups, families below the poverty line with women heads of household. Medicaid is a federally

**transfer payments** expenditures for which no goods or services are exchanged. Welfare, Social Security, and unemployment compensation are government transfer payments.

**entitlement program** government benefits which qualified recipients are entitled to by law, e.g., Social Security old-age benefits.

**food stamps** certificates that can be used in place of money to purchase food items.

**Aid to Families With Dependent Children (AFDC)** a federally subsidized, public assistance program to provide income maintenance and social services to needy families with dependent children.

**Medicaid** a federally subsidized, state-administered program to pay for medical and hospital costs of low-income families.

financed program to provide adequate health care for low-income families. There are also subsidies that assist the poor in obtaining more or less adequate housing.

Transfer payments substantially reduce the portion of the nation that is poverty-stricken. When the pre-transfer incidence of poverty is 21% for the population as a whole, it is only 12% after the distribution of antipoverty transfer payments and non-monetary benefits. The poverty programs have sometimes been criticized for "throwing money at the problem." Long-term solutions to poverty such as increased opportunities are essential, but in the short run "throwing money at the problem" raises millions of people out of poverty.

**Negative income tax** A proposed alternative to the multiplicity of income transfer programs for the poor is the negative income tax. Under the negative income tax plan, the government would establish a minimum basic income level, similar to the present poverty line but more realistic in providing an adequate living standard. Those with incomes at that level would pay zero income tax. Those with higher incomes would pay the usual tax rates. But those whose incomes fell below the basic income level would receive payments in the form of a negative income tax. The further their incomes fell below the basic level, the higher would be the rate of negative tax received.

Among the advantages claimed for the negative income tax plan over the existing welfare and other income transfer programs are that it would be simple to administer and would dispense with the costly "welfare industry" of agencies and administrators. Also, it would have the advantage of encouraging the poor to earn more income if they can. Under present welfare programs, an additional dollar of earnings can result in a reduction of an equal amount in income supplements. This removes the incentive to earn more income. Under the negative income tax proposal, there would always be an income incentive to increase earnings from work. A dollar of additional income from employment would not reduce income supplements by one dollar as now.

The earned income tax credit (EITC) has become a type of negative income tax for the working poor, who comprise 60% of all those in poverty. It was originally instituted in 1975 as a way to offset the federal tax liabilities of the poor. But the 1986 tax reform bill, increasing the maximum amount of the tax credit and providing an adjustment for inflation, entitles many low-income families to credits that exceed their tax liabilities—a negative income tax subsidy. In 1989 some 10 million families received EITC's worth an average of $552.

**negative income tax** an income maintenance plan that would provide a guaranteed minimum income for eligible families with no other income, and a supplement for families with incomes below a predetermined level.
**earned income tax credit (EITC)** a federal tax credit for poor families with earnings that offsets their tax liabilities and, for the poorest, provides a tax subsidy.

The term workfare covers a number of different programs that enable people to enter or reenter the job market. Above, one workfare recipient helps clean up a park in the East Bay Region Park District in Oakland, California.

By raising the minimum income on which taxes must be paid and increasing the standard deduction, the 1986 tax bill also elevated millions of low-income households above the poverty line. The change removed more than 6 million low-income households from the tax rolls altogether.

**Workfare**  Another alternative to the ordinary income transfer programs is workfare. Originally, workfare referred to programs that required public assistance recipients to "work off" the value of their checks—perhaps $100 a month—by community service in government or nonprofit organizations. Several states adopted such programs under the Aid to Families with Dependent Children program, though recipients who were unable to work or had pre-school children were typically exempt from the requirements.

More recently, workfare has been used to refer to a variety of education, training, work experience, and job placement programs designed to increase the self-sufficiency of public assistance recipients. Federal laws authorize such programs for AFDC recipients, and several states—most notably California and Massachusetts—have mounted major programs. Child care and transportation expenses may be subsidized to enable public assistance recipients to participate in the programs. Some states have also experimented with "grant diversion," under which the assistance payments are diverted to serve as wage subsidies to support on-the-job training by employers who hire welfare recipients.

**workfare**  originally a program that required nonexempt welfare recipients to work at public service jobs for a given number of hours a month; now may also include job training and wage subsidies.

# case application

## The Rich Get Richer and the Poor Get Ketchup

Income distribution has become more un-equal in the last decade, as shown in Table 2 on page 246. Adjusting for inflation, families in the lowest 20% of income receivers have less purchasing power now than they did 10 years ago. A typical family in the top 20%, by contrast, has seen their real earnings rise by a healthy 12%.

These average figures for income classes do not show the income changes that partic-ular groups have experienced, which in many cases are even more inequitable. Be-cause of the low average earnings of women, for example, families exclusively dependent on the income of a female householder con-stitute almost half of the families below the poverty line, although such families are only 10% of the population. Altogether, 38% of single-mother families are poor, over three times the incidence of poverty among mem-bers of other families (Figure 10). Looked at another way, nearly three-fourths of all the poor are women and children.

Racial and ethnic minorities are also dis-proportionately represented among those people below the poverty threshold. One-third of the black population is classified as poor. The incidence of poverty among minor-ities in general is two to three times that of the white population. Families with black female householders have the highest inci-dence of poverty, with more than one-half such families below the poverty level.

Families below the poverty line are more likely to include children under 18 than fami-lies above the poverty line. More than one

child in five lives in poverty. Nearly half of all black and Hispanic children live below the poverty level. The younger the children, the more likely they are to be poor: more than one of every two black children under the age of six lives in poverty. Children are now the poorest group in the country, having displaced the elderly from this unfavorable distinction as far back as 1974 when 15% were below the poverty level. Since then their economic position has deteriorated further and now over 20% are living in poverty.

According to the Children's Defense Fund, the average real income of families headed by people under 30 has declined by 14% since 1973 and their poverty rate has nearly dou-bled. This high poverty rate among young families foreshadows a continuation of this problem well into the future. Poverty tends to reproduce itself, creating a self-perpetuat-ing underclass. For example, 36% of girls from welfare families end up on welfare in later years themselves, compared to 9% from nonwelfare families.

A 1989 congressional analysis of the causes of the increase in poverty found that nearly one-half of the increase was attributable to cutbacks in state and federal aid. Decreased funding for antipoverty programs during the Reagan years affected the range of anti-poverty programs. Living stipends paid to welfare families with children fell 35% below the 1970 level, adjusted for inflation. A mil-lion people were eliminated from the food stamp program. Two million children were dropped from eligibility for school lunches. One cutback that was reversed by public reaction was the attempt to save money on the school lunch program by classifying ketchup as a vegetable in satisfying nutri-tional requirements.

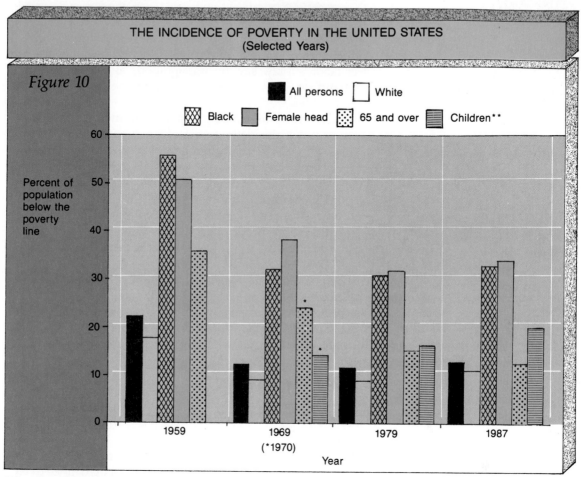

THE INCIDENCE OF POVERTY IN THE UNITED STATES
(Selected Years)

*Figure 10*

Legend: ■ All persons  □ White  ▨ Black  ▨ Female head  ▦ 65 and over  ▦ Children**

Percent of population below the poverty line

Year
1959
1969 (*1970)
1979
1987

**Data for children in 1959 not available.

Source: U.S. Bureau of the Census, *Current Population Reports*.

The percentages of the total population and each population subgroup falling below the poverty line have been reduced since 1959, but over one-third of all blacks and those in single-mother families are still living in poverty. In the 1980s there was a reversal of the antipoverty trend, putting more of all groups below the poverty level except those 65 and over.

## Economic Reasoning

1. What group experienced the largest increase in the percentage of the group below the poverty line between 1979 and 1989?
2. How do government programs such as the school lunch program increase opportunities for rising out of poverty?
3. Do you think women receiving AFDC should be required to participate in workfare? Why or why not?

# Putting It Together

Wages are determined basically the same way other prices are, by demand and supply. The demand for labor is a *derived demand* because it depends upon consumer demand for goods and services. The value of what a worker produces, after subtracting the costs of the other inputs, determines the demand for that worker's services. An increase in the labor supply, say, by immigration, also increases the demand for labor as a result of greater spending on goods and services.

The amount and quality of capital equipment available per worker is a major determinant of productivity and wages. More workers will be hired in an industry as long as the *net value* of an additional worker's output exceeds the wage rate.

*Minimum wage laws* may increase wages by accelerating capital investment. When wages are thus pushed up, in the long run either the number of workers in the industry will decline or labor productivity will be increased so that the last worker hired brings in as much added revenue as the wage paid.

Under *collective bargaining*, established by the National Labor Relations (Wagner) Act in 1935, agreements are negotiated between a firm and a labor union to determine wages and working conditions. If agreement on a contract cannot be reached, the union may resort to *job actions* such as a *strike* or boycott.

According to the traditional theory of wage determination, in a free labor market wages fall to the level at which all workers are employed. But modern economics holds that wages are "sticky" in the downward direction. They do not readily fall when there is unemployment. This is one difference between the price of labor and the price of most things: a surplus of labor often does not cause a fall in its price to an equilibrium level where the surplus is eliminated. When unions hold wages above the free market level, higher labor costs accelerate the introduction of laborsaving equipment, as in the case of minimum wages.

*Functional income distribution* reflects the way income is distributed according to its source: labor, land, capital, or entrepreneurship. Wages and salaries are paid for labor. Rent is payment for the use of land, which includes not only real estate but everything provided by nature. The payment for the use of financial capital is interest, and the income from entrepreneurship is profit. In addition to being the source of people's income, factor payments ration productive resources to their most valuable uses and serve as an incentive to produce.

Immigrant workers represent one controversial issue in the discussion of how income distribution is affected by labor—the most important factor of production.

Most income, about three-quarters of the total, is composed of wages and salaries. Although rent income, as such, is less than 1% of total income, some other incomes are similar to rent in that the supply of the factor is fixed. A unique human skill or ability that cannot be replicated by education, training, or practice earns an income that is more similar to rent than to wages. When the factor supply is perfectly inelastic, the factor price depends entirely on the level of demand. An increase in demand is accommodated exclusively by a rise in price, since the quantity supplied cannot increase.

From the standpoint of their economic function, proprietors' accounting profits consist to a large extent of *implicit interest* returns on the owners' capital, including a premium for risktaking, and *implicit wages* for the owners' labor. These are not economic profits. In competitive markets, economic profits tend to disappear. If economic profits persist, it is because of monopolistic power in the market.

*Personal income distribution* is the proportion of income going to different groups of income receivers. The most usual measure of income distribution is the percentage of total income received by each fifth of income receivers. A *Lorenz curve* plots this data on a diagram. The further the curve deviates from a straight diagonal line, the more unequally is income distributed.

Unequal income distribution results from differences in productivity, differences in economic opportunity, and differences in the amount of income-earning assets owned. Productivity differences are due to varying amounts of capital equipment per worker and variations in the training and skills of workers. Opportunity differences are often due to lack of access to education and lack of access to higher-paying jobs in industry and the professions. The Civil Rights

Act of 1964 prohibits discrimination in job opportunities. The widest variations in income result from earnings on financial assets, of which *capital gains* are the most significant for the highest income receivers.

The *poverty line* is the income level below which people are officially designated as poor. The poverty line is based on the amount of money that a family needs to spend on an economical food budget. That amount is multiplied by three to determine the total income needed for a family's basic living costs. Each year it is adjusted upward to reflect rising prices.

During the 1960s and early 1970s the number of people below the poverty line was decreasing. Since 1973 the number has been increasing. The majority of families below the poverty line are those in which women are the head of household, although such families are only 10% of the total population. Racial and ethnic minorities are also disproportionately represented among the poor, with two or three times the proportion of minority families falling below the poverty line as white families. Children constitute a disproportionately large share of those below the poverty line.

Government programs to increase the economic opportunities of poor people include job training programs, child-care facilities for working mothers, higher education grants and student loans, early-childhood education programs, and *affirmative action program* requirements for employment and education. *Transfer payments* to increase the real income of poor people include *entitlement programs* such as *food stamps, Aid to Families With Dependent Children, Medicaid,* housing subsidies, and food programs for school children and the elderly.

The proposed *negative income tax* would replace existing income transfer programs with a revision of the income tax system to provide direct government payments to families below a basic income level. The further families fall below this income level, the higher would be the rate of negative income taxes paid by the government. Under the negative income tax proposal, those receiving subsidies would have an incentive to earn more of their income. There would not be a one hundred percent trade-off between additional earnings and transfer payment income as there is with current programs. *Earned income tax credits* constitute a type of negative income tax.

Many states have initiated *workfare* programs for those on welfare, requiring a given number of hours of work per month in public service agency jobs. Some states incorporate job training in their programs to get welfare recipients into private sector jobs or provide wage subsidies to employers hiring someone on welfare.

# Perspective

## The Haymarket Affair

The Haymarket Square riot in Chicago, 1886. A dynamite bomb exploding among the police touched off large-scale bloodshed.

Additional information on The Haymarket Affair and labor union history can be found in *The Haymarket Tragedy* by Paul Avrich (Princeton, N.J.: Princeton University Press, 1984); *Labor in America: A History* by Foster Dulles (New York: Crowell, 1966); *History of the Labor Movement in the United States* by Philip Foner (New York: International Publishers, 1947); and *Working Men: The Story of Labor* by Sidney Lenz (New York: Putnam's, 1960).

On the evening of May 4, 1886, a rally was held in Chicago's Haymarket Square to protest the deaths of six striking workers, killed the previous day by police at the McCormick Harvester factory. The events were the outgrowth of a nationwide demonstration held on May 1 to reinforce labor demands for an 8-hour day to replace the average 10- or 11-hour workday existing at the time.

The Haymarket Square demonstration was attended by about 1500 people, and as police were attempting to disperse them a bomb was thrown killing and wounding a number of policemen. The police then opened fire on the crowd, inflicting over 200 casualties. It was never determined who threw the bomb, but eight labor organizers were arrested, tried, and convicted of murder. Only one of the eight had been at the demonstration, and he was speaking on the platform at the time the bomb was thrown. Nevertheless, all were found guilty of contributing to the crime because of inflammatory speeches they had made on other occasions. One of the condemned men committed suicide in prison, four were hanged, and the other three were eventually pardoned after serving seven years in prison. John Altgeld, the Illinois governor who pardoned them, stated that all eight were completely innocent and had been the victims of a biased judge and packed jury.

The Haymarket Affair was a turning point in labor union history. Before then unions had been weak and transitory. If a union was defeated in a strike, it generally went out of existence. Economic depressions virtually wiped out the whole union movement. Union organizers were blacklisted by employers, and could not get jobs. Job applicants were required to sign pledges that they would not join a union. The extensive use of children and immigrant labor in the factories undercut the unions. Immigrant workers were recruited from other countries, and many strikes were broken by pitting one nationality group against another.

Prior to the Haymarket Affair, no national union had ever lasted. But a few months after that episode, the American Federation of Labor was formed under the leadership of Samuel Gompers. It was the first federation of unions that proved able to survive depressions. In the 1930s a second national union was organized, the Congress of Industrial Organizations, and in 1955 the two merged to form the AFL-CIO.

# For Further Study and Analysis

## Study Questions

1. How would an increase in the demand for a product affect the wages of workers in that industry? Why?
2. What effects does the use of more capital equipment have on the productivity of labor in a particular industry? How can increased investment in capital equipment sometimes result in less demand for labor and at other times result in more demand for labor?
3. For most things, a higher price results in a larger quantity being supplied, but higher wages for labor have led to shorter workweeks. How do you account for this?
4. How do minimum wage laws affect youth employment? What would be the effects of reducing or abolishing minimum wage laws for people under 20?
5. In what ways might labor unions affect the rate of technological development?
6. What differences between U.S. industries result in some being high-wage industries and others being low-wage industries?
7. If the proprietor of a dry-cleaning establishment has $200,000 in personal capital invested in the business, works an average of 60 hours a week running the firm, and has an average $35,000 proprietor's income a year, would you estimate the proprietor's economic profits to be positive or negative? Why?
8. Are the high prices paid for admission to professional games the result of high players' salaries or the cause of high players' salaries? Or are these high salaries not related at all to high ticket prices? Why?
9. Has the relative income of the middle fifth of income receivers improved or worsened compared with other income receivers since 1960? What explanations might be found for the change in the relative income of middle-income earners?
10. Why do workers who work with large amounts of capital equipment generally earn more than workers who do not use large amounts of capital equipment?

## Exercises in Analysis

1. By researching the labor movement in your state or province, determine if "union shops" are legal. Then prepare a position paper supporting either the concept of the "union shop" or the reasoning behind "right-to-work" laws.
2. In what ways, if any, do government workers differ from workers in private industry in their right to organize unions and enforce their demands with strikes? Prepare a position paper defending or attacking the right of public employees to organize unions and to strike.
3. Draw a Lorenz curve based on the following data:

| *Percent of Population* | *Percent of Income* |
| --- | --- |
| Lowest 20% | 6% |
| Next 20% | 12% |
| Next 20% | 18% |
| Next 20% | 24% |
| Highest 20% | 40% |

4. Using the latest census data available, create a line graph reflecting the income level of American women as compared to American men for the past ten years.

## Further Reading

Acker, Joan. *Doing Comparable Worth: Gender, Class, and Pay Equity.* Philadelphia: Temple University Press, 1989. Based on an Oregon comparable worth project, this book examines the reform of gender-based pay scales and the effect on poverty relief.

Borjas, George J. *Friends or Strangers: The Impact of Immigrants on the U.S. Economy.* New York: Basic Books, 1990. Examines the impact of immigrants on earnings and employment, immigrant poverty and government programs, immigrant entrepreneurship, and international competition for immigrants.

Böhning, W. R. *Studies in International Labour Migration.* New York: St. Martin's Press, 1984. "It would be ridiculous to attempt to show whether the effects of immigration are a 'good thing' or a 'bad thing.' . . . There can be no peremptory conclusion to a controversy in which there are so many factors and so many intermingled and conflicting interests" (page 61, quoting M. Allefresde).

Easterlin, Richard A. *Birth and Fortune: The Impact of Numbers on Personal Welfare.* New York: Basic Books, 1980. A study of the effects of generation size on personal income and on society and the economy.

Freeman, Richard B., and James S. Metdoff. *What Do Unions Do?* New York: Basic Books, 1984. Covers the effects of unions on wages, wage inequality, nonorganized labor, productivity, and profits.

Haveman, Robert. *Starting Even: An Equal Opportunity Program to Combat the Nation's New Poverty.* New York: Simon & Schuster, 1988. Discusses the relationship between inequality of income distribution and efficiency, the effect government has had on inequality, and a program for equality with efficiency.

Kozol, Jonathan. *Rachel and Her Children: Homeless Families in America.* New York: Crown Publishers, 1988. Case studies of poverty in contemporary U.S. society.

Osterman, Paul. *Employment Futures: Reorganization, Dislocation, and Public Policy.* New York: Oxford University Press, 1988. A study of developments in the labor market, U.S. employment policy, and the effect on poverty.

Piore, Michael. *Birds of Passage: Migrant Labor and Industrial Societies.* Cambridge, U.K.: Cambridge University Press, 1979. Discusses migrant labor markets in general and the United States in particular, concluding with a chapter on "The Dilemmas of Current U.S. Immigration Policy."

Rees, Albert. *The Economics of Work and Pay.* New York: Harper & Row, 1979. A systematic treatment of the labor market, including labor demand and supply, wage differentials, and macroeconomic aspects.

Schiller, Bradley R. *The Economics of Poverty and Discrimination,* 5th ed. Englewood Cliffs, N.J.: Prentice Hall, 1989. A textbook treatment of poverty, the working poor, discrimination, and public policy.

Simon, Julian L. *The Economic Consequences of Immigration.* Cambridge, Mass.: Basil Blackwood, 1989. A technical treatment of the consequences of immigration for public finance, native workers' incomes, productivity, and the environment.

# Unit III

# MACROECONOMICS

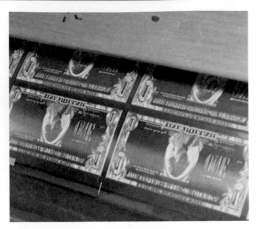

## Chapter 10. Money

Money comes in different forms and serves various purposes. The ways in which it is created and controlled have a major effect on the economy.

## Chapter 11. Unemployment and Inflation

The two big problems that macroeconomics has to deal with are unemployment and inflation. There are three different types of unemployment and a similar number of causes of inflation. The trade-off between unemployment and inflation changes at different times.

Macroeconomics covers the overall aspects of the economy. It deals with the total performance of the economy rather than with the behavior of individual units.

## Chapter 12. The Economy's Output

There are two different ways of measuring the total output of the economy, giving the same result. There are also two different explanations for what determines the level of total output—demand-side economics and supply-side economics—which do not come to the same conclusions.

## Chapter 13. Public Finance

Spending by the three levels of government—federal, state, and local—equals about one-third of total spending in the economy and accounts for one-fifth of total output. What this money is spent on and what its sources are depend on the level of government concerned. The way in which government spending is financed affects households and the economy.

## Chapter 14. Policies for Economic Stability and Growth

The government attempts to solve the unemployment and inflation problems and simultaneously maximize total output through the use of monetary and fiscal policies. The goal of economic growth can be achieved by increasing capital investment and capital efficiency and by improvements in the quality of the labor force.

## chapter 10

# MONEY

*People often associate economics with money. As we have seen in the first half of this book, economics deals with much more than just money, but now it is necessary to take a closer look at money. The introductory article examines its origins.*

## That Curious Commodity

Money is a curious commodity. Cattle were commonly used as money in pre-Christian times, and even recently by some primitive tribes. In fact, our word "pecuniary," which means "related to money," comes from the Latin word *pectus* meaning cattle. Cloth, corn, slaves, knives, and even beer have been used as money in different places at various times. These were types of money that had a value in exchange. But that was not true of all forms of money used in the past. Seashells, porpoise teeth, and woodpecker scalps have little practical use; but, at one time or other, in various places, all of these items have been used as money.

Metal coins were first used as money in the seventh century B.C. in ancient Lydia, which was located in what is now Turkey. Lydian coins were stamped with the head of a lion. Coins from other places sported turtles, owls, and horses with wings. These coins were usually made from an alloy of gold and silver.

Paper money originated with goldsmiths during the seventeenth century in London. Because the goldsmiths had safes in which to keep the precious metals that they worked with, people would bring them coins and gold and silver for safekeeping. The gold-smith gave the "depositors" receipts for their coins and precious metals.

It developed that these receipts would then be transferred from person to person as a means of payment. And if a wily goldsmith made out a few extra receipts and used them as a means of payment, no one would know it as long as everyone with receipts did not come to claim his or her precious metals or coins at the same time.

In the United States, after the Revolutionary War and during the next century, paper money in the form of bank notes was issued by privately owned banks. These banks were chartered by the federal government and the state governments. The state-chartered banks tended to be reckless in creating money. If someone presented a bank note for redemption, it had to be redeemed in gold or silver. Since the banks, following the example of the goldsmiths, issued more paper money than they had reserves of gold and silver, they preferred that the notes not be redeemed. Some banks made it difficult for people to find them by locating in out-of-the-way places. These hard-to-find locations were out in the "wilds," and this gave rise to the term "wildcat banking."

When the Civil War broke out, the federal government put an end to the freewheeling practices of state-chartered banks. The federal government printed paper money it-self—"greenbacks"—to help finance the war. But it was not until 1913, when the Federal Reserve System was established, that the federal government monopolized the issuance of bank notes.

Today, the production of currency is a big operation. There is a factory in Washington, D.C., that prints tens of millions of dollars in paper money every day. Tight security measures are used to protect this operation. Closed-circuit television cameras monitor production and inventory, and each employee has a security clearance. This factory, the Bureau of Printing and Engraving, operates 24 hours a day, seven days a week, including holidays.

New currency leaves the Bureau of Printing and Engraving in armored trucks for distribution to the 12 Federal Reserve banks around the country. The Federal Reserve banks act as wholesalers in passing the currency to commercial banks and other financial institutions. It is from these that the public obtains currency.

If we used currency for all of our money transactions, the printing presses in the Washington printing factory couldn't possibly keep up with the demand. But we don't use currency for all our money transactions. In terms of the total amount paid, 90% of all our monetary transactions are paid by check rather than currency.

The way we pay for goods and services is undergoing another change. One indication of this change is the increasing use of credit cards. Another aspect is the emerging use of electronic transfers of funds to replace writing checks for making payments. In some supermarkets you can pay for grocery purchases with a bank debit card. The card is inserted in a "reading" machine attached to the cash register and electronically transfers money from your bank account to the store's account. This point-of-sale (POS) system has spread to gas stations and other businesses as well. The next step is home banking. Already some tens of thousands of households in the United States are able to pay bills

and switch their funds among accounts by means of their home computers.

These changes are altering the nature of banking. Handling currency becomes unnecessary. When Dallas's Lone Star National Bank opened its doors in August 1984, it became the nation's first cashless bank. It kept no currency on hand. Among other advantages, this eliminated any danger of holdups. On the sides of the bank were signs announcing "No cash on premises."

The volume of electronic payments will likely exceed the amount paid by checks in the future. Even the paper symbols of money payments are being replaced by invisible electrical impulses. Money, that curious commodity, has come a long way from seashells and woodpecker scalps.

## Chapter Preview

*Although you can use a dollar bill to clean the lenses of your glasses or a coin as an emergency screwdriver, modern money is not a very useful commodity. Its only value is that other people have confidence in it and are willing to accept it in exchange for goods and services. This chapter explores the behavior of money by examining the following questions:* What is money? What does money do? How is money created? How is the supply of money controlled?

## Learning Objectives

*After completing this chapter, you should be able to:*

1. *Discuss the history of money.*
2. *Define the M1 money supply and describe its components.*
3. *Explain how near money differs from money and discuss how near money relates to the broader money definitions of M2, M3, and L.*
4. *List the three functions of money and explain the characteristics money must have in order to be functional.*
5. *Discuss how currency is affected by public demand and explain money creation.*
6. *Describe the Federal Reserve System.*
7. *Explain how the Federal Reserve System controls the money supply.*

# What Is Money?

As we have seen, money has taken many forms throughout the centuries. It can be anything that society generally accepts as payment for goods and services. This section will discuss what serves as money in our contemporary economy.

**Currency**   In the United States today, only about one-fourth of our money supply is currency. The amount of currency in circulation increases each year by varying amounts. After regularly increasing 9–10% a year during the last half of the 1970s, the rate of growth slowed to an average of less than 8% during the 1980s. The amount of currency in circulation depends on how much is desired by individuals and businesses. In April 1990 it totaled $230 billion. Individual and business withdrawal of currency from banks determines how much the banks will order from the Federal Reserve System. The government mints enough coins and prints sufficient paper money to satisfy this demand. Currency held by the government or by banks is not considered part of the money supply.

At one time federal law required that the amount of currency in circulation be limited to a legally fixed ratio to the value of the banking system's gold reserves. In 1968 this requirement was eliminated. The value of currency today depends only on people's confidence in the stability of the United States' economy.

The percentage of currency in the money supply increased gradually from 20% in 1960 to 28% in 1980. This currency component of the money supply stabilized in the

**currency** that part of the money supply consisting of coins and paper bills.
**Federal Reserve System (Fed)** the central bank of the United States; a system established by the Federal Reserve Act of 1913 to issue paper currency, supervise the nation's banking system, and implement monetary policy.

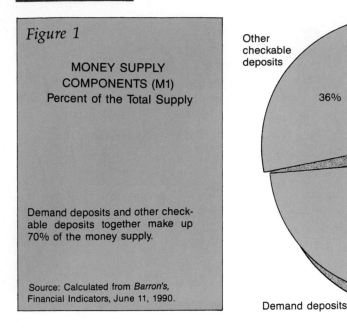

**Figure 1**

MONEY SUPPLY
COMPONENTS (M1)
Percent of the Total Supply

Demand deposits and other checkable deposits together make up
70% of the money supply.

Source: Calculated from *Barron's,*
Financial Indicators, June 11, 1990.

Other checkable deposits 36%

Currency 29%

34%

Travelers checks 1%

Demand deposits

1980s, and by 1990 was only 0.5% greater than it was 10 years earlier. Monetary experts are not sure why there are variations in the demand for currency. One view is that the percentage of currency in the money supply always rises whenever there is a publicized failure of a business or bank. In the year following the failure of Oklahoma's Penn Square Bank in 1982, the growth of currency in circulation temporarily increased, lending support to that idea. On the other hand, widespread failures of savings and loan institutions in the late 1980s (chapter 11, p. 295) had no appreciable effect on the currency component of the money supply.

There are also variations in the amount of currency in circulation during the year, especially around December when it reaches a peak to accommodate the holiday buying rush. At any given time, a number of factors can affect how much of their wealth people desire to hold in the form of currency.

**Demand deposits**  The largest part of the money supply is not currency but demand deposits and other checkable deposits—the obligations of a financial institution that are payable whenever the depositor writes a check. These deposits, which may be in either commercial banks, savings banks, savings and loan associations, or credit unions, do not consist of currency. A deposit is a liability, a sum that the bank must stand ready to pay immediately upon request. A check is a written order instructing the institution to do so, to transfer funds from one account to another. In this

**demand deposits (checking accounts)**  liabilities of depository institutions to their customers that are payable on demand.
**other checkable deposits**  accounts, other than demand deposit accounts in commercial banks, on which checks can be drawn, principally negotiable order of withdrawal (NOW) accounts in savings and loan banks.
**check**  a written order to a depository institution to pay a person or institution named on it a specified sum of money.

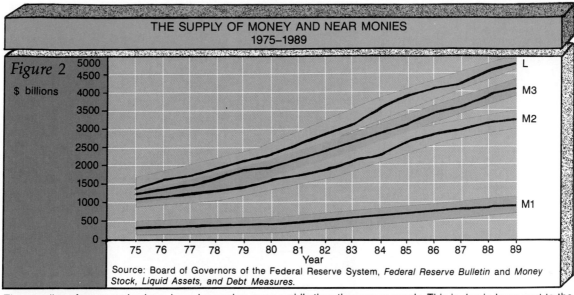

**Figure 2**

**$ billions**

THE SUPPLY OF MONEY AND NEAR MONIES
1975–1989

Source: Board of Governors of the Federal Reserve System, *Federal Reserve Bulletin* and *Money Stock, Liquid Assets, and Debt Measures.*

The supplies of near monies have been increasing more rapidly than the money supply. This is due in large part to the rapid growth of new financial instruments, such as money market funds and money market accounts, that combine high liquidity with higher returns.

respect, it is similar to an I.O.U. given to a friend in exchange for a cash loan. Checks written on demand deposits differ from personal I.O.U.s in their widespread general acceptability as money. Unlike a check written on a demand deposit, a personal I.O.U. normally cannot be used for purchases.

Because checks drawn on deposit accounts are used to pay for goods and services, these deposits are considered money. When people make cash withdrawals from their checking accounts to pay for purchases, or when they deposit cash into their checking accounts, the money supply is not changed. One type of money is exchanged for another type, the total remaining the same.

The most commonly used measurement of the money supply includes currency, travelers' checks, demand deposits, and other checkable deposits such as NOW accounts. This measurement of the money supply is known as Ml. Demand and other checkable deposits constitute 70% of the money supply (see Figure 1).

**Near money** There are various types of financial assets which can be turned into money more or less easily. These assets are considered near monies. They include savings deposits, certificates of deposit (CDs), and shares in money market mutual funds. The ease with which near monies can

**negotiable order of withdrawal (NOW) accounts** savings and loan bank customer accounts on which checks can be drawn.

**M1** a measure of the money supply that includes currency in circulation, demand deposit accounts, negotiable order of withdrawal (NOW) accounts, automatic transfer savings (ATS) accounts, travelers' checks, and checkable money market accounts.

**near money** assets with a specified monetary value that can be readily redeemable as money; savings accounts, certificates of deposit, and shares in money market mutual funds.

**savings deposits** liabilities of depository institutions to their customers which are not transferable by check and for which the institution may require advance notice before withdrawal.

**certificate of deposit (CD)** a deposit of a specified sum of money for a specified period of time which cannot be redeemed prior to the date specified.

**money market mutual fund** an investment fund that pools the assets of investors and puts the cash into debt securities that mature in less than one year: short-term bank CDs, commercial paper of corporations, and 6-month Treasury bills.

When people withdraw cash from their checking accounts to pay for purchases, the money supply is not changed.

**liquidity** the degree of ease with which an asset can be converted into cash without appreciable loss in value.

**M2** a measure of the money supply which includes M1 plus savings deposits, small time deposits (CDs), and certain money market mutual funds.

**M3** a measure of the money supply which includes M2 plus large time deposits (CDs).

**L** a measure of the money supply which includes M3 plus commercial paper, savings bonds, and government securities with maturities of 18 months or less.

**automatic transfer services (ATS)** a type of account which provides for the depository institution to automatically transfer funds from the depositor's savings account to her or his checking account when it has been drawn down.

be converted into money is called their liquidity. Depending upon how liquid these various financial assets are, they may be included in broader definitions of the money supply referred to as M2, M3, and L.

With the deregulation of the banking system and the evolution of new types of financial assets, the line between money and near monies has become blurred. Banks now provide automatic transfer services (ATS) from savings deposits to demand deposits. Money market funds permit investors to write checks on their fund accounts. These new types of accounts cross over the line from near money to money.

## Dealing the Cards

The stakes in the plastic card game are high and everybody wants in on the action. There are over 4,000 banks and other companies issuing universal credit cards. With these types of cards you can buy anything from a toothbrush to an automobile. The most widely used universal cards are Visa and MasterCard, which are issued by banks, while American Express and Sears's Discover cards are expanding rapidly. The total number of universal charge cards in the United States is approaching 300 million, more than double the number existing 10 years ago. Besides the universal cards, there are also innumerable specialized credit cards issued by oil companies, department stores, airlines, hotels, and the telephone companies.

From the standpoint of the customer, the explosion in the popularity of credit cards is due to a number of attractions: their convenience, the chance to spread out the payments over a period of time, the "float" (the delay between the date of the purchase and the date when the credit card payment is due), and the reduced risk of having cash lost or stolen. For some transactions—renting a car, ordering merchandise over the phone—a credit card is a virtual necessity. Most bank cards offer the cardholder the option of paying all bills in one lump sum or stretching out payments.

From the standpoint of the banks issuing the cards, the attraction is the high rate of interest they earn on outstanding balances. Interest charges on credit card balances are typically 18–20%, substantially higher than the 12–13% banks charge on other types of personal loans. The banks maintain that the costs of credit-card fraud and defaults necessitate the high interest rates. Furthermore, they claim, card holders are not concerned about what interest they pay, but only about the convenience of their charge cards.

The evidence suggests that they may be right about the claim that card holders generally are not concerned about the interest they pay. They are wrong, however, about the claim that it is economically necessary for them to charge such high rates. According to Federal Reserve data, since 1982 the profit margin on credit card business has been higher than for any other type of bank lending. Further evidence of the profitability of credit cards is the premium price paid when one bank buys the credit-card business of another bank. In 10 such transactions for which the price was publicly disclosed, the accounts sold at an average premium of 17% above their value, reflecting the expected future profitability of the accounts.

Despite the high interest rates, some people are credit-card junkies. Like compulsive gamblers, they are unable to control their use of the credit cards. They find themselves over their heads in debt, and unable to meet their payments. This often means that the cards are cancelled and the cardholder gets a bad credit rating. Other people choose to make minimum use of credit cards in order to keep their spending under control. If they can pay off the balance each month, as about one-third of all cardholders do, they benefit from the convenience of credit cards but avoid the high interest charges. The issuing banks don't like this much, but they still make a profit from the annual fees paid by the cardholder plus the amounts they collect from merchants for processing charge slips.

Some credit card users elect to carry only a few cards so that in case the cards get lost or stolen it won't be difficult to notify the companies. At the other extreme are the credit

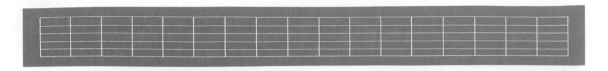

Walter Cavanagh, also known as "Mr. Plastic Fantastic," displays some of his 1,200 different credit cards. Even with his record-breaking collection, however, Mr. Cavanagh possesses only 12% of the different kinds of credit cards that are available.

card collectors. According to the *Guinness Book of World Records*, the champion cardholder is Walter Cavanagh, who has over 1,200 valid credit cards. He has the nickname of Mr. Plastic Fantastic. He keeps his credit cards in a fold-out wallet 250 feet long, weighing 35 pounds. The total amount of credit available to him with the cards is over $1.5 million. However, he makes a practice of paying off all of his bills each month.

## Economic Reasoning

1. Is "plastic money" included in the money supply measured by M1? How can you tell whether it is?
2. If credit cards are not money, can their use lead to an increase in the money supply? How?
3. Should the government tighten restrictions on credit card companies? What kinds of restrictions might be imposed?

# What Does Money Do?

Not only does money take different forms, it also serves various functions. In this section, we'll examine the different functions of money.

**Medium of exchange**   One function of money is that it is used as a medium of exchange, something that people will accept in exchange for goods or services.

The use of money to pay for things evolved as an alternative to barter. Using money as a medium of exchange for goods and services of all kinds is much easier than attempting to trade those goods and services directly for each other. Money generally simplifies the exchange process. There is no need in a monetary economy to waste time looking for someone who has exactly that good or service you want and who wants exactly what you have to trade. The use of money greatly simplifies exchange.

In order to serve well as a medium of exchange, whatever is used as money should be universally recognized, have an adequate but limited supply, not be easily reproduced (forged), be easily portable, and be durable. The evolution of money from seashells to bank drafts has been one long attempt to satisfy these requirements.

**Unit of measurement**   Some of the earlier forms of money did not serve very well as a medium of exchange. Cows, for example, are not exactly portable. However, they did serve another function of money, that of providing a unit of measurement. The money unit serves as a common denominator that can specify the value of something else. In societies where cattle were used for money, everyone knew pretty well the value of a cow. The value of other things could therefore be expressed in terms of how much of each was equivalent to the value of a cow.

**medium of exchange**   a commodity accepted by common consent in payment for goods and services and as settlement of debts and contracts.
**barter**   direct exchange of goods and services without the use of money.
**unit of measurement (standard of value or unit of account)**   a common denominator of value in which prices are stated and accounts recorded.

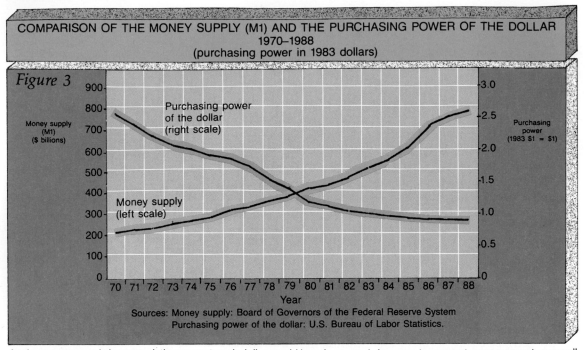

**COMPARISON OF THE MONEY SUPPLY (M1) AND THE PURCHASING POWER OF THE DOLLAR**
1970–1988
(purchasing power in 1983 dollars)

*Figure 3*

Money supply
(M1)
($ billions)

Purchasing power
of the dollar
(right scale)

Money supply
(left scale)

Purchasing
power
(1983 $1 = $1)

Year

Sources: Money supply: Board of Governors of the Federal Reserve System
Purchasing power of the dollar: U.S. Bureau of Labor Statistics.

As the money supply increased, the amount each dollar would buy decreased. As a result, money has not served very well as a store of value. Inflation diminishes this function of money.

Normally, the unit of measurement is the same as the medium of exchange, but not always. In international transactions where countries use different mediums of exchange (French francs, German marks, British pounds), the American dollar is frequently used as a unit of measurement. The price of OPEC oil, for example, is quoted in U.S. dollars per barrel all over the world.

A unit of measurement should itself be stable in value. Because of fluctuations in the value of the dollar, there have been suggestions that the world adopt a new unit of measurement. It would be based on the value of <u>commodities</u> rather than on the value of the dollar or any other currency.

**Store of value** The third function of money is to serve as a store of value, a form in which wealth can be held. Any form of wealth may be used as a <u>store of value</u>, but money has the advantage of being more liquid than other forms of wealth. Near monies are not perfectly liquid because in order to use them for purchases they must normally be converted into currency or a demand deposit. You run the risk that converting them at a particular time may result in a loss. Holding money itself, however, results in a loss during times of rising prices. As prices rise, the real purchasing power of money declines.

**commodity** an economic good.
**store of value** a means of conserving purchasing power for a future time.

# case application

## P.O.W. Money

During World War II, captured servicemen in prisoner of war (P.O.W.) camps in Germany and Italy created a simple but complete economic system to serve their needs. The prisoners received Red Cross rations, which included canned milk, chocolate bars, jam, sugar, crackers, and cigarettes. Some also received gift packages from home through the mail. These rations and gifts comprised a flow of real income to the prisoners, although they had no money.

The Red Cross rations were fairly standardized, and a P.O.W. would likely find himself with a shortage of his favorite commodities and an excess of other commodities that he did not want.

The prisoners soon began to make exchanges. Out of these exchanges a market system was born. The essence of exchange is that both parties benefit. A nonsmoker gives up cigarettes he does not value for chocolate, which he does like. So the smoker gets the cigarettes and the candy lover gets the chocolate.

Exchanges at first were made through a simple barter procedure, whereby one item was swapped for another. But this process was awkward and time-consuming. If one P.O.W. had some crackers and chocolate bars and wished to exchange the chocolate bars for jam to eat with the crackers, he would have to find someone else who had jam but preferred to have chocolate bars instead. Some prisoners in the camp became very good at making advantageous swaps and made a business venture of it—P.O.W. capitalists.

To get around the inconvenience of barter, a money economy gradually developed in the camps, complete with buyers, sellers, and even a merchant class. Cigarettes were used

as money, and the prices of all other items were quoted in terms of how many cigarettes they were worth.

## Economic Reasoning

1. Which functions of money did cigarettes perform in the P.O.W. camp?
2. Heavy air raids in the vicinity of the camp increased the consumption of cigarettes. What effect did this have on the prices of things?
3. Sometimes the successful P.O.W. capitalists who profited from buying and selling things were resented by other prisoners. Was the hostility directed toward them justified? Were they providing a useful service or were they merely leeches on the P.O.W. society?

The Lydians of western Anatolia minted the first gold and silver coins and set up the first permanent retail stores in the seventh century B.C.

# How Is Money Created?

The manner in which money is created has evolved quite a bit since the Lydians stamped out their lion-headed coins 26 centuries ago. In this section we will look at how money is created in a modern economy.

**Currency** As we have seen, this part of the money supply is produced by the federal government, which supplies coins and paper money in the amounts required by the public. Currency enters businesses and households through banks. An increase in the amount of currency in circulation, however, does not necessarily mean an increase in the money supply. People who need more currency buy it from their banks by writing checks on their deposits for the bills or coins desired. The increase in currency has been offset by a decrease in demand deposits, leaving the total money supply unchanged.

It would be possible for the federal government to increase the money supply by printing more currency if it used the currency directly to pay government bills rather than selling the currency to the public through the banking system. This is not the usual practice in this country, however, and the government normally produces currency only in response to the demands from businesses and the general public.

**Private borrowing** Borrowing from a bank increases the supply of money by increasing the amount of demand deposits. The borrower, in exchange for promising to repay a given sum (usually this promise is represented by a promissory note), receives the amount in his or her checking account. This added deposit does not reduce anyone else's deposit and, as such, represents a net increase in the supply of money. The individual is then able to use that money to purchase goods and services by writing a check on the account. The new money created by the loan is thereby transferred to someone else who in turn may use it for other purchases.

If the borrower repays the loan from the bank when the note comes due, the money supply is reduced by that amount. Changes in the money supply depend on the amount of new loans relative to the amount of repayment of previous loans. When the volume of new lending by banks exceeds the repayment of previous loans, the money supply increases.

**Government borrowing** When the local, state, or federal government borrows from a bank, the initial effect upon the money supply is much the same as in the case of private

**promissory note** (IOU) a written obligation to pay a specified amount at a specified time.

In a throwback to earlier forms of money, these cumbersome stones, while not easily portable, serve as a unit of measurement on the islands of Yap.

borrowing. New deposits are created. A government borrows by promising future repayment in return for a current deposit. The government can then write checks on the deposit to cover its expenditures. <u>Treasury bills</u> and <u>bonds</u> are government promises to repay its loans.

Thus the federal government does not customarily increase the money supply by printing money. It increases the money supply in the same way businesses and individuals increase the money supply—by borrowing.

**Treasury bill** a short-term, marketable, federal government security with a maturity of one year or less.
**bond** a long-term, interest-bearing certificate issued by a business firm or by a government that promises to pay the bondholder a specified sum of money on a specified date.

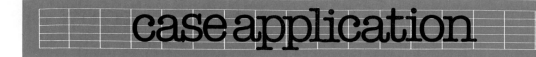

# case application

## How to Create Money

One way you can create money is to print it on a printing press in your basement. But if you were to do that you could get into a lot of trouble. A perfectly legal way you can create money, however, is to take out a loan at a bank. Imagine that you have decided that you will buy a computer that costs $700. You go to the bank for a loan, and if the bank approves your loan for $700, you sign a promissory note. The banker makes out a deposit slip to be credited to your demand deposit account, and you can then write a check to pay for the computer.

When the purchase is made and the computer dealer deposits your check in the bank, it is presented to your bank for payment. Your demand deposit account is decreased by the amount of the check. What has happened to your personal wealth? You now own a computer worth $700. You have also increased your liability by the amount of the loan ($700), so your personal wealth has not changed. Your assets and liabilities from this transaction are equal. But you have succeeded in increasing the money supply in the economy. That money is now in the computer dealer's checking account. When the computer dealer spends it, it will move to someone else's account.

*Economic Reasoning*

1. If you borrowed the $700 in cash rather than having it credited to your checking account, would the effect on the money supply be the same? Why or why not?
2. When you pay off your bank loan, what happens to the money supply? Is the effect on the money supply any different whether you pay the bank by check or with currency?
3. There is an old adage that bankers are only willing to loan money to people who don't need it. Those who have plenty of financial assets that can readily be turned into cash have little trouble getting a loan, whereas those who have no assets have a great deal of difficulty. Should bankers make loans only to those who have enough assets to guarantee repayment of the loan? What are the consequences of making loans to people who are not good credit risks?

# How Is the Supply of Money Controlled?

In order for our monetary system to function successfully, people must have confidence in the value of money. This confidence can be maintained only if the quantity of money in circulation does not fluctuate excessively. Here we will examine how the money supply is controlled to prevent excessive variations in the quantity and value of money.

**The Federal Reserve System**   Banks in the nineteenth century, by their unrestrained issuance of currency and their lending behavior, caused wild fluctuations in the money supply. Excessive creation of money alternated with bank failures and the collapse of the monetary system. Finally, after the panic of 1907, when a run on banks by people attempting to withdraw their deposits forced many banks to close, the government established a National Monetary Commission to formulate a plan for a new American banking system. The recommendations in its report led to the establishment of the Federal Reserve System in 1913. The Federal Reserve, commonly referred to as "the Fed," is the central bank of the United States. It is a government institution that acts as a "banker's bank," serves the monetary needs of the federal government, and controls the monetary system.

There are 12 regional Federal Reserve banks in the country. Each one services and regulates the banks in its district. The Federal Reserve Districts are shown in Figure 4 on page 283. The system is under the overall authority of the Board of Governors in Washington, D.C. The seven members of the Board are appointed by the president of the United States and confirmed by the Senate for staggered 14-year terms. The Board's Chairman and Vice Chairman are named by the president, confirmed by the Senate, from among the members of the Board. They are appointed to serve for 4-year terms, with the possibility of reappointment so long as their Board terms have not expired.

Only about one-third of the nation's banks, some 5,000, are members of the Federal Reserve System. However, the Depository Institutions Deregulation and Monetary Control Act of 1980 (more simply referred to as the Monetary Control Act) made nonmember banks and other depository institutions such as savings banks, savings and loan associations, and credit unions subject to the same conditions as Fed

**Fed**   Federal Reserve System.
**central bank**   a government institution that controls the issuance of currency, provides banking services to the government and to the other banks, and implements the nation's monetary policy; in the United States the Federal Reserve is the central bank.
**Fed Board of Governors**   the governing body of the Federal Reserve System consisting of seven members appointed by the president for 14-year terms.
**depository institutions**   financial institutions that maintain deposit account obligations to their customers; includes commercial banks, savings banks, savings and loan associations, and credit unions.

## Table 1     ORGANIZATION OF THE FEDERAL RESERVE SYSTEM

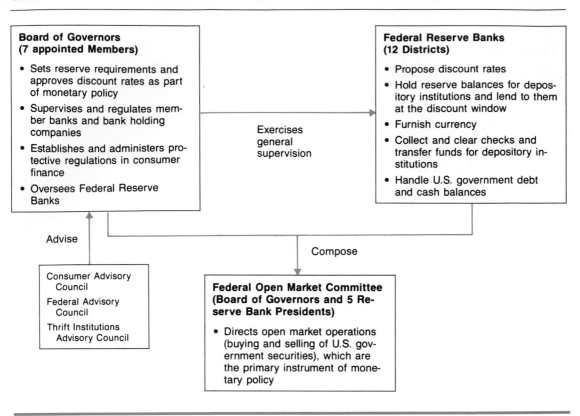

**Board of Governors (7 appointed Members)**

- Sets reserve requirements and approves discount rates as part of monetary policy
- Supervises and regulates member banks and bank holding companies
- Establishes and administers protective regulations in consumer finance
- Oversees Federal Reserve Banks

Exercises general supervision

**Federal Reserve Banks (12 Districts)**

- Propose discount rates
- Hold reserve balances for depository institutions and lend to them at the discount window
- Furnish currency
- Collect and clear checks and transfer funds for depository institutions
- Handle U.S. government debt and cash balances

Advise

**Consumer Advisory Council**

**Federal Advisory Council**

**Thrift Institutions Advisory Council**

Compose

**Federal Open Market Committee (Board of Governors and 5 Reserve Bank Presidents)**

- Directs open market operations (buying and selling of U.S. government securities), which are the primary instrument of monetary policy

Source: Board of Governors of the Federal Reserve System, Division of Support Services, *Purposes & Functions*, 1984.

---

**legal reserve requirement (required reserves)** the minimum amount of reserves that a depository institution must have on deposit with the Federal Reserve bank, stated as a percentage of its deposit liabilities.

**discount rate** the interest rate charged by the Federal Reserve on loans to depository institutions.

**open market operations** the purchase or sale of government securities by the Federal Reserve to implement monetary policy.

**required reserves** see legal reserve requirement.

---

member banks. There are about 33,000 other financial institutions, in addition to the 5,000 commercial bank members of the system, that are subject to the Fed's reserve requirements. The Fed provides these nonmember institutions with the same services that it provides to member banks. The nonmember institutions must pay the Fed a fee to cover the costs of the services. In this chapter the term "banks" has been used to refer to depository institutions in general.

The most important function of the Federal Reserve System is to control the creation of money by depository institutions. There are three ways by which it accomplishes this: (1) by setting legal reserve requirements; (2) by varying the discount rate; (3) by open market operations.

**Reserve requirements** All banks are required to have a reserve on deposit with the Federal Reserve bank in their district. These deposits are the banks' required reserves. A bank may have in its reserve account more than the legal

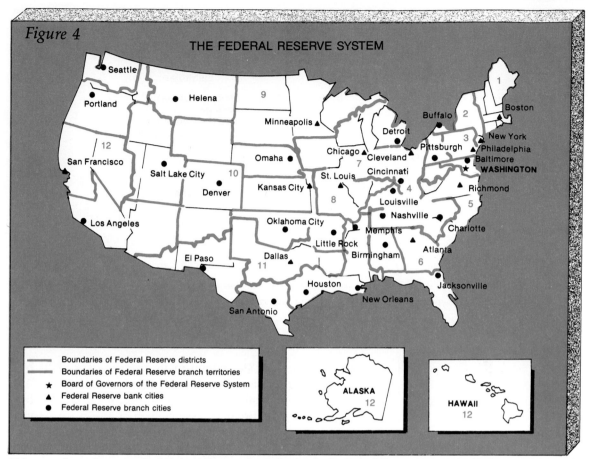

**Figure 4**

**THE FEDERAL RESERVE SYSTEM**

- —— Boundaries of Federal Reserve districts
- —— Boundaries of Federal Reserve branch territories
- ★ Board of Governors of the Federal Reserve System
- ▲ Federal Reserve bank cities
- ● Federal Reserve branch cities

ALASKA 12

HAWAII 12

This map shows the network of Federal Reserve bank districts in the United States. Before the Fed's establishment in 1913, bank failures and monetary collapse threatened the economic system.

minimum specified, but it is not allowed to operate with less. Reserves over the legal minimum are referred to as excess reserves.

Under the Monetary Control Act, the Federal Reserve Board specifies the legal reserve requirements of all banks as a percentage of the bank's customer deposits—whether checking, savings, or time deposits. These reserve requirements can be varied by the Fed within statutory limits. The highest reserve requirements are imposed on checking and "checkable" savings (NOW and ATS) accounts, and can vary from 8 to 14%.

Let us assume for illustration that the reserve requirement ratio is 10%. This means that the bank must have on deposit in its reserve account with the Fed at least $1 for every $10 in customer deposits on its books. If the balance sheet of the bank shows deposit liabilities of $100 million the bank must

**excess reserves** reserves of depository institutions over and above the legally required minimum on deposit with the Federal Reserve.
**reserve requirement ratio** the percentage of a depository institution's deposit obligations to its depositors that must be maintained in reserves.
**deposit liabilities** the amount that a depository institution is obligated to pay out to its depositors.

## Table 2     SEVENTH BANK OF COMMERCE YEAR-END BALANCE SHEET
### (thousands of dollars)

| Assets | | Liabilities | |
|---|---|---|---|
| Reserves at Federal Reserve | $ 15,843 | Demand deposits (private) | $ 91,145 |
| Vault cash | 3,721 | Time deposits (private) | 63,025 |
| Deposits at other banks | 12,210 | Deposits of U.S. Government | 1,670 |
| Checks in process of collection | 5,776 | Deposits of state & local gov'ts | 26,145 |
| U.S. Government securities | 23,680 | Due to financial institutions | 7,445 |
| Securities of state & local gov'ts | 24,370 | Other liabilities | 6,760 |
| Other securities | 2,420 | Total Liabilities | $196,190 |
| Loans and discounts | 114,155 | | |
| Bank premises | 5,305 | **Capital** | |
| Other assets | 3,310 | Common stock | $ 2,265 |
| Total Assets | $210,790 | Capital surplus | 5,360 |
| | | Undivided profits | 4,700 |
| | | Reserves | 2,205 |
| | | Total Capital | $ 14,600 |
| | | Total Liabilities and Capital | $210,790 |

The balance sheet of a hypothetical bank. Required and excess reserves are an asset. Deposits are liabilities.

have no less than $10 million in its reserve deposit. If by some chance the bank's reserves stand at less than $10 million, it must obtain additional reserves. It can do this by selling some of its financial assets, such as the government securities it owns, or by borrowing funds from the Fed or from other banks. If the bank wants to avoid doing one of these things, which might be costly, it must reduce its deposit liabilities to a level that does not exceed ten times its reserves.

How does the Fed control the supply of money by altering the legal reserve requirements? Let us assume that the bank we are discussing has not loaned all the money it was allowed to loan. Instead of having $10 million in reserves, it has $12 million. In addition to its $10 million required reserves, it has $2 million in excess reserves. The bank could profit by expanding its credit business and making new loans. If the Fed Board of Governors does not want banks to expand their lending because the money supply is growing too rapidly, it can prevent the bank from making new loans by raising the reserve requirement to 12%. Since the bank's $12 million reserve is 12% of its demand deposit liabilities, the bank has made as many loans as it can. It cannot extend additional loans to borrowers without first increasing its reserves. Thus the money supply has been prevented from growing.

The reserve requirement ratio determines by how much the banking system can expand the money supply. If the

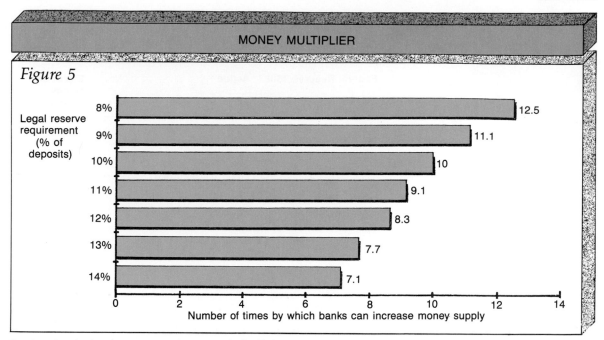

**MONEY MULTIPLIER**

*Figure 5*

Legal reserve requirement (% of deposits)

| | |
|---|---|
| 8% | 12.5 |
| 9% | 11.1 |
| 10% | 10 |
| 11% | 9.1 |
| 12% | 8.3 |
| 13% | 7.7 |
| 14% | 7.1 |

Number of times by which banks can increase money supply

By changing the legal reserve requirement ratio the Fed can control the supply of money. The lower the required reserve ratio, the more money banks can create by making loans.

reserve requirement is 10%, the maximum expansion of the money supply is ten times the increase in bank reserves. If the reserve requirement is 12.5%, the maximum expansion of the money supply is only eight times the amount of the increase in bank reserves. The ratio of maximum money supply creation to bank required reserves is the money multiplier. If the reserve requirement was 100%, commercial banks would be unable to expand the money supply at all. This would make it very difficult for businesses to borrow money, and would seriously hamper economic activity.

**Discounting**  If a bank wishes to expand its lending activity but has no excess reserves, or if it finds itself below the legal reserve requirement, it may add to its reserves by borrowing from the Fed. Federal Reserve lending to commercial banks is called discounting, and the interest charged by the Fed for such loans is the discount rate. By increasing this rate, the Fed can discourage banks from coming to the "discount window" and asking for a loan. On the other hand, if the Fed wishes to see an expansion of the money supply, it can lower the discount rate and thereby lessen the cost of the loan. This makes borrowing additional reserves a more attractive possibility for the bank.

A bank can also supplement its reserves by borrowing the

**money multiplier**  the ratio of the maximum increase in the money supply to an increase in bank reserves. Determined by the required reserve ratio.

**discounting**  assigning a present value to future returns; making a loan with the interest subtracted in advance from the principal.

*Table 3*   MAJOR TOOLS OF FEDERAL RESERVE
MONETARY CONTROL

| Federal Reserve Tool | Action | Effect on Money Supply |
|---|---|---|
| Reserve Requirement | Raise required reserve ratio<br>Lower required reserve ratio | Decreases<br>Increases |
| Discount Rate | Raise discount rate<br>Lower discount rate | Decreases<br>Increases |
| Open Market Operations | Buy U.S. Treasury securities<br>Sell U.S. Treasury securities | Increases<br>Decreases |

excess reserves of another bank. This type of borrowing is referred to as the Federal Funds market. Such inter-bank lending is typically only overnight or for a few days at most to cover the bank's short-term reserve needs. The interest rate that banks charge each other for these loans is called the Federal Funds rate. It is one of the most closely watched interest rates because of its effect on other interest rates.

**Open market operations**   The third way in which the Fed influences the money-creating power of banks is through open market operations. This means that the Fed purchases or sells United States government securities (bonds or Treasury bills) in the government-securities market. The decision to buy or sell such securities is made by the Federal Open Market Committee. This committee is made up of the seven members of the Board of Governors together with presidents of five of the Federal Reserve banks.

When the Fed purchases government securities, the amount it pays for them ends up as new reserves for the banks. The new excess reserves in turn make it possible for these banks to create more demand deposits by making new loans. When the Fed sells securities, the opposite happens. Reserves flow out of the banks' Federal Reserve accounts, and bank-deposit creation is curtailed.

In practice, open market operations are the tool most commonly used by the Fed to control the money supply. The reason that this is the most popular instrument of monetary policy is that it is the most flexible. It permits the banks the greatest amount of leeway in adjusting to their individual circumstances.

**Federal Funds market**   the market among depository institutions for temporary transfer of excess reserves from one institution to another.
**Federal Funds rate**   the interest rate paid on Federal Funds borrowed.
**Federal Open Market Committee**   a committee consisting of the Federal Reserve Board and the presidents of five regional Federal Reserve banks that decides on the purchase or sale of government securities by the Federal Reserve to implement monetary policy.

# case application

## Cheap Money

Money is a real bargain in the United States. The price of money is the interest rate. But the actual cost of money is less than the quoted interest rate, the so-called "nominal rate."

One reason interest costs are less than the nominal rate is inflation. As a result of inflation, when you pay back a loan the dollars that you use to make the payment are not worth as much as the dollars that you borrowed. The real rate of interest is the nominal rate minus the rate of inflation. If the interest rate is 10% and the inflation rate is 10%, you get the use of the money free.

The real interest rate is the actual cost of money to the borrower in purchasing power. Figure 6 shows the prime interest rates and the corresponding real interest rates, after subtracting the rate of inflation, for the years 1970 to 1989. As you see, the real interest rate was less than zero in 1974 and 1975. This means that lenders were subsidizing borrowers to use the lenders' money.

Of course, only the most successful, most

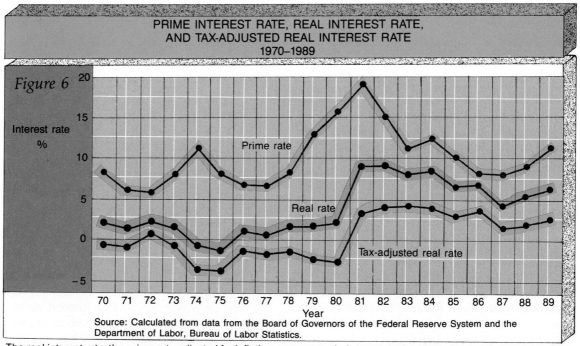

**Figure 6**

PRIME INTEREST RATE, REAL INTEREST RATE, AND TAX-ADJUSTED REAL INTEREST RATE 1970–1989

Interest rate %

Prime rate

Real rate

Tax-adjusted real rate

Year

Source: Calculated from data from the Board of Governors of the Federal Reserve System and the Department of Labor, Bureau of Labor Statistics.

The real interest rate, the prime rate adjusted for inflation, was near or below zero in the 1970s. In recent years it has been around 5%. The tax-adjusted real interest rate for those in the 30% tax bracket was negative in the 1970s and, for loans on real estate equity, below 5% in the 1980s.

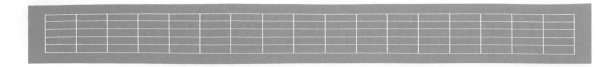

credit-worthy businesses can borrow money at the prime rate. Individuals and most businesses must pay higher rates, reflecting the higher loan risks. Nonetheless, real interest rates were quite low during the 1970s.

This situation changed in the 1980s as a result of a variety of factors. One was the realization by lenders, after a succession of years of high inflation rates, that inflation was apparently going to persist and the rates they charged should take this into account. Reinforcing this movement to higher rates was the deregulation of the banking system that eliminated interest ceilings on bank deposits. Competition for customers among banks and other financial institutions, such as money market funds, raised the cost of money to lenders, which they passed on in higher interest rates charged to borrowers.

The rise in nominal interest rates actually began in 1977, but real interest rates remained low until 1980 because of increasing inflation. The subsequent rise in real interest rates resulted from a change in Federal Reserve policy. In 1979 the Fed changed its monetary target from control of interest rates to control of the supply of money. It restricted money growth to stop inflation. This caused a further rise in nominal rates and brought on a recession which halted the inflation. As a result, real interest rates increased and remained high despite the sharp decrease in nominal rates that followed.

Nominal and real interest rates in some countries, Japan for example, are lower than in the United States. But, in this country, the real interest rate is not the "really real" interest rate. The real interest rate takes into account only inflation. It does not take into account the tax benefits to borrowers. Unlike the tax systems in other countries, our tax laws have allowed taxpayers to deduct certain interest payments from their incomes before computing their taxes. The 1986 tax reform phased out deductions for interest paid by individuals, excepting mortgage interest. But individuals can borrow on the equity in their homes and use the proceeds of the loan for any purpose, receiving a tax subsidy on the interest charges.

This means that the government continues to subsidize much consumer borrowing. If the borrower's combined federal and state marginal income tax rate is 30%, government picks up 30% of the nominal interest cost on eligible loans. The tax-adjusted real prime interest rates for borrowers in the 30% tax bracket are shown in Figure 6. From 1973 to 1980 they were negative, and since then they have been less than 5%. The government has, in effect, bribed people to borrow money. At the same time, it discourages people from saving by charging them taxes on their interest earnings.

## Economic Reasoning

1. What effect would an increase in the Fed discount rate have on the money supply? Why?
2. What effect would it have on the interest rates shown in Figure 6? Why?
3. Should the tax laws stop subsidizing all borrowing by individuals? By businesses? Why or why not? Should interest earnings on savings be exempt from taxation? What effect would this have on income distribution between the wealthy and the poor?

# Putting It Together

Money can be anything that society generally accepts as payment for goods and services. What we consider money today includes not only *currency*, but also travelers' checks, *demand deposits* and other checkable deposits such as *negotiable orders of withdrawal*. Currency, which consists of coins and bills not held by the banking system, constitutes just over one-fourth of the country's money supply. The remainder is principally made up of bank deposits on which people can write *checks*. The measurement of the money supply, referred to as *M1*, includes *other checkable deposits* in depository institutions such as savings banks and credit unions, as well as those in commercial banks. Other types of financial assets which are not used directly to pay for goods and services, but which can be turned into money quickly and easily are called *near money*. Near monies with a high degree of *liquidity* are *savings deposits, certificates of deposit,* and shares in *money market mutual funds.*

Money serves three distinct functions. First, it serves as a *medium of exchange* in conducting transactions. It is much more efficient in facilitating the transfer of goods and services than a *barter* system would be. The second function of money is that it serves as a *unit of measurement*. Whether or not any transactions take place, the value of goods and services is measured in units of money. The unit of measurement within each country is the currency of that country. The unit of measurement in international transactions is quite often the American dollar. Finally, money can be used as a *store of value*. During periods of rapidly rising prices, however, it does not serve this function well.

Currency is produced by the government in response to the demand for it by businesses and the general public. The currency enters the economic system when people purchase it from banks, paying for it by check. Therefore, an increase in currency in circulation does not increase the money supply. It is merely exchanged for a different form of money—demand deposits. The money supply is increased when banks lend funds to businesses, individuals, or governments. The bank loans are in the form of demand deposits which borrowers can then transfer to someone else by writing checks. The amount borrowed continues to circulate in the banking system as additional money until the loan is repaid.

The responsibility for controlling the money supply is in the hands of the *Federal Reserve System*. The Fed has three tools of monetary control. First, it can limit or expand the ability of banks to make loans by raising or lowering banks'

All of this money would be mere paper if it were not for the fact that people are willing to accept it in exchange for goods and services.

reserve requirements. The *required reserves* are equal to a specified percentage of the bank's total *deposit liabilities* which must be deposited with the regional Federal Reserve bank. Any reserves that a bank has deposited over and above the required minimum are *excess reserves* and can form the basis for an increase in loans extended by the bank to borrowers. The ratio of the maximum increase in the money supply to an increase in bank reserves is the *money multiplier*. Its size is determined by the required reserve ratio. The second instrument of the Federal Reserve monetary control is the *discount rate*. This is the interest rate that banks must pay on funds borrowed from the Fed. Lowering the discount rate encourages banks to borrow from the Federal Reserve to acquire excess reserves in order to expand loan business. Raising the discount rate discourages them from making new loans. The third and most often employed monetary tool of the Federal Reserve is *open market operations*. This is the purchase and sale of U.S. government securities by the Fed in order to increase or decrease bank reserves. When the Fed purchases a bond in the government securities market, the amount of the check that it issues to pay for the bond becomes an addition to the reserves of the banking system. If the Fed sells a bond, the amount that it receives from the sale diminishes bank reserves.

# Perspective

## The Big Bank Controversy

An engraving of the Bank of the United States in Philadelphia about 1799.

Further information on the evolution of the nation's banking system can be found in *The Second Bank of the United States* by R. C. H. Caterall (Chicago: University of Chicago Press, 1960); *The Theory and History of Banking* by Charles Dunbar (New York: G. P. Putnams, 1917); and *Money: Whence It Came, Where It Went* by John Kenneth Galbraith (Boston: Houghton Mifflin, 1975).

From the earliest days of the American republic there has been conflict over states' rights versus the power of the federal government. One of the first important battles in this conflict was over the control of the nation's banking system. The Federalists, led by Alexander Hamilton, wanted a strong national banking system to finance the expansion of industry. The Anti-Federalists, under the leadership of Thomas Jefferson, wanted to minimize the power of the banking system, which they did not trust to protect the predominantly agricultural interests of the country.

The initial victory went to Hamilton and the Federalists when Congress chartered the First Bank of the United States in 1791 for a period of 20 years. One-fifth of the capital needed to finance the bank was provided by the federal government and the remaining four-fifths by private investors. The national bank established branches in major cities and engaged in commercial banking activities and central bank functions. It accepted deposits from and made loans to private borrowers. It also lent money to the federal government and acted as the depository for government funds. It issued bank notes of its own and acted to curb the issuance of bank notes by state-chartered or private banks.

This latter activity generated a great deal of hostility on the part of the state banks. When the charter of the First Bank of the United States expired, it was not renewed by Congress. Freed from the restraints imposed by the national bank, state banks went on a note-issuing spree. They more than doubled their note issue in 5 years. Most of them stopped redeeming their notes for gold and silver. As a result, the notes of many banks became practically worthless. There was chaos in the banking system and numerous bank failures and alternating periods of excessive money expansion and contraction.

As a result, the Second Bank of the United States was chartered in 1816. It was similar in its financing and operations to the First Bank. It also had a similar fate, its charter allowed to lapse in 1836. The state banks again had the banking field to themselves until the National Banking Act of 1864. The Act provided for a system of federally chartered banks to take over the note-issuing function of the state banks. Congress also intended these national banks to help finance government spending for the Civil War. It was not, however, until the establishment of the Federal Reserve System in 1913 that a true central bank was created.

# For Further Study and Analysis

## Study Questions

1. Have you ever transformed near money into money? How?
2. Are there any barter transactions that take place in today's economy? Why would anyone prefer barter to money transactions?
3. Using the criteria by which money is judged, how well would each of the following serve as a medium of exchange? (1) empty beer cans, (2) four-leaf clovers, (3) I.O.U.s written on cards with the name and address of the writer, (4) fresh fish.
4. Which of the above items could serve one or both of the other two functions of money, even if it isn't a good medium of exchange?
5. Because many people take vacations in the summer, there is an increased demand for currency. How is this additional demand satisfied? Does it increase the money supply? Why or why not?
6. Suppose that in one week the First National Bank made loans of $217,000. During that same week repayment on earlier loans amounted to $220,000. What happened to the money supply as a result?
7. Which would have a more expansionary effect on the money supply, the Treas-

ury's sale of securities to the banks or to the general public? Why?

8. If banks have no excess reserves, what happens when the Fed raises the required reserve ratio?
9. Since bank interest rates are always higher than the Fed discount rate, why does a rise in the discount rate discourage banks from making new loans?
10. Why does appointing members of the Federal Reserve Board of Governors for terms of 14 years make the Board independent? Why was this provision put in when the Federal Reserve System was established?

## Exercises in Analysis

1. Determine what Federal Reserve district you live in and write a short paper on the Federal Reserve bank that serves the district. Include such information as what states are served by the bank, the bank's capitalization, assets and liabilities. This information can be obtained from the bank or from the *Federal Reserve Bulletin.*
2. Assume the banking system is fully loaned up and the required reserve ratio is 12.5%. If the Fed then purchases $10

billion worth of U.S. Treasury securities from the banks, what is the effect on bank reserves? What is the total potential effect on the money supply?

3. Make a table showing current interest rates for different types of borrowing. Include interest rates on the following types of bank accounts, loans, and investments: deposit accounts; automobile loans; mortgage loans; 90-day certificates of deposit; money market funds; prime rate; Fed discount rate; Federal Funds rate; 26-week Treasury bills. (The first three rates can be obtained at local banking institutions and may vary from one to the other; the remainder can be found in the *Wall Street Journal* or other financial publications.)

4. From issues of the *Wall Street Journal,* or another source, plot the money supply for each month for the past year. Write a brief description of changes.

## Further Reading

DeRosa, Paul, and Gary H. Stern. *In the Name of Money.* New York: McGraw-Hill, 1981. How the Fed implements monetary policy.

Galbraith, John Kenneth. *Money: Whence It Came, Where It Went.* Boston: Houghton Mifflin, 1975. A history of money and money management and its effects on the economy.

Garcia, Gillian, and Elizabeth Plautz. *The Federal Reserve: Lender of Last Resort.* Cambridge, Mass.: Ballinger, 1988. Discusses the need for the Fed as a lender of last resort and its effectiveness in handling crises.

Graziano, Loretta. *Interpreting the Money Supply.* New York: Quorum Books, 1987. The author takes the position that "the money supply is in the eye of the beholder." She discusses the pitfalls in interpreting data on the money supply. She draws conclusions regarding the relationship between the money supply and interest rates and the money supply and inflation.

Hendrickson, Robert A. *The Cashless Society.* New York: Dodd, Mead, 1972. An examination of the relationship between credit cards and money.

Mayer, Martin. *The Money Bazaars.* New York: E. P. Dutton, 1984. Banks are being replaced by "financial services institutions." How the new system works and how it is changing the country's financial operations are examined.

Melton, William C. *Inside the Fed: Making Monetary Policy.* Homewood, Ill.: Dow Jones-Irwin, 1985. Examines how the Fed operates, how to interpret its behavior, and the results of its actions.

Ritter, Lawrence S., and William L. Silber. *Money,* 5th ed. New York: Basic Books, 1984. The first three chapters discuss what money is, what it does, and the role of the Fed. The epilogue raises the question of whether money is becoming obsolete and the implications for the economy.

## chapter 11

# ECONOMIC INSTABILITY

*Money and the institutions that create it are vital to the smooth functioning of a modern economy. But their mismanagement can result in economic disruption and instability, as is shown in the following article introducing the chapter.*

## Fallout From the S&L Meltdown

The savings and loan industry, an institution as American as apple pie, disintegrated in 1986. What at first appeared to be a difficult but manageable $40 billion blowup rapidly increased to the size of a financial nuclear meltdown. As many as 1,000 thrifts—40% of the industry—could fail, with an ultimate cost to taxpayers of $500 billion. This amount or more may be needed to pay for government-insured deposits in failed savings and loan institutions (S&Ls), direct subsidies and tax subsidies to investors willing to take over insolvent thrifts, and the interest costs on bonds sold to pay for the bailout.

How was the savings and loan industry transformed into the swindle and moan industry? It wasn't easy. It took the combined forces of a negligent congress, an administration that purposely swept the problem under the rug, an army of fast-buck-artist financiers, and even the Mafia to bring it off.

The sordid details of the S&L fiasco are related in *Inside Job: The Looting of America's Savings and Loans* by Stephen Pizzo, Mary Fricker, and Paul Muolo (see Further Reading). The authors received an award for the best investigative book in the nation for 1989. Among their revelations are:

- That thrift industry regulators were prevented from doing their jobs until it was too late, both by staffers in the White House that opposed government regulation and by lawmakers allied with the S&Ls.
- That the Reagan administration kept the S&L crisis under wraps until after the 1988 elections in order not to jeopardize the chances of Republican presidential candidate George Bush.
- That mobsters turned to the S&L industry for a source of funding after they were cut off from their access to the Teamster's Pension Fund in 1982.
- That properties taken over by the government from failed S&Ls were later purchased at bargain prices with funds looted from those S&Ls.

Economic developments also played a part in the S&L meltdown. In the years after World War II, the thrift business was a stable and comfortably profitable regulated industry. S&L executives lived by the 3-6-3 rule: Take in deposits at 3% interest, lend the money to home buyers at 6%, and be on the golf course by 3 P.M.

In the late 1970s, however, inflation disrupted this tidy arrangement. Inflation drove interest rates above 20%. Depositors drew their money out of the low-interest thrifts and put it into high-yield money market mutual funds.

In 1980, Congress removed the legal cap on interest rates the S&Ls could pay on deposits. At the same time, it raised the limit on the maximum amount of a deposit account that was federally insured from $40,000 to $100,000. This encouraged the thrifts to compete for funds by paying high interest on deposits. The problem was that they were stuck with existing mortgage loans earning only 6–9% interest while they were paying more to depositors.

Congress further deregulated the industry two years later when it loosened restrictions on the types of investments open to thrift institutions. They were allowed to make commercial and consumer loans, finance construction projects, and make direct investments in development projects.

The relaxed regulatory environment attracted numbers of ambitious operators into the industry, some merely inexperienced in banking and others outright crooked. One common scam began by attracting deposits from money brokers with above-market interest rates. Deposit money was then lent to a company controlled by an associate of the S&L. The loan was secured by a new office or condominium project. With the help of a "cooperative" appraiser, the project was appraised at a value much higher than its actual worth. By this means, the amount of the loan far exceeded the construction costs of the project, with a great deal of money left over. The excess money was shared among the S&L officers and the project developers, with something for the helpful appraiser.

This system produced a number of millionaires, along with a surplus of cheaply-built commercial properties. The system collapsed in 1986 when a decline in petroleum prices sent the economies of the Oil Patch—Texas, Louisiana, Oklahoma, and Colorado—into a nosedive. Many of the high-flying S&Ls were located in those states, and they accounted for more than half of all bank failures nationwide in 1987.

The decline in the Oil Patch economies resulted in those new office buildings and condominiums financed by the S&Ls standing vacant. Real estate prices fell sharply. There were no buyers. Properties went into

receivership, and their inflated appraisal values in S&L portfolios were adjusted to their actual values. The banks' deposit liabilities exceeded the value of their assets. The banks were insolvent. On the average, the assets of failing thrifts were worth only about 75 cents for every dollar due depositors.

The federal government was pledged to make up the difference. It stood behind the semigovernmental Federal Savings and Loan Insurance Corporation, whose reserves were soon exhausted, with taxpayer money. The FSLIC was dissolved and its responsibilities have been turned over to the stronger Federal Deposit Insurance Corporation. The FDIC previously only insured deposits in commercial banks.

Other reforms to strengthen the S&L industry include increasing the amount of capital that the owners of a thrift must invest in it from 3% of deposits to 6%, requiring that 70% of the thrift business be in mortgages, prohibiting investment in high-yield junk bonds, and putting a $500,000 limit on loans to one borrower except with special permission of the Office of Thrift Supervision.

The job of recovering as much as possible of the government's losses in the S&L collapse is up to the Resolution Trust Corporation. The RTC was set up to dispose of the assets of failed S&Ls. As of 1990, it held mortgages for $76.3 billion, other loans of $11.8 billion, securities worth $26.2 billion, real estate with a book value of $15.7 billion, and other assets worth $9.7 billion.

The RTC is in the tricky position of having to dispose of over $100 billion worth of assets in a short period of time without causing a sharp decline in the market prices of those assets. Every day that it holds on to the assets costs the taxpayers millions of dollars. But if its sales cause a further decline in prices, more thrift institutions could fail. It is in a no-win situation.

Its problem will be much greater if there is an economic decline nationally. The Oil Patch has been showing signs of recovery, while previously vigorous economies in New England are slumping. Nationwide, there has

This condominium building in Garland, Texas, is in the process of being demolished as a result of the failure of the S&L that financed it.

been an economic expansion since 1982. This is an unusually long time for a continuous expansion, and there are indications that it may be coming to an end.

The S&L meltdown could be one additional factor in bringing the expansion to a halt. Its fallout could include a deflation of real estate values, a credit crunch, and a diversion of the "peace dividend" (chapter 2) from new investment and rebuilding the infrastructure to paying for the bailout.

The deregulation of the thrift industry in the early 1980s resulted in an increase in the interest earnings of depositors by an estimated $100 billion or more. But at what cost?

## Chapter Preview

*The S&L meltdown was primed by inflation. Inflation and its accompanying high interest rates forced a change in the industry. The fallout from the S&L explosion has resulted in a deflation of real estate prices. So far, its effects on economic activity have been localized, mainly in the Oil Patch. But it may have macroeconomic consequences that will affect the whole economy. The*

*S&L case provides a background for discussing the following questions of economic instability: What causes unemployment? What causes inflation? Is there a trade-off between unemployment and inflation? What are the consequences of unemployment and inflation?*

## Learning Objectives

*After completing this chapter, you should be able to:*

1. *Describe the three major causes of unemployment.*
2. *Explain why some unemployment is hidden.*
3. *State the meaning of inflation and the CPI.*
4. *Describe three causes of inflation and explain the usage of the quantity equation.*
5. *Explain the relationship between unemployment and inflation and use the Phillips curve to show this relationship.*
6. *Define stagflation and relate the price level to output and employment levels by use of the aggregate supply and aggregate demand curves.*
7. *Explain the consequences of unemployment and inflation.*

## What Causes Unemployment?

A market system operates on the assumption that people who want to work can obtain employment to earn the income necessary for consumption. This chapter analysis section looks at the reasons why this assumption isn't always fulfilled.

**Frictional unemployment**  It is expected that in a market economy a certain number of people will be changing jobs at any given time. They may have quit their jobs to find better ones, or they may have lost their jobs because they were laid off, or their firms may have relocated. In a dynamic economy there will always be some workers between jobs. This type of unemployment is called frictional unemployment. However, in a healthy economy, workers who are experiencing frictional unemployment should be able to find other jobs within a few weeks.

From the end of World War II until the 1970s, 3% to 4% frictional unemployment was considered normal. If no more than 4% of the labor force was without a job, the economy was considered to be at full employment. Even under these conditions, there were some people who, because of lack of skills or opportunity, were unable to find work. For the past decade the economy has had an unemployment rate that ranged between 5.2% and 9.5%.

**Structural unemployment**  Employment in the Oil Patch was hit hard by the decline in petroleum prices in the 1980s. Workers in this major industry were put out of work and many could not find other jobs. The ranks of the unemployed were swelled by construction workers when the building boom that was fueled by S&L speculation came to an abrupt halt. The type of unemployment that was experi-

**frictional unemployment**  the lack of work that occurs from time lost changing jobs.

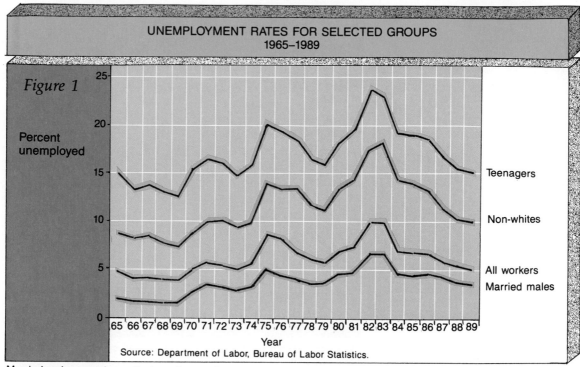

UNEMPLOYMENT RATES FOR SELECTED GROUPS
1965–1989

*Figure 1*

Percent
unemployed

Teenagers

Non-whites

All workers
Married males

Year
Source: Department of Labor, Bureau of Labor Statistics.

Married males experience the lowest unemployment rates and teenagers the highest. Unemployment rates for all groups have been higher in the past two decades than they were during the preceding 20 years.

enced by the oil and construction workers is called <u>structural</u> <u>unemployment</u>. It results from changes in the market conditions of a particular industry or geographic region.

Structural unemployment occurs when the quantity demanded of particular kinds of labor falls short of the quantity offered in the job market at the going wage rate. When a large number of workers in an industry lose their jobs it may be difficult or impossible to absorb them into other industries, even in the best of times. Skills and work experience in one line of work are not always easily transferred to another line of work. The skilled oil-field worker who is laid off is not automatically employable in the field of medical technology, even though there are numerous jobs in that field. Even if workers have transferable skills, they may not know about available jobs or may not be able to take them. Unemployed workers in Houston may not be aware that they have the qualifications for job openings in Atlanta, Georgia. Even if they knew about a job in Atlanta, they might not be in a position to pull up stakes and move there.

**Inadequate aggregate (total) demand**   Frictional and structural unemployment are not usually considered serious economic problems, except for the particular individuals and communities affected. In order for an economy to be

**structural unemployment**   the lack of work that occurs because of changes in the basic characteristics of a market, such as a new substitute product, a change in consumer tastes, or new technology in production.

There are different types of unemployment, and several reasons why those who want work cannot always find it.

efficient, there must be flexibility in the allocation of resources. Changing consumer tastes and the development of new production technologies require a continual reallocation of resources, including labor. Losing a job and having to find another one may be a problem for the individual, but it is one of the processes that are necessary in order for a market economy to be efficient.

In a robust economy, the average length of time a laid-off worker is without a job is short, usually a matter of a few weeks. The most serious unemployment, both for the individual worker and for the economy, is cyclical unemployment associated with inadequate total demand. In contrast to frictional and structural unemployment, when demand is down in the whole economy, there are simply not enough jobs to employ the labor force fully.

The total spending for all types of goods and services is called aggregate demand. When aggregate demand is below the full employment level, people will be out of work, some of them for long periods of time. Full employment aggregate demand is the amount of goods and services that the economy can produce when it is using all of its capacity. During a recession the economy is operating far below its capacity.

Figure 2 illustrates the relationship between unemploy-

**cyclical unemployment**  the lack of work that occurs because the total effective demand for goods and services is insufficient to employ all workers in the labor force.

**aggregate demand**  the total effective demand for the nation's output of goods and services.

**full employment aggregate demand**  the level of total effective demand which is just sufficient to employ all workers in the labor force.

**recession**  a decline for at least two successive quarters in the nation's total output of goods and services.

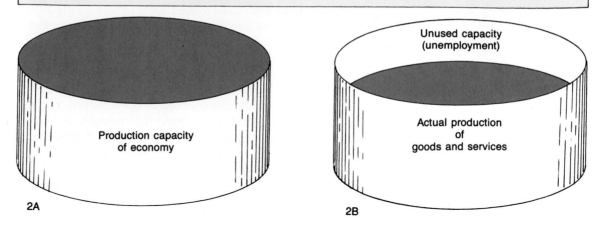

**Figure 2**  PRODUCTION CAPACITY AND UNEMPLOYMENT

2A

2B

When aggregate demand is at the full employment level the production capacity is fully utilized (2A). However, when aggregate demand falls below the full employment level it causes unused production capacity creating unemployment (2B).

ment and aggregate demand. It shows a tank much like a water tank. The size of the tank represents the capacity of the economy to produce goods and services, and the purple represents the aggregate demand for those goods and services. When aggregate demand reaches the top of the tank, as shown on the left, full employment results. When aggregate demand is not sufficient to employ all of the labor, capital, and other resources of the economy a recession occurs; or, if the excess capacity is very large, a depression. This situation is illustrated on the right in Figure 2. The white space between the purple and the top of the tank is unemployment.

In a recession there is too little buying to keep the economic wheels turning at a rate that will provide full use of the available resources. A recession tends to spread throughout the system and affect all parts of the nation's economy. It may be aggravated by structural problems, such as those in the petroleum and construction industries, but the main problem is inadequate total spending. When workers are unemployed, they have less to spend and therefore reduce their purchases. This results in more workers being laid off and spending less, and aggregate demand falls even further. A downward spiral is created which, if it isn't stopped, leads to a depression.

**Hidden unemployment**  The labor force is made up of persons who are either working or unemployed but actively looking for work. Someone who would like to have a job but is not actively looking for work is not counted among the

**depression**  a severe and prolonged period of decline in the level of business activity.

unemployed. Such individuals are part of the hidden unemployment in the United States.

Some of those who have looked for a job for a long time without finding one become discouraged. They decide that it is useless to look for work and stop trying to find employment. In the employment statistics they are then no longer counted as unemployed. In 1987 the number of discouraged workers reached 7.4 million, greater than the number of workers officially counted as unemployed. Favorable employment conditions draw discouraged workers back into the market, and by the first quarter of 1990 their number had shrunk to less than 1 million.

Another form of hidden unemployment is represented by the workers who have had their work hours reduced involuntarily. If a factory cuts back from a 40-hour workweek to a 30-hour week as a result of slow sales, the official measure of unemployment is not affected. For the workers involved, however, this situation is the same as a 25% drop in their employment level, and a change from a full-time job to a part-time one. The term underemployed has been used to describe those workers who can find only part-time work or jobs beneath those for which they are qualified. The number of involuntary part-time workers was 5.1 million in 1987, over 4% of the labor force.

**hidden unemployment** that part of the unemployed population not reflected in official unemployment figures.
**underemployed** workers who cannot obtain full-time employment or who are working at jobs for which they are overqualified.

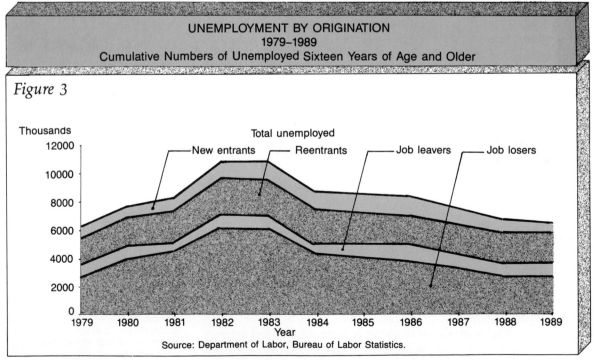

Figure 3

**UNEMPLOYMENT BY ORIGINATION**
**1979–1989**
Cumulative Numbers of Unemployed Sixteen Years of Age and Older

Source: Department of Labor, Bureau of Labor Statistics.

Most of the unemployed have lost their jobs, but many are reentering the labor force or are new entrants.

# case application

## "Go West, Young Man, Go West"

A noted nineteenth-century New York newspaper editor by the name of Horace Greeley advised ambitious youths of the day to "Go West, young man, go West" to earn their fortunes. He believed that the expanding economies of the western states provided the best opportunities for young people to further their careers. (In addressing only the young men Greeley reflected the sexist view regarding careers by women that existed at the time.)

Today that would once again be good advice. As recently as 1988 New England was the place to be if you needed a job. There was such a shortage of workers that some businesses were busing them in from as far away as New York City. The jobless rate in the region was less than 3%, below the full employment level.

How quickly fortunes change. Unemployment in New England states is now above the national average. The higher unemployment levels are the result of a slowdown in the construction, financial, and business-service industries. Reduced spending in the defense industry, an important part of the New England economy, will likely prolong the recession.

Employment opportunities have gravitated west. In March 1990 Nebraska had the lowest unemployment rate in the country with 2.8%, followed by Hawaii at 3% (see Figure 4). Even the Rocky Mountain states are making a comeback from depressed employment levels. Firms in the area have invested heavily in new plant and equipment. The rate of growth in the Rocky Mountain states is now greater than the average for the nation.

New Hampshire's economic decline pushed increasing numbers of people into unexpected poverty, such as Cecilia Fernandez, above. In 1990 applications for welfare in New Hampshire jumped by 38%, and food stamp applications by 54%, the highest rise of any in the country.

Although some regions are doing better than others, all around the country there is a mismatch between where the unemployed workers are concentrated and where the jobs are. The big cities have the workers and the suburbs have the jobs. More and more service industries are moving from big cities to the suburbs where land, rents, utilities, and taxes are less costly. Job openings outside the major metropolitan areas are growing at rates 2 to 10 times the growth rate of employment in the cities. In some large cities, St. Louis

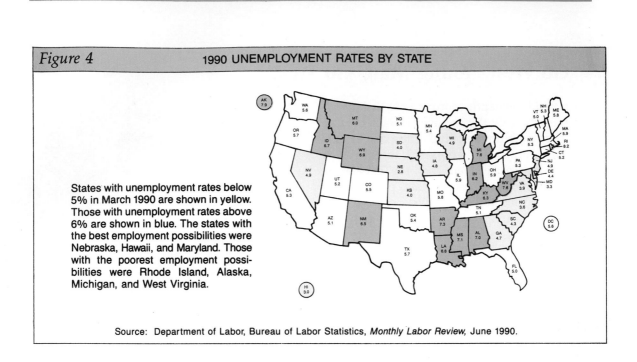

## Figure 4 — 1990 UNEMPLOYMENT RATES BY STATE

States with unemployment rates below 5% in March 1990 are shown in yellow. Those with unemployment rates above 6% are shown in blue. The states with the best employment possibilities were Nebraska, Hawaii, and Maryland. Those with the poorest employment possibilities were Rhode Island, Alaska, Michigan, and West Virginia.

Source: Department of Labor, Bureau of Labor Statistics, *Monthly Labor Review*, June 1990.

and Philadelphia for example, job openings suffered an actual decline in the 1980s. In others, such as Baltimore, Detroit, and San Francisco, they were nearly static. In the outlying areas of these cities, on the other hand, employment increased by amounts ranging from 9% to 15% during the same time period.

There is a gradual shift of the population to where the jobs are, but the disparity continues. One of the major problems is the mismatch between the skills needed for the service and high-tech jobs in the suburbs and the blue-collar or inexperienced and untrained labor force in the big cities. Another problem is the lack of adequate public transportation, which traps the lower-skilled workers inside the cities. They can't afford a move to the suburbs and can't afford the cost and upkeep of a car for commuting to a low-paid unskilled service job.

## *Economic Reasoning*

1. If there are job openings in the suburbs but the jobless blue-collar workers in the cities don't have the necessary skills to fill them, what type of unemployment is this?

2. Explain how the situation in this case application is illustrated by Figure 2B. What changes would bring about conditions such as those illustrated by Figure 2A?

3. What can be done to solve the problem of the mismatch between where the jobs are and where the unemployed workers are? Does government have a responsibility in the solution of this problem or should it be left strictly to industry and the unemployed individuals to solve on their own? Why?

# What Causes Inflation?

One of the twin devils of economic instability is unemployment and the other is inflation. This section sheds some light on the forces that give rise to inflation, forces that can arise on the demand side of the economy or on the supply side. First we will examine what inflation is and how it is measured.

**Measuring inflation**  Inflation is a period of generally rising prices in the economy as a whole. In a market economy it is normal for the prices of some things to rise and others to fall because of changing demand and supply. But when the prices of nearly everything rise inflation occurs. This increases the cost of living. Each dollar spent buys fewer goods and services.

The consumer price index (CPI) is the most commonly used measure of changes in the general price level. This index is a statistic issued monthly by the Bureau of Labor Statistics of the U.S. Department of Labor. It is popularly known as the cost of living index, although it actually measures changes in a specific group of prices rather than people's living costs. Costs of living are affected by changes in buying habits as well as by price changes.

The CPI expresses the price of consumer goods in a given month as a percentage of the price prevailing in some earlier period, known as the base period. In computing the index, the total cost of a representative sample of 205 household purchases during the base period is calculated. The cost of that same "market basket" of goods and services is then computed in subsequent months. The base period price level has an index number of 100. If the current cost of the "market basket" is 25% greater than in the base period, the CPI is 125. Figure 5 on page 306 shows the CPI for the period from 1960 to 1989, with 1982–84 as the base period.

**Demand-pull inflation**  A basic cause of inflation is excessive demand. In the most extreme cases, when the demand for goods and services exceeds the production capacity of the economy, we have pure demand-pull inflation. This is illustrated in Figure 6A, where we again have a tank representing the capacity output of the economy. The amount of purchasing power attempting to buy goods and services is shown in purple. When demand reaches the top of the tank, the economy is unable to produce additional goods and services in the short run. As a result, the purchasing power overflows the tank and is reflected in the economy as a general rise in prices, or inflation.

**consumer price index (CPI)**  a statistical measure of changes in the prices of a representative sample of urban family purchases relative to a previous period.
**base period (base year)**  the reference period for comparison of subsequent changes in an index series; set equal to 100.
**demand-pull inflation**  a continuing rise in the general price level which occurs when aggregate demand exceeds the full-employment output capacity of the economy.

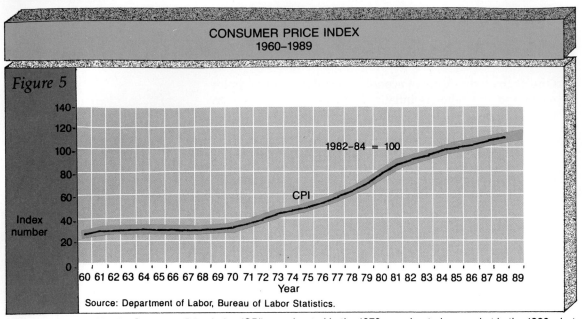

**CONSUMER PRICE INDEX**
1960–1989

Figure 5

1982–84 = 100

CPI

Index number

Source: Department of Labor, Bureau of Labor Statistics.

Inflation, measured by the Consumer Price Index (CPI), accelerated in the 1970s, moderated somewhat in the 1980s, but remained high compared to previous norms.

When the increase in demand is not too rapid, the economy can adjust. In the long run, producers can expand their capacity to produce more goods and services. If the increase in demand occurs gradually over a period of time, it can be matched by an enlargement of the output capacity of the economy without causing inflation. This is shown in Figure 6B. But when demand increases rapidly at or near full employment, as during a war, the excess purchasing power overflows in the form of inflation as in Figure 6A.

When inflation gets started, it is likely to be self-reinforcing. If people see that prices are going up, they may attempt to stock up on goods before prices rise even further. This boosts demand and accelerates the inflation. Speculators also contribute to inflation. With prices rising rapidly, it is profitable to buy something, hold it for a while, and then sell it. This fuels inflation, not only by adding speculative demand to the market, but also by holding supplies of goods off the market. These factors contributed to the inflation in the 1970s shown in Figure 5.

**Cost-push inflation**   Inflation can also result from reduced supplies of production inputs as well as from increased total demand. When inflation comes from the supply side, it is called cost-push inflation.

A major cause of high inflation in the late 1970s was the increase in energy costs brought on by the OPEC oil cartel. Because energy is an important factor input in the produc-

**speculators** people who purchase goods or financial assets in anticipation that prices will rise and they can sell at a profit; speculators can also speculate on a fall in prices.
**cost-push inflation** a continuing rise in the general price level which results from increases in production costs.

306

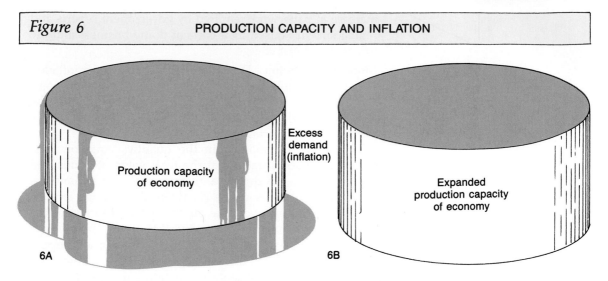

**Figure 6**  PRODUCTION CAPACITY AND INFLATION

Excess demand (inflation)

Production capacity of economy

Expanded production capacity of economy

6A

6B

When aggregate demand exceeds the full employment level it causes inflation (6A). However, over a period of time, increased aggregate demand can be satisfied without inflation by increasing the production capacity of the economy (6B).

tion of so many goods and services, the rise in energy prices increased production costs. Prices rose throughout the economy. The increase in oil prices also raised the demand for oil substitutes, such as coke, a coal residue. Industries that use coke for fuel, the steel industry for instance, found that they had to pay more for it. Because of the increase in this production cost, steel prices went up. This price rise, in turn, resulted in price increases for all of the goods using steel.

There is often an interaction between demand-pull and cost-push inflation forces, each feeding the other. When the cost of living goes up, labor unions demand higher wages so that their workers can maintain their real incomes and living standards. The wage increases raise production costs, causing producers to increase prices again. Workers try to catch up with the cost of living by higher wage demands, which again increases production costs and the cost of living. Sometimes this wage inflation is built into labor union contracts with a cost of living adjustment (COLA) clause. The COLA clause calls for automatic wage increases when the consumer price index goes up a specified number of percentage points.

The government has been accused of contributing to cost-push inflation by its environmental controls and other regulations. Government-imposed emission controls and safety requirements for automobiles have increased car prices by several hundred dollars. Smokestack emission controls on industries have increased their production costs, which raises the price of products. Businesses complain that the

**cost of living adjustment (COLA)** a frequently used provision of labor contracts that grants wage increases based on changes in the Consumer Price Index; often referred to in negotiations as the "escalator clause."

increase in paperwork required by government reports and regulations has raised their costs of doing business and the prices they must charge.

**Monetary inflation** Demand-pull and cost-push inflation are attributed to changed demand and supply conditions. An alternative view of the cause of inflation is held by the monetarists, who believe that changes in the money supply are the most important factor in inflation.

This view is embodied in the quantity equation. The quantity equation states that the total value of goods and services purchased during a given period, say a month, is the number of transactions (T) times the average level of prices (P). This value of total purchases (T x P) must be the same as the quantity of money (M) times the average number of times that each dollar of the money supply changes hands, called the velocity of money circulation (V). In other words, the quantity equation says that the total spending during a period must be the same as the total value of goods and services transacted. Stated in shorthand equation form it is $M \times V = T \times P$. If the volume of transactions (T) remains the same, as it would at full employment, and the rate of turnover of money (V) is constant, an increase in the money supply (M) necessarily results in a rise in the price level (P). This relationship between the money supply and the price level is summarized in the quantity equation below.

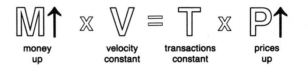

money up — velocity constant — transactions constant — prices up

The quantity equation is a truism rather than a statement of economic analysis since the total amount spent must always necessarily be the same as the total amount received. For some time the quantity equation was out of fashion in economic theory because it was not considered important to solving economic problems. Economists noted that you could have full employment and stable prices with any given money supply, whether it be large or small, because the monetary unit itself is arbitrary. In recent years, however, the quantity theory of money has made a comeback and the monetarists have a large influence on policy. While it is true that in the long run it doesn't make any difference what the quantity of money is, short-term changes in the money supply can have a significant impact on the economy. They influence the economy through their effect on the availability of credit, interest rates, and the demand for goods and services.

**monetarists** those who believe that changes in the money supply have a determinative effect on economic conditions.

**quantity equation (equation of exchange)** the quantity of money **(M)** times the velocity of its circulation **(V)** equals the quantity of goods and services transacted **(T)** times their average price **(P)**; $M \times V = T \times P$.

**velocity of money circulation (V)** the average rate at which money changes hands.

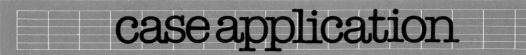

# case application

## The High Cost of Loving

The increase in the cost of living has been bad enough, but it hasn't been nearly as bad as the increase in the cost of loving. Raymond F. DeVoe, Jr., who writes a stock market newsletter, has been calculating a cost of loving (COL) index since 1955. (Please note that the COL index is not the same as COLA, the cost of living adjustment.) Since that time, the general price level of consumer goods and services has increased 4.7 times the level in 1955. In other words, if 1955 were the base period, the CPI would have risen from 100 to 470.

To figure the COL, we take a representative sample of goods and services involved in the mating game and compare their prices in 1955 with the prices today. A cost of loving index might be calculated as shown below. The 1990 COL index was 665.

The cost of loving has gone up much more than the CPI. The COL assumes that young men still court young women the same way they did in 1955. Today's courting practices may include fewer candlelight dinners and fewer birthday gifts of expensive perfume.

The same type of problem affects the CPI. Changes in life-styles and consumption habits make comparisons of the cost of living over a number of years difficult. For this reason, the base period and the contents of the market basket of goods for the CPI are periodically updated.

1. The most inflationary item in the COL was the increase in diamond prices. The price of diamonds increased because people were buying them as a hedge against inflation, and for speculation. Would you call the inflation of diamond prices a demand-pull or a cost-push type of inflation? Why?
2. Which index is a better measure of our purchasing power, the CPI or the COL? Why?
3. Do you think that the high cost of loving has actually affected dating practices? How? Do price changes affect our buying habits in general? What implication does this have for the validity of the CPI?

### COST OF LOVING INDEX

| Item | Number purchased (Q) | Price 1955 ($P_0$) | $P_0 \times Q$ | Price 1990 ($P_1$) | $P_1 \times Q$ |
|------|------|------|------|------|------|
| Wine for picnic | 4 | $1.55 | $6.20 | $5.45 | $21.80 |
| First run movie | 14 | 1.00 | 14.00 | 6.50 | 91.00 |
| Candlelight dinner | 6 | 2.75 | 16.50 | 70.00 | 420.00 |
| Silver bracelet | 2 | 1.29 | 2.58 | 14.00 | 28.00 |
| Dozen roses | 2 | 5.00 | 10.00 | 40.00 | 80.00 |
| Perfume | 1 | 35.00 | 35.00 | 95.00 | 95.00 |
| Diamond ring | 1 | 400.00 | 400.00 | 2500.00 | 2500.00 |
| Blood test | 1 | 7.00 | 7.00 | 25.00 | 25.00 |
| Marriage license | 1 | 2.00 | 2.00 | 20.00 | 20.00 |
| | | | $493.28 | | $3,280.80 |

$$\text{COL (1990)} = \frac{P_1 \times Q}{P_0 \times Q} \times 100 = \frac{\$3,280.80}{\$493.28} \times 100 = 665$$

*This index is based on but not identical to the one devised by Raymond F. DeVoe, Jr.

# Is There a Trade-off Between Unemployment and Inflation?

Unemployment and inflation have plagued economic systems since the beginning of market economies. Until recently, however, they alternated. They did not appear together. In this analysis section we will examine the question of whether we necessarily have less of one when we have more of the other.

**Phillips curve** Economic data for various periods in the past suggest that there is a trade-off between unemployment and inflation. The higher the rate of inflation, the lower the rate of unemployment and vice versa. Historically, economic booms result in full employment, and the high level of aggregate demand causes shortages of goods and services. As a consequence, prices rise. When the boom collapses, demand falls off, surpluses of goods appear, and workers are laid off. Prices and unemployment generally move in opposite directions. A diagram of this trade-off is called a Phillips curve, named after the British economist, A. W. Phillips.

The Phillips curve in the 1960s is shown in Figure 7. The unemployment rate is on the horizontal axis and the infla-

**Phillips curve** a statistical relationship between increases in the general price level and unemployment.

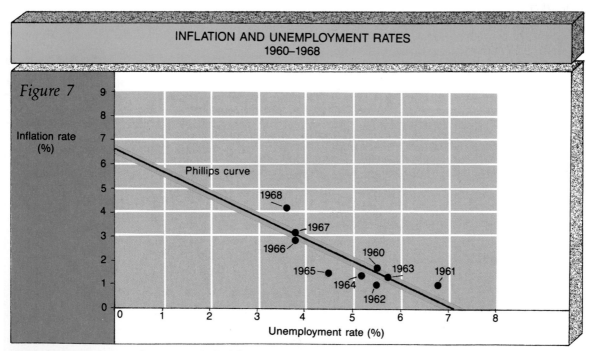

INFLATION AND UNEMPLOYMENT RATES
1960–1968

*Figure 7*

Source: Department of Labor, Bureau of Labor Statistics.

The Phillips curve in the 1960s showed the historic trade-off between inflation and unemployment.

tion rate is on the vertical axis. When the unemployment rate was over 4%, the inflation rate was less than 2%. The higher the unemployment, the lower the inflation. In 1961 when unemployment reached 6.7% of the work force, the inflation rate was negligible, only 0.7%. On the other hand, when unemployment fell below 4%, the inflation rate rose sharply. In 1968 when unemployment was only 3.6%—full employment—the inflation rate reached 4.2%. This does not seem like a high inflation rate in view of what followed in the 1970s, but at that time it was considered quite high.

**Stagflation**   In the 1970s the inflation-unemployment relation saw a dramatic change. Instead of having *either* high unemployment or high inflation rates as we had in the 1960s and earlier periods, we had *both* high unemployment and high inflation. When we have a combination of high unemployment and high inflation rates the situation is called stagflation—a combination of stagnation and inflation.

This led some economists to say that there was no longer a Phillips curve trade-off. But the Phillips curve for 1974–1982, the blue line in Figure 8, shows that a trade-off between inflation and unemployment did exist, although at a different level than in the 1960s. Both variables had shifted upwards and the trade-off was not as definitive. Nevertheless, it appears that the Phillips curve still represented the

**stagflation**  a term created to describe a situation of simultaneous economic stagnation, high unemployment, and inflation.

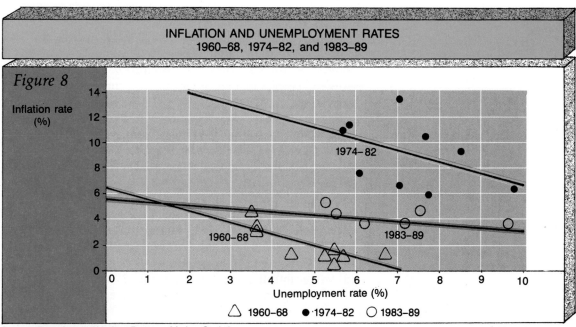

Figure 8

**INFLATION AND UNEMPLOYMENT RATES**
**1960–68, 1974–82, and 1983–89**

Inflation rate (%) / Unemployment rate (%)

△ 1960–68   ● 1974–82   ○ 1983–89

Source: Department of Labor, Bureau of Labor Statistics.

The Phillips curve showing the trade-off between inflation and unemployment is not constant over time. It shifts according to economic expectations and other factors. But under any given conditions, the greater the amount of unemployment, the less inflation is likely to be and vice versa.

relationship between inflation and unemployment in the short run, even under conditions of stagflation.

Stagflation is very unpleasant, both for the public suffering from it and for the economic policymakers trying to cure it. How did the economy get into that situation in the 1970s? Traditionally inflation was not supposed to become a problem until the economy was producing at full capacity. The situation represented in Figure 2B on page 301, where there is excess production capacity, provides no reason for prices to go up. Only when aggregate demand exceeded capacity was there expected to be a spillover into inflation, as in Figure 6A on page 307.

Why wasn't this true in the 1970s? Why did the Phillips curve shift upwards? To help us with the answers to these questions, let us look at another set of diagrams that relate aggregate supply to demand. Figure 9A shows the same simplified conditions as the output tanks we saw earlier in Figures 2 and 6, but in a different way by using aggregate demand and supply curves. The aggregate supply curve (AS) is assumed to be perfectly elastic (horizontal) at the existing price level as long as the economy is operating at less than full capacity. When output reaches the full employment level, however, the aggregate supply curve becomes perfectly inelastic (vertical). When aggregate demand is on the elastic part of the supply curve, as it is in demand curves $AD_1$ and $AD_2$, demand can increase with no rise in the price level. However, when demand increases beyond the full employment level, as shown by $AD_3$, inflation occurs.

The actual supply curve in the 1960s was more like that shown in Figure 9B. When the economy was operating well below full employment as it was in 1961, the price level was nearly constant. This is indicated by the point where the aggregate demand curve $AD_1$ intersects the aggregate supply curve in Figure 9B. When the economy was operating at a higher level of output as in 1965, prices rose as indicated to the point where $AD_2$ intersects AS. When demand was near full capacity output as it was from 1966 to 1968, the price level rose sharply. This is represented by the intersection of demand curve $AD_3$ and AS.

The Phillips curve in Figure 7 and the aggregate supply curve in Figure 9B show the normal relationship between unemployment and inflation prior to the 1970s. How, then, did we get into the stagflation situation? There was apparently a change of the sort shown by the aggregate supply curve in Figure 9C. The price level was no longer stable, even when the economy was operating well below capacity with high unemployment, as with demand $AD_1$. Higher levels of demand $AD_2$ and $AD_3$ created even more extreme inflation.

**aggregate supply**   the total amount of goods and services available from all industries in the economy.

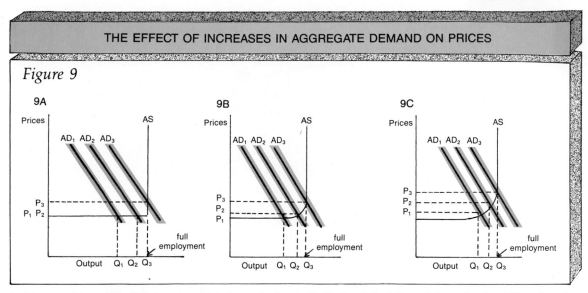

THE EFFECT OF INCREASES IN AGGREGATE DEMAND ON PRICES

*Figure 9*

In 9A aggregate supply (AS) is assumed to be perfectly elastic (horizontal) at the existing price level ($P_1$) when the economy is operating below its full production capacity. However, when output reaches the full employment level ($Q_3$) the aggregate supply curve (AS) becomes perfectly inelastic (vertical). When aggregate demand is on the elastic part of AS as with $AD_1$ and $AD_2$, demand can increase with no rise in the price level. When demand increases beyond the full employment level, as with $AD_3$, inflation occurs.

In 9B the situation in which factor prices rise somewhat as production output approaches the full employment level is illustrated. This is similar to the occurrences of the 1960s. When the economy is operating well below full employment, the price level is nearly constant as indicated by the point where $AD_1$ intersects AS. At a higher output level prices rise slightly as indicated by the intersection of AS by $AD_2$. When demand is near full capacity ($Q_3$), the price level rises sharply as illustrated by the intersection of $AD_3$ with AS.

In 9C factor prices rise substantially before output reaches full employment. This illustrates the occurrences of the 1970s.

The aggregate supply curve in Figure 9C indicates what happened in the 1970s to the relationship between employment and output on the one hand and inflation on the other. But it doesn't explain why it happened. The stagflation problem of the 1970s originated in the second half of the 1960s when the war in Vietnam escalated at the same time that major new domestic social programs got under way. Additional demand resulted from increased government expenditures for these activities. The increased government spending was not offset by higher taxes, thus generating inflationary conditions. A surge in oil prices and resulting energy shortage in the 1970s drove prices higher.

A succession of economic stabilization programs failed to stem the inflation. This failure created expectations in the minds of consumers, workers, and businessmen that prices would continue to rise. Inflationary expectations probably played a large role in what happened during the decade. When the public loses faith in a stable price level, prices are bid up by people stocking up in anticipation of even higher

The increased military spending during the Vietnam war, which was not offset by higher taxes, was one of many factors that caused both high inflation and high unemployment in the 1970s.

prices to come. Attempts by labor unions to keep wages in step with, or ahead of, increases in the cost of living and attempts by producers to beat rising production costs result in ever-increasing prices.

It took the shock treatment of a severe recession in the early 1980s to break the inflationary psychology. The Phillips curve shifted back to a lower level (red line, Figure 8), but not as low as during the 1960s. The economy experienced a decade of continuous but moderate expansion. However, both the inflation rate and the unemployment rate remained higher than was previously considered normal for economic stability. The standard of what is normal may now have to include conditions of mini-stagflation.

During the 1980s the trade-off between inflation and unemployment was not as pronounced as it was in the 1960s. Figure 8 illustrates the differences in the two periods. The red Phillips curve for 1983–89 is flatter than the green Phillips curve for 1960–68. This shows that reductions in unemployment in the 1980s were associated with only moderate increases in prices. The price increases, however, started from a higher level.

What happens to inflation and unemployment in the 1990s may resolve the debate about whether or not there is a significant trade-off between the two.

# case application

## The Roller Coaster Ride

The historical course of economic activity has been similar to a roller coaster ride, with its climbing, peaking, plunging downward, and bottoming out. Let us take a figurative ride on the business cycle.

We start at the bottom, as one does on roller coasters. The first part of the ride up is not steep. The economy is getting in gear, picking up speed. Factories have a great deal of unused capacity. As demand increases, output can be expanded easily without increasing average production costs. Interest rates are unusually low, making it easy for producers and merchants to obtain capital. This is the recovery phase of the business cycle.

The climb begins to get steeper. More jobs, larger incomes, increased spending, and higher profits create an enthusiastic atmosphere. A confident buying public goes into debt to acquire new cars, appliances, and other consumer durable goods. Would-be entrepreneurs see the profits being made by others and decide to undertake new business ventures. This is the expansion phase of the business cycle. In the rosy glow of prosperity, speculation replaces real investment and price increases accelerate, creating an economic "boom."

After a while the steep climb begins to level off. As labor and other resources become fully employed, production costs rise and cut profit margins. The banking system has become fully loaned up and interest rates increase, making credit hard to obtain. Consumers reach their debt limits and demand for durable goods decreases. This is the peak or downturn phase. Some firms fail, affect-

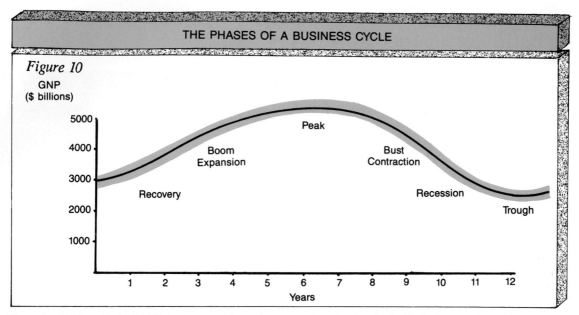

### THE PHASES OF A BUSINESS CYCLE

*Figure 10*

**GNP ($ billions)**

Peak

Boom
Expansion

Bust
Contraction

Recovery

Recession

Trough

Years

Throughout history, the United States has experienced a succession of swings in the level of economic activity more or less following the phases of this typical business cycle.

ing the financial situation of their suppliers and creditors, which leads to more failures, resulting in an economic "bust."

As the economy starts its downward plunge, it rapidly gains momentum. Widespread bankruptcies result in a collapse of the credit market. Worker layoffs and falling incomes result in declining sales in all industries. This is the contraction phase of the cycle, which leads to a recession or, if it is severe, a depression.

The ride down seems as if it will never stop, but it does. The economy bottoms out. The rate of business failures slows. Inventories are reduced. Consumer purchases begin to increase. Due to the small amount of lending in the slump, banks have an in-

creased amount of liquidity and interest rates are lowered. The stage is set for the trough or upturn, the last phase of our cyclical roller coaster ride.

*Economic Reasoning*

1. At what phase of the business cycle would you expect conditions to be at the upper left end of the Phillips curve? At the lower right end?
2. How does stagflation differ from the traditional business cycle?
3. Which do you think is worse, stagflation or the traditional business cycle? Why?

# What Are the Consequences of Unemployment and Inflation?

Having examined the nature and causes of unemployment and inflation and their relationship to each other, we will now take a look at their economic and social consequences.

**Income effects of unemployment**  Unemployed people and their families must continue to pay living costs when their income is cut. Nondiscretionary expenditures such as insurance, housing payments, utility bills, and taxes take a large part of some unemployed people's savings, especially after their eligibility for unemployment compensation is exhausted. The loss of medical insurance coverage resulting from unemployment is a major financial problem for families in case of illness, accident, or pregnancy. The loss of income means a reduction in buying power and living standards for the unemployed and their dependents.

The drop in income of the unemployed also hurts others who are not unemployed. Reduced spending means lower receipts for retail merchants, manufacturers, workers, and others in the chain of production. As we have seen, each person's income generally depends on someone else's spending.

Unemployment reduces the revenues of federal, state, and local governments while at the same time adding to their outlays for unemployment compensation and welfare support. When unemployment increases 1%, the federal treasury alone loses $30 billion in tax revenue and increased welfare and unemployment compensation payments.

**Real output effects of unemployment**  From the standpoint of the overall economy, a rise in unemployment means a decline in the nation's production. For each 1% of unemployment, the country loses over $100 billion in output. Goods and services not produced because of unemployment are gone forever. This means that the nation as a whole is poorer by $100 billion, not just the unemployed.

The real output effects of unemployment continue into the future. Some of the goods not produced during a period of high unemployment are capital goods. The result is reduced growth in the production capacity of the economy that will affect the amount of future output of goods and services. Although the economy resumes growing after a recession, it is on a lower growth path than it would have been. This reduces future production and standards of living.

**Social effects of unemployment**  Unemployment has social as well as economic costs. When people lose their jobs,

**real output**  the value of output adjusted for changes in prices; the volume of output.

Unemployment can lead to many difficulties, even imprisonment for some. These inmates line up outside the barber shop at Sumter County Correctional Institution in Bushnell, Florida.

especially when they cannot find another for an extended period, they tend to become depressed and their health suffers. Suicides increase, families break up, and there is more child abuse. A study by Harvey Brenner of Johns Hopkins University School of Hygiene and Public Health shows that for every 1% increase in the unemployment rate, there is a 1.9% increase in deaths from stress-related diseases, a 4.1% increase in suicides, a 5.7% increase in homicides, and a 4% increase in commitments to state prisons.

Other studies have found that the mental and physical health of the spouses and children of unemployed workers are also affected. Children in families where one or both parents have lost their jobs are more likely to suffer from malnutrition, child abuse, and behavior problems than children of working parents.

**Income effects of inflation**   During the 1980s the purchasing power of the dollar fell by over 40%. Taking 1979 as the base year, when $1.00 would buy a dollar's worth of goods and services, that same dollar in 1989 would buy only $0.58 worth of goods and services. For people whose money income did not keep pace with the rise in prices, these inflated dollars meant a decline in real income.

The income effects of inflation are not the same for everyone. Those on a fixed money income are bound to suffer during periods of inflation. One of the great ironies of inflation is that it often penalizes thriftiness. Many people who have worked hard and lived frugally over a working lifetime and who planned to live off their savings in old age have found the purchasing power of their savings has declined substantially as a result of inflation.

But not everyone is hurt by inflation. Those whose dollar incomes rise faster than the general price level enjoy a rise in real income. Chief executives of major corporations have been among the big winners in the inflation race, with their income from salaries and bonuses going up much faster

**real income** money income adjusted for changes in the prices of goods and services.

than prices. Asset owners also do well in inflationary times. Property owners see the value of their properties rise. Owners of scarce resources and speculators receive windfall profits.

Debtors are another group benefiting substantially from inflation. When the time comes to pay off their loans, they pay them off with dollars that are worth less than the dollars that they borrowed. Because of this, the federal government, with its $3-trillion-plus debt, stands to be the biggest beneficiary of inflation. However, as people come to anticipate continuing inflation and these inflationary expectations are reflected in higher interest rates, the advantage of incurring new debt disappears.

**Real output effects of inflation**  The rise of aggregate demand associated with demand-pull inflation tends to increase the real output of the economy up to the full employment level. An increase in demand, given some slack or unused productive capacity, stimulates production. Idle resources are put to work, and idle plant capacity is utilized more fully. These developments may favorably affect business profit expectations and lead to increased investment spending on new plants, equipment, inventories of raw materials, and goods in process.

This is only part of the story, however. As inflation continues and as the system moves closer to full employment, cost-push inflation forces strengthen. Though on the average all prices are rising in a period of inflation, not all individual prices are rising at the same time. Firms that feel reasonably confident that the prices of the things they are selling will rise faster than the prices of what they must buy will have an incentive to expand by investing. Others may find that their costs are rising faster than their selling prices, or they may fear that this will happen. This causes considerable differences in supply responses. The patterns of production change.

Inflation is tricky. It may stimulate production in some areas and simultaneously create bottlenecks, uncertainties, or other difficulties that can hold back production in other areas. Inflation may induce some producers to anticipate future needs for materials, to buy more heavily than they otherwise would, and to hoard the materials.

As inflationary expectations strengthen, interest rates rise well above normal levels, making business investment in plant and equipment too costly. This discourages further expansion of output and thus contributes to higher inflation by creating shortages. On balance, it appears that the higher the inflation rate and the longer the period of time the inflation goes on, the greater will be the negative effects on output.

*Figure 11*

# AMERICAN BUSINESS ACTIVITY FROM 1878 TO TODAY

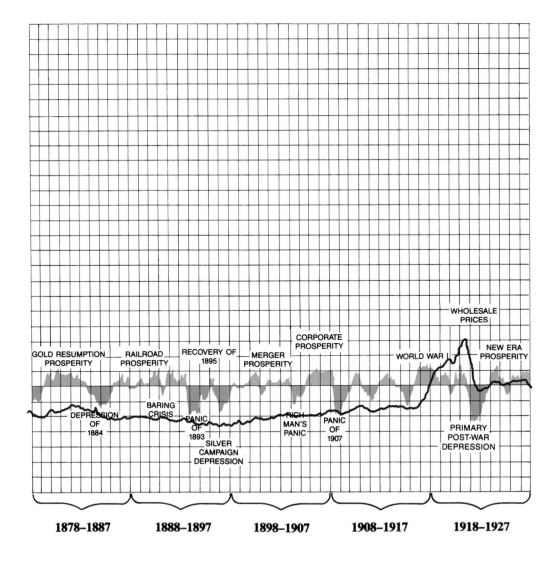

WHOLESALE PRICES

GOLD RESUMPTION PROSPERITY

RAILROAD PROSPERITY

RECOVERY OF 1895

MERGER PROSPERITY

CORPORATE PROSPERITY

WORLD WAR I

NEW ERA PROSPERITY

DEPRESSION OF 1884

BARING CRISIS

PANIC OF 1893

SILVER CAMPAIGN DEPRESSION

RICH MAN'S PANIC

PANIC OF 1907

PRIMARY POST-WAR DEPRESSION

**1878–1887**   **1888–1897**   **1898–1907**   **1908–1917**   **1918–1927**

The cyclical behavior of the U.S. economy since 1878 is shown by the shaded areas above and below the horizontal base line. The base line has been adjusted to eliminate growth of the economy over time, thus leaving only the short-term fluctuations around the long-term trend of economic activity. The shaded areas above the line in blue are periods of prosperity. The green areas below the line are periods of recession or depression. The red line represents the changes in wholesale commodity prices.

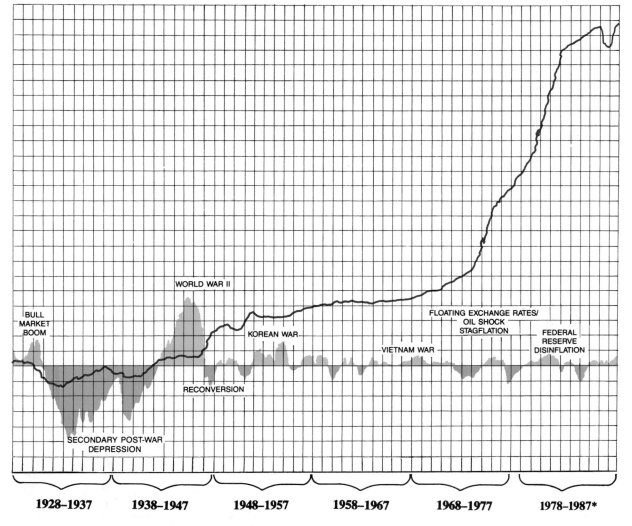

BULL MARKET BOOM

WORLD WAR II

KOREAN WAR

RECONVERSION

SECONDARY POST-WAR DEPRESSION

VIETNAM WAR

FLOATING EXCHANGE RATES/ OIL SHOCK STAGFLATION

FEDERAL RESERVE DISINFLATION

| 1928–1937 | 1938–1947 | 1948–1957 | 1958–1967 | 1968–1977 | 1978–1987* |

*Latest figures available.

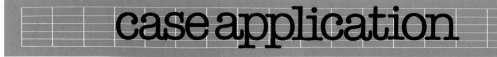

# case application

## Inflation—How High Is Up?

America's experience with inflation in the 1970s was a problem. But here the inflation rate reached "only" 13.3% a year at its height in 1979. In other places inflation has fed on itself to such an extent that it exploded, a condition called hyperinflation. Extreme inflation can paralyze an economy. The bad effects—hoarding, uncertainty, loss of confidence in the value of money, production bottlenecks—may so greatly override the investment-stimulating and output-expanding effects that they virtually halt production.

A classic example of this was the hyperinflation experienced in Germany during the early 1920s. The acceleration in the rate of inflation became so great that firms had to pay workers by the day. If firms refused to pay their workers daily, they would refuse to work at all. Why should they put in a week's work for an agreed-upon wage of 100,000 marks, the workers argued, if prices were rising at such an unpredictable rate that by the end of the week they couldn't be sure 100,000 marks would buy a kilogram of bratwurst and a loaf of bread? The rate of inflation became so extreme by 1923 that prices were literally rising by the hour and workers had to be paid twice a day. As soon as a worker received his morning's pay he would rush out to the entrance and thrust the large bundle of marks into his wife's hands. She would rush off to spend them within the hour, for in a few hours perhaps that bundle of marks would buy only half as much. With the institution of money shattered, market-directed activity all but collapsed.

That was the most extreme case of inflation in this century, but in recent years there have been other countries that experienced hyperinflation rates. In 1984–85 Bolivia had hyperinflation that reached an incredible annual rate of 11,750%, and a number of other Latin

In post–World War I Germany, hyperinflation made some paper money only good for lighting fires with.

American and African countries have experienced runaway inflation. They include Brazil (682%), Argentina (672%), and Israel (374%). In these countries, as in Germany in the 1920s, prices of some goods rose daily or even twice a day. This situation greatly complicates life for consumers and producers alike.

## *Economic Reasoning*

1. Which effects of inflation does the case of hyperinflation in Germany during the 1920s illustrate?

2. The German government was unable to sell bonds, so it had to resort to "printing press" money. Why would no one buy German government bonds in the early 1920s?

3. Do you think that hyperinflation could happen in this country? Why do you think it might, or what do you think would prevent it?

# Putting It Together

Normal adjustments to changing demand and supply conditions for different products and services in a market economy result in the loss of jobs for some people. Other workers quit their jobs because of dissatisfaction or for other personal reasons. In a healthy economy, these people should be able to find new jobs within a few weeks. While they are seeking employment, they constitute a *frictional unemployment* bloc in the labor force. Unemployment levels of 3–4% were in the past considered normal due to frictional unemployment and those unemployable for one reason or another.

When a whole industry or region has less business because of changing consumer tastes or changing cost conditions, some workers lose their jobs. There may not be enough jobs immediately available in other industries to re-employ them, or they may not have the skills and training necessary to take jobs in other industries. This *structural unemployment* may result in extended periods without work for some people.

The most serious and widespread unemployment, however, is *cyclical unemployment*, which occurs when there is inadequate *aggregate (total) demand* for goods and services. If there is insufficient spending in the economy to purchase all of the goods and services that could be produced, workers will not be able to find jobs. Those workers without jobs are forced to cut back on their consumption, and this results in a further decline in output and a further increase in unemployment.

When unemployment is high for a prolonged period of time, some workers who have been unable to find a job become discouraged and stop looking. Since they are not actively seeking employment, they are not included in the unemployment statistics. They constitute a segment of *hidden unemployment*. Other workers forced to work only part-time are part of this segment as well.

Just as unemployment may be caused by insufficient demand, *inflation* may be the result of too much demand. If demand exceeds the capacity of the economy to produce at full employment, prices will rise. Inflationary expectations and speculation tend to accelerate *demand-pull inflation* even more.

Another cause of inflation can be an increase in the costs of production. Shortages of raw materials, higher wages, or government regulations raise prices. The interaction between demand-pull and *cost-push inflation* can result in an inflationary spiral.

According to the *monetarists*, increases in the money

The institutions that create and distribute money are vital to the functioning of a modern economy. Their mismanagement is just one of the causes of economic instability.

supply are inflationary because of the relationship between the quantity of money and the price level. This is expressed by the *quantity equation*, $M \times V = T \times P$, where M is the money supply, V is the velocity of circulation of money, T is the number of transactions during the period, and P is the average price level. If output (T) and the rate at which money turns over (V) are constant, there is a direct ratio between changes in the money supply and changes in the price level.

There has historically been a trade-off between the rate of unemployment and the rate of inflation. This relationship is shown by the *Phillips curve*. Phillips curves based on data from earlier periods show that when unemployment was high the inflation rate was low, and vice versa. During the 1970s, however, the economy had simultaneously both high unemployment and high inflation. This situation is referred to as *stagflation*.

Unemployment has an effect upon income, real output, and social conditions. The *income effects* result in lower living standards for those who are unemployed, their families, and those who supply them with goods and services. The *real output effects* result in smaller production, investment, and growth for the whole economy. The *social effects* include health problems, family disintegration, and higher crime levels.

Inflation, too, has income effects and real output effects. The income effects vary for different groups. Some, especially those on fixed incomes, lose, while others, such as debtors, gain. When inflation rates are low, the real output effect of a small rise in prices may be to stimulate production. But when inflation rates are high, speculation takes precedence over production, and rising production costs discourage output. The high interest rates that accompany inflation deter new investment, and productivity and economic growth decline.

# Perspective

## Black Thursday and the Great Crash

Crowds gathered on Wall Street on Black Thursday as stock prices declined. The Great Depression was soon to follow.

More on the crash and the Great Depression can be found in *The Great Depression* by David A. Shannon, ed. (Englewood Cliffs, N.J.: Prentice Hall, 1960); *The Great Crash* by John Kenneth Galbraith (Boston: Houghton Mifflin, 1988); *America's Great Depression* by Murray N. Rothbard (Oakland, Calif.: Liberty Tree Press, 1983); *The Great Slump* by Goronwy Rees (New York: Harper & Row, 1971); and *The World in Depression, 1929–1939* by C. P. Kindleberger (London: Allen Lane, 1973).

Black Thursday, as it is called, was Thursday, October 24, 1929. It was a truly black day for stock market investors, and for the nation as a whole. Stock prices declined rapidly during the morning hours in a panic of selling. The market volume was so large that the stock market ticker did not finish reporting the day's transactions until after midnight.

People's savings were wiped out and many stock speculators were bankrupted within a few hours. Among the many rumors that spread on Wall Street that day was the story that 11 stock speculators had committed suicide. According to a report in the next day's *New York Times*, "A peaceful workman atop a Wall Street building looked down and saw a big crowd watching him, for the rumor had spread that he was going to jump off." Humorist Will Rogers wrote in his newspaper column, "When Wall St. took that tail spin, you had to stand in line to get a window to jump out of." (Actually, the legend of suicide leaps by ruined Wall Street financiers is largely myth. There were only two such suicides from Black Thursday up until the end of the year, while a few other investors took their lives in alternate ways.)

Significant and dramatic as the events on Wall Street were, they were not "the" cause of the Great Depression that followed. The causes were in the fundamental weaknesses in the economy, not just in the excesses of speculation in the stock market. Although the decade of the 1920s was a period of prosperity and growth, not all sectors of the economy participated in the prosperity. The farmers, who constituted a large proportion of the population, were suffering from overproduction and low prices throughout the second half of the decade. The farm population and the low-paid unskilled workers had insufficient purchasing power to absorb all of the goods that were produced by the large investment in production facilities during the boom.

Excessive financial speculation was founded on a weak banking structure. There was not yet a Federal Deposit Insurance Corporation, so when defaults by debtors created liquidity problems for some banks and forced them to close, panic withdrawal of deposits from other banks took place, forcing them to close too.

The significance of Black Thursday and the Great Crash was that the events in the stock market revealed the fallacy of faith in endless prosperity. This loss of faith did not happen all at once. For a time there were assurances from many "experts" that the setbacks were only temporary, that the economy was basically sound and would soon turn up again. Instead, it sank further and further into depression until universal pessimism in the 1930s replaced the unbounded optimism of the 1920s.

For
Further
Study
and
Analysis

## Study Questions

1. Mr. Jones was disabled in an accident in 1981 and has not been able to work since. Is he included in the unemployment statistics? Why or why not?

2. If the average propensity to consume (chapter 5) increased, how might the price level be affected? Under what circumstances would such an increase be inflationary? Under what circumstances would it not necessarily be inflationary?

3. A reduction in space exploration programs has resulted in a loss of jobs in the aerospace industry. This situation is an example of what type of unemployment?

4. Judging from the quantity equation, could the money supply go down and prices go up at the same time? What would have to happen for this to come about?

5. The economy is currently in what phase of business conditions—recovery, boom, peak, bust, contraction, recession, trough, or stagflation? How can you tell?

6. How can the production capacity of the economy expand from the amount shown in Figure 6A to the amount shown in Figure 6B?

7. If an anticipation of price inflation leads business firms to build up inventories of raw materials and semifinished goods, what effect does this have on economic conditions? Why?

8. Assuming an inflation rate of 10% per year for the next five years, what would be the effect on the purchasing power of the dollar at the end of that time?

9. If Mrs. Sawyer were living on a fixed pension of $500 a month, how would she fare if inflation occurred at the rate indicated in question 8 above?

10. Why did homeowners who bought houses in the 1970s benefit from inflation?

## Exercises in Analysis

1. Write a short paper on employment conditions in your area.

2. Assume that inflation is taking place and that it appears it will continue for the foreseeable future. You have a nest egg from an inheritance of $25,000. Write a short paper on what you would do with the money and why.

3. From the following data, calculate the student cost of living (SCOL) index for 1991 with 1978 as the base year.

| Item | # Purchased per Semester | 1978 Price | 1991 Price |
|---|---|---|---|
| Hamburgers | 50 | $ 1.25 | $ 3.00 |
| Jeans | 2 | 20.00 | 30.00 |
| Books | 3 | 15.00 | 35.00 |
| Movie tickets | 10 | 4.00 | 6.00 |

4. From the statistical tables in the most recent Economic Report of the President (see Further Reading below), find the unemployment and inflation rates for the past four years. Plot them on a diagram similar to the one in Figure 9 in this chapter.

## Further Reading

Adams, James Ring. *The Big Fix: Inside the S&L Scandal.* New York: John Wiley & Sons, 1990. This exposé describes "how an unholy alliance of politics and money destroyed America's banking system."

Case, John. *Understanding Inflation.* New York: William Morrow, 1981. "This book is for people who want to know why prices keep going up. It is not—rest assured—an economics textbook. It contains no equations, one graph, and only a few statistics" (p. 7). Includes an appendix on how the inflation rate is calculated.

Cleveland, Harold Van B., and W. H. Bruce Brittain. *The Great Inflation: A Monetarist View.* Washington, D.C.: National Planning Association, 1976. The causes of inflation from an international monetary perspective.

*Economic Report of the President.* Washington, D.C.: Superintendent of Documents, annual. A report by the president to Congress on the state of the nation's economy. Includes the annual report of the Council of Economic Advisers, which covers a number of macroeconomic subjects such as inflation and unemployment. Also includes an appendix of statistical tables relating to income, employment, and production.

Eichler, Ned. *The Thrift Debacle.* Berkeley, Calif.: University of California Press, 1989. This is not the same sort of exposé treatment of the S&L collapse as the Adams and Pizzo-Fricker-Muolo books. It explores the historical development of the S&L industry and the process of its demise.

Kelvin, Peter, and Joanna E. Jarrett. *Unemployment: Its Social Psychological Effects.* Cambridge, U.K.: Cambridge University Press, 1985. Examines the ways in which unemployment affects individuals in terms of how the unemployed see themselves and how others see them.

Kristensen, Thorkil. *Inflation and Unemployment in Modern Society.* New York: Praeger, 1981. An analysis of the causes of stagflation and the global policy issues raised by it.

Massey, Doreen, and Richard Meegan. *The Anatomy of Job Loss: The How, Why, and Where of Employment Decline.* New York: Methuen, 1982. A study of unemployment related to technological and geographic changes in production in specific industries.

Pizzo, Stephen, Mary Fricker, and Paul Muolo. *Inside Job: The Looting of America's Savings and Loans.* New York: McGraw-Hill, 1989. From bank and court documents and interviews with Justice Department officials and the culprits involved, the authors describe the process by which the savings and loan industry was transformed into the swindle and moan industry.

## chapter 12

# THE ECONOMY'S OUTPUT

*In order to deal with economic instability, we must know what to expect in the economy's behavior. The introductory article discusses the difficulties of predicting where the economy is going.*

## Forecasting or Fortunetelling?

Citizens of ancient Greece could get a prophecy about a military campaign or a long, dangerous sea trip by going to the oracle at the temple of Apollo at Delphi. The oracle predicted future events by examining the intestines of a goat or by asking for a sign from Apollo. The prophecy was often so vague that no matter what happened the oracle could claim the prophecy had been fulfilled.

The demand for prophecies still flourishes. Businesses and governments go to present-day oracles for help in planning for the future. Increasingly, the oracles to which they go are those of economic model builders such as Chase Econometrics, Wharton Econometric Forecast Associates, Evans Economics, and McGraw-Hill's Data Resources. Complex systems of equations, rather than mystical signs, are the sources of modern prophecy.

A great quantity of statistical data is cranked into their computer models. The data deal with economic variables whose interrelationships are shown by sets of mathematical equations. The more complex your economic view, the more equations you must use to forecast the results of changes in variables. For example, the Wharton Quarterly Model of the U.S. economy uses 1,100 equations to forecast hundreds of specific economic changes—in prices, interest rates, automobile sales, retail sales, tax collections, unemployment, and so on.

The track record of the leading forecasting establishments has been far from perfect. In October of 1981 Evans Economics predicted that the economy would grow 3.3% in 1982, Wharton Associates predicted 2.2% growth, and Chase Econometrics forecast a 2% growth rate. In actuality, economic growth *fell* by 2.5% in 1982. As a group, they greatly underestimated the strength and duration of the economic expansion following 1983. And none of them foresaw the high federal government deficits, import surpluses, and high real interest rates that marked the 1980s. Even when individual forecasters or forecasting companies have been right in a particular instance, they have not been able to repeat their success consistently.

Why have modern economic oracles not been more successful? One of the problems of the forecasters is caused by the accuracy—or lack of it—of the original data that go into the forecasting models. The figures published by the agencies responsible for gathering the data are almost never correct when they first appear. Sometimes they are off by a factor of 10. As more accurate data become available, the figures are revised; but it may be 2 years before the final figures are available. Even after revisions the data may not be reliable. According to the Congressional Office of Technology Assessment, "As much as 30% of the productivity decline after 1973 is the result of errors in measuring both outputs and inputs."

And why are the economic data so unreliable? Collecting the raw data is not the job of the forecasting businesses. Their function is to determine what the data mean for the industries and firms who are their clients and for the economy as a whole. Only the federal government is in a position to collect and organize economic data on the huge scale needed. But, according to Courtney Slater, former chief economist of the Commerce Department, "Too many statistical series are outmoded, and there are too many data gaps. Information about new industries and rapidly growing economic sectors is often scanty and sometimes misleading." Cuts in the budget for data collection and reporting during the Reagan administration made the problem worse.

The unreliablity of data is just one problem in economic forecasting. Another problem is understanding what effects a change in one economic variable will have on other variables. Forecasting models are based on past relationships of the variables—for example, the Phillips curve discussed in the last chapter. But, as we saw, those relationships may change over time, resulting in inaccurate predictions. The pace of such shifts in relationships seems to be accelerating. Management consultant Peter Drucker describes this as an "age of discontinuity" in which old rules and relationships do not apply any more.

It is possible to compensate somewhat for unreliable data and inexact models by putting predictions in the form of a range of possibilities rather than as an exact figure. This approach, however, may be too wimpy to impress potential clients and others. According to Herbert Stein, former chairman of the Council of Economic Advisers, "Certitude pays money. It pays in attention, influence. . . . There is no 'don't know' school to which you can belong."

A difficulty that has plagued forecasters from ancient Greece to modern days is the effect of external forces on developments. Wars, disasters, shifts in government policies, all types of unforeseen occurrences can play havoc with even the most astute predictions. For example, there was a run-up in oil prices in the 1970s as a result of OPEC manipulations of the petroleum market. That changed the economic picture so much that the forecasters were left with models that were no longer relevant.

Despite their fallibility, the forecasting companies are handsomely rewarded for their services. Not all forecasting involves computers and fat fees, however. The Delphic oracle of old has many contemporary imitators. A Chicago pawnbroker, for instance, indexes economic trends by the percentage of pawnshop items that are redeemed. A psychologist predicts economic ups and downs by the number of patients signing up for expensive therapy. And a Los Angeles pet store operator believes that an important economic omen is the number of rhinestone-studded poodle collars the store sells.

## Chapter Preview

*The statistical models used in economic forecasting were originally developed as tools for understanding what happens in the economy. Only later did they become devices for predicting what may happen in the future. In this chapter we will use the most basic formulation of the national income model to explain the following:* How much does the economy produce? What determines domestic output from the demand-side point of view? What determines domestic output from the supply-side point of view?

## Learning Objectives

*After completing this chapter, you should be able to:*

1. *Define the GNP and explain the two ways of measuring it and why they give the same result.*
2. *Explain the four types of expenditures that make up the total demand for goods and services.*
3. *Define National Income and discuss how it differs from GNP.*
4. *Define constant dollar GNP and show how it relates to current dollar GNP.*
5. *Explain the Keynesian economic model and show under what conditions the output of the economy is at equilibrium.*
6. *Describe the meaning of Say's Law.*
7. *Explain how supply-side economics differs from demand-side economics.*

# How Much Does the Economy Produce?

There are two methods of measuring the total output of the economy. We can measure the sales value of the output of goods and services, or we can measure the incomes received by the workers and the owners of other factors used in production. These two measurements should give us the same figure because the value of what is sold ends up in the pockets of those who produced and distributed it. Income should be the same as the value of the output.

**Expenditure categories**   In 1989, the national output of the United States totaled $5,233.2 billion in goods and services. This was the sum of four types of spending: consumer purchases, investment outlays for new capital goods, government spending, and net exports. The total of those expenditures was the Gross National Product (GNP). The 1989 GNP consisted of the outlays shown in Table 1 on page 332. The largest class of spending, shown in the left column of the chart, was personal consumption expenditures (C). They comprised all household outlays for durable goods such as automobiles, nondurable goods such as food and clothing, and services such as medical care, repairs, and entertainment.

Gross private domestic investment (I) refers to outlays for capital goods. Such spending enables businesses to maintain and expand their production capacity. The two main types of investment spending are for fixed investment in buildings and for capital equipment, such as machinery. Increases in inventories of goods in the hands of producers or on the shelves of dealers are also considered investments. If inventories were to fall during the year it would be disinvestment, a reduction in (I). In addition, in the United States' system of accounts, new residences sold during the year are included in fixed investment.

**Gross National Product (GNP)**   the sum of the values of all goods and services produced during the year.
**personal consumption expenditures (C)**   spending by households on goods and services.
**gross private domestic investment (I)**   private-sector spending on capital equipment, increased stocks of inventories, and new residential housing.
**inventories**   the value of finished and semi-finished goods and raw materials in the hands of producers and distributors.

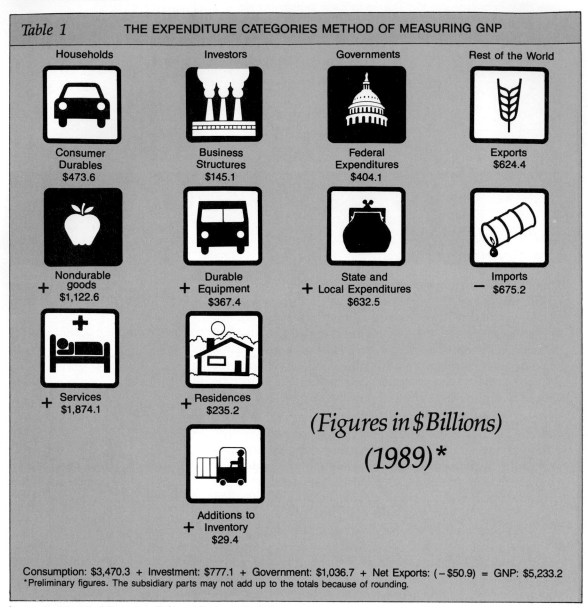

| Table 1 | THE EXPENDITURE CATEGORIES METHOD OF MEASURING GNP |
|---|---|

Households

Consumer Durables
$473.6

Nondurable goods
+ $1,122.6

Services
+ $1,874.1

Investors

Business Structures
$145.1

Durable Equipment
+ $367.4

Residences
+ $235.2

Additions to Inventory
+ $29.4

Governments

Federal Expenditures
$404.1

State and Local Expenditures
+ $632.5

Rest of the World

Exports
$624.4

Imports
− $675.2

*(Figures in $ Billions) (1989)\**

Consumption: $3,470.3 + Investment: $777.1 + Government: $1,036.7 + Net Exports: (−$50.9) = GNP: $5,233.2
*Preliminary figures. The subsidiary parts may not add up to the totals because of rounding.

*Source:* Department of Commerce, Bureau of Economic Analysis.

In 1989, by using the expenditure categories method (the total sales value of the output of goods and services), the Gross National Product of the United States was $5,233.2 billion.

**government sector spending (G)** spending by the various levels of government on goods and services, including public investment.

The government sector spending (G) includes both purchases from the private sector (for example, purchase of military equipment) and the costs of government itself (for example, salaries paid to government workers). Government spending is a mixture of consumer-type purchases, such as school lunches, and investment-type purchases, such as hydroelectric dams.

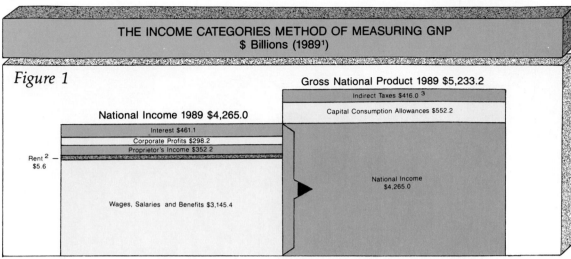

**THE INCOME CATEGORIES METHOD OF MEASURING GNP**
**$ Billions (1989[1])**

*Figure 1*

Gross National Product 1989 $5,233.2

Indirect Taxes $416.0 [3]

Capital Consumption Allowances $552.2

National Income 1989 $4,265.0

Interest $461.1

Corporate Profits $298.2

Proprietor's Income $352.2

Rent [2] — $5.6

National Income $4,265.0

Wages, Salaries and Benefits $3,145.4

[1] Preliminary figures   [2] Rental income of persons less depreciation.   [3] Includes other business transfers.

The individual parts may not add up to the total because of rounding.

Source: Department of Commerce, Bureau of Economic Analysis.

In 1989, by using the income categories method (the sum of all incomes earned plus capital consumption allowances [depreciation] and indirect taxes with other business transfer payments), the Gross National Product of the United States was $5,233.2 billion.

The GNP also includes the net value of U.S. international trade. Since GNP measures only what is produced domestically, we subtract imports (M) from exports (X). The difference is net exports (X − M), and is added into the GNP.

Adding these various expenditure categories, the GNP measures the current output of our economy as the grand total of final spending (aggregate demand). It is the sum of spending by the nation's households (C), investors (I), governments (G), and the excess, if any, of the nation's exports over its imports (X − M). Thus,

$$GNP = C + I + G + (X − M)$$

**Income categories**   The second method of measuring GNP is to add together all of the incomes earned in production: labor earnings, business profits, interest, and rent payments. This total of income earnings is called National Income (NI). The GNP measurement by income categories is the sum of National Income plus non-income costs of production, including depreciation on capital goods and business transfer payments such as excise taxes. The components of NI and GNP for 1989 are shown in Figure 1.

The largest part of National Income consists of the earnings of labor, including professional and managerial salaries. Other income components are proprietors' net income, corporate profits, interest, and rent. The National Income in 1989 totaled $4,265.0 billion. In addition to National Income,

**net exports (X − M)**   the value of goods and services exported minus the amount spent on imported goods and services.

**National Income (NI)**   the total of all incomes earned in producing the GNP.

**business transfer payments**   outlay by business for which no good or service is exchanged, such as excise taxes, payouts under deferred compensation arrangements, gifts, and donations.

**excise taxes**   a tax on a particular type of good or service; a sales tax.

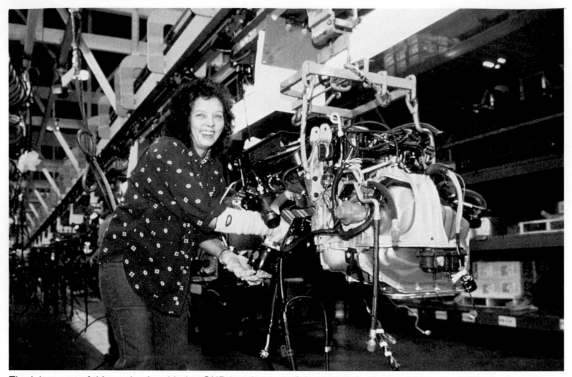

The labor cost of this worker is added to GNP, but the cost of the materials she is working on, which were purchased from other suppliers, is not added to GNP because that would result in double-counting.

GNP also includes cost allocations to cover the depreciation of plant and equipment, listed in Figure 1 as capital consumption allowances. It further includes indirect taxes such as business excise taxes and other business transfer payments, which are not a part of earnings but do constitute a cost of production. When we add these non-income costs to National Income we obtain the same GNP figure that we arrived at using the expenditures approach in Table 1, $5,233.2 billion.

**Value added**   The GNP is a measure of the total goods and services produced by a nation's economy in a given year. To avoid overstating the real output, the same good must not be counted more than once. For example, if we count the sale of iron ore used in making steel, then count the value of the steel sold, and finally count the selling price of an automobile in which the steel is used, we would be counting the value of the iron ore three times. To avoid double-counting, only the value added at each stage of production is counted. The final sale price includes and is equal to all the individual values added at each intermediate stage of production. The worth of production that actually takes place in the industries making goods like automobiles is

**capital consumption allowances** the costs of capital assets consumed in producing GNP.

**indirect taxes**   taxes collected from businesses that are ultimately paid in full or in part by someone other than the business from which the tax is collected; not income taxes.

**value added**   the difference between the value of a firm's sales and its purchases of materials and semi-finished inputs.

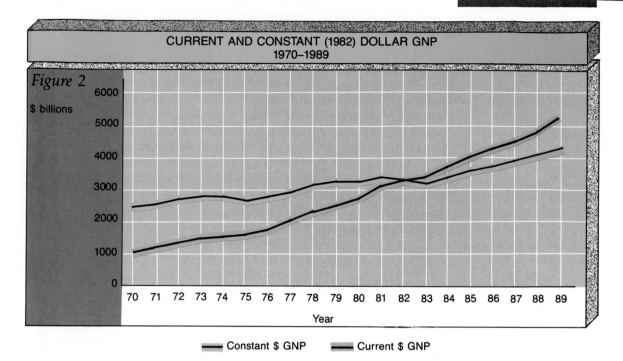

**CURRENT AND CONSTANT (1982) DOLLAR GNP
1970–1989**

*Figure 2*

$ billions

Source: Department of Commerce, Bureau of Economic Analysis.

Removing the effect of inflation by using 1982 constant dollar measurement gives a real GNP for 1989 of $4,142.6 billion as compared to the current 1989 dollar GNP of $5,233.2 billion.

indicated by the sum of values added. It is not the total prices of intermediate and final sales.

**Current and constant dollar GNP**   In estimating GNP, an item's current worth is the price paid for it. A current dollar GNP reflects the current price level of goods and services. Current dollar GNP may increase over time because of inflation.

A real or constant dollar GNP is used to remove the effects of inflation in order to see the real change in output. This measure indicates what the GNP would be if the purchasing power of the dollar had not changed from what it was in the base year (see chapter 11, p. 305). The United States' national income accounts now use 1982 as the base year. Figure 2 shows the real or constant dollar GNP for the years 1970–89, measured in the value of 1982 dollars (blue line), compared to the GNP measured in current year dollar values for those years (green line). It shows that the real or constant dollar GNP for 1989 was only $4,142.6 billion as compared to the 1989 current dollar GNP of $5,233.2 billion. The difference reflects price increases since 1982.

**current dollar GNP**  the value of GNP as measured by figures unadjusted for inflation.
**constant dollar GNP (real GNP)** the value of GNP adjusted for changes in the price level since a base period.
**national income accounts**  the collective name for various macroeconomic measurements such as GNP and National Income.

# case application

## Harry's Sub Shop

Harry's Sub Shop opened for business in 1989 in a good location near a college campus. By pricing his submarine sandwiches at the competitive level of $2.25, Harry soon had all the business he could handle. By year's end, he had sold 34,600 sandwiches and taken in $77,850.

From his revenues, of course, Harry had to pay for the expenses of making and selling the subs. The salami, cheese, pickles, onions, tomatoes, lettuce, rolls, and other ingredients used in the subs had cost $31,240. Out of the difference between the $77,850 taken in and the $31,240 paid for supplies, Harry had to pay an assistant, make the mortgage payments on the building, cover the depreciation on his equipment, and pay a city license fee. In addition to the costs of utilities and advertising, this amounted to a total of $24,000 in additional business expenses. After deducting these business expenses from his revenues, Harry was left with a net income of $22,610. This wasn't much, but the Sub Shop was only open 25 hours a week, and Harry also ran a catering business on the side.

How much did Harry's Sub Shop add to the current dollar 1989 GNP? One way to look at the answer is to examine how much people spent on Harry's subs. They spent $77,850. The other way to look at it is to add up all of the expenses of producing the subs, including Harry's proprietary income. The $31,240 that Harry paid to his suppliers became wages, rent, interest, profits, and depreciation allowances for all the intermediate firms in the supply chain.

Due to an increase in the cost of ingredients, Harry had to raise the price of his subs to $2.50 in 1990. Because the prices at other eating places in the area also went up, Harry did not lose any sales. He sold the same number of subs in 1990 as he had the year before.

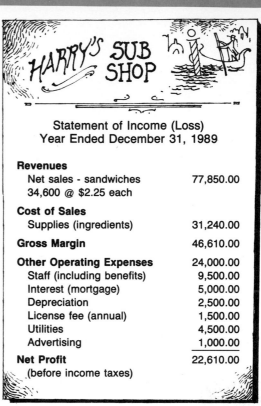

**Statement of Income (Loss)**
**Year Ended December 31, 1989**

| | |
|---|---:|
| **Revenues** | |
| Net sales - sandwiches | 77,850.00 |
| 34,600 @ $2.25 each | |
| **Cost of Sales** | |
| Supplies (ingredients) | 31,240.00 |
| **Gross Margin** | 46,610.00 |
| **Other Operating Expenses** | 24,000.00 |
| Staff (including benefits) | 9,500.00 |
| Interest (mortgage) | 5,000.00 |
| Depreciation | 2,500.00 |
| License fee (annual) | 1,500.00 |
| Utilities | 4,500.00 |
| Advertising | 1,000.00 |
| **Net Profit** | 22,610.00 |
| (before income taxes) | |

*Economic Reasoning*

1. What was the value added to national output by Harry's Sub Shop in 1989?
2. What happened to the firm's contribution to the current dollar GNP in 1990 compared to 1989? What happened to its contribution to real or constant dollar GNP in that year compared with the previous year?
3. While Harry was running his two businesses, his wife Margaret was taking care of their three children and the house. Since she didn't get paid for this, she was not contributing to GNP. Was she actually making no contribution to the nation's output? What might be the arguments for and against including housework in GNP?

# What Determines Domestic Output from the Demand-Side Point of View?

There are two principal interpretations of what determines total output. One emphasizes the role of demand in determining how much will be produced; the other emphasizes the role of supply. The demand-side analysis dominated economic thinking and planning from World War II to the 1980s. It stems from the writings of British economist John Maynard Keynes. The model he developed of how the economy works is called Keynesian economics.

The Keynesian economic model can be illustrated with the use of the production capacity tank introduced in the previous chapter. As you will recall, the size of the tank represents the maximum capacity of the economy to produce goods and services. Since the total output of goods and services for the year is Gross National Product and the contents of the tank represent that output, we will refer to the tank as the GNP tank. The GNP tank is shown in Figure 3A on the next page with the flow of consumer spending.

**Keynesian economics** the body of macroeconomic theories and policies that stem from the model developed by John Maynard Keynes.

According to Keynes, police do more than keep ducks in line. Their wages, and other government spending, also add to demand in the economy.

*Figure 3A*   GNP TANK WITH CONSUMER SPENDING

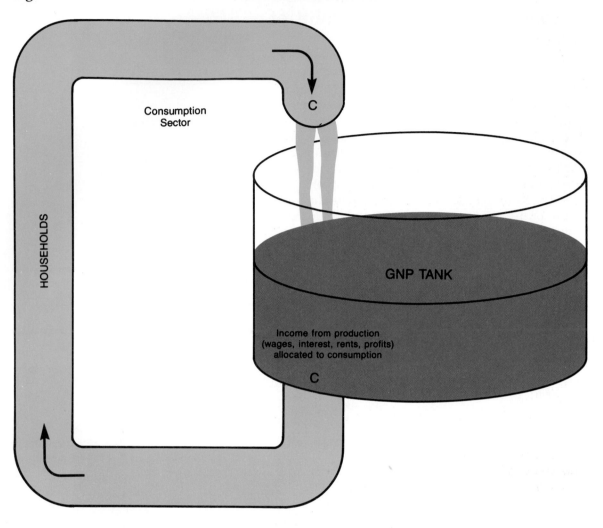

The GNP tank represents the nation's output of goods and services. Consumption demand by households takes the largest part of that output. Purchasing power flows into the top of the tank in the form of consumer spending. It becomes income to the households in payment for their productive services. The income that households allocate to purchase additional consumption goods and services flows out of the bottom of the tank and is returned in the form of new purchasing power.

**Consumption demand** The GNP tank model with consumer spending is related to the circular flow model from chapter 3, shown in Figure 3B. The rent, wage, and interest payments from business to households for their productive services that are allocated by the households to consumption purchases are shown in the GNP tank model by the outflow from the bottom of the tank to the consumption sector.

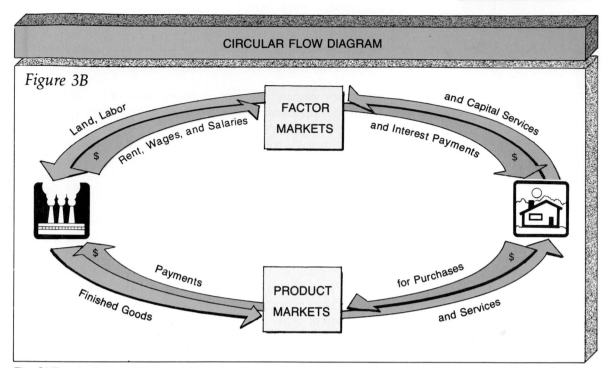

CIRCULAR FLOW DIAGRAM

Figure 3B

FACTOR MARKETS

Land, Labor

Rent, Wages, and Salaries

and Capital Services

and Interest Payments

PRODUCT MARKETS

Payments

Finished Goods

for Purchases

and Services

The GNP tank diagram with consumer spending (Figure 3A) shows the same flow of purchasing power through the economy as the circular flow diagram from chapter 3 (p. 00). Households use the income that they receive from the sale of their labor, land, and capital services in production to purchase the consumption goods and services produced by the firms. The GNP tank diagram, however, is better than the circular flow diagram for showing the effects of the other sectors of the economy, as follows.

The outflow is marked "C." This is the amount of income generated by production that is allocated to purchase new consumer goods and services. It flows back into the tank where it again becomes income to the producers of those goods and services. The inflow, the amount spent, is also marked "C" because it is equal to the outflow, the amount of their income households allocate to consumption.

The amount of consumer spending depends basically on people's disposable income. Disposable income is income received minus taxes. Most of this disposable income is spent on consumption. In 1989 disposable personal income was $3,780.0 billion. Of this amount, households spent $3,470.3 billion on consumption goods and services. This is the amount shown in the first column of Table 1 (see p. 332) and the amount represented by "C" in the GNP tank model.

The consumption sector is the largest part of aggregate demand, making up nearly two-thirds of GNP in 1989. But it is not the most important sector as far as economic instability is concerned. The other sectors, although smaller, account for more instability. These other sources of demand

**disposable income**  the amount of after-tax income that households have available for consumption or saving.

are investment demand, government demand, and foreign demand. We will add the first two of these demand sectors to the GNP tank model in this chapter and consider the effects of the foreign sector in chapter 16.

**Investment demand**   A second determinant of the amount of output is investment demand. Private investment spending, shown in Figure 4 in green, flows into the GNP tank from the pipe marked "I." This is spending by businesses for equipment, factories, office buildings, and inventories. It also includes spending on new residences. As shown in the second column of Table 1, investment demand in 1989 was $777.1 billion.

Investment spending comes principally from savings. The amount of income generated in producing GNP which is allocated to savings is shown flowing out of the GNP tank from the pipe at the bottom market "S." The savings outflow, however, is not directly connected to the investment inflow. Instead, most savings flow through the banking system or other parts of the financial marketplace. This financial marketplace is represented in Figure 4 by the investment sector holding tank to the right of the GNP tank. Savings flow into the financial markets and are then drawn out to be invested in capital equipment, structures, and inventories. (This does not apply to that part of business investment which is financed out of retained earnings. In that case the savings flows directly from the company's earnings into capital spending without passing through financial markets.)

The amount of savings flowing into the financial markets through pipe "S" is not necessarily the same as the amount of investment spending flowing out of the financial markets through pipe "I." As we saw in chapter 10, the banking system can create money by making loans. In that way investment spending can be greater than intended savings. It would also be possible for the financial markets to absorb more savings than the amount of new investment spending. In that case, the amount of income flowing out of the GNP tank in the form of savings would be larger than the amount of purchasing power flowing into the tank in the form of investment.

Unlike the rate of consumption spending, which normally has a fairly consistent relationship to disposable income and tends to be rather stable, investment spending may be quite unstable. It depends a lot on expectations of future economic conditions, which may be influenced by all kinds of events and are likely to change frequently and violently. Inventory investment is an especially unstable component of investment.

*Figure 4*                   GNP TANK WITH INVESTMENT SPENDING

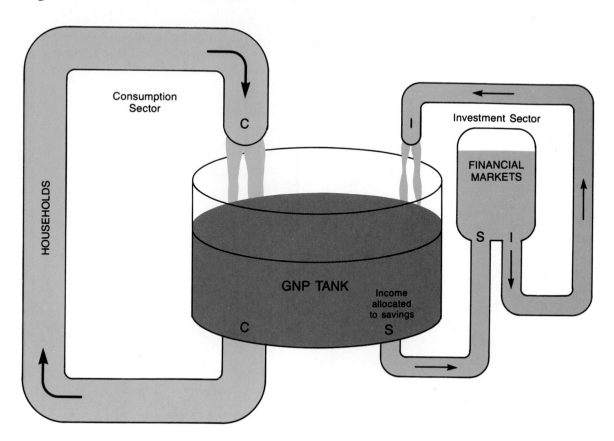

Whereas all of the income that households allocate to consumption is spent on consumer goods and services, the income allocated to savings may or may not all be spent on investment goods. Savings go into financial markets; and that amount, or less, or more, may be returned to the economy in the form of investment spending.

**Government demand**   A third source of demand is federal, state, and local government purchases of goods and services. These purchases include armaments, highways, police and fire protection, and schools, among other things. Government spending is added to consumption and investment demand for GNP in Figure 5 on the next page. It is shown by the red flow from the pipe at the top of the GNP tank marked "G." This amounted to $1,036.7 billion in 1989, as shown in the third column of Table 1.

At the bottom of the tank, income is drawn off by government in the form of taxes through the pipe labeled "T." As with the relation between savings and investment, the amount of income drawn off in taxes is not necessarily the same as the amount of government spending going back into the economy. If the government has a <u>deficit</u> in its

**deficit**   a negative balance after expenditures are subtracted from revenues.

*Figure 5*           GNP TANK WITH GOVERNMENT SPENDING

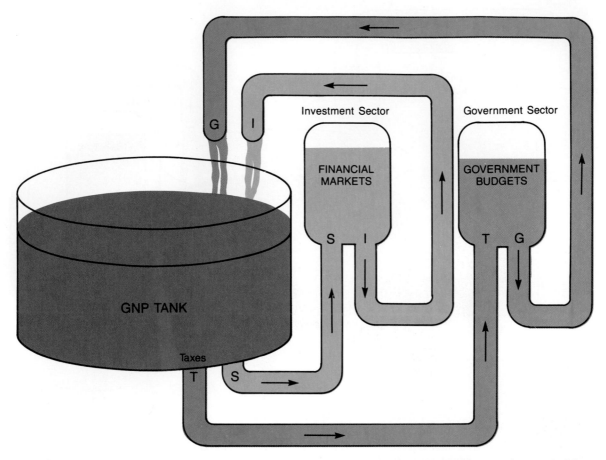

Government spending is funded by taxes; but, as with the investment sector, the amount of income drawn out of the economy in taxes is not necessarily the same as the amount returned to the economy in government spending. Generally, government spending, especially federal government spending, is greater than tax receipts; and government budgets are in the red.

budget (spending more than it takes in), it is pumping more purchasing power into the economy than it is drawing off in taxes. If, on the other hand, the government has a surplus (spending less than it takes in), there is an accumulation in the government sector red holding tank. The flow of purchasing power back into the economy is reduced. For the most part, state and local governments must keep their budgets in balance, except for spending on long-term capital projects. It is mainly the federal government deficits or surpluses that affect changes in the income stream.

**Equilibrium output**  Aggregate demand in the domestic sectors of the economy is the total of consumption (C),

**surplus**  a positive balance after expenditures are subtracted from revenues.

Savings that flow out of the GNP and into financial markets are used by businesses to invest in capital equipment, such as these computers.

investment (I), and government (G) spending. The flow of purchasing power from these three sectors determines the quantity of goods and services that can be sold. (The foreign sector is excluded for the present. It will be incorporated in the model in chapter 16.)

The quantity of goods and services demanded in turn determines how much output firms will produce. If the flow of purchasing power from one or more of these sectors is reduced, output and employment will go down. When the expenditure flows are increased, output and employment go up, unless the economy is already at full capacity production. In that case, as we saw in Figure 6A in chapter 11, on

*Figure 6A*      EFFECT OF A DECREASE IN INVESTMENT SPENDING

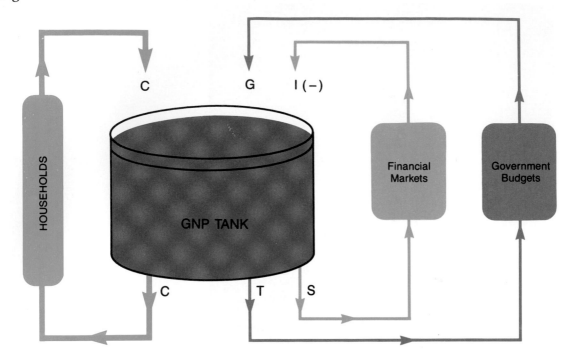

If there is a reduction in the amount of investment spending, as indicated by I( – ), there will be a decline in aggregate demand. The amount of purchasing power flowing into the economy (C + G + I) will be less than the amount flowing out (C + T + S). This will lower the level of economic activity, as shown in Figure 6B.

**equilibrium output level** the level of GNP at which aggregate demand (C + I + G + X) is just equal to aggregate supply (C + S + T + M); where income leakages (S + T + M) are exactly equal to income additions (I + G + X).

page 307, the increased demand results in demand-pull inflation rather than increased output.

Production will be at the equilibrium output level, whether at full employment or below it, when the additions to purchasing power from domestic consumption (C), investment (I), and government spending (G) are just equal to the leakages from the income tank. These leakages are the income generated in the tank and allocated to consumption (C), intended savings (S), and taxes (T). Since the amount of income allocated to consumption of domestic goods (C) is always the same as the amount of purchasing power returned to the tank in consumer spending (C), only the other two sectors can get out of equilibrium. GNP will be constant when all of the income that is *drawn out* of GNP in the form of savings (S) and taxes (T) is *returned* to GNP in the form of investment (I) and government (G) spending. When I + G = S + T, output is at an equilibrium level. Output, employment, and income will remain the same as long as there is no change in one of those variables.

## Figure 6B

### NEW EQUILIBRIUM LEVEL OF GNP

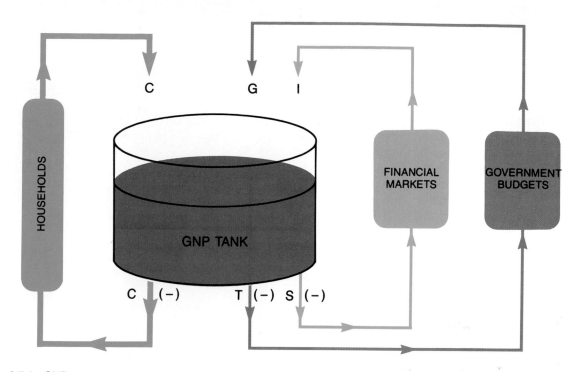

The fall in GNP resulting from reduced investment spending will decrease incomes. This will result in reduced consumption, taxes, and savings, as shown by C ( – ), T ( – ), and S ( – ). There will be a new lower equilibrium level of GNP when the reduced T + S equals the reduced G + I.

If there is a change in one of the demand sectors, there will be a change in the level of GNP. For example, if there is a decrease in investment, purchasing power flowing into the GNP tank from investment and government demand will be less than the outflow into savings and taxes (I + G < S + T). This causes production to decline as shown in Figure 6A. (This figure is a schematic version of the GNP tank model in Figure 5.) The resulting fall in output and employment reduces people's income.

When their income is reduced, households save less and pay less taxes, as well as reducing consumption of goods and services. Output, employment, and income will continue to fall until the reduction in investment spending is offset by a comparable decline in savings and taxes, so that inflows again equal outflows (I + G = S + T). A new equilibrium GNP results, with a lower level of output and income accompanied by higher unemployment and unused production capacity. This outcome is shown in Figure 6B above.

# case application

## The Inventory Paradox

In the third quarter of 1981 (July, August, and September), the American economy was in a recession, but manufacturing inventories increased over 2%. Why did businesses increase their inventories during a recession? That seems like rather strange behavior. When businesses are selling less, why would they want to keep a larger stock of goods for sale?

The answer is that they actually did not want to increase their inventories, especially in 1981 when interest rates were exceptionally high and it cost so much to have money tied up in inventories. The increase in inventories was unintentional. Due to the recession, sales were falling, and goods previously ordered and produced were being added to inventories faster than the inventories were being depleted by sales.

Because of the cost of carrying these inventories, businesses naturally wanted to reduce them. Therefore, they cut back on new orders for additional goods. Despite this, inventories continued to go up. The production declines due to reductions in new orders caused further falls in employment, incomes and sales. The more businesses attempted to reduce inventories, the higher those inventories went.

This seemingly paradoxical development is also found at the other end of the business cycle. As a result of rapidly rising sales during the expansion phase of a boom, businesses are not able to get deliveries of new orders fast enough to restock their shelves. Sometimes they lose out on sales because they can't fill customers' orders immediately. They may place duplicate orders with different suppliers in order to get deliveries of much-needed items. This leads to over-ex-

By trying to reduce inventories, businesses can cause unemployment that lessens demand—and leads to even greater inventory backlogs.

pansion of production during the boom phase of the cycle, which contributes to the subsequent collapse in the bust.

### Economic Reasoning

1. Which of the demand sectors incorporates inventory accumulation?
2. Why does the inventory paradox tend to make business cycles worse?
3. Some economic fluctuations since World War II have consisted almost exclusively of changes in inventory investment and are known as "inventory cycles." Under what conditions do you think an inventory cycle could touch off a major business cycle and under what conditions would it be unlikely to?

# What Determines Domestic Output From the Supply-Side Point of View?

The demand-side national income model was developed by Keynes in the 1930s and refined after World War II by his intellectual heirs, the neo-Keynesians. It emphasized the importance of aggregate demand in determining the levels of output, employment, and prices. Government macroeconomic policies have been based largely on Keynesian economics. From the 1940s to the 1960s those policies worked quite well. The economy was more stable than it had been during the 1930s and before.

However, the stagflation of the 1970s raised doubts about Keynesian economic policies. Some economists and politicians advocated a different approach based on supply-side economics. Their ideas were the foundation for "Reaganomics," the economic program on which Ronald Reagan campaigned in 1980 and introduced as president. Supply-side economics is more an approach to economic policy than it is a model of how the economy operates. In fact, supply-side proponents use the Keynesian model of how the economy works to analyze and explain the effects of their supply-side policies.

**Say's Law** Supply-side economics is not entirely new. Its roots go back at least as far as the early nineteenth century when a French economist by the name of J. B. Say formulated Say's Law of Markets. Say's Law states simply that "supply creates its own demand." In a money economy, this means that when an entrepreneur produces something, enough income is created in payments for wages, raw materials, capital, and other costs to purchase what was produced.

The prevailing idea prior to the Keynesian revolution in economic thinking was that overproduction or underproduction would not be a problem because demand would always be equal to the amount supplied. If there were a temporary glut, prices would fall and permit the excess goods to be purchased. Full employment would automatically be restored.

The Keynesian model showed that this was not the case. A decrease in investment spending, for example, would mean that some goods that were produced would not be sold, as indicated in Figures 6A and 6B on pages 344 and 345. There is a good deal of institutional resistance to reducing prices. There is especially resistance by labor unions to a reduction in the price of labor (wages). Demand therefore remains insufficient for full employment. As a

**supply-side economics** an approach to macroeconomic problems that focuses on the importance of increasing the supply of goods and services.
**Say's Law of Markets** A theory of the French economist J. B. Say, which holds that when goods or services are produced, enough income is generated to purchase what is produced, thereby eliminating the problem of overproduction.
**Keynesian revolution** the name given to the transformation in macroeconomic theory and policy that resulted from the ideas of Keynes.

result, high unemployment could last for a long time. The experience of the 1930s depression discredited Say's Law and led to the acceptance of Keynes's theories.

**Incentives** The emphasis in modern supply-side economics is on the importance of incentives in determining output. Keynesian economics assumes that an increase in aggregate demand automatically results in more goods and services being produced, as long as there is excess capacity in the economy. Supply-side proponents, on the other hand, maintain that increased production will not take place if costs are too high. These high costs include high interest rates and high tax rates.

Today's supply-side economists believe that there is a basis of truth in Say's Law. They believe that a reduction of costs, especially taxes, increases the incentive to produce, and that this increased production will create jobs and income. Increasing the net returns to producers by reducing taxes and other costs provides an incentive for them to produce more. They believe that reducing taxes also will cause households to save more, thereby making additional funds available to businesses for investment in new capital equipment. This additional investment will increase aggregate supply, as shown in Figure 7. The expansion of production capacity will shift aggregate supply from $AS_1$ to $AS_2$. As a result, there will be a decrease in inflation and unemployment as the general price level falls from $P_1$ to $P_2$ and output increases from $Q_1$ to $Q_2$.

The advocates of supply-side economics believe that increased monetary incentives can affect the supply of labor as well as the supply of capital. They maintain that reducing marginal tax rates will induce managers and workers to increase their labor input. Worker absenteeism will decline; workers will seek more overtime and second jobs; there will be less voluntary unemployment.

It is true that a reduction in tax rates means an increase in real wages, and the Law of Supply states that an increase in the price of a good or service will increase the amount offered for sale. However, there is some question as to whether this applies to the supply of labor, and under what conditions. If real wages increase, does this cause people to seek more work, or does it cause them to work less and take more leisure time? Studies show that the effect varies among different groups of workers. Many workers prefer more vacation time to higher wages, which suggests that greater real income might actually reduce the amount of labor that they supply.

**Government deficits** Supply-side economics also differs from demand-side economics another way. It emphasizes

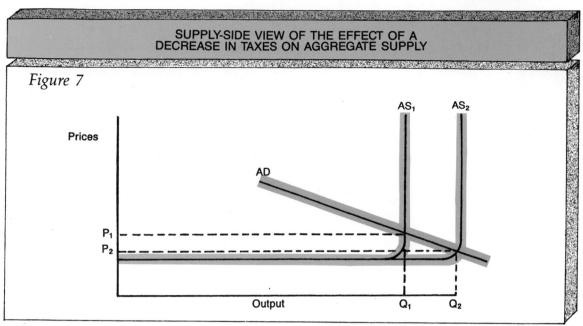

## SUPPLY-SIDE VIEW OF THE EFFECT OF A DECREASE IN TAXES ON AGGREGATE SUPPLY

**Figure 7**

Supply-side economics believes a reduction in taxes on businesses will provide an incentive to expand production. This expansion will shift aggregate supply from $AS_1$ to $AS_2$ and prices will fall from $P_1$ to $P_2$ as output increases from $Q_1$ to $Q_2$.

the effect of government deficits on the availability and cost of capital to investors in the private sector. When government spends more than it collects in taxes, it finances the difference by borrowing money in the financial markets. State and local governments sell revenue bonds to finance major projects, and the federal government sells Treasury bills and bonds to finance federal deficits. The sale of these government securities draws large quantities of capital out of the private capital market and raises interest rates. This process is illustrated in Figure 8 on page 350. It is the same as the previous GNP tank models except that government budgets are connected to the financial markets out of which governments siphon off investment capital.

Figure 8 shows current GNP, the colored area in the GNP tank, at less than full employment. Some supply-siders argue that the reason for the unemployment is that the government is crowding out private investment, depriving it of capital. (The crowding-out effect is exaggerated in Figure 8 by showing a complete elimination of private investment flow from the financial sector.)

If the private investors had access to this capital, supply-siders say, they would invest it in new plants and equipment, thereby creating jobs and increasing GNP. But the government returns some of its payments to the economy in the form of income transfers which are nonproductive and

**revenue bond**   a financial obligation issued by a branch of state or local government that has the receipts from a specific revenue source pledged to the obligation's interest and redemption payments.
**crowding out**   the term given to the effect government has in reducing the amount of financial capital available for private investment.

*Figure 8*     EFFECT OF GOVERNMENT BORROWING CROWDING OUT PRIVATE INVESTMENT

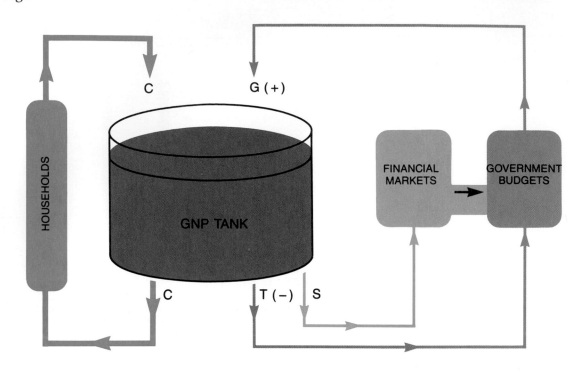

When an increase in government spending, G ( + ), or a decrease in taxes, T ( – ), is financed by government borrowing, investment sector funds may be diverted from private investment to the government sector. This is the "crowding out" effect shown by the connecting flow between the financial markets (green) and government budgets (red). The effect is exaggerated in the diagram by completely eliminating the investment flow.

only tend to raise prices and not output. This is the rationale for reducing government spending and balancing the budget.

There has been a controversy among supply-siders between those who believe in the need for tax cuts to provide production incentives and those who fear that the resulting government deficits will crowd out private investment. However, even with the record government deficits of the 1980s, this did not occur. It did not occur in part because the demand by businesses for investment funds was moderate and in part because a large amount of funds was supplied to the U.S. capital market by foreigners, especially the Japanese. But the danger is that if foreign investors pull their money out of the country while the government is running large deficits, it will result in crowding out private investment. This would raise interest rates and choke off economic expansion.

# case application

## Spending Like There Is No Tomorrow

Americans did not show much interest in saving during the 1980s. The private savings rate fell from an average between 7% and 8% of disposable income in the 1960s and 1970s to a low of 3.2% in 1987. By 1989 it recovered to 5.5%. This is a much lower savings rate than in other industrialized countries. Why is the savings rate so low?

A study by Joel Slemrod, a University of Michigan economist, found a correlation between personal savings rates and the perceived threat of nuclear war. The more likely nuclear war seemed to the public at a given time, the lower the personal savings rate. Other researchers have come up with similar findings. The fear that there is no tomorrow partly explains our spending binge in the 1980s. But only partly. The influence of the nuclear threat on spending was positive but small. Other factors were more important.

One of the other explanations for a low savings rate is the income security provided by our social security system. The Japanese, for instance, must depend much more on lifetime savings to provide for retirement income. Another reason is the ready availability of credit in this country.

The reasons for the especially low savings rate in the 1980s, however, may be found in particular economic circumstances of the time. The rise in the values of real estate and of stock portfolios encouraged spending. Owners of those assets could spend more of their income and yet see an increase in worth of their assets at the same time. This affected the spending habits of some 20% of the population with substantial assets.

The other 80% of the population did not, in fact, go on a consumption binge. Their real standard of living actually declined during the decade, according to most economists.

The Baby Boom generation has been saving 2% to 3% less of their income at age 35, the prime saving years, than did their parents at the same age. One view is that they are starting families at a later age than previous generations did, and that their savings rate will increase as they assume family responsibilities.

And to the extent that the fear of a nuclear holocaust does influence people's decisions to spend rather than save, the end of the cold war should have a small positive effect on the savings rate.

### *Economic Reasoning*

1. According to Say's Law, what would be the effect of an increase in investment on consumption? Why?
2. A supply-side argument for the 1981 tax cut was that it would increase savings, making more money available in the financial sector for investment. Show with a schematic GNP tank diagram what was expected to happen. Show what happened instead.
3. Should the government levy consumption taxes on goods and services to discourage consumption spending and raise revenue for the government as European governments do? Why or why not?

There are different ways to measure the output of the economy, and different models to explain its operation.

# Putting It Together

The total output of the economy, *Gross National Product (GNP)*, can be measured either by the sales value of the output of goods and services or by the total incomes received in producing these goods and services. In measuring sales, there are four sources of demand for goods and services: *consumption demand, investment demand, government demand,* and *net export demand.* The total expenditures by these four sectors constitute GNP.

In measuring GNP as the total of incomes, we first determine *National Income,* which is the sum of wages, rents, interest, and profits. To arrive at GNP, the amount of capital equipment used up during the year (depreciation) plus *indirect business taxes* and other *business transfer payments* are then added to National Income.

In measuring the value of GNP, we do not include the total sales for each industry. That is because the value of goods produced by finished goods industries already includes the value of the semi-finished goods used to produce the finished products. To avoid double-counting, only the *value added* by each industry in the production process is included. In order to compare changes in real output from year to year, the effects of inflation are removed from the figures. This is done by adjusting *current dollar GNP* to eliminate the effect of higher prices. Deflating current dollar GNP by the price index gives us *constant dollar GNP.*

The *Keynesian economic model* is the basis for demand-side economics. The model, including only the domestic sectors for the present, holds that consumption (C), investment (I), and government (G) spending determine an economy's total output. When purchasing power going into the economy from investment and government spending is exactly offset by the allocation (leakages) of income into savings (S) and taxes (T), an economy's output will be at equilibrium level. On the other hand, if the income leakages into S and T are greater than the injections of purchasing power from I and G, then output, employment, and income will fall. Or if spending injections exceed leakages, output will rise, unless the economy is already at full employment.

Keynes's model demonstrated that the economy could be at equilibrium even though it was operating at less than full employment. This contradicted classical theories of economics, including *Say's Law of Markets,* which states that "supply creates its own demand."

Say's Law was an early formulation of *supply-side economics.* Modern supply-side economists claim that Keynesian economic policies are misguided because they ignore the effects of these policies on supply. In order to induce producers to risk their capital, it is necessary to provide adequate profit incentives. Adding to aggregate demand without providing incentives to producers only drives up prices. Supply-siders call for a reduction in tax rates, both on investment income and on labor services, a decrease in government spending by cutting back on government services and transfer payments, and a reduction in cost-increasing government regulations.

# Perspective

## The Keynesian Revolution

**John Maynard Keynes (1883–1946)**
Keynes was raised in the intellectual environment of Cambridge University where his father, a noted writer on political economy and logic, taught and where his mother was mayor of the city of Cambridge. Upon graduation from the university, he took the examinations for entry into the British Civil Service and received his lowest mark in the economics part of the examinations. His explanation for the low grade was that "the examiners presumably knew less than I did" about economics. His career alternated between government service, teaching, writing, editing, and business, including making a fortune in the commodities market. He was a patron of the arts and married a star ballerina of the Russian Imperial Ballet. In 1942 he was made a peer and became Lord Keynes. He died of a heart attack in 1946.

In addition to *The General Theory*, his other important publications include *The Economic Consequences of the Peace* (1919), in which he predicted the results of the heavy war reparations imposed on Germany which later contributed to the rise of Hitler; *A Treatise on Probability* (1921); and *A Treatise on Money* (1930).

In a 1935 letter to Irish playwright George Bernard Shaw, British economist John Maynard Keynes predicted that the book he was working on would revolutionize the way people thought about economic problems. That book, *The General Theory of Employment, Interest and Money,* was published in 1936. Keynes was prophetic. *The General Theory* did revolutionize economic thinking, and the transformation became known as the "Keynesian revolution," sometimes capitalized as "Keynesian Revolution" to dramatize its significance.

Prior to the publication of *The General Theory,* the working hypothesis of macroeconomics was that the economy had a natural tendency to full employment. Unemployment was assumed to be the result of a *temporary* malfunction. The depth and length of the Great Depression, however, appeared to belie this assumption. In the United States, output fell by almost one-half and prices dropped nearly as much. Unemployment reached as high as one out of every four in the working population. By the time *The General Theory* appeared, the depression had been gong on for over half a decade and it continued, only somewhat abated, until the outbreak of World War II.

The revolutionary model which Keynes presented in *The General Theory* showed how an economy can be stuck at an equilibrium output level far below full employment because of insufficient aggregate demand. The policy implication of the model was that government should take an active role in bringing the economy out of a depression by injecting government spending into the income stream. This increased spending by government at a time of declining tax revenues would, of course, result in large budget deficits. To those who were concerned about the long-run consequences of such policies Keynes's response was, "In the long run we are all dead."

Keynes wrote in his letter to Shaw that the revolution in economic thinking would not take place overnight. Keynes's theory was elaborated on by a number of other economists, including Joan Robinson (See chapter 6 Perspective). Perhaps the final triumph of the Keynesian revolution was reached when conservative Republican president Richard Nixon said, "I am a Keynesian." Ironically, this triumph of the Keynesian revolution came at a time when the structure of the economy had changed so much that Keynesian economics no longer seemed to provide an adequate solution to our economic problems.

**For Further Study and Analysis**

## Study Questions

1. If you tutored a classmate for 10 hours at $8 an hour, what would be the effect on the National Income?

2. In the above case, if you had no expenses, what would be the effect on the nation's output as measured by GNP?

3. Assuming in the above case that you had to spend 50 cents on gas to drive to each 1-hour tutoring session, what would be the value added to GNP by your tutoring?

4. On January 1, 1990, a grocery store had on hand an inventory valued at $240,000. During 1990 the store had bought groceries worth $600,000. Sales for that year came to $800,000. How much did this firm contribute to the investment component of GNP for 1990?

5. If you had a $200,000 "dream house" built, what would be the effect on GNP? What component of aggregate demand would be affected?

6. You are working at a job with a take-home pay of $200 a week. You have been putting $15 into a savings account every week, but you want to build up your savings faster, so you increase it to $25. What effect would this have on GNP?

7. Assuming the economy is at an equilibrium level of output, what are three examples of changes that would cause output to fall?

8. If output were not at the full employment level, what are three examples of changes that would increase GNP?

9. According to Keynesian economics, what would happen to output, employment, and income if government spending was reduced by 50% and taxes by 25%?

10. According to supply-side economics, what would happen to equilibrium GNP if government spending and taxes were both reduced by 50%?

## Exercises in Analysis

1. In the *Economic Report of the President* (see Further Reading at the end of chapter 11) or another source, find the changes in current dollar GNP for the most recent year reported compared to the preceding year. Then write a short paper on which components of GNP were principally responsible for the changes.

2. The following are GNP figures for a hypothetical country: Consumption—$2,000; Investment—$300; Government spending—$400; Exports—$150; Savings—$400; Taxes—$400; Imports—$100. From these figures calculate the aggregate demand in the economy. Does the total demand equal the value of current output? If not, what would you expect to happen to output? Why?

3. Write a short paper on what has happened to investment spending, government spending, savings, taxes, output, and employment in the past year. Illustrate with a GNP tank diagram.

4. Write a short paper on whether demand-side economics or supply-side economics is, in your opinion, a better explanation of how the economy behaves and why.

## Further Reading

Evans, Michael K. *The Truth About Supply-Side Economics*. New York: Basic Books, 1981. The myths, the truths, and the policy implications of supply-side economics.

Hailstones, Thomas J. *A Guide to Supply-Side Economics*. New York: Prentice Hall, 1983. Compares the evolution and policies of Keynesian and supply-side economics.

Hall, Peter A. *The Political Power of Economic Ideas: Keynesianism Across Nations*. Princeton, N.J.: Princeton University Press, 1989. Explores the spread of the Keynesian Revolution from country to country and the effect it had on politics and policies.

Hillard, John, ed. *J. M. Keynes in Retrospect: The Legacy of the Keynesian Revolution*. Aldershot, U.K.: Edward Elgar, 1988. This book is a collection of articles on the Keynesian Revolution in the past and where it stands today.

Kotlikoff, Laurence J. *What Determines Savings?* Cambridge, Mass.: MIT Press, 1989. There are sections on the motives for savings, the relation of fiscal policy to savings, and how social security and demographics affect savings.

O'Laughlin, Carleen. *National Economic Accounting*. New York: Pergamon Press, 1971. An explanation of the methodology used in devising the national accounts and of the sources of data.

Roberts, Paul Craig. *The Supply-Side Revolution*. Cambridge, Mass.: Harvard University Press, 1984. A description and evaluation of how supply-side economics was implemented during the Reagan years by one of supply-side economics' leading proponents.

Rousseas, Stephen. *The Political Economy of Reaganomics*. New York: M.E. Sharp, 1982. An examination of classical supply-side economics, demand-side economics, monetarist supply-side economics, and how "Reaganomics" fits into these schools of thought.

Schwartz, Thomas R., Frank J. Bonello, and Andrew F. Kozak. *The Supply Side: Debating Current Economic Policies*. Guilford, Conn.: The Dushkin Publishing Group, 1983.

# PUBLIC FINANCE

*Government spending and taxing have a large effect on the economy. The government sector is where economic stabilization policies are implemented. Sometimes there is a conflict between our spending and taxing goals and our economic stability goals, as the following article shows.*

## Lessons in Lip Reading

During the 1988 campaign George Bush emphasized his commitment to oppose higher taxes if he were elected president by saying, "Read my lips: no new taxes!" He pledged to continue the tax policies of the Reagan administrations, in which he served as vice president. In 1981 personal income taxes were cut 23% and tax breaks given to businesses. In 1986 the maximum income tax rate was reduced to 28%.

Those tax reductions followed the principles of supply-side economics. Supply-side theory maintains that lower taxes provide incentives to producers and investors to increase capital investment and output. It holds that lowering taxes also makes available the investment funds for new plant and equipment. Supply-siders argued that the growth of investment and output resulting from lower tax rates actually increases total tax receipts.

Federal tax revenue from personal and corporate income taxes did grow by $29 billion, in constant dollar value, between 1981 and 1988. However, that was less than half the real growth rate of income tax receipts in the preceding 8 years and not nearly enough to cover increases in government spending. Defense spending alone grew by $63 billion in constant value dollars from 1981–88.

As a result of tax receipts falling short of expenditures, federal budget deficits piled up. From a deficit of $79 billion in fiscal year (FY) 1981, the federal deficit increased to a record $221 billion in FY 1986 and was nearly as high at over $220 billion for FY 1990. (The

federal budget fiscal year ends on September 30.) The total budget deficits from FY 1982 through FY 1990 amounted to over $1.6 trillion, resulting in more than doubling the national debt to $3 trillion.

In order to stanch the flow of red ink, Congress passed the Balanced Budget and Emergency Deficit Control Act of 1985, familiarly known as the Gramm-Rudman bill after its two initial sponsors. This legislation aimed at bringing federal spending in line with receipts by reducing the deficit each year over a 5-year period. According to the 1985 act, the federal budget was to be balanced by FY 1991.

The Gramm-Rudman bill provided that if Congress and the president did not agree on a budget for the coming year that met the targets set by the bill, automatic spending reductions would be imposed. Automatic cuts have been avoided in various ways, however, despite repeated failures to actually meet the deficit reduction goals. In 1987 Congress postponed the date specified for bringing the budget into balance from 1991 to 1993, making the annual goals less restrictive.

The projected deficit each year was reduced by including in the budget calculation the annual surpluses added to the Social Security trust funds. Those surpluses are intended to cover the higher Social Security payments after 2010 when the baby boom generation retires (see p. 238). The Treasury borrows the trust fund surpluses to help cover the federal deficit. In the budget calculations, however, the Social Security surpluses were counted as income. If the Social Security fund surplus had not been counted as income in 1990, the deficit would have been

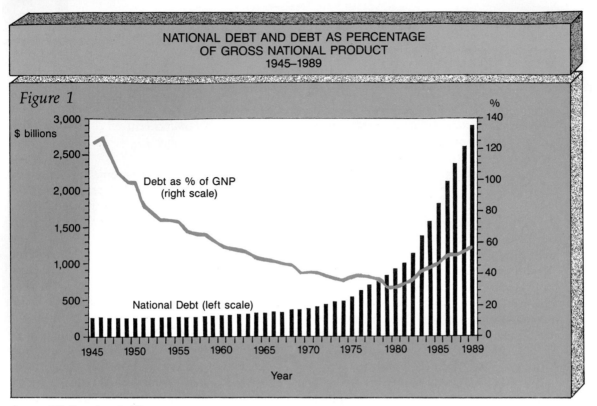

**NATIONAL DEBT AND DEBT AS PERCENTAGE
OF GROSS NATIONAL PRODUCT
1945–1989**

*Figure 1*

Debt as % of GNP
(right scale)

National Debt (left scale)

Year

Source: U.S. Department of Treasury.

As a result of record budget deficits, the national debt has more than doubled since 1981. However, as a percentage of Gross National Product, it is not as high as it was between World War II and 1960.

$68 billion higher. (The practice of including the Social Security trust funds in the general budget is proposed to be discontinued.)

Postponing the day of reckoning and counting the Social Security surplus as revenue helped to avoid the politically painful adjustment to a balanced budget. But the last-resort method for avoiding Gramm-Rudman restraints was an annual ritual of budget magic. What appeared to be deficits for the coming year that exceeded the Gramm-Rudman limits were made to disappear by "smoke and mirrors."

The difference between the target deficit mandated by Gramm-Rudman and the actual deficit increased each year. The Gramm-Rudman deficit limit for FY 1990 was $100 billion. The budget adopted in the fall of 1989 was within this limit and automatic cuts thus avoided. However, the actual 1990 deficit

turned out to be $220.4 billion, more than twice the Gramm-Rudman limit. And that did not even include $67 billion in S&L bailout costs that were excluded from the budget calculations.

How can it happen that every year the budget deficit exceeded the legal maximum? For purposes of satisfying the Gramm-Rudman requirements, it is the projected deficit for the coming year that counts, not what the deficit actually turns out to be. Consequently, Congress and the administration "cooked the books" to make it appear that the proposed budget met the legal requirement. They engage in accounting trickery that a private business could never get away with.

One of the tricks employed for the FY 1990 budget was shifting the October 1, 1989, payday for our military personnel to September 29. This moved the spending from the FY

1990 budget to the FY 1989 budget. That change increased the actual 1989 deficit, of course; but in Gramm-Rudman requirements the actual deficit doesn't count, only the proposed deficit. The same sleight-of-hand transfer was performed with the farm subsidy payments.

Other ways the budget numbers were manipulated to meet the target were in overestimating revenues by projecting a higher economic growth rate, in underestimating interest costs by projecting a fall in the interest rates on government borrowing, and in assuming unspecified revenue increases and spending decreases.

By the summer of 1990, however, it was apparent that no amount of accounting tricks could reduce the deficit from more than $220 billion in FY 1990 to the $64 billion mandated by Gramm-Rudman for FY 1991. Large reductions in spending or increased revenues were required, or both. But neither Congress nor the president wanted to take the blame for initiating program cuts or tax hikes. As one congressional leader noted, "If there's going to be a tax increase, we're all going to have to join hands and jump off the bridge together."

"Bridge-jumping" summit meetings on the budget were held between congressional leaders and the president, resulting in the president retracting his "no new taxes" pledge. After protracted discussion and angry disagreements, a FY 1991 budget was brought forth and signed into law—4 weeks after the beginning of the fiscal year. It was opposed by conservatives, who objected to the tax increases it contained, and by liberals, who objected to cuts in Medicare and other social programs. It passed with bare majorities in the House and Senate and was treated as an illegitimate child by all concerned. Politicians from the president down denied parentage. Read my lips: The only thing more politically distasteful than large deficits is getting rid of them.

Economists also had reservations about the budget. The multi-year budget agreement purported to reduce deficits by a projected total of $490 billion over 5 years. However, this was based on exaggerated estimates of economic growth. Many economists expressed concern that the 1991 budget, with its tax increases and spending cuts, would actually push the economy over the brink into recession. The resulting decrease in tax receipts and increase in government income supplement payments would drive the deficits even higher. In fact, a decline in business activity in the early months of FY 1991 erased all of the deficit reduction hammered out so painfully at the budget summit meetings and, combined with the military costs of the Persian Gulf action, threatened to push the 1991 deficit to between $300 and $400 billion.

## Chapter Preview

*The size of government deficits and the growing national debt have been of increasing concern to the public. People want the programs government provides, but they do not want the country to go broke paying for them. In this chapter we will examine the problem of government finance by asking these questions: On what do governments spend money? Where do governments get the money to spend? Who pays for government spending?*

## Learning Objectives

*After completing this chapter, you should be able to:*

1. *Describe the size of government debt and deficits.*
2. *Discuss the relative size of government economic activity.*
3. *List the most important types of federal government spending.*
4. *List the most important types of state and local government spending.*
5. *Identify the principal sources of revenue for the federal, state, and local governments respectively.*
6. *Explain the criteria for equity in taxation.*
7. *Describe how "bad" taxes decrease economic efficiency.*
8. *Define what is meant by the incidence of a tax.*

# On What Do Governments Spend Money?

According to public opinion polls, people are not as much concerned about the amount of taxes collected as they are about the efficiency with which their tax dollars are spent. This section examines the allocations of spending by the different levels of government.

**Size of government spending** Just how big is "big government"? About one-third of all money flow in the U.S. economy is channeled through governments. The budgets of all levels of government—federal, state, and local—together equal 34% of the Gross National Product. This is similar to or less than the share of government spending in other advanced economies (33% in Japan and 47% in what was West Germany).

However, this overstates the impact of government spending on the economy because a large part of government payments, especially in the federal budget, are not purchases but rather income transfers. In 1989, about two-thirds of all federal expenditures were transfer payments. If we subtract transfer payments from the total of all government expenditures, then government spending at all levels accounts for one-fifth of total spending. The various levels of government purchase about 20% of the nation's yearly output of goods and services, of which the federal government accounts for just under 8%.

During the last two decades, total government spending has increased by 36% after adjustment for inflation. Two-thirds of the increase in federal spending was for defense, with the remainder accounted for by larger transfer payments. The increase in state and local spending has been primarily for government services.

*Figure 2*

GNP ALLOCATION BY SECTORS
1989

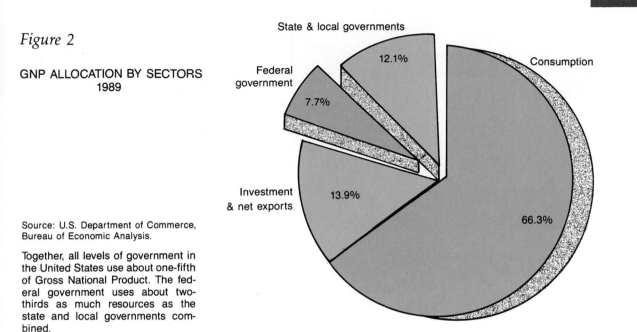

State & local governments

Federal
government

Consumption

12.1%

7.7%

Investment
& net exports

13.9%

66.3%

Source: U.S. Department of Commerce,
Bureau of Economic Analysis.

Together, all levels of government in
the United States use about one-fifth
of Gross National Product. The federal government uses about two-
thirds as much resources as the
state and local governments combined.

As a result of transfer payments, the federal budget is 70%
greater than the total of state and local government budgets.
But state and local governments employ four and a half
times as many people as the federal government because
they provide the bulk of public services. Nearly 13% of all
civilian employees in the country work for state and local
governments, while the federal government employs less
than 3%. The size of the federal work force has been
virtually constant for the last two decades and has actually
declined by one-fourth as a percentage of the total labor
force. Meanwhile, the number of employees in state and
local governments has doubled.

**Federal spending**   Figure 3 shows the allocation of federal
outlays in 1989. The federal budget is divided between
purchases of goods and services and transfer payments. The
largest single expenditure item in 1989 was for national
defense, as it is each year, accounting for over one-fourth of
the total budget. All other direct expenditures—for running
the executive, legislative, and judicial branches of the government, protecting and developing natural resources,
space, technology, energy, etc.—accounted for less than 5%
of the budget. It is direct spending that makes up the
government sector (G) in determining the level of national
output (GNP) discussed in the last chapter.

The rest of the budget consists of transfer payments of
various sorts. The largest of these in 1989 was Social Secu-

## *Figure 3*

FEDERAL GOVERNMENT
SPENDING
1989

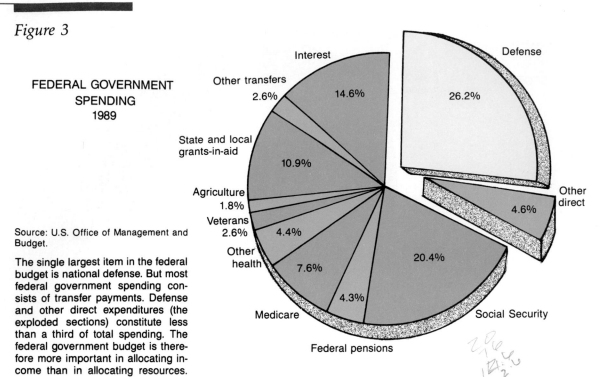

Interest

Other transfers
2.6%

State and local
grants-in-aid

10.9%

Agriculture
1.8%

Veterans
2.6%

Other
health

Medicare

Federal pensions

14.6%

Defense

26.2%

Other
direct

4.6%

4.4%

7.6%

4.3%

20.4%

Social Security

Source: U.S. Office of Management and Budget.

The single largest item in the federal budget is national defense. But most federal government spending consists of transfer payments. Defense and other direct expenditures (the exploded sections) constitute less than a third of total spending. The federal government budget is therefore more important in allocating income than in allocating resources.

**grants-in-aid**    federal government allocations of funds to states to finance programs, frequently programs mandated by the federal government.

rity pension and disability benefits. (For a full discussion of Social Security, see the Case Application for the second analysis section of this chapter, page 370.) Next in size was interest on the national debt, the third largest expenditure in the budget and growing. In 1980 it was only 8.9% of the budget compared with 14.6% in 1989. Other major transfers are for Medicare and other health programs and for grants-in-aid to state and local governments to assist them in carrying out federally mandated programs. Since transfer payments account for over two-thirds of the budget, the federal government is more important in allocating income in the economy than it is in allocating resources through its purchases.

It is obvious from these figures that reducing "waste and inefficiency in government," insofar as federal government civilian activities are concerned, cannot accomplish a great deal in reducing the deficit. Eliminating the direct costs of all federal government non-defense departments and agencies completely would reduce the size of the federal budget by less than 5%. Preserving the programs but making them more efficient can reduce government spending by only a negligible amount. Furthermore, since interest on the national debt cannot be evaded, that leaves defense spending and the various income transfer programs as the only possible areas of significant federal budget reduction.

Most of these income transfer programs are entitlements,

## Figure 4

### STATE AND LOCAL GOVERNMENT SPENDING 1987

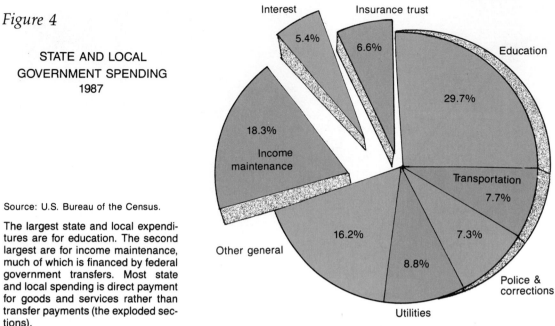

Source: U.S. Bureau of the Census.

The largest state and local expenditures are for education. The second largest are for income maintenance, much of which is financed by federal government transfers. Most state and local spending is direct payment for goods and services rather than transfer payments (the exploded sections).

which means that eligible recipients are legally entitled to the payments or services from the government. These entitlements include Social Security benefits, federal employee retirement benefits, Medicaid, Medicare, veterans' benefits, and unemployment assistance. Anyone who is eligible to receive these benefits, is, by law, entitled to them, and more and more people have become eligible in recent years. The total number of beneficiaries of these various entitlement programs now is over 70 million, or about one of every three persons in the population. These recipients constitute a very large group in support of continuation of these programs. As the age distribution of the population becomes older, more people become eligible for these programs, and some programs become more expensive because their benefits are indexed to the cost of living. This creates a built-in pressure for continuing increases in transfer payments.

**State and local expenditures**  As shown in Figure 4, state and local governments spend more on education than in any other area. Education absorbs about 30% of state and local budgets. In contrast to the federal budget, most state and local expenditures are direct rather than transfer payments.

The interest costs on the debt of state and local governments amount to only about 5% of their budgets, much less than for the federal government. This is because state and local governments in general are legally prevented from running deficits in their current spending. Except for capital

Free public education accounts for over one-third of state and local government expenditures. Tax reduction initiatives and higher costs have led to smaller budgets and cutbacks in many classrooms.

expenditures such as construction projects which are funded by specific bond issues, most state and local government budgets must be in annual balance.

Because state and local governments cannot run current budget deficits and because of a "taxpayers' revolt" against rising taxes, there was a shortage of funds for providing services in the 1980s. School buildings deteriorated, teachers' salaries were held down, and some schools were forced to close before the end of the school year because they ran out of money. Transportation was another area hard hit by budget reductions. There has been widespread deterioration of city streets because of lack of maintenance—an estimated 1 million potholes in the streets of Chicago alone. Highway construction projects have been cancelled or postponed because of lack of funds. Traffic on many bridges is restricted because of their dangerous condition. About 45% of the nation's bridges are considered structurally deficient or functionally obsolete. Public transportation systems in many places have been affected even more seriously than private transportation. Water and sewage systems are badly deteriorated.

Two areas of state spending have been increasing: prisons and health care. In 1980 states spent about 7% of their budgets on Medicaid, the federal-state health-care program for the poor. By 1989 Medicaid costs had risen to nearly 11% of state spending. Congress has required states to expand health care and welfare benefits but failed to provide additional money to pay for them.

# case application

## Privatization

In an attempt save money, state and local governments have been turning more of their functions over to private for-profit companies. Private contracting of public services has long been used for some services such as garbage collection and road repair. But as budget pressures have forced city, county, and state governments to seek cost reductions, some are hiring private firms to take over a variety of government services.

A number of cities in Los Angeles County have opted for contracting out such functions as janitorial services, public works inspections, operating the parks and recreation department, providing day-care, tree trimming, and even prosecuting offenders in municipal court. Grants Pass, Oregon, has contracted with privately owned Valley Fire to provide fire protection services to a part of the city rather than expand the municipal fire department.

This movement toward turning traditional government services over to private enterprise has been termed "privatization." In many instances it has been successful, in others not. Among the failures was the private contracting of the administration of Arizona's health-care system, which had to be taken back by the state because of cost overruns and other problems. New York City cut its janitorial and printing costs in half by performing the work using city employees rather than private contractors.

In the last century many public services were provided by private firms, but because the services were not satisfactory they were

The New Mexico Women's Correctional Facility, shown above, is run for profit by Correctional Corporation of America. Prisons run by private companies supervise over 3,000 inmates in 24 state and county institutions, and represent a controversial type of privatization.

adopted as functions of government. An example is the for-profit fire departments discussed in chapter 8 (see p. 209). Some critics of privatization, especially the unions representing government employees, claim that the public will become disenchanted with privatization when the quality of services declines as the private firms attempt to increase their profit margins.

The biggest controversy over state privatization of services is the privatization of prisons. The prison population has doubled in the last decade, nearing 1 million inmates. Faced with swelling costs for prison construction and inmate maintenance, some states have turned to for-profit prison management companies. Such firms as Corrections Corporation of America,

U.S. Corrections, and Wackenhut supervise over 3,000 inmates in 24 state and county institutions.

Privatization of prisons can reduce costs 5% to 10%. But critics of the system argue that for-profit prison corporations are only interested in warehousing inmates, not in rehabilitating them. If inmates of private prisons are more likely to return to crime when released than those of public institutions, it could cost society more in the long run. Critics are also concerned about prison security and the possibility of escapes from private prisons. This has been particularly an issue in some communities where the private prison companies have proposed building new prisons.

State legislatures that have opted for prison privatization believe that private firms can do the job as well as or better than state institutions, at least with minimum-security prisoners, and at lower cost.

## Economic Reasoning

1. Does privatization affect mainly direct government spending or transfer payments? Explain.
2. Why is privatization more applicable at the state and local level than at the federal level?
3. Should states privatize the imprisonment of criminals? Why or why not?

# Where Do Governments Get the Money to Spend?

In the preceding section, we saw that there are major differences in what the federal government spends money on and what state and local governments spend money on. In this section we will see that there are also major differences in the sources of their funds.

*Federal, Excise taxes: on*
*- gasoline*
*- alcohol*
*- cigarettes*
*- public utility services.*

**Federal government revenues**   The largest source of revenue for the federal government is individual income taxes. As shown in Figure 5, the tax on personal incomes provided nearly half of the federal government's revenue in 1989.

Next to income taxes, the largest government revenue—over one-third—comes from Social Security payroll taxes and federal and other pension contributions. Social Security taxes have been steadily increasing, and over half of the nation's workers, those at the lower end of the income scale, pay more in Social Security contributions than in income taxes.

Corporate income taxes generated just over one-tenth of federal revenues in 1989. Excise taxes—the federal taxes on gasoline, alcohol, cigarettes, and public utility services—customs duties on imports, and miscellaneous receipts such as user fees and earnings by the Federal Reserve System accounted for the balance.

**payroll tax**   a tax on wages and salaries to finance Social Security and Medicare costs, with equal amounts paid by employee and employer—the 1990 tax rate on each was 7.65%.

*Figure 5*

FEDERAL GOVERNMENT
REVENUE
1989

Sources: U.S. Department of the Treasury and Office of Management and Budget.

The largest source of federal government revenue is personal income taxes. The second largest is payroll taxes from Social Security and federal pension contributions. The largest item of miscellaneous receipts is the deposits of earnings by the Federal Reserve System.

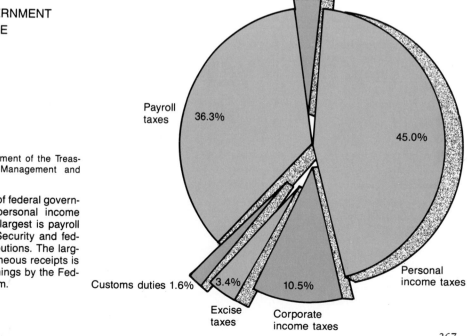

Miscellaneous 3.2%

Payroll taxes 36.3%

45.0%

Customs duties 1.6%

Excise taxes 3.4%

Corporate income taxes 10.5%

Personal income taxes

**State and local government revenues**   As Figure 6 shows, the largest sources of state and local government revenues come from sales taxes (states), property taxes (local governments), and grants-in-aid and other federal transfers (both).

The federal income transfers are referred to as fiscal federalism, by which a lower branch of government is financed by revenues collected at a higher level of government. Under the 1982 "new federalism" program introduced by the Reagan administration, more of this funding was in the form of block grants over which the state and local government units have discretion in how the money is to be used. This was a change from previous practice under which the spending was specified in detail by the federal government. The opponents of the "new federalism" maintain that the level and standards of public services should be equally available to all Americans, whatever the area in which they live, and that a role of the federal government is to assure this by stipulating how federal funds to states and local governments should be spent. The amounts of federal transfers to each state in 1988 are shown in Table 1.

State and local governments are caught in a financial squeeze. They face increasingly vocal demands from their citizens for improvements in highways, transportation, and other infrastructure; better schools; and pollution control. They are required by mandated federal programs to spend

**fiscal federalism**  tax collection and disbursement of funds by a higher level of government to lower jurisdictions.
**block grants**  funds allocated by the federal government to the states for discretionary state spending rather than for specified use.

*Figure 6*

STATE AND LOCAL
GOVERNMENT REVENUE
1987

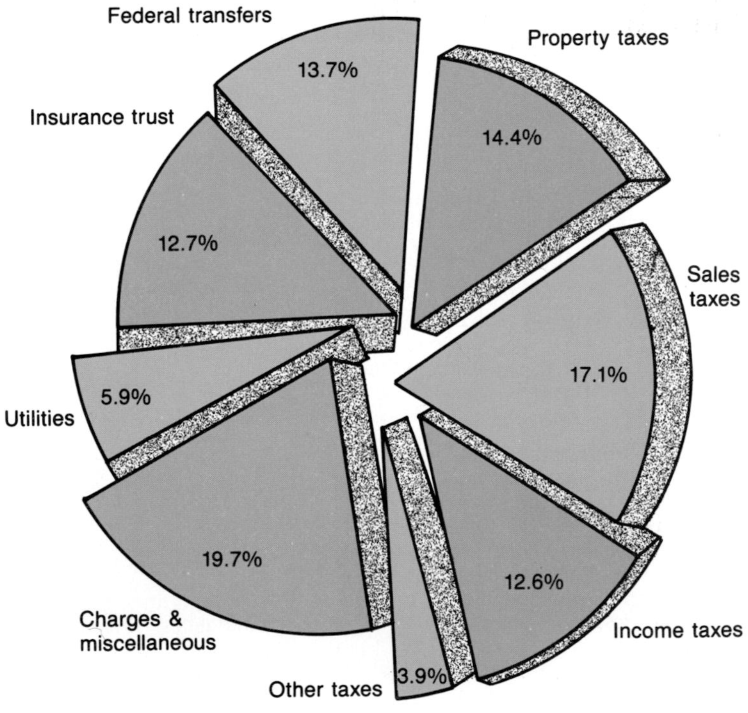

Source: U.S. Bureau of the Census.

The largest single source of revenue for the states is sales taxes. For local governments it is property taxes. Grants-in-aid and other federal government transfers are important to both state and local governments. Also important is the income from investment of insurance trust funds for employee pensions, etc.

Federal transfers 13.7%
Property taxes 14.4%
Insurance trust 12.7%
Sales taxes 17.1%
Utilities 5.9%
Charges & miscellaneous 19.7%
Other taxes 3.9%
Income taxes 12.6%

## Table 1

### FEDERAL INCOME TRANSFERS TO STATES
### In Order of Amounts per Capita—1988

| State | Federal Aid ($ billions) | Per Capita | State | Federal Aid ($ billions) | Per Capita |
|---|---|---|---|---|---|
| Dist. of Columbia | $ 1.6 | $ 2,605 | Michigan | $ 4.2 | $ 456 |
| Alaska | $ 0.6 | $ 1,156 | Tennessee | $ 2.2 | $ 452 |
| Wyoming | $ 0.4 | $ 950 | Nebraska | $ 0.7 | $ 445 |
| New York | $ 12.5 | $ 698 | Maryland | $ 2.0 | $ 442 |
| North Dakota | $ 0.5 | $ 679 | Hawaii | $ 0.5 | $ 436 |
| Montana | $ 0.5 | $ 679 | Ohio | $ 4.7 | $ 432 |
| Rhode Island | $ 0.6 | $ 647 | New Jersey | $ 4.3 | $ 431 |
| South Dakota | $ 0.4 | $ 620 | Oklahoma | $ 1.4 | $ 431 |
| Vermont | $ 0.3 | $ 582 | Utah | $ 0.7 | $ 429 |
| Massachusetts | $ 3.3 | $ 567 | Iowa | $ 1.2 | $ 423 |
| West Virginia | $ 1.1 | $ 561 | Alabama | $ 1.7 | $ 417 |
| Maine | $ 0.7 | $ 551 | Arkansas | $ 1.0 | $ 417 |
| New Mexico | $ 0.8 | $ 550 | California | $ 11.7 | $ 415 |
| Mississippi | $ 1.3 | $ 504 | Illinois | $ 4.7 | $ 405 |
| Minnesota | $ 2.1 | $ 492 | South Carolina | $ 1.4 | $ 388 |
| Louisiana | $ 2.1 | $ 483 | Missouri | $ 1.9 | $ 378 |
| Delaware | $ 0.3 | $ 483 | Colorado | $ 1.2 | $ 377 |
| Pennsylvania | $ 5.8 | $ 482 | New Hampshire | $ 0.4 | $ 363 |
| Oregon | $ 1.3 | $ 482 | Kansas | $ 0.9 | $ 354 |
| Idaho | $ 4.8 | $ 477 | North Carolina | $ 2.3 | $ 352 |
| Connecticut | $ 1.5 | $ 476 | Indiana | $ 2.0 | $ 352 |
| Kentucky | $ 1.8 | $ 474 | Arizona | $ 1.2 | $ 339 |
| Washington | $ 2.2 | $ 470 | Virginia | $ 2.0 | $ 327 |
| Georgia | $ 3.0 | $ 463 | Nevada | $ 0.3 | $ 317 |
| **National** | **$114.6** | **$ 460** | Texas | $ 5.2 | $ 308 |
| Wisconsin | $ 2.2 | $ 459 | Florida | $ 3.4 | $ 276 |

Source: U.S. Bureau of the Census.

The federal government provides grants-in-aid and other income transfers to state and local governments under a system of fiscal federalism. Other than the District of Columbia, which is financed by the federal government, the largest federal aid per capita in 1988 went to Alaska—$1,156 per Alaskan. The smallest amount went to Florida—only $276 for each Floridian.

more on Medicaid, social services, and income maintenance. At the same time, federal aid to the states is limited by the Gramm-Rudman pressure on federal spending and has been declining as a percentage of state revenues. State taxes, meanwhile, have been restricted by the taxpayers' revolt of the 1980s.

There are some indications at the beginning of the new decade, however, that voters are willing to pay more to get the improved services that they want. In California, where the taxpayer revolt began, and Florida, Massachusetts, Montana, Nevada, Oklahoma, Texas, and Vermont, either state voters or local governments have recently passed tax increases to fund specific programs. Voters are apparently willing to accept targeted taxes earmarked for specific purposes that they feel are needed.

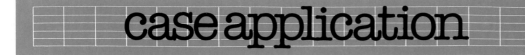

## Social Insecurity

Is the Social Security system going broke? Will there be any money left to pay retirement benefits to the young workers who are contributing to the system now? These are troublesome questions because, since the passage of the Social Security Act in 1935, the Social Security system has become the cornerstone of our society's method of providing economic security to older Americans.

The magazine *U.S. News & World Report* commissioned a study in 1985 to discover what people believed would happen to Social Security in their lifetimes. The survey found that most, especially the young, were pessimistic about the future of the system and the benefits they would receive from it (*U.S. News & World Report*, Aug. 12, 1985, p. 40). Are those pessimistic views justified?

There are actually four separate trust funds under the Social Security program. The principal fund pays *retirement benefits* to those who are past retirement age, or to their survivors, and a second fund provides *disability payments* to those who are unable to work any longer for physical or psychological reasons, although they have not reached retirement age. The other two funds are for *hospital* and *supplementary medical* care for the aged—the Medicare program.

The funds—especially the retirement fund—were nearing exhaustion in the early 1980s. To rescue the funds from running out of money, Congress enacted legislation in 1983 that increased Social Security revenues and reduced benefits. The bill accelerated scheduled increases in payroll taxes, raised the tax rate on the self-employed, and subjected some Social Security retirement benefits to income taxation. On the side of benefits, the most important change was to delay from 65 to 67 the age at which workers could retire with full benefits. That change will not come

into effect until the year 2000, when it will be phased in gradually up to the year 2027. Other benefit changes include a reduction in the percentage received by those who retire early, also effective at the turn of the century.

The Medicare fund was saved from insolvency by cost-containment measures imposed on hospitals and doctors. Also, Medicare patients have had to pay an increasing share of their health care costs.

As described in the chapter's introductory article (p. 357), the trust funds are now piling up surpluses. The surpluses are helping the government to balance the federal budget because the Social Security accounts are included in the government's overall budget.

Wait a minute. Does this mean that the government can tap the Social Security trust funds to pay its other bills? Not exactly. It borrows from the trust funds in the same way it borrows from others—by selling them Treasury bonds. By law, the reserves of the funds can only be used to purchase U.S. government securities. The Social Security surpluses thus reduce the government's need to go into the private capital market to finance the deficit. But the government is obligated to repay the funds borrowed, and the total assets of the funds remain intact.

Surpluses in the Social Security trust funds are projected to continue accumulating well into the next century in the case of the pension and disability funds and at least until the end of this century in the case of Medicare. The exact dates at which the funds might again become depleted, under the current provisions, depend on future economic conditions and demographic factors such as longevity and birth rates. The date most commonly given for future funding problems is 2020.

The long-run problem that must be re-

solved is the relationship between the number of retirees entitled to Social Security pensions and the number of workers making contributions to the system. This problem will become especially acute when the members of the baby boom generation begin to retire in large numbers. Unlike private pension plans, the Social Security system does not pay benefits out of returns on investments made with the contributions to the fund. Instead, the current contributions of workers pay the benefits to present retirees. This system worked very well during the time that the labor force was expanding more rapidly than the number of people collecting benefits. But since 1950, the ratio of workers to retirees has been steadily declining. In 1950 there were 16 workers paying Social Security taxes for every person collecting retirement benefits. By 1960, the ratio had been reduced to 5 to 1. Today, it is just over 3 to 1. This ratio of workers to retirees is expected to remain fairly constant until about the year 2020 when the baby boom generation will begin to retire. The ratio is then expected to decline to only two workers for each retiree.

To continue benefits at their present levels after that time might require Social Security tax rates of 35% or more. This would probably not be politically acceptable. Even now there is discussion of an emerging intergenerational conflict between younger workers. An average couple retiring now at age 65 can expect cash benefits worth over 3 times the amount they and their employer put in (plus interest). The same couple retiring in 2025 would get only about 1.75 times the original investment. And most young people starting work now can expect to collect less than they pay in over their working lifetimes.

Various suggestions have been put forth for solutions to the long-run problems of the Social Security system. One proposal has

been to change the method of calculating cost-of-living increases in benefit payments. Since Social Security benefits were indexed to the cost of living in 1975, the real income of retirees has actually increased faster than that of workers. Proposed changes in the method of calculating cost-of-living increases and raising taxes on benefits could result in decreasing real income for retirees.

More radical solutions would involve changing the very basis of financing the Social Security system. One proposal is to change it over into an investment fund like private pension plans rather than a pay-as-you-go system. A modified version of this solution has been put forth which would provide for a sort of "super IRA," allowing workers to contribute to their own tax-sheltered pension plan to supplement Social Security benefits. Another proposal is to eliminate the payroll tax method of financing and pay Social Security benefits out of general tax revenues just as other transfer payments are made. At the least, it is argued, the amount of any future deficits in the trust funds should be covered out of general tax revenues rather than further increasing the already substantial payroll tax.

## Economic Reasoning

1. How does the financing of Social Security differ from the financing of other government programs?

2. It has been said that Medicare is not properly a part of the Social Security system and should be transferred to the U.S. Department of Health and Human Services. What would be the effects of such a change on the budget?

3. What changes do you think should be made in the Social Security system and why?

# Who Pays for Government Spending?

The question of who should pay how much of the cost of government—how the burden should be shared—is a continuing subject of debate. Economics can help enlighten this debate by providing certain criteria that are presented in this analysis section.

**Equity**  In a democracy, governments can only tax people with their agreement, and people will only agree to be taxed if they perceive the tax system to be fair. One of the conditions of fairness is that people who are equally able to pay should bear the same tax burden. This is horizontal equity. An example of this condition which was not being fulfilled was the so-called "marriage penalty." Because their joint return put them in a higher bracket, a married couple paid more taxes on a given income than two people who were not married. The income tax rate structure has been changed to diminish this marriage penalty. Another question of horizontal equity is the relationship between tax rates on earned income, such as wages and salaries, and tax rates on such non-earned income as capital gains. Previously, capital gains was taxed at a lower rate than earned income, but the differential in the tax rates for these two types of income was eliminated by tax reform legislation in 1986.

Another criterion of a fair tax structure is vertical equity, which is based on the concept that those with higher incomes are in a better position to pay taxes with less sacrifice and should therefore pay a larger percentage in taxes. It is felt that the larger the income, the smaller the sacrifice for each dollar paid in taxes. Those below a certain income level, for whom the marginal utility of money is very high because they are living in poverty, pay zero income taxes.

Just what constitutes vertical equity is one of the most heated questions in the subject of taxation. The 1986 tax bill made federal income taxes less progressive, reducing the maximum marginal tax rate from 50% to 33%. The 33% rate, however, did not apply to the highest income earners, who paid only a 28% marginal rate. For example, couples with taxable income between $80,000 and $200,000 paid a 33% rate on all income over $80,000. But those with incomes over $200,000 paid a marginal tax rate of only 28% on all income over $200,000.

This tax rate "bubble" appeared to violate the principle of vertical equity, with higher income earners paying a lesser marginal tax rate (though not a smaller average tax rate) than those with lower incomes. One of the most heated

**horizontal equity**  equality of treatment for all individuals at the same level.

**earned income**  wages, salaries, and other employee compensation plus earnings from self-employment.

**non-earned income**  dividends, interest, capital gains, and other non-labor income.

**vertical equity**  fair differentiations of treatment of individuals at different levels.

**marginal tax rate**  the tax rate applied to the last or additional income received.

controversies in putting together the 1991 tax bill was over the "bubble." It was finally resolved by a compromise 31% rate on all income above a certain level.

A different approach to tax equity is applied in some cases where the proceeds of a tax are directly allocated to a corresponding government service. An example of this is the highway trust fund which is used to finance the construction and maintenance of our highway system and is financed by gasoline sales taxes and motor vehicle fees. This represents the benefits principle of equity in taxation.

As can be seen from Table 2, the residents of Alaska pay much more in state and local taxes per person than the residents of other states. Alaska, with its harsh winters and vast distances, is an expensive state to maintain. As a consequence, the state and local tax burden on its residents is greater than that paid by the inhabitants of "the lower 49."

**benefits principle** levy of a tax on an individual to pay the costs of government service in proportion to the individual's benefit from the service.

**Table 2**     DIFFERENCES AMONG THE STATES IN STATE AND LOCAL TAXES
1987

| State | Taxes Per Capita | State | Taxes Per Capita |
|---|---|---|---|
| Alaska | $ 3,162 | Iowa | $ 1,530 |
| Dist. of Columbia | $ 3,078 | Ohio | $ 1,509 |
| New York | $ 2,773 | Kansas | $ 1,508 |
| Wyoming | $ 2,293 | Nebraska | $ 1,460 |
| Connecticut | $ 2,216 | New Hampshire | $ 1,389 |
| Massachusetts | $ 2,105 | Georgia | $ 1,372 |
| New Jersey | $ 2,099 | Montana | $ 1,366 |
| Hawaii | $ 1,965 | Florida | $ 1,365 |
| California | $ 1,926 | North Carolina | $ 1,363 |
| Minnesota | $ 1,904 | Utah | $ 1,360 |
| Maryland | $ 1,904 | Texas | $ 1,329 |
| Wisconsin | $ 1,787 | New Mexico | $ 1,308 |
| Michigan | $ 1,776 | Indiana | $ 1,304 |
| Delaware | $ 1,753 | North Dakota | $ 1,276 |
| Rhode Island | $ 1,720 | Missouri | $ 1,247 |
| Washington | $ 1,697 | South Carolina | $ 1,233 |
| **National avg.** | **$1,665** | West Virginia | $ 1,231 |
| Illinois | $ 1,650 | Louisiana | $ 1,227 |
| Vermont | $ 1,631 | Oklahoma | $ 1,218 |
| Nevada | $ 1,622 | Kentucky | $ 1,210 |
| Maine | $ 1,614 | South Dakota | $ 1,194 |
| Oregon | $ 1,612 | Idaho | $ 1,178 |
| Colorado | $ 1,602 | Tennessee | $ 1,156 |
| Arizona | $ 1,595 | Alabama | $ 1,088 |
| Pennsylvania | $ 1,554 | Arkansas | $ 1,037 |
| Virginia | $ 1,548 | Mississippi | $ 990 |

Source: U.S. Bureau of the Census.

There are wide variations among the states in the amount of state and local taxes collected per capita. The highest taxed state by far is Alaska, which also receives the largest federal transfers per capita of the states (see Table 1, p. 369).

**Efficiency**   Along with their effect on equity, taxes are also judged for their effect on economic efficiency. To be efficient, the tax should neither interfere with the way resources are allocated nor discourage production. An exception to this rule is made in the case of sin taxes such as those levied on tobacco and alcohol, in part to reduce their consumption in the public interest.

It is, of course, impossible to levy taxes which are completely neutral in their effects on output, but taxes should be avoided which produce inefficiency. A classic example of a "bad" tax was one that was levied in medieval England on the window space of houses. Glass windows were considered a luxury at the time, and those who could afford large houses with lots of windows were assumed to be able to afford the taxes. The result of the tax, however, was that new houses were constructed without windows. This was not a sensible way to build houses. The window tax was inefficient. It was inefficient, not because it didn't produce much tax revenue, although that happened to be the case, but rather because of the adverse effect it had on the allocation of resources. Building houses without windows resulted in lowering the utility from a given amount of output.

All taxes are to some extent inefficient, and there is frequently a conflict between the principles of equity and efficiency in taxation. Finding the right mix of taxes which best satisfies these criteria and also provides the necessary revenue for the functions of government is a perpetual problem.

**Incidence**   One of the major obstacles to devising an equitable and efficient tax system lies in the difficulty of determining who ultimately pays the tax. The incidence of a tax is not necessarily determined by those on whom the tax is levied by the government. Frequently those who pay the tax to the government actually shift it to someone else. Personal income taxes cannot be shifted, and the incidence of the tax falls on the person who pays it. However, this is not the case with most other taxes. Excise taxes and property taxes on rental and business property, for example, are shifted to consumers. Even employer payroll taxes are shifted—to consumers in the form of higher prices and to workers in the form of lower wages.

The federal personal income tax has historically been a progressive tax because the tax paid as a percentage of income increased as income rose. Tax changes over the last two decades have made it much less progressive. Progressiveness has been eliminated for higher incomes, with the 1991 tax bill establishing a flat 31% tax rate on incomes above a certain level.

---

**sin tax**   an excise tax levied on commodities that public policy deems undesirable in order to limit their consumption, such as taxes on cigarettes and alcohol.

**incidence of a tax**   the amount of a tax that ultimately falls on households, irrespective of who initially pays the tax.

**progressive tax**   a tax rate that increases as the income on which the tax is based grows larger.

"STEP UP TO THE CAPTAIN'S OFFICE AND SETTLE!"

In the caption under this cartoon of 1895, during President Grover Cleveland's administration, Uncle Sam says: "I'm sorry for you, my unfortunate friends;——I know the Income Tax is 'inquisitorial and oppressive'; but I've *got* to meet the one hundred and sixty million dollars of pension appropriation somehow!"

Most taxes, other than income taxes, are regressive taxes as a result of shifting the incidence of the tax to consumers. This is due to the fact that the lower a person's income, the larger a percentage of that income is spent on the goods and services whose prices include the taxes. As a result, low-income consumers pay a larger percentage of their income on sales taxes, gasoline taxes, utility taxes, and so forth. Even though they may not own property, property taxes take a higher percentage of their income as property owners shift the tax to renters in the form of higher rents.

A proportional tax would take the same percentage of income from taxpayers at all income levels. When the federal income tax was more progressive, the total of all types of taxes in the country—federal, state, and local—was considered roughly proportional.

**regressive tax**   a levy that takes a higher proportion from low incomes in taxes than it takes from high incomes.
**proportional tax**   a levy that takes the same proportion in taxes from low and high incomes.

# Whose Goose Is Getting Plucked?

Prior to the 1980s, studies of the net effect on income distribution of all taxes taken together indicated that the tax burden was approximately proportional for most income earners, having little effect on income distribution. A report delivered at the December 1989 American Economics Association meetings, however, shows that the tax system now makes after-tax incomes more unequal than income distribution before taxes are paid. The study was done by the economist and tax expert Joseph A. Pechman before his death, and his paper was presented at the meetings by a colleague.

According to Pechman's study, the increased regressiveness of the tax system has been due to higher payroll taxes, reductions in corporation income taxes and property taxes, and less progressive federal income taxes. High-income individuals paid an effec-

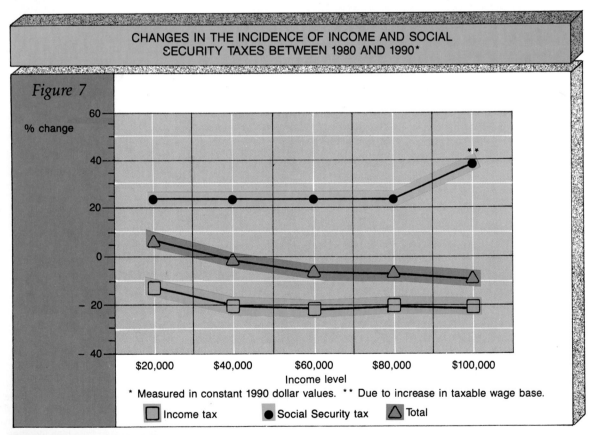

Source: Congressional Budget Office.

Reductions in income tax rates and increases in payroll taxes in the 1980s affected different income groups differently. Those earning $20,000 a year experienced a net increase in their real tax burden. Those earning over $40,000 had their real taxes decreased.

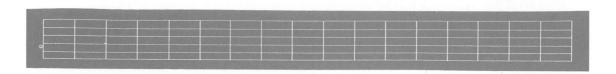

tive tax rate of 27.4% in 1988, far below the level they paid in the 1960s and 1970s. In 1966 the tax burden on capital income was almost twice as large as it is now.

The net effect on different income levels of changes in income and Social Security taxes during the 1980s is shown in Figure 7. The green line shows the percentage change in income taxes at different income levels between 1980 and 1990; the blue line shows the percentage change in Social Security taxes; and the red line shows the net effect on total taxes paid as a result of those changes. Constant value 1990 dollars are used in the measurements.

As indicated by the red line, showing the total impact of changes in the income and Social Security taxes, the tax burden increased in the 1980s for those earning $20,000. For those earning $40,000 and more

the tax burden decreased. The largest decrease was for $100,000 income earners.

Looking at changes in real income compared to changes in the federal tax rates shows what has happened to the incidence of the tax burden in recent years. In Table 3, the income classes are given for those in the lowest, middle, and highest 20% of income earners and for those in the highest 5% and highest 1% classes. From 1977 to 1990, the richest income receivers did best in real income increases and lowering of their federal tax rates.

But that does not tell the full story of the increasing regressiveness of the tax system. As federal spending has been restrained by Gramm-Rudman and administration policies, more of the burden has been put on state and local governments to provide social services.

*Table 3*      PERCENTAGE CHANGES IN REAL INCOME AND FEDERAL TAX RATES
1977–1990

| Income Class | Real Income (% change) | Federal Tax Rate* (% change) |
|---|---|---|
| Poorest 20% | − 9.0% | + 2.6% |
| Middle 20% | + 6.1% | + 3.6% |
| Richest 20% | + 34.4% | − 4.6% |
| Richest 5% | + 52.7% | − 12.5% |
| Richest 1% | + 91.2% | − 23.2% |

*Includes payroll taxes.

Source: *U.S. News & World Report*, August 13, 1990, p. 49. Copyright 1990.

Between 1977 and 1990 the tax system became more regressive as federal tax rates increased for lower and middle income earners and decreased on the highest incomes.

In raising revenues to meet these increased demands, state and local governing bodies have followed the advice of a seventeenth-century French finance minister, Jean-Baptiste Colbert, who said that the art of taxation was in "plucking the goose so as to obtain the largest amount of feathers with the least possible amount of hissing." Legislators have discovered that the least amount of taxpayer hissing comes from raising miscellaneous taxes and fees.

As a result, we have seen increases in state and local taxes on such things as utilities, gasoline, cigarettes, entertainment, and hotel and motel rooms. States have also extended the collection of sales taxes to additional goods and services, including mail-order goods from out of state. Fees have been increased on everything from parks to home and building construction permits. These excise taxes and fees are regressive because they take a larger percentage of the income of low-income families than they do of higher-income families.

One new revenue source that states have found produces little hissing—in fact is greeted by public cheers—is the state lottery. Thirty-three states have introduced lotteries in recent years, and others are considering them. Generally, about half of the amount wagered on the lotteries is returned as prizes. Another 10%, more or less, goes for administrative expenses. The remaining 40% is, in effect, a tax. It is a particularly regressive tax because this form of gambling is indulged in mainly by low-income earners looking for a miraculous escape from their

Approximately 40% of the price of lottery tickets is, in effect, a tax on gambling.

poverty. (Wealthier individuals tend to do their gambling in the stock and commodities markets, where they do not have to pay a tax of 40% for the privilege.) Since the purchase of lottery tickets is voluntary, however, state lottery revenue is not a tax that generates any hissing, except from social "do-gooders."

## Economic Reasoning

1. Are state and local tax systems progressive, proportional, or regressive? Why?
2. What has happened to the vertical equity of the overall tax burden in the past two decades? Why?
3. Are state lotteries a good way to raise revenue? Why or why not?

# Putting It Together

Total government spending—federal, state, and local—amounts to about one-third of GNP. A large part of this represents *transfer payments* of income to individuals rather than government purchases or salaries for government employees. If these transfer payments are subtracted, government spending at all levels accounts for one-fifth of the nation's economic activity.

The largest item in the federal budget is national defense, which accounts for over one-fourth of the total budget. All other direct expenditures account for less than 5%. All of the rest of federal government spending consists of transfer payments, the largest of which is Social Security. Next largest in size and growing is interest on the national debt. For state and local governments, the major expense is education. Most state and local government spending is for direct purchases rather than transfer payments.

The largest revenue source for the federal government is *personal income taxes*. After that come *payroll taxes* for Social Security, unemployment insurance, and federal pensions. State and local governments obtain nearly 14% of their revenues from federal *grants-in-aid* under a system of *fiscal federalism*. They obtain roughly similar portions of their revenues from *sales taxes*, the largest revenue producer for the states, and *property taxes*, the largest for local governments.

To make the tax system work, the public must perceive it as being fair. One criterion for fairness would be that people in similar economic situations pay similar amounts in taxes. This is referred to as *horizontal equity*. Another criterion would be that people with higher incomes pay proportionally more taxes than people with lower incomes. This is referred to as *vertical equity*. A third criterion, applied to certain government programs, would be that those who benefit from a government service pay directly for that service. This is the *benefits principle* of equity.

Taxes should be levied in a way that least affects the allocation of resources and least discourages economic activity. If a tax results in some goods not being produced that otherwise would be produced, it is a "bad" tax. Public policy makes an exception in the case of *sin taxes,* such as alcohol and tobacco excise taxes, which are levied in part to reduce the consumption of items which society wishes to discourage.

Taxes frequently are not borne by the person who initially pays the tax. Taxes, other than income taxes, are shifted to consumers in the form of higher prices or to workers in the form of lower wages. How the tax burden is allocated is the *incidence of the tax.* Taxes that take a larger percentage of higher incomes than lower incomes are *progressive.* Those that take the same percentage from all income levels are *proportional,* and those that take a larger percentage from low incomes are *regressive.*

Among the 110 million individual income tax returns filed in 1990 was one from the president of the United States and the first lady.

## Perspective

# The Growth of Big Government

More information on the growth of government spending can be found in *Growth of Government in the West* (1978) by G. Warren Nutler; *Public Sector Economics* (1979) by Robin W. Broadway, *The National Income and Product Accounts of the United States, 1929–74* (1977) issued by the U.S. Department of Commerce, and *Democracy in Deficit* (1977) by James M. Buchanan and Richard Wagner.

At the end of the 1920s total expenditures for all levels of government amounted to less than 10% of GNP. For the past 23 years they have been 30% to 35%. How did government grow so much in the second half of this century? Where is the growth of government taking us?

These are just some of the questions raised by the debate over "big government."

The size of government relative to GNP doubled in the early 1930s, due primarily to the decline in GNP during the Great Depression rather than to an increase in government spending. The ratio of government expenditures to total output doubled again during World War II, but dropped back to less than 20% after the war. It rose above 25% during the Korean War and the "cold war" years of the early 1950s. It remained around 27–28% until 1968 when a combination of the Vietnam War expansion and increased domestic social spending on the "War on Poverty" raised government outlays above 30% of GNP. Since then government spending has hovered around one-third of total spending in the economy.

These figures on total government spending, however, do not reveal the important changes that have been occurring in the types of government spending. One significant change has been in the proportions of total government spending accounted for by the three levels of government. In the 1920s local government spending accounted for about half of the total. It fell to below 10% in the 1940s and today is over 22%. State government spending is almost the same amount. Meanwhile, the federal government's share reached a peak during World War II, and has gradually declined since. Although federal outlays are greater than the combined spending of state and local governments, part of that federal government spending goes for funding state and local government programs under fiscal federalism.

The picture is also affected by changes in the makeup of federal spending. In the 1920s only about 10% of federal expenditures were transfer payments. This has increased over the years until today transfer payments account for over half of the federal budget. As a result, state and local government spending plays a larger part in economic allocations than does federal spending. In terms of economic activity and the number of employees, the growth of "big government" is now personified not so much by the federal government as by the growth in state and local spending.

**For Further Study and Analysis**

## Study Questions

1. What types of government spending are included in GNP? What types are most readily subject to cost-cutting?

2. How many people in your family and how many friends with whom you are acquainted are receiving transfer payments? What type of transfer payments are they receiving?

3. Have there been any recent reductions in government services in your area? What were they? In which level of government did they occur?

4. If a candidate for national office promised, if elected, to double the efficiency of federal government operations and thereby reduce taxes by half, why might you question that promise? What promises might that candidate make about tax reduction that you would find feasible?

5. Approximately how much have you paid in excise taxes (taxes other than on income) in the past three days? On what items?

6. What revenues do state (province) and local governments receive, other than taxes? What is the impact on various income groups of these revenue sources?

7. What is the current outlook for the Social Security system? Do you believe that you will benefit from it in the future?

8. Why is it assumed that wealthier people have a smaller marginal utility for money than people with lower incomes?

9. What are three things, other than cigarettes and liquor, whose production is affected by a tax? What is the effect of the tax? What is the incidence of the tax?

10. How did the most recent tax legislation affect the equity of the tax burden?

## Exercises in Analysis

1. Write a report on changes in the federal, state (or province), and local funding of your school over the last five years. Have the funds increased at a greater rate, the same, or a lesser rate than the inflation rate? What adjustments have been made in school expenditures as a consequence?

2. Write a report on the sources of funding for your state or provincial budget.

3. From a taxpayer's guide, list five personal income tax deductions and five business tax deductions. Why do you think these deductions are allowed?

4. Write a short paper on the problems of the Social Security system and the best solution of those problems.

## Further Reading

Aaron, Henry J. *Economic Effects of Social Security*. Washington, D.C.: Brookings Institution, 1982. An exploration of the effects of the Social Security program on savings, the labor supply, and income distribution.

Aaron, Henry J., and Harvey Galper. *Assessing Tax Reform*. Washington, D.C.: Brookings Institution, 1985. Examines the need for tax reform and assesses the merits of the various options.

Ackerman, Frank. *Hazardous to Our Wealth*. Boston: South End Press, 1984. The book contains useful tables on The Effects of an Across-the-Board Tax Cut, The Federal Tax Burden Before and After the Reagan Tax Cuts, Unemployment and Social Welfare Programs Spending Per Unemployed Person, 1981–1984, and others.

Crystal, Stephen. *America's Old Age Crisis*. New York: Basic Books, 1982. Discusses the conflict between the increasing needs of an aging population and the inadequacy of existing programs to meet those needs. Proposes a more focused system that integrates the various programs to serve those elderly who are in actual need.

Friedman, Benjamin. *Day of Reckoning*. New York: Random House, 1988. "This book is about debt: debt and the material and moral impoverishment that inevitably follow, no less for a nation than for an individual or family, from continually borrowing for no purpose other than to live beyond one's means." (From page vii.)

Kuttner, Robert. *Revolt of the Haves: Tax Rebellions and Hard Times*. New York: Simon & Schuster, 1980. An examination of the reasons for the popular revolt against taxes in the late 1970s and how taxes affect society.

Lindholm, Richard W. *A New Federal Tax System*. New York: Praeger, 1984. Explores the economic effects of various types of taxes and discusses the proposals for shifting from the income tax to taxes on expenditures, such as the Value Added Tax, or taxes on wealth.

Lindsey, Lawrence. *The Growth Experiment: How the New Tax Policy Is Transforming the U.S. Economy*. New York: Basic Books, 1990. This is a justification for supply-side tax policy. It maintains that the tax cuts of the 1980s were not the cause of the federal deficits, although conceding that they contributed to making the deficits greater than they would otherwise have been.

Meyers, Robert J. *Social Security* (3rd edition). Homewood, Ill.: Irwin, 1985. A comprehensive explanation of the Social Security system.

Pechman, Joseph A. *Who Paid the Taxes, 1966–1985?* Washington, D.C.: Brookings Institution, 1985. A study of the effects of taxes and transfers on income distribution, the burdens of federal versus state and local taxes, and changes in the distribution of tax burdens.

Peterson, Peter G., and Neil Howe. *On Borrowed Time: How the Growth in Entitlement Spending Threatens America's Future*. San Francisco, Calif.: ICS Press, 1988. An alarmist view of where Social Security, federal pensions, and inflation of health-care costs are leading the country.

Stockman, David A. *The Triumph of Politics: Why the Reagan Revolution Failed*. New York: Harper & Row, 1986. A controversial and revealing book by President Reagan's director of the Office of Management and the Budget about why the "supply-side revolution" led to record deficits rather than a balanced budget.

# POLICIES FOR ECONOMIC STABILITY AND GROWTH

*The economic policies followed in the 1980s were dubbed "Reaganomics" because they reflected the supply-side philosophy of Ronald Reagan. His successor, George Bush, promised to continue the same policies. This introductory article looks at the outcome of the "Reagan revolution."*

## The Legacy of Reaganomics

Ronald Reagan campaigned for the presidency in 1980 on an economic platform of reducing government spending, lowering taxes, balancing the budget, maintaining a slow and steady growth of the money supply, and reducing government regulation of business. How well did he succeed in achieving these objectives?

Total federal spending as a percentage of GNP was exactly the same when he left office in 1988 as it was the year before he took office (23%, including federal transfers to state and local governments). Whether or not that means he failed in his objective of reducing government spending is subject to interpretation. During the preceding 10 years the ratio of government spending to GNP had increased by 2 percentage points. Reaganomics halted a further rise in the ratio.

Also, the composition of government spending changed during the Reagan years. An additional objective of his administration was to strengthen the country's military power. When he took office defense spending was 23% of total federal spending. By the end of his administration it had grown to 27%.

With respect to taxes, total tax receipts as a percentage of GNP were reduced 1% during the 8 years of the Reagan administration. Again, the bare figures do not tell the whole story. Shifting some of the financial burden of social services to state and local governments accounted for about half of the federal tax reduction, with an offsetting increase in the revenues collected at the lower government levels.

There was also a change in the composition of federal revenues. Income taxes, personal and corporate, made up 60% of total tax receipts the year President Reagan took office and 57% when he left. Meanwhile, payroll taxes increased from 30% of the total to 38%. (Excise and estate and gift taxes accounted for the remainder.) As a consequence, wage earners in general paid more taxes under Reaganomics while those who received their income from capital paid less.

While Reaganomics could claim limited success in its objectives of reducing government spending and lowering taxes, it failed altogether in balancing the budget. As described in the last chapter, federal budget deficits bloated to record levels, doubling the national debt. The hope for achieving a balanced budget was based on supply-side as-

The monetary policy of the United States is under the control of the Federal Reserve Board, which uses its power of regulating required and excess reserves to manage the supply of money. Shown above is the Federal Reserve Bank in Charlotte, North Carolina, part of the Federal Reserve System.

sumptions. Reducing income tax rates was supposed to provide the incentives and investment capital that would increase economic growth sufficiently to provide enough government revenues to balance the budget.

Instead, consumers went on a spending spree, resulting in unprecedented low levels of savings. And investment capital was used to finance leveraged buyouts of existing firms, rather than adding to the nation's stock of new plant and equipment. Gross private investment accounted for 15.9% of GNP during the Reagan years, down from 17.5 % in the preceding Carter administration. The average annual rate of growth in constant dollar GNP was identical under the Reagan and Carter administrations—3% per year.

The real money supply—the money supply adjusted for inflation—increased 6 times as much in the Reagan period as in the previous 20 years. Changes in the money supply are not under the control of the president but under the Federal Reserve, which is intended to be independent of the administration in power. The president does have some leverage over the Fed, particularly in his power to appoint or deny reappointment to the chairman of the Board of Governors and to fill empty seats on the Board. The chairman during most of Reagan's presidency was Paul Volcker, a man noted for his independent policies and actions, whom Reagan reappointed to the chairmanship. In 1984 President Reagan appointed Martha Segar, someone who favored a faster growth of the money supply than did Volker, to the Board of Governors.

Deregulation of the banking, trucking, and

airline industries was already under way when Reagan assumed the presidency. The deregulation process was continued and extended under his administration. Deregulation made pricing in the affected industries more competitive. This helped to restrain inflation and increase job opportunities. Deregulation, however, can have a downside if not carefully managed, as evidenced, for example, in the savings and loan meltdown discussed in chapter 11.

Surveying the results of Reaganomics, there are pluses and minuses. One of the pluses was bringing the stagflation of the late 1970s under control. The inflation rate, as measured by changes in the consumer price index, fell from 13.5% in 1980 to a low of 1.9% in 1986. This was accomplished by means of a sharp recession, the most severe since the Great Depression of the 1930s. The trigger for the recession was a tightening of the money supply by the Fed.

The recession set the stage for the second longest continuous economic expansion since World War II. One of the key elements in the expansion was the annual federal deficits. This "fiscal stimulus" added about 3% on the average to each year's GNP, which would account for the entire growth of the economy during the Reagan years.

The accumulation of national debt resulting from the deficits is one of the minuses of Reaganomics. Doubling the size of the debt more than doubled the interest costs of carrying the debt and made the goal of a balanced budget that much more difficult to achieve.

Other legacies of the Reagan era, though not necessarily the results of Reaganomics, were record deficits in our international payments, turning the United States from the world's largest creditor into its largest debtor (see chapter 16, p. 456); large increases in household and business indebtedness, followed by higher bankruptcy rates; scandals in the Housing and Urban Development Department, toxic waste management, and savings and loan industry regulation; deterioration of the nation's infrastructure; and greater inequality of income distribution, lowering the real income of most of the population and increasing the number below the poverty level.

## Chapter Preview

*According to the Employment Act of 1946 and the Full Employment and Balanced Growth Act of 1978, the government has a responsibility to maintain full employment, reasonably stable prices, and economic growth. Under Reaganomics these goals were achieved to some extent. The legacy of Reaganomics, however, may make it difficult to achieve the goals in coming years. This chapter will examine the specific tools that the government has at its disposal for influencing economic activity by asking the following questions: What can the government do about unemployment and inflation? How can fiscal policy help stabilize the economy? How can monetary policy help stabilize the economy? How can economic growth be increased?*

## Learning Objectives

*After completing this chapter, you should be able to:*

1. *Discuss economic policies in the 1980s and their consequences.*
2. *Identify the government's two major instruments of stabilization policy.*
3. *Differentiate between annually balanced budgets, cyclically balanced budgets, and functional finance.*
4. *Explain how discretionary fiscal policy works from the Keynesian and supply-side viewpoints.*
5. *Describe the multiplier effect.*
6. *Define and give examples of automatic stabilizers.*
7. *Explain how monetary policy is implemented.*
8. *Explain the investment/GNP ratio and the capital/output ratio and describe their importance.*
9. *Describe the effects on economic growth of the labor-force participation rate and investment in human capital.*

## What Can the Government Do About Unemployment and Inflation?

The government's two principal instruments for managing the economy are fiscal policy and monetary policy. Fiscal policy involves taxing and spending by the government, while monetary policy involves control of the money supply and interest rates.

**Fiscal policy**  In 1980 and in 1981–1982, the country experienced back-to-back recessions, the only time since World War II that we have had three successive years of recession. One of the measures to get out of recession is to reduce taxes, and this was done in 1981. But the tax cuts enacted in the 1981 tax bill represented a new direction in the government's fiscal policy. Earlier major tax cuts, such as those in 1964, had been aimed at stimulating demand by increasing disposable income. A tax reduction leaves people with more purchasing power and thus increases aggregate demand. The 1981 tax bill, on the other hand, was intended to increase output by making production and investment profitable for any level of demand and stimulating savings to finance the investment. It was a supply-side tax bill, designed to leave more money in the hands of those with a higher propensity to save rather than those with a higher propensity to consume.

The difference between Keynesian and supply-side fiscal policy also showed up in the treatment of government expenditures. Supply-side economics called for a reduction in government spending in order to reduce the government's

**fiscal policy**  the use of federal government spending, taxing, and debt management to influence general economic activity.

competition with the private sector of the economy for labor, capital, and other resources. Reducing the growth of government spending during a time of high unemployment is exactly opposite the Keynesian policies that the United States pursued since World War II. According to demand-side economics, a recession should be offset by increasing government spending.

The policy of combining increased spending with reduced taxes to combat a recession results in government budget deficits. Before the experiences of the 1930s and before the writings of Keynes, it was traditionally held that the government should have an annually balanced budget. If the federal government took $25 out of the spending stream in taxes in a given fiscal year, it should put $25 into the spending stream through its purchases of goods and services. However, such a budgetary policy can be destabilizing. As an economy moves into a recession, tax receipts fall as production, employment, and income decline. If an annually balanced budget policy is followed, the government must then cut spending, or raise taxes, or do both. Such policies would make a recession worse by reducing aggregate demand.

On the other side of the business cycle, during a period of economic expansion, tax receipts automatically rise as sales, price, and income increases generate more taxes. To balance the budget, a tax cut or spending increase would be necessary. Either action would tend to be inflationary by increasing aggregate demand.

Instead of an annually balanced budget, a cyclically balanced budget would allow active fiscal policy to stabilize the economy. Short-run deficits and surpluses would be used to stabilize recessions and booms, but the deficits would offset the surpluses and the budget would balance over the course of the business cycle. There are problems, however, with this approach. Financially, recessions and booms may not cancel each other out, and the budget may not balance over the long run. Also, it is politically far more popular to reduce taxes and increase spending than to increase taxes or cut spending. Fiscal policy under these conditions might thus have an inflation bias.

A third budget philosophy, functional finance, sees non-inflationary full employment as the most important economic goal; balancing the budget becomes a secondary objective. Under this philosophy, taxes and spending should be administered at whatever level is necessary to promote full employment without increasing prices. This policy might leave the budget permanently out of balance.

**Monetary policy**  Neither the president nor Congress has control over monetary policy; rather it is under the control of the Federal Reserve Board. The money supply is managed indirectly by the Fed through its direction of financial institutions' required and excess reserves. By employing the control

**annually balanced budget**  a budgetary principle calling for the revenue and expenditures of a government to be equal during the course of a year.
**cyclically balanced budget**  a budgetary principle calling for the balancing of the budget over the course of a complete business cycle rather than in a particular fiscal or calendar year; over the course of the cycle, tax receipts and expenditures would balance.
**functional finance**  the use of fiscal policy to stabilize the economy without regard to the policy's effect on a balanced government budget.
**monetary policy**  actions of the Federal Reserve Board to produce changes in the money supply, the availability of loanable funds, or the level of interest rates in an attempt to influence general economic activity.

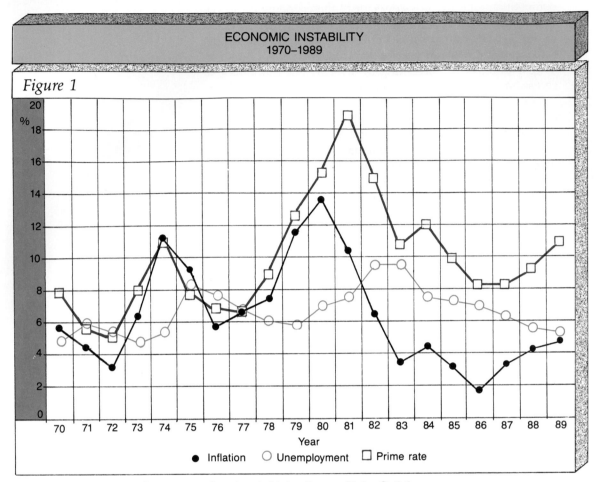

ECONOMIC INSTABILITY
1970–1989

*Figure 1*

Sources: Inflation and unemployment rates: Department of Labor, Bureau of Labor Statistics.
Prime interest rates: Board of Governors of the Federal Reserve System.

The magnitude of economic fluctuations in the 1980s was greater than at any time in the last 40 years. Achieving economic stability has become more difficult because of the effects of external events and the unanticipated reactions of the public to policy measures.

techniques described in chapter 10, the Fed can vary the volume of excess reserves. This action affects the ability of lending institutions to grant loans and thereby their ability to increase the money supply.

In a recession, the level of aggregate demand is below that necessary for full employment. In that situation, the Fed through its monetary policy actions would bring about an increase in the volume of bank reserves. Bankers could then grant more loans. The loans stimulate higher total spending in the economy, and income and employment would rise. Conversely, to combat inflation, the Fed would use its controls to decrease the volume of bank reserves. Bankers would grant fewer loans, and there would be less total spending in the economy.

## Who's at the Wheel?

The economy has been on a wild ride in the past decade. It plunged to the worst recession since the Great Depression of the 1930s and rose to the second longest economic expansion since World War II. It experienced record-breaking inflation, record-breaking interest rates, and record-breaking government deficits and national debt. Most of these developments came as a surprise.

As the introductory article for chapter 12 showed (p. 329), predicting where the economy is going has always been more or less a guessing game. But these days the pace of change seems to have speeded up, while our ability to anticipate and correct for changes in direction has diminished. It is as if we were at the wheel of a speeding car with the gas pedal pressed to the floor and the windshield painted black.

Just who *is* at the wheel in control of the economy? The Full Employment Act, passed in 1946 and amended in 1978, assigns to the federal government a legal responsibility to ensure maximum employment, production, and purchasing power. In order to accomplish this, the Council of Economic Advisers is designated to advise the president on economic policy and to submit a yearly report to Congress on the state of the economy. The Federal Reserve Board has the responsibility for pursuing a monetary policy that is stabilizing. But the best-laid plans of those responsible for maintaining full employment and stable prices are subject to two types of forces that may defeat them: unforeseen, uncontrollable external events and the behavior of you, me, and the rest of the public.

While external events, such as increases in petroleum prices, complicate the job of stabilizing the U.S. economy, an even bigger problem for policymakers is the unpredictable behavior of the public. If we decide to spend less, we can cause a recession or make an existing one worse. If we spend more, we may contribute to inflation.

Attempts to make us behave in a particular way have been less than successful. In the 1980s income tax rates were cut and Individual Retirement Accounts were established, allowing people to shelter part of their income from taxes. These measures were expected to motivate the public to save more. The United States has a savings rate far below that of other industrialized countries. We generally save only 5%–6% of our income, compared to 18% in Japan and 12% in Germany. But instead of the savings rate increasing in this country as the policymakers expected, the rate fell below 3%.

Individuals watch government policy for clues as to what actions they should take to protect and promote their personal economic well-being. For example, if the Federal Reserve increases the money supply to encourage more production and investment, people take this as an indicator that inflation is coming. The result of these "rational expectations" is a rise in long-term interest rates to compensate for the anticipated inflation, thereby discouraging new investment and checkmating the Fed's move.

## *Economic Reasoning*

1. When income tax rates were cut in the 1980s in the hopes that the public would increase their savings, was this an example of fiscal policy or monetary policy?
2. Why do people take an increase in the money supply as an indication that inflation is coming?
3. Should the government get around the problem of public behavior that negates stabilization policies by, for example, forcing people to save more or imposing a ceiling on interest rates? Why or why not?

# How Does Fiscal Policy Help Stabilize the Economy?

Stabilizing the economy is not the principal reason for government taxing and spending, but rather to provide the services that citizens require from government. However, the fiscal activities of government can be managed to counteract cyclical fluctuations.

**Discretionary fiscal policy** Decisions about increasing or decreasing taxes and decreasing or increasing government spending are referred to as discretionary fiscal policy. Keynesian and supply-side economists differ on how discretionary fiscal policy should be implemented.

Keynesians focus on the use of fiscal policy to compensate for inadequate or excessive demand in the private sector. How Keynesian fiscal policy is used to combat unemployment can be traced in the GNP tank diagram in Figure 2.

If the amount of purchasing power flowing into the economy from consumption (C), government (G), and investment (I) demand is not sufficient to provide full employ-

**discretionary fiscal policy**   fiscal policy measures activated by overt decisions.

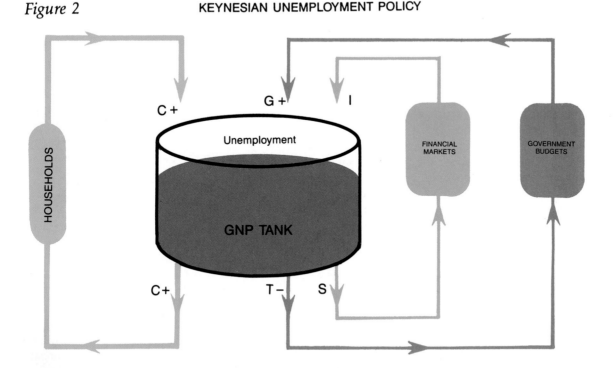

*Figure 2*                    KEYNESIAN UNEMPLOYMENT POLICY

Keynesian fiscal policy to increase GNP and reduce unemployment is to lower taxes (T –) and increase spending (G +) in the government sector (red). This results in an increase in purchasing power and demand (C +) in the consumption sector (blue). The increased demand raises the GNP level (purple) and reduces unemployment.

ment, as indicated by the level in the tank, the government can increase demand by larger expenditures, causing more purchasing power to flow from government (G+), and/or by reducing taxes (T−), taking less from the income stream. If the tax cuts are directed primarily at the lower-income groups, which have the highest propensity to consume, nearly all of the tax savings will be allocated to increased consumption (C+), which stimulates production and employment.

Supply-side fiscal policy also calls for a reduction in taxes when aggregate demand is too low. But government spending is reduced rather than increased in order not to put the government in competition with the private sector for productive resources and financial capital. The purpose of reducing the leakage into taxes (T−) in the supply-side approach is not to increase consumption (C) but rather to increase savings (S+) and investment (I+), as shown in Figure 3. Therefore, the tax cuts are directed toward busi-

*Figure 3*  **SUPPLY-SIDE UNEMPLOYMENT POLICY**

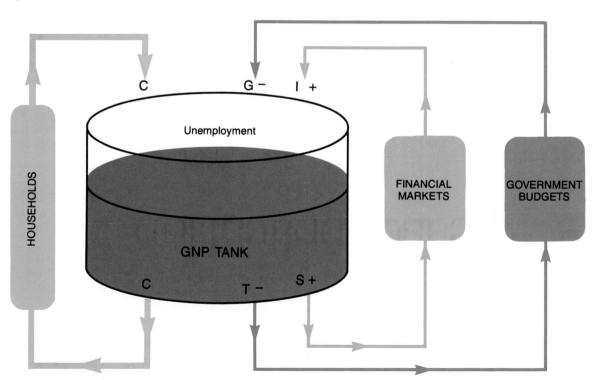

Supply-side fiscal policy to reduce unemployment is to lower taxes T(−) and spending (G−) in the government sector (red) in order to increase savings (S+) and investment (I+) in the investment sector (green). The reduction in taxes provides incentives and financial capital for increased investment. The added investment increases the level of GNP and reduces unemployment. At the same time, lower government spending reduces competition in the factor markets for real and financial resources, helping to hold down prices and interest rates.

nesses and toward individuals in high tax brackets who save more, rather than toward consumers.

The use of discretionary fiscal policy to combat recession at a time when the government is already running large deficits is difficult. When the economy falls into recession, the Gramm-Rudman law provides for a suspension of the requirement to reduce the deficit. However, with deficits already at record levels, there is a danger in increasing them further to combat the recession. It could lead to a loss of confidence in the financial security of the U.S. government on the part of the American public, business, and foreign investors. Interest rates would have to be raised to sell the government securities necessary to finance the deficit. Higher interest rates are the opposite of the monetary policy needed to overcome recession. This problem is one of the most troublesome legacies of Reaganomics.

**The multiplier effect** Fiscal policy can be used not only to combat unemployment caused by insufficient aggregate demand, but also to combat inflation caused by too much demand. In either case, fiscal policy is more effective as a result of the multiplier effect. The multiplier effect refers to the magnified impact on national income of an initial increase or decrease in spending. It is similar in principle to the money multiplier in chapter 10 (page 285).

Suppose, for example, an outsider comes into your community and spends $100 on a single purchase. Someone's income would increase by $100 with that expenditure. The income receiver would probably not hold onto the $100 very long, but would spend most of it, say, four-fifths ($80), on increased consumption of goods and services. The rest would go to taxes and into savings. Those who receive the $80 that was spent would now spend four-fifths of that amount, or $64. The process, as shown in Table 1, would continue until the original influx of $100 has generated additional income to the community of another $400 for a total of $500.

The multiplier effect is based on the assumption that people, on the average, spend a certain fraction of any increase in income after taxes and put the rest into savings. The smaller the amount that leaks into savings in each round of spending, the larger will be the multiplier. In the above example, the multiplier was 5 since an initial increase in spending of $100 resulted finally in a total increase in spending of $500. The size of the multiplier is easy to calculate if you know the percentage of new income that goes into taxes and savings. The multiplier is found by dividing the savings rate plus the tax rate, expressed in decimal form, into 1. If savings plus taxes are 20% of new income, you divide 1 by .20, which gives a multiplier of 5.

**multiplier effect** the process by which an initial increase in income results in a total income increase that is a multiple of the initial increase.
**multiplier** the ratio of the ultimate increase in income, caused by an initial increase in spending, to that initial increase.

Table 1
### THE MULTIPLIER EFFECT
Initial Spending Increase $100

| | C | S + T |
|---|---|---|
| Person 1 | $ 80.00 | $ 20.00 |
| Person 2 | $ 64.00 | $ 16.00 |
| Person 3 | $ 51.20 | $ 12.80 |
| All others | $204.80 | $ 51.20 |
| Total (including initial $100) | $500.00 | $100.00 |

An initial increase in spending of $100 (when leakage to savings and taxes is 20%) will multiply through the community until it has generated an additional $400 in consumption spending (C) for a total of $500. Total leakages to savings and taxes (S + T) will be $100.

$$\text{Multiplier} = \frac{1}{\text{savings rate} + \text{tax rate}} = \frac{1}{.20} = 5$$

The multiplier process takes time to work. It is usually a matter of a few months before the major part of the effect is completed.

**Automatic stabilizers**  In order to put discretionary fiscal policy to work, the government must do something—must take some action. But there is another type of stabilization that takes effect as a result of automatic changes in government spending and revenue collections. These automatic stabilizers help increase incomes in a depressed economy and decrease incomes in an inflationary economy.

Automatic stabilizers consist of taxes, which automatically rise and fall with changes in income, or some form of payments designed to redistribute income. Most types of welfare and other government transfer payments, such as Aid for Dependent Children and unemployment compensation, are based on the income of the recipient. When a person's income falls to a designated level, government expenditures provide income supplements. These supplements add to the spending stream, pushing aggregate demand up. By themselves, automatic stabilizers are not strong enough to reverse a trend, but they do cushion the economic shock until discretionary fiscal policy can be implemented.

**automatic stabilizers** changes in government payments and tax receipts that automatically result from fluctuations in national income and act to aid in offsetting those fluctuations.

# case application

## Investment Incentives or Tax Loopholes?

Reaganomics gave large tax breaks to businesses to raise investment incentives. It contained provisions for accelerated tax write-offs on investment purchases, investment tax credits, and the sale of tax credits to other companies by firms unable to use them because they were not paying any taxes even without them. This enabled some profitable companies not only to avoid paying taxes but to receive tax subsidies. The loss of revenues to the government from such tax incentives, referred to as "tax expenditures," equaled some $100 billion in the 1986 tax year, about half of the government deficit in that year.

At first glance, the investment incentives seemed to be working since business investment spending increased, promoting an economic revival. But two studies, one which analyzed which companies increased their investments and the other which analyzed which types of investment increased, raised doubts that the tax incentive programs were responsible for the high level of investment. In an article by Robert S. McIntyre and Dean C. Tipps ("Exploding the Investment-Incentive Myth," *Challenge: The Magazine of Economic Affairs*, May-June, 1985), the authors reported on the investment levels of 238 profitable corporations relative to the amount of taxes they paid. The authors found that between 1981 and 1983 the 50 companies that paid the lowest tax rates—an average 8.4% of their profits—actually reduced their investment spending more than the average company. On the other hand, the 50 companies that paid the highest tax rates—33.1% of their profits—increased their investments. The writers concluded that the amount of investment spending by a company depends on the market for its products and is not determined by tax breaks.

It was found that the 5 companies with the largest tax rebates during the 3-year period covered by the study each increased their dividend payments to stockholders rather than spending the tax savings on investment. General Electric earned $6.5 billion in profits over 3 years, paid no taxes, and claimed tax rebates of $283 million on taxes paid in earlier years. Between 1981 and 1983 it decreased its investment spending by 15% and increased its dividends by 19%. The Union Carbide company earned $613 million, received net tax benefits of $70 million (resulting in a minus 11.4% tax rate), reduced investment spending by 35.8%, and increased stockholder dividends 7.1%.

Among the 50 most highly taxed companies, ABC earned $818 million in profits on which it paid 38.7% taxes while increasing investment by a whopping 133.1%. It raised dividends only 3.1%. IBM increased its investment spending 15.3% despite paying a 28.2% tax rate on its $14.1 billion profits.

McIntyre and Tipps concluded that doing away with the tax incentives for businesses "can help strengthen our economy by forcing our corporations to stop relying on lobbyists and loopholes to bolster profits and, instead, to go back to making money the old-fashioned way: earning it."

The other study, by Barry Bosworth of the Brookings Institution, took a different approach to the question of tax incentives by examining what types of investments increased from 1979 to 1984. He found that 93% of the increase in investment spending on equipment went for automobiles and office machinery, including computers. These were investment items that did not significantly benefit from the investment tax incentives. The types of investment that would have

These companies increased their investment spending between 1981 and 1983, despite paying high tax rates. Other companies that paid lower tax rates—or even received tax money back from the government—reduced their investment spending, contrary to the expectations of Reaganomics.

benefited most from the tax incentives actually grew the least.

The 1986 tax reform bill did away with most of the tax incentives given to businesses. There nevertheless have been recent proposals to restore investment tax credits.

## Economic Reasoning

1. Did the investment tax incentives for business represent Keynesian fiscal policy or supply-side fiscal policy? Show the intended effects with a GNP tank diagram.

2. If taxes were increased so that individuals' take-home pay decreased by $14 billion, what would be the potential multiplier effect on total spending with a savings rate of 5% and a tax rate of 20%?

3. Do you think that the government should use the tax system to provide investment incentives? Why or why not? How about tax incentives to purchase a house (mortgage interest deductions) or save for retirement (IRAs)? How do you feel about government incentives for education (student assistance and student loans)?

# How Can Monetary Policy Help Stabilize the Economy?

The three measures available to the Federal Reserve for affecting bank reserves—changing legal reserve requirements, discounting, and open market operations—were discussed in chapter 10 on pages 282–286. Now we will look at the way these monetary controls are used in stabilization policy and examine what the targets of monetary policy are.

**Monetary policy tools**   Open market operations are the Fed's most flexible tool of monetary control and the most utilized. If the Fed undertakes to curb inflation, it offers U.S. government securities, which it has in its possession as a result of earlier purchases, for sale at an attractive price. Financial institutions, other businesses, or individuals buy these securities. Regardless of who purchases them, reserves are transferred from commercial banks' reserve accounts to the Fed to pay for the securities. This reduces the ability of the banks to expand their lending activity and may even force them to contract credit. The resulting limitation on the money supply raises interest rates, thus reducing aggregate demand, especially for capital goods, new housing, and consumer credit purchases of durable goods such as new cars.

If the problem is too little aggregate demand rather than too much, the Fed purchases government securities from banks, other businesses, or individuals. This action by the Fed pumps more reserves into the banking system and has an expansionary effect on the economy.

As an alternative to or in addition to selling securities to combat inflation, the Fed can also raise the discount rate it charges on loans to financial institutions. A rise in the discount rate is contractionary because it limits the money supply and raises other interest rates, while a reduction in the discount rate is expansionary.

The most forceful monetary tool the Fed has is its power to change the required reserve ratio. Because it is also the least flexible, it is infrequently used. Raising the reserve ratio from, say, 10% to 12% of banks' deposit liabilities would wipe out a large portion of their excess reserves and force them to contract credit. That would have a deflationary effect on economic activity. Lowering the legal reserve requirement, on the other hand, would make it possible for banks to extend more credit on easier terms. This might have an expansionary effect on economic activity, depending on economic conditions. If the economic outlook is very poor, businesses still might not borrow and invest—even at low interest rates. Consequently, although monetary policy

*Table 2*    HOW THE FEDERAL RESERVE ATTEMPTS TO COMBAT INFLATION

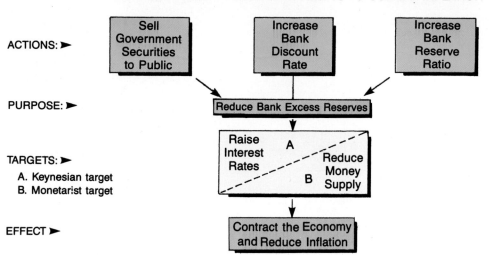

ACTIONS: ►

PURPOSE: ►

TARGETS: ►
  A. Keynesian target
  B. Monetarist target

EFFECT ►

In times of high unemployment the Federal Reserve might try to expand the economy by taking these actions in the opposite manner.

can contract excessive aggregate demand in a boom period, it may be powerless to stimulate demand to bring about a recovery at the bottom of the cycle.

Monetary policy, as well as fiscal policy, is constrained by the existing budget deficits and large national debt. For example, tightening the money supply and raising interest rates to curb inflation would have consequences for the federal budget. An increase in interest rates raises the cost of carrying the debt. This would increase government outlays at a time when when spending should be reduced.

**Controlling interest rates**   Prior to October 1979 the target of Federal Reserve monetary policy was the control of interest rates. Specifically, it attempted to control the Federal Funds rate, the interest rate banks charge each other on short-term lending of excess reserves. By controlling the Federal Funds rate, the Fed could influence the various other interest rates which are charged on loans. By causing interest rates to rise, the Fed would have a deflationary effect on economic activity and prices, and by causing interest rates to fall it would have an expansionary effect.

The Fed came under a great deal of criticism for mistakes in the timing of its actions. It often seemed to wait too long before putting on the brakes in a boom period, allowing the inflation rate to become exceedingly high before raising interest rates sufficiently to cool the economy. When it finally did act, the results of this action too often appeared after the turning point in the economy, and resulted in emphasizing the severity of the downturn. These mistakes in timing were due partly to time

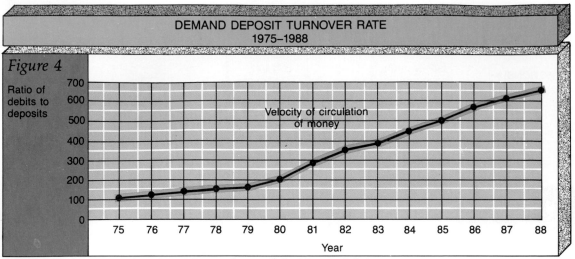

**DEMAND DEPOSIT TURNOVER RATE**
**1975–1988**

*Figure 4*

Ratio of debits to deposits

Velocity of circulation of money

Year

Source: Board of Governors of the Federal Reserve System, *Federal Reserve Bulletin.*

The bank deposit turnover rate, one measure of the velocity of circulation of money, indicates the number of times a deposit dollar is used during a period. It is not constant as assumed by the quantity theory of money (quantity equation).

lags in receiving and evaluating data on what was actually happening in the economy.

**Control of the money supply** Criticisms of the effectiveness of Federal Reserve monetary policy led to a change in the policy target. In October 1979 the newly appointed chairman of the Federal Reserve Board of Governors, Paul Volcker, announced that instead of attempting to control interest rates, the Fed would concentrate on keeping the money supply growth at a predetermined level. According to the quantity theory of money, $M \times V = T \times P$, if the money supply (M) goes up at the same rate as the increase in transactions (T), the price level (P) will remain constant and we will not have inflation—that is, if the velocity of circulation of money (V) does not change (see chapter 11, p. 308).

Actually, the velocity has been on a long-term rising trend since the Great Depression. This in itself would not be a problem since it could be taken into account in setting the growth rate of M. But problems arise when V jumps around unpredictably, and when it moves in a destabilizing direction. Studies indicate that when we have inflation and high interest rates, V accelerates. This offsets the stabilizing effects of limiting M, and thus makes it difficult for a monetarist approach to stability to achieve satisfactory results.

A strict monetarist approach, as advocated by its foremost proponent, Milton Friedman (see Perspective, p. 413), would have a "monetary rule" setting annual increases in the money supply equal to the average long-run increase in real GNP.

# case application

## Target Practice at the Fed

For the Federal Reserve, controlling the money supply today is like playing an electronic game in which you have a number of targets moving in different directions and only one shot. The main target of the Fed is the money supply, M1. Because of the new types of money accounts that have appeared and rapidly grown—the NOW and ATS accounts and money market funds that are somewhere in between the traditional demand deposit and savings accounts—managing the money supply is more complicated and more difficult than it was previously.

Although NOW and ATS accounts can be used like demand deposit accounts to make payments, the Fed estimates that 20% to 25% of the money in those accounts is bona fide savings, rarely used for transactions. On the other hand, M1 does not include money market funds, which some people use for large purchases. (Money market funds normally set a minimum amount, say $500, for checks written on the account.) If money market funds increase, the Fed does not count that as an increase in the money supply even though people can use the funds directly to make payments.

Although since 1979 the Fed has had a professed policy of controlling the money supply rather than controlling interest rates, it apparently still feels that it has a responsibility for maintaining stability in the financial markets. To do this, the Fed attempts to control sharp swings in interest rates. Since the money supply affects interest rates and vice versa, when the Fed chooses to shoot at one target, it's bound to miss the other. If it hits the lower money supply target, it is bound to miss the stable interest rate target when the lower money supply causes a rise in interest rates.

Whether the reason is because it has not been able to decide which target it is shooting at or because it is simply unable to hit the target, the Fed has been heavily criticized for its failure to control the money supply adequately. There have been proposals to make the Federal Reserve more directly accountable to the president and/or Congress. Instead of having the Board of Governors appointed for periods of 14 years as at present, one of the more extreme proposals would require all of the governors to submit their resignations to the president if the Fed missed its monetary target by more than one percentage point during the year. The resignations would be submitted along with an explanation of what went wrong. The president would then have the choice of accepting the explanation and sharing the blame or accepting the resignations.

*Economic Reasoning*

1. What initial target is the Fed aiming at when it attempts to affect the Federal Funds rate?
2. One of the explanations given for the Fed's inability to hit its money supply target is the time lag involved in the response of the economy to changes in Fed policies. Why don't the tools of monetary policy immediately affect the money supply?
3. Do you think that the Federal Reserve ought to be made more directly responsible to the president and Congress? What would be the advantages and disadvantages of this?

# How Can Economic Growth Be Increased?

Reaganomics, with its emphasis on increasing the rate of investment, was more appropriate for increasing long-term growth rather than improving short-term stability. Increases in savings-investment and in factor supplies are a means for increasing our economy's output over a period of time.

**Importance of economic growth** Our standard of living is largely determined by the rate of economic growth. At the 3% real growth rate that characterized the U.S. economy in the last 15 years, our standard of living would double in 24 years with a constant population. If the growth rate were as fast as the 4.58% achieved by the Japanese economy, where the population size actually *is* static, the standard of living would double in just two-thirds the time—less than 16 years.

Figure 5A shows the inflation-adjusted GNP growth of the United States for 1940 to 1989. Since a dollar of GNP growth is less significant the higher is GNP, Figure 5B gives a better idea of the relative growth rate over those years. It shows real GNP on a log scale that displays relative rather than absolute changes.

A higher growth rate makes it easier to solve many economic problems, from balancing the budget to stabilizing the economy to overcoming poverty.

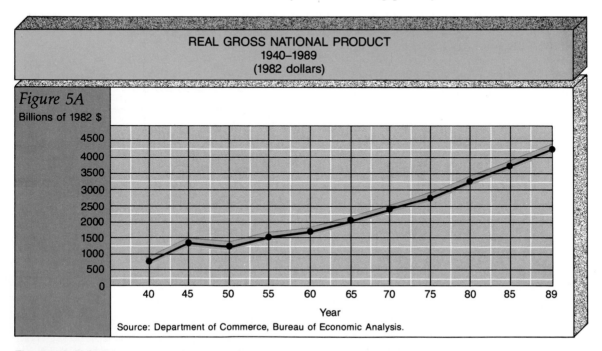

**REAL GROSS NATIONAL PRODUCT**
**1940–1989**
**(1982 dollars)**

*Figure 5A*

Billions of 1982 $

Source: Department of Commerce, Bureau of Economic Analysis.

The growth of GNP is the main determinant of increases in our standard of living. Since 1975 the economy has been growing at a 3% growth rate. This is slighly below the average of the last 40 years.

**Increasing capital investment**  The proportion of a nation's output that goes into capital formation—buildings, equipment, and public works such as highways—is an important determinant of growth. The measure of that proportion is the investment/GNP ratio, the fraction of each year's GNP that is allocated to investment goods.

Figure 6 shows the U.S. investment/GNP ratio for the years 1960–1989, expressed as a percentage. In the 1960s and 1970s we were putting about 9%–11% of our output into fixed, nonresidential investment (which excludes investment in inventories and housing). This was less than the investment/GNP ratios in the countries of Western Europe, especially West Germany where it was almost 50% greater than here, and Japan where it was twice as great. As a result those countries grew more rapidly than the United States.

United States investment rates increased during the 1980s, but the rate of growth of output did not. On the basis of historical experience, it is not surprising that we have as yet not seen the productivity payoff from the new investment. There is a lag of some years between the introduction of new technology and the resulting growth which it generates. For example, productivity failed to grow much for 20 years after the introduction of the assembly line in 1901. It will take companies time to assimilate the new technologies and make the best use of them. Some firms that have automated

**investment/GNP ratio**  the proportion of GNP which is allocated to private investment.

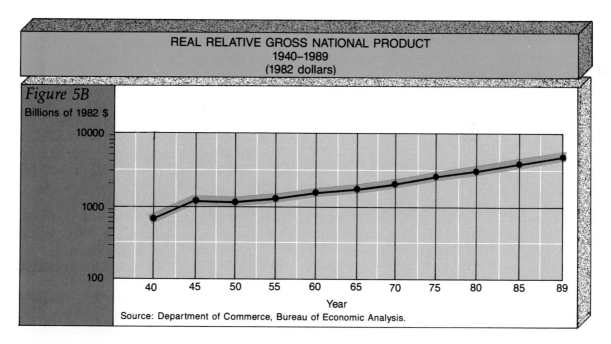

**REAL RELATIVE GROSS NATIONAL PRODUCT**
**1940–1989**
**(1982 dollars)**

*Figure 5B*

Billions of 1982 $

Year

Source: Department of Commerce, Bureau of Economic Analysis.

If growth in real GNP is shown relative to the size of GNP, the growth rate is not as steep. Changes in GNP of equal size are not as significant at higher levels of GNP as they are at lower levels.

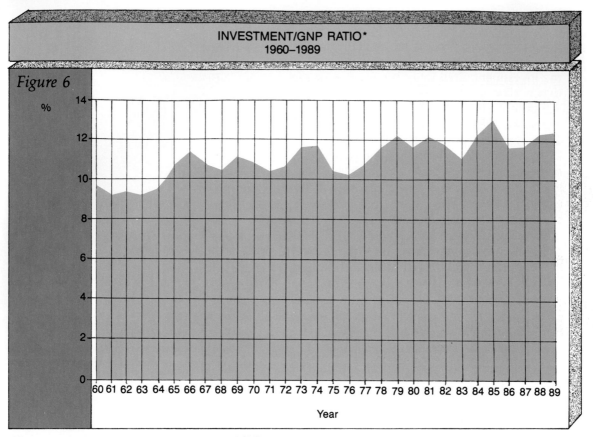

*Figure 6*

**INVESTMENT/GNP RATIO***
**1960–1989**

*Fixed nonresidential investment as a percentage of GNP.

Source: Calculated from data from the Department of Commerce, Bureau of Economic Analysis.

The rate of investment has been increasing since the 1960s. It has not, however, produced higher growth rates of output. The reasons may be decreasing capital efficiency and inadequate investment in human capital.

their operations have realized significant productivity gains while others have not. For some reason, office automation has led to less of a reduction in white-collar staffing than factory automation has led to displacement of blue-collar labor. As a result, productivity gains have been much larger in manufacturing than in services.

The effects of increasing the investment/GNP ratio are shown in Figures 7A and 7B. In Figure 7A there is an initial reduction in consumption spending (C−) to finance increased savings-investment (S+ and I+). This results in increasing the production capacity of the economy, shown in Figure 7B by an expanded GNP tank. More production means more consumption (C+) and higher levels of savings and tax receipts (S+ and T+), which make possible more investment and government services (I+ and G+).

*Figure 7A*

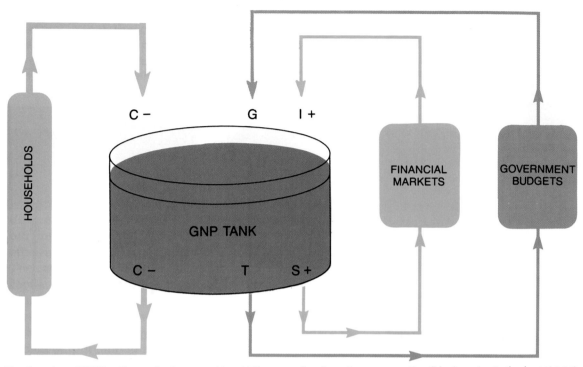

INCREASING INVESTMENT/GNP RATIO

The investment/GNP ratio can be increased by shifting spending from the consumption (blue) sector to the investment (green) sector to finance the production of more investment goods (I +).

The real cost of economic growth is the current consumption which must be given up in order to save for investment in new capital formation. One of the controversial questions in public policy is, "Whose consumption is going to be reduced in order to free the resources for increased investment?" Government policies can make the solution to this problem easier by reducing the unemployment level, increasing the total of resources engaged in production.

Another way in which stabilization policies and growth policies are interconnected is through interest rates. For example, anything that causes higher interest rates, such as large government deficits, discourages investment in increased production capacity. As another example, the hoped-for peace dividend discussed in the chapter 2 introductory article "Swords Into Plowshares" would benefit economic growth in two ways. It would lower the deficit and thus reduce upward pressure on interest rates. At the same time it would free up resources from military production, especially scarce scientific and technical labor, encouraging investment in civilian production facilities that are more productive of real growth.

# case application

## Investing in the Future

Policies to promote economic growth call for a longer time horizon than stabilization policies. Some growth measures may have a relatively quick payoff. For instance, increased investment in production plant and equipment can expand output in a matter of months. However, if the investment does not raise productivity as well as production, the output may not be competitive.

Advances in technology that do raise productivity take time to yield results. Studies of the learning curve (chapter 7, p. 176) show that the harvest period for technological innovations in U.S. firms is longer than in some other countries. Particularly in the service industries, the increase in computer technology put in place in the 1980s showed little productivity improvement by 1990.

The growth instrument with the longest period for results is investment in human capital. But the fact that it has a long payoff interval does not mean that it should not be given high priority in national policy. Technological advances will not produce results without a work force that has the skills to make use of sophisticated equipment. Automated equipment that is designed for very simple work tasks, referred to as "idiot-proof" machines, does not provide the high-productivity growth that raises living standards.

A 1990 study by the Commission on the Skills of the American Workforce compared the education-training systems in the United States, West Germany, Japan, Sweden, Denmark, Ireland, and Singapore. It found that all of the other countries except Ireland provide far better schooling and job training than the U.S. for those youth not going on to college.

It also found that the other countries have much more effective national systems for facilitating high school graduates' movement into industry. It characterizes the system in the United States, or virtual absence of any system, as "the worst of any industrialized country."

The commission study recommended a drastic overhaul in the way that the nation educates and trains that portion of its citizens who will not graduate from a four-year college, some 70%. One proposal of the study was for a national fund to upgrade worker skills. The fund would be financed by a 1% tax on business payrolls. Employers could avoid the tax by spending an equivalent amount on their own company training programs.

*Economic Reasoning*

1. Of the factors that affect economic growth, which one produces results in the shortest period of time and which one takes the longest to increase the growth rate?

2. Why is the growth measure that takes effect most quickly not necessarily the one that public policy should concentrate on?

3. Should the recommendation of the Commission on the Skills of the American Workforce that employers be required to spend an amount equal to 1% of their payroll on in-house or national training programs be adopted into law? Why or why not?

# Putting It Together

Since the 1930s, the federal government has used *fiscal policy* and *monetary policy* as the principal means to stabilize prices and maintain full employment. In implementing fiscal policy, the government adapts its spending and taxing activities in order to increase aggregate demand when there is unemployment and to decrease aggregate demand when there is inflation. Prior to the 1930s, government policy was an *annually balanced budget*. The Great Depression and the spread of the ideas of John Maynard Keynes led the government to adopt new policies which purposely created deficits in the budget to compensate for inadequate demand in the private sector and to provide for full employment.

It would be well for the government to have budget surpluses at times to counteract inflation. Over the whole business cycle, if the surpluses offset the deficits, we would have a *cyclically balanced budget*. Some economists argue that balancing the budget either annually or cyclically is not important. What is important is to do what is required for stabilization at any given time. This is *functional finance.*

The Keynesian method of solving unemployment by use of *discretionary fiscal policy* is to increase government spending on goods and services in order to expand aggregate demand, raise production, and thus stimulate employment. By increasing transfer payments, for example with cash subsidies to lower income families, the government provides larger purchasing power to the private sector, which also increases aggregate demand. On the taxation side, the Keynesians would cut taxes to boost consumption spending, thus increasing production and stimulating employment.

The amount of increased government spending and/or decreased taxes necessary to bring about full employment depends on the *multiplier.* Any increase in sales provides purchasing power to those producing the goods and services, most of which they in turn use to purchase additional goods and services. The total increase in spending is a multiple of the original increase in sales. The smaller the propensity to save, the larger is the *multiplier effect.*

The Federal Reserve System regulates the United States' monetary policy. The president and Congress control fiscal policy. Together, these institutions work to stabilize the economy and increase economic growth.

Supply-side economic policy also involves the use of tax cuts, but with a different purpose. The objective of supply-side tax cuts is to make production and investment more profitable and thereby provide incentives to businesses, workers, and other factor inputs to make more of these inputs available for production. The resulting increase in economic activity would create more jobs, and the rising output of goods and services would reduce or eliminate price increases by reducing scarcity.

In addition to the discretionary fiscal policy tools used by the federal government, there are *automatic stabilizers* built into the economy. These are tax provisions and government expenditures, such as unemployment insurance payments, that help counteract cyclical fluctuations.

The principal tools of Federal Reserve monetary policy are open market operations, changes in the discount rate, and changes in the required reserve ratio. Prior to 1979, Fed policy was targeted on the control of interest rates. Since then, the target has been the control of the money supply itself.

The monetarist approach assumes that if the money supply is only allowed to rise at the rate of the average long-run increase in real output, the price level will be stabilized. Monetarist theory is based on a constant velocity of circulation of money, which may not be the case. If the money supply is held constant while taxes are cut and defense expenditures are increased, resulting in large government deficits, interest rates can skyrocket, creating massive unemployment and widespread business failures, especially in interest-sensitive industries.

Economic growth is promoted by having a higher proportion of total output flow into new investment—raising the *investment/GNP ratio* . Another determinant of growth is the ratio between the amount of new capital spending in an industry and the increase in output resulting from that investment—the *capital/output ratio*. If the capital/output ratio is low, there is a larger increase in output for a given amount of capital spending, and the profit incentives for investment are greater.

Raising the *labor-force participation rate*, while it may in the short run reduce labor productivity, increases total and per capita output and is a significant growth factor. In the United States in the last two decades, increased participation by women in the labor force has contributed to intensive growth and raised per capita income. Growth also results from upgrading human capital through additional education and occupational training.

# Perspective

## Monetarism—Does Money Matter?

**Milton Friedman (born 1912)**
Friedman was born in Brooklyn, New York, and attended the University of Chicago and Rutgers University. He received a Ph.D. from Columbia University in 1946. During his schooling Friedman worked on the research staff of the National Bureau for Economic Research and in the tax research division of the U.S. Treasury Department. He taught for one year at the University of Minnesota before returning to the University of Chicago where he spent the rest of his teaching career, becoming the Paul Snowden Russell Distinguished Service Professor of Economics. In 1977 he became a senior Research Fellow at the Hoover Institution at Stanford University. Friedman served as the president of the American Economics Association in 1967 and was awarded the Nobel Prize in economics in 1976. He has repeatedly proven to be a formidable opponent in his numerous public debates with liberal economists because of the great amount of data he has developed from his prodigious research. He is not only the leading spokesman for monetarism but also for the conservative economic viewpoint associated with the Chicago School. Among his publications are *Essays in Positive Economics* (1953), *Inflation: Cause and Consequences* (1963), *A Theoretical Framework for Monetary Analysis* (1972), *There's No Such Thing as A Free Lunch* (1975), and *Price Theory* (1976).

In the early years of the Keynesian revolution, during the 1940s and early 1950s, the role of money in determining the level of economic activity was generally dismissed as having no relevance to economic stabilization policy. Keynes's discussion of the role of prices in *The General Theory* was interpreted by many of his followers to mean that wage rates were rigid, except at full employment when increasing demand would cause inflation of wages and other prices. Some latter-day Keynesian followers (neo-Keynesians) have noted that the assumption about fixed wages and prices was only a simplifying assumption which Keynes dropped in later chapters when he discussed the effects of price changes. Still others say that what he meant was that wages *should* be rigid to prevent even greater economic instability.

In any event, the role of prices and money was largely ignored in discussions of macroeconomic theory and economic stabilization policy. Everywhere, that is, except at the University of Chicago where the quantity theory of money ($M \times V = T \times P$) was kept alive and nurtured by a group of economists that came to be known as "The Chicago School." The foremost member of the Chicago School of economists was Milton Friedman.

In his monumental study (with Anna Schwartz), *A Monetary History of the United States 1867–1960*, Friedman demonstrated a close correlation between changes in the money supply on the one hand and inflation and the level of economic activity on the other. In his view, it was fiscal policy that was irrelevant. Promoted by Friedman and other Chicago School economists and reinforced by the persistent inflation of the 1970s, monetarism had a strong influence on both theory and policy in the early 1980s.

The rise of monetarism to the forefront of macroeconomics did not last long, however. In the area of theory, monetarism proved unable to explain what was happening any better than, or as well as, Keynesian economics. On the basis of monetarist analysis, Friedman predicted a recession in early 1984, followed by renewed inflation. Neither of these things happened, either then or for some years after.

On the policy side, the implementation of monetarist policies by the Fed did put a halt to inflation in 1981–1982 by contracting the money supply and bringing about the most severe recession since the depression of the 1930s, but that was no great trick. The real trick is to restrain inflation and at the same time provide full employment and a healthy growth rate. Monetarist policies were not any more successful in accomplishing this than previous approaches.

# Unit IV

# WORLD ECONOMICS

## Chapter 15. International Trade

Trading with other nations enables us to increase our living standards, but some people are hurt in the process. Restricting the amount of foreign trade is a subject of continuing controversy.

## Chapter 16. International Finance and the National Economy

International payments are made and exchange rates of currencies determined in the foreign-exchange market. There is a close interconnection between the international payments balance and domestic equilibrium.

The economy of the United States is closely integrated into the world economy. Our economic policies have a major impact on other countries and vice versa.

# Chapter 17. Alternative Economic Systems

Contrasting types of economic systems around the world have to resolve the same basic economic questions, but they do it in quite different ways. Comparing the performance of these systems is difficult, but they achieve the economic and socioeconomic goals with varying degrees of success.

# Chapter 18. World Economic Development

Two-thirds of the people in the world live in countries with low living standards and numerous obstacles to development. The prospects for overcoming poverty in less-developed countries depend to a large extent on how the world meets the population, debt, and environmental threats.

## chapter 15

# INTERNATIONAL TRADE

*The motivations for international trade are basically no different from those for trade within a country, but nations impose special regulations and restrictions on foreign trade. In order to escape the resulting limitations on commerce, they sometimes form trade blocs of neighboring countries. Now recently established trade blocs may drastically change the international trade system.*

## New Kid on the Bloc

A new economic entity has been conceived that will have a dramatic impact on international trade. The newborn weighs in at $5 trillion plus, comparable in size to the U.S. economy and nearly twice as large as that of Japan. It has 12 proud parents—the 12 members of the European Economic Community. In order of economic size they are: Germany, France, Italy, the United Kingdom, Spain, the Netherlands, Belgium, Denmark, Greece, Portugal, Ireland, and Luxembourg. Their populations total 320 million, compared to the United States' 250 million. The name given to this huge infant is "EC92"—European Community, 1992—the year of its arrival.

EC92 is an outgrowth of the European Economic Community, first established in 1957. The purpose of EC92 is to unify the economies of the 12 Common Market countries into one internal market by abolishing economic borders between the countries. This means no tariffs on sales of goods and services between the countries, no limits on the movement of labor or financial capital between countries, and no currency restrictions.

Unification of the individual national markets was not simple. In 1985 the European Commission, located in Brussels, Belgium, issued a "white paper" setting forth 300 directives. These directives spelled out issues that would have to be resolved and the resolutions adopted by the member countries to harmonize their economic policies in order to make EC92 work. The directives covered such things as industrial standards (product specifications, safety requirements), regulation of financial services (to avoid any European equivalent of the United States' S&L meltdown), excise taxes, labor laws, environmental policies, and immigration regulations. Since each country already had its own standards, laws, and regulations covering these areas and many others, differences had to be reconciled in order to provide a level playing field for the producers in all countries.

For example, excise tax rates that differed widely between countries had to be brought into line. (The tax on a bottle of whisky in Denmark, for instance, was 35 times higher than in Greece.) Otherwise, consumers would simply buy the products in the country with the lowest tax rates, putting firms in high-tax countries out of business.

The anticipated advantages of this enormous market-without-internal-frontiers outweighed the difficulties and the sacrifices of national sovereignty. Even before the actual birth of EC92, the stimulus to investment, production efficiency, and economic growth was apparent. European companies have invested heavily in new plants and equipment, both to exploit the EC market and to reduce production costs in order to meet the new competition in their domestic markets. Firms from outside Europe, especially U.S. and Japanese firms, have also invested in Europe to get a foothold in the new market and make sure that they were not left on the outside looking in.

EC92 has generated a mixed reaction in the business circles of non-European countries. On one hand, foreign companies were happy to see the standardization of product specifications and regulations among the European countries. That made it easier and less costly to produce export goods for the European market. On the other hand, they feared that the elimination of internal trade barriers among the EC92 countries would be accompanied by increased external trade walls. The pressure of more intra-European competition on their firms might cause the EC countries to adopt a "fortress Europe" approach to external competition, protecting the new market by means of tariffs and trade regulations on goods and services from outside Europe.

Large as the EC92 baby is, it is growing even bigger. The countries of the affiliated European Free Trade Agreement (EFTA)—Norway, Sweden, Finland, Switzerland, Austria, and Iceland—have free trade access to the EC market, although no political or administrative ties with it. And since the dramatic liberation of the Eastern European economies, there has been speculation that they too might be included in the free-trade zone, either through membership in EFTA or otherwise. If they and the Soviet Union were to come under the EC trade umbrella, it would constitute a free-trade area of 25 countries with 850 million people.

Whether in response to the challenge posed by EC92 or independently motivated, the United States and Canada signed a Free Trade Agreement (FTA) in 1989. It phases out all tariffs between the two countries over a period of 10 years. There is now discussion of bringing Mexico into the U.S.–Canada FTA to form a North American Common Market.

The danger of such trading blocs is that they will adopt external barriers to trade with the rest of the world that are as high as the most restrictive existing in any one of the countries before formation of the bloc. Increased trade among the countries of the bloc would thus be offset by reductions in trade with other countries. From the standpoint of world trade, economic growth, and living standards, the ideal solution would be for the EC, the North American FTA, and other trade blocs to become trading partners rather than trade opponents.

## Chapter Preview

*Foreign trade is the subject of much controversy, but in this chapter we shall see that the basic logic of international trade does not differ from the basic logic of domestic trade. We shall examine international trade by dealing with the following questions: Why do we trade with other countries? Who benefits and who is hurt by foreign trade? How do we restrict foreign trade? Should foreign trade be restricted?*

## Learning Objectives

*After completing this chapter, you should be able to:*

1. *Explain the difference between absolute and comparative advantage.*
2. *Explain why specialization is sometimes complete but normally is limited.*
3. *Compare the types of goods exported by the United States with the types of goods imported.*
4. *Describe the effects of foreign trade on economies.*
5. *Specify who benefits and who loses as a result of foreign trade.*
6. *Compare the different types of restrictions imposed on foreign trade.*
7. *Discuss the different vehicles for trade negotiations and define "most-favored nation" treatment.*
8. *Evaluate the arguments in favor of trade restrictions.*

# Why Do We Trade with Other Countries?

Trade between countries results from specialization of production. In chapter 3 absolute and comparative advantage were introduced to explain specialization in the use of resources. These concepts are especially applicable to international trade. It might be useful for you to review the explanation on pages 62 and 63 before taking up the discussion that follows.

**Absolute advantage**   The South American country of Ecuador has excellent climate and terrain for growing coffee, cocoa, and bananas. It has an absolute advantage over the United States in the production of these goods. The United States, on the other hand, has an absolute advantage over Ecuador in many manufactured goods such as computers, airplanes, and electric razors. Ecuador does not have the capital equipment, technology, or trained personnel to produce these things economically. Thus there is trade between the two countries, based on their respective absolute advantages, that benefits each country.

**Comparative advantage**   Many people in the textile industry are strong advocates of increased trade restrictions. Textile imports from Hong Kong, Taiwan, and South Korea have eliminated a large part of the market for U.S. textiles. The United States is an efficient producer of textiles, but labor and capital in this country are more efficient in the production of other goods. As an example, let us assume that the United States has an absolute advantage over Taiwan in the production of both electric drills and raincoats. However, the efficiency advantage of the United States is greater in producing drills than producing raincoats. The United States has a comparative advantage in drills with respect to Taiwan. The advantage of a cheaper labor supply

*Figure 2*

**U.S. IMPORTS BY TYPE
1988**

The largest category of U.S. imports is machinery. This includes such things as office machines and data processing equipment, telecommunications apparatus, and semiconductors.

*[handwritten: MACHINERY: - office machinery - data processing - telecom apparatus - semiconductors]*

Source: U.S. Bureau of the Census, *U.S. General Imports and Imports for Consumption.*

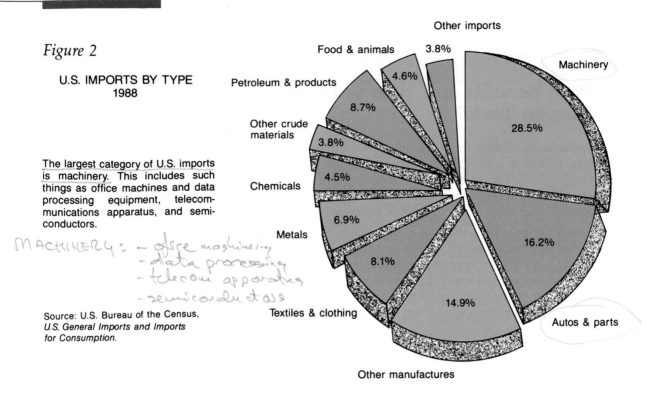

Other imports 3.8%
Food & animals 4.6%
Petroleum & products 8.7%
Other crude materials 3.8%
Chemicals 4.5%
Metals 6.9%
Textiles & clothing 8.1%
Machinery 28.5%
Autos & parts 16.2%
Other manufactures 14.9%

*[handwritten left margin: Producer & Worker Benefits? • provides markets for export industries • create jobs • increase incomes • profits to the owners
1988: • $319.3 billion civilian goods exported • 8.1% for national income]*

every four dollars. For the United States, however, this amount of import spending is much higher than it has been historically.

**Producer and worker benefits** Many industries and workers also benefit in various ways from foreign trade. Some American industries depend on raw materials that can only be acquired abroad. Other firms purchase semi-finished components for their products from foreign sources, including both independent producers and subsidiaries of American firms abroad.

Perhaps the most important benefit of foreign trade to producers and workers, however, is providing markets for our export industries. The United States exported $319.3 billion worth of civilian goods in 1988. The major merchandise export industries are shown in Figure 3. Machinery, including computers and power generators, accounted for more than a quarter of all merchandise exports.

Our exports create jobs and increase the income of all the suppliers of the export industries as well as provide profits to the owners. Merchandise exports generated 8.1% of our national income in 1988. The leading U.S. export firms are shown in Table 1 opposite.

## Figure 3

### U.S. EXPORTS BY TYPE
### 1988

The largest category of U.S. exports, as with imports, is machinery. The most important items in that category are computers and accessories. The world economic system is highly integrated, with most trade taking place between industrialized countries that have similar economies.

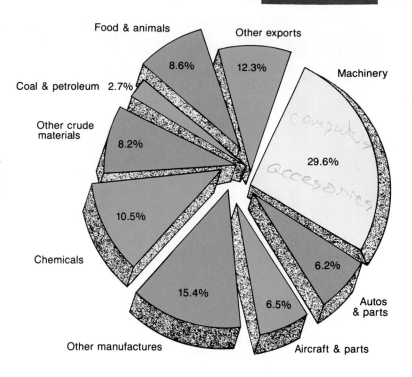

Source: U.S. Bureau of the Census, *U.S. Exports.*

## Table 1     LEADING U.S. EXPORTERS - 1989

| Company | Exports ($ billions) | Exports as % of Sales |
|---|---|---|
| 1.  Boeing | 11.0 | 54.4 |
| 2.  General Motors | 10.2 | 8.0 |
| 3.  Ford Motor | 8.6 | 8.9 |
| 4.  General Electric | 7.3 | 13.2 |
| 5.  IBM | 5.5 | 8.6 |
| 6.  Du Pont | 4.8 | 13.8 |
| 7.  Chrysler | 4.6 | 12.9 |
| 8.  United Technologies | 3.3 | 16.7 |
| 9.  Caterpillar | 3.3 | 29.6 |
| 10. McDonnell Douglas | 2.9 | 19.3 |
| 11. Eastman Kodak | 2.9 | 15.6 |
| 12. Hewlett-Packard | 2.6 | 22.1 |
| 13. Unisys | 2.4 | 23.8 |
| 14. Motorola | 2.3 | 24.1 |
| 15. Philip Morris | 2.3 | 5.9 |

Source: *Fortune* magazine, July 16, 1990, p. 77.

Although American automobile producers have been hurt by imports of foreign cars, they are at the same time among the country's largest exporters, ranking second, third, and seventh in export sales in 1989. The firms that depend most on exports for a large percentage of their sales, however, are aircraft, tractor, and computer/electronics manufacturers.

Appealing to pride in domestic manufacture has become an important sales strategy for firms in import-competing industries.

In addition to merchandise exports, the country transferred $10 billion worth of military goods under military agency sales contracts. Foreigners also spent $57 billion on U.S. travel and transportation and $35.7 billion on miscellaneous services.

**Import-competing firms' and workers' losses**   The heavy pressure exerted by some industries on Congress for protection from imports is a good indication of which groups are hurt by foreign trade. The automobile industry and the United Auto Workers' union have reversed their earlier free trade attitudes and have demanded restrictions on automobile imports. The textile and steel industries plead for more protection. The closing of plants and loss of jobs in these industries have caused hardships.

Free trade can be costly to workers and owners in import-competing industries. But these costs are no different from the costs resulting from domestic competition. For example, a once-thriving U.S. railroad industry has been devastated by competition from the automobile and trucking industries. The market mechanism allocates resources to their most efficient employment in accordance with costs and consumer demand.

**Mobility of capital and labor**   If sales of the textile industry are reduced because of imports, while sales of electrical equipment are increased because of export demand, capital and labor should move from the textile industry to the electrical-equipment industry. The difficulty is that these factors of production are not perfect substitutes for one another, and the transfer of some factors from one employment activity to another can cause hardships. Workers in one industry may not want or be able to move to another industry in a different region. Fixed capital has even less mobility: textile industry machinery, for example, cannot be used to produce electrical equipment.

**Domestic consumers of export industries**   International trade equalizes the prices of products. Before trade, the price of electric drills was relatively low in the United States and relatively high in Taiwan. With trade, the price of drills tends to rise in the United States and fall in Taiwan as some of the U.S. output is exported. Eventually, this adjustment process leads to equal prices in both countries, except for transportation costs and import taxes. The American consumer of drills finally pays a higher price for domestically produced drills.

**free trade**   international trade that is unrestricted by government protectionist measures.

# case application

## Steel Industry Does an About Face

For years, the United States steel industry led the fight *for* free trade. Today, it is fighting *against* free trade.

The emergence of a mature, efficient steel industry in Germany, Japan, South Korea, and elsewhere has tipped the scales. Not only have U.S. steel firms been priced out of many foreign markets, they are in a struggle with foreign competitors for the profitable North American steel market.

The steel industry is suffering from lagging productivity and the higher costs associated with environmental protection regulations. As a result of rising production costs, the price of a ton of domestic steel is so high that American steel users are finding it more cost-effective to import larger and larger quantities from foreign suppliers. In order to reduce the price differentials of domestic steel compared to foreign steel, U.S. steel firms have pleaded for relief from environmental controls as well as new restrictions on the importation of foreign steel.

Both labor and management in the steel industry are now far more sensitive to the implications of their low productivity. Steel output in the United States declined from a peak of 116.6 million tons in 1978 to 83.5 million tons in 1983. Cumulative losses of the industry from 1982 through 1984 amounted to $5.8 billion. But some small steel plants using advanced smelting technology, the so-called minimills, have been able to undersell imported steel and are increasing their sales.

The steel industry claims that the problem is not so much high production costs in the United States as it is unfair competition from foreign producers, subsidized by their governments. In June 1982 the Commerce Department declared that steel imported in 1981 from nine countries was, in fact, subsidized

The U.S. steel industry, suffering from lagging productivity and the high costs of government regulation, is fighting for protection from foreign competition.

and being sold in the United States at unfairly low prices. As a result, the government imposed an additional tax on foreign steel that ran as high as $250 a ton on some imports. Higher steel prices as a result cost U.S. consumers at least $5 billion annually.

### Economic Reasoning

1. Who will gain and who will lose as a result of the higher taxes on steel imports?
2. Why was the steel industry at one time in favor of free trade?
3. Do you think that the steel industry should get more protection from imports? Why or why not?

# How Do We Restrict Foreign Trade?

International trade would be larger than it is if it were not for the restrictions countries put on it. These restrictions take various forms.

**Tariffs** Tariffs are a tax on imports either on the value of the imports or per unit of quantity imported. Tariffs could be used for revenue purposes, but in recent times their principal purpose has been to shelter domestic firms from foreign competition. United States tariffs historically have been imposed on selective goods and have been relatively high. High tariffs result in a small quantity of imports, and as a consequence do not generate much tax revenue.

Empowered by the Reciprocal Trade Agreement Act of 1934 and its extensions, U.S. presidents have steadily reduced tariffs through bilateral trade negotiations (see Figure 4). These negotiated reductions depended upon the willingness of other countries to lower tariffs imposed on United States exports. Because bilateral negotiations can create confusing multiple tariff rates for different nations, most-favored nation clauses in trade agreements extend the benefits of tariff reductions negotiated with one country to all other countries which accord the United States similar treatment. The United States has been reluctant to extend the benefits of the most-favored nation treatment to some countries, notably the Soviet Union. Trade negotiations with these countries continue on a purely bilateral basis.

In 1947, the United States and 22 other nations signed the General Agreement on Tariffs and Trade (GATT). It provided for nondiscrimination among the cooperating nations. It also set a pattern for multilateral trade negotiations as a substitute for bilateral trade negotiations. When all of the participating countries negotiate simultaneously, the possibilities for making deals for tariff reductions are greatly expanded. Through GATT, which now includes some 70 countries, tariffs have been markedly reduced. Although some significant exceptions exist, trade between the United States and the rest of the world is much more free today than it has ever been.

**Quotas** Restrictions on the quantity of a good that may be imported or exported during a given time period are called quotas. They are established either in physical terms—a set number of tons of a commodity, for example—or in value terms—a set number of dollars' worth of a commodity. Quotas may be directed toward one or a number of specific countries, or they can be established without regard to the country of origin. The quota may be stated in absolute terms; that is, a fixed quantity or value of a commodity may

**tariff** a tax placed on an imported good; also, the whole schedule of a country's import duties.

**bilateral trade negotiations** trade negotiations between two countries only.

**most-favored nation clause** a provision in trade agreements that extends lower tariff concessions granted to one country to all other countries that are accorded most-favored nation treatment.

**multilateral trade negotiations** simultaneous trade negotiations between a number of countries.

**quota** a limit on the quantity or value of a good that can be imported in a given time period.

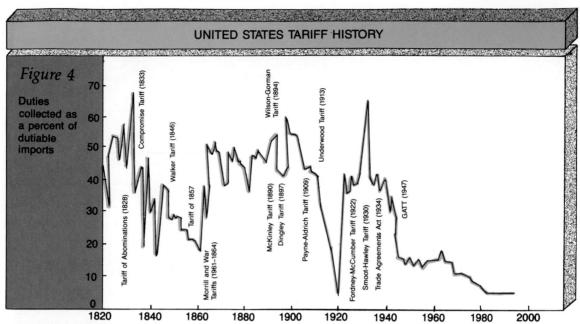

**UNITED STATES TARIFF HISTORY**

*Figure 4*

Duties collected as a percent of dutiable imports

Tariff of Abominations (1828)
Compromise Tariff (1833)
Walker Tariff (1846)
Tariff of 1857
Morrill and War Tariffs (1961–1864)
McKinley Tariff (1890)
Wilson-Gorman Tariff (1894)
Dingley Tariff (1897)
Payne-Aldrich Tariff (1909)
Underwood Tariff (1913)
Fordney-McCumber Tariff (1922)
Smoot-Hawley Tariff (1930)
Trade Agreements Act (1934)
GATT (1947)

Since the early 1800s average tariff rates have fluctuated widely. Since the early 1930s, however, the trend has been downward.

be allowed to enter a country. Alternatively, the quota may be stated as a tariff quota, which allows a given quantity or value of commodity to enter a country duty-free or at a low tariff, with larger quantities or values entering at a higher rate of duty.

Quotas have been largely responsible for limiting Japanese auto penetration in European markets. France restricted Japanese cars to 3% of total sales, and tough quotas in Italy and Spain held Japan's share of their markets to less than 1%.

The main difference in the effect of a tariff and a quota—at least an absolute quota—is that the tariff still allows the price system in the importing country to allocate goods and resources. Quotas, on the other hand, set an absolute limit and, no matter how high the domestic price is above the price abroad, no more can be imported.

**Non-tariff barriers** Besides tariffs and quotas, there are a number of other ways of restricting imports. These are termed non-tariff barriers. If industries lobbying for protection are unable to get high tariffs or import quotas imposed, they still have other weapons. For example, a requirement may be imposed that all goods that have foreign components must have labels affixed. This labeling can serve to encourage nationalistic sentiments. In addition, labeling adds to the costs of the foreign producer.

**non-tariff barriers** restrictions on imports resulting from requirements for special marking, test, or standards enforced on imported goods or the time delays in clearing them for importation.

Foreign trade is sometimes restricted for political reasons. Members of the United Nations Security Council are shown here voting on September 9, 1990, in favor of an air traffic embargo on Iraq to retaliate for that country's invasion of Kuwait. Voting, from left to right, are then–Soviet foreign minister Eduard Shevardnadze, British foreign minister Douglas Hurd, and U.S. secretary of state James A. Baker III.

An informal type of barrier to foreign imports is to make the clearing of foreign goods through customs difficult, time-consuming, and therefore expensive. Imported goods can be made subject to a series of tests and inspections for reasons of safety, health, and general public welfare. These non-tariff barriers when applied and enforced can be very effective in discouraging imports.

**Export embargoes**   Export embargoes are prohibitions on the export of commodities, capital, or technology. They are sometimes imposed for political reasons, such as the 1980 embargo on exports of U.S. grain to the Soviet Union because of the Soviet invasion of Afghanistan. The United Nations imposed a total import-export embargo on Iraq in 1990 to force it to withdraw from its occupation of Kuwait.

Export embargoes might instead be used to prevent other countries from having access to valuable new technologies. They could also be imposed to block the outflow of important raw materials and thus keep down their prices to domestic producers.

**export embargo**   a prohibition of the export of a commodity, capital, or technology.

# case application

## Protection Japanese Style

American producers regularly complain that the Japanese market is particularly tough to crack. Public officials in the United States insist that the enormous trade deficit with Japan—$52 billion in 1988—must be reduced.

The Japanese, for their part, claim that they have greatly reduced their tariffs in recent years; the average tariff level of Japan is in fact below that of the United States. If Japanese tariffs are not especially high, why is it so difficult for U.S. businesses to penetrate the Japanese market?

One area in which Japan does have stiff import restrictions is on agricultural products. Quotas on imports of meat and fruit create large price differences between the Japanese market and the American market—$20 a pound for steak and $35 for melons in Tokyo, for example.

However, the main obstacles to selling more American products in Japan are not formal trade barriers. One of them is Japanese government red tape. For instance, documentation and testing of American cars sold in Japan add as much as $500 to the price of each car. Testing for the safety of U.S. health care products is required in Japan, even if similar tests have already been performed for the same products marketed in the United States.

Another problem for foreigners in penetrating the Japanese market is the existence of giant integrated Japanese firms that produce goods all the way from the raw material stage to the finished product (see the introductory article to chapter 7). Foreign suppliers of intermediate products have no chance of selling them to the vertically integrated Japanese firms. Even the smaller Japanese producers are frozen out of their own domestic markets in this way. As a result, some of them are now entering into joint production and marketing arrangements with American and other foreign firms to take advantage of the Japanese government's efforts to open the Japanese market more to foreigners in order that they can gain an entry into their *own country's* markets!

But perhaps the greatest barrier American business has to overcome is cultural. The formalities and informalities of Japanese business conduct are significantly different from those in the West. Personal relationships are more important in Japanese business dealings. Socializing over a cup of tea is an essential ingredient in business negotiations. The Japanese characterize such business dealings as "wet," in contrast to the "dry," more businesslike and less personal practices in the United States and other Western countries.

It takes considerable time for U.S. firms to develop a market in Japan. American business has been criticized for having a too-short profit horizon. Any proposed business activity that doesn't promise to show profits within a few months is rejected. The small number of American businesspeople who take the time to learn the Japanese language attests to a lack of commitment to nurturing the Japanese market. By comparison, a Japanese business representative may spend 10–15 years in the United States making contacts and learning the language. Some American firms that have put forth the effort have had success with sales in Japan; included among these firms are IBM, Schick, Coca-Cola, and McDonald's.

A Japanese youth rushes past "The American Train in Japan," which toured the major cities of Japan in 1988 and 1989 promoting American products.

## *Economic Reasoning*

1. What type of non-tariff barriers, other than quotas, restrict imports into Japan? Can you think of any similar barriers that restrict imports into the United States?

2. Would U.S. farmers and ranchers be able to export more to Japan if the Japanese applied tariffs rather than quotas to imports of agricultural products? What are the assumptions underlying your answer?

3. Americans' lack of ability in speaking foreign languages is said to hamper the country in business dealings, international understanding, and cultural growth. Do you think that more study of foreign languages should be required of American students? What would be the trade-off of increased language requirements in our schools?

# Should Foreign Trade Be Restricted?

As can be seen in Figure 4 on page 431, the level of protectionist sentiment in this country has fluctuated widely, though over the years protectionism has generally been high. Since the GATT agreement in 1947, trade barriers have been greatly reduced. But there is currently a resurgence of protectionism. Why does the protectionist movement keep reappearing? This analysis section examines some of the arguments over free trade versus protectionism.

**Traditional protectionist arguments**  The most common justification given for protectionism is that it is supposed to increase domestic employment by protecting the U.S. worker from the unfair competition of cheap foreign labor. But trade is based on comparative, not absolute, advantage. Low foreign wages do not necessarily create comparative advantage for those countries. The wage issue, in essence, ignores the productivity of workers. Wages of American workers are high because of their high productivity. The low wages of foreign workers are due to their low productivity. When their productivity increases, so do their wages, as has happened in Japan. Imports, as a result of specialization according to comparative advantage, increase the real wages of American workers.

A second argument for protectionism is that imports represent a leakage of spending from the economic system and that a reduction in spending for imports would increase domestic aggregate demand. This argument is true as far as it goes, but one country's imports are another's exports. The imposition of tariffs generally causes retaliation, reducing employment in U.S. export industries as much or more than the increased employment in import-competing industries.

One situation in which protection can be justified for a period of time is where a *new industry* could be efficient and competitive if it had a chance to mature and achieve economies of scale. This argument holds that newly established industries need to be protected until they reach levels of production that allow them to be competitive in the world market. The costs of temporary trade restrictions might be worth paying in order to gain a long-run benefit. This infant industry argument may have limited validity for under-developed countries, but it generally has little applicability in the United States or other mature economies.

**Terms of trade**  The average price of exports relative to the price of imports is called the terms of trade. It shows how many units of imports can be purchased with a given amount of exports.

Countries may desire to improve the terms of trade in

**protectionism**  measures taken by the government in order to limit or exclude imports which compete with domestic production.
**infant industry argument**  the contention that it is economically justified to provide trade protection to a new industry in a country to enable it to grow to a size that would result in production costs competitive with foreign producers.
**terms of trade**  the ratio of average export prices to average import prices.

order to increase their purchasing power in the international marketplace. They want the value of the goods they export to increase relative to the value of the goods they import. They would then be able to buy more imports for the same quantity of exports, thus raising their standard of living.

The terms of trade can be altered either by a reduced price for imports or an increased price of exports. For example, the prices paid to foreign exporters may be forced down by imposing tariffs or quotas. The higher retail prices resulting from import restrictions cause the quantity demanded in the importing country to fall. In response to the lower demand, foreign producers will reduce their export prices, resulting in an increase in the terms of trade for the country imposing the tariff or quota. However, when one country attempts to turn the terms of trade in its favor in this fashion, it invites retaliation from others.

**Neomercantilist arguments** The mercantilists around the time of Queen Elizabeth I believed that the strength of a nation lay in how much gold and other precious metals it held. They believed a country must export more than it imported. For if there is an excess of exports over imports, goods and services will flow out of the country; and in payment, gold will flow into the country. An exception to their export drive was the export of machinery. England prohibited the export of textile machinery, or even the plans for constructing it, because that would have enabled France and other rivals to compete with English textiles.

The neomercantilists of today are reviving the ideas of the seventeenth-century mercantilists. They argue that, whereas in the past comparative advantage came in large part from the basic resources of a country, comparative advantage for a modern industrialized economy is primarily a function of technology. Thus, a country will retain a comparative advantage only as long as it retains a technological lead over other countries. When technology is being rapidly exported, as it is now, a domestic industry has less time to capitalize on any comparative advantage that it might have due to superior technology. If the industry loses this comparative advantage, it is faced with resource dislocation and the accompanying structural unemployment.

No one can deny that technology is more mobile today than it has ever been. A country can lose its comparative advantage if it does not remain technologically superior. A major strength of the United States economy has been its ability to generate technology. Many claim that to be its fundamental comparative advantage. The question is should it—or can it—prevent the export of its technology to Japan and other countries? Or, failing that, should it restrict the importation of the products of that technology?

**mercantilists** those who advocated mercantilism, a doctrine that dominated policies in many countries from the sixteenth to the eighteenth centuries. It held that exports should be maximized and imports minimized to generate an inflow of gold, and exports of machinery and technology should be prohibited to prevent competition from foreign producers.

**neomercantilists** contemporary advocates of mercantilist trade policies to restrict imports, maximize exports of consumer products, and restrict exports of capital equipment and technology to prevent competition from foreign producers.

Neomercantilists contend that exporting high technology can cause a country to lose its competitive advantage.

Protectionist arguments fail to take into account the basic rationale for trade—to raise standards of living by maximizing the efficiency of resource allocation through comparative advantage. Furthermore, the matter of technology transfer is becoming a two-way street as Japan and Western Europe devote more resources to research and development.

However, since the nation as a whole benefits from the advantages of foreign competition and new technology, it must be prepared to compensate those who are injured in the process. In the United States, trade adjustment assistance is given by the government to industries injured by foreign competition to help capital and labor shift to new products.

**Restrictions to solve foreign payments problems**   If a country's imports exceed its exports, it will have a deficit in its foreign payments. The method of correcting the deficit under free trade and free currency conditions would be to let the value of the country's currency fall relative to other countries until its exports became inexpensive enough to compete in world markets. The protectionist method would be to restrict imports and perhaps also restrict investments in foreign countries. This solution to the problem of a foreign deficit could only work if other countries did not retaliate.

**trade adjustment assistance** supplementary unemployment payments to workers who have lost their jobs because of import competition and assistance to firms in shifting to other types of production.

# case application

## Bastiat's Petition

The controversy between protectionists and free traders has remained very much alive, as the current pressure for increased protection from foreign competition shows. The most extreme protectionist position was neatly satirized in the nineteenth century by French economist Frederic Bastiat (1801–1850) in his famous "Petition of the Manufacturers of Candles, Waxlights, Lamps, Candlesticks, Strut Lamps, Snuffers, Extinguishers, and the Producers of Oil, Tallow, Resin, Alcohol, and Generally Everything Connected with Lighting" which was addressed to the French parliament.

"Gentlemen:

We are suffering from the intolerable competition of a foreign rival, placed, it would seem, in a condition so far superior to our own for the production of light, that he absolutely *inundates* our *national market* with it at a price fabulously reduced. . . . This rival . . . is no other than the sun.

What we pray for is . . . a law ordering the shutting up of all windows, skylights . . . in a word of all openings, holes, chinks, and fissures. . . . If you shut up as much as possible all access to natural light and create a demand for artificial light, which of our French manufacturers will not benefit by it?

Make your choice, but be logical; for as long as you exclude, as you do, iron, corn, foreign fabrics, *in proportion* as their prices approximate to zero, what inconsistency it would be to admit the light of the sun, the price of which is already at zero during the entire day!"

*Economic Reasoning*

1. What type of protectionist argument was Bastiat satirizing?

2. If the French parliament had adopted Bastiat's petition, what effect would this have had on the manufacturers of candles, wax lights, lamps, and candlesticks? What would have been the effect on the French economy?

3. Do you think that the U.S. industries which are suffering from import competition should be accorded protection? Why or why not? Is there a difference between the argument for restricting the imports of textiles, steel, or Japanese automobiles and Bastiat's petition to restrict the competition from the sun?

# Putting It Together

Specialization according to absolute or comparative advantage means that resources are employed efficiently and total world output increases. Specialization may be complete, especially in smaller countries with a limited variety of resources. But most often specialization is *limited*. Countries both produce and import a specific item. The reason they do not produce enough for their needs, even though they are capable of producing the item, is because of *increasing costs*. Increasing the output of the industry would raise costs due to a limited supply of factor inputs. It is resource availability that determines the nature and extent of specialization.

Consumers are the greatest beneficiaries of foreign trade. Because goods are made where they can be produced most inexpensively, consumers' real purchasing power is maximized. Production firms that use imported raw material and components are also beneficiaries of trade. Export industries and their workers also benefit. Losses are sustained by firms that must compete with imports. These losses are more lasting and severe when the mobility of capital and labor between different industries is limited. Domestic consumers of the products of export industries will also suffer to the extent that the export demand raises the prices of the products.

*Tariffs* and *quotas* are methods of restricting imports. *Nontariff barriers*, such as regulations on labeling, packaging, and testing, also restrict imports. On rare occasions, exports may be taxed or prohibited when the authorities believe that it is in the best interest of the country to do so.

In order to reduce trade barriers, nations negotiate mutual concessions in *bilateral* or *multilateral trade negotiations*. When a nation grants a tariff reduction or other trade concession on imports of a good from one country through these negotiations, it automatically extends the concession to all other countries to whom it extends *most-favored nation* treatment.

Among the older *protectionist* arguments are the "cheap foreign labor" argument, which maintains that the wages of American workers are held down by competition from low-wage workers abroad, notwithstanding that the foreign wages are low because the foreign labor is not very productive. Other current justifications for protection such as to stimulate domestic employment or improve the terms of trade usually ignore the likelihood of retaliation.

*Neomercantilist* arguments for restricting exports of American capital and technology contradict the principle of comparative advantage. Another reason given for imposing

International trade follows the same basic logic as domestic trade; it is based on comparative, not absolute, advantage. Shown here is one artist's conception of what a common unit of currency (an ecu) for EC92 might look like.

import restrictions is to attempt to eliminate a deficit in the nation's foreign payments. Under free trade and currency conditions, however, this should not be necessary because the deficit should be corrected by a fall in the value of the country's currency, which would stimulate exports and curb imports.

The only protectionist argument which has received limited approval by most economists is the *infant industry* argument. This argument holds that a country which has the resource endowment for a particular industry to be efficient can justifiably protect that industry from foreign competition during the industry's early growth period. The assumption is that import restrictions will be removed when the industry matures. This argument may have validity for underdeveloped nations but generally has little application to developed economies.

Unemployed men stand in a breadline at the New York Municipal Lodging House during the Depression in 1930. The effects of the Depression were made worse by the strongly protectionist Smoot-Hawley Tariff of 1930, the subject of the Perspective on the opposite page.

# Perspective

## Smoot-Hawley Revisited

The Smoot-Hawley Tariff was especially hard on farmers, who depended on foreign markets for export income.

For additional information on Smoot-Hawley and U.S. tariff history, see John M. Dobson, *Two Centuries of Tariffs* (Washington, D.C.: United States Trade Commission, 1976); David A. Lake, *Power, Protection, and Free Trade* (Ithaca, N.Y.: Cornell University Press, 1988); Stefanie Ann Lenway, *The Politics of U.S. International Trade* (Boston: Pitman, 1985); and F. W. Taussig, *The Tariff History of the United States* (New York: Augustus M. Kelley, 1967).

In 1930, a thousand members of the American Economics Association begged Congress to defeat the Smoot-Hawley Tariff Bill. However, their petitions fell on deaf ears. Unemployment was rising, and Congress reasoned that if workers were displaced because of cheap foreign imports, then why not curtail the imports and protect the United States worker? It proceeded to enact the most restrictive set of import duties ever adopted in the United States.

Passage of this legislation turned some economists' worst fears into reality. It set in motion massive, worldwide trade restrictions. The powerful and not-so-powerful nations of the world responded to the Smoot-Hawley Tariff of 1930 out of self-protection and self-interest. They did not have enough dollars or gold to continue to pay for U.S. goods if the United States bought less from them. And they reasoned that if it was advantageous for the United States to protect its industries from foreign competition, then it was equally advantageous for them to protect their industries from American competition. The result was a marked reduction in world trade—a reduction that left the export industries of most countries in shambles. Incomes fell. Unemployment grew. The intensity of the Great Depression increased.

The loss of export markets was especially hard on farmers. The farm economy had been in a depression since the mid-1920s, years before the crash hit industry and commerce. Exports were an outlet for excess American farm production prior to Smoot-Hawley.

The irony of Smoot-Hawley was that all during the preceding decade the United States had an excess of exports over imports. In 1928 the export surplus was over $1 billion, more than $9 billion in today's dollars. During the years leading up to Smoot-Hawley, the United States on balance gained, not lost, jobs from foreign trade.

Raising the barriers against the import of goods from abroad made it impossible for other countries to pay their accumulated debts to American banks and other lenders. The consequent defaults added more pressure on the crumbling U.S. financial structure.

Once the international trading system was virtually destroyed by the protectionist policies of the early 1930s, it was slow to recover. The lessons learned as a result of Smoot-Hawley and its aftermath conditioned the international approach to trade following World War II. Led by the United States, the western countries adopted GATT and other agreements intended to liberalize trade and avoid in the future the havoc that followed Smoot-Hawley.

For
Further
Study
and
Analysis

## Study Questions

1. If the United States has an absolute advantage in the production of rubber boots, does it necessarily follow that it will also have a comparative advantage in producing rubber boots? Explain.
2. Why could a country have a comparative advantage in the production of a certain quantity of a good, but a comparative disadvantage in producing larger quantities of that same good?
3. If all countries followed their comparative advantage and world output increased, who would get this increased output?
4. Does your state or province have any export industries? What are they? Does it have any import-competing industries? Which ones?
5. Since some people benefit from an increase in foreign trade while others lose, although the total benefits exceed the total losses, how could the benefits be redistributed so that everybody gains?
6. Approximately what was the 1989 level of U.S. tariffs as a percentage of dutiable imports? Was it ever that low before? When?
7. Why do quotas result in less efficient resource use than do tariffs?

8. How could the United States take better advantage of its technological innovation?
9. Why are small countries not as likely to encounter retaliation when they increase trade restrictions as large countries are?
10. A U.S. Congressman favoring trade restrictions on textile imports released figures showing that foreign-made apparel cost 97% of the average retail price for U.S.–made goods. Does this indicate that consumers would not be much affected by restrictions on imports of apparel? Explain.

## Exercises in Analysis

1. Locate 5 imported items in stores in your area. List the items, where they were produced, what materials were used in their manufacture, and whether competing products manufactured in the United States were also available. For those items in which foreign-made and U.S. goods competed, compare the prices. If the prices differed, explain why. If the prices were identical or nearly the same, explain why.

2. Write a short paper on the impact of foreign trade on your area. Include such information as: what local businesses export all or part of their production; what local businesses are in direct competition with imported products; what local businesses use imported raw materials; and whether any local businesses provide tourist services to foreigners.

3. In the *Readers' Guide to Periodical Literature* in the library, or another source, find a recent article on U.S. trade policy. Write a short paper summarizing the article and explaining what effects the trade policies discussed are likely to have on the economy.

4. Write a brief paper arguing for or against increased protection for U.S. industries.

## Further Reading

Adams, John. *International Economics: A Self-Teaching Introduction to the Basic Concepts* (3rd edition). New York: St. Martin's Press, 1989. A programmed instruction primer on classical and modern trade theory and international finance.

Calingaert, Michael. *The 1992 Challenge From Europe: Development of the European Community's Internal Market.* Washington, D.C.: National Planning Association, 1988. Part I sets forth the specifics of the EC92 integration plan. Part II examines the implications of EC92 for the United States, including its impact on specific industry sectors.

Destler, I. M. *American Trade Politics.* Washington, D.C.: Institute for International Economics, 1986. Discusses the politics of protectionism, the pressures on Congress, and prescriptions for dealing with trade problems.

Emerson, Michael, et al. *The Economics of 1992: The E. C. Commission's Assessment of the Economic Effects of Completing the Internal Market.* Oxford, U.K.: Oxford University Press, 1988. An examination of European market barriers and the expected effects of market integration.

Hufbauer, Gary Clyde, ed. *Europe 1992: An American Perspective.* Washington, D.C.: The Brookings Institution, 1990. This book examines the likely effect of EC92 on various U.S. industries and what it implies for American policies.

Overturf, Stephen Frank. *The Economic Principles of European Integration.* New York: Praeger, 1986. Discusses the institutions, theory, and mechanics of European integration. Also covers the effect on trade relations with other countries.

Schott, Jeffrey J., and Murray G. Smith, eds. *The Canada–United States Free Trade Agreement: The Global Impact.* Washington, D.C.: Institute for International Economics, 1988. Contains conference reports covering various aspects of the agreement.

Silva, Michael, and Bertil Sjögren. *Europe 1992 and the New World Power Game.* New York: John Wiley & Sons, 1990. This book proposes that the internationalization of consumption is shifting the locus of economic power and that European integration will make it the major power because it will have the largest market. The authors maintain that changes in the Japanese society and economy, such as consumer revolt against monopolistic pricing, reduce the international economic power of Japan. They predict that the American economy, on the other hand, will regain some of its lost glory.

*Tariffs, Quotas, and Trade: The Politics of Protectionism.* San Francisco, Calif.: Institute for Contemporary Studies, 1979. An examination of free trade vs. protectionism, divergence between theory and practice, the changing international monetary system, adjustment assistance, Japan's trade surplus, and the international macroeconomy.

## chapter 16

# INTERNATIONAL FINANCE AND THE NATIONAL ECONOMY

*International transactions impact the domestic economy in a variety of ways. The effects can be positive or negative—or both, depending on your viewpoint. The following introductory article takes a satirical look at the contradictions posed by international transactions, with the help of Lewis Carroll's familiar characters.*

## Alice in the Wonderland of International Finance

According to the *Economist*, a British journal of political economy, there are only some 600 people in the world who really understand how the international monetary system works. The editors of the *Economist* believe it is unfortunate the rest of us don't take more interest in the subject because it "affects everybody's everyday lives. What happens to exchange rates, trade, interest rates, and debt translates into jobs, the safety of a nest egg, the cost of a foreign holiday. For millions, it can mean the difference between tolerable and intolerable poverty" (*Economist*, October 5, 1985, p. 5).

What the magazine did not reveal is that,

in addition to the 600 academic economists, government officials, and commercial moneymen, there is another "expert" on the workings of the international monetary system—a little girl by the name of Alice who learned the secrets of international finance while on a visit to Wonderland, one of the few places where it is understood.

The subject first came to Alice's attention when the Queen of Hearts announced that her land would make war on the Land of the Rising Sun. The reason for the war, it seemed, was that the Land of the Rising Sun was sending them too many things.

"Are these things it is sending you things that you don't want?" asked Alice.

"Don't ask impudent questions, little girl," said the Queen.

The helpful White Rabbit pulled on Alice's sleeve and whispered in her ear, "Oh, no, we like the things they send us very much. They are better than the things we have here, but they are sending too many things and won't take enough from us in return."

Alice thought this a peculiar reason for starting a war, but before she could ask any more questions, the Dormouse came running up, all out of breath, exclaiming, "The dollar is sinking. The dollar is sinking."

Upon hearing this news, some of those in attendance cheered and others moaned. The March Hare scampered off to see his broker.

"Why is the dollar sinking?" inquired Alice.

"Don't ask stupid questions," said the Queen. "The dollar is sinking because of the floating exchange rate system."

"Oh, dear," said Alice, "I hope no one is hurt when the dollar sinks."

"Lots of people will be hurt," replied the King, gleefully. "The importers will get killed. So much the worse for them. Consumers will have to pay more for all of those things from the Land of the Rising Sun and won't be able to afford them. So much the worse for them. Producers will have to pay more for imported raw materials and will have to raise their selling prices. So much the worse for them."

"But that is terrible," Alice said. "What caused the dollar to sink? Can't we rescue it?"

"Get that ninny of a girl out of my sight," screamed the Queen, "or I'll have her head."

The White Rabbit took Alice aside where he could explain to her the facts of international exchange rate policy. "We purposely caused the dollar to sink so that we would have to pay more for the things we get from the Land of the Rising Sun and other lands," he said. "The other lands will, of course, pay less for what we send them. They weren't very happy about it, but we threatened them with a trade war if they didn't go along. So the finance ministers of the other six lands in the Group of Seven agreed to cooperate with us in sinking the dollar."

"How do you sink the dollar?" asked Alice.

"The Queen was right. You are a ninny," said the Rabbit. "You sink the dollar by floating more of them. The more dollars you float, the lower the dollar sinks."

"This gets curiouser and curiouser," thought Alice. "Everything in the World of International Finance seems to be upside-down."

Just then she heard a commotion and went to see what the cause of it was. There was the Queen, purple with rage, shouting "Cut off their heads! Cut off their heads!"

"Oh, my, whose head does she want to cut off now?" asked Alice.

"She has proof that the foreign exporters of hats are being subsidized by their governments to sell us hats below their costs of production," responded the Gryphon. "It has made the Queen furious and the Mad Hatter even madder."

"But if they are selling us hats below the costs of producing them, aren't they giving us something for nothing?" puzzled Alice. "Shouldn't we thank them instead of cutting off their heads?"

"You might at first think so," replied the Gryphon, "but if we took their low-priced hats, what would the Mad Hatter do?"

"Couldn't he make something else that no one wants to give us?" asked Alice.

The Gryphon, normally quite polite, looked at her with visible disdain. "But then he wouldn't be the Mad Hatter any more, would he?

"Oh, my," sighed Alice. "I don't think that I will ever understand international finance. The more you have to pay for something the better. If somebody outside your land wants to give you something, they should have their head cut off. If they send you too much of what you want, you declare war on them. If your currency floats too high, you try to sink it. It seems to me that in the World of International Finance nothing is the way it's supposed to be."

At this, she heard a chuckle. Turning in the direction from which it came, Alice saw the Cheshire Cat grinning at her from the bough of a tree. "When you understand that, you understand everything there is to know about international finance." said the Cat. Having pronounced that bit of wisdom, the Cat grinned even wider and gradually began to disappear, from its tail forward, until all that was left behind was its smile.

## Chapter Preview

*The Cheshire Cat was smiling at the contradictions in our attitudes and policies with regard to international trade and finance. These contradictions partly are inherent in the problems posed by the foreign sector of the economy. But they are also in part the result of a lack of understanding of how the international financial system works and how it impacts the national economy. This chapter will attempt to make it more understandable by covering the following questions:* How do we pay for imports? What happens when exports and imports do not balance? What is the relationship between international finance and the national economy?

## Learning Objectives

*After completing this chapter, you should be able to:*

1. *Explain how payments are made for imports.*
2. *Distinguish between fixed and freely fluctuating exchange rates and explain how the rate of exchange is determined under each system.*
3. *Differentiate between currency depreciation, currency appreciation, devaluation, and revaluation.*
4. *Define balance of payments and list the different accounts in the balance of payments.*
5. *Distinguish between a favorable and an unfavorable balance of trade.*
6. *Explain basic deficit and the role of the residual accounts in the balance of payments.*
7. *Explain national economic equilibrium and illustrate with a schematic GNP tank diagram.*
8. *Show how an import surplus allows the economy to consume more than it produces.*
9. *Describe the role of foreign investment in compensating for insufficient domestic savings and taxes.*

## How Do We Pay for Imports?

One answer to the question, "How do we pay for imports?" is that we pay for imports with exports. But, although bartering is more common in international trade than in domestic trade, most imports are paid for with a medium of exchange. The problem is that a different medium of exchange and unit of measurement is used in each country: dollars in the United States, pounds in the United Kingdom, marks in Germany, and yen in Japan. How can importers pay in their currency and at the same time exporters receive payment in theirs?

**Foreign-exchange market** The conversion of U.S. dollars into foreign currency occurs in the foreign-exchange market. Here the price of any one money in terms of another is set either by market forces of demand and supply, or by government price fixing, or by a combination of both. Once the price has been set, a foreign currency can be bought very easily through a bank.

Local banks obtain foreign money from centrally located correspondent banks that deal in the foreign-exchange market. These are generally the larger banks in principal trading centers such as New York, London, Frankfurt, and Tokyo. Such banks supply their customers and other banks with foreign money from balances they hold abroad. For example, the Chase Manhattan Bank may have an account with the Midlands Bank in London. If an American cloth importer needs British pounds to pay for a shipment of English woolens, the Chase Manhattan Bank will sell the importer some pounds in its London account. The American importer can use these pounds to pay the British exporter. The

**foreign-exchange market** a set of institutions, including large banks in the world's financial centers, private brokers, and government central banks and other agencies, that deal in the exchange of one country's money for another's.

**correspondent bank** a bank in another city or country that a bank has an arrangement with to provide deposit transfer or other services.

account balance held in Britain by the Chase bank was created by payments made by Britons for U.S. goods or in settlement of accounts owed to American citizens from other transactions.

**Exchange rates**  The foreign exchange rate expresses the price of one money in terms of another. Like any price, an exchange rate may vary in the free play of market forces. For example, the British pound was priced at $2.40 in 1970. It declined to $1.30 in 1985 and then rose to near $2.00 in 1990.

Exchange rates were not always allowed to fluctuate in that fashion. From the end of World War II to the early 1970s, the major Western countries maintained a system of fixed exchange rates. For the system to work, each country had to accept or supply money at the fixed rate. If a nation ran short of a particular foreign money, it could resort to short-term loans from the International Monetary Fund (IMF) to maintain the fixed price. But because of chronic imbalances in the demand and supply of various countries' currencies (especially the United States dollar), the system of fixed rates was abandoned.

**fixed exchange rates** exchange rates between currencies that are legally set by the respective countries. **International Monetary Fund (IMF)** an organization established in 1946 to assist in operation of the world monetary system by regulating the exchange practices of countries and providing liquidity to member countries that have payment problems.

## EXCHANGE RATES

Wednesday, January 9, 1991

The New York foreign exchange selling rates below apply to trading among banks in amounts of $1 million and more, as quoted at 3 p.m. Eastern time by Bankers Trust Co. Retail transactions provide fewer units of foreign currency per dollar.

| Country | U.S. $ equiv. Wed. | Tues. | Currency per U.S. $ Wed. | Tues. |
|---|---|---|---|---|
| Argentina (Austral) ... | .0001809 | .0001816 | 5527.20 | 5507.60 |
| Australia (Dollar) ...... | .7733 | .7767 | 1.2932 | 1.2875 |
| Austria (Schilling) ..... | .09242 | .09217 | 10.82 | 10.85 |
| Bahrain (Dinar) ........ | 2.6525 | 2.6525 | .3770 | .3770 |
| Belgium (Franc) | | | | |
| Commercial rate .... | .03156 | .03148 | 31.69 | 31.77 |
| Brazil (Cruzeiro) ....... | .00570 | .00580 | 175.57 | 172.27 |
| Britain (Pound) ......... | 1.8975 | 1.8960 | .5270 | .5274 |
| 30-Day Forward .... | 1.8870 | 1.8855 | .5299 | .5304 |
| 90-Day Forward .... | 1.8689 | 1.8683 | .5351 | .5352 |
| 180-Day Forward ... | 1.8448 | 1.8453 | .5421 | .5419 |
| Canada (Dollar) ....... | .8677 | .8678 | 1.1525 | 1.1523 |
| 30-Day Forward .... | .8645 | .8648 | 1.1568 | 1.1563 |
| 90-Day Forward .... | .8598 | .8599 | 1.1631 | 1.1629 |
| 180-Day Forward ... | .8525 | .8527 | 1.1730 | 1.1728 |
| Chile (Official rate) ... | .003060 | .003061 | 326.76 | 326.67 |
| China (Renminbi) ..... | .191205 | .191205 | 5.2300 | 5.2300 |
| Colombia (Peso) ...... | .001797 | .001799 | 556.35 | 555.86 |
| Denmark (Krone) ...... | .1688 | .1679 | 5.9244 | 5.9544 |
| Ecuador (Sucre) | | | | |
| Floating rate ......... | .001142 | .001142 | 876.00 | 876.00 |
| Finland (Markka) ...... | .27056 | .27005 | 3.6960 | 3.7030 |
| France (Franc) ........ | .19183 | .19099 | 5.2130 | 5.2360 |
| 30-Day Forward .... | .19154 | .19070 | 5.2208 | 5.2438 |
| 90-Day Forward .... | .19069 | .18986 | 5.2440 | 5.2670 |
| 180-Day Forward ... | .18929 | .18847 | 5.2830 | 5.3060 |
| Germany (Mark) ....... | .6504 | .6481 | 1.5375 | 1.5430 |
| 30-Day Forward .... | .6495 | .6473 | 1.5397 | 1.5449 |
| 90-Day Forward .... | .6472 | .6452 | 1.5450 | 1.5498 |
| 180-Day Forward ... | .6436 | .6419 | 1.5537 | 1.5578 |
| Greece (Drachma) .... | .006190 | .006179 | 161.55 | 161.85 |
| Hong Kong (Dollar) ... | .12823 | .12823 | 7.7985 | 7.7985 |
| India (Rupee) ........... | .05507 | .05507 | 18.16 | 18.16 |
| Indonesia (Rupiah) .... | .0005299 | .0005299 | 1887.01 | 1887.01 |
| Ireland (Punt) .......... | 1.7362 | 1.7355 | .5760 | .5762 |
| Israel (Shekel) .......... | .4962 | .4972 | 2.0153 | 2.0114 |
| Italy (Lira) .............. | .0008647 | .0008628 | 1156.51 | 1159.00 |
| Japan (Yen) ............. | .007302 | .007326 | 136.95 | 136.50 |
| 30-Day Forward .... | .007299 | .007323 | 137.01 | 136.55 |
| 90-Day Forward .... | .007291 | .007318 | 137.16 | 136.65 |
| 180-Day Forward .... | .007289 | .007319 | 137.19 | 136.64 |
| Jordan (Dinar) ......... | 1.4995 | 1.4995 | .6669 | .6669 |
| Kuwait (Dinar) ......... | z | z | z | z |
| Lebanon (Pound) ...... | .001146 | .001146 | 872.50 | 872.50 |
| Malaysia (Ringgit) .... | .3668 | .3673 | 2.7260 | 2.7225 |
| Malta (Lira) .............. | 3.3445 | 3.3445 | .2990 | .2990 |
| Mexico (Peso) | | | | |
| Floating rate ......... | .0003393 | .0003393 | 2947.00 | 2947.00 |
| Netherland (Guilder) .. | .5774 | .5752 | 1.7320 | 1.7385 |
| New Zealand (Dollar) . | .5901 | .5930 | 1.6946 | 1.6863 |
| Norway (Krone) ........ | .1662 | .1656 | 6.0166 | 6.0373 |
| Pakistan (Rupee) ...... | .0459 | .0459 | 21.80 | 21.80 |
| Peru (Inti) ............... | .00000190 | .00000190 | 524934.38 | 524934.38 |
| Philippines (Peso) ..... | .03676 | .03676 | 27.20 | 27.20 |
| Portugal (Escudo) ..... | .007297 | .007297 | 137.05 | 137.01 |
| Saudi Arabia (Riyal) .. | .26667 | .26667 | 3.7500 | 3.7500 |
| Singapore (Dollar) .... | .5682 | .5680 | 1.7600 | 1.7605 |
| South Africa (Rand) | | | | |
| Commercial rate .... | .3887 | .3870 | 2.5725 | 2.5843 |
| Financial rate ........ | .2946 | .2924 | 3.3950 | 3.4200 |
| South Korea (Won) .... | .0013996 | .0013996 | 714.50 | 714.50 |
| Spain (Peseta) ......... | .010320 | .010262 | 96.90 | 97.45 |
| Sweden (Krona) ........ | .1746 | .1742 | 5.7290 | 5.7390 |
| Switzerland (Franc) .. | .7743 | .7710 | 1.2915 | 1.2970 |
| 30-Day Forward .... | .7732 | .7701 | 1.2933 | 1.2986 |
| 90-Day Forward .... | .7716 | .7684 | 1.2960 | 1.3014 |
| 180-Day Forward .... | .7691 | .7663 | 1.3002 | 1.3050 |
| Taiwan (Dollar) ........ | .037502 | .037530 | 26.67 | 26.65 |
| Thailand (Baht) ........ | .03959 | .03959 | 25.26 | 25.26 |
| Turkey (Lira) ........... | .0003380 | .0003391 | 2959.00 | 2949.00 |
| United Arab (Dirham) . | .2723 | .2723 | 3.6725 | 3.6725 |
| Uruguay (New Peso) | | | | |
| Financial .............. | .000616 | .000616 | 1623.00 | 1623.00 |
| Venezuela (Bolivar) | | | | |
| Floating rate ......... | .01932 | .01912 | 51.76 | 52.30 |
| SDR ...................... | 1.41304 | 1.40727 | .70769 | .71060 |
| ECU ...................... | 1.34552 | 1.33462 | .... | .... |

Special Drawing Rights (SDR) are based on exchange rates for the U.S., German, British, French and Japanese currencies. Source: International Monetary Fund.

European Currency Unit (ECU) is based on a basket of community currencies. Source: European Community Commission.

z-Not quoted.

The exchange rates of currencies on the international market change daily in response to the forces of demand and supply. This newspaper clipping shows one day's values of various currencies in relation to the U.S. dollar.

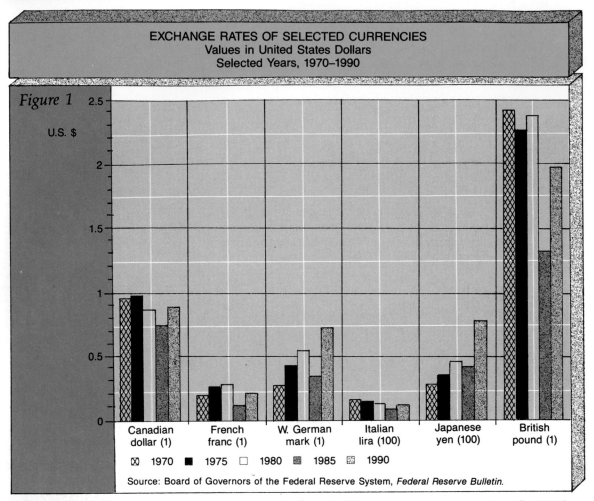

**EXCHANGE RATES OF SELECTED CURRENCIES**
Values in United States Dollars
Selected Years, 1970–1990

*Figure 1*

U.S. $

Canadian dollar (1) · French franc (1) · W. German mark (1) · Italian lira (100) · Japanese yen (100) · British pound (1)

⊠ 1970   ■ 1975   □ 1980   ▨ 1985   ▦ 1990

Source: Board of Governors of the Federal Reserve System, *Federal Reserve Bulletin*.

Since the system of fixed exchange rates was abandoned in the early 1970s, currency exchange rates have fluctuated widely. The exchange rates are dependent on foreign trade and investments.

**freely fluctuating exchange rates** an exchange-rate system by which the relative values of different currencies are determined by demand and supply rather than by government fiat.

**currency depreciation** a decline in the value of a country's currency relative to other currencies as a result of an increase in its supply relative to the demand for it.

The opposite of a fixed-rate system is one of freely fluctuating exchange rates that vary daily in response to demand and supply. With such rates, increased demand for a foreign money results in a rise in its price in terms of domestic currency. Conversely, increased supplies of a particular national currency depress its price. Such price changes increase the uncertainty and risk of international transactions.

If the supply of a country's currency in the foreign exchange market is greater than the demand for that currency, the currency will depreciate. Depreciation means that a unit of the country's currency will buy less of other currencies than it did previously. One common reason for currency depreciation is domestic inflation. If the general level of prices is going up faster in one country than in others, that country will find it difficult to export goods, while at the same time it will be importing more from overseas. This results in a surplus of the country's currency on the foreign exchange market, which lowers its exchange rate value. The opposite of depreciation is currency appreciation, an increase in the foreign value of currency.

Under a fixed exchange rate system, with exchange rates set by the government, a lowering of the exchange rate by government regulation is a devaluation. If the government raises the exchange rate of its currency under a fixed exchange rate system, that is termed revaluation.

Even under a freely fluctuating exchange rate system, government central banks may attempt to control exchange rate movements within limits or otherwise manipulate the rate. For example, if a country's currency is exchanging at such a high rate that it hurts exports, as was the case with the U.S. dollar in the mid-1980s, the central bank may lower the rate by selling its own currency on the foreign-exchange market. As the White Rabbit explained to Alice in the chapter introduction, the added supply floated on the market results in lowering the currency's exchange rate.

**currency appreciation**   an increase in the value of a country's currency relative to other currencies as a result of a decrease in its supply relative to the demand for it.
**devaluation**   a decrease in the value of a country's currency relative to other currencies due to an official government reduction in the exchange rate under a fixed rate system.
**revaluation**   an increase in the value of a country's currency relative to other currencies due to an official government increase in the exchange rate under a fixed rate system.

The imports that this ship brings to the United States are represented by the flow marked M on the GNP tank diagram on page 459. To continue the metaphor used in the text above, by floating more dollars a country can increase its exports.

# The Hunt for the Elusive Ecu

Have you ever seen an ecu? Before you answer, you should be warned that this is a trick question—no one has ever seen an ecu. But that does not mean they do not exist; they most assuredly do.

The ecu is the European Currency Unit. It was established in 1981 as the official unit of account (unit of measurement) for the European Economic Community. It was originally intended only to serve administrative purposes in defining the relationships among the various EC currencies. But the ecu proved so useful in financial markets that, by 1990, transactions in ecus reached an estimated value of ECU200 billion. This included mortgages, life-insurance policies, travelers' checks, certificates of deposit, corporate and government bonds, and even Visa and MasterCard payments, all denominated in ecus. The menu of Luxembourg's elegant La Gaichel restaurant goes so far as to list the prices of its dishes in ecus rather than Luxembourg francs.

The worth of an ecu is determined by a basket of the EC currencies, each one contributing a fraction of the ecu's value. The amount of each currency that goes into determining the value of the ecu is shown in Table 1.

Column 1 shows the ratio of the column 2 currency that is used in making up the ecu. To get the ecu value in any particular currency, say the U.S. dollar, the ratio of each currency in the basket is multiplied times its current dollar exchange rate, and the results are added. Column 3 shows the U.S. dollar exchange rate for the EC currencies on October 12, 1990. The ecu ratio in column 1 times the exchange rate in column 3 is shown in column 4. The sum of the ratios times the individual exchange rates gives the ecu/dollar exchange rate. On October 12, 1990, it was $1.36.

The values of the individual EC currencies are maintained at a fixed rate to the ecu, with a possible fluctuation of plus or minus 2.25%

*Table 1*       VALUE OF THE EUROPEAN CURRENCY UNIT
October 12, 1990

| ECU Ratio | Currency | $ Exchange Rate | ECU $ Value |
|---|---|---|---|
| 0.08784 | British pound | 1.972 | 0.1732 |
| 0.1976 | Danish krone | 0.1734 | 0.0343 |
| 1.332 | French franc | 0.1964 | 0.2616 |
| 1.440 | Greek drachma | 0.006547 | 0.0094 |
| 0.00852 | Irish pound | 1.766 | 0.0150 |
| 151.8 | Italian lira | 0.000878 | 0.1333 |
| 0.2198 | Dutch guilder | 0.5834 | 0.1282 |
| 0.6242 | Deutsche mark | 0.6562 | 0.4096 |
| 3.301 | Belgian franc | 0.0319 | 0.1053 |
| 0.130 | Luxembourg franc | 0.0319 | 0.0042 |
| 6.885 | Spanish peseta | 0.01046 | 0.0720 |
| 1.393 | Portuguese escudo | 0.00749 | 0.0104 |
| | Value of the ecu in U.S. dollars | | 1.3565 |

# case application

(plus or minus 6% for the Spanish peseta). If any currency deviates from its fixed ecu value by more than that, the EC central banks must intervene to bring the currency's value back to par. This helps to eliminate the uncertainty of exchange rate instability for EC businesses and investors.

The ecu has been useful as a unit of measurement for trade and investments among the EC countries. But with the coming of EC92 (chapter 15, p. 419) and the near total integration of their economies, there is discussion of the need for a common European currency—a unit of exchange. In the not-too-distant future you may actually see an ecu.

## Economic Reasoning

1. Why is the ecu ratio so much larger for the Italian lira than it is for the French franc? (Hint: compare their exchange rates.)
2. What could cause the peseta to depreciate more than 6%? What could the central banks do to bring it back to its ecu par value?
3. If a North American Common Market is established (chapter 15, p. 420), should the dollar be replaced by a nacu (North American Currency Unit)? Why or why not?

The stamp shown here presents a glimpse of the probable future of economic cooperation in Europe. When Italy issued this 500-lira stamp to commemorate the elections for the 12-member European Parliament in 1989, it printed the stamp's equivalent value in ecus. Europe does not yet have a single currency, and thus ecus are still a technical measure rather than a spendable currency. Still, the European Community is working toward monetary union, and the ecu may well soon supplement, or even supplant, the British pound, German mark, French franc, and other national currencies.

# What Happens When Exports and Imports Do Not Balance?

Under a system of freely fluctuating exchange rates, the exchange rate for a currency is determined by the demand for and supply of that currency in the foreign-exchange market. If a country's international transactions are out of balance, the exchange rate for the country's currency will be unstable.

**Balance of payments**   The accounting record of all international transactions between the residents of one country and the residents of the rest of the world is the country's balance of payments. When a country imports something, the cost shows up in its balance of payments. Similarly, when a country exports something, the receipts from the sale are recorded in the balance of payments.

The balance of payments is divided into different types of transactions. The imports and exports of goods and services are recorded in the current account section of the balance of payments. Take, for example, the importation of French cheese. This is a merchandise import in the current account section. The difference between merchandise imports and merchandise exports is the balance of trade. If merchandise exports during the year are greater than merchandise imports, the balance of trade is said to be favorable. If imports are greater than exports, the balance of trade is said to be unfavorable.

But the current account includes more than just merchandise trade. It also includes services. One major type of service "import" is foreign travel. If the French cheese had been consumed by an American tourist in a Paris cafe, the effect on the U.S. balance of payments would have been the same as if it had been imported. The consumption of the cheese gave rise to a foreign claim on American dollars, which in this case would presumably have to be paid before the tourist left the cafe.

Military assistance, foreign aid, government remittances, and private gifts are special types of current transactions for which there may be no actual material import. The "import" may be national security or goodwill. But note the basic rule: If it results in a money outflow, it is an import-type transaction. Profits, dividends, and interest earned by Americans on foreign assets are export-type transactions. What is exported is the use of American capital.

**International capital flows**   At the time when capital is transferred abroad, it appears in the balance of payments in the long-term or short-term capital accounts. The long-term capital account summarizes the flow of public and private

**balance of payments** an annual summary of all economic transactions between a country and the rest of the world during the year.

**current account**  those transactions in the balance of payments consisting of merchandise and service imports and exports and unilateral transfers (gifts).

**balance of trade**  the net deficit or surplus in a country's merchandise trade; the difference between merchandise imports and exports.

**favorable balance of trade**  the surplus in a country's merchandise trade when exports during the year are greater than imports.

**unfavorable balance of trade**  the deficit in a country's merchandise trade when imports during the year are greater than exports.

**long-term capital**  direct investment in plant and equipment or portfolio investments in stocks and bonds.

**short-term capital**  transfers of demand deposits or liquid investments such as money market funds, CDs, or Treasury bills.

investment into and out of the country. This includes only those new investments undertaken during the year. If an American firm builds a plant abroad or if an individual buys stock in a foreign company, these are import-type transactions.

The short-term capital account consists of liquid funds transferred from one country to another, such as transfers of bank deposits. The greater part of this type of transfer consists of money payments for merchandise, service, and investment transactions. The purchase of English woolens in the example on page 448 constituted an import entry in the U.S. current account. Then when the U.S. importer paid the British exporter by transferring funds to the exporter from an account at the Midlands Bank in London, an export-type entry in the U.S. short-term capital account occurred. The two entries offset each other in the balance of payments.

In the sense that for every transaction there is an import or export on one side of the balance of payments and an offsetting transfer of the payment on the other side, the balance of payments always balances. What, then, is meant by a deficit or a surplus in the balance of payments? The current account transactions, the long-term capital account transactions, and certain short-term capital account transactions, such as foreigners investing in U.S. money market funds, are considered spontaneous transactions motivated by market conditions. If a country's total import-type payments are greater than its total export-type receipts for these transactions, the difference is the country's basic deficit. It is this deficit that we read about in the newspapers.

The balance of payments system has two means to offset a basic deficit and bring the accounts into balance. Either foreigners can, in effect, extend credit to the deficit country by holding larger amounts of the country's currency, which are in the nature of IOUs, or the deficit can be covered by an export of gold. Short-term capital and gold movements constitute the residual accounts that bring the balance of payments into balance. If the deficit country does not have gold to export and foreigners are not willing to accept more of its money, it can turn to the International Monetary Fund for a loan to temporarily solve its balance of payments problem while it attempts to eliminate its basic deficit.

Under a freely fluctuating exchange rate system, the existence of a basic deficit results in a depreciation of the country's currency. An excess of imports over exports results in more of the country's currency going into the foreign exchange market than is demanded. As a result of the excess supply, the exchange rate falls. The lower exchange rate helps to eliminate the basic deficit by increasing exports and decreasing imports.

**basic deficit** the excess of import-type transactions over export-type transactions in a country's current, long-term capital and noninduced, short-term capital movements in the balance of payments.

**residual accounts** the short-term capital transfers and monetary gold transactions that compensate for the imbalance in a country's basic balance in its international payments.

# case application

## The World's Biggest Debtor

Very large foreign debts have been piled up in recent years by countries such as Brazil, Mexico, and Argentina. But in 1986 the United States became the biggest debtor of all. Its net foreign indebtedness—the amount owed to foreigners minus the amount owed by foreigners—reached $268 billion. The foreign debt continued to grow rapidly and by 1989 exceeded $600 billion. At that rate, it will pass $1 trillion in the early 1990s. The foreign earnings on that debt may reach 2% of the United States GNP.

It was only in 1985 that the United States became a net debtor for the first time since 1914. During all the intervening years, as befits a prosperous, capital-rich nation, the country had lent abroad much more than it borrowed. Countries in need of more investment capital than they could muster from their domestic sources borrowed from the United States in various ways. There was private capital flow to other countries in the form of direct investment by U.S. companies in foreign subsidiaries. There was additional private lending by purchases of foreign stocks and bonds and by commercial bank loans to foreign firms or governments. Besides these private capital flows, there was U.S. government lending to less-developed countries both directly and channeled through international lending agencies.

In 1982, however, the positive net foreign asset position of the United States began to decline as a result of rising foreign investment in this country relative to U.S. investment abroad. Up to 1985 the total amount of foreign assets held by U.S. residents was greater than the total claims by foreigners against the assets of this country. Since then the United States has had an increasing net foreign debt (see Figure 2 on the opposite page). The reasons were the large balance of trade deficits run up by the United States and the attractiveness of U.S. securities to foreign investors.

These two causes were related. The low savings rate in the United States resulted in a high propensity to consume, including the consumption of imported goods. This resulted in growing trade deficits. The low savings rate and large government budget deficits also meant high interest rates, which made U.S. securities attractive to foreign investors. The United States has long been a desirable place for foreigners to invest their funds because of its political stability.

In a sense, then, the increasing foreign debt of the U.S. was due in part to the strength of its economy rather than its weakness—foreigners wanted to invest here because returns were greater and more secure. For the United States, the inflow of foreign capital was very useful in helping to finance its record federal budget deficits, compensating for the low savings rate of the U.S. population. Foreigners increased their holdings of U.S. Treasury securities by $114.8 billion between 1984 and 1988—thus financing over 15% of our federal government deficits during those years.

Nevertheless, it created an uneasy situation because foreign funds can be withdrawn very rapidly if the outlook changes. If there were a flight of capital from the country, the international value of the dollar would come tumbling down, and a shortage of domestic capital would make it difficult for the government and businesses to raise money, driving

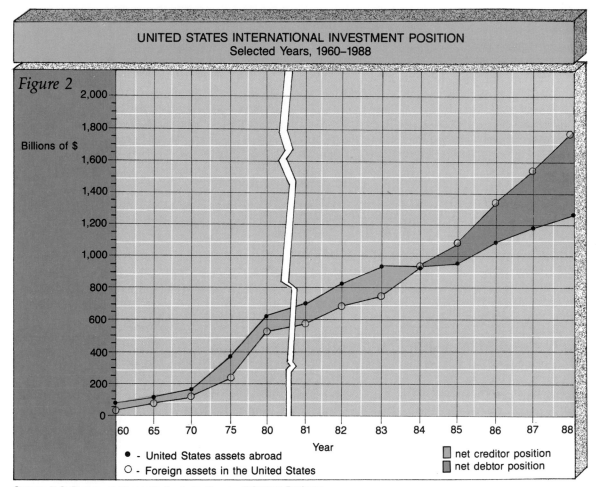

*Figure 2*

**UNITED STATES INTERNATIONAL INVESTMENT POSITION**
Selected Years, 1960–1988

Billions of $

- ● - United States assets abroad
- ○ - Foreign assets in the United States

□ net creditor position
■ net debtor position

Source: U.S. Bureau of Economic Analysis, *Survey of Current Business*.

Between 1914 and 1985 the United States was a net creditor with respect to the rest of the world (green shaded area). Since then it has had a rapidly increasing net foreign debt (red shaded area).

interest rates higher. The danger of that happening became more apparent when the crisis in the Middle East caused foreign capital to flow out of the country, rather than flowing in as was customary in previous world crises. With its large government and foreign deficits and the deteriorating value of the dollar, the United States no longer appeared to be the safe haven for world capital that it had been in the past.

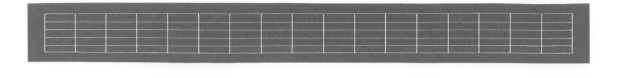

*Table 2*   SIMPLIFIED HYPOTHETICAL BALANCE OF PAYMENTS FOR COUNTRY A
FOR A GIVEN YEAR (BILLIONS OF DOLLARS)

| Credit Items | | Debit Items | |
|---|---|---|---|
| **(Foreign earnings by Country A)** | | **(Liabilities of Country A to Foreigners)** | |
| Current Account | | Current Account | |
| Exports of merchandise | $224 | Imports of merchandise | $249 |
| Tourist expenditures in Country A | 22 | Country A tourist expenditures abroad | 30 |
| Earnings from investments abroad | 75 | Earnings by foreign investments in Country A | 33 |
| Military & economic aid from abroad | 0 | Military & economic aid to other countries | 17 |
| Capital Account | | Capital Account | |
| New foreign investments in Country A | 20 | New investments by Country A abroad | 45 |
| Basic Balance Total | $341 | Basic Balance Total | $374 |

**Basic deficit ($374 – $341) = $33**

| | | | |
|---|---|---|---|
| Residual Account | | | |
| New bank deposits by foreigners in Country A | $30 | | |
| Gold exports | 1 | | |
| International Monetary Fund loan | 2 | | |
| Balancing Items Total | $33 | | |
| Balance of Payments Total | $374 | Balance of Payments Total | $374 |

*Economic Reasoning*

1. How do foreign investments in the United States affect the U.S. balance of payments? If Table 2 above was the balance of payments statement for the United States, in what account would the sales of Treasury securities to foreign buyers appear?

2. How will the earnings of foreigners on their U.S. investments affect the exchange rate of the dollar in the future? Why?

3. Is it a good thing to have foreigners finance part of our federal budget deficits? Why or why not?

# What Is the Relationship Between International Finance and the National Economy?

In chapter 12 we examined the conditions of national economic equilibrium when considering the domestic sectors of the economy. In this analysis section we will see how the foreign sector affects it.

**The foreign sector in the national economy**   In discussing gross national product (chapter 12, p. 333), we noted that aggregate demand was the sum of consumer demand (C), investment demand (I), government demand (G), and net foreign demand (X – M). The first three sectors were included in the GNP tank model in chapter 12 showing domestic equilibrium. Figure 3 adds the foreign sector (pictured in orange) to the three domestic sectors of the economy in the GNP tank diagram.

*Figure 3*

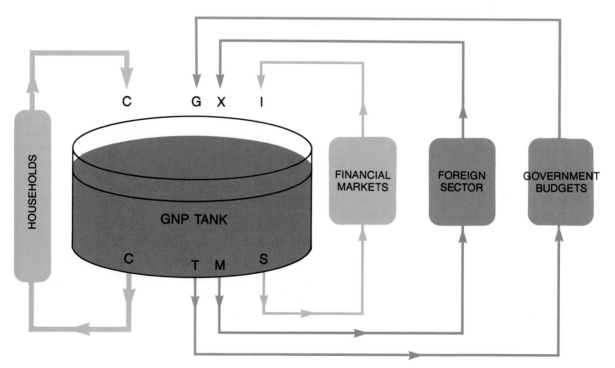

GNP TANK NATIONAL INCOME MODEL
INCLUDING THE FOREIGN SECTOR

Economic equilibrium requires that the allocations of GNP income to savings (S), taxes (T), and imports (M) be equal to the purchasing power flowing back into the economy from investment (I), government spending (G), and exports (X). In the United States in recent years, the amount of savings and taxes has been less than investment and government spending (S + T < I + G). The difference has been compensated by an excess of imports over exports (M > X) so that savings, taxes, and imports together equal the total of investment, government spending, and exports (S + T + M = I + G + X).

The amount of income that consumers and businesses allocate to imports, indicated by M, flows out of the tank into the foreign sector. The expenditures by foreigners on U.S. exports flow from the foreign sector into the GNP tank as demand for goods and services, shown by X. As was the case with the investment and government sectors, the amount of purchasing power flowing out of the economy for imports is not necessarily the same as the amount of purchasing power flowing into the economy for export purchases.

If the balance of trade is unfavorable, as it has been for the United States in recent years, there are more dollars flowing out of the economy into the foreign sector in payment for imports than there are flowing into the economy from the foreign sector in payment for exports. The excess dollars accumulated by foreigners could be held as deposit balances in U.S. banks. Or they could be used to buy monetary gold. But most of the excess dollars from the foreign sector have been used for capital investment in the United States. They have been used to buy securities, both government and private, and to purchase or create real assets such as office buildings, chemical plants, and automobile factories.

**The foreign sector and national economic equilibrium**   The economy is in equilibrium when aggregate demand equals aggregate supply (review the discussion of equilibrium output in chapter 12, pp. 342–345). Considering only the domestic sectors, the U.S. economy has not been in equilibrium for some time. Saving has been less than investment and taxes have been less than government spending. As a result, the amount of funds flowing into the investment and government sectors has been less than the amounts flowing from those sectors into the demand for goods and services.

The difference between the amounts allocated to savings and taxes and the total of investment and government spending ($S + T < I + G$) has been made up by an excess of imports over exports ($M > X$). In other words, the U.S. import surplus has compensated for the deficiency in our savings and taxes. This results in savings, taxes, and imports equaling investment, government spending, and exports ($S + T + M = I + G + X$). Since aggregate demand ($I + G + X$) equals aggregate supply ($S + T + M$), the national economy is in equilibrium.

The United States has been living beyond its means, consuming and investing more than it has been producing. But the foreign sector has balanced the domestic sectors. Foreigners made it possible for aggregate demand to exceed aggregate supply in the domestic sectors by sending us more goods and services than we send them and lending the accumulated dollars back to us to finance our deficits.

## FOREIGN SECTOR FINANCING
## OF UNITED STATES DOMESTIC DEFICITS

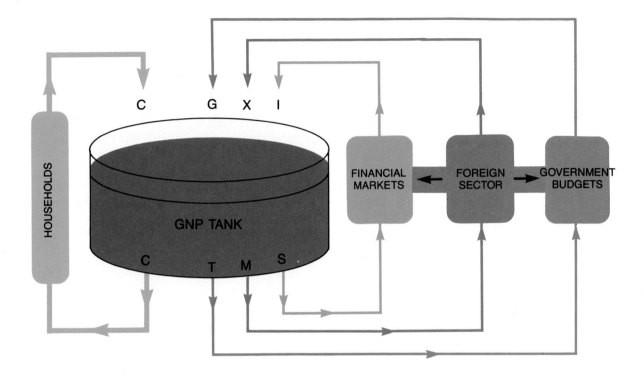

There is more income going to the foreign sector from imports (M) than is being returned to the economy in export demand (X). The excess dollars in the foreign sector (orange) are invested in U.S. private financial markets (green) and U.S. Treasury securities (red). The import surplus has permitted the economy to consume (including I and G) more than it produces. It also has been the source of foreign capital to finance domestic deficits.

This process is shown in Figure 4. A portion of the funds flowing out of the economy in payments for imports (the M outflow from the bottom of the tank) are channeled from the foreign sector into U.S. financial markets (the green sector) and into financing government deficits (red). The flow to the private sector consists of both portfolio investments in corporate stocks and bonds and direct investments in new plant and equipment, as well as the acquisition of existing companies and other real assets. The flow into the government sector consists principally of the purchase of U.S. Treasury securities.

These investments compensated for the imbalance in aggregate demand and supply in the domestic sectors of the economy. The import surpluses gave rise to dollar balances in the hands of foreigners. When those dollars were invested they paid for our excess domestic spending. The American banking system can create money to finance investments and fund government deficits, as we discovered in chapter 10 (p. 278). But the banking system cannot provide the economy with additional resources and products that allow us to consume (including I and G) more than we produce. Only the foreign sector can do that.

Although the Queen of Hearts in the introductory story wanted to make war on the Land of the Rising Sun for not buying as much from us as it sold to us, the fact is that it was only by means of our import surplus that we had the level of consumption, investment, and government spending that we did in the 1980s. Of course, we will have to pay the piper for our dance in the 1980s in the form of future interest and dividends on the foreign debt. Unless we continue increasing our foreign debt indefinitely, which the rest of the world will not permit, this will mean consuming less than we produce in the future.

*Table 3*   FOREIGN DIRECT INVESTMENTS IN
THE UNITED STATES BY COUNTRY
1988

| Country | Total Investments ($ millions) |
|---------|-------------------------------|
| United Kingdom | 101,909 |
| Japan | 53,354 |
| Netherlands | 48,991 |
| Canada | 27,363 |
| West Germany | 23,845 |
| Switzerland | 15,896 |

Foreign direct investments in the United States played an important role in compensating for the domestic deficits of the 1980s. The influence that these foreign investments have on the U.S. economy is discussed in the following Case Application.

## Selling America

Rockefeller Center in New York bears the name of one of the most powerful financial dynasties in American history. But there is now a different name on the ownership papers—Mitsubishi Estate Co. Mitsubishi owns the controlling interest in Rockefeller Center. Mamma Leone's restaurant, a well-known New York tourist spot, now belongs to Kyotaru Co., a Japanese restaurant company.

These, along with such purchases as Columbia Pictures, San Francisco's Mark Hopkins Hotel, and exclusive Beverly Hills real estate, are some recent Japanese acquisitions that have made news. Less newsworthy but more important are sizeable foreign investments in such basic industries as chemicals; glass, stone, and clay; primary metals; printing and publishing; and electrical machinery. Foreign ownership of these industries ranges from 12% of the electrical machinery industry to 32% of the chemical industry.

Of particular concern is the current movement of foreign capital, mainly Japanese, into U.S. high-tech acquisitions. Hitachi purchased 80% of National Advanced Systems, manufacturers of mainframe computers, for $309 million; Canon acquired a 16.7% interest in NEXT (computer work stations) for $100 million; and TDK took over all of disk drive chip producer Silicon Systems for $200 million.

Although the focus of attention has been on Japanese acquisition of American companies and property, Japan is only in second place as a foreign owner of U.S. assets. It trails far behind investments from the United Kingdom (see Table 3, opposite).

The rising foreign ownership of United States assets has alarmed many Americans. Do foreigners have too much power over our economy? Can they use their ownership of American business to injure the country? Are we losing control of our destiny?

For the most part, these fears are groundless. The government can always intervene if there is any hostile intent. However, there is a danger of another sort. It does not arise because of any ill intentions on the part of foreign investors, but only out of self-protection on their part. If there should appear to be further sizeable depreciation of the dollar coming, that might cause a flight of capital out of the United States to avoid future exchange losses. Or if there should be a serious recession abroad and a drop in the value of Japanese domestic investments in real estate and the Tokyo stock market, it might force Japanese investors to pull their funds out of U.S. investments. If there were a sizeable withdrawal of foreign investment from the United States, it would cause a drop in the value of the dollar and a sharp rise in U.S. interest rates. The danger of foreign investments in the United States is not that they are here, but that they could suddenly be withdrawn.

### Economic Reasoning

1. Referring to Figure 4, where did the funds come from for the Mitsubishi purchase of Rockefeller Center and the Kyotaru purchase of Mamma Leone's?
2. If foreign investment is withdrawn from the United States, what compensating change or changes must there be in the domestic sectors of the economy? Show the changes on a schematic GNP tank diagram.
3. Should the United States restrict foreigners from acquiring assets in this country such as businesses, real estate, and financial securities? Why or why not?

The Cheshire Cat was smiling at the contradictions in our attitudes and policies with regard to international trade and finance. These contradictions partly are inherent in the problems posed by the foreign sector of the economy. But they are also in part the result of a lack of understanding of how the international financial system works and how it impacts the national economy.

# Putting It Together

Payments for international transactions are made through the *foreign-exchange market*, which consists mainly of major banks in the financial capitals of the world, plus some other foreign exchange dealers and brokers. *Correspondent banks*, which possess deposit accounts in banks overseas, facilitate the purchase of foreign exchange.

Under the *freely fluctuating exchange rate system* currently in existence, the exchange rate for a country's currency is determined by the demand for and supply of the country's currency in the foreign-exchange market. An increase in the supply of a country's currency on the exchange market will cause the currency to depreciate in value. An increase in the value of a country's currency is called *appreciation*; a decrease is called *depreciation*. Under a system of *fixed exchange rates*, governments set the rates of exchange for their currencies. If the government lowers the international value of its currency, it is *devaluation*; raising the value is *revaluation*.

The summation of foreign transactions of a country is its *balance of payments*. The net of merchandise imports and exports is the *balance of trade*. If exports are larger than imports, the balance of trade is said to be *favorable*; if imports are larger, it is *unfavorable*.

In addition to merchandise exports and imports, the balance of payments includes service exports and imports in the *current account*, foreign investments in the *long-term capital* account, and short-term capital movements and monetary gold in the *residual accounts*. When receipts from abroad in the current and long-term capital accounts are less than foreign spending, there is a *basic deficit*. This basic deficit is covered by a short-term capital inflow or gold exports so that the balance of payments balances.

Export demand added to consumption, investment, and government demand makes up aggregate demand for the nation's output. If imports exceed exports, the excess dollars in the foreign sector are used to finance foreign investments in the United States.

The economy is in equilibrium when aggregate demand equals aggregate supply. Since demand in U.S. domestic sectors has been greater than supply, the foreign sector made up the difference. Imports have been greater than exports, offsetting the deficiency in savings and taxes and making $S + T + M$ equal to $I + G + X$. The foreign sector has provided the additional resources and products that have allowed the United States to consume more than it produced. The excess dollars in the foreign sector have been channeled into investments and the purchase of U.S. Treasury securities.

# Perspective

## Bring Back Gold?

For additional information on the gold standard, see *The International Gold Standard Re-interpreted* (1940) by W. A. Brown, Jr., *The Downfall of the Gold Standard* (1936) by C. G. Cassel, *Gold or Credit* (1965) by Francis Cassel, *The Gold Standard in Theory and Practice* (1947) by Sir R. G. Hautrey, *Gold and the Gold Standard* (1944) by E. W. Kemmerer, *Gold and the Dollar Crisis* (1961) by Robert Triffin, *The Rise and Fall of the Gold Standard* (1934) by Sir C. M. Webb, and *A Tool of Power: The Political History of Money* (1977) by W. Wiseley.

The extreme fluctuations of currency values under the system of freely fluctuating exchange rates (see Figure 1, p. 450) has given rise to calls for a return to the gold standard. Under the gold standard, which was in effect from the 1830s to the 1930s and in a modified form in the United States up to 1971, the value of a currency was defined by how much gold it was worth. The U.S. government specified the value of the dollar at $35 per ounce of gold. It maintained this value of the dollar by offering to both buy and sell gold at that price, thereby assuring that the value of the dollar would be stable with respect to gold and other gold standard currencies.

Those advocating a return to the gold standard believe that it would stabilize exchange rates and prevent a return of inflation by imposing a monetary discipline on our government that the current paper money standard does not. If a country were to permit inflation, its imports would exceed its exports and the surplus of its currency on the foreign exchange market would be used by foreigners to buy its gold. The resulting drain on its gold reserves would force the government to reduce the domestic money supply and stop the inflation.

The problem with the gold standard when it was in effect was that it made the domestic economy a slave to what happened abroad. If, for example, other countries were in a recession, exports to those countries would fall. This resulted in an outflow of gold to cover the difference between export earnings and import spending. Following the "rules of the game" for the gold standard, the government would permit the outflow of gold to deflate the domestic economy. In this way, recessions would be "imported." That is basically why the world-wide depression in the 1930s put an end to the international gold standard.

After the depression, the United States continued to value its currency in gold, but restricted its sales of gold only to official transactions, not to private gold dealers. Other countries valued their currencies either in terms of the dollar or the British pound. In 1971, with the foreign trade deficit threatening to deplete its gold supply, the United States first devalued the dollar and later abandoned any ties to gold, setting the U.S. dollar free to fluctuate according to demand and supply in the foreign exchange market.

For those who today advocate a return to the gold standard, it should be noted that during the time that the gold standard was previously in effect there were periods that were highly inflationary as well as periods of severe depression.

For
Further
Study
and
Analysis

## Study Questions

1. Assuming that the price of the Swiss franc is 80 cents (U.S.), if there is a large increase in the demand for Swiss watches in this country, what would you expect to happen to the franc-dollar exchange rate under a system of freely fluctuating exchange rates?

2. How does inflation affect the international value of a country's currency? Does it cause the currency to appreciate or depreciate?

3. Why does a rise in U.S. interest rates affect the foreign exchange rate of the dollar? Would it cause the dollar to appreciate or depreciate?

4. In what sense is an export surplus favorable to the exporting country? In what way might an export surplus not be favorable?

5. If a Japanese investor redeems (cashes in) a U.S. Treasury bond, is that an export-type transaction in the U.S. balance of payments or an import-type transaction? How can you tell?

6. Can a country have a surplus in its balance of trade and at the same time have a basic deficit in its balance of payments? How?

7. What determines the amount of income that consumers allocate to imports? What determines the level of exports?

8. If foreigners reduced their investments in the United States, how would this be shown in the GNP tank diagram? What effect would it have on exports and/or imports? Why?

9. Why do dollars earned by foreign exporters always return to (or never leave) the United States?

10. Under the gold standard, if the U.S. dollar was valued at $35 per ounce of gold and the French franc was 700 francs per ounce of gold, what was the exchange rate between the dollar and the franc?

## Exercises in Analysis

1. Call or visit a local bank and ask if they sell bank drafts drawn in French francs. Ask what exchange rate they give. Compare the exchange rate quoted by the bank with the exchange rate listed for French francs in the *Wall Street Journal* or the business section of your newspaper. Put the information you gathered in a report along with your explanation of the difference, if any, in the exchange rate

quoted by your bank and the exchange rate listed in the paper.

2. Do a report on what has happened to the foreign exchange rate of the dollar since 1990. If the exchange rate has gone up or down since then, explain why.

3. From the most recent Economic Report of the President or other sources, find the U.S. balance of payments for the last year

reported. Write a brief analysis of the balance of trade position and the balance of payments position of the United States.

4. Make a report on the current equilibrium position of the U.S. economy. Show what has happened to the investment, government, and foreign sectors. Illustrate with a schematic GNP tank diagram.

## Further Reading

Aliber, Robert Z. *The International Money Game* (5th edition). New York: Basic Books, 1987. A lively treatment of the world monetary system, including discussions of the gold standard, the effects of OPEC money, multinational corporations, the rise of Japan as an international economic power, and monetary reform.

Bergsten, C. Fred. *America in the World Economy: A Strategy for the 1990s.* Washington D.C.: Institute for International Economics, 1988. Discusses how the current account deficit can be eliminated, domestic politics in trade policy, foreign direct investment in the United States, and international monetary reform, among other topics.

Blake, David H., and Robert S. Walters. *The Politics of Global Economic Relations* (3rd edition). Englewood Cliffs, N.J.: Prentice Hall, 1987. An examination of international trade and monetary issues in their political context.

Edwards, Richard W., Jr., *International Monetary Collaboration.* Dobbs Ferry, N.Y.: Transnational Publishers, 1985. Thoroughly explains the operations of international financial institutions and how the international payments and debt settlement system works.

Frieden, Jeffry A. *Banking on the World: The Politics of American International Finance.* New York: Harper & Row, 1987. "International finance is the pivot around which the world economy twists and turns, and it affects politics and economics in every nation" (p. 1). Discusses the effects of foreign borrowing,

the future of international finance, and its effect on American politics.

Gilbert, Milton, *Quest for World Monetary Order: The Gold-Dollar System and Its Aftermath.* New York: John Wiley & Sons, 1980. A study of the international monetary system and balance of payments adjustment under the gold standard and with the dollar serving as the key currency, the monetary reforms of the 1970s, and the experience under a floating exchange rate system.

Kindleberger, Charles P. *The International Economic Order.* Cambridge, Mass.: MIT Press, 1988. Part I of the book contains essays on the international capital and foreign-exchange markets. The author discusses distress in international financial markets and whether there is going to be a global depression. Contained in Part II are essays on the European Community, economic development, and international public goods.

Rosow, Jerome M., ed. *The Global Marketplace.* New York: Facts on File, 1988. A collection of essays by chief executives of corporations engaged in international trade and finance.

Tolchin, Martin, and Susan Tolchin. *Buying Into America: How Foreign Money Is Changing the Face of Our Nation.* New York: Times Books, 1988. Examines the effects, both positive and negative, of foreign investment in the United States. Specific cases are studied to show the changes resulting from foreign investment.

## chapter 17

# ALTERNATIVE ECONOMIC SYSTEMS

*Market economies such as that of the United States have a lot of problems to deal with, as we have seen in the preceding chapters. Those problems, however, are eclipsed by the problems that have beset some other systems. The economy of the Soviet Union is practically a basket case. This introductory article to the chapter looks at its problems and the program for rescuing it.*

## Revolution from Above

The Soviet Union, which had the most influential revolution in the twentieth century, is undergoing another. The first one, the Bolshevik revolution of 1917, led to the establishment of the ultimate in centrally planned economies. Under the Soviet system, virtually all decisions regarding what, how, and for whom to produce were decided by the central government authorities. Highest in priority of production were heavy industry, defense, and total output, while consumer goods and services were ranked low on the scale of priorities for resource use.

Not until the early 1970s was growth in the production of consumer goods designed to exceed growth in producer goods. This switch in emphasis took place because the increase in the size and complexity of the Soviet economy created problems for planning authorities. There were constant shortages of raw materials and semi-finished products that made it difficult for plants to meet their production targets.

Productivity was low. Among Soviet workers, not known for their industriousness, there is little sense of a work ethic, little effort to produce quality, little initiative. According to Leonid Abalkin, director of the Soviet Institute of the Economy, "People have become accustomed to working at a pace that isn't too demanding." Furthermore, the system of traded favors and outright bribes pervading Soviet society created a cynical populace. Employees often use work time for personal business.

The growth rate of the Soviet economy, which had been exceptionally high during the period of industrialization, fell from over 5% per year in the 1950s to near 2% per year in the 1980s. As the traditional sources of Soviet growth—increases in the quantities of labor and capital—became more scarce, the Soviets tried to compensate for this loss by increasing workers' purchasing power. It was hoped that this would motivate the workers to higher productivity. However, their income was increased much more than the availability of goods and services. As a result, long lines formed at stores to buy everything from meat to soap.

The slowdown in economic growth, increasing shortages, and rising disaffection of the population produced irresistible pressures for change. Mikhail S. Gorbachev became the Soviet Union head of state in 1985 and initiated new reforms. These reforms were characterized as *glasnost* (openness) and *perestroika* (restructuring). Under *glasnost*

This Soviet automobile factory worker waits for the assembly line to resume. It has stopped because of a lack of parts.

However, *perestroika,* as an attempt to restructure the economic system by providing production incentives and eliminating bureaucratic inefficiency, was less successful. While the Soviet people were highly dissatisfied with the existing economic situation, they feared radical change. Workers did not want to give up government subsidies of food prices, cheap rents, or job security. They preferred the long lines for buying scarce items to the alternative of sharp price increases that would make the items unaffordable.

A prominent Soviet historian and writer, Nathan Eidelman, has said about *perestroika,* "Frankly, it's a revolution from above. Naturally, it stimulates movement at the grass roots level, without which there would never be success, but still, it's a revolution from above. . . . During a revolution from above, society is often more conservative than the governing forces."

At first, *perestroika* was proposed as a gradual transition to a socialist market economy. It was conceived of as a compromise between a centrally directed and a market system. It was termed a "regulated market economy." Individual enterprises would be given the freedom and responsibility to decide what and how to produce. The market would decide which firms would expand and which would decline or go out of production. Private enterprise would be encouraged in the service and light production sectors by liberalizing the rules regulating cooperatives. However, large enterprises and natural resources would remain in the hands of the central government, with the state still controlling 40% of production. Those economic activities most important to the state would still be controlled by the central authorities. Those included the structure of industry, the exploitation of natural resources, the rate of savings and investment, the balance of payments.

By 1990 it was obvious that the gradual, limited transition was not working. Shortages worsened, extending to goods that had not previously been in short supply—matches, salt,

individuals and the media were free to criticize the system, and the government was more forthcoming with information. These were dramatic changes from the repression and secretiveness that existed previously. The Soviet people embraced their new freedoms enthusiastically, and there was an explosion of political activism.

vegetable oil, tea, mayonnaise, even toilet paper. Inflation increased from a rate of 4% in 1987 when *perestroika* was introduced to over 10% in 1990. The value of the Russian ruble, which had an official exchange rate of $1.67, fell to as little as $0.04 on the currency black market. The government deficit soared to over 100 billion rubles, equal to 11–12% of Soviet GNP (compared to a U.S. government deficit, including off-budget spending, equaling 4–5% of GNP). The country's infrastructure, such as roads and buildings, deteriorated even further below its already substandard level, as did its factories.

Radical reformers, led by Gorbachev's chief political rival, Boris Yeltsin, and including a number of economists, called for the abandonment of halfway measures. They urged rapid introduction of free market pricing in all sectors of economic activity, private ownership of all production facilities, and the immediate removal of all power from the central control authorities. They claimed that bureaucrats in the ministries and other government agencies were sabotaging *perestroika* because it would end their privileged positions.

During August 1990 a team of 13 economists met in nonstop sessions at a secluded house in the woods outside Moscow to work out a plan for rapid conversion to a market economy. Twice they adjourned to meet with Yeltsin and three times for meetings with Gorbachev. They came up with a 500-day plan for reforming the economy. It called for the government to auction off collective farms and state lands to farm workers, dispose of large government enterprises by selling shares to the workers for a nominal price, establish a central banking system modeled on the U.S. Federal Reserve, end restrictions on internal migration to enable workers to seek jobs wherever available, and allow nearly all prices to be set by demand and supply.

In a meeting that lasted six hours, the economists convinced Gorbachev to accept their radical plan. The plan, however, met with strong opposition from conservatives in the central government, and Gorbachev backed away from it. However, it was adopted by the Congress of People's Deputies of the Russian Republic, largest by far of the 15 republics that make up the Soviet Union. The Russian Republic contains three-quarters of the land area of the U.S.S.R., half of the total population, and produces two-thirds of the GNP. In 1990, Yeltsin, an advocate of independence for the Russian Republic, was elected president of the republic. Russia and the other Soviet republics are asserting their sovereignty and putting pressure on the central government to move faster in reforming the economy.

## Chapter Preview

*As we saw in chapter 2, an economic system is a set of arrangements by which a society answers the basic economic questions—what shall be produced, how, and for whom. Dramatic changes in their economic systems have recently been undertaken by the Soviet Union and Eastern European countries. Those changes form the background for examining the following questions:* What are the alternatives to capitalism? How do alternative economic systems resolve the basic economic questions? How does the performance of alternative economic systems compare?

## Learning Objectives

*After completing this chapter, you should be able to:*

1. *Explain the distinctions between capitalism, state socialism, market socialism, and the welfare state.*
2. *Compare the way in which a system of state socialism answers the basic economic questions of what, how, and for whom to produce with the way a market system answers those questions.*
3. *Evaluate the relative performance of state socialist and market economies in terms of each of the following: efficiency, price stability, unemployment, and growth.*
4. *Compare the alternative economic systems in how well they achieve socioeconomic goals.*

471

# What Are the Alternatives to Capitalism?

In the preceding chapters we have examined how capitalistic systems work, that of the United States in particular. In this section of the chapter we will examine the alternatives to capitalism.

**State socialism** From 1929, when the U.S.S.R. undertook total central planning and forced collectivization of agriculture, the Soviet Union installed the first system of state socialism in the modern world. The Soviet system was most commonly referred to as communism. It was not, however, true communism as envisioned by Karl Marx (Perspective, p. 495). Marx proposed communism as the system that would result after a "withering away" of the state. Then workers would have direct control of the means of production. He saw state socialism as a stage in the transition from feudalism and capitalism to communism, a transition which the U.S.S.R. never completed and showed no signs of ever completing.

Under state socialism, sometimes called authoritarian socialism, the government owns the means of production—the factories, stores, farms, and natural resources. Economic decisions are centrally directed by government planning authorities.

As noted in chapter 3, all real-world economies are to some extent mixed systems. In the U.S.S.R. a small amount of private enterprise was allowed, notably in the private plots of land allocated to some farmers. When the farmers were not working at their regular jobs on the government

**capitalism** an economic system based on the right of private ownership of most of the means of production, such as businesses, farms, mines, and natural resources, as well as private property, such as homes and automobiles.

**central planning** a method of resource allocation in which the top leadership makes the major decisions on production, distribution, and coordination.

**state (authoritarian) socialism** a command economy in which virtually all of the means of production are in the hands of the state and decision-making is centralized.

**communism** according to Karl Marx, the last stage of economic development after the state has withered away and work and consumption are engaged in communally; today frequently used to designate state socialist economies.

farms they could work their private plots and sell the produce in the local market. In recent times, there was also a good deal of illegal private production and black market activity ("Capitalists in the U.S.S.R.," p. 70). With these exceptions, all production in the Soviet Union was centrally directed.

The U.S.S.R. system of state socialism was imposed on the countries of Eastern Europe when they came under Soviet domination after World War II. It was also adopted by the People's Republic of China following the 1949 communist revolution victory, by Cuba under Castro, and by North Korea, Vietnam, Angola, and Nicaragua, among others. Most state socialist countries have now rejected state socialism in favor of a less rigid, less centrally controlled, more market-oriented economic system.

**Market socialism**  Under market socialism the government retains more control of the economy than under capitalism but less than under state socialism. The government owns most of the means of production, but resource allocation is determined to a large extent in the marketplace, based on demand and supply. The advantages of a market system over central planning are the wealth of information that markets provide to producers and consumers and the incentives offered to workers and managers. Although central planners and plant managers under state socialism could theoretically have access to the demand and supply information necessary for efficient decision-making, in practice it was not available to them. Nor did they have any motivation to attempt to acquire it.

The market socialist model was developed in the 1930s by the Polish economist Oskar Lange and others in order to answer the critics of socialism who said that it could not achieve a rational allocation of resources. In Lange's model, the means of production are socially owned but are run by managers who select their inputs and determine their outputs according to the usual decision-making rules of competitive enterprises. The prices of consumer goods and labor are determined by market forces, while the central planning board tries to set the prices of producers' goods by trial and error to equate demand and supply. The central planning board would also take action on the rate of investment to achieve growth and stability.

Setting prices by trial and error, however, is not effective in a dynamic economy where demand and supply functions are constantly changing. An alternative model has been proposed under which the central planners would constantly measure demand and supply functions by means of market surveys for the demand functions and gathering

**market socialism (regulated market economy)** an economic system in which the means of production are publicly or collectively owned, and the allocation of resources follows the rules of the market.

information on resource availability and production costs for the supply functions. The necessary demand and supply information could conceivably be assembled and processed with the use of powerful computers. The objective would be to simulate a market system but leave pricing and allocation decisions under control of the central authorities.

Such a system has never been put into practice. The information processing power to implement it was not available until recently. And even with the use of supercomputers, the bureaucratic costs of acquiring and disseminating such an immense amount of information would be enormous. Free markets, on the other hand, automatically take all of the relevant demand and supply information into account at zero cost.

**Welfare state**   The efficiency of a market system has been one of the great advantages of capitalism. But a market system leads to great inequalities in income. In order to take advantage of the efficiency of markets but avoid the extreme differences in income levels that result, a number of western countries following World War II adopted a welfare state system. Under the welfare state, income is distributed more equally than under pure capitalism. This is accomplished by means of high marginal tax rates on upper incomes, government transfer payments to low-income persons, and large-scale social welfare programs. The welfare state systems of Western Europe have also been called democratic socialism because they have democratic political institutions.

In welfare states the governments customarily own the utility, communications, and public transportation systems and frequently also such basic industries as steel and mining. Most industries are privately owned, however, and operated for a profit. The government may guide the investment decisions made by private firms through indicative planning. The government publishes forecasts or targets for industries, but compliance with them is voluntary. Tax incentives, relaxation of antitrust regulations, or other encouragement may be provided to selected industries. Indicative planning is not exclusive to welfare states. It has been used in capitalistic Japan by the Ministry of International Trade and Industry to promote the development of export industries (chapter 7, p. 189). However, its use has been rejected in the United States by recent administrations—in the case of high-definition television, for example—on the basis that it constituted government interference in the marketplace.

The first country to install a welfare state system was Sweden. In 1932 the Swedish Social Democratic Party was elected to office and adopted measures to provide economic security for all of its citizens. The Swedish system was

**welfare state (democratic socialism)**   an economic system that combines state ownership of some basic industries with a market system, income redistribution, and democratic political institutions.

**indicative planning**   a method used by governments to improve the performance of the economy by providing economic information in the form of forecasts or targets for industries and, possibly, providing incentives for selected industries.

Day-care for Swedish children, such as this baby in Stockholm, is subsidized by the government.

termed the "third way" because it differed from both the capitalism of the United States and the state socialism of the Soviet Union. Sweden is definitely a free-enterprise economy, with the government owning only 13% of the nation's production facilities. At the same time, however, the government offers high-quality medical care for all, subsidizes modern housing, provides excellent transportation, communication, and child-care services, guarantees income security for the aged and others who cannot work, and assists the unemployed through worker retraining and make-work programs.

Whereas in the United States the various levels of government spend an amount equal to 34% of GNP, the Swedish government spends some 60% of GNP. This government spending is paid for by value-added taxes that amount to 23.5% of the prices consumers pay for products and by income taxes with marginal tax rates of 72% on higher incomes. This has resulted in a very egalitarian after-tax income distribution.

It is expected that the system care for the basic needs of all of its citizens from the cradle to the grave. Among the entitlements of Swedish citizens are 18 months of parental leave following the birth of a child, benefits of 90% of income lost due to illness of a worker or time lost to care for a sick child, and pensions equal to two-thirds of a retiree's highest average earnings over 15 years.

Under its welfare state system, Sweden for a time attained the world's highest living standard, surpassing that of the United States. It is not surprising that the economic reformers in the U.S.S.R. and Eastern Europe look to Sweden as a model of "capitalism with a human face." It is ironic, however, that the Swedish system has been getting so much favorable attention from abroad at a time when it is experiencing economic difficulties—inflation, a slowdown in productivity gains and growth—and a loss of political support at home.

| *Table 1* | ALTERNATIVE ECONOMIC SYSTEMS |
|---|---|
| System | Characteristics |
| Capitalism (Free Enterprise) | *Production:*  The means of production (farms, factories, stores, natural resources) are, with few exceptions, owned by private individuals and firms that produce for a profit. Resource allocation and production methods are determined by market forces.<br><br>*Income distribution:*  Income to labor and other factors is determined in factor markets, with labor unions often playing a role in negotiations between employees and employers. Income distribution is also affected by taxation and other government policies.<br><br>*Government:*  Democratically elected. Regulates industries to a limited extent and acts to stabilize economy, but does not engage in comprehensive planning. Government provides some public services and income security.<br><br>*Leading examples:*  United States, Japan. |
| State Socialism (Communism, Authoritarian Socialism) | *Production:*  The means of production are virtually all in the hands of the government. Allocation and pricing decisions are made by a central planning authority.<br><br>*Income distribution:*  Money income, with minor exceptions, is all from wages and salaries set by the government. There are no free unions. Incomes are supposed to be relatively equal, but government and ruling party officials have benefits and privileges that raise their real income far above that of the workers.<br><br>*Government:*  Self-perpetuating government by the ruling party. Close direction of all economic activity. Government provides extensive public services and income security.<br><br>*Leading examples:*  Soviet Union before *perestroika,* China. |
| Market Socialism (Regulated Market Economy) | *Production:*  The basic means of production are owned and operated by the government, excepting family farms, service businesses, and small production enterprises. Major allocation decisions are made by the central authorities, while production methods and the mix of consumer goods are left to market determination.<br><br>*Income distribution:*  Income incentives are provided by the market, but real income is determined by government wage policies, taxation, subsidies, and public services. Sometimes labor unions are able to force policy changes by striking.<br><br>*Government:*  Market socialist governments until recently have been authoritarian, but some have turned to democratic elections while maintaining a market socialist system. Government provides extensive public services and income security.<br><br>*Leading examples:*  Soviet Union after *perestroika,* Hungary. |
| Welfare State (Democratic Socialism) | *Production:*  The means of production are predominantly in private hands, except for a few basic industries. Pricing, allocation, and production methods are mainly determined by market forces. The government may intervene for specific objectives.<br><br>*Income distribution:*  Money incomes are determined by market forces, with strong labor unions playing a large part in the process. Real after-tax incomes are quite egalitarian as a result of government taxation, income transfers, and social services.<br><br>*Government:*  Democratically elected. Engages in planning for industrial development and stability, implemented by industry regulation and economic incentives. Government provides extensive public services and income security.<br><br>*Leading examples:*  Great Britain, Sweden. |

# case application

## The Yugoslavian Way

After the Yugoslavs drove the Germans out of Yugoslavia at the end of World War II, they established an economic system modeled on the centrally planned economy of the U.S.S.R. All production was controlled. Central planning could not have been more restrictive.

Then in 1948 Yugoslavia broke political ties with the U.S.S.R. and established its own type of socialism. It abandoned collectivization and in 1950 introduced a program of "the factories to the workers." It gave up central planning in favor of a market economy, though the state continued to exert a great deal of control over the markets.

Previously nationalized industries were transformed into self-managed enterprises. The assets of the enterprises remain the property of the state, but the workers are given use of the assets and, within limits, control over their use. Workers form a council for self-management in order to decide both what will be produced and how it will be produced. They determine pay and prices, hire new workers, and certify annual reports.

One problem with workers' councils is that they frequently opt for more of the enterprise profits to be allocated to worker incomes, thus reducing investment and sacrificing long-run growth. According to one Yugoslavian critic of the workers' councils, they frequently want to "put the future in their pockets now"—just the opposite of former Soviet practices.

The manager of an enterprise usually makes the strictly business management decisions. But managers are constrained by the enterprise workers' councils in matters relating to hiring and layoffs, which have a direct impact on the personal lives of workers and their council representatives. A manager is not allowed to fire anyone.

Along with the socially owned enterprises,

there is also a private sector of the economy. It consists of small farmers, retail businesses, restaurants, and other service and small production workshops.

This decentralized, worker-controlled variation of the socialist model worked very well for the Yugoslavs until the late 1970s. From 1950 to 1979 output grew at a rate of 6.3% a year. Exports increased over 7% a year, more than 70% of them to noncommunist countries. Car ownership rose faster than in any other country in Europe. Shops in major cities displayed a full line of major appliances.

After 1979 the economic situation rapidly deteriorated. Growth slowed to less than 1% a year. This may in part have been a consequence of the workers' councils "putting the future in their pockets." But more directly, like most other countries Yugoslavia was hard hit by the 1970s OPEC oil price increases and the world recession in the early 1980s. Its foreign debt ballooned from $4 billion to over $20 billion, nearly $1,000 per Yugoslav. The interest payments on that debt totaled over $4.5 billion a year, or nearly one-fourth of Yugoslavia's total export earnings. Inflation hit rates of 50% and more a year. Because of rising prices and rising unemployment, up to 15% of the work force, workers' real wages have fallen by over 20%.

## *Economic Reasoning*

1. Would you describe the economic system of Yugoslavia as state socialism, market socialism, or a welfare state?
2. The Yugoslavian system has been described as more communistic than the old Soviet system. What would lead to such a conclusion?
3. Would you expect Yugoslavia's worker management of enterprises to be efficient? Why or why not?

# How Do Alternative Economic Systems Resolve the Basic Economic Questions?

The following discussion is organized according to the framework laid out in chapter 2, here examining the way a socialist system resolves the what, how, and for whom to produce questions.

**What to produce**   To accomplish their goal of transforming the U.S.S.R. into an advanced industrial and military power, the Soviet leaders turned to state socialism in the 1920s and adopted a command method of allocating resources. Central planning permitted them to decide directly on the allocation of key commodities. Planning authorities coordinated the production and distribution of goods and services without using prices as indicators of economic scarcity.

Production allocations were made by Gosplan, the central planning authority, based on goals set forth in five-year plans. Each year Gosplan gathered information about the state of the economy and the priorities of leadership concerning such things as the consumption-investment mix, the funding of new military projects, and the growth of key industries, including steel, coal, oil, cars, and computers.

Once the major goals were decided, the planning agencies created detailed directives. Gosplan worked out a set of control figures for about 2,000 major commodity groups. The central planners sent these control figures to the 40 or so economic ministries, which broke them down into rough approximations of production targets for individual enterprises. The targets were revealed to those enterprises—the factories, collective farms, mines, and so forth.

Each enterprise then had to estimate the amount of raw materials, labor, and capital goods needed to produce the proposed output. Its plan went to its ministry and included requests for the factors required to meet the production quota. There was constant pressure on enterprises from Soviet leaders to decrease these requests. The enterprises, however, attempted to inflate their needs in order to protect themselves and to make their jobs easier. Thus a bargaining process took place as the plan went back up the line.

The ministries forwarded the requests to Gosplan, which attempted to achieve an overall balance. It compared the sums of requests (uses) for each major commodity with the available supplies (sources) to see if the plan was feasible.

If planning worked perfectly, the result would be a well-balanced plan in which sources were consistent with the use of them in every sector of the economy. Generally speaking, Soviet planners were not able to achieve consistency. But

**Gosplan**   the highest level Soviet planning agency.

**Five-Year Plan**   the basic planning document in the Soviet Union which established the economic objectives for a 5-year period.

**consumption-investment mix**   the percentage of shares of the national product going respectively to consumption and investment.

**control figures**   the aggregate targets established by Gosplan to reflect the priorities of the authorities.

When economic decisions are made by a central planning authority a tremendous flow of paperwork is inevitable. In the Soviet Union under state socialism, planners, ministers, industrial managers, and bureaucrats at all levels had to constantly exchange information.

this problem did not concern them much because their major concern was the fulfillment of the plan for the specific priority sectors of the economy.

One of the priority sectors was investment to maximize economic growth. A high percentage of GNP was devoted to investment (about 30% compared to about 15%, including public investment, in the United States). Consumption generally was controlled through adjustments in retail prices, including the so-called turnover tax. The other priority sector was military production. The military absorbed 14% of GNP in the U.S.S.R., compared to 7% of GNP in the United States. Equally or more important, 75% of all research and development spending went into military-related research programs, starving the research needs of the civilian sector.

After approval, the production plan was controlled by individual ministries and supervised by statistical and financial agencies. Gosbank, the state bank, handled all financial transactions among the enterprises, which were required to pay on time and prove that their purchases were authorized. Thus, Gosbank could monitor both input use and production output. Incentives, including both bonuses and penalties, were also used to keep things moving according to plan. But the effect of complex incentive schemes on managers, combined with the tremendous pressure on those managers to fulfill their leaders' ambitious production quotas, resulted in major economic problems for the Soviet economy.

Under market socialism, this elaborate system of central control is largely abandoned. As under capitalism, most

**priority sectors** those parts of the economy that decisionmakers want to expand most rapidly and therefore favor with scarce inputs.
**Gosbank** the Soviet state bank that handles all financial transactions between firms, extends credit to firms to purchase production inputs, and audits firms' plan fulfillment.

resource allocation decisions are left to the forces of the marketplace to determine what will be produced. However, the government plays a larger role in decisions regarding the investment mix, natural resource extraction, and foreign trade than in a capitalistic system.

**How to produce**   In a system of state socialism, how goods are produced is to a large extent determined by central planners. When planning authorities decide on the quantity and type of capital goods that are produced, they consequently dictate production methods.

One of the problems that arose under the Soviet system was with regard to innovation and technical change. Managers tended to avoid change because it made plan fulfillment more difficult. They were reluctant to shut down production to change over to more sophisticated technology because of the risk of underachievement of the goal, lost bonuses, and missed promotions. The result tended to be an emphasis on the short run and a disregard for the long-run consequences of decisions.

Agriculture was not a priority sector under Soviet central planning and, therefore, it had to make do with old methods and equipment. Agriculture suffered from many of the same innovation and incentive problems that the rest of the economy did. That sector of the Soviet economy in particular was not modern or productive. Under Gorbachev, however, more capital was allocated to the agricultural sector to modernize it. Fully 27% of all new investment was directed into agriculture, considerably more than before, and a far higher percentage than in other industrial countries.

Changing to a system of market socialism in the U.S.S.R. allows the market to determine how goods are to be produced as well as what goods are to be produced. It encourages innovation because inefficient production methods make a firm uncompetitive in the marketplace.

**For whom to produce**   Under state socialism as practiced in the Soviet Union, labor income did not fare well. The Soviet Union paid its work force only 37% of the GNP in salaries—about half the proportion of GNP that other industrial nations allocate to labor compensation. Offsetting the low compensation, however, were large government subsidies of basic necessities such as food, housing, and medical care.

Managers, bureaucrats, and party leaders in the U.S.S.R. were rewarded in various ways. First, the managerial base pay was higher than that of the average production worker's. Second, managers' bonus payments could range as high as 69% of their base pay, although actual bonuses earned seemed to be about half of that. Party officials, professional people, and bureaucrats had their own fringe benefits. One was the so-called "thirteenth month," a bonus of an extra month's pay for high-ranking individuals. Officials were also entitled to special medical care. Top officials in Moscow were able to buy quality Soviet products or imported luxuries at low prices in special stores where the ordinary citizen was not admitted.

The Soviets built a highly structured, differentiated wage system to allocate and motivate labor. Industrial wages were set by the central authorities. In each sector, base rates established the actual wage of the lowest occupation. Next, a schedule was set, giving the wages of higher-grade occupations as percentages of the lowest grade rate. By changing the base rate, labor could then be directed into or out of industries. By altering the schedule, workers could be motivated to obtain needed skills. Regional wage differentials were used to encourage workers to move to areas of the country, such as Siberia, with high development potential but a harsh climate and few of the advantages found in a city like Moscow. Workers also received a number of bonus and incentive payments. Finally, the Soviet worker had access to the enterprise's recreational and dining facilities, purchasing arrangements, and sometimes even housing facilities.

Under the Gorbachev reforms, plant managers have increased flexibility in paying workers. Out of the total wage fund allocated to a plant by the ministry and any cost savings of the firm, the manager can give raises to those workers who work better. The manager can also reward workers who come up with innovative ideas with bonuses of up to 50% of their salaries.

The system of privileges for those in high positions in the government and the party generated a great deal of resentment among the general populace. Those privileges were especially angering as shortages of goods became worse and the lines became longer. One of Gorbachev's first efforts at reform was putting an end to the system of special privileges. However, bureaucrats are tenacious in holding on to their prerogatives.

In welfare state systems, on the other hand, the lower ranks of the work force share very well in the nation's output. Even pre-tax incomes tend to be distributed more equally in welfare states than under either capitalism or the state socialism of the U.S.S.R. In Sweden the difference between the pay of workers and the pay of government officials is moderate. Income differences in the private sector are held in check by strong labor unions and public policy.

The main distinction in the resolution of the "for whom" question in welfare states, however, is the redistribution of income that results from highly progressive tax rates, income transfers, and social services.

## Little Lions?

We have the so-called "little tigers" of Asia, the small economic dynamos—Hong Kong, South Korea, Taiwan, Singapore—that are giving Japan a great deal of competition. Now, with freedom for the countries of Eastern Europe, we may see the emergence of a group of "little lions" there. Hungary, Czechoslovakia, Poland, and other countries of Eastern Europe are moving fast to transform their economies from state socialism to democratic socialism and are outpacing reforms in the U.S.S.R. However, the legacies of 40 years of state socialism and the problems of transition have worsened their current economic plight.

Hungary turned toward market socialism years ago. The sophisticated Hungarians were less willing than the Soviet population to suffer the low living standards provided by Soviet-style central planning. Although a popular uprising in 1956 was crushed by Soviet tanks, it made the Hungarian communist government realize that changes were necessary to pacify the civil unrest.

The most important changes were introduced in 1968 in the New Economic Mechanism. It included a number of reforms in the planning system. The central authorities no longer dictated production quotas in detail to the individual plants. They permitted plant managers to determine their own output mix and to negotiate sales contracts with their customers. Many firms were able to set their own prices, although prices were still centrally fixed in some sectors of the economy. Firms could undertake small projects out of retained profits, but they had to apply for investment credits from the central bank to finance medium- or large-scale projects.

The New Economic Mechanism reduced the role of central planning in the allocation of resources. Vertical negotiations between the production units and the bureaucracy were replaced in some degree by horizontal negotiations between the producers and their suppliers on one side and the users of their output on the other. This improved the efficiency of the system.

Even before its liberation from Soviet control in 1990, there was a good deal of private enterprise in Hungary. Hundreds of state enterprises had been transformed into stock companies. The Hungarian stock market had reopened and arranged for the London Stock Exchange to install an electronic trading system. The government offered university graduates low-interest loans to start their own businesses.

Hungary's so-called "goulash communism" was so much more successful than the rigid central planning in the U.S.S.R. that its example paved the way for the Soviet radical reformers. Now that the external restraints imposed on Hungarian policies by the Soviet Union are removed, the Hungarian economy is expected to become even more productive.

Another of Eastern Europe's little lions is Czechoslovakia, now renamed the Czech and Slovak Federal Republic, which has been industrialized for more than a century. The Czech government is denationalizing its industries, and ended price controls as of January 1, 1991. One of the advantages Czechoslovakia has in moving to a market economy is its past experience. Prior to Hitler's seizure of the country in 1939, Czechoslovakia had a modern economic system with a thriving entrepreneur class. The country's economic progress was interrupted by 50 years of Nazi and Soviet occupation, but its entrepreneurial spirit lives on. The Blahoslav family, which owned a small manufacturing enterprise before it was taken by the government in 1948, recovered the firm in 1990 and went back into business.

Hungary and Poland also have the advan-

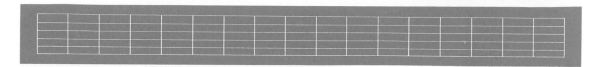

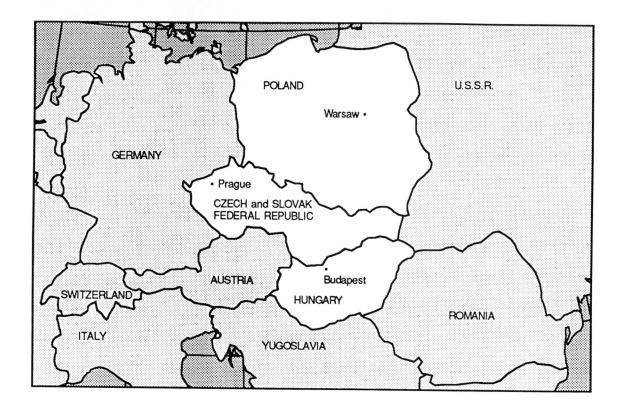

tage of previous experience with a thriving market economy, entrepreneurship, and competition. However, reestablishing those attitudes after 40 years of authoritarian socialist practices is a formidable task. Absenteeism is high and labor productivity low. In Czechoslovakia about 19% of the labor force does not show up for work each day. In Hungary it might take 3 weeks for a bank check to clear. Work habits as well as technology will have to change if the little lions of Eastern Europe are to compete successfully in world markets. In the meantime, they are experiencing rising unemployment and inflation.

*Economic Reasoning*

1. How was the "what to produce" question resolved in Hungary?
2. Why was production more efficient after introduction of the New Economic Mechanism than it was before?
3. Is it all right for the Blahoslavs to again become a wealthy family from the ownership of their enterprise while their workers have a hard time making ends meet? Why or why not?

# How Does the Performance of Alternative Economic Systems Compare?

In chapter 2 we listed the goals of an economic system. While there is a difference in emphasis in different countries, the goals of socialist economies are pretty much the same as those of market economies. We have examined in previous chapters the performance of the U.S. economy in achieving the principal economic goals of efficiency, price stability, full employment, and economic growth, as well as certain socioeconomic goals. Here we will examine the performance of alternative economic systems with respect to these criteria.

**Efficiency** Efficiency describes how well an economy makes use of its scarce resources. Roughly, it is how much output is obtained per unit of input. Efficiency can be measured at a particular time—static efficiency—or it can be estimated over a period of time—dynamic efficiency. Usually, economists take the level of productivity of labor and capital as an approximate measure of static efficiency and the growth of productivity as a measure of dynamic efficiency. A system can be dynamically efficient and yet not be statically efficient. We will look at the dynamic efficiency of Soviet state socialism in the subsection concerned with growth. Here we look at static efficiency.

There are many reports of a lack of static efficiency in the Soviet Union. Imagine the problem of a manager of a sporting goods store in Kiev who finally receives on June 1 the shipment of ice skates and toboggans ordered the previous September. How about the manager of a warehouse full of faulty electrical appliances who finds another whole shipment on the way? What about the nail factory that only produces big, heavy nails because that makes it easier to meet its output quota given in weight of nails produced? Many Soviet factories set up their own shops to make tools, equipment, and other materials because they cannot depend on other factories to produce quality items or to deliver on schedule. This practice may work, but economies of scale are lost. Soviet managers are known for hoarding materials, fuel, and even workers.

With an average wage of 200 rubles a month, a Soviet worker could buy 2 pairs of Russian-made jeans or 1 pair of Calvin Klein jeans in the black market, with 50 rubles left from the month's pay. The quality of Soviet products is notoriously poor. Fully 60% of all television sets produced and 50% of refrigerators need repair in the first year.

**static efficiency** efficiency in resource allocation at a given time with a given amount of resources and level of technology.
**dynamic efficiency** efficiency over a period of time with changing resources and levels of technology.

This electronics shop in Leningrad sells Soviet-made television sets—60% of which need repair in the first year.

Of course, static efficiency is frequently lacking in our capitalist economy as well, as noted in chapter 7. The millions of U.S. automobiles recalled for factory defects, the buttons that fall off shirts the second time they are worn, the nuclear reactor breakdowns, and similar experiences show that centrally planned economies have no monopoly on inefficiency. For example, it is difficult to think of any aspect of the North American transportation system that is without problems. By contrast, the Moscow subway system is one of the best-run in the world, and the Soviet intercity railroads (like most government-owned trains in Europe), transport people on time and in comfort.

Nonetheless, the relative inefficiency of the Soviet system overall is apparent. It, like the United States, is a vast country with large population and a wealth of natural resources. It is third in the size of its total production (GNP). But it does not rank highly among the industrialized countries in output per person (see Figure 1 on p. 486). It even trails its former satellite Czechoslovakia in GNP per capita.

One of the claims made for market socialism, on the other hand, is that it avoids the costs of the market failures that are

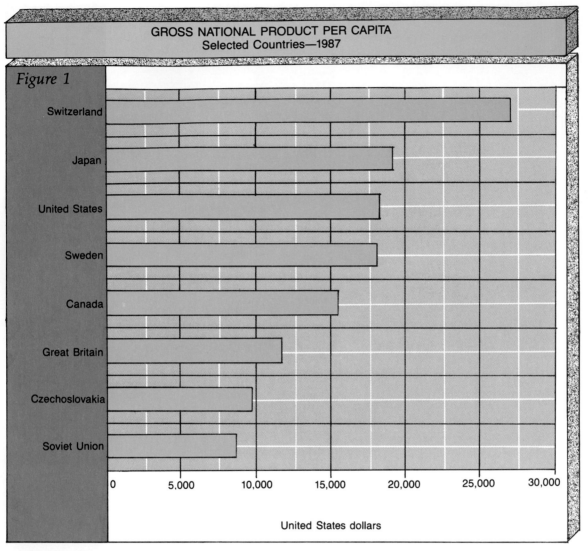

**GROSS NATIONAL PRODUCT PER CAPITA**
Selected Countries—1987

*Figure 1*

|  | |
| --- | --- |
| Switzerland | |
| Japan | |
| United States | |
| Sweden | |
| Canada | |
| Great Britain | |
| Czechoslovakia | |
| Soviet Union | |

0   5,000   10,000   15,000   20,000   25,000   30,000

United States dollars

Sources: International Bank for Reconstruction and Development and U.S. Central Intelligence Agency.

Although the Soviet Union has the third largest economy in the world, it ranks low among industrialized countries in per capita Gross National Product.

characteristic of capitalism. These market failures include monopoly, external costs, and failure to take advantage of external benefits.

**Price stability**   Centrally planned economies supposedly do not suffer from inflation, since prices are not determined in the marketplace. But when gasoline prices were increased by 100% and coffee prices by 300% in the Soviet Union in one year, it was difficult for the Soviet consumer to tell the difference between such "price adjustments" and Western-style inflation.

Theoretically, state socialist governments can keep prices almost perfectly stable because most prices are established by state agencies. In earlier times, when the Soviet government was not as concerned about shortages of consumer goods as it is now, prices were quite stable. The official Soviet price index changed by less than 1% in 15 years.

However, the government subsequently adopted a more rational price system that more closely reflected supply conditions. Prices for many products—gasoline, coffee, paper products—were raised to reflect their higher world prices. The authorities referred to price increases as "correcting distortions" in the price system. But it is obvious, from the long line of anxious buyers and the numbers of discouraged buyers who give up trying to buy some items because of shortages, that the prices of numerous goods are still below their equilibrium level. The lines and waiting lists for purchases are evidence of suppressed inflation.

Further evidence is the large accumulation of savings. Because of the unavailability of goods, Soviet consumers have accumulated an estimated 165 billion rubles in "forced savings." If prices are freed to seek their equilibrium level, that amount of pent-up purchasing power can be expected to drive prices through the roof. Among other consequences, such inflation would be very hard on the Soviet Union's 60 million pensioners living on fixed incomes.

Market systems tend to have unstable prices. It is part of the adjustment mechanism. High prices call forth more resources and production. The increased output stops further price increases and may bring about price reductions. But for the mechanism to work, there must be a smoothly functioning vertical network of suppliers and distributors. Since such a network does not exist in the U.S.S.R., the nation may be in for severe inflation.

**Full employment**  Unemployment in the Soviet Union was officially declared abolished in 1930. The official policy was that any able-bodied person who wanted to work could find a job to match his or her training, skill, and preference. Because workers could not be laid off even when not needed, there were excess workers in some plants, while at the same time there were shortages elsewhere.

Under the system of state socialism, the number of unemployed in the U.S.S.R. was only 1–3%. With the transition to a market system, unemployment is expected to multiply 5 times that. By 1992 it is anticipated that there will be at least 10 million, and perhaps as many as 25 million, unemployed workers.

As in the case of prices, market systems are characterized by unstable employment. A guaranteed job was one of the advantages over capitalism touted by communist authorities

Women fill important roles in every sector of the Soviet economy. Above, radiologist Dr. Natalya Goltseva analyzes a patient's condition at a hospital in Moscow.

and prized by the workers. However, as Sweden has shown, with determined efforts a market system can have as low an unemployment rate as did the Soviet Union's state socialism and still produce efficiently. With its labor retraining and make-work programs, the Swedish welfare state had a 1990 unemployment rate of only 1.4%.

**Growth**　The Soviet record in annual growth in real GNP was exceptional during the decades of its industrial development. The long-run average growth rate for the U.S.S.R., starting in 1928 with the first Five-Year Plan and lasting to the 1960s, excluding the war years, has not been matched by any other country over such a period of time, either in aggregate or per capita terms.

The labor-force participation rate, which is probably higher in the U.S.S.R. than in any other industrial nation, has played a major role in accounting for the high Soviet growth rate. The Soviets were very successful in moving people from the countryside to the city and into the active labor force. Furthermore, the economic role of women in the Soviet economy has been greater than anywhere in the West. Women are important in every sector of the Soviet economy, including manual labor in construction, transportation, and in professions such as medicine. The Soviet leadership has placed a high priority on education, which can be viewed as an investment in human capital for growth. Soviet precollege students rank first in the world in tests on physics. Thus the opportunities for labor force participation and the emphasis on education, especially

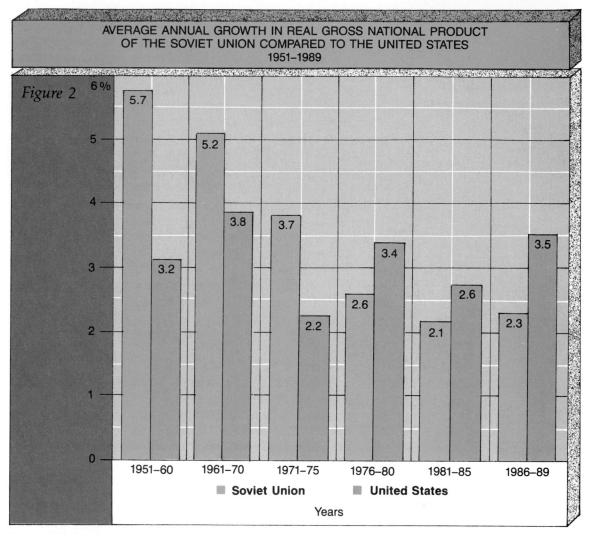

AVERAGE ANNUAL GROWTH IN REAL GROSS NATIONAL PRODUCT
OF THE SOVIET UNION COMPARED TO THE UNITED STATES
1951–1989

*Figure 2*

Sources: U.S. Department of Commerce and Council of Economic Advisors.

The period of exceptionally high economic growth rates in the Soviet Union came to a halt in the 1970s. The factors that had previously sustained growth—an increasing industrial work force and high investment/GNP ratio—ended and were not replaced by such new growth factors as improved technology and higher labor productivity.

scientific education, have contributed to dynamic efficiency in the Soviet Union.

The period of exceptional growth in the Soviet Union came to a halt in the 1970s. Growth factors such as the increasing industrial labor force and the high investment/ GNP ratio that had powered the earlier growth period were played out. They have not been replaced by such other growth factors as improved technology (except in the high-priority military and space industries), or increased labor productivity. When development of heavy industry held priority, increases in total output came quickly. When more resources were allocated to consumer goods and services, productivity gains did not come as easily.

With the exception of the Central Asiatic region, the labor force has stopped growing. Raw materials must increasingly come from Siberia where the costs of extracting them are very high. The Soviet armament buildup has been a drain on the economy, especially since it absorbs the high-technology resources that are necessary to increase productivity. The complexity of and breakdowns in planning and directing the immense economic apparatus of the Soviet Union led to the situation that required *perestroika*.

**Socioeconomic goals** Since the ultimate purpose of economic activity is to raise living standards and improve the life of the people, socioeconomic goals are as important in evaluating a country's performance as the more strictly economic goals. For some socioeconomic goals, income security and equity for example, socialist systems are superior to capitalism. For others, such as economic freedom, capitalism is the foremost system. And in the case of environmental protection, neither capitalism nor state socialism have done well.

*Glasnost* has brought to light some real environmental horrors in the U.S.S.R. An example is Lake Baikal, one of the largest and deepest freshwater lakes in the world. This lake, which has an exceptional variety of living organisms, some of which can be found nowhere else, has suffered serious damage from logging operations, pulp and paper mills, and nearby construction. Large cities also have pollution problems because water treatment facilities are conspicuously lacking. In the nation's second largest city, Leningrad, you can't drink the tap water, just as in an underdeveloped country. The nation's capital, Moscow, has tried to limit population congestion for years with little success. Industrialization, historically the source of Soviet growth, is today the major source of pollution.

In a planned economy, pollution is the result of failures in those plans that do not automatically include costs of environmental damage in their calculation. The worst single instance of environmental devastation in the U.S.S.R. resulted from the nuclear power plant explosion at Chernobyl in 1986. It contaminated more than 1,000 square miles of the countryside around—valuable land in the Ukraine, the breadbasket of the Soviet Union—making much of it uninhabitable for an indefinite period. According to the official Soviet report, the accident resulted from inadequate planning and a failure of those in control to exert responsible supervision. Some Western experts believe that it was also due in part to design deficiencies of that particular type of

Lake Baikal in the U.S.S.R., one of the largest and deepest freshwater lakes in the world, has suffered serious pollution damage. Above, scientists bring up a sample of water from a 1-kilometer depth for testing.

Soviet nuclear reactor, with unwarranted reliance on a supposedly fail-safe system of controls.

With respect to the goal of economic security, citizens in the Soviet Union had a high degree of job security under state socialism. Everyone was guaranteed a job. Job security was higher in the Soviet Union than in most market economies because workers could not be laid off. The Soviet social security system was and is paid for entirely by the state, but benefits are low compared to Western countries. Soviet people were also protected by disability pay, maternity leave, maternity grants, family allowances, free medical care, and a family income supplement for low-income families. Thus, there was no reason for Soviet workers to save for either retirement or emergencies. However, despite the extensive social services, the life expectancy of Soviet citizens has been decreasing, an unheard-of occurrence for nations in modern societies.

*Glasnost* has gone a long way in providing social and political freedom to Soviet citizens. Economic freedom, however, is still curtailed. Even the new privately owned cooperative enterprises have been constrained by restrictive regulations, sometimes arbitrarily enforced by local authorities, and high taxes. Some individuals in the U.S.S.R. have shown an eagerness to make use of economic freedom to prosper, but the mass of the people do not appear eager either for the right to fail themselves or for the prospect of others succeeding in exploiting free markets.

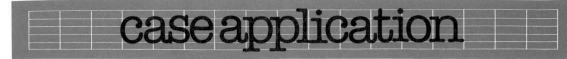

## Exploiting the Environment

One of the major criticisms leveled at capitalism by proponents of alternative systems is the alleged exploitation of the worker under capitalism. When it comes to exploiting the environment, however, the state socialist systems proved themselves to be every bit as ruthless as the most greedy capitalists.

In addition to despoiling Lake Baikal and poisoning large tracts of land with radiation fallout from Chernobyl, shortsighted Soviet planners polluted Lake Ladoga, once even more pure than was Lake Baikal. They permitted the pollution of the mighty Volga river with sewage—some untreated—and drastically reduced its flow by draining off water for irrigation. They turned one-third of the landlocked Aral Sea into a sea of sand, threatening to dry it up totally by the year 2000.

The Soviets were equally wasteful of air resources. In one year the Ukraine Republic alone emitted 22 billion pounds of toxic substances. This was 8 times the rate of air pollution in the United States. On one occasion, air in the industrial center of Nizhniy Tagil in the Russian Republic became so polluted that car drivers had to drive with headlights on in the middle of the day. People became dizzy and fell ill.

Ecological damage was equally bad under central planning in the smaller Eastern European countries. Decades of pushing industrial output without any environmental controls has led to costs in human health. To satisfy the demands of heavy industry for plentiful power, governments subsidized electric power production and ignored conservation. As a result, Poland, for example, emits 6 times as much air pollutants for each unit of output produced as the countries of Western Europe. Air pollution from Eastern European countries is killing the forests of Western Europe, and toxic wastes are poisoning the Baltic Sea.

East Germany was one of the worst polluters—all the while its government engaged in a massive cover-up of the environmental damage. In fact, all of the information gathered on pollution was declared to be state secrets. Any Ralph Naders of Eastern Europe attempting to expose the environmental crimes inflicted on the public would doubtless have been promptly silenced.

Even the more progressive Eastern European countries such as Hungary and Czechoslovakia have serious environmental damage to clean up before they can achieve their potential in a market system. However, according to Boldrich Moldan, the Czech and Slovak Federal Republic's new Environment Minister, "We know what we need to do, but we don't have the money to do it."

*Economic Reasoning*

1. How did ignoring the pollution caused by industry affect the static efficiency of the system? How did it affect dynamic efficiency?
2. Which economic goal may be helped by the massive environmental cleanup needed in Eastern Europe over the next few years? Why? Which goals may be set back by the cleanup needs? Why?
3. It has been proposed that the Western European countries subsidize the environmental cleanup in East Europe. If you were a German or Danish taxpayer, would you approve of that use of your tax money? Why or why not?

# Putting It Together

One of the alternatives to *capitalism* is *state socialism*, which makes use of extensive *central planning*. State socialism has commonly been called *communism*, but true communism as described by Karl Marx is the system that would follow state socialism after a "withering away" of the state. The government owns the means of production under a system of state socialism, and planning authorities make virtually all economic decisions.

Another alternative system is *market socialism*. In that system, the government also owns most of the means of production, but resource allocation is determined in the marketplace.

A *welfare state* system is one in which the means of production, with the exception of some basic industries, are privately owned, while income distribution is determined by government policy. This is accomplished by highly progressive tax rates, income transfers, and extensive public services.

Alternative economic systems resolve the basic economic questions of what, how, and for whom to produce in different ways, depending on the system. In the Soviet Union before *perestroika* when it was practicing state socialism, the state planning agency, *Gosplan*, decided in broad categories what goods and services would be produced and in what volume, depending on the priorities ordered by the Soviet leadership. The various economic ministries then worked out with the firms under their control the details of implementing the plan. In order to coordinate inputs with outputs in the various parts of the economy, Gosplan drew up a material balance for each major commodity produced. Heavy industry and the military goods sectors had top priority and until the 1970s received the bulk of capital investment. Since then the consumer goods sector has received greater emphasis. Because agriculture had a low priority for so long, it lags behind other sectors of the Soviet economy in technology and efficiency.

The state bank, *Gosbank*, controlled the activities of the firms to ensure the overall economic plan was carried out. By monitoring payments for inputs and finished products, Gosbank could compare the actual uses of materials and labor with those specified in the plan.

Changing to a market system will put the decisions concerning both what to produce and how to produce to the determination of market forces. The Soviet government, however, intends to retain control of some of the fundamental economic parameters.

Soviet soldiers attempt to control a mass of shoppers at a shoe store. When goods have become difficult to obtain, the government has called on the militia to regulate admittance to stores.

Under state socialism, wages were set by central authorities, and the base rate and schedule for higher skills in each industry were changed when necessary to direct labor into or out of industries or to motivate workers to obtain higher skills when needed. Incomes of those in the elite leadership positions were augmented greatly by nonwage benefits.

Welfare states, such as Sweden, follow policies of income redistribution and have smaller income differences than under either pure capitalism or the state socialism of the Soviet Union.

The Soviet Union placed great stress on economic growth and, by emphasizing capital accumulation at the expense of consumption, it achieved a higher level of growth from the 1930s to the 1960s than any other country. *Dynamic efficiency* was high during that period, but it paid a price for economic growth in terms of *static efficiency*, economic freedom, environmental pollution, and morale of the people.

Centrally controlled economies generally do better than market systems in providing economic security for workers, but Sweden's welfare state has maintained as low an unemployment rate as the U.S.S.R. had under state socialism. In reforming their economies, the Soviet Union and the smaller countries of Eastern Europe are examining the Swedish example as a model.

# Perspective

## Marx on Capitalism

**Karl Marx**

Marx was born in Germany, the son of a lawyer. Entering Bonn University at the age of 17, he intended to be a lawyer, too. However, after being arrested for public intoxication, he was transferred by his father to Berlin University, which was a more academic institution. There he became a brilliant student and developed a passionate interest in philosophy. After receiving a doctorate from the University of Jena in 1841, he turned to journalism. In 1843 he married the daughter of an aristocratic family from his home town and moved to Paris. It was there that his interest in communism began. There also he began a collaboration with Frederick Engels that would continue for a lifetime. Together they wrote the *Manifesto of the Communist Party* in 1848. They went to Cologne, Germany, to edit a liberal paper backing the German revolution. The revolution failed and Marx, having been exiled from Paris, moved to London. There he spent the remainder of his life, most of it without funds and in poor health, studying, writing, and organizing the Communist International. The first volume of his major work, *Capital (Das Kapital)*, was published in 1867. The second and third volumes were compiled and published by Engels from Marx's unfinished manuscripts after his death in 1883.

In 1867 Karl Marx predicted the demise of capitalism. He did not say just when capitalism would expire, but he did explain why and how. Capitalism had to be replaced, according to Marx, because the evolution of society's institutions is a natural and inevitable process of history. This evolution takes place as a result of class struggles—the struggle of lower socioeconomic classes with higher socioeconomic classes over the fruits of production.

According to Marx, all history can be explained by the conflict between opposing forces, thesis and antithesis. Out of this conflict change emerges through synthesis. Marx contended that the direction of social change is determined by such concrete things as machinery. This philosophy of the inevitability of change resulting from the struggle of opposites and determined by concrete realities rather than ideas is called dialectical materialism. It is the basic philosophy of communism.

The evolution of society into capitalism resulted from the arrival of machines and the factory system. It created two contending forces—the capitalist class or bourgeoisie, which owns the means of production, and the wage workers or proletariat class, which has to sell its labor to live.

Marx seized on the labor theory of value of the classical economists to explain why labor is the source of all surplus value (profit) which is appropriated by capitalists and invested in more machinery. The increasing accumulation of capital equipment, according to Marx, results in increasing output with a smaller labor force. As a result, the workers do not have enough purchasing power to remove from the market all of the output of goods produced by the increasing stock of capital. The consequence, he thought, would be cyclical depressions of increasing severity, leading to revolution.

Marx expected the new synthesis to be socialism. He predicted that there would be two phases of the transition from capitalism to the new synthesis. In the first phase, there would be a "dictatorship of the proletariat" in which the workers would take power. This government by the working class would subsequently give way to a communal society, in which the slogan, "From each according to his ability, to each according to his needs," could at last be realized.

The collapse of communist, actually state socialist, systems in the U.S.S.R. and elsewhere has dimmed the reputation of Marx as a prophet, but his place in history as a social critic and a major influence on events in the twentieth century is secure.

**For Further Study and Analysis**

## Study Questions

1. In what ways is the economic system of United States similar to a welfare state? In what ways is it different?
2. Why does a market system result in more innovation than a centrally planned system?
3. Was there a difference in the way pipeline workers in Siberia were convinced to endure harsh working conditions compared to the way workers are induced to work in Alaska?
4. Since according to Marxian economics labor is the only factor input that should be paid and there is no justification for paying interest on the use of capital, why were Soviet firms charged interest on the capital they used, even though the interest payment came from and ended up in Gosbank?
5. How would a state socialist economy and the U.S. economic system handle each of the following problems? (a) determining the mix between the production of machinery and the building of houses; (b) setting the relative pay for doctors and plumbers; (c) fighting inflation; (d) keeping unemployment down.
6. Why was it difficult for the Soviet Union to engage profitably in foreign trade based on comparative advantage?

7. Why is a market system thought to be more efficient in allocating resources than a centrally planned system?
8. Why is the Soviet public's high rate of savings accumulation an indication of suppressed inflation?
9. Why did the increased emphasis on providing more consumer goods and services slow down the Soviet growth rate?
10. Since the paper mills around Lake Baikal are not owned by profit-minded capitalists, why did they pollute the lake by disposing of their waste in the streams that feed it?

## Exercises in Analysis

1. Under the headings of the four alternative economic systems discussed, make lists of those countries that currently fit the descriptions of each system.
2. List the types of information that you would need as a top official in Gosplan in order to draw up a Five-Year Plan.
3. There is a story about what happens to a farmer and his two cows under alternative types of economics systems: Under capitalism, the farmer trades one of the

cows for a bull. Under a welfare state, the government takes the cows and gives the farmer the milk. Under market socialism, the government shoots the cows and gives the farmer the meat. Under state socialism, the government shoots the farmer and takes the cows. Write an essay explaining why you think this story does or does not accurately illustrate the difference between the various systems.

4. Write a short paper on why you believe market economies are superior to centrally planned economies or vice versa.

## Further Reading

Berend, Ivan T. *The Hungarian Economic Reforms, 1953–1988*. Cambridge, U.K.: Cambridge University Press, 1990. Traces the various stages of reforms in Hungary and the debates that accompanied them.

Coates, Ken, ed. Perestroika: *Global Challenge*. Nottingham, U.K.: Russell Press, 1988. Articles on various aspects of *perestroika*—its effects on economic security, international relations, research and science, and the environment, among others—including an article from *Pravda* by Gorbachev.

Desai, Padma. *Perestroika in Perspective: The Design and Dilemmas of Soviet Reform*. Princeton, N.J.: Princeton University Press, 1989. Discusses the reasons why reforms were needed in the Soviet system, the likelihood of their success, and how long Gorbachev is likely to last.

Heilbroner, Robert L. *Between Capitalism and Socialism*. New York: Random House, 1970. A look at capitalism, socialism, Marxian economics, and alternative economic futures by one of the most prolific and readable of economists.

Ioffe, Olimpiad Solomonovich. *Gorbachev's Economic Dilemma: An Insider's View*. St. Paul, Minn.: Merrill/Magnus, 1989. An examination of the three sectors in the new Soviet system—the state, cooperative, and individual economies—and their interconnections.

Lane, David. *Soviet Economy and Society*. Oxford, U.K.: Basil Blackwell, 1985. An examination of the administration of the Soviet economy, its performance, economic reforms, and social relations in the U.S.S.R.

Le Grand, Julian, and Saul Estrin. *Market Socialism*. Oxford, U.K.: Clarendon Press, 1989. Contains articles on how markets can be used to achieve socialist ends.

Lekachman, Robert, and Borin Van Loon. *Capitalism for Beginners*. New York: Pantheon Books, 1981. A lively treatment of capitalism, Marxism, Keynesian and post-Keynesian economics, with humorous illustrations.

Lydall, Harold. *Yugoslavia in Crisis*. Oxford, U.K.: Clarendon Press, 1989. Examines the causes of the sharp decline of the Yugoslav economy after 1979.

Mandel, Ernest. *Beyond Perestroika: The Future of Gorbachev's U.S.S.R.* London: Verso, 1989. Discusses *perestroika* and *glasnost* in the context of socialist theory and politics.

Miller, James R. *The ABCs of Soviet Socialism*. Urbana, Ill.: University of Illinois Press, 1981. A study of the history, organization, and performance of the Soviet system.

Prout, Christopher. *Market Socialism in Yugoslavia*. Oxford, U.K.: Oxford University Press, 1985. An examination of the origins of market socialism in Yugoslavia and how the capital, labor, and goods markets operate.

Wright, Anthony. *Socialisms: Theories and Practices*. Oxford, U.K.: Oxford University Press, 1986. Covers the evolution of socialism, its arguments, doctrines, and methods.

## chapter 18

# WORLD ECONOMIC DEVELOPMENT

*The earth has been compared to a spaceship whose occupants depend on each other for survival. In this spaceship Earth, about one-fifth of the ship's crew and passengers are Chinese. How they fare could have a major impact on the spaceship's other occupants. Here we examine what and how the Chinese passengers are doing.*

## China's Great Leap Backward

The communist government of China announced the Great Leap Forward in 1958. It was a program that shifted emphasis from production in large-scale factories, following the Soviet model, to small-scale production in communes. It was characterized in the West as a "steel furnace in every backyard" concept. This was carrying the "small is beautiful" development strategy to the extreme. It sacrificed economies of scale, and the economy promptly fell flat on its face. Since then the path to economic development in China has been full of twists and turns. The Great Leap Forward program was abandoned in 1961 in favor of a pragmatic approach to what worked. Then the Great Proletarian Cultural Revolution was launched in 1965, which attacked scientists and intellectuals, closed universities, and sent professors into the fields to pick crops. In addition, reformers like Deng Xiaoping were alternately purged and rehabilitated.

The economic position of China differs from that of the Soviet Union in that it is predominantly an agricultural country with a per capita income that puts it among the world's poorer countries. However, a reform program begun in the late 1970s and led by Deng produced an exceptionally high growth rate. From 1981 to 1988 the average growth in output of the Chinese economy was 9.9%. By comparison, the growth of output of the Soviet Union averaged only 2.2% in those years and 3% in the United States. Only one other country, the small African nation of Botswana, had a higher rate of economic growth during that period.

A key to the increase in China's output was the contract system. In the agricultural sector, collectives were given production quotas that they had to fulfill and sell to the government at a fixed price. The individual farmers in the collective contracted to provide a portion of the quota. Any output that they produced above the contracted amount they could sell in the free markets at whatever price it would bring. By 1985 there were 60,000 agricultural free markets in China. This contract system was a more liberal version of the practice of allowing private plots in Soviet agriculture. Under the system, China, a country with over 1 billion people to feed, became a food exporter!

In industry China got the jump on the Soviet Union in economic reform by allowing and encouraging profit-making enterprises. Those businesses, originally operated by individuals or collectives as a sideline to farming, were encouraged beginning in 1978. They engaged in a wide range of services such as restaurants, tailoring, and retail merchandising, and in consumer goods manu-

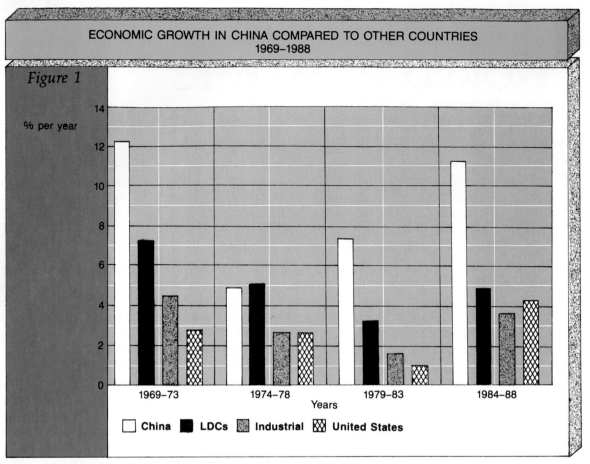

ECONOMIC GROWTH IN CHINA COMPARED TO OTHER COUNTRIES
1969–1988

Figure 1

% per year

China   LDCs   Industrial   United States

Source: World Bank, *World Tables, 1989–90.*

During the past 20 years China's economic growth rate has customarily greatly exceeded the average growth rates of the other less-developed countries as well as the growth rates of the industrialized nations, including the United States.

facturing including clothing, furniture, and spare automobile parts, sometimes in competition with government businesses. There were also arrangements by which individuals could lease state-owned enterprises.

Businesses run by private enterprise were allowed to hire paid employees, in direct conflict with Marxist ideology which holds that one person working for another's profits constitutes exploitation. By 1989, the private and collective enterprises produced 37% of China's industrial output and employed over 100 million workers. In industry as in agriculture, the enterprises had to contract production of a quota of output for sale to the government at a set low price. Additional production could be sold on the open market at much higher prices. In many cases, however, the contract quotas were not fulfilled.

There was an explosion of entrepreneurial activity, especially in the south of China which had close contacts with Hong Kong. Per capita income doubled between 1980 and 1989. However, a rising emphasis on materialism resulted in a wave of corruption and profiteering by officials connected with government enterprises and the emergence of such banned activities as prostitution and pornography. The *People's Daily* reported that half of all state and collectively run enterprises were cheating on their taxes. There were grumblings among that part of the population not benefiting from the new economic activities about profiteering and price gouging. Envy of the "yuan millionaires" engaged in private economic activities created a backlash of resentment in a nation accustomed to everyone "eating from the big pot," that is, receiving the same income.

Initially nearly all of the early private enterprises, about 90%, were located in rural areas. Beginning in the early 1980s the government cautiously undertook an expansion of free enterprise in the cities as well. It was hesitant because of the fear of overheating the economy, causing shortages and inflation. Indeed, by 1989 prices were rising at a rate of 18% to 20% a year.

In China, economic reform was not coupled with political reform as it was in the Soviet Union under Gorbachev. There was no equivalent of *glasnost* in China. Consequently, there emerged growing social unrest and increasing demonstrations, especially by students, for political liberalization as well as more rapid economic reforms.

To control the unrest and stem the rising inflation, corruption, and black market activities the central authorities reined in the reform movement. An austerity program was adopted in 1989 that imposed new taxes on private enterprises, stopped development loans to new businesses, and reexerted central control.

The conflict between the liberalization movement, led by the students, and the con-

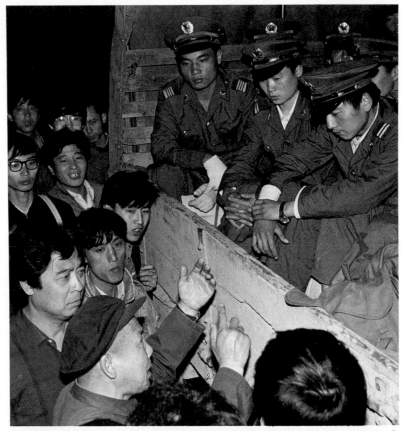

On May 20, 1989, demonstrators blocked the advance of troops sent to quell antigovernment protests in Tiananmen Square. "You cannot go and hurt your brothers and sisters," one resident of Beijing admonishes the soldiers in the photo above.

servative central government authorities came to a head on June 3 and 4, 1989, in Tiananmen Square. The giant square in the center of Beijing had been occupied by student demonstrators to call attention to government repression of the reform movement. Deng the reformer became Deng the repressor as army troops from outlying areas were moved into the city and attacked the students and their supporters. There were a great many casualties. In the following weeks, liberal reformers were rounded up all over the country and jailed.

Outrage abroad over this brutal suppression resulted in trade, diplomatic, and other sanctions being imposed by the United States and other Western nations. Foreign

On May 13, 1989, this Chinese student was one of many who went on a hunger strike in protest of government policies, as his hand-painted shirt proclaims. On January 26, 1991, a Chinese court in Beijing sentenced one member of a group of already imprisoned human rights activists to 7 years in jail. Many other protesters were executed or given longer sentences.

investors and companies doing business in China were frightened off by the instability and future uncertainty created by the government's actions. The Chinese economy took a giant leap backward. Production dropped sharply, unemployment mounted, and consumer spending dried up. The production of color televisions, for example, dropped 40% between January 1989 and January 1990.

Reviving the Chinese economy, getting it back on the road to development, apparently will take time and a change in the old-guard leadership.

## Chapter Preview

*As part of the "developed" world, it is difficult for us to appreciate fully the vast gap between our way of life and the way of life that exists in the less-developed two-thirds of the world. Even in those countries that have begun to break the poverty cycle, the average worker earns a bare subsistence wage. China, for example, has made significant economic gains in recent years. Yet, by Western standards, incomes remain very low. This chapter will address the problem of economic development by examining three basic questions: How do standards of living compare? What makes countries poor? What are the prospects for world economic development?*

## Learning Objectives

*After completing this chapter, you should be able to:*

1. *Discuss the ways of comparing living standards among countries and explain how China compares with other less-developed countries.*
2. *Name the regions where poverty is most prevalent and list four low-income countries in those regions.*
3. *Explain the problems that cause countries to be poor.*
4. *Explain the significance of the population growth rate in economic development.*
5. *Describe the role of foreign indebtedness with respect to the LDCs.*
6. *Discuss the relationship between economic development and environmental pollution.*

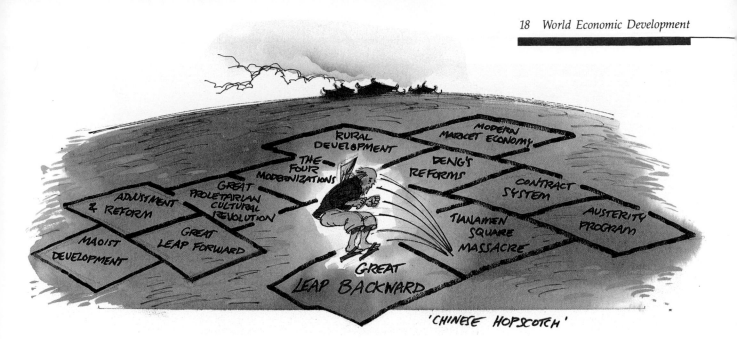

'CHINESE HOPSCOTCH'

# How Do Standards of Living Compare?

Most of the world's peoples do not live in the types of countries whose economies have been discussed in the preceding chapters. Two-thirds of the world's population live in nonindustrialized countries. These countries are referred to by various designations, the most common and inclusive being less-developed countries (LDCs). However, there are wide differences among the various LDCs in their living standards, potential for development, rate of development, and problems to be overcome in achieving development. In this analysis section we will examine living standards in the LDCs.

**Poverty**   Most of the world's population is found in countries with a per capita income of only a few hundred dollars a year. These countries are located in Asia, Africa, and Latin America. They are largely agricultural—as much as 80% of the population engaged in agriculture—with only small and inefficient manufacturing sectors. This subjects their income earnings to the wide price fluctuations characteristic of commodity markets.

The World Bank classifies countries as low-income, lower-middle-income, upper-middle-income, and high-income economies. Despite its economic advances in recent years, China is still one of the low-income economies, with a per capita GNP of only $330.

The low-income countries are mainly in South Asia and sub-Saharan Africa (African countries that lie south of the

**less-developed countries (LDC)** a non-industrialized country, generally characterized by a poverty income level, a labor force primarily employed in agriculture, extensive underemployment, illiteracy, and located in Africa, Asia, or Latin America.
**per capita income** total National Income (or GNP) divided by the population size.
**World Bank (International Bank for Reconstruction and Development—IBRD)** a specialized agency of the United Nations which began operations in 1945 first to help countries rebuild facilities destroyed in World War II and subsequently to help finance development of the LDCs.

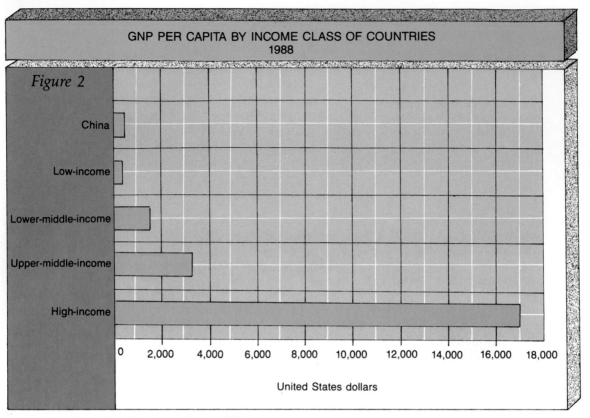

*Figure 2*

**GNP PER CAPITA BY INCOME CLASS OF COUNTRIES**
**1988**

China

Low-income

Lower-middle-income

Upper-middle-income

High-income

0    2,000    4,000    6,000    8,000    10,000    12,000    14,000    16,000    18,000

United States dollars

Source: World Bank, *World Development Report, 1990.*

China's GNP per capita is just slightly above the average of low-income countries in general. The great gap in incomes is between the less-developed economies and the industrialized high-income countries.

**headcount index**   the percentage of the population below the poverty line.

Sahara desert). They have an average per capita output of only $320 a year. The World Bank has established a poverty line—or rather a poverty line range—of $275 to $370 income per person per year. It bases this range on studies of countries with low average incomes and the amount required for a minimum standard of nutrition and other basic necessities plus minimum amenities acceptable in particular countries (for example, whether or not indoor plumbing is considered a necessity).

The percentage of the population that falls below the poverty line is termed the headcount index of poverty. According to this index, over 1 billion people fall below the poverty line worldwide, more than half of whom are extremely poor with incomes below $275 per year. The largest concentrations of poor are in rural areas with high population densities and in areas lacking productive natural resources.

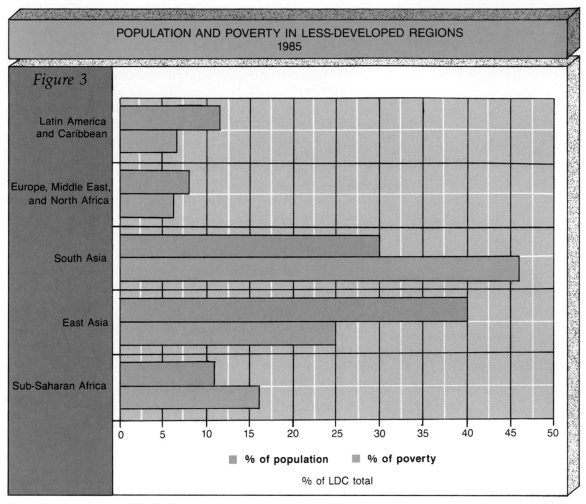

**POPULATION AND POVERTY IN LESS-DEVELOPED REGIONS
1985**

*Figure 3*

- Latin America and Caribbean
- Europe, Middle East, and North Africa
- South Asia
- East Asia
- Sub-Saharan Africa

0  5  10  15  20  25  30  35  40  45  50

■ **% of population**    ■ **% of poverty**

% of LDC total

Source: World Bank, *World Development Report, 1990.*

Among the less-developed regions, South Asia and sub-Saharan Africa have more than their share of poverty relative to population size. The largest concentrations of the poor are in rural areas with high population densities and in areas that have few natural resources.

The headcount index gives the number of people in poverty, but it does not show how far incomes would have to be raised to take them out of poverty. To provide this information, the World Bank has devised a supplementary index called the <u>poverty gap</u>. According to the poverty gap index, China is in a much better position than the average low-income country. India, for instance, although its per capita GNP is slightly higher than that of China, has four times the income shortfall of the poor. In other words, the poor in India require four times as large an aggregate income increase to bring them up to the poverty line as do the poor in China.

**poverty gap**  the aggregate income shortfall of the poor as a percentage of aggregate consumption.

**Income distribution** One of the reasons why the head-count index does not fully reflect the extent of poverty is the pattern of income distribution in different countries. Many LDCs have highly skewed income distributions, with a large percentage of total income going to a small percentage of the population. In Brazil the highest 10% of income receivers get 46% of the total income while the poorest 20% share less than 3%. In Sri Lanka the top 10% receive 43% of the income, the bottom 20% only 5%. In Botswana the figures are 43% and 3%; in Guatemala, 41% and 6%.

Figures on income distribution are not available for China, but income has customarily been distributed much more equally—everyone "eating from the big pot"—than is typical for a low-income country. The breaking down of this custom was at the heart of much public dissatisfaction with the outcome of Chinese reforms in the 1980s.

There is a difference, however, in the type of unequal income distribution that results from inherited wealth, particularly land ownership, which is typical of LDC agrarian societies, and the inequality in income distribution that results from development activities. The former perpetuates poverty, while the latter results in increasing demand for labor, thereby raising incomes down the line.

**Social indicators** Per capita output and per capita income are the most direct measures of poverty. However, they do not give a complete picture of the comparison of living standards in different countries. Table 1 shows some basic economic and <u>social indicators</u> for each income class of countries and data for the largest five countries in each group. The table lists their population, per capita GNP, growth in per capita GNP, adult illiteracy rate, life expectancy at birth, and infant mortality rate.

Although China is among the low-income countries, a newborn Chinese baby has a life expectancy of 70 years. That is higher than most of the world outside of the high-income industrialized countries (see Table 1). Also, the infant mortality rate in China is a fraction of that in other low-income countries. China is similarly in a much more favorable position relative to most low-income countries with respect to literacy. As shown in Table 1, only 31% of the adult Chinese population is illiterate, compared to 57% in India and an average of 44% in all low-income countries. An amazing 93% of China's primary-age children are enrolled in school. The average for sub-Saharan African countries is only 56%.

Another social indicator of the standard of living in a country is the nutrition level. The daily per capita calorie supply in China is 2,630 calories. This is greater than the

Ninety-three percent of China's primary-age children are enrolled in school, like this kindergarten student at a factory school in Beijing. The daily per capita calorie intake for China, however, is only about two-thirds that of the United States.

**social indicators** noneconomic statistics that reflect a country's standard of living.

## Table 1

### BASIC INDICATORS

| Country | Population (millions) 1988 | GNP per Capita | | Adult Illiteracy (%) 1985 | Life Expectancy at Birth 1988 | Infant Mortality (per 1,000 live births) 1988 |
|---|---|---|---|---|---|---|
| | | Dollars 1988 | Growth (%) Average 1965–88 | | | |
| **Low-income** | 2,884 | 320 | 3.1 | 44 | 60 | 72 |
| China | 1,088 | 330 | 5.4 | 31 | 70 | 31 |
| India | 816 | 340 | 1.8 | 57 | 58 | 97 |
| Indonesia | 175 | 440 | 4.3 | 26 | 61 | 68 |
| Nigeria | 110 | 290 | 0.9 | 58 | 51 | 103 |
| Bangladesh | 109 | 170 | 0.4 | 67 | 51 | 118 |
| **Lower-middle-income** | 742 | 1,380 | 2.6 | 27 | 65 | 57 |
| Brazil | 144 | 2,160 | 3.6 | 22 | 65 | 61 |
| Mexico | 84 | 1,760 | 2.3 | 10 | 69 | 46 |
| Phillipines | 60 | 630 | 1.6 | 14 | 64 | 44 |
| Thailand | 55 | 1,000 | 4.0 | 9 | 65 | 30 |
| Turkey | 54 | 1,280 | 2.6 | 26 | 64 | 75 |
| **Upper-middle-income** | 326 | 3,240 | 2.3 | 24 | 68 | 42 |
| Iran | 49 | NA | NA | 49 | 63 | 64 |
| S. Korea | 42 | 3,600 | 6.8 | NA | 70 | 24 |
| S. Africa | 34 | 2,290 | 0.8 | NA | 61 | 70 |
| Algeria | 24 | 2,360 | 2.7 | 50 | 64 | 72 |
| Yugoslavia | 24 | 2,520 | 3.4 | 9 | 72 | 25 |
| **High-income** | 784 | 17,080 | 2.3 | NA | 76 | 9 |
| United States | 246 | 19,840 | 1.6 | * | 76 | 10 |
| W. Germany | 61 | 18,480 | 2.5 | * | 75 | 8 |
| Italy | 57 | 13,330 | 3.0 | * | 77 | 10 |
| U.K. | 57 | 12,810 | 1.8 | * | 75 | 9 |
| France | 56 | 16,090 | 2.5 | * | 76 | 8 |

*Less than 5%

Source: World Bank, *World Development Report, 1990.*

average calorie supply for low-income countries, 2,384 calories, but just over two-thirds of the calories consumed by residents of the United States (3,645 calories) and other high-income countries (average 3,376 calories). Since, from a health standpoint, we are said to consume too many calories ("Dieting—The National Pastime," p. 43), the lower average consumption level of the Chinese may leave them better off. The problem in poor economies is the distribution of the available food—millions of children in Africa are malnourished—and periodic famines that reduce the food supply below subsistence levels.

# case application

## A Tale of Two Countries

Kenya and Tanzania are two sub-Saharan African countries that have much in common. They share a common border in East Africa. It was near this border, in the Olduvai Gorge of Tanzania, that British paleontologist Louis B. Leakey discovered the remains of our earliest ancestors who lived there about 1.75 million years ago. You might say that this part of the world got a head start in economic development. However, today it is among the world's poorest areas.

In addition to their common border and ancestry, Kenya and Tanzania have other similarities. They are similar in population size—about 25 million—and high population growth rates—3.8% for Kenya and 3.5% for Tanzania. They were both administered as colonies by Great Britain until they gained their independence in the early 1960s. Each of them has a one-party democratic political system, disrupted by strife among the various tribal factions.

Kenya has 40 separate ethnic groups, the largest of which are the Kikuyu that dominate the political scene. Jomo Samiburati ("Call me Sammy") is a Kikuyu. He was named after the father of Kenya's independence movement and its first president, Jomo Kenyatta. Sammy is not interested in politics, however. He is interested in making money. He is a driver and guide for tourist groups on safari to Kenya's game preserves. In addition to his native Bantu dialect, he speaks Swahili, the official language of Kenya, fluent English, and some French, German, and Italian. He learned the foreign languages from movies and tourists; he never went further than the primary grades in school. His income is far above the average for Kenya, but he will not say just how much.

However, his expenses are also far above average. Nairobi, the capital of Kenya, is a very expensive city to live in compared to his native village. He is the father of six children under the age of 10, four of whom are in school. He also has two nephews living with him whose schooling he is paying for; they are sons of a brother still living in their home village where secondary school is not available. Most weeks that Sammy is on safari he drives for six days; he gets home to see his wife and children and recuperate for only one day before going out again. It is a tough life, but he is ambitious for himself and his children.

Across the border in Tanzania, 200 miles to the southwest, lives Mkwamasi, a Maasai tribesman. Mkwamasi follows the traditional Maasai occupation of herding cattle. Over 7 feet tall, he makes an imposing figure striding across the plain in bright orange-red flowing dress, carrying a spear for protection from the lions and other wild animals. He grazes his cattle over the vast Serengeti Plain, sometimes following the seasonal grass up into Kenya. The land the Maasai tribe have traditionally inhabited is now divided between Kenya and Tanzania. If Sammy were to cross the Tanzanian border without a passport, he would be arrested. But Mkwamasi has no passport, nor for that matter any document of any sort—no driver's license, no Social Security card, no birth certificate. He has virtually no money income. The cattle herd provides the principal subsistence for him and his village. He drinks their milk, frequently mixed with their blood, and eats their meat. Some Maasai are now turning to farming, but not his village. The village is much different from the native village of Samiburati in Kenya with its houses and streets. The Maasai village is a

**Table 2**  BASIC INDICATORS FOR KENYA AND TANZANIA

| Country | GNP per Capita | | Inflation Rate (%) Average 1980–88 | Agriculture as % of GNP 1988 | Life Expectancy at Birth 1988 | Infant Mortality (per 1,000 live births) 1988 |
| | Dollars 1988 | Growth (%) Average 1965–88 | | | | |
| --- | --- | --- | --- | --- | --- | --- |
| Kenya | 370 | 1.9 | 9.6 | 31 | 59 | 70 |
| Tanzania | 160 | – 0.5 | 25.7 | 66 | 53 | 104 |

Source: World Bank, *World Development Report, 1990.*

circle of 15 low thatched-roof huts made of sticks and mud, surrounded by a fence of bushes and woven branches. The huts have dirt floors, crawling with insects, and are pitch black inside except for the glow of charcoal embers in the cooking fire and a small ventilation hole in one wall. The entrance is a baffled maze to keep out the weather and unwelcome intruders, animal or human. In the center of the village is a stick enclosure for animals. But mainly the central area is full of children, none of whom attend school, and their mothers. Five of the children, ranging in age from 6 months to 11 years old, are those of Mkwamasi. Two older sons are with him herding the cattle.

The life-styles of Samiburati and Mkwamasi are not typical of Kenya and Tanzania respectively, but they do symbolize the differences between the two countries and, in fact, the contrasts between traditional and developing societies in Africa and elsewhere. Despite their similar backgrounds, the economies of Kenya and Tanzania perform quite differently. Both countries are classified as low-income countries, but the per capita GNP of Kenya is more than twice that of Tanzania. More significantly, the average an-

nual per capita real growth of GNP from 1965–88 was 1.9% in Kenya and a minus 0.5% in Tanzania. The Tanzanian economy actually lost ground during those years. Economic and social indicators for the two countries are given in Table 2 above.

The social indicators of life expectancy and infant mortality confirm the economic indicators. Kenya is doing better than Tanzania on the road to escaping poverty.

*Economic Reasoning*

1. Are Kenya and Tanzania above or below the average of low-income economies in respect to GNP per capita and the rate of growth in GNP per capita?
2. What differences between the economies of the two countries are shown in Table 2 that might explain the better performance of the Kenyan economy in the 1980s? Why?
3. Do you think that the Kenya and Tanzania economies would perform better under multiparty political systems than with only one legal party in each country? Why?

# What Makes Countries Poor?

Why are more than 1 billion people living below the poverty level? Why, after 40 years of World Bank and country-to-country development assistance, are two-thirds of the world population still in LDCs? These questions do not have clear answers. The path to economic development is difficult and complicated. But there are certain basic development lessons that are clear—certain problems that must be overcome in order for countries to achieve self-sustaining growth.

**Lack of capital, technology, and human capital**   In order to grow and develop, a low-income country must surmount a number of severe problems. Perhaps the most difficult of these is breaking the vicious circle of poverty. Per capita output in LDCs is close to the subsistence level. There is no economic surplus to allocate to capital accumulation or technological progress. As a result, productivity remains low and the subsistence standard of living is perpetuated.

In prerevolutionary China, the vast majority of people lived in poverty. A rich minority hoarded its wealth or put it into conspicuous display. Surplus production above subsistence needs was not invested to generate future growth. Nor was it used to raise the standard of living of the masses. In an attempt

**vicious circle of poverty**   the pattern of economic stagnation resulting from a lack of surplus of production to invest in capital goods to increase productivity.

**economic surplus**   a margin of output over and above consumption needs which can be allocated to investment for intensive growth.

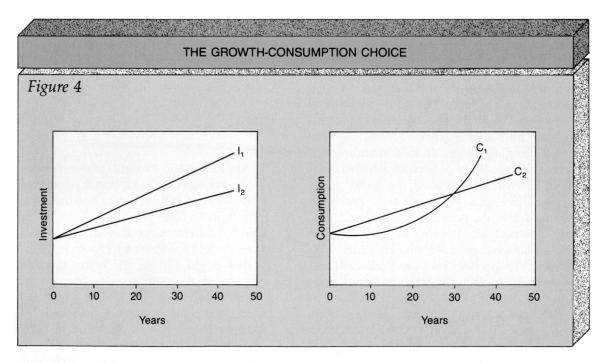

**THE GROWTH-CONSUMPTION CHOICE**

*Figure 4*

By sacrificing present consumption (C₁), an economy will be able to invest more (I₁) and be able to grow more rapidly than at consumption level (C₂) and investment level (I₂). This long-term strategy eventually creates more consumption.

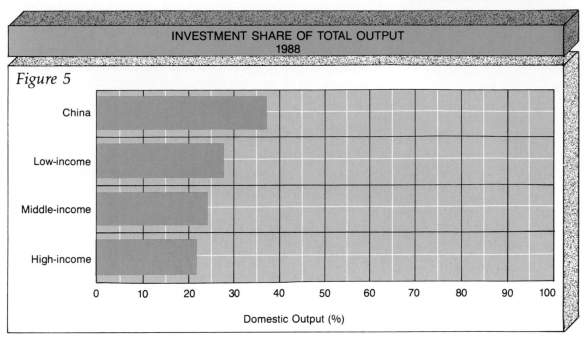

**INVESTMENT SHARE OF TOTAL OUTPUT**
**1988**

*Figure 5*

Source: World Bank, *World Tables, 1989–90.*

China allocates a much larger share of total output to investment capital than most countries. Gross domestic investment as a percentage of total domestic output in China is the greatest of any large country.

to maximize industrial growth after the 1949 Communist take-over, the rate of capital formation was pushed to a punishing 44% of total output. There were 355,000 factories constructed in the 30 years following the revolution.

Subsequently, the investment rate was reduced, but it remains the highest of any large nation and well above the average of other LDCs. Figure 5 shows gross domestic investment as a percentage of total domestic output for China and for other countries grouped by income classes.

As for productive human capital, China has increased it by tapping the masses of unemployed or underemployed people in the countryside. In contrast to other LDCs, the factories to a large extent have been taken to the workers in rural areas rather than moving farm workers to the cities. Migration from rural to urban areas, a typical occurrence in developing countries, has been limited. Approximately 80% of the population still resides in the countryside.

One of the major obstacles to economic development in most LDCs is the lack of literate, skilled labor. To overcome this obstacle, China now has almost as many children enrolled in school as the total population of the United States. However, there is little opportunity for higher education. Only 2% of Chinese youths are able to attend college, compared to over 50% in the United States.

**Overpopulation**  Educated and trained human capital is an asset to economic growth. Increased numbers of mouths to feed are not. A nation's standard of living is determined by the amount of food, housing, and other goods and services available to each person. The number of people and the rate of population increase are important factors in this measure. For many developing nations, overpopulation can be a major obstacle to improving living standards.

China's population is over 1 billion—one-fifth of the world's population living on 7% of the world's land area. At first, the leaders of communist China regarded a huge population as a resource that could be used to develop the economy rapidly. Today, however, they recognize the cost of a high population growth rate. Between 1953 and 1978 a sizeable 58% of the increase in output was allocated for the additions to the population, leaving only 42% for investment and improved living standards. In 1979 a one-child-per-family policy was initiated. There is an effective program for population control that combines education in family planning and birth-control clinics with government propaganda and community pressure for smaller families. There are rewards for those who adhere to family planning regulations and penalties for those who do not. If a newly married couple agrees to have only one child,

A couple and their son take a ride in Sichuan Province in China. Since 1979 the Chinese government has promoted policies to encourage one-child families.

they receive a lump sum reward of rice and money, the child gets a full adult grain ration and a double fruit and vegetable ration, and the child is allotted a private plot of 75 square meters instead of the usual 50. If the child dies, the couple is allowed to have another. However, if they break their promise and have two children, they must repay all of the rewards they received.

Because of this program, the rate of population growth was reduced from 30 per thousand in the 1960s to 13 per thousand in 1989, a dramatic change unprecedented in history. But because of the large numbers of young people approaching the age of establishing families, the size of the population will continue to increase for some time to come despite the lower birthrate. Present policy calls for reductions in population increases until zero population growth is reached by the year 2000. The birthrate restrictions are not considered permanent, however. A falling population growth rate has its own problems, mainly what it does to the age structure of the population. Now each 100 workers support 14 retired persons, but by the middle of the next century 40% of the population will be over the age of 65.

Other developing countries have made headway in bringing population growth under control, but about one-fourth of the world, mainly the poorest countries such as Bangladesh and a number of nations in Africa, still have explosive population growth. The average fertility rate for the African continent is 6.3 children per woman. The problem of providing the necessities of life for ever-increasing numbers of population is one of the most serious facing all developing countries.

**Exploitation**   Another barrier that underdeveloped countries must overcome is exploitation, external and internal. Many of the LDCs were previously colonies of other countries. The intended purpose of the colonies was to provide the mother country with a supply of raw materials and to buy its processed goods. Other nations, such as China, although not formally colonies, were frequently used by more powerful states for their own purposes.

The Opium War is a good example of foreign exploitation. This war between China and Great Britain began in 1842 when the Chinese government attempted to regulate opium imports into the country, which accounted for nearly 60% of all imports. The opium imports provided the British East India Company with the currency to pay for much of the tea and silk that it purchased. Thus China was trading her valuable tea and silk for a socially worthless item, opium. China lost the war, and because of it Great Britain acquired a colony at Hong Kong in addition to many trade concessions. In a series of treaties following the war, China was forced to

**exploitation**   obtaining labor services, raw materials, or finished goods for a price that is less than their true value.

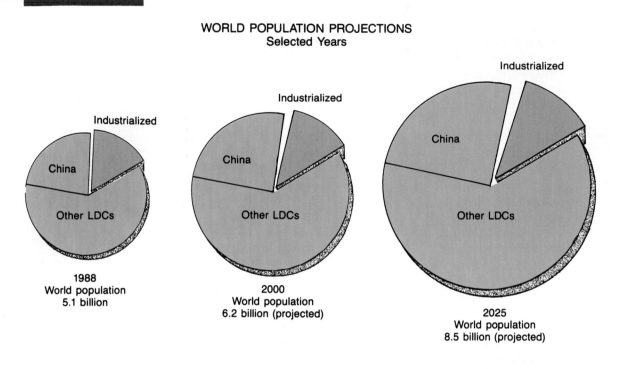

WORLD POPULATION PROJECTIONS
Selected Years

Industrialized

China

Other LDCs

1988
World population
5.1 billion

Industrialized

China

Other LDCs

2000
World population
6.2 billion (projected)

Industrialized

China

Other LDCs

2025
World population
8.5 billion (projected)

Source: World Bank, *World Development Report, 1990.*

China will continue to have the same percentage of world population between now and the year 2025, about 23%. The percentage of the population in the other LDCs will increase from 60% currently to 66% in 2025, while the percentage in the presently industrialized countries will relatively decrease from 17% now to 11%.

grant foreigners substantial rights to mining, navigation, manufacturing, and commerce in parts of China. Today, some developing countries still feel they are suffering similar, if less overt, exploitation.

Perhaps a greater obstacle to development is the internal exploitation of one class by another. LDCs are predominantly agricultural, with ownership of the land usually concentrated in the hands of a wealthy elite class that also controls the government. The landless peasants are kept at a subsistence level. In prerevolutionary China, less than 10% of the population owned 70%–80% of the land, with landowners extracting from peasants rent and crop shares, levying taxes and taking graft from their taxes, and charging them exorbitant interest rates on their debts. The landowners could even seize the children of a poor family in payment of the family's debt.

This type of exploitation of the masses was overthrown by the 1949 revolution. Land reform, income redistribution programs, rural development, and education programs all have contributed to improving the conditions of the peasants. Famine, a regular recurrence in China throughout history, has been eliminated. But the 1989 repression of the liberalization movement demonstrates that the pattern of authoritarian control of the Chinese people continues still.

**Economic policies**  Misguided government policies frequently contribute to the difficulties of LDCs. China's Great Leap Forward program in 1958 and its Great Proletarian Cultural Revolution in 1965 were ideologically motivated policies that did much damage to the Chinese economy.

Government priorities may not accord with the most favorable development practices. According to a report on the attempt of an American automobile firm to produce in China, "The Western executives placed the highest possible value on economic efficiency, even if it led to differentials in income or unemployment; by contrast, they found that Chinese state enterprises were more willing to tolerate inefficiency for the sake of equality of income, full employment, and social order" (*Beijing Jeep*, p. 307; see Further Reading at the end of this chapter).

There have been a number of government strategies pursued by other LDCs that have undermined their economic development in the long run. One common strategy, particularly among African countries, has been the exploitation of agriculture to provide cheap food for the growing urban populations. Holding down agricultural prices is popular with the politically powerful urban areas, but has often resulted in a decrease in agricultural output so that countries which historically were self-sufficient had to begin importing food. The food imports absorb scarce foreign exchange needed to pay for machinery imports to modernize production.

Another policy frequently adopted by LDCs, including many in Latin America, has been a concentration on developing import-substitution industries. Protectionist measures are enacted to keep out imported manufactured goods, leaving the market to high-cost domestic producers. This policy is popular both with the producers and with labor unions. However, it results in inflation and inefficient production.

Peru provides a good example of the consequences of following a highly protectionist trade policy, accompanied by large government deficit spending. At the end of 1988 the inflation rate in Peru was more than 100% a month, and the economy contracted 8.5% during the year.

Successful government development strategies in LDCs are not policies that are politically popular in the short run. Successful development strategies call for government budget restraint—avoiding grandiose projects and large military spending in favor of strengthening the country's basic infrastructure—encouraging competition in industry, and maintaining a stable environment for investment.

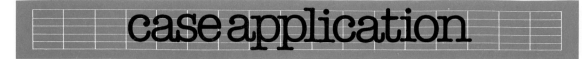

# case application

## The Example of India

India, with the world's second largest population (after China), illustrates the problems facing an LDC and how not to handle them. The economic development policy of India has concentrated on expanding basic industry in order to make the country self-sufficient in fields that are fundamental to industrialization. These include metals and machinery, chemicals, energy, and transportation and communication. This policy has been criticized because it meant the neglect of rural development and consumer goods industries and resulted in a high-cost heavy industry sector that has had to be protected from foreign competition.

The modern industrial sector employs only about 10% of the work force and absorbs only 1.5 million of the 6.5 million Indian youths who enter the labor market each year. The overall growth rate of the economy has consistently fallen short of the 5% growth target, averaging less than 4% a year over the last 25 years. Growth could have been greater if it were not for bottlenecks in the supplies of fuel, power, and transport.

There are 420 million people classified as poor in India, more than half of the population, of whom 250 million are extremely poor. Among the agricultural population, 40% own no land or less than one and a quarter acres. Farm output is subject to large climatic disasters of monsoons and droughts. Although increased agricultural production in the most fertile Indian states has overcome the famines of earlier periods and the country has a large subsidized wheat surplus, it is estimated that 40% of the population remains underfed as a result of high food costs and poor distribution of food supplies.

Life expectancy is less than the average for low-income countries and much less than that of China. The infant mortality rate is three times China's, and its adult illiteracy almost twice as high. This high illiteracy is surprising because one advantage that India has over the typical LDC is in having a large number of college-educated people, a legacy of the British colonial period which emphasized education. This provides a source of white-collar and professional workers, including a large supply of teachers.

An aggressive government birth control program, which at one time even resorted to forced sterilization, has reduced the population growth rate to 2.2%, quite low relative to most LDCs. Nevertheless, the population is projected to reach 1 billion by the year 2000 and surpass the population size of China before stabilizing.

The Indian government employs a system of planning control that is extremely bureaucratic. Key prices are centrally administered; large investments are licensed; critical materials, credit, and foreign exchange are rationed; taxes are complex and tax rates high; and labor laws are very protective. The industrial regulations have been relaxed to some extent in recent years, but India is still said to be the most regulated economy with the exception of the communist countries. The restrictive policies have retarded economic growth; but even so, India, unlike nations of sub-Saharan Africa, is making progress.

## Economic Reasoning

1. What are some of the causes of poverty in India?
2. What are the similarities and differences in the development problems of India and China?
3. Which system do you think will be most successful in achieving economic development, China or India? Why?

# What Are the Prospects for World Economic Development?

In order to accomplish economic development, LDCs have to overcome the problems hindering their economic growth and mobilize their resources effectively. Some of the factors limiting economic development, however, are worldwide in scope and require international cooperation.

**The population bomb**   World population, which stands at over 5 billion, is climbing at the rate of 1.7% per year. Total population is projected to double in the next 40 years. It is possible for food production to double in that time, also, but whether it will is problematical. There is the problem of the high costs of energy required to increase productivity per acre. Up to now, the world's total food production capacity has been more than sufficient to feed all of the world's people. The problems that have arisen have been the result of poor distribution of the food supplies relative to population needs and inadequate transportation and distribution mechanisms.

Since 1965, the population growth in the industrial nations has fallen from a rate of 1.2% per year to 0.6% per year. The populations of less-developed countries, however, are still expanding at a much faster pace—around 2% annually, 2.8% excluding China and India. Even if birth rates are reduced, the LDC populations will continue to grow rapidly for some time to come because of their large numbers of young people. The LDCs are adding 80 times as many young people to the world's population as are the developed countries. Three-fourths of the world's population are of childbearing age or will enter their reproductive years within the next 15 years.

The countries of sub-Saharan Africa have population growth rates averaging 3.2% per year, more than half again as large as the average for all LDCs. At this rate, their populations will double in just 23 years. In many LDCs, especially those in Africa, virtually all economic gains from development efforts are cancelled out by population growth. In the poorest countries, malnutrition results in illness, blindness, and death of large numbers of children. Starvation is a costly and cruel form of population control.

The world population boom will strain not only food resources, but international relations. According to reports by Georgetown University's Center for Strategic and International Studies, overpopulation is already a major factor underlying and aggravating political turmoil in Africa and

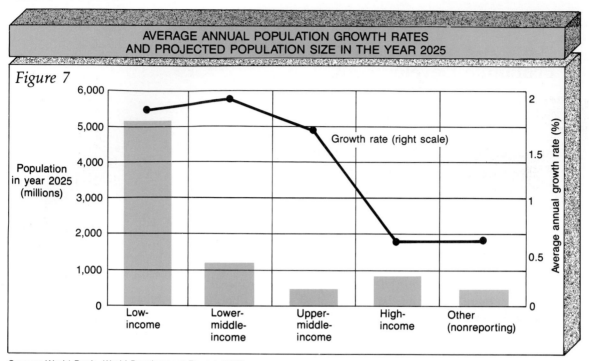

**AVERAGE ANNUAL POPULATION GROWTH RATES
AND PROJECTED POPULATION SIZE IN THE YEAR 2025**

*Figure 7*

Source: World Bank, *World Development Report, 1990.*

The populations of the less-developed countries are growing at much higher rates than populations of the industrialized nations. This hampers development of the LDCs and may cause economic, environmental, and political problems for the whole world.

the Near East. Population growth also increases the pressure on nonfood resources, on energy, and on the environment.

But resource use does not depend just on numbers. Those mainly responsible for using up the world's resources are the populations of the industrialized countries. It has been estimated that the average resident in a developed country uses up 50 times more of the world's natural and environmental resources than does the average LDC resident. In the industrialized West, the average annual per capita energy consumption is 120 times as much as in the poorest LDCs. If, as the developing countries industrialize, they use as great amounts of energy and raw materials as the industrialized countries already do, the world's resource base will be insufficient to sustain the growth.

**The debt bomb** Of more immediate concern to many LDCs than the overpopulation problem is their debt crisis. The two problems are not unrelated. In order to provide for the food and other needs of their growing populations and at the same time invest to expand and modernize their production capacity, developing countries have borrowed to the hilt from foreign banks and international lending institutions. In 1989 the 39 major debtor nations owed foreign creditors some $1.23 trillion dollars. This would be an overwhelming amount of debt even for countries with healthy economies, much more so for nations with subsistence economies. The yearly interest cost to the debtors of carrying the loans was over $140 billion. Almost 30% of their exports were required just to service the foreign debt.

Most of this debt was incurred by the LDCs when their income from petroleum and other commodity exports was high and growing. They—and the lenders—expected them to have no trouble paying the interest and paying off the loans out of earnings from their raw materials, which were in short supply. With the collapse of many primary products markets in the 1980s, the borrowing countries were unable to meet their interest payments. This has created a financial crisis which threatens the international financial structure. If the largest debtor nations default on their loans—declaring that they will no longer make payments on the interest and principal—some of the West's largest commercial banks that have extended the loans could be in difficulty and might collapse.

This boy sits on a mat in a Sudanese hospital that is far different from the kind of medical facility found in developed countries. A civil war and years of drought have added to the economic plight of the Sudanese population.

In order to avoid this happening, there have been a number of international meetings of monetary authorities from the debtor nations with representatives of the commercial banks and the International Monetary Fund and World Bank, with the United States playing a leading role. The most recent program adopted to enable the debtor nations to survive the debt crisis, and at the same time enable foreign lenders to recover at least a part of their investments, is the Brady Plan, proposed by U.S. treasury secretary Nicholas Brady and targeted especially at Latin America. Under the Brady Plan, the indebtedness of the LDCs will be written down by the lenders by 20%. The countries will receive additional loans from the World Bank, the IMF, and whichever foreign banks can be induced to risk further lending. This will enable them to continue interest and principal repayments on their earlier loans rather than defaulting. In return, the governments of the LDCs participating in the plan must agree to economic reforms and bring discipline to their economies. These reforms include curbing government spending and the inflation rate, freeing up markets, and disposing of money-losing nationalized industries.

The conditions imposed on the debtor countries have meant cutbacks in social programs, higher unemployment, and shortages of imported goods. These austerity measures have caused social unrest which threatens to topple the governments in some countries. Their leaders are walking a tightrope between defaulting on the loans—thereby alienating the creditors, cutting off future financial assistance and foreign investment and even essential imports—and economically squeezing their populations to the point of revolution. The fuse continues to burn on the LDC debt bomb.

**The environmental bomb** Less-developed countries attempting to industrialize rapidly—China, India, Brazil, Mexico—are running into severe environmental problems. Their skies are choked with soot and fumes, their waterways are poisoned with chemical wastes, and their lands are denuded of trees. The increase in mineral fuel prices (oil, kerosene, coal) in the 1970s forced millions of people in the underdeveloped nations to resort to using wood as their principal fuel for cooking and heating. The result was a massive denuding of the land of trees. This, in turn, caused erosion of the topsoil, reducing agricultural output.

The external costs of industrialization in the LDCs are enormous. Few efforts have been made to internalize those external costs because of the economic burden of doing so (see chapter 8, pp. 218–219). With insufficient capital for normal investment purposes, the LDCs have been unwilling to divert resources into environmental protection. Furthermore, they lack the technology needed to cure such environmental problems as smokestack emissions.

The growing concern over global warming in the industrialized countries leaves the developing world indifferent. After all, they argue, the high-income nations became wealthy exploiting the environment. Is it fair now to ask the LDCs to sacrifice their own growth to satisfy world environmental concerns? In view of the consequences of global warming for everyone on spaceship Earth (chapter 1, p. 5), it may be in the interest of the wealthy countries to subsidize such measures as the preservation of tropical rain forests in the LDCs. The United States, rather than taking a leading role and setting a good example, has itself been dragging its feet on international agreements to reduce the gas emissions that contribute to global warming.

**Utopia or apocalypse**   What does the future hold in store for the LDCs? The futurologists are busy writing scenarios and most of them are rather grim. They have presented a super-inflation scenario, a worldwide depression scenario, a World War III scenario, and a wars of redistribution scenario. The pessimists far outnumber the optimists because there is so little evidence that anything significant is being done to change the present course.

The optimists, however, claim that we have the technological and organizational tools to overcome the problems. They point out that there have been many earlier predictions of impending doom, but although there have been periodic catastrophes such as famine and depression, the world's economy and standards of living have continued to improve. Many economists are optimists because they believe in a system that is self-adjusting, self-correcting. They believe in the "invisible hand" (Adam Smith's term) directing the adjustments necessary to solve the problems.

Preserving the rain forests is in the economic interest of all people; but the fact that these forests are located primarily in less-developed or developing countries makes the question of how this can be accomplished a controversial one.

## South of the Border

One instructive case in economic development is close at hand, just south of the border—Mexico. It is a case which is of great importance to the United States. If Mexico should fail to achieve development and rising living standards, the consequences for the United States would be at best increased illegal immigration or at worst a Mexican revolution and the emergence of a hostile, terroristic nation on our border.

Mexico is faced with the whole range of problems discussed above—rapid population growth, a huge foreign debt, and severe environmental pollution. Air pollution in Mexico City is the worst of any city in the world. Mexico is 11th in the world in population and has the highest birthrate of any country of its size. Every newborn baby stretches the nation's resources that much farther. The baby must be fed, clothed, and educated. Eventually, that baby will join the long line of those already waiting to be employed.

It is this last problem that most worries the economic planners in Mexico. Until mid-1982, when it was hit by a currency crisis resulting from its foreign indebtedness, the Mexican economy was growing at the healthy rate of 8% a year. It was one of the few success stories among the LDCs. Even so, it has been unable to create the more than 1 million new jobs needed each year to accommodate the young workers entering the job market. As a result, hundreds of thousands annually join the ranks of the unemployed. The unemployment rate is conservatively estimated at 15% with many more underemployed. For those without work, life is hard. Public welfare programs are nearly nonexistent. Many of the poor crowd into the cities and some must

beg for their livelihood. Others head for the United States border in an attempt to escape the poverty of their homeland.

The collapse of world oil prices put Mexico into a financial crisis. During the years of rising oil prices it had borrowed heavily from foreign banks and the World Bank to finance its expansion, counting on oil revenues to pay the interest on the loans and repay the debt. When its petroleum income shrank drastically, it was no longer able to meet its obligations. In 1985 oil revenues were $14 billion, of which half were used to pay interest on the foreign debt and the other half to finance government services. The following year, due to falling petroleum prices, oil revenues shrank by 50%.

In 1988, Mexico's total foreign debt amounted to $106–$107 billion, of which half was owed to commercial banks. The interest it had to pay on its foreign debt was 52% of its export earnings, and the nation's per capita output fell by 13%. Mexico became the Brady Plan's first test. The IMF advanced Mexico $3.64 billion, including more than $1 billion for interest and principal payments on old debt.

For its part, Mexico cut its budget deficit by 20%, sold off two-thirds of the 1,200 businesses it owned to private investors, and pressured labor and business to restrain wage and price increases in order to reduce the inflation rate. The consequences of its economic difficulties and the austerity program included a 20% fall in the standard of living for the average Mexican family and a deterioration of public services. The telephone system, for example, was devastated by lack of maintenance and investment. To make a call, it required up to 10 tries to get a line that worked.

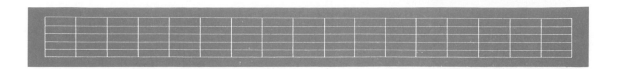

As part of the reform program, Mexico turned away from its traditional protectionist trade policies by eliminating some tariffs, reducing other obstacles to trade, and inviting in foreign investment without the previous restrictions such as requiring Mexican partners. The result of its reforms has been a turnaround of the economy and a resumption of economic growth, reaching 3%.

But even if the country gets through its present difficulties, it must still find a way to cope with the population problem if it is to achieve long-run prosperity. Fully half of Mexico's population is under 20 years old. The spread of family planning, notably in the cities, has reduced the birthrate by 1% in the past two decades. However, even if the birthrate can be reduced further, Mexico's population will nevertheless double in the next 26 years.

*Economic Reasoning*

1. How does the rate of economic growth per capita in Mexico compare with that of the other largest LDCs?
2. How could Mexico's large population of young people be turned into a human capital asset rather than a liability?
3. Should U.S. banks that have lent money to Mexico "forgive" a portion of the debt on condition that Mexico does not default on the major part? Should they lend Mexico additional funds? Why or why not?

Air pollution in Mexico City (above) is the worst of any city in the world.

# Putting It Together

A Chinese People's Liberation Army soldier and tank stand guard in front of the Gate of Heavenly Peace and a portrait of Chairman Mao in Tiananmen Square on June 10, 1989.

Two-thirds of the world's people live in poverty in the *less-developed countries (LDCs)* of Asia, Africa, and Latin America. These countries are largely agricultural with small, inefficient manufacturing sectors and *per capita incomes* of only a few hundred dollars a year. The *World Bank* measures the extent of poverty by the *headcount index* and the *poverty gap*.

Income distribution in the LDCs is generally skewed so that a small percentage of income receivers have most of the income. Various *social indicators* such as illiteracy, life expectancy at birth, and infant mortality, along with the economic indicators, reveal a country's standard of living.

The poverty in developing countries stems from a number of factors. The *vicious circle of poverty* perpetuates low productivity because a lack of capital and the resulting low incomes do not provide an *economic surplus* with which to create capital. The lack of capital, modern technology, and productive human capital result in low GNP per capita.

Rapid population growth compounds the problem of insufficient capital by consuming virtually all production. This prevents the accumulation of a sufficient quantity of capital upon which growth and development can build.

Colonialism left a legacy of economic and social effects in these developing countries. Though some things left by colonial powers are beneficial, many effects of colonialism have had a negative impact. The world economic system prior to World War II was based on taking raw materials from the colonies to use in the industries of Western countries. This did not give Third World countries a chance to develop industries on their own. Today, domestic exploitation of one class by another retards development.

Misguided government policies have also interfered with growth. Many LDCs have embarked on ambitious industrialization programs, neglecting agriculture. The results of these programs too often were high-cost, poor-quality manufactured goods, food shortages, and serious balance of payments problems. Protectionist trade policies have frequently resulted in high-cost production and inflation with falling real income.

There is a race between world population growth—the population bomb—and increased food production. The long-run specter of food shortages, resource depletion, and environmental pollution is a threat not only to LDCs, but to the industrialized countries as well. The world's resources may be insufficient to satisfy demand if the developing countries begin to use them up at the same per capita rate as the industrialized countries do now.

A pressing problem for many LDCs is meeting the payments on their large external debt—the debt bomb. If they default they will lose international credit, foreign investment, and perhaps have their imports cut off. But if the governments tighten their domestic economic belts in order to avoid defaulting, their citizens may revolt.

# Perspective

## The Malthusian Dilemma

**Thomas Robert Malthus (1766–1834)**
Robert Malthus was born in Surrey, England. He studied for the ministry at Cambridge, from which was derived the deprecatory reference to him by some of his later critics as "Parson Malthus." He was appointed professor of modern history and political economy at the Haileybury College of the East India Company where he remained until his death. He was a friend and frequent correspondent of David Ricardo, who occasionally passed on to him tips on good investments in the commodities markets. Malthus did not act on the advice given by his successful friend, and lived a life of genteel penury. In addition to six editions of the *Essay on Population*, Malthus wrote a text on the *Principles of Political Economy* (1820) and a number of pamphlets on such topics as prices, money, gold, rent, and foreign trade policy.

In his *Essay on Population* (1798), Thomas Robert Malthus predicted that the growth of population was bound to outrun the world's food supply. According to his calculations, population grew at a geometric ratio (1, 2, 4, 8, 16, etc.) while food production at most grew at an arithmetic ratio (1, 2, 3, 4, 5, etc.).

As a result, population would always push against the limit of food supplies and would be held in check by famine, as well as war and disease. Under these circumstances, there could be no improvement in living standards.

In the second edition of the *Essay on Population*, Malthus suggested that there might be a way to avoid mass starvation. He recognized that "moral restraint" might serve as a preventive check on population growth. He defined moral restraint as postponing marriage and also strict sexual continence prior to marriage. He was not, however, very hopeful that sufficient moral restraint would be practiced by the British working class to alleviate the population problem.

It was Malthus's very gloomy prediction of worldwide mass starvation that gave economics the designation of "the dismal science." So far, Malthus's expectations have not been fulfilled. On the whole, the world's population is better fed now than it has ever been in history. Malthus did not foresee the vast new areas that would be brought under cultivation in the New World and elsewhere, nor could he foresee the dramatic improvements in transportation that would make the New World's produce available throughout the world. Even less could he foresee the improvements in agricultural productivity that were to result from the agricultural revolution of the late nineteenth and early twentieth centuries and the "green revolution" that has resulted in more productive seed hybrids and improved irrigation and fertilization in the last three decades.

However, there are many today who believe that Malthus was basically right and only his timing was mistaken. These "neo-Malthusians" maintain that at the present rates of reproduction in many countries throughout the world, the population is bound to outrun the food-producing capacity of the earth, perhaps early in the next century. Even today the balance between food and population is precarious, with no reserve of staples in storage that could sustain the world over a series of shortfall production years resulting from drought or other production interruptions in major growing areas.

# For Further Study and Analysis

## Study Questions

1. How does China compare with other LDCs in progressing toward the goal of economic development?
2. How can the LDCs increase the amount of capital available for investment in development projects to increase their rate of economic growth?
3. Why are educational and health programs important to economic growth?
4. What would it mean for a country if its population growth rate was higher than the growth rate of the GNP?
5. How does the existence of large amounts of unemployment and underemployment in LDCs affect their decisions about development strategies? What economic sectors might be stressed and what kind of technology might be used in those circumstances?
6. Why does a poor country typically have a much higher birth rate than a developed country? What causes the birth rate to fall as income levels rise?
7. How does income distribution in the LDCs compare with the income distribution figures given for the United States in chapter 9 (p. 246)?
8. What policies should the governments of LDCs pursue in order to bring about economic development?
9. Why do LDCs accumulate so much international debt?
10. Why does environmental pollution get worse as a country begins to develop?

## Exercises in Analysis

1. Based on the data in Table 1, write a paper on the relative incomes and rate of growth in the different types of countries. Include an analysis of what explains the differences.
2. Select an LDC that interests you, other than the ones discussed in this chapter, and write a paper on its economy and prospects for development.
3. Write a paper on world population growth, the problems it poses, the possible solutions to those problems, and the prospects for the future.
4. Write an essay on one or all of the international problems hindering economic development, and the international cooperation to overcome them.

## Further Reading

Ehrlich, Paul. *The Population Bomb,* new revised edition. New York: Ballantine, 1986. The most popular and influential book on the problems attendant to unchecked population growth.

Feinberg, Richard E., et al. *Economic Reform in Three Giants: U.S. Foreign Policy and the USSR, China, and India.* New Brunswick, N.J.: Transaction Books, 1990. Covers recent economic reforms in three of the world's largest countries and discusses the international political ramifications.

Kirkpatrick, C. H., N. Lee, and F. I. Nixson. *Industrial Structure and Policy in Less Developed Countries.* London: Allen & Unwin, 1984. Studies the role of the private business sector in economic development, including domestic firms and international investment.

Leonard, H. Jeffrey, ed. *Divesting Nature's Capital: The Political Economy of Environmental Abuse in the Third World.* New York: Holmes and Meier, 1985. Articles on the role of natural resources and the environment in economic development and the policies that have resulted in environmental degradation.

Leonard, H. Jeffrey. *Pollution and the Struggle for the World Product: Multinational Corporations, Environment, and International Comparative Advantage.* Cambridge, U.K.: Cambridge University Press, 1988. A more technical treatment than the preceding book, it examines the relationship between industrial strategy and environmental pollution in both advanced and industrializing economies.

Little, Ian M. *Economic Development: Theory, Policy, and International Relations.* New York: Basic Books, 1982. Reviews the conflicting policies and politics of development.

Lombardi, Richard W. *Debt Trap: Rethinking the Logic of Development.* New York: Praeger, 1985. The impact of multinational banking in the Third World and the debt crisis.

Mann, Jim. *Beijing Jeep: The Short, Unhappy Romance of American Business in China.* New York: Simon and Schuster, 1989. A newspaper reporter's account of trials and tribulations accompanying American Motors' and, after its takeover of American Motors, Chrysler's attempts to produce Cherokee jeeps in China prior to the Tiananmen Square massacre.

Meier, Gerald M. *Emerging From Poverty.* New York: Oxford University Press, 1984. "I have wanted to distinguish [this book] from other development books by writing in readily understandable language for the nonspecialist" (Preface, page vii). Discusses current development problems in the light of the experiences of the past four decades.

Simon, Julian L. *The Ultimate Resource.* Princeton, N.J.: Princeton University Press, 1981. An optimistic view on the future availability of food, energy, and other resources relative to population size. Holds that, in the long run, people, the ultimate resource, will solve the short-run problems.

Tidrick, Gene, and Chen Jiyuan, eds. *China's Industrial Reform.* New York: Oxford University Press, 1987. Contains articles on factor allocation and enterprise incentives; planning, supply, and marketing; and enterprise organization in China.

Todaro, Michael, *Economic Development in the Third World.* 4th edition. New York: Longman, 1989. Describes the characteristics of LDCs, the problems and policies of development, and foreign aid and investment.

Woods, Richard G., ed. *Future Dimensions of World Food and Population.* Boulder, Colo.: Westview Press, 1981. Covers many aspects of the problem of balancing food supplies with population.

# GLOSSARY

This glossary has been prepared to provide you with a convenient and ready reference as you encounter terms in *The Study of Economics* you wish to review. It includes the definition of each of the economic concepts contained in the text's marginal glossary along with definitions of a number of other important economic terms, theories, and institutions.

All together there are a total of 378 items contained here. The number in *italics* following the **boldface** entry is the page number on which the item is first discussed in the text. For other references to each term in the text you should consult the index which begins on page xxxv.

## —A—

**absolute advantage** *62;* when each of two producers can produce a different good or service more efficiently than can the other producer, each of the producers has an absolute advantage in the good or service that he produces most efficiently.

**affirmative action program** *252;* a program devised by employers to increase their hiring of women and minorities; frequently mandated by government regulations.

**aggregate concentration** *186;* a measure of the proportion of the total sales of all industries accounted for by the largest firms in the country. There is no common standard for measuring the aggregate concentration ratio.

**aggregate demand** *300;* the total effective demand for the nation's output of goods and services.

**aggregate supply** *312;* the total amount of goods and services available from all industries in the economy.

**Aid to Families With Dependent Children (AFDC)** *253;* a federally subsidized, public assistance program to provide income maintenance and social services to needy families with dependent children.

**annually balanced budget** *389;* a budgetary principle calling for the revenue and expenditures of a government to be equal during the course of a year.

**antitrust legislation** *201;* laws which prohibit or limit monopolies or monopolistic practices.

**area chart** *21;* a chart in which filled areas compare the magnitude of data series, frequently over time.

**automatic stabilizers** *395;* changes in government payments and tax receipts that automatically result from fluctuations in national income and act to aid in offsetting those fluctuations.

**automatic transfer services (ATS)** *272;* a type of account which provides for the depository institution to automatically transfer funds from the depositor's savings account to her or his checking account when it has been drawn down.

**automation** *179;* production techniques that adjust automatically to the needs of the processing operation by the use of control devices.

**average costs** *143;* total costs divided by the number of units produced.

**average propensity to consume** *114;* the percentage of after-tax income which, on the average, consumers spend on goods and services.

**average propensity to save** *114;* the percentage of after-tax income which, on the average, consumers save.

# —B—

**balance of payments** *454;* an annual summary of all economic transactions between a country and the rest of the world during the year.

**balance of trade** *454;* the net deficit or surplus in a country's merchandise trade; the difference between merchandise imports and exports.

**bar chart** *21;* a chart, similar to a column chart turned on its side, used to compare sizes and amounts or emphasize differences in amounts, usually at the same point in time.

**barrier to entry** *187;* an obstacle to the entry of new firms into an industry.

**barter** *275;* direct exchange of goods and services without the use of money.

**base period (base year)** *305;* the reference period for comparison of subsequent changes in an index series; set equal to 100.

**basic deficit** *455;* the excess of import-type transactions over export-type transactions in a country's current, long-term capital and noninduced, short-term capital movements in the balance of payments.

**benefits principle** *373;* levy of a tax on an individual to pay the costs of government service in proportion to the individual's benefit from the service.

**bilateral trade negotiations** *430;* trade negotiations between two countries only.

**block grants** *368;* funds allocated by the federal government to the states for discretionary state spending rather than for specified use.

**bond** *279;* a long-term, interest-bearing certificate issued by a business firm or by a government that promises to pay the bondholder a specified sum of money on a specified date.

**boycott** *170;* refusal by consumers to buy the products or services of a firm.

**break-even point** *148;* the output level of a firm where total revenue equals total costs (TR = TC).

**business transfer payments** *333;* outlay by business for which no good or service is exchanged, such as excise taxes, payouts under deferred compensation arrangements, gifts, and donations.

# —C—

**capital** *8;* the means of production including factories, office buildings, machinery, tools, and equipment; alternatively, it can mean financial capital, the money to acquire the foregoing and employ land and labor resources.

**capital consumption allowances** *334;* the costs of capital assets consumed in producing GNP.

**capital equipment** *173;* the machinery and tools used to produce goods and services.

**capital gain** *249;* net income realized from an increase in the market value of a real or financial asset when it is sold.

**capitalism** *472;* an economic system based on the right of private ownership of most of the means of production, such as businesses, farms, mines, and natural resources, as well as private property, such as homes and automobiles.

**capital/output ratio** *407;* the ratio of the cost of new investment goods to the value of the annual output produced by those investment goods.

**cartel** *153;* an industry in which the firms have an agreement to set prices and/or divide the market among members of the cartel.

**central bank** *281;* a government institution that controls the issuance of currency, provides banking services to the government and to the other banks, and implements the nation's monetary policy; in the United States the Federal Reserve is the central bank.

**central planning** *472;* a method of resource allocation in which the top leadership makes the major decisions on production, distribution, and coordination.

**centrally directed (command) economy** *66;* an economic system in which the basic questions of what, how, and for whom to produce are resolved primarily by governmental authority.

**certificate of deposit (CD)** *271;* a deposit of a specified sum of money for a specified period of time which cannot be redeemed prior to the date specified.

**chart** *19;* a graphic representation of statistical data or other information.

**check** *270;* a written order to a depository institution to pay a person or institution named on it a specified sum of money.

**circular flow diagram** *73;* a schematic drawing showing the economic relationships between the major sectors of an economic system.

**collective bargaining** *233;* a process by which decisions regarding the wages, hours, and conditions of employment are determined by the interaction of workers acting through their unions and employers.

**collective good (public good)** *209;* an economic good (includes services) that is supplied by the government either with no direct payment by the recipient or at a price less than the cost of providing it.

**column chart** *20;* a chart in which the height of columns compares one item to another or compares items over a period of time.

**command-and-control regulations** *219;* a system of administrative or statutory rules that requires the use of specific control devices to reduce pollution.

**commodity** *276;* an economic good.

**communism** *472;* according to Karl Marx, the last stage of economic development after the state has withered away and work and consumption are engaged in communally; today frequently used to designate state socialist economies.

**community demand schedule** *85;* the sum of all the individual demand schedules in a particular market showing the total quantities demanded by the buyers in the market at each of the various possible prices.

**comparative advantage** *63;* when one producer has an efficiency advantage over another producer in both of two products, but has a greater relative advantage in one product than in the other, the efficient producer has a comparative advantage in the product in which he has the greater relative efficiency; and the inefficient producer has a comparative advantage in the product in which he has the lesser relative efficiency.

**complement** *91;* a product that is employed jointly in conjunction with another product.

**computer-integrated manufacturing (CIM)** *179;* a system of integrating all the operations of different departments in a plant by means of a central computer and a network of workstation computers.

**concentration ratio** *185;* the percentage of total sales of an industry accounted for by the largest four firms. An alternative measure is the percentage of sales accounted for by the largest eight firms.

**constant dollar GNP (real GNP)** *335;* the value of GNP adjusted for changes in the price level since a base period.

**consumer equilibrium** *118;* the condition in which consumers allocate their income in such a way that the last dollar spent on each good or service and the last dollar saved provide equal amounts of utility.

**consumer price index (CPI)** *305;* a statistical measure of changes in the prices of a representative sample of urban family purchases relative to a previous period.

**consumer sovereignty** *114;* the condition in a market economy by which consumer decisions about which goods and services to purchase determine resource allocation.

**consumer tastes and preferences** *90;* individual liking or partiality for specific goods or services.

**consumption-investment mix** *478;* the percentage of shares of the national product going respectively to consumption and investment.

**control figures** *478;* the aggregate targets established by Gosplan to reflect the priorities of the authorities.

**cooperative** *132;* producer and worker cooperatives are associations in which the members join in production and marketing and share the profits. Consumer cooperatives are associations of consumers engaged in retail trade, sharing the profits as a dividend among the members.

**corporation** *132;* a business enterprise that is chartered by a state government or, occasionally, by the federal government to do business as a legal entity.

**correspondent bank** *448;* a bank in another city or country that a bank has an arrangement with to provide deposit transfer or other services.

**cost of living adjustment (COLA)** *307;* a frequently used provision of labor contracts that grants wage increases based on changes in the Consumer Price Index; often referred to in negotiations as the "escalator clause."

**cost-push inflation** *306;* a continuing rise in the general price level which results from increases in production costs.

**cross-training** *177;* giving workers training in performing more than one task.

**crowding out** *349;* the term given to the effect government has in reducing the amount of financial capital available for private investment.

**currency** *269;* that part of the money supply consisting of coins and paper bills.

**currency appreciation** *451;* an increase in the value of a country's currency relative to other currencies as a result of a decrease in its supply relative to the demand for it.

**currency depreciation** *450;* a decline in the value of a country's currency relative to other currencies as a result of an increase in its supply relative to the demand for it.

**current account** *454;* those transactions in the balance of payments consisting of merchandise and service imports and exports and unilateral transfers (gifts).

**current dollar GNP** *335;* the value of GNP as measured by figures unadjusted for inflation.

**cyclical unemployment** *300;* the lack of work that occurs because the total effective demand for goods and services is insufficient to employ all workers in the labor force.

**cyclically balanced budget** *389;* a budgetary principle calling for the balancing of the budget over the course of a complete business cycle rather than in a particular fiscal or calendar year; over the course of the cycle, tax receipts and expenditures would balance.

# —D—

**deficit** *341;* a negative balance after expenditures are subtracted from revenues.

**demand** *84;* the relationship between the quantities of a good or service that consumers desire to purchase at any particular time and the various prices that can exist for the good or service.

**demand curve** *84;* a graphic representation of the relationship between price and quantity demanded.

**demand deposits (checking accounts)** *270;* liabilities of depository institutions to their customers that are payable on demand.

**demand schedule** *84;* a table recording the number of units of a good or service demanded at various possible prices.

**demand-pull inflation** *305;* a continuing rise in the general price level which occurs when aggregate demand exceeds the full-employment output capacity of the economy.

**deposit liabilities** *283;* the amount that a depository institution is obligated to pay out to its depositors.

**depository institutions** *281;* financial institutions which maintain deposit account obligations to customers; includes commercial banks, savings banks, savings and loan associations, and credit unions.

**depreciation** *141;* the costs of buildings, machinery, tools, and equipment which are allocated to output during a given production period.

**depression** *301;* a severe and prolonged period of decline in the level of business activity.

**deregulation** *204;* the process of eliminating government regulations and reducing the scope and power of regulatory bodies.

**derived demand** *230;* the demand for a factor of production, not because it directly provides utility, but because it is needed to produce finished products which do provide utility.

**design for manufacturability and assembly (DFMA)** *179;* a system of designing products in which the design engineers consult with manufacturing personnel during the designing process to avoid designs that will be difficult or costly to manufacture.

**devaluation** *451;* a decrease in the value of a country's currency relative to other currencies due to an official government reduction in the exchange rate under a fixed rate system.

**diagram** *21;* a graph that shows the relationship between two or more variables that may or may not have values that can actually be measured; a graphic model.

**differentiated competition** *154;* an industry in which there are a large number of firms producing similar but not identical products; sometimes called monopolistic competition.

**differentiated products** *153;* similar but not identical products produced by different firms.

**diminishing marginal utility** *116;* the common condition in which the marginal utility obtained from consuming an additional unit of a good or service is smaller than the marginal utility obtained from consuming the preceding unit of the good or service.

**diminishing returns** *148;* the common condition in which additional inputs produce successively smaller increments of output.

**direct relationship** *22;* a relationship between two variables in which their values increase and decrease together.

**discount rate** *282;* the interest rate charged by the Federal Reserve on loans to depository institutions.

**discounting** *285;* assigning a present value to future returns; making a loan with the interest subtracted in advance from the principal.

**discretionary fiscal policy** *392;* fiscal policy measures activated by overt decisions.

**disposable income** *339;* the amount of after-tax income that households have available for consumption or saving.

**dynamic efficiency** *484;* efficiency over a period of time with changing resources and levels of technology.

## —E—

**earned income** *372;* wages, salaries, and other employee compensation plus earnings from self-employment.

**earned income tax credit (EITC)** *254, 372;* a federal tax credit for poor families with earnings that offset their tax liabilities and, for the poorest, provides a tax subsidy.

**economic concept** *15;* a word or phrase that conveys an economic idea.

**economic good** *12;* any good or service which sells for a price; that is, not a free good.

**economic growth** *50;* an increase in the production capacity of the economy.

**economic model** *15;* a simplified representation of the cause and effect relationships in a particular situation. Models may be in verbal, graphic, or equation form.

**economic profits** *144;* earnings on invested capital that are in excess of the normal rate of return.

**economic reasoning** *12;* the application of theoretical and factual tools of economic analysis to explaining economic developments or solving economic problems.

**economic surplus** *510;* a margin of output over and above consumption needs which can be allocated to investment for intensive growth.

**economies of scale** *187;* decreasing costs per unit as plant size increases.

**eco-tax** *219;* a fee levied by the government on each unit of pollutant emitted.

**effective demand** *90;* the desire and the ability to purchase a certain number of units of a good or service at a given price.

**efficiency** *48;* maximizing the amount of output obtained from a given amount of resources or minimizing the amount of resources used for a given amount of output.

**elastic** *109;* a demand condition in which the relative size of the change in quantity demanded is greater than the size of the price change.

**elasticity ratio** *112;* a measurement of the degree of the response of a change in quantity to a change in price.

$$\text{Elasticity Ratio} = \frac{\%\text{ change in Q (quantity)}}{\%\text{ change in P (price)}}$$

**employee involvement (EI)** *180;* various programs for incorporating hourly-wage workers in decision-making; may involve decisions on production methods, work scheduling, purchase of capital equipment, etc.

**entitlement program** *253;* government benefits which qualified recipients are entitled to by law, e.g., Social Security old-age benefits.

**entrepreneur** *8;* a business innovator who sees the opportunity to make a profit from a new product, new process, or unexploited raw material and then brings together the land, labor, and capital to exploit the opportunity, risking failure.

**equilibrium output level** *344;* the level of GNP at which aggregate demand $(C+I+G+X)$ is just equal to aggregate supply $(C+S+T+M)$; where income leakages $(S+T+M)$ are exactly equal to income additions $(I+G+X)$.

**equilibrium price** *88;* the price at which the quantity of a good or service offered by suppliers is exactly equal to the quantity that is demanded by purchasers in a particular period of time.

**equity** *114;* the owner's share of the value of property or other assets, net of mortages or other liabilities.

**excess reserves** *283;* reserves of depository institutions over and above the legally required minimum on deposit with the Federal Reserve.

**excise taxes** *333;* a tax on a particular type of good or service; a sales tax.

**exploitation** *513;* obtaining labor services, raw materials, or finished goods for a price that is less than their true value.

**export embargo** *432;* a prohibition of the export of a commodity, capital, or technology.

**external costs** *218;* costs of the production process that are not carried by the producer unit or by the purchaser of the product and are therefore not taken into consideration in production and consumption decisions.

**external economies** *210;* benefits which accrue to parties other than the producer and purchaser of the good or service; benefits for which payment is not collected.

**externalities** *211;* external economies or external dis-economies (external costs).

## —F—

**factor incomes** *73;* the return to factors of production as a reward for productive activity.

**factor market** *71;* a market in which resources and semifinished products are exchanged.

**factor share** *342;* the part of national income received by a particular factor of production.

**factors of production** *8;* another name for the production resources of land (natural resources), labor, and capital (machinery and buildings).

**favorable balance of trade** *454;* the surplus in a country's merchandise trade when exports during the year are greater than imports.

**Fed** *281;* Federal Reserve System.

**Fed Board of Governors** *281;* the governing body of the Federal Reserve System consisting of seven members appointed by the president for 14-year terms.

**Federal Funds market** *286;* the market among depository institutions for temporary transfer of excess reserves from one institution to another.

**Federal Funds rate** *286;* the interest rate paid on Federal Funds borrowed.

**Federal Open Market Committee** *286;* a committee consisting of the Federal Reserve Board and the presidents of five regional Federal Reserve banks that decides on the purchase or sale of government securities by the Federal Reserve to implement monetary policy.

**Federal Reserve System (Fed)** *269;* the central bank of the United States; a system established by the Federal Reserve Act of 1913 to issue paper currency, supervise the nation's banking system, and implement monetary policy.

**financial capital** *8;* the money to acquire the factors of production.

**fiscal federalism** *368;* tax collection and disbursement of funds by a higher level of government to lower jurisdictions.

**fiscal policy** *388;* the use of federal government spending, taxing, and debt management to influence general economic activity

**Five-Year Plan** *478;* the basic planning document in the Soviet Union which established the economic objectives for a 5-year period.

**fixed costs** *141;* production costs which do not change with changes in the quantity of output.

**fixed exchange rates** *449;* exchange rates between currencies that are legally set by the respective countries.

**flexible manufacturing systems (FMS)** *179;* the use of computer-controlled capital equipment that can be readily shifted from the production of one part to a different part.

**food stamps** *253;* certificates that can be used in place of money to purchase food items.

**"for whom" question** *45;* the question concerning the decisions made by an economy about income distribution—who gets how much of the goods and services produced.

**foreign-exchange market** *448;* a set of institutions, including large banks in the world's financial centers, private brokers, and government central banks and other agencies, that deal in the exchange of one country's money for another's.

**free good** *12;* a production or consumption good that does not have a direct cost.

**free trade** *428;* international trade that is unrestricted by government protectionist measures.

**freely fluctuating exchange rates** *450;* an exchange-rate system by which the relative values of different currencies are determined by demand and supply rather than by government fiat.

**frictional unemployment** *298;* the lack of work that occurs from time lost changing jobs.

**full employment** *49;* employment of nearly everyone who desires to work. In practice, an unemployment level of not more than 4–5% is considered full employment.

**full employment aggregate demand** *300;* the level of total effective demand which is just sufficient to employ all workers in the labor force.

**functional finance** *389;* the use of fiscal policy to stabilize the economy without regard to the policy's effect on a balanced government budget.

**functional income distribution** *240;* the shares of total income distributed according to the type of factor service for which they are paid, e.g., rent as a payment for land, wages for labor, and interest for capital.

**Gosbank** *479;* the Soviet state bank that handles all financial transactions between firms, extends credit to firms to purchase production inputs, and audits firms' plan fulfillment.

**Gosplan** *478;* the highest level Soviet planning agency.

**government sector spending (G)** *332;* spending by the various levels of government on goods and services, including public investment.

**grants-in-aid** *362;* federal government allocations of funds to states to finance programs, frequently programs mandated by the federal government.

**Gross National Product (GNP)** *331;* the sum of the values of all goods and services produced during the year.

**gross private domestic investment (I)** *331;* private sector spending on capital equipment, increased stocks of inventories, and new residential housing.

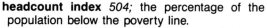

# —H—

**headcount index** *504;* the percentage of the population below the poverty line.

**hidden unemployment** *302;* that part of the unemployed population not reflected in official unemployment figures.

**homogeneous products** *153;* identical products produced by different firms.

**horizontal equity** *372;* equality of treatment for all individuals at the same level.

**household** *72;* an economic unit consisting of an individual or a family.

**"how" question** *44;* the question concerning the decisions made by an economy about the technology used to produce goods and services.

**human capital** *175;* labor which is literate, skilled, trained, healthy, and economically motivated.

**hypothesis** *10;* a tentative explanation of an event; used as a basis for further research.

# —I—

**implicit interest** *243;* income which derives from the use of capital but is not paid as interest but rather as a part of accounting profits.

**implicit wages** *240;* income which is the result of labor input but is not received in the form of wages or salaries, but in some other form such as net proprietor's income (profits).

**import-competing industry** *425;* a domestic industry that produces the same or a close substitute good that competes in the domestic market with imports.

**incentive** *72;* a motivation to undertake an action or to refrain from undertaking an action; in a market economy profits are the incentive to produce.

**incidence of a tax** *374;* the amount of a tax that ultimately falls on households, irrespective of who initially pays the tax.

**income effect** *83;* the effect of a change in the price of a good or service on the amount purchased which results from a change in purchasing power of the consumer's income due to the price change.

**increasing costs** *423;* a rise in average production costs as the quantity of output of the good increases.

**indicative planning** *474;* a method used by governments to improve the performance of the economy by providing economic information in the form of forecasts or targets for industries and, possibly, providing incentives for selected industries.

**indirect taxes** *334;* taxes collected from businesses that are ultimately paid in full or in part by someone other than the business from which the tax is collected; not income taxes.

**industry consortium** *202;* a combination of firms in an industry to carry out a common purpose.

**inelastic** *110;* a demand condition in which the relative size of the change in the quantity demanded is less than the size of the price change.

**infant industry argument** *435;* the contention that it is economically justified to provide trade protection to a new industry in a country to enable it to grow to a size that would result in production costs competitive with foreign producers.

**inflation** *49;* a continuously rising general price level, resulting in a loss of the purchasing power of money.

**infrastructure** *45;* an economy's stock of capital—much of it publicly owned—that provides basic services to producers and consumers. Includes highways, electric power, water supplies, educational facilities, health services, etc.

**institutions** *14;* decision-making units, established practices, or laws.

**interdependence** *63;* the relationship between individuals and institutions in a country or between countries that arises because of specialization of production.

**interest** *72;* a factor payment for the use of capital.

**internalize external costs** *218;* the process of transforming external costs into internal costs so that the producer and consumer of a good pay the full cost of its production.

**International Monetary Fund (IMF)** *449;* an organization established in 1946 to assist in operation of the world monetary system by regulating the exchange practices of countries and providing liquidity to member countries that have payment problems.

**inventories** *331;* the value of finished and semi-finished goods and raw materials in the hands of producers and distributors.

**inverse relationship** *22;* a relationship between two variables in which the value of one decreases as the value of the other increases.

**investment/GNP ratio** *403;* the proportion of GNP which is allocated to private investment.

**job action** *233;* a concerted action by employees to disrupt production or distribution in order to put pressure on employers to grant concessions. They may consist of lesser actions such as work slowdowns or work-to-rule (performing the minimum tasks stipulated in the job description) as an alternative to a strike.

**junk bonds** *175;* bonds that are issued paying higher than normal interest rates because they have a greater risk of default.

**just-in-time** *179;* a system that provides for raw materials and subassemblies to be delivered by suppliers to the location where they will be processed at the time they are needed rather than being stored in inventories.

— K —

**Keynesian economics** *337;* the body of macroeconomic theories and policies that stem from the model developed by John Maynard Keynes.

**Keynesian revolution** *347;* the name given to the transformation in macroeconomic theory and policy that resulted from the ideas of Keynes.

**kickback** *187;* the return of a portion of a payment or commission in accordance with a secret agreement.

**L** *272;* a measure of the money supply which includes M3 plus commercial paper, savings bonds, and government securities with maturities of 18 months or less.

**labor** *8;* all human resources including manual, clerical, technical, professional, and managerial labor.

**labor-force participation rate** *407;* the percentage of the working-age population, or a subgroup of the population, that is in the labor force.

**labor-intensive** *422;* production processes that employ a large amount of labor relative to the amount of capital equipment.

**land** *8;* all natural resources including fields, forests, mineral deposits, the sea, and other gifts of nature.

**law of demand** *83;* the quantity demanded of a good or service varies inversely with its price; the lower the price the larger the quantity demanded, and the higher the price the smaller the quantity demanded.

**law of supply** *86;* the quantity supplied of a good or service varies directly with its price; the lower the price the smaller the quantity supplied, and the higher the price the larger the quantity supplied.

**learning curve** *176;* a diagram showing how labor productivity or labor costs change as the total number of units produced by a new plant or with new technology increases over time.

**legal reserve requirement (required reserves)** *282;* the minimum amount of reserves that a depository institution must have on deposit with the Federal Reserve bank, stated as a percentage of its deposit liabilities.

**less-developed countries (LDC)** *503;* a non-industrialized country, generally characterized by a poverty income level, a labor force primarily employed in agriculture, extensive underemployment, illiteracy, and located in Africa, Asia, or Latin America.

**limited liability** *135;* a legal provision that protects individual stockholders of a corporation from being sued by creditors of the corporation to collect unpaid debts of the firm.

**limited specialization** *423;* specialization in producing goods or services according to comparative advantage when the specialization is not complete due to increasing costs (decreasing returns).

**line graph** *19;* a graph in which points on a line show the relationship of two variables.

**liquidity** *272;* the degree of ease with which an asset can be converted into cash without appreciable loss in value.

**long run** *93;* a period of time sufficiently long that the amount of all factor inputs can be varied.

**long-term capital** *454;* direct investment in plant and equipment or portfolio investments in stocks and bonds.

**Lorenz curve** *246;* a diagram showing the distribution of income among groups of people; an indicator of the degree of inequality of income distribution.

**luxury** *109;* a good or service which increases satisfaction but is not considered essential to well-being.

— M —

**M1** *271;* a measure of the money supply that includes currency in circulation, demand deposit accounts, negotiable order of withdrawal (NOW) accounts, automatic transfer savings (ATS) accounts, traveler's checks, and checkable money market accounts.

**M2** *272;* a measure of the money supply which includes M1 plus savings deposits, small time deposits (CDs), and certain money market mutual funds.

**M3** *272;* a measure of the money supply which includes M2 plus large time deposits (CDs).

**macroeconomics** *xv;* the area of economic studies that deals with the overall functioning of an economy, total production output, employment, the price level.

**marginal cost** *153;* the addition to total cost from the production of an additional unit of output.

**marginal revenue** *153;* the addition to total revenue from the sale of an additional unit of output.

**marginal tax rate** *372;* the tax rate applied to the last or additional income received.

**marginal utility** *116;* the amount of satisfaction a consumer derives from consuming one additional unit (or the last unit consumed) of a particular good or service.

**market** see marketplace

**market concentration** *185;* a measure of the number of firms in an industry.

**market economy** *65;* an economic system in which the basic questions of what, how, and for whom to produce are resolved primarily by buyers and sellers interacting in markets.

**market socialism (regulated market economy)** *473;* an economic system in which the means of production are publicly or collectively owned, and the allocation of resources follows the rules of the market.

**marketplace (market)** *65;* a network of dealings between buyers and sellers of a resource or product (good or service); the dealings may take place at a particular location or they may take place by communicating at a distance with no face-to-face contact between buyers and sellers.

**maximum profit level** *148;* the output level of a firm where the revenue from one additional unit of production (marginal revenue) is equal to the cost of producing that unit (marginal cost).

**Medicaid** *253;* a federally subsidized, state-administered program to pay for medical and hospital costs of low-income families.

**medium of exchange** *275;* a commodity accepted by common consent in payment for goods and services and as settlement of debts and contracts.

**mercantilists** *436;* those who advocated mercantilism, a doctrine that dominated policies in many countries from the sixteenth to the eighteenth centuries which held that exports should be maximized and imports minimized to generate an inflow of gold, and exports of machinery and

technology should be prohibited to prevent competition from foreign producers.

**merger** *187;* a contractual joining of the assets of one formerly independent company with another; may be a horizontal merger of companies producing the same product, a vertical merger of companies producing different stages of a product in the same industry, or a conglomerate merger of companies producing in different industries.

**merit goods** *211;* goods (including services) which have a social value over and above their utility for the individual consumer.

**microeconomics** *xv;* the area of economic studies that deals with individual units in an economy, households, business firms, labor unions, and workers.

**minimum wage laws** *233;* federal or state laws that prohibit employers from paying less than a specified hourly wage to their employees.

**misallocation of resources** *187;* not producing the mix of products and services that would maximize consumer satisfaction.

**mixed economy** *68;* an economic system in which the basic questions of what, how, and for whom to produce are resolved by a mixture of market forces with governmental direction and/or custom and tradition.

**monetarists** *308;* those who believe that changes in the money supply have a determinative effect on economic conditions.

**monetary policy** *389;* actions of the Federal Reserve Board to produce changes in the money supply, the availability of loanable funds, or the level of interest rates in an attempt to influence general economic activity.

**money market mutual fund** *271;* an investment fund that pools the assets of investors and puts the cash into debt securities that mature in less than one year; short-term bank CDs, commercial paper of corporations, 6-month Treasury bills.

**money multiplier** *285;* the ratio of the maximum increase in the money supply to an increase in bank reserves. Determined by the required reserve ratio.

**monopolistic pricing** *187;* setting a price above the level necessary to bring a product to market by restricting the supply of the product.

**most-favored nation clause** *430;* a provision in trade agreements that extends lower tariff concessions granted to one country to all other countries that are accorded most-favored nation treatment.

**multilateral trade negotiations** *430;* simultaneous trade negotiations between a number of countries.

**multiplier** *394;* the ratio of the ultimate increase in income, caused by an initial increase in spending, to that initial increase.

**multiplier effect** *394;* the process by which an initial increase in income results in a total income increase that is a multiple of the initial increase.

## —N—

**National Income (NI)** *333;* the total of all incomes earned in producing the GNP.

**national income accounts** *335;* the collective name for various macroeconomics measurements such as GNP and National Income.

**natural monopoly** *202;* an industry in which the economies of scale are so extensive that a single firm can supply the whole market more efficiently than two or more firms could; natural monopolies are generally public utilities.

**near money** *271;* assets with a specified monetary value that can be readily redeemable as money; savings accounts, certificates of deposit, and shares in money market mutual funds.

**necessity** *109;* a good or service which is considered essential to a person's well-being.

**negative income tax** *254;* an income maintenance plan that would provide a guaranteed minimum income for eligible families with no other income, and a supplement for families with incomes below a predetermined level.

**negotiable order of withdrawal (NOW) accounts** *271;* savings and loan bank customer accounts on which checks can be drawn.

**neomercantilists** *436;* contemporary advocates of mercantilist trade policies to restrict imports, maximize exports of consumer products, and restrict exports of capital equipment and technology to prevent competition from foreign producers.

**net exports (X – M)** *333;* the value of goods and services exported minus the amount spent on imported goods and services.

**net value** *232;* the market value of a worker's output after subtracting the other production costs, such as raw materials.

**non-earned income** *372;* dividends, interest, capital gains, and other non-labor income.

**non-tariff barriers** *431;* restrictions on imports resulting from requirements for special marking, test, or standards enforced on imported goods or the time delays in clearing them for importation.

**normal rate of return** *144;* the rate of earnings on invested capital that is normal for a given degree of risk.

## —O—

**oligopoly** *153;* a shared monopoly in which there is no explicit agreement among the firms.

**open market operations** *282;* the purchase or sale of government securities by the Federal Reserve to implement monetary policy.

**opportunity cost** *39;* real economic cost of a good or service produced measured by the value of the sacrificed alternative.

**other checkable deposits** *270;* accounts, other than demand deposit accounts in commercial banks, on which checks can be drawn, principally negotiable order of withdrawal (NOW) accounts in savings and loan banks.

## —P—

**partnership** *132;* a nonincorporated business enterprise with two or more owners.

**payroll tax** *367;* a tax on wages and salaries to finance Social Security and Medicare costs, with equal amounts paid by employee and employer— the 1990 tax rate on each was 7.65%.

**per capita income** *503;* total National Income (or GNP) divided by the population size.

**perfectly elastic** *111;* a demand condition in which the quantity demanded varies from zero to infinity when there is a change in the price.

**perfectly inelastic** *111;* a demand condition in which there is no change in the quantity demanded when price changes.

**personal consumption expenditures (C)** *331;* spending by households on goods and services.

**personal income distribution** *246;* the pattern of income distribution according to the relative size of people's income.

**Phillips curve** *310;* a statistical relationship between increases in the general price level and unemployment.

**pie chart** *19;* a graph in the form of a pie that shows the relationship of parts to the whole.

**poverty gap** *505;* the aggregate income shortfall of the poor as a percentage of aggregate consumption.

**poverty line** *251;* the family income level below which people are officially classified as poor.

**predatory business practice** *187;* any action on the part of a firm carried out solely to interfere with a competitor.

**price discrimination** *187;* selling a product to two different buyers at different prices where all other conditions are the same.

**price elasticity of demand** *109;* the relative size of the change in the quantity demanded of a good or service as a result of a small change in its price.

**price leadership** *154;* a common practice in shared monopoly industries by which one of the firms in the industry, normally one of the largest, changes its prices, and the other firms follow its lead.

**price stability** *48;* a constant average level of prices for all goods and services.

**priority sectors** *479;* those parts of the economy that decisionmakers want to expand most rapidly and therefore favor with scarce inputs.

**privatization** *209;* the process of selling government assets to private buyers and/or relinquishing government services to the private sector.

**process innovation** *179;* introducing improved methods of organizing production.

**product differentiation** *188;* a device used by business firms to distinguish their product from the products of other firms in the same industry.

**product market** *71;* a market in which finished goods and services are exchanged.

**production inputs (inputs)** *72;* the factors of production used in producing a good or service.

**production possibility frontier (PPF)** *39;* the line on a graph showing the different maximum output combinations of goods or services that can be obtained from a fixed amount of resources.

**productivity** *166;* a ratio of the amount of output per unit of input; denotes the efficiency with which resources—people, tools, knowledge, and energy—are used to produce goods and services; usually measured as output per hour of labor.

**profits** *143;* the net returns after subtracting total costs from total revenue. If costs are greater than revenue, profits are negative.

**progressive tax** *374;* a tax rate that increases as the income on which the tax is based grows larger.

**promissory note** *278;* (IOU) a written obligation to pay a specified amount at a specified time.

**proportional tax** *375;* a levy that takes the same proportion in taxes from low and high incomes.

**proprietorship** *132;* a business enterprise with a single private owner.

**protectionism** *435;* measures taken by the government in order to limit or exclude imports which compete with domestic production.

**public utility** *150;* an industry that produces an essential public service such as electricity, gas, water, and telephone service; normally, a single firm is granted a local monopoly to provide the service.

**public utility commission** *203;* a regulatory body whose members are appointed by government to set rates and services provided by public utility firms.

**pure competition** *146;* a condition prevailing in an industry in which there are such a large number of firms producing a standardized product that no single firm can noticeably affect the market price by changing its output; also an industry in which firms can easily enter or leave.

**pure monopoly** *150;* an industry in which there is only one firm.

**quantity demanded** *83;* the amount of a good or service that consumers would purchase at a particular price.

**quantity equation (equation of exchange)** *308;* the quantity of money (M) times the velocity of its circulation (V) equals the quantity of goods and services transacted (T) times their average price (P); $M \times V = T \times P$.

**quota** *430;* a limit on the quantity or value of a good that can be imported in a given time period.

**rate discrimination (price discrimination)** *200;* charging different customers different rates for services of equal production cost.

**real capital** *137;* the buildings, machinery, tools, and equipment used in production.

**real income** *318;* money income adjusted for changes in the prices of goods and services.

**real interest rate** *120;* the quoted interest rate calculated on an annual basis and adjusted for changes in the purchasing power of money during the duration of the loan.

**real investment** *173;* the purchase of business structures and capital equipment; investment measured in dollars of constant value to adjust for inflation.

**real output** *317;* the value of output adjusted for changes in prices; the volume of output.

**recession** *300;* a decline for at least two successive quarters in the nation's total output of goods and services.

**regressive tax** *375;* a levy that takes a higher proportion from low incomes in taxes than it takes from high incomes.

**rent** *72;* a factor payment for the use of land.

**required reserves** *282;* see legal reserve requirement.

**reserve requirement ratio** *283;* the percentage of a depository institution's deposit obligations to its depositors that must be maintained in reserves.

**residual accounts** *455;* short-term capital transfers and monetary gold transactions that compensate for the imbalance in a country's basic balance in its international payments.

**resources** *8;* the inputs that are used in production. Includes natural resources (minerals, timber, rivers), labor (blue collar, white collar), and capital (machinery, buildings).

**revaluation** *451;* an increase in the value of a country's currency relative to other currencies due to an official government increase in the exchange rate under a fixed rate system.

**revenue** *143;* the receipts from sales of goods and services.

**revenue bond** *349;* a financial obligation issued by a branch of state or local government that has the receipts from a specific revenue source pledged to the obligation's interest and redemption payments.

—S—

**savings deposits** *271;* liabilities of depository institutions to their customers which are not transferable by check and for which the institution may require advance notice before withdrawal.

**Say's Law of Markets** *347;* a theory of the French economist J. B. Say, which holds that when goods or services are produced, enough income is generated to purchase what is produced, thereby eliminating the problem of overproduction.

**scarcity** *8;* the limited resources for production relative to the wants for goods and services.

**scientific method** *10;* a procedure used by scientists to develop explanations for events and test the validity of those explanations.

**shared monopoly** *153;* an industry in which there are only a few firms; more specifically, an industry in which four or fewer firms account for more than 50% of industry sales.

**shift in demand** *95;* a change in the quantity of a good or service that would be purchased at each possible price.

**shift in supply** *96;* a change in the quantity of a good or service that would be offered for sale at each possible price.

**short run** *93;* a period of time so short that the amount of some factor inputs cannot be varied.

**short-term capital** *454;* transfers of demand deposits or liquid investments such as money market funds, CDs, or Treasury bills.

**sin tax** *374;* an excise tax levied on commodities that public policy deems undesirable in order to limit their consumption, such as taxes on cigarettes and alcohol.

**social indicators** *506;* noneconomic statistics that reflect a country's standard of living.

**socioeconomic goal** *51;* the type of social goal that has important economic dimensions.

**specialization** *61;* concentrating the activity of a unit of a production resource—especially labor—on a single task or production operation. Also applies to the specialization of nations in producing those goods and services that their resources are best suited to produce.

**speculators** *306;* people who purchase goods or financial assets in anticipation that prices will rise and they can sell at a profit; speculators can also speculate on a fall in prices.

**stagflation** *311;* a term created to describe a situation of simultaneous economic stagnation, high unemployment, and inflation.

**state (authoritarian) socialism** *472;* a command economy in which virtually all of the means of production are in the hands of the state and decision-making is centralized.

**static efficiency** *484;* efficiency in resource allocation at a given time with a given amount of resources and level of technology.

**statistics** *14;* the data on economic variables; also the techniques of analyzing, interpreting, and presenting data.

**stock option** *406;* the right to purchase a specific amount of a corporation's stock at a fixed price. Often part of the compensation package for a company's top executives.

**store of value** *276;* a means of conserving purchasing power for a future time.

**strike** *233;* a collective refusal by employees to work.

**structural unemployment** *299;* the lack of work that occurs because of changes in the basic characteristics of a market, such as a new substitute product, a change in consumer tastes, or new technology in production.

**substitute** *91;* a product that is interchangeable in use with another product.

**substitution effect** *83;* the effect of a change in the price of a good or service on the amount purchased which results from the consumer substituting a relatively less expensive alternative.

**supply** *85;* the relationship between the quantities of a good or service that sellers wish to market at any particular time and the various prices that can exist for the good or service.

**supply curve** *86;* a graphic representation of the relationship between price and quantity supplied.

**supply schedule** *85;* a table recording the number of units of a good or service supplied at various possible prices.

**supply-side economics** *347;* an approach to macroeconomic problems that focuses on the importance of increasing the supply of goods and services.

**surplus** *342;* a positive balance after expenditures are subtracted from revenues.

— T —

**tariff** *430;* a tax placed on an imported good; also, the whole schedule of a country's import duties.

**technology** *8;* the body of skills and knowledge that comprises the processes used in production.

**terms of trade** *435;* the ratio of average export prices to average import prices.

**time series** *19;* the changes in the values of a variable over time; a chart in which time—generally years—is one of the variables.

**total costs** *142;* the sum of fixed costs and variable costs.

**total revenue** *143;* the sum of receipts from all of the units sold; price × quantity.

**total utility** *116;* the amount of satisfaction a consumer derives from all of the units of a particular good or service consumed in a given time period.

**trade adjustment assistance** *437;* supplementary unemployment payments to workers who have lost their jobs because of import competition and assistance to firms in shifting to other types of production.

**trade-off** *38;* the choice between alternative uses for a given quantity of a resource.

**traditional economy** *67;* an economic system in which the basic questions of what, how, and for whom to produce are resolved primarily by custom and tradition.

**transfer payments** *253;* expenditures for which no goods or services are exchanged. Welfare, Social Security, and unemployment compensation are government transfer payments.

**Treasury bill** *279;* a short-term, marketable, federal government security with a maturity of one year or less.

**trust** *200;* a combination of producers in the same industry under one direction for the purpose of exerting monopoly power.

## —U—

**underemployed** *302;* workers who cannot obtain full-time employment or who are working at jobs for which they are overqualified.

**unfavorable balance of trade** *454;* the deficit in a country's merchandise trade when imports during the year are greater than exports.

**unit of measurement (standard of value or unit of account)** *275;* a common denominator of value in which prices are stated and accounts recorded.

**unitary elasticity** *112;* a demand condition in which the relative change in the quantity demanded is the same as the size of the price change.

**utility** *116;* the amount of satisfaction a consumer derives from consumption of a good or service.

## —V—

**value added** *334;* the difference between the value of a firm's sales and its purchases of materials and semi-finished inputs.

**variable** *19;* a quantity—such as number of workers, amount of carbon dioxide, interest rate, amount of cropland, etc.—whose value changes in relationship to changes in the values of other associated items.

**variable costs** *142;* production costs that change with changes in the quantity of output.

**velocity of money circulation (V)** *308;* the average rate at which money changes hands.

**vertical equity** *372;* fair differentiations of treatment of individuals at different levels.

**vertically integrated** *189;* separate divisions of one company producing the different stages of a product and marketing their output to one another.

**vicious circle of poverty** *510;* the pattern of economic stagnation that results from a lack of surplus of production to invest in capital goods to increase productivity.

## —W—

**wage or salary** *72;* a factor payment for labor service.

**welfare state (democratic socialism)** *474;* an economic system that combines state ownership of some basic industries with a market system, income redistribution, and democratic political institutions.

**"what" question** *44;* the question concerning the decisions made by an economy about how much of the different alternative goods and services will be produced with the available resources.

**workfare** *255;* a program that requires nonexempt welfare recipients to work at public service jobs for a given number of hours a month.

**World Bank (International Bank for Reconstruction and Development—IBRD)** *503;* a specialized agency of the United Nations which began operations in 1945 first to help countries rebuild facilities destroyed in World War II and subsequently to help finance development of the LDCs.

# INDEX

This index has been prepared to help you easily find important information contained in *The Study of Economics*. It includes names, literary references, and subject entries.

The index is alphabetically arranged by *principal entry*. Each principal entry is immediately followed by the page or page numbers of the text on which it appears or by a *subentry* or series of *subentries* with page references to enable you to find the discussion of a particular aspect of the principal entry. **Bold face** page numbers are references to marginal glossary items. These items can also be found in the general glossary beginning on page xvii.

*(continued from page iv)*

411 Federal Reserve Bank, Charlotte Branch; 413 UPI/Bettmann

**Chapter 15** 418 Karen Stolper; 421 Mike Eagle; 422 Pamela Carley Petersen—DPG; 428 Crafted with Pride in America; 429 courtesy American Iron & Steel Institute; 432 UPI/Bettmann; 434 Reuters/Bettmann; 437 EPA Documerica; 438 EPA Documerica; 440 UPI/Bettmann; 441 Library of Congress

**Chapter 16** 444 Mike Eagle; 447–448 Mike Eagle; 451 courtesy the Port Authority of New York and New Jersey; 464 Mike Eagle; courtesy Chase Manhattan Archives

**Chapter 17** 468 Tass/Sovfoto; 470 Robert Wallis/SIPA; 472 Mike Eagle; 475 UN photo by W. A. Graham; 485 Fotokronika/Tass; 488 Fotokronika/Tass; 491 Fotokronika/Tass; 494 Tass/Sovfoto; 495 Library of Congress

**Chapter 18** 498 Reuters/Bettmann; 501 Reuters/Bettmann; 502 Reuters/Bettmann; 503 Mike Eagle; 506 UN photo by John Isaac; 512 UN photo by John Isaac; 519 UN photo; 521 Pamela Carley Petersen—DPG; 523 UN photo; 524 Reuters/Bettmann; 525 The Bettmann Archive, Inc.

**Editor** John S. L. Holland
**Copy Editor** Robert Mill
**Production Manager** Brenda S. Filley
**Designers** Charles Vitelli and Whit Vye
**Typesetting Supervisor** Libra Ann Cusack
**Typesetter** Juliana Arbo
**Systems Coordinator** Richard Tietjen
**Editorial Assistant** Diane Barker
**Graphics** Tom Goddard
**Art Editor** Pamela Carley Petersen
**Photo Researcher** Wendy Connal

Manufactured in compliance with NASTA specifications.
The body of the text was set in CG Palacio.
Charts and graphs were rendered by Whit Vye. Cartoons were drawn by Mike Eagle.
The text was printed in web offset lithography and bound by Ringier America, Inc., at New Berlin, WI.
Text paper is 45# Mead Pub Matte. The end sheets are 80# Publisher's White Winnebago.
The cover material is a laminated Corvon II, non-woven stock.
Cover design by Whit Vye.